Lecture Notes in Computer Science 11729

More information about this series at http://www.springer.com/series/7407

Igor V. Tetko · Věra Kůrková ·
Pavel Karpov · Fabian Theis (Eds.)

Artificial Neural Networks and Machine Learning – ICANN 2019

Image Processing

28th International Conference on Artificial Neural Networks
Munich, Germany, September 17–19, 2019
Proceedings, Part III

Springer

Editors
Igor V. Tetko
Helmholtz Zentrum München - Deutsches
Forschungszentrum für Gesundheit
und Umwelt (GmbH)
Neuherberg, Germany

Pavel Karpov
Helmholtz Zentrum München - Deutsches
Forschungszentrum für Gesundheit
und Umwelt (GmbH)
Neuherberg, Germany

Věra Kůrková
Institute of Computer Science
Czech Academy of Sciences
Prague 8, Czech Republic

Fabian Theis
Helmholtz Zentrum München - Deutsches
Forschungszentrum für Gesundheit
und Umwelt (GmbH)
Neuherberg, Germany

ISSN 0302-9743   ISSN 1611-3349   (electronic)
Lecture Notes in Computer Science
ISBN 978-3-030-30507-9   ISBN 978-3-030-30508-6   (eBook)
https://doi.org/10.1007/978-3-030-30508-6

LNCS Sublibrary: SL1 – Theoretical Computer Science and General Issues

This Springer imprint is published by the registered company Springer Nature Switzerland AG
The registered company address is: Gewerbestrasse 11, 6330 Cham, Switzerland

Preface

The fast development of machine learning methods is influencing all aspects of our life and reaching new horizons of what we have previously considered being Artificial Intelligence (AI). Examples include autonomous car driving, virtual assistants, automated customer support, clinical decision support, healthcare data analytics, financial forecast, and smart devices in the home, to name a few, which contribute to the dramatic improvement in the quality of our lives. These developments, however, also bring risks for significant hazards, which were not imaginable previously, e.g., falsification of voice, videos, or even manipulation of people's opinions during elections. Many such developments become possible due to the appearance of large volumes of data ("Big Data"). These proceedings include the theory and applications of algorithms behind these developments, many of which were inspired by the functioning of the brain.

The International Conference on Artificial Neural Networks (ICANN) is the annual flagship conference of the European Neural Network Society (ENNS). The 28th International Conference on Artificial Neural Networks (ICANN 2019) was co-organized with the final conference of the Marie Skłodowska-Curie Innovative Training Network European Industrial Doctorate "Big Data in Chemistry" (http://bigchem.eu) project coordinated by Helmholtz Zentrum München (GmbH) to promote the use of machine learning in Chemistry. The conference featured the main tracks "Brain-Inspired Computing" and "Machine Learning Research." Within the conference the First International Workshop on Reservoir Computing as well as five special sessions were organized, namely:

Artificial Intelligence in Medicine
Informed and Explainable Methods for Machine Learning
Deep Learning in Image Reconstruction
Machine Learning with Graphs: Algorithms and Applications
BIGCHEM: Big Data and AI in chemistry

A Challenge for Automatic Dog Age Estimation (DogAge) also took place as part of the conference. The conference covered all main research fields dealing with neural networks. ICANN 2019 was held during September 17–19, 2019, at Klinikum rechts der Isar der Technische Universität München, Munich, Germany.

Following a long-standing tradition, the proceedings of the conference were published as Springer volumes belonging to the *Lecture Notes in Computer Science* series. The conference had a historical record of 494 article submissions. The papers went through a two-step peer-review process by at least two and in majority of cases by three or four independent referees. In total, 503 Program Committee (PC) members and reviewers participated in this process. The majority of PC members had Doctoral degrees (88%) and 52% of them were also Professors. These reviewers were assigned 46 articles. The others were PhD students in the last years of their studies, who reviewed one to two articles each. In total, for the 323 accepted articles, 975 and 985 reports were submitted for the first and the second revision sessions. Thus, on average, each accepted article received 6.1 reports. A list of reviewers/PC Members, who agreed to publish their names, are included in these proceedings.

Based on the reviewers' comments, 202 articles were accepted and more than 100 articles were rejected after the first review. The remaining articles received an undecided status. The authors of the accepted articles as well as of those with undecided status were requested to address the reviewers' comments within two weeks. On the basis of second reviewers' feedback, another 121 articles were accepted and the authors were requested to include reviewers' remarks into the final upload. Based on these evaluations, diversity of topics, as well as recommendations of reviewers, special session organizers, and PC Chairs, 120 articles were selected for oral presentations. Out of the total number of 323 accepted articles (65% of initially submitted), 46 manuscripts were short articles with a length of five pages each, while the others were full articles with an average length of 13 pages.

The accepted papers of the 28th ICANN conference were published as five volumes:

Volume I Theoretical Neural Computation
Volume II Deep Learning
Volume III Image Processing
Volume IV Text and Time series analysis
Volume V Workshop and Special Sessions

The authors of accepted articles came from 50 different countries. While the majority of the articles were from academic researchers, the conference also attracted contributions from manifold industries including automobile (Volkswagen, BMW, Honda, Toyota), multinational conglomerates (Hitachi, Mitsubishi), electronics (Philips), electrical systems (Thales), mobile (Samsung, Huawei, Nokia, Orange), software (Microsoft), multinational (Amazon) and global travel technology (Expedia), information (IBM), large (AstraZeneca, Boehringer Ingelheim) and medium (Idorsia Pharmaceuticals Ltd.) pharma companies, fragrance and flavor (Firmenich), architectural (Shimizu), weather forecast (Beijing Giant Weather Co.), robotics (UBTECH Robotics Corp., SoftBank Robotics Group Corp.), contract research organization (Lead Discovery Center GmbH), private credit bureau (Schufa), as well as multiple startups. This wide involvement of companies reflects the increasing use of artificial neural networks by the industry. Five keynote speakers were invited to give lectures on the timely aspects of intelligent robot design (gentle robots), nonlinear dynamical analysis of brain activity, deep learning in biology and biomedicine, explainable AI, artificial curiosity, and meta-learning machines.

These proceedings provide a comprehensive and up-to-date coverage of the dynamically developing field of Artificial Neural Networks. They are of major interest both for theoreticians as well as for applied scientists who are looking for new innovative approaches to solve their practical problems. We sincerely thank the Program and Steering Committee and the reviewers for their invaluable work.

September 2019

Igor V. Tetko
Fabian Theis
Pavel Karpov
Věra Kůrková

Organization

General Chairs

Igor V. Tetko   Helmholtz Zentrum München (GmbH), Germany
Fabian Theis   Helmholtz Zentrum München (GmbH), Germany

Honorary Chair

Věra Kůrková   Czech Academy of Sciences, Czech Republic
(ENNS President)

Publication Chair

Pavel Karpov   Helmholtz Zentrum München (GmbH), Germany

Local Organizing Committee Chairs

Monica Campillos   Helmholtz Zentrum München (GmbH), Germany
Alessandra Lintas   University of Lausanne, Switzerland

Communication Chair

Paolo Masulli   Technical University of Denmark, Denmark

Steering Committee

Erkki Oja   Aalto University, Finland
Wlodzislaw Duch   Nicolaus Copernicus University, Poland
Alessandro Villa   University of Lausanne, Switzerland
Cesare Alippi   Politecnico di Milano, Italy, and Università della
     Svizzera italiana, Switzerland
Jérémie Cabessa   Université Paris 2 Panthéon-Assas, France
Maxim Fedorov   Skoltech, Russia
Barbara Hammer   Bielefeld University, Germany
Lazaros Iliadis   Democritus University of Thrace, Greece
Petia Koprinkova-Hristova   Bulgarian Academy of Sciences, Bulgaria
Antonis Papaleonidas   Democritus University of Thrace, Greece
Jaakko Peltonen   University of Tampere, Finland
Antonio Javier Pons Rivero   Universitat Politècnica de Catalunya, Spain
Yifat Prut   The Hebrew University Jerusalem, Israel
Paul F. M. J. Verschure   Catalan Institute of Advanced Studies, Spain
Francisco Zamora-Martínez   Veridas Digital Authentication Solutions SL, Spain

Program Committee

Nesreen Ahmed	Intel Labs, USA
Narges Ahmidi	Helmholtz Zentrum München (GmbH), Germany
Tetiana Aksenova	Commissariat à l'énergie atomique et aux énergies alternatives, France
Elie Aljalbout	Technical University Munich, Germany
Piotr Antonik	CentraleSupélec, France
Juan Manuel Moreno-Arostegui	Universitat Politècnica de Catalunya, Spain
Michael Aupetit	Qatar Computing Research Institute, Qatar
Cristian Axenie	Huawei German Research Center Munich, Germany
Davide Bacciu	University of Pisa, Italy
Noa Barbiro	Booking.com, Israel
Igor Baskin	Moscow State University, Russia
Christian Bauckhage	Fraunhofer IAIS, Germany
Costas Bekas	IBM Research, Switzerland
Barry Bentley	The Open University, UK
Daniel Berrar	Tokyo Institute of Technology, Japan
Soma Bhattacharya	Expedia, USA
Monica Bianchini	Università degli Studi di Siena, Italy
François Blayo	NeoInstinct, Switzerland
Sander Bohte	Centrum Wiskunde & Informatica, The Netherlands
András P. Borosy	QualySense AG, Switzerland
Giosuè Lo Bosco	Universita' di Palermo, Italy
Farah Bouakrif	University of Jijel, Algeria
Larbi Boubchir	University Paris 8, France
Maria Paula Brito	University of Porto, Portugal
Evgeny Burnaev	Skoltech, Russia
Mikhail Burtsev	Moscow Institute of Physics and Technology, Russia
Jérémie Cabessa	Université Panthéon Assas (Paris II), France
Francisco de Assis Tenório de Carvalho	Universidade Federal de Pernambuco, Brazil
Wolfgang Graf zu Castell-Ruedenhausen	Helmholtz Zentrum München (GmbH), Germany
Stephan Chalup	University of Newcastle, Australia
Hongming Chen	AstraZeneca, Sweden
Artem Cherkasov	University of British Columbia, Canada
Sylvain Chevallier	Université de Versailles, France
Vladimir Chupakhin	Janssen Pharmaceutical Companies, USA
Djork-Arné Clevert	Bayer, Germany
Paulo Cortez	University of Minho, Portugal
Gennady Cymbalyuk	Georgia State University, USA
Maximilien Danisch	Pierre and Marie Curie University, France
Tirtharaj Dash	Birla Institute of Technology and Science Pilani, India
Tyler Derr	Michigan State University, USA

Sergey Dolenko	Moscow State University, Russia
Shirin Dora	University of Amsterdam, The Netherlands
Werner Dubitzky	Helmholtz Zentrum München (GmbH), Germany
Wlodzislaw Duch	Nicolaus Copernicus University, Poland
Ujjal Kr Dutta	Indian Institute of Technology Madras, India
Mohamed El-Sharkawy	Purdue School of Engineering and Technology, USA
Mohamed Elati	Université de Lille, France
Reda Elbasiony	Tanta University, Egypt
Mark Embrechts	Rensselaer Polytechnic Institute, USA
Sebastian Engelke	University of Geneva, Switzerland
Ola Engkvist	AstraZeneca, Sweden
Manfred Eppe	University of Hamburg, Germany
Peter Erdi	Kalamazoo College, USA
Peter Ertl	Novartis Institutes for BioMedical Research, Switzerland
Igor Farkaš	Comenius University in Bratislava, Slovakia
Maxim Fedorov	Skoltech, Russia
Maurizio Fiasché	F-engineering Consulting, Italy
Marco Frasca	University of Milan, Italy
Benoît Frénay	Université de Namur, Belgium
Claudio Gallicchio	Università di Pisa, Italy
Udayan Ganguly	Indian Institute of Technology at Bombay, India
Tiantian Gao	Stony Brook University, USA
Juantomás García	Sngular, Spain
José García-Rodríguez	University of Alicante, Spain
Erol Gelenbe	Institute of Theoretical and Applied Informatics, Poland
Petia Georgieva	University of Aveiro, Portugal
Sajjad Gharaghani	University of Tehran, Iran
Evgin Goceri	Akdeniz University, Turkey
Alexander Gorban	University of Leicester, UK
Marco Gori	Università degli Studi di Siena, Italy
Denise Gorse	University College London, UK
Lyudmila Grigoryeva	University of Konstanz, Germany
Xiaodong Gu	Fudan University, China
Michael Guckert	Technische Hochschule Mittelhessen, Germany
Benjamin Guedj	Inria, France, and UCL, UK
Tatiana Valentine Guy	Institute of Information Theory and Automation, Czech Republic
Fabian Hadiji	Goedle.io, Germany
Abir Hadriche	University of Sfax, Tunisia
Barbara Hammer	Bielefeld University, Germany
Stefan Haufe	ERC Research Group Leader at Charité, Germany
Dominik Heider	Philipps-University of Marburg, Germany
Matthias Heinig	Helmholtz Zentrum München (GmbH), Germany
Christoph Henkelmann	DIVISIO GmbH, Germany

Spiros Likothanassis	University of Patras, Greece
Christian Limberg	Universität Bielefeld, Germany
Alessandra Lintas	University of Lausanne, Switzerland
Viktor Liviniuk	MIT, USA, and Skoltech, Russia
Doina Logofatu	Frankfurt University of Applied Sciences, Germany
Vincenzo Lomonaco	Università di Bologna, Italy
Sock Ching Low	Institute for Bioengineering of Catalonia, Spain
Abhijit Mahalunkar	Technological University Dublin, Ireland
Mufti Mahmud	Nottingham Trent University, UK
Alexander Makarenko	National Technical University of Ukraine - Kiev Polytechnic Institute, Ukraine
Kleanthis Malialis	University of Cyprus, Cyprus
Fragkiskos Malliaros	University of Paris-Saclay, France
Gilles Marcou	University of Strasbourg, France
Urszula Markowska-Kaczmar	Wroclaw University of Technology, Poland
Carsten Marr	Helmholtz Zentrum München (GmbH), Germany
Giuseppe Marra	University of Firenze, Italy
Paolo Masulli	Technical University of Denmark, Denmark
Siamak Mehrkanoon	Maastricht University, The Netherlands
Stefano Melacci	Università degli Studi di Siena, Italy
Michael Menden	Helmholtz Zentrum München (GmbH), Germany
Sebastian Mika	Comtravo, Germany
Nikolaos Mitianoudis	Democritus University of Thrace, Greece
Valeri Mladenov	Technical University of Sofia, Bulgaria
Hebatallah Mohamed	Università degli Studi Roma, Italy
Figlu Mohanty	International Institute of Information Technology at Bhubaneswar, India
Francesco Carlo Morabito	University of Reggio Calabria, Italy
Jerzy Mościński	Silesian University of Technology, Poland
Henning Müller	University of Applied Sciences Western Switzerland, Switzerland
Maria-Viorela Muntean	University of Alba-Iulia, Romania
Phivos Mylonas	Ionian University, Greece
Shinichi Nakajima	Technische Universität Berlin, Germany
Kohei Nakajima	University of Tokyo, Japan
Chi Nhan Nguyen	Itemis, Germany
Florian Nigsch	Novartis Institutes for BioMedical Research, Switzerland
Giannis Nikolentzos	École Polytechnique, France
Ikuko Nishikawa	Ritsumeikan University, Japan
Harri Niska	University of Eastern Finland
Hasna Njah	ISIM-Sfax, Tunisia
Dimitri Nowicki	Institute of Cybernetics of NASU, Ukraine
Alessandro Di Nuovo	Sheffield Hallam University, UK
Stefan Oehmcke	University of Copenhagen, Denmark

Axel Sauer	Munich School of Robotics and Machine Intelligence, Germany
Konstantin Savenkov	Intento, Inc., USA
Hanno Scharr	Forschungszentrum Jülich, Germany
Tjeerd olde Scheper	Oxford Brookes University, UK
Rafal Scherer	Czestochowa University of Technology, Poland
Maria Secrier	University College London, UK
Thomas Seidl	Ludwig-Maximilians-Universität München, Germany
Rafet Sifa	Fraunhofer IAIS, Germany
Pekka Siirtola	University of Oulu, Finland
Prashant Singh	Uppsala University, Sweden
Patrick van der Smagt	Volkswagen AG, Germany
Maximilian Soelch	Volkswagen Machine Learning Research Lab, Germany
Miguel Cornelles Soriano	Campus Universitat de les Illes Balears, Spain
Miguel Angelo Abreu Sousa	Institute of Education Science and Technology, Brazil
Michael Stiber	University of Washington Bothell, USA
Alessandro Sperduti	Università degli Studi di Padova, Italy
Ruxandra Stoean	University of Craiova, Romania
Nicola Strisciuglio	University of Groningen, The Netherlands
Irene Sturm	Deutsche Bahn AG, Germany
Jérémie Sublime	ISEP, France
Martin Swain	Aberystwyth University, UK
Zoltan Szabo	Ecole Polytechnique, France
Kazuhiko Takahashi	Doshisha University, Japan
Fabian Theis	Helmholtz Zentrum München (GmbH), Germany
Philippe Thomas	Universite de Lorraine, France
Matteo Tiezzi	University of Siena, Italy
Ruben Tikidji-Hamburyan	Louisiana State University, USA
Yancho Todorov	VTT, Finland
Andrei Tolstikov	Merck Group, Germany
Matthias Treder	Cardiff University, UK
Anton Tsitsulin	Rheinische Friedrich-Wilhelms-Universität Bonn, Germany
Yury Tsoy	Solidware Co. Ltd., South Korea
Antoni Valencia	Independent Consultant, Spain
Carlos Magno Valle	Technical University Munich, Germany
Marley Vellasco	Pontifícia Universidade Católica do Rio de Janeiro, Brazil
Sagar Verma	Université Paris-Saclay, France
Paul Verschure	Institute for Bioengineering of Catalonia, Spain
Varvara Vetrova	University of Canterbury, New Zealand
Ricardo Vigário	University Nova's School of Science and Technology, Portugal
Alessandro Villa	University of Lausanne, Switzerland
Bruno Villoutreix	Molecular informatics for Health, France

Paolo Viviani	Università degli Studi di Torino, Italy
George Vouros	University of Piraeus, Greece
Christian Wallraven	Korea University, South Korea
Tinghuai Wang	Nokia, Finland
Yu Wang	Leibniz Supercomputing Centre (LRZ), Germany
Roseli S. Wedemann	Universidade do Estado do Rio de Janeiro, Brazil
Thomas Wennekers	University of Plymouth, UK
Stefan Wermter	University of Hamburg, Germany
Heiko Wersing	Honda Research Institute and Bielefeld University, Germany
Tadeusz Wieczorek	Silesian University of Technology, Poland
Christoph Windheuser	ThoughtWorks Inc., Germany
Borys Wróbel	Adam Mickiewicz University in Poznan, Poland
Jianhong Wu	York University, Canada
Xia Xiao	University of Connecticut, USA
Takaharu Yaguchi	Kobe University, Japan
Seul-Ki Yeom	Technische Universität Berlin, Germany
Hujun Yin	University of Manchester, UK
Junichiro Yoshimoto	Nara Institute of Science and Technology, Japan
Qiang Yu	Tianjin University, China
Shigang Yue	University of Lincoln, UK
Wlodek Zadrozny	University of North Carolina Charlotte, USA
Danuta Zakrzewska	Technical University of Lodz, Poland
Francisco Zamora-Martínez	Veridas Digital Authentication Solutions SL, Spain
Gerson Zaverucha	Federal University of Rio de Janeiro, Brazil
Junge Zhang	Institute of Automation, China
Zhongnan Zhang	Xiamen University, China
Pengsheng Zheng	Daimler AG, Germany
Samson Zhou	Indiana University, USA
Riccardo Zucca	Institute for Bioengineering of Catalonia, Spain
Dietlind Zühlke	Horn & Company Data Analytics GmbH, Germany

Exclusive Platinum Sponsor for the Automotive Branch

∧RGMAX.ai

VOLKSWAGEN GROUP ML RESEARCH

Keynote Talks

Recurrent Patterns of Brain Activity Associated with Cognitive Tasks and Attractor Dynamics (John Taylor Memorial Lecture)

Alessandro E. P. Villa

NeuroHeuristic Research Group, University of Lausanne,
Quartier UNIL-Chamberonne, 1015 Lausanne, Switzerland
alessandro.villa@unil.ch
http://www.neuroheuristic.org

The simultaneous recording of the time series formed by the sequences of neuronal discharges reveals important features of the dynamics of information processing in the brain. Experimental evidence of firing sequences with a precision of a few milliseconds have been observed in the brain of behaving animals. We review some critical findings showing that this activity is likely to be associated with higher order neural (mental) processes, such as predictive guesses of a coming stimulus in a complex sensorimotor discrimination task, in primates as well as in rats. We discuss some models of evolvable neural networks and their nonlinear deterministic dynamics and how such complex spatiotemporal patterns of firing may emerge. The attractors of such networks correspond precisely to the cycles in the graphs of their corresponding automata, and can thus be computed explicitly and exhaustively. We investigate further the effects of network topology on the dynamical activity of hierarchically organized networks of simulated spiking neurons. We describe how the activation and the biologically-inspired processes of plasticity on the network shape its topology using invariants based on algebro-topological constructions. General features of a brain theory based on these results is presented for discussion.

Unsupervised Learning: Passive and Active

Jürgen Schmidhuber

Co-founder and Chief Scientist, NNAISENSE, Scientific Director,
Swiss AI Lab IDSIA and Professor of AI, USI & SUPSI, Lugano, Switzerland

I'll start with a concept of 1990 that has become popular: unsupervised learning without a teacher through two adversarial neural networks (NNs) that duel in a mini-max game, where one NN minimizes the objective function maximized by the other. The first NN generates data through its output actions while the second NN predicts the data. The second NN minimizes its error, thus becoming a better predictor. But it is a zero sum game: the first NN tries to find actions that maximize the error of the second NN. The system exhibits what I called "artificial curiosity" because the first NN is motivated to invent actions that yield data that the second NN still finds surprising, until the data becomes familiar and eventually boring. A similar adversarial zero sum game was used for another unsupervised method called "predictability minimization," where two NNs fight each other to discover a disentangled code of the incoming data (since 1991), remarkably similar to codes found in biological brains. I'll also discuss passive unsupervised learning through predictive coding of an agent's observation stream (since 1991) to overcome the fundamental deep learning problem through data compression. I'll offer thoughts as to why most current commercial applications don't use unsupervised learning, and whether that will change in the future.

Machine Learning and AI for the Sciences—Towards Understanding

Klaus-Robert Müller

Machine Learning Group, Technical University of Berlin, Germany

In recent years machine learning (ML) and Artificial Intelligence (AI) methods have begun to play a more and more enabling role in the sciences and in industry. In particular, the advent of large and/or complex data corpora has given rise to new technological challenges and possibilities.

The talk will connect two topics (1) explainable AI (XAI) and (2) ML applications in sciences (e.g. Medicine and Quantum Chemistry) for gaining new insight. Specifically I will first introduce XAI methods (such as LRP) that are now readily available and allow for an understanding of the inner workings of nonlinear ML methods ranging from kernel methods to deep learning methods including LSTMs. In particular XAI allows unmasking clever Hans predictors. Then, ML for Quantum Chemistry is discussed, showing that ML methods can lead to highly useful predictors of quantum mechanical properties of molecules (and materials) reaching quantum chemical accuracies both across chemical compound space and in molecular dynamics simulations. Notably, these ML models do not only speed up computation by several orders of magnitude but can give rise to novel chemical insight. Finally, I will analyze morphological and molecular data for cancer diagnosis, also here highly interesting novel insights can be obtained.

Note that while XAI is used for gaining a better understanding in the sciences, the introduced XAI techniques are readily useful in other application domains and industry as well.

Large-Scale Lineage and Latent-Space Learning in Single-Cell Genomic

Fabian Theis

Institute of Computational Biology, Helmholtz Zentrum München (GmbH),
Germany
http://comp.bio

Accurately modeling single cell state changes e.g. during differentiation or in response to perturbations is a central goal of computational biology. Single-cell technologies now give us easy and large-scale access to state observations on the transcriptomic and more recently also epigenomic level, separately for each single cell. In particular they allow resolving potential heterogeneities due to asynchronicity of differentiating or responding cells, and profiles across multiple conditions such as time points and replicates are being generated.

Typical questions asked to such data are how cells develop over time and after perturbation such as disease. The statistical tools to address these questions are techniques from pseudo-temporal ordering and lineage estimation, or more broadly latent space learning. In this talk I will give a short review of such approaches, in particular focusing on recent extensions towards large-scale data integration using single-cell graph mapping or neural networks, and finish with a perspective towards learning perturbations using variational autoencoders.

The Gentle Robot

Sami Haddadin

Technical University of Munich, Germany

Enabling robots for interaction with humans and unknown environments has been one of the primary goals of robotics research over decades. I will outline how human-centered robot design, nonlinear soft-robotics control inspired by human neuromechanics and physics grounded learning algorithms will let robots become a commodity in our near-future society. In particular, compliant and energy-controlled ultra-lightweight systems capable of complex collision handling enable high-performance human assistance over a wide variety of application domains. Together with novel methods for dynamics and skill learning, flexible and easy-to-use robotic power tools and systems can be designed. Recently, our work has led to the first next generation robot Franka Emika that has recently become commercially available. The system is able to safely interact with humans, execute and even learn sensitive manipulation skills, is affordable and designed as a distributed interconnected system.

Contents – Part III

Image Segmentation

Occluded Object Recognition

Gesture Recognition

Saliency Detection

Perception

Motion Analysis

Generating Images

Attacks on Images

Image Denoising

Unsharp Masking Layer: Injecting Prior Knowledge in Convolutional Networks for Image Classification

Jose Carranza-Rojas[1], Saul Calderon-Ramirez[1(✉)], Adán Mora-Fallas[1], Michael Granados-Menani[1], and Jordina Torrents-Barrena[2]

[1] Instituto Tecnologico de Costa Rica,
PAttern Recognition and MAchine Learning Group, Cartago, Costa Rica
{jcarranza,sacalderon}@tec.ac.cr,
{adamora,migranados}@ic-itcr.ac.cr
[2] Rovira i Virgili University, Tarragona, Spain
jordina.torrents@urv.cat

Abstract. Image enhancement refers to the enrichment of certain image features such as edges, boundaries, or contrast. The main objective is to process the original image so that the overall performance of visualization, classification and segmentation tasks is considerably improved. Traditional techniques require manual fine-tuning of the parameters to control enhancement behavior. To date, recent Convolutional Neural Network (CNN) approaches frequently employ the aforementioned techniques as an enriched pre-processing step. In this work, we present the first intrinsic CNN pre-processing layer based on the well-known unsharp masking algorithm. The proposed layer injects prior knowledge about how to enhance the image, by adding high frequency information to the input, to subsequently emphasize meaningful image features. The layer optimizes the unsharp masking parameters during model training, without any manual intervention. We evaluate the network performance and impact on two applications: CIFAR100 image classification, and the PlantCLEF identification challenge. Results obtained show a significant improvement over popular CNNs, yielding 9.49% and 2.42% for Plant-CLEF and general-purpose CIFAR100, respectively. The design of an unsharp enhancement layer plainly boosts the accuracy with negligible performance cost on simple CNN models, as prior knowledge is directly injected to improve its robustness.

Keywords: Convolutional Neural Networks · Unsharp masking · Prior knowledge injection · PlantCLEF · Preprocessing

1 Introduction

Image enhancement refers to the intensification of meaningful signal energy to considerably improve the performance of image visualization [33], segmentation [5] or classification [4] tasks. Furthermore, image denoising methods aim

© Springer Nature Switzerland AG 2019
I. V. Tetko et al. (Eds.): ICANN 2019, LNCS 11729, pp. 3–16, 2019.
https://doi.org/10.1007/978-3-030-30508-6_1

to attenuate or eliminate irrelevant signal energy. Performed as an initial stage, both image enhancement and denoising are commonly referred as image pre-processing techniques.

Several pre-processing techniques are covered in literature, namely spatial weighted filters Unsharp Masking (USM), collaborative [8], bilateral [35] and non-local means filters [3]), contrast equalization [9], partial derivative operators [36], morphological operators [30], variational [28] and transformation based methods [6]. These approaches are often designed to attenuate or emphasize signal features, and are quantitatively evaluated with a number of metrics such as the peak signal to noise ratio or the structure similarity index [2,27], usually designed for visualization enhancement. Pre-processing behavior is controlled by several parameters, tuned by the user depending on the given needs and the dataset. This implies the user has to manually calibrate them requiring further experimentation, and often preventing to yield optimal results [4]. Furthermore, the aforementioned calibration is frequently biased by the use of general purpose metrics or visual qualitative judgments [27] to assess its performance.

State-of-the-art CNN models are trainable end-to-end to learn automatically a large set of parameters for a number of image filters. These networks theoretically learn optimum filter parameters from the training data, which allows the manipulation of different image characteristics [14]. Together with pooling layers, feature extraction or dimensionality reduction operators can also be learned. However, little has been explored about the usage and influence of manually handcrafted pre-processing techniques [4] in CNN models, as well as the integration of such algorithms into a CNN architecture [11,18].

In this paper, we integrate the USM filter into a CNN architecture as a novel pre-processing layer. The λ parameter which controls the amount of image sharpening is tuned in a data-driven manner during the CNN training phase, avoiding manual fine-tuning. This parameter is estimated to converge to a semantically meaningful value, given the fixed Laplacian of Gaussian (LoG) kernel used for image sharpening. We hypothesize that datasets with high visual inter-similarity between classes will improve both its accuracy and convergence speed with the implementation of an USM layer, given the prior known sharpening behavior of the filter, which might enhance important details to boost class discrimination. We perform a multi-domain assessment to evaluate the impact of this layer in two different datasets: the CIFAR100 and PlantCLEF.

2   Related Work

Image enhancement and denoising techniques are widely explored in the literature, usually making more emphasis on visualization enhancement, employing general purpose metrics [32,37]. Enhancement methods designed for domain-specific imaging (*i.e.,* medical data) also rely on these metrics [1,22], which are frequently inspired on the human visual system. Previous work as seen in [1,22] encouraged the implementation of image pre-processing methodologies to improve segmentation and classification pipelines. However, pre-processing parameters are still empirically tuned, using often general purpose metrics, as the peak signal to noise ratio, which do not necessarily measure the overall impact of the preprocessing parameters on the model. Also, often the most suitable values are not reported appropriately [21] due to the burden of describing the collateral effects of each parameter, which is often not the main focus of work.

Measuring the impact of pre-processing on image analysis tasks contributes to study the influence of different image degradation phenomena [7,10,25,31] in modern image analysis pipelines. For instance, quantitative assessments of image pre-processing in handcrafted approaches such as local binary patterns and statistical texture features were presented in [7,31]. Both works concluded that image degradation hinders classification accuracy by a large margin, whereas popular pre-processing methods can partially overcome such performance degradation.

Recent deep CNN architectures outperformed handcrafted methods on a wide variety of image analysis tasks [29]. CNN based techniques learn image transformations and feature extractors from data, which requires a large amount of training images. Dodge [10] and Nazare [25] evaluated the influence of image degradation and pre-processing in CNN classification models. The former found that the CNN performance is more sensitive to blur and noise degradation rather than poor contrast. The latter explored the impact of Gaussian and Salt and Pepper (SP) noise, along with median and non-local means denoising filters using the MNIST and CIFAR10 datasets. Among the findings in this work, CNN models trained with SP noisy samples performed better when test data was affected by different noise conditions, increasing the model resilience to noise. However, tested CNN models shown higher accuracy when the median filter was applied to reduce the SP noise, when test images were not contaminated by noise. Authors also reported lower accuracy when the non-local means filter was used for attenuating Gaussian noise in training and test samples. However, authors pointed the need of further parameter tuning for the non-local means filter. To address further assessment on image pre-processing, Calderon [4] employed the deceived non-local means filter on bone age estimation to denoise and enhance X-ray images in a CNN model, with different parameter combinations tested. Authors yielded a large accuracy boost over 42% with a specific set of parameters, showing a high impact of image pre-processing technique in a CNN model, along with the importance of pre-processing parameter tuning.

Based on previous literature, pre-processing parameters need to be carefully adjusted to increase the overall performance of an image analysis pipeline. This improvement depends on both the application and dataset, even with CNN based approaches. Few works were reported towards automatic parameter optimization of pre-processing techniques as part of the CNN back-propagation process. Gadde [11] implement the bilateral filter for upsampling enhancement rather than a pre-processing step within the CNN architecture. The filter parameters are learned during training.

Authors in [23] also injected prior knowledge in a CNN model. A wavelet-based layer increased the segmentation consistency and accuracy by capturing texture information and improving robustness to noise through the traditional pooling process. Jampani [18] proposed a high dimensional convolution to learn and approximate the parameters of the bilateral filter from data. The bilateral kernel window size is adjusted during training, with the new layer named as Bilateral Convolution Layer (BCL). Both works in [11,18] based the proposed layers in the popular edge preserving bilateral filter [35], designed to attenuate Gaussian noise. To the best of our knowledge, no CNN layers with prior aim to enhance the input signal has not been proposed in the literature.

A simple and popular approach for image enhancement is Unsharp Masking (USM) [17]. The USM is a spatial filter consisting of two steps. The first step calculates the *base* and *detail* layers. The base B layer corresponds to the original input image U or the low-pass filtered image U_{lp}. The detail layer D contains high frequency energy associated with fine details from U or U_{lp}. It is usually calculated by convolving a fixed Laplacian or LoG kernel L, making $D = U * L$, through a Difference of Gaussians (DoG), or by substracting the base layer U_{lp} to the original image U. In the second step, the detail layer is added to the base layer. The conventional USM scales the detail layer by a factor λ that controls sharpening and contrast enhancement [37]. The USM output F_{USM} is shown in Eq. 1.

$$F_{\mathrm{USM}} = B + \lambda D \tag{1}$$

The USM can be thought as a skip connection with the convolution of a fixed kernel scaled by λ, similar to what is proposed in the ResNet architecture for dealing with the vanishing gradient problem [15]. As detailed in [37], several more sophisticated USM approaches can be found in literature, addressing over-enhancement of details, overshoot artifacts and noise amplification.

3   Methodology

3.1   Unsharp Masking (USM) Layer

We propose the implementation of an Unsharp Masking layer using the Eq. 1, with a fixed LoG kernel L, making λ a learnable parameter during error back-propagation of a CNN model. The Gaussian parameter σ for the LoG kernel is fixed, given it is less important for boosting CNN performance, as it is related to sample denoising, which often has a negligible impact in the overall model accuracy [25]. The layer implementation as CNN layer is straightforward, as the filter is differentiable and cheap to compute. To keep the computational cost low, the filter dimensions are fixed.

We implement the USM filter as the first layer of several tested CNN models, to emulate its impact as a pre-processing stage. We aim to test its impact across different CNN models and datasets, to further assess its influence in models with different number of parameters, and using training samples with different difficulties to discriminate. We focused on testing the filter impact in the original image dimensionality space, to measure its influence as a pre-processing step, however, the filter can be used in further layers and learn its optimal λ_i for each layer i, similar to the proposed CNN architecture devised in [18].

3.2   Datasets

We selected the CIFAR100 [19] dataset as it contains general class categories. This dataset allows us to test the behavior of the USM layer with small image resolutions, and consequently, less visual details.

For more specific domain data, we selected the PlantCLEF (PC) dataset developed for the PlantCLEF challenge 2015. It is composed of 1,000 species with 91,759 fixed training samples, and 21,446 fixed testing samples [12]. Images are sampled from plants taken *in-situ*, which contain different organs such as flowers, fruits, leaves, among others. We used the PlantCLEF (PC) dataset since plant species have inter and intra-specific variability and similarity [24]. To the human eye, different species may look similar, whereas images of the same species may look different as they may differ visually depending on the organs present in the image, the region where it was taken, etc. This scenario is significantly challenging to test the effects of the USM layer.

3.3   Deep Learning Models

Table 1 summarizes the models used to study the effects of the USM layer. The models were selected based on the dataset at hand. For CIFAR100 we selected smaller models since the dataset itself has smaller dimensionality and fewer classes. The smallest model selected was LeNet [20]. Our focus on using LeNet is not to obtain state-of-the-art results, but to give room for potential accuracy and convergence improvements with the USM layer. We also test ResNet20 as a middle-sized model [15]. In low resource environments such as embedded computing, smaller models are appealing.

For the PlantCLEF (PC) dataset, the smallest model used was SqueezeNet with 1,000 categories [16], and ResNet18 was selected as a middle-sized model. ResNet has been the winner architecture in the PlantCLEF 2017 competition [13], as well in the ImageNet 2015 challenge [29]. Finally, the largest model used was InceptionV3 [34].

We used PyTorch to implement the selected CNN models due to its automatic differentiation capabilities [26]. A new layer was created to integrate the USM filter in the forward pass. The auto-grad functionality takes care of the gradient calculation during back-propagation. Our code implementation is available online[1]. Our experiments ran in a NVIDIA Tesla K40 using CUDA in Linux.

4   Experiments and Results

The experiments conducted on both CIFAR100 and PC datasets measure the convergence speed, top-1 and top-5 accuracy. We use different deep learning

---

[1] https://github.com/maeotaku/pytorch_usm.

Table 1. Models and their amount of parameters (with USM layer) used in our experiments.

Model	Parameter # (plus USM λ)	Dataset
LeNet	69,656	CIFAR100
ResNet20	278,325	CIFAR100
SqueezeNet (1K Classes)	1,235,497	PC 2015
ResNet18	11,689,514	PC 2015
InceptionV3	27,161,265	PC 2015

Table 2. Best accuracy results obtained during the experiments of USM with the CIFAR100 dataset. The last four columns are given in %.

Model	Phase	λ Median	Epochs/Batch size	Baseline Top-1	USM Top-1/Boost	Baseline Top-5	USM Top-5/Boost
LeNet	Train.	0.39	300/128	36.64	**41.01**/4.37	68.26	**72.35**/4.08
LeNet	Test.	0.39	300/128	37.00	**39.42**/2.42	67.73	**70.23**/2.50
ResNet20	Train.	0.24	300/128	**88.75**	86.42/−2.33	**99.07**	98.58/−0.49
ResNet20	Test.	0.24	300/128	**63.81**	60.36/−3.45	**88.61**	86.51/−2.10

architectures without the USM layer, which are named *baseline*. The *baseline* results are compared with the same architectures with the USM layer integrated just before the original first layer. The number of epochs and batch size varies in each experiment. Tables 2 and 3 show the selected hyper-parameters for each dataset. The USM layer σ is initialized to 1.667, with a kernel size of 5. In all cases, we provide the optimal λ found by the USM layer upon model optimization. In addition, we tried to relocate the USM layer between the original layers of the aforementioned architectures, or even concatenate them. However, no significant accuracy improvement was achieved, thus we only present results using the USM as a first layer.

4.1   Results on CIFAR100

Figure 1a presents how the USM layer integrated into the LeNet architecture improves the training precision of top-1 and top-5 by 4.37% and 4.08%, respectively. Table 2 and Fig. 1b also show a slight accuracy improvement of 2.42% and 2.50% in both top-1 and top-5, respectively, during testing. The λ parameter was optimized automatically to a median value of 0.39. Moreover, Table 2 reveals that the ResNet20 *baseline* provides better results than its USM counterpart, therefore ignoring the usefulness of the prior USM knowledge. This suggests as Resnet20 architecture is bigger than LeNet, it allows the model to learn more complex filters by itself.

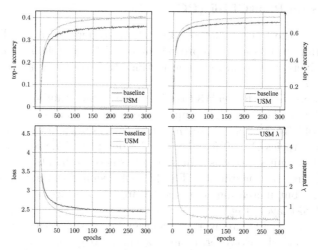

(a) Training top-1 and top-5 accuracy and losses. Accuracy improvements are noticed with respect to the baseline. The λ parameter automatic optimization during training is shown to converge.

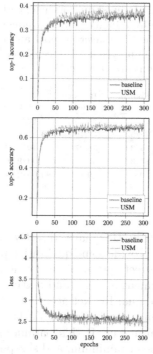

(b) Testing top-1 and top-5 accuracy and losses. Slight accuracy improvements can be noticed when using the USM layer.

Fig. 1. Training and testing results of LeNet (baseline = blue, USM = red) and the CIFAR100 dataset. (Color figure online)

4.2   Results on PlantCLEF (PC)

Table 3 provides the SqueezeNet results, among others, with the PC dataset. During the training phase, an improvement of 5.54% and 4.99% for top-1 and top-5, respectively, was achieved. The testing stage obtained a similar gain of 3.36% and 4.05%.

Figure 2a depicts the ResNet18 *baseline* versus USM training results with the PC dataset. Particularly, a slight improvement can be noticed on top-1 with a mean λ value of 0.54. The largest testing accuracy is shown in Fig. 2b, with a top-1 and top-5 accuracies of 9.49% and 8.18%, respectively. The convergence of the USM ResNet18 architecture was achieved in less epochs than the *baseline* during both training and testing phases. The fact of keeping the accuracy constant during training but increasing it in the testing step, suggests a regularization effect of the USM layer (Fig. 3).

The USM layer yielded an average accuracy boost of 3.9% and 3.2% for top-1 and top-5, respectively. However, a small accuracy degradation is yielded when using the more complex InceptionV3 model (see Table 3).

Table 3. Best accuracy results obtained during the experiments of USM with the PC dataset, using transfer learning from ImageNet. An average accuracy boost of 3.9% and 3.2% is obtained when using the USM layer in top-1 and top-5 accuracy, respectively. The only model that shows no improvement is InceptionV3 during testing, the largest one tested. The last four columns are given in %.

Model	Phase	λ Median	Epochs/ Batch Size	Baseline Top-1	USM Top-1/Boost	Baseline Top-5	USM Top-5/ Boost
SqueezeNet	Training	0.82	74/32	41.55	**47.10**/5.54	65.81	**70.80**/4.99
SqueezeNet	Testing	0.82	74/32	30.16	**33.52**/3.36	53.21	**57.26**/4.05
ResNet18	Training	0.54	83/32	78.27	**81.49**/3.22	92.99	**94.35**/1.36
ResNet18	Testing	0.54	83/32	45.54	**55.03**/9.49	68.75	**76.94**/8.18
InceptionV3	Training	0.19	50/32	79.81	**82.05**/2.24	93.43	**94.31**/0.88
InceptionV3	Testing	0.19	50/32	**60.20**	59.99/−0.21	**81.23**	80.91/−0.33

Since the λ parameter of the USM layer directly affects the image representation and visualization, we provide some qualitative plant examples (see Fig. 4) to clearly demonstrate its correct optimization through a ResNet18 architecture. A prominent visual enhancement of edges and textures is appreciated as epochs progress, thus improving the final ResNet accuracy.

One of the benefits of implementing an USM layer in a CNN model is the interpretability of the λ parameter. If this parameter is zero or near-zero, it means the filter effect is none or minimum, and sharpening of the input samples is not needed. For instance, Table 3 shows a mean λ of 0.19 (close to zero) for InceptionV3, which suggests that the USM layer does not provide any relevant or new information to the model. However, the ResNet18 results present a mean λ of 0.54, which causes the model to improve accuracy and robustness. Importantly, during our experiments the λ never converged to negative values.

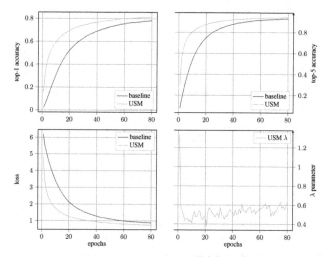

(a) Training top-1 and top-5 accuracy, loss and λ parameter optimization results. Accuracy is similar but convergence is faster with USM.

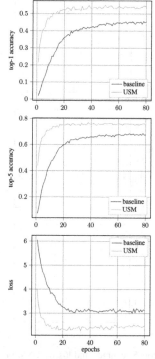

(b) Testing top-1 and top-5 accuracy and losses. USM provides accuracy improvements in both top-1 and top-5.

Fig. 2. Training and testing results of ResNet18 (baseline = blue, USM = red) and the PC dataset. (Color figure online)

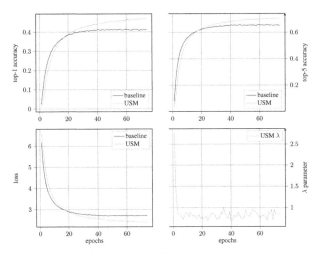

(a) Training top-1 and top-5 accuracy, loss and λ parameter optimization results. Accuracy is better with USM.

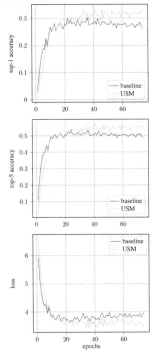

(b) Testing top-1 and top-5 accuracy and losses. USM provides accuracy improvements in both top-1 and top-5. Additionally loss becomes smaller than the baseline.

Fig. 3. Training and testing results of SqueezeNet (baseline = blue, USM = red) and the PC dataset. (Color figure online)

Fig. 4. Visual results of the USM layer parameter convergence during training, taken from the PC 2015 dataset. Figure shows the original images and the enhanced image with $\lambda = 0.61$ from the last epoch when using ResNet18 with USM.

5   Conclusions and Future Work

The integration of an USM layer into a CNN framework opens a new line of research toward improved image denoising and enhancement methodologies in CNN models. Prior knowledge is injected to enhance the input, learn the most suitable λ value, and consequently, reduce the number of parameters through a 5×5 filtering. In most cases, the proposed layer improves both top-1 and top-5 identification performances. More specifically, the challenging PlantCLEF (PC) dataset achieved higher accuracy although an important inter-class similarity is present. Depending on the problem at hand, there is also a tendency of smaller models to gain larger accuracy improvements with USM compared to bigger models, which suggests that in resource constrained scenarios where smaller models need to be used, USM layer might boost its accuracy. The USM layer boosts the accuracy of more simple and less expensive models, making them efficient and useful in embedded or real-time processing scenarios.

A major characteristic of the proposed approach is the simple interpretability of the optimized λ parameter found during error back-propagation. High λ values suggest that input samples enhancement is needed, whereas values close to zero suggest that there is no sharpening needed given the model complexity and the dataset.

Complex CNN models seem capable to learn the USM behavior, or at least overlook it, as suggested by the results obtained. The USM layer has a positive effect when the ratio between model complexity and discrimination difficulty is higher. Although the implemented USM approach is rather simple, we think it opens an interesting research line of designing more sophisticated, non-linear, adaptive [37] and custom pre-processing layers for deep learning models.

References

1. Al-Ameen, Z.: Sharpness improvement for medical images using a new nimble filter. 3D Res. **9**(2), 12 (2018)
2. Buades, A., Coll, B., Morel, J.-M.: A non-local algorithm for image denoising. In: IEEE Computer Society Conference on Computer Vision and Pattern Recognition, CVPR 2005, vol. 2, pp. 60–65. IEEE (2005)
3. Buades, A., Coll, B., Morel, J.M.: Neighborhood filters and pdes. Numer. Math. **105**(1), 1–34 (2006)
4. Calderon, S., et al.: Assessing the impact of the deceived non local means filter as a preprocessing stage in a convolutional neural network based approach for age estimation using digital hand x-ray images. In: 2018 25th IEEE International Conference on Image Processing (ICIP), pp. 1752–1756. IEEE (2018)
5. Calderón, S., Moya, D., Cruz, J.C., Valverde, J.M.: A first glance on the enhancement of digital cell activity videos from glioblastoma cells with nuclear staining. In: 2016 IEEE 36th Central American and Panama Convention (CONCAPAN XXXVI), pp. 1–6. IEEE (2016)
6. Chan, T.F., Shen, J.J.: Image processing and analysis: variational, PDE, wavelet, and stochastic methods, vol. 94. SIAM (2005)
7. da Costa, G.B.P., Contato, W.A., Nazare, T.S., Neto, J., Ponti, M.: An empirical study on the effects of different types of noise in image classification tasks. In: Iberoamerican Conference on Pattern Recognition 2017, abs/1609.02781, pp. 416–424 (2016)
8. Dabov, K., Foi, A., Katkovnik, V., Egiazarian, K.: Image denoising by sparse 3-D transform-domain collaborative filtering. IEEE Trans. Image Process. **16**(8), 2080–2095 (2007)
9. Deserno, T.M.: Fundamentals of biomedical image processing. In: Deserno, T. (ed.) Biomedical Image Processing, pp. 1–51. Springer, Heidelberg (2010). https://doi.org/10.1007/978-3-642-15816-2_1
10. Dodge, S., Karam, L.: Understanding how image quality affects deep neural networks. In: 2016 Eighth International Conference on Quality of Multimedia Experience (QoMEX), pp. 1–6. IEEE (2016)
11. Gadde, R., Jampani, V., Kiefel, M., Kappler, D., Gehler, P.V.: Superpixel convolutional networks using bilateral inceptions. In: Leibe, B., Matas, J., Sebe, N., Welling, M. (eds.) ECCV 2016. LNCS, vol. 9905, pp. 597–613. Springer, Cham (2016). https://doi.org/10.1007/978-3-319-46448-0_36
12. Goëau, H., Bonnet, P., Joly, A.: LifeCLEF plant identification task 2015. In: CLEF: Conference and Labs of the Evaluation forum. CLEF 2015 Working notes, vol. 1391, Toulouse, France. CEUR-WS, September 2015
13. Goeau, H., Bonnet, P., Joly, A.: Plant identification based on noisy web data: the amazing performance of deep learning (LifeCLEF 2017). In: CLEF 2017 - Conference and Labs of the Evaluation Forum, Dublin, Ireland, pp. 1–13, September 2017
14. Goodfellow, I., Bengio, Y., Courville, A.: Deep Learning. MIT Press, Cambridge (2016)

15. He, K., Zhang, X., Ren, S., Sun, J.: Deep residual learning for image recognition. In: 2016 IEEE Conference on Computer Vision and Pattern Recognition (CVPR), pp. 770–778 (2016)
16. Iandola, F.N., Moskewicz, M.W., Ashraf, K., Han, S., Dally, W.J., Keutzer, K.: Squeezenet: alexnet-level accuracy with 50x fewer parameters and <1 MB model size. CoRR, abs/1602.07360 (2016)
17. Jain, A.K.: Fundamentals of Digital Image Processing. Prentice Hall, Englewood Cliffs (1989)
18. Jampani, V., Kiefel, M., Gehler, P.V.: Learning sparse high dimensional filters: image filtering, dense CRFs and bilateral neural networks. In: 2016 IEEE Conference on Computer Vision and Pattern Recognition (CVPR), pp. 4452–4461 (2016)
19. Krizhevsky, A., Nair, V., Hinton, G.: CIFAR-100 (Canadian Institute for Advanced Research)
20. Lecun, Y., Bottou, L., Bengio, Y., Haffner, P.: Gradient-based learning applied to document recognition. In: Proceedings of the IEEE, pp. 2278–2324 (1998)
21. Lee, H., et al.: Fully automated deep learning system for bone age assessment. J. Digit. Imaging **30**, 1–15 (2017)
22. Lee, M.S., Park, C.H., Kang, M.G.: Edge enhancement algorithm for low-dose X-ray fluoroscopic imaging. Comput. Methods Programs Biomed. **152**, 45–52 (2017)
23. Lu, H., Wang, H., Zhang, Q., Won, D., Yoon, S.W.: A dual-tree complex wavelet transform based convolutional neural network for human thyroid medical image segmentation. In: 2018 IEEE International Conference on Healthcare Informatics (ICHI), pp. 191–198. IEEE (2018)
24. Mata-Montero, E., Carranza-Rojas, J.: Automated plant species identification: challenges and opportunities. In: Mata, F.J., Pont, A. (eds.) WITFOR 2016. IAICT, vol. 481, pp. 26–36. Springer, Cham (2016). https://doi.org/10.1007/978-3-319-44447-5_3
25. Nazaré, T.S., da Costa, G.B.P., Contato, W.A., Ponti, M.: Deep convolutional neural networks and noisy images. In: Mendoza, M., Velastín, S. (eds.) CIARP 2017. LNCS, vol. 10657, pp. 416–424. Springer, Cham (2018). https://doi.org/10.1007/978-3-319-75193-1_50
26. Paszke, A., et al.: Automatic differentiation in pytorch (2017)
27. Polesel, A., Ramponi, G., Mathews, V.J.: Image enhancement via adaptive unsharp masking. IEEE Trans. Image Process. **9**(3), 505–510 (2000)
28. Rudin, L.I., Osher, S., Fatemi, E.: Nonlinear total variation based noise removal algorithms. Physica D **60**(1–4), 259–268 (1992)
29. Russakovsky, O., et al.: ImageNet large scale visual recognition challenge. Int. J. Comput. Vis. (IJCV) **115**(3), 211–252 (2015)
30. Serra, J., Soille, P.: Mathematical Morphology and Its Applications to Image Processing, vol. 2. Springer, Dordrecht (2012). https://doi.org/10.1007/978-94-011-1040-2
31. Sharmila, T.S., Ramar, K., Raja, T.S.R.: Impact of applying pre-processing techniques for improving classification accuracy. SIViP **8**(1), 149–157 (2014)
32. Singh, N.K., Sunaniya, A.K.: An adaptive image sharpening scheme based on local intensity variations. SIViP **11**(5), 777–784 (2017)
33. Strobel, N., Mitra, S.K.: Quadratic filters for image contrast enhancement. In: 1994 Conference Record of the Twenty-Eighth Asilomar Conference on Signals, Systems and Computers, vol. 1, pp. 208–212. IEEE (1994)
34. Szegedy, C., Vanhoucke, V., Ioffe, S., Shlens, J., Wojna, Z.: Rethinking the inception architecture for computer vision. In: 2016 IEEE Conference on Computer Vision and Pattern Recognition (CVPR), pp. 2818–2826, June 2016

35. Tomasi, C., Manduchi, R.: Bilateral filtering for gray and color images. In: Sixth International Conference on Computer Vision, pp. 839–846. IEEE (1998)
36. Weickert, J.: Anisotropic Diffusion in Image Processing, vol. 1. Teubner Stuttgart (1998)
37. Ye, W., Ma, K.-K.: Blurriness-guided unsharp masking. IEEE Trans. Image Process. **27**(9), 4465–4477 (2018)

Distortion Estimation Through Explicit Modeling of the Refractive Surface

Szabolcs Pável[1,2(✉)], Csanád Sándor[1,2], and Lehel Csató[1]

[1] Faculty of Mathematics and Informatics, Babeş-Bolyai University,
Kogălniceanu 1, Cluj-Napoca, Romania
[2] Robert Bosch SRL, Someşului 14, Cluj-Napoca, Romania
{szabolcs.pavel,csanad.sandor,lehel.csato}@cs.ubbcluj.ro

Abstract. Precise calibration is a must for high reliance 3D computer vision algorithms. A challenging case is when the camera is behind a protective glass or transparent object: due to refraction, the image is heavily distorted; the pinhole camera model alone can not be used and a distortion correction step is required. By directly modeling the geometry of the refractive media, we build the image generation process by tracing individual light rays from the camera to a target. Comparing the generated images to their distorted – observed – counterparts, we estimate the geometry parameters of the refractive surface via model inversion by employing an RBF neural network. We present an image collection methodology that produces data suited for finding the distortion parameters and test our algorithm on synthetic and real-world data. We analyze the results of the algorithm.

Keywords: Inverse models · Image distortions · Calibration

1 Introduction

Video-cameras are widely used in different robotic and automated driving applications. These applications frequently employ the pinhole camera model to make the association between the outside world and image pixels. The parameters of the model are found using a camera calibration procedure: done either statically, using calibration patterns (e.g. checkerboards, see Fig. 4), or with self-calibration, where the geometric constraints of the scene are leveraged. The camera model is a first step towards image analysis [17]: it considers the way a 3D scene – including geometry, lights, materials, etc. – is mapped to a 2D image. This complex mapping is further split into three stages: a geometric, a photo-metric and a sampling stage. Our work considers the first stage, the geometric part: the association of 3D points with 2D pixels by explicitly modeling the refraction caused by a refractive material present between the camera and the object (e.g. protective covers made out of glass or transparent plastic materials). To find this association, we have to follow light rays hitting a given pixel of the sensor. Due to the refractive material, tracing is more complex: as light enters or leaves

© Springer Nature Switzerland AG 2019
I. V. Tetko et al. (Eds.): ICANN 2019, LNCS 11729, pp. 17–28, 2019.
https://doi.org/10.1007/978-3-030-30508-6_2

a denser media, it changes direction, resulting in deviations from the pinhole model; called *image distortions*, as shown in Fig. 1(a). We construct the *forward model* $f_\theta(\boldsymbol{p}) : \Omega \to \mathbb{R}^3$, where – knowing the camera parameters, the refractive media and scene characteristics, jointly denoted as θ – we map a pixel $\boldsymbol{p}$ from the image $\Omega \subset \mathbb{R}^2$ to a point in the scene. We implement this function as a raycasting algorithm – see Sect. 4 –, allowing us to generate images given a set of parameters. After constructing the forward model, by using model inversion, we fit the parameters of the refractive media to a set of observations, given as displaced points. We build an RBF-network [11] based parametric model of the thickness of the refractive media and use ML estimation [2] to infer the optimal parameters that generated the distortions.

Our contribution in this work is three-fold: (1) we introduce a parametric model of the refractive media and derive the geometric image formation process in the presence of the refractive media (2) we provide a methodology to estimate the model parameters using a static calibration setup with checkerboard patterns (3) we present our experiments where we estimate the image distortions induced by a conic glass surface in a synthetic, as well as in a real-world scenario.

2   Related Work

Most 3D computer vision algorithms assume that the pinhole camera model precisely describes image optics but this is not the case in the presence of *geometric* image distortions, where pixels are displaced compared to their expected positions. Without estimating and correcting the images subject to these distortions, 3D computer vision algorithms often loose performance or simply fail to produce meaningful results. To put our work into context, we review some methods for correcting image distortions.

Estimating image distortions is usually a building block of the **camera calibration algorithm**. These algorithms can be static or can use self-calibration. Static calibration [18,19] techniques use objects with previously known patterns and sizes to extract camera – distortion – parameters. These algorithms provide the highest accuracy, but require the presence of a calibration object. Self-calibration methods [4,7,8] use geometric constraints of the imaging system to estimate camera parameters. These methods are less accurate then static methods, but are more flexible and can be used for online calibration. In our method we perform static calibration using a checkerboard pattern.

Specific algorithms use explicit **distortion models** of differing complexity; the most popular being Brown's polynomial distortion model [3] for radial and tangential distortions. The division model [8] uses an even simpler model with a single parameter to estimate radial distortions only. Using the radial distortion model as above, one can estimate the center of the distortions [10]. Fish-eye lenses create specific image distortions and the *field of view* model explicitly considers those distortions [7], describing the FOV of an ideal fish-eye lens. Lastly, we mention the *rational function* distortion model [6], the most similar to our model, as they lift the 2D pixels into the 3D space and associate rays to individual pixels.

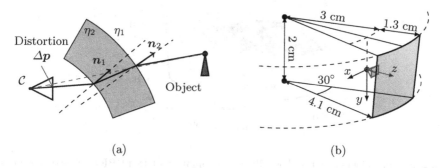

(a)   (b)

Fig. 1. Refraction (a): as light enters or leaves a material, it changes direction; governed by incident angles and normal vectors n_1 and n_2, leading to a "shift" Δp in pixel position. In our **experiment (b):** the camera is inside a conical glass object. The blue area denotes the 30 degree by 2 cm patch where we consider the uneven surface, see Sect. 3 (best viewed in color).

Our method also traces 3D light rays, but we instead directly parameterize the refractive surfaces which generate the distortions.

The work of Agrawal et al. [1] sets up distortions for images taken through flat refractive surfaces (they use a water tank for their experiments), therefore modeling explicitly the **distortions from light refraction.** They use the theory of non-central cameras [16] and multi-view geometry in the presence of refractive media [5]. Morinaka et al. [12] presents static camera calibration and 3D reconstruction in challenging setups like images taken through a wine glass. They use the "raxel" imaging model [9] with two calibration planes, with polynomial mappings between image pixels and corresponding points on the planes. This model is closest to ours, the main difference being that in their method the refractive media is treated as a black box, while we directly model the refractive surface, giving us a global model.

3   Refractive Surface Model

We model our refractive media as a "thick" cone slice, as in Fig. 1(a). The inner and outer cones have the same aperture, and the centers are such that the thickness Δr of the media is constant. We constrain the position of the cone such that the main axis is parallel with the y-axis of the camera coordinate system and that the cones shrink in the positive (downwards pointing) y direction, shown in Fig. 1(b). We parameterize the cone surface with its height relative to the apex $s_1 \in [0, h]$ and a polar angle $s_2 \in [-\pi, \pi]$, where a polar angle of 0 describes the points on the YOZ plane, with positive z values. We use bold notation for the two-dimensional vectors: $\boldsymbol{s} = (s_1, s_2)$.

To model the uneven refractive media – implicit the distortions – we add a parametric surface in the radial direction to the cone; this radial offset is defined as a Radial Basis Function network (RBF) [13] where the inputs are

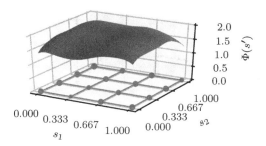

Fig. 2. Sample offsets generated as a linear combination of 4×4 RBF kernels distributed on a regular grid. Dot sizes denote the – positive – kernel amplitudes.

the cone coordinates. We choose an RBF network because they are universal function approximators given a sufficient number of centers, and can be used to estimate arbitrary surfaces. In practice we show that a relatively small number of parameters is enough to model complex surfaces – see Sect. 6.1. The RBF centers $\{s_{ij}\}$, $i, j = \overline{1,N}$ are on a regular grid over the input region, as shown in Fig. 1(b). We keep the RBF centers fixed and tune the amplitudes $a_{ij} \in \mathbb{R}$. The radial offset $\Phi(s')$ at a given normalized cone point s' is defined as the output of the RBF network with Gaussian kernels, an example of which is shown in Fig. 2:

$$\Phi(s') = \sum_{i,j=1}^{N} a_{ij}\mathrm{RBF}(s_{ij}, s'), \quad \text{where } \mathrm{RBF}(s, s') = \exp\left(-\frac{\|s - s'\|^2}{2\beta}\right) \quad (1)$$

When computing the Cartesian coordinates for a point on the cone, parameterized by a height s_1 and an angle s_2, first we compute the RBF offset $\Phi(s')$, and then add this offset to the radius. The surface normals of the outer cone can be computed as the cross product of the two partial derivatives of the Cartesian coordinates w.r.t. the parameters. This cross product also has a dependence on the amplitudes associated with the RBF centers, which will be used as the model parameters during minimization. Changing the RBF amplitudes causes a change in the surface normals, which in turn changes the direction of the refracted light rays, and by a consequence the direction and length of the distortion vectors.

4   Raycasting Model

The ray casting model describes how we associate a pixel from the image with a 3D point on an object, in our case on a checkerboard pattern. In a distortion-free setup this can be achieved using the pinhole camera model, which uses a perspective projection and a set of linear operations to describe this relationship. In the presence of a refractive surface this simple perspective geometric description does not hold, and we need additional steps to associate pixels with world points. The complete computational graph can be seen on Fig. 3. Each ray starts at the camera center and we assume that the intrinsic camera parameters

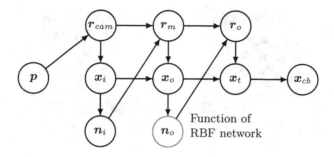

Fig. 3. The computation graph of raycasting: given a pixel p, we compute the 3D point x_t on the checkerboard plane, respectively the local coordinate x_{cb} of the corners. Notation: r – ray direction, x – Cartesian coordinate vector, and n – normal vectors.

– the focal lengths and the principal point, ie. the intrinsic camera matrix – are known. All 3D points are expressed in the camera coordinate system. Using the camera intrinsics, we can convert any pixel coordinate p to metric coordinates, which after normalization correspond to the direction vector r_{cam} of the light ray that passes through the selected pixel.

The light ray coming from the camera first hits the inner side of the refractive surface. Using the fact that the inner surface is a regular cone, we first compute the intersection with the cone x_i and its normal n_i. The direction r_m of the refracted light-ray inside the media is computed using Snell's law [15]. Knowing the geometry of the refractive body and the new direction of the refracted ray, we first identify the location x_o where the ray hits the outer surface, and is refracted for the second time. Using the surface normal n_o at this point we compute the direction of the outgoing light-ray, which we denote with r_o. Note that this second refraction is modulated by the *direction* of the normal, that is parameterized by the RBF network. At the same time, we ignore the changes caused by the RBF network in the *thickness* of the material when computing x_o and we argue that this approximation holds, as the offsets are significantly smaller than the distance between the two cones (the thickness of the media), and the difference is negligible.

Finally, this outgoing light ray hits the calibration target – in our case the checkerboard pattern – whose position is defined through a 3D rotation and the 3D translation of the board center relative to the camera coordinate system. The intersection point x_t is computed as an intersection of a line and a plane. For an easier handling of the checkerboard, we define a local 2D coordinate system on the object plane, with its origin at the board center, and the two axes being the horizontal and vertical directions of the square grid. We denote the local coordinates of a 3D point x_t as x_{cb}.

(a)   (b)

Fig. 4. Samples of (a) rendered and (b) real images used in our experiments.

5   Optimization of the Surface Parameters

The estimation of image distortions is equivalent to finding the surface parameters that generated a set of calibration images. We use a square checkerboard pattern as calibration target, and take multiple images of the same target in different positions. We use gradient descent minimization to find the amplitudes $a = \{a_{ij}\}$, $i, j = \overline{1, N}$, of the RBF centers, the parameters of the refractive surface. During the minimization all other parameters, including the camera intrinsics, the sizes of the inner and outer cones, as well as the calibration pattern pose and size are assumed to be known.

For each calibration image I^k, $k = \overline{1, N_i}$ we find the pixel coordinates and ordering of the checkerboard pattern corners $\{p_{ij}^k\}$, $i, j = \overline{1, N_c}$. The corresponding local coordinates of the detected corners on the object plane – denoted with $\{x_{ij}^{cb}\}$, $i, j = \overline{1, N_c}$ – are given by their distance from the board center. Let $f_{a,k}(\cdot)$ be the raycasting function described in Sect. 4, parameterized by the RBF amplitudes a, which takes an input pixel, and computes the local coordinates of the corresponding world point on the $k-th$ target checkerboard pattern. Then the loss function used for the minimization is the $\mathcal{L}_2$ loss between the local coordinates of a corner estimated by the raycast function, and the ground-truth local coordinates of the corners:

$$\mathcal{L}(a) = \sum_{k=1}^{N_i} \sum_{i,j=1}^{N_c} \left\| f_{a,k}\left(p_{ij}^k\right) - x_{ij}^{cb} \right\|^2 \tag{2}$$

The optimal parameters $a^\star$ are found through a Gradient Descent minimization of the loss function:

$$a^\star = \arg\min_a \mathcal{L}(a) \tag{3}$$

The optimization algorithm including the ray-casting model is implemented using the PyTorch [14] deep learning framework. This framework makes the implementation easier as it provides backward automatic differentiation and implements gradient descent minimization.

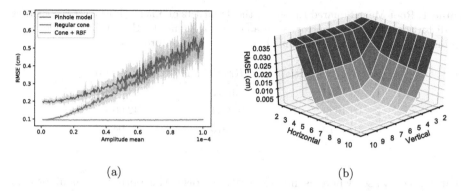

(a)   (b)

Fig. 5. Results for synthetic data. (a) Errors for different refraction complexity: *Pinhole model* disregards distortions, *Regular cone* uses a perfect cone, and *Cone + RBF* uses optimization. (b) Errors for varying RBF complexities: as the number of RBF centers increases, the estimation error drops.

6   Experiments

We evaluate our algorithm on two data sets: a noise-free synthetic one and a real experimental setup. In the synthetic case we show that our algorithm is capable of finding the optimal parameters that generated a given image even for large irregularities on the outer surface. In the second case we present an experimental setup, and show that the algorithm is able to reduce reconstruction errors in real-world scenarios.

6.1   Synthetic Dataset

In a first set of experiments we applied the forward image generation model to render synthetic images. We set the parameters of the camera, refractive surface, and the checkerboard pattern to similar values as in the real-world experiment, as shown in Fig. 4(a).

In our first synthetic experiment, using an RBF grid of size 4×4, we sample the amplitudes $\boldsymbol{a}$ from a Gaussian with mean $\mu_a \in [1 \times 10^{-6}, 1 \times 10^{-4}]$ and standard deviation $\sigma_a = \mu_a/4$. With the sampled surface we generate 10 synthetic images using random positions for the calibration target – as shown in Fig. 4. Using the batch of 10 images we run the optimization from Sect. 5 for 500 steps and store the final error as the *root mean squared error* between the predicted and ground-truth checkerboard corners.

For each amplitude distribution we repeat the whole process 10 times and show the results in Fig. 5(a): *Pinhole model* is the error without any distortion model, while *Regular cone* and *Cone + RBF* show the results using a *perfect* cone and one where parameters are inferred. We see that with small RBF amplitudes the error is a result of the cone geometry, while with higher amplitudes the errors due to the uneven surface dominate the distortion. An important conclusion is

Table 1. Root Mean Squared Errors for the 3 real sets of images. Initial error considers no distortion model, final error is obtained using Cone + RBF surface model with optimized parameters. Last column shows the relative improvement.

Set	$RMSE$ initial (cm)	$RMSE$ final (cm)	Rel. imp
1	0.1364	0.0772	43.35%
2	0.1649	0.0941	42.90%
3	0.1570	0.0973	38.04%

that for this case, where is no observation noise, the optimization algorithm works well, reducing the errors almost to zero.

In the second experiment we generate random refraction patterns using 10×10 RBF centers with amplitudes drawn randomly from Gaussian distributions, and show the errors after performing the optimization – corresponding to the *Cone + RBF* case from Fig. 5(a). Instead of changing the amplitudes, we vary the numbers of RBF centers – both horizontally and vertically, results are shown in Fig. 5(b). We observe that – in this artificial setup – the refractive surface is well approximated with a smaller complexity model: 7×5 parameters are enough to approximate the generated surface (the asymmetry is due to our setup of the refractive surface, which is a cone with larger horizontal curvature).

6.2   Real Dataset

For a real-world experiment we use a Raspberry Pi Camera Module v2 to capture the checkerboard images. The camera has a 3.68×2.76 mm sensor and registers images on a 3280×2464 pixel resolution. Prior to the experiment we calibrated the camera using Zhang's method [19] and we registered a 2558.36 pixel focal length and a principal point at the $(1666.03, 1273.65)$ location. After calibration we placed a cone shaped glass in the front of the camera, with approximate parameters shown on Fig. 1(b). In our experiments we use 45 images of a checkerboard pattern that were randomly split into 3 non-overlapping sets of 15 items each, which we will refer to as Sets 1, 2 and 3.

Since the positions of the checkerboard patterns are unknown, we have to estimate them. We do this in two steps: (1) we estimate the object pose by running Zhang's method on the distorted images, while we fix the camera intrinsic parameters to the calibrated values; and (2) we apply the *perfect* cone refraction model and with the same objective function we minimize for the calibration pattern positions. Keeping the above values fixed, we then run the optimizer for the RBF center amplitudes.

With our real dataset we use 8×8 RBF centers – found using experimentation as in Fig. 5 – and run the minimization for 1000 steps and we report results for the different sets separately. Table 1 shows the RMSE for the 3 sets of images. The errors can be interpreted as the 3D distance in centimeters between the ground-truth and the predicted position of the same corner on the checkerboard

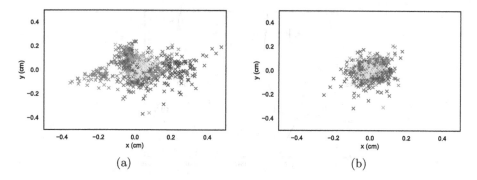

(a)   (b)

Fig. 6. Scatter plots of all the checkerboard corner errors. x and y are the axis in the local coordinate system of the checkerboard patterns (different for each image). Different colors correspond to different images when (a) no distortion model is used, and when (b) the optimized distortion model is used.

pattern. The first column shows the mean error in the case where we consider no distortion model at all, while the second column shows the results after the minimization using the *Cone + RBF* surface model. Last column shows the relative improvements between the two error values. Our method is able to improve the 3D distances in each case, resulting in a more precise generative model of the image formation process. Figure 6 shows all corner errors in the 2D local coordinate system of the checkerboard, with different colors for different images. We see that in the uncorrected scatter plot (a) for each image – denoted by the color – there is a dominant direction, which is caused by the horizontal curvature of the cone. We highlight that the effect of minimization – right subplot in Fig. 6 – is that the errors are around zero, without dominant directions for individual images.

6.3 Analyzing Distortions

Most of the distortion estimation methods directly model the pixel displacements on the image plane, and define a single, fixed distortion map for a given camera. In contrast, our model estimates the distortion map by explicitly modeling the refractive material and using a ray-tracing. We consider this advantageous since the – usually separate directional distortions – are given a unified and *consistent* generative model. A consequence is that the physical model introduces a depth-dependent component in the distortion map, where the distance of a 3D point has to be known in order to find the image distortion, that is usually expressed in pixels.

In order to compute the image distortion vector, we start from a distorted pixel on the image. Using the distorted pixel $\boldsymbol{p}_d$, we use the ray-casting algorithm to obtain a 3D coordinate $\boldsymbol{x}_t$ of the object point at a given distance. The undistorted pixel coordinates $\boldsymbol{p}_u$ for an object point can be computed using the pinhole camera model. The distortion vector $\varDelta\boldsymbol{p}$ for a given pixel $\boldsymbol{p}_d$ is

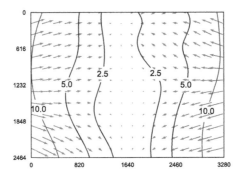

Fig. 7. Distortion vectors for Set 1 for a fixed object distance of 1 m with contour lines for distortions of 2.5, 5, and 10 pixels. The curvature of the cone shaped glass object introduces large horizontal distortions on the two lateral image sides.

given by the difference between the distorted and undistorted coordinates, i.e. $\Delta p = p_u - p_d$.

Figure 7 shows the image distortion vector field using the optimal parameters for the images from Set 1. To better visualize our model and to be able to compute a distortion field, we fixed the object distance to 1 m for the whole scene; this is comparable to the range of the calibration objects on the images. Rays corresponding to the middle pixels are almost orthogonal to the refractive surface, resulting in little or no distortion, while the rays located on the two lateral sides have a large angle compared to the surface normal, resulting in large refraction and large image distortions.

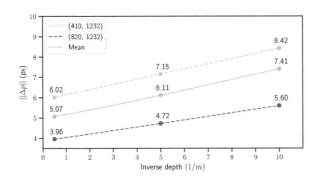

Fig. 8. Individual and average pixel distortions as a function of the *inverse depth*. We see a linear dependence between the inverse depth and the distortion norm.

A consequence of the physical *generative* model is the possibility to inspect the dependence of the distortions on pixel depth, as shown in Fig. 8. The image shows the change of distortion norm for two individual pixels with coordinates $(820, 1232)$ and $(410, 1232)$, as well as the change of the mean distortion norm.

We can observe, that the distortion norm shows a linear dependence on the inverse depth of the pixel. The figure shows the distortions for the inverse depth interval of 0.5 (corresponding to a depth of 2 m) to 10 (depth of 10 cm). We can also observe that the slope of the line showing the change of distortion increases as we get closer to the edges of the image, where the change of distortion is 2.4 pixels over the analyzed interval, compared to the change of 1.64 pixels for the point closer to the image center.

7   Conclusions

In our work we presented a model for geometric image distortions caused by refractive surfaces being placed between the camera and the scene. Based on an explicit model of the refractive surface, we presented a forward generative model of the distortions and the image generation; the generating process used the ray-casting mechanism. We assumed a conic refractive surface and used an additive model for the imperfections of the surface; the used model was a restricted Radial Basis Function network. Using model inversion and automated differentiation, we estimated the refractive surface with a set of checkerboard calibration target images. We validated our algorithm on synthetic and real-world data, and analyzed the observed image distortions.

The benefit of the method is that the model we proposed *is parametric*: despite being strongly non-linear and complex, using a small set of calibration images, the algorithm is able to find the global distortion map. A second important aspect is that the data collection methodology allows for heterogeneous data: by estimating the view angles, we can use the *whole* dataset for estimation.

A weak limitation of our method is the fixed base shape, which in the current formulation was a cone. We chose this shape as it was the closest to the actual object used in the experiments. A work-around to the strict constraint of the shape is to parameterize it and – added to the parameters of the irregularities – to optimize for an extended set of parameters. Evidently, as the number of free parameters grows, this introduces further modeling difficulties, as the degree of freedom increases and the optimization can be much harder.

Future work will focus on (1) developing a model that is general enough to be suitable for a wide range of applications without significant changes, and (2) will explore whether there is a possibility for our method to infer distortions using other types of inputs to the system. An extension possibility is to use – under specific constraints – other data, like the estimated optical flows with certain constraints on the collection procedure.

References

1. Agrawal, A., Ramalingam, S., Taguchi, Y., Chari, V.: A theory of multi-layer flat refractive geometry. In: 2012 IEEE Conference on Computer Vision and Pattern Recognition (CVPR), pp. 3346–3353. IEEE (2012). https://doi.org/10.1109/CVPR.2012.6248073

2. Bishop, C.: Pattern Recognition and Machine Learning. Springer, New York (2006)
3. Brown, D.C.: Decentering distortion of lenses. Photogram. Eng. Remote Sens. **32**(3), 444–462 (1966)
4. Cefalu, A., Haala, N., Fritsch, D.: Structureless bundle adjustment with self-calibration using accumulated constraints. ISPRS Ann. Photogram. Remote Sens. Spatial Inf. Sci. **3**(3), 3–9 (2016). https://doi.org/10.5194/isprs-annals-iii-3-3-2016
5. Chari, V., Sturm, P.: Multiple-view geometry of the refractive plane. In: BMVC 2009-20th British Machine Vision Conference, pp. 1–11. The British Machine Vision Association (BMVA) (2009). https://doi.org/10.5244/c.23.56
6. Claus, D., Fitzgibbon, A.W.: A rational function lens distortion model for general cameras. In: 2005 IEEE Computer Society Conference on Computer Vision and Pattern Recognition (CVPR 2005), vol. 1, pp. 213–219. IEEE (2005). https://doi.org/10.1109/cvpr.2005.43
7. Devernay, F., Faugeras, O.: Straight lines have to be straight. Mach. Vis. Appl. **13**(1), 14–24 (2001). https://doi.org/10.1007/pl00013269
8. Fitzgibbon, A.W.: Simultaneous linear estimation of multiple view geometry and lens distortion. In: Proceedings of the 2001 IEEE Computer Society Conference on Computer Vision and Pattern Recognition, CVPR 2001, vol. 1, pp. I-125–I-132. IEEE (2001). https://doi.org/10.1109/CVPR.2001.990465
9. Grossberg, M.D., Nayar, S.K.: The raxel imaging model and ray-based calibration. Int. J. Comput. Vision **61**(2), 119–137 (2005). https://doi.org/10.1023/b:visi.0000043754.56350.10
10. Hartley, R., Kang, S.B.: Parameter-free radial distortion correction with center of distortion estimation. IEEE Trans. Pattern Anal. Mach. Intell. **29**(8), 1309–1321 (2007). https://doi.org/10.1109/iccv.2005.184
11. Haykin, S.O.: Neural Networks and Learning Machines, 3rd edn. Pearson Education, London (2009)
12. Morinaka, S., Sakaue, F., Sato, J., Ishimaru, K., Kawasaki, N.: 3D reconstruction under light ray distortion from parametric focal cameras. Pattern Recogn. Lett. 16–54 (2018). https://doi.org/10.1016/j.patrec.2018.11.007
13. Park, J., Sandberg, I.W.: Universal approximation using radial-basis-function networks. Neural Comput. **3**(2), 246–257 (1991). https://doi.org/10.1162/neco.1991.3.2.246
14. Paszke, A., et al.: Automatic differentiation in pytorch. In: NIPS-W (2017)
15. Pharr, M., Jakob, W., Humphreys, G.: Physically Based Rendering: From Theory to Implementation. Morgan Kaufmann, Burlington (2016). https://doi.org/10.1016/c2013-0-15557-2
16. Sturm, P., Ramalingam, S.: A generic concept for camera calibration. In: Pajdla, T., Matas, J. (eds.) ECCV 2004. LNCS, vol. 3022, pp. 1–13. Springer, Heidelberg (2004). https://doi.org/10.1007/978-3-540-24671-8_1
17. Szeliski, R.: Computer vision: algorithms and applications. Springer Science & Business Media (2010). https://doi.org/10.1007/978-1-84882-935-0
18. Tsai, R.: A versatile camera calibration technique for high-accuracy 3D machine vision metrology using off-the-shelf tv cameras and lenses. IEEE Journal on Robotics and Automation **3**(4), 323–344 (1987). https://doi.org/10.1109/JRA.1987.1087109
19. Zhang, Z.: A flexible new technique for camera calibration. IEEE Trans. Pattern Anal. Mach. Intell. **22**, 1330–1334 (2000). https://doi.org/10.1109/34.888718

Eye Movement-Based Analysis on Methodologies and Efficiency in the Process of Image Noise Evaluation

Cheng Peng[1], Qing Xu[1(✉)] [iD], Yuejun Guo[2], and Klaus Schoeffmann[3]

[1] College of Intelligence and Computing, Tianjin University, Tianjin, China
qingxu@tju.edu.cn
[2] Institute of Informatics, University of Girona, Girona, Spain
[3] Institute of Information Technology, Klagenfurt University, Klagenfurt, Austria

Abstract. Noise level (image quality) evaluation is an important and popular topic in many applications. However, the knowledge of how people visually explore distorted images for making decision on noise evaluation is rather limited. In this paper, we conducted psychophysical eye-tracking studies to deeply understand the process of image noise evaluation. We identified two different types of methodologies in the evaluation processing, speed-driven and accuracy-driven respectively, in terms of both evaluation time and decision error. The speed-driven methodology, compared with the accuracy-driven one, uses less time to give evaluation results, with shorter fixation duration and stronger central bias. Furthermore, based on the utilization of temporal-spatial entropy analysis on eye movement data, a quantitative measure is obtained to show significant correlation with the decision-making efficiency of evaluation processing, which is characterized by evaluation time and decision error. As a result, the new measure may be used as a proxy definition for this decision-making efficiency.

Keywords: Noise level evaluation ·
Temporal-spatial entropy analysis · Reduced redundant information ·
Decision-making efficiency

1 Introduction

In multimedia processing domain, impulse noise is an important and widely researched issue [1]. However, the knowledge of how people explore noisy images and make noise evaluations is rather limited [2]. Eye movement data analysis is a valuable research tool, and it is helpful for us to obtain the knowledge of human

This work has been funded by Natural Science Foundation of China under Grants No. 61471261 and No. 61771335. The author Yuejun Guo acknowledges support from Secretaria dUniversitats i Recerca del Departament dEmpresa i Coneixement de la Generalitat de Catalunya and the European Social Fund.

© Springer Nature Switzerland AG 2019
I. V. Tetko et al. (Eds.): ICANN 2019, LNCS 11729, pp. 29–40, 2019.
https://doi.org/10.1007/978-3-030-30508-6_3

environment interaction [3]. By now, a handful of fundamental and path-breaking psychophysical studies have been conducted to analyze the bottom-up impacts of image noise on eye movement patterns. For instance, in [4] an eye-tracking study discussed the impact of image distortion and content on the viewing behaviors in quality assessment task. The result showed that the image content seems to play a major role compared to the image distortion. Another study indicated that human perceptual processing strategy could change in different external noise level conditions [5]. A research investigation gave the influence of JPEG compression artifacts on saliency and found that higher compression levels impact visual attention more [6]. Also, a recent study discussed the impact of image noise on gaze allocation in assessing image quality [7], and its result indicated that the noise intensity, compared to noise type, has a stronger impact. These empirical findings have made important contributions to understanding eye movement patterns for noise level (image quality) evaluation.

Recently, more and more studies begin to analyze the relationship between top-down impacts and eye movement data in the decision-making process [8,9]. Note that noise evaluation is a kind of decision-making processing, and the top-down analysis on this processing is necessary. However, the studies mentioned above lack top-down analysis of eye movement patterns. In decision-making tasks, including noise evaluation, evaluation time and decision error are two major factors which would indicate the information processing methodologies influencing how people make their decisions [9]. Few works have analyzed the differences between eye movement patterns corresponding to different evaluation methodologies. Moreover, the decision-making efficiency, which is characterized by evaluation time and decision error, have rarely been discussed in the process of image noise.evaluation. The knowledge of the correlation between the decision-making efficiency and eye movement data is few touched.

In this paper, based on the combination of temporal and spatial dimensions, we utilize temporal-spatial entropy analysis to provide enough insights for understanding the process of impulse image noise evaluation. Two different types of evaluation methodologies, speed-driven and accuracy-driven, are identified and their different eye movement patterns are analyzed. More importantly, we found that eye movement data shows significant correlation with decision-making efficiency of evaluation processing. As a result, we obtain a quantitative measure which may be a proxy for this decision-making efficiency.

This paper is organized as follows: Sect. 1 shows the introduction. Section 2 explains the experiment we conducted. The gaze data analysis is presented in Sect. 3. Discussion and conclusion are provided in Sects. 4 and 5, respectively.

2   Psychophysical Method

2.1   Participants

Thirty students (14 female; age range: 21–29, Mean = 23.4, SD = 1.56) from Tianjin University volunteered to participate in this study. All participants had

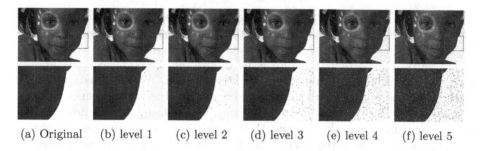

(a) Original   (b) level 1   (c) level 2   (d) level 3   (e) level 4   (f) level 5

Fig. 1. Examples of original image and its five noisy level variants.

normal/corrected-to-normal visual acuity and normal color vision, and they were inexperienced to the study.

2.2 Stimuli

Original images along with impulse noise distortion images (distortion type No. 6) in dataset TID2013 [10] were chosen as our experiment materials (see Fig. 1 for examples). The dataset contains 25 original images and its impulse noise distortion has five levels. One original image and its five noisy variants were randomly chosen from the dataset for training session. Five noisy variants of the remaining 24 original images (five noise levels) set up our stimuli set with totally 120 images for testing session.

2.3 Procedure

If participants have viewed multiple variations of the same original image, carryover effects would cause biased gaze data [2]. To avoid undesirable effects that would potentially influence the result, we randomly assigned five noisy images of each original image to five different partitions. In this case, each original image in one partition has only one noisy variant. Participants were randomly divided into five groups of equal size, and the five groups of participants were then randomly assigned to evaluate five partitions. As a result, each participant evaluated only one noisy variant of the same original image and each noise image was evaluated by six participants. In this paper, a trial represents the eye movement data recorded per participant per noise image. Totally, we got 720 trials.

The eye-tracking system (7INVENSUN Instrument aGlass DKII) was used for data collection, with a 90 Hz sampling rate and a gaze position accuracy of 0.5°. In this paper, one degree of visual angle represents 12 pixels. Before the experiment, each participant was introduced with the study purpose and procedure of the experiment. A 9-point calibration was taken for each participant. After that, a training session was carried out for participants to get familiar with the whole evaluation procedure. The training session was repeatable if desired by a participant. When participants were ready, the testing session started. The testing session was divided into 24 subtasks. In one single subtask, one of the original images was presented for 10 s firstly followed by a white blank picture for 2 s. After that, only one noisy variant of the current original image was shown for at most 10 s. The participants were asked to give the subjective perceived noise level and meanwhile, the evaluation time was recorded. When evaluation results were given, the noisy images disappeared immediately. If participants did not give their evaluation results in 10 s, the noisy image disappeared automatically and participants were asked to give their evaluations. The rating results of the perceived image noise levels range from 1 (least) to 5 (most). The next subtask started when the participant was ready. Each participant made evaluations, in all, on 24 noise images.

3   Gaze Data Analysis

3.1   Temporal-Spatial Entropy Analysis Method

Spatial gaze allocation reveals human attention distribution and it is widely researched in the works mentioned above. Fixation map is a widely used tool to analyze the spatial distribution of gaze allocation. In this paper, we made aggregation of all the fixations to obtain a single gaze allocation map for the evaluation processing per participant per noise image. A Gaussian kernel filter with a standard deviation of 1° of visual angle was applied when producing the map. All maps were normalized, resulting in probability density functions. After that, the gaze allocation map entropy was computed as the definition of Shannon entropy [11]:

$$H = -\sum_{x \in \chi} p(x) \log_2 p(x), \tag{1}$$

where χ is the set of all spatial locations in the image, and $p(x)$ is the spatial probability distribution of gaze allocation. For each participant, 24 gaze allocation map entropies were obtained. Actually, the Aggregation Entropy (AE) of each participant was defined by calculating an arithmetic average for 24 gaze allocation map entropies. Based on the information theory, entropy is a measure of the amount of information [11,12]. In fact, this AE indicates the effective information a participant consumes for using informative noise feature to obtain evaluation results, because image noise influences human gaze allocation in image noise evaluation [7].

Actually, people need a period of time to give their evaluations, and the evolution of gaze allocation over time could reveal the human perceptual processing of noise level evaluation. In this case, fixation map can evolve over time, resulting in map sequences [13]. In this paper, we calculated the entropy of each item in the map sequence to generate the temporal-spatial entropy plot (TSEP) for describing the evolution of gaze allocation over time:

$$H(t) = -\sum_{x \in \chi} p_t(x) \log_2 p_t(x), \tag{2}$$

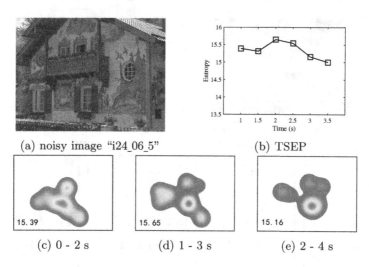

(a) noisy image "i24_06_5"   (b) TSEP

15. 39   15. 65   15. 16

(c) 0 - 2 s   (d) 1 - 3 s   (e) 2 - 4 s

Fig. 2. A participant (No. 10, belonging to speed-driven methodology group) was evaluating a noisy image (a) with high temporal-spatial entropy (b), and had relatively dispersed gaze allocation all the time (c–e).

where χ is the set of all spatial locations in the image, and $p_t(x)$ is the spatial probability distribution of gaze allocation in the time interval $[t - \Delta t, t + \Delta t]$. To this end, we have drawn the map sequences from raw data recorded over a sliding 2-s window (i.e. $\Delta t = 1$) at 0.5-s time step size for each participant per noise image. All maps were smoothed by a Gaussian kernel filter and then normalized. After that, we calculated the entropy of each normalized map as Eq. 2 and obtained a TSEP. For all 720 trials, we computed their temporal-spatial entropy and obtained 720 TSEPs. The mean entropy of a TSEP is the mean value of all entropies of this plot. This mean entropy represents the statistical dispersion of the gaze allocation during noise evaluation per participant per image. As mentioned in Sect. 2.3, each participant made evaluations on 24 noise images and obtained 24 TSEPs. For each participant, an arithmetic average for the mean entropy values of the 24 TSEPs was obtained, called Evaluation Entropy (EE) in this paper. This EE represents the amount of information of fixation distribution during the processing of noise evaluation.

For exemplification, there are two typical trials shown in Figs. 2 and 3. These two figures display TSEPs and heatmaps resulted from the map sequences respectively by participant No. 10 on the image "i24_06_5" and by No. 5 on "i24_06_2". The warmer color area has higher probability of gaze allocation. For the sake of clarity, we do not show all the maps, and we present them in a temporally uniform sampling way. Two temporal-spatial entropy plots are shown in Figs. 2b and 3b. Each point in TSEP, presented in the lower left corner of each heatmap figure, represents the degree of dispersion of gaze allocation within a certain time interval. For instance, in Fig. 2b, the first point at 1 s gives the temporal-spatial entropy value of the map in the 0–2 s interval (Fig. 2c). The

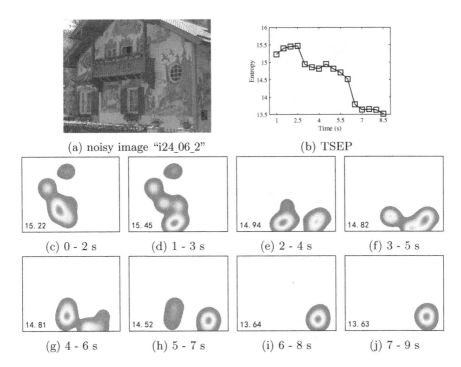

Fig. 3. A participant (No. 5, belonging to accuracy-driven methodology group) was evaluating a noisy image (a) with temporal-spatial entropy decreasing from high to low (b), and his gaze allocation changed from dispersion to concentration (c–j).

length of the TSEP points out the evaluation time. The longer the plot, the longer the evaluation time. As we can see in Fig. 2c–e, participant No. 10 generated relatively dispersed gaze allocations while doing the evaluation. Whereas the gaze allocations of participant No. 5 changed from dispersion to concentration, see Figs. 3c–j.

3.2   Speed-Driven and Accuracy-Driven Methodologies

Evaluation time and decision error are two impact factors on the human performance of image noise evaluation [9]. People need to make choices for obtaining a trade-off between these two factors. For each participant, we calculate their average evaluation time, and Root Mean Squared Error between subjective perceived image noise level and the actual noise level. Decision error of evaluation processing is characterized by the Root Mean Squared Error. All the evaluation performances of participants, along with the limit situation (i.e. the values of evaluation time and decision error are equal to zero), were presented in Fig. 4a (yellow point denotes the limit situation). Evaluation time and decision error were standardized by min-max normalization. In this case, depending on whether time or accuracy the participants focus on, participants data

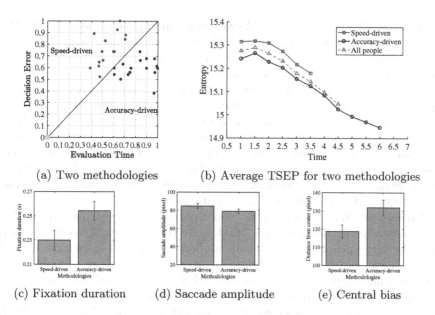

(a) Two methodologies   (b) Average TSEP for two methodologies

(c) Fixation duration   (d) Saccade amplitude   (e) Central bias

Fig. 4. Identification (a), average TSEP (b) and eye movement statistic features (c–e) for different evaluation methodologies. Error bars represent standard error of mean. (Color figure online)

can be divided into two groups, which indicate two evaluation methodologies, speed-driven and accuracy-driven, respectively (see Fig. 4a). People adopting the speed-driven methodology tend to finish the task quickly, whereas those using the accuracy-driven methodology are willing to spend more time ensuring the accuracy of the answer.

The gaze patterns of two different types of evaluation methodologies were analyzed for statistical significance. One-way ANOVAs with different gaze statistic features were conducted and some significant differences in gaze statistic features were found between different evaluation methodologies. Note that Welch's ANOVA was applied when the data show a lot of heteroscedasticity. We used the fixation distance from image center to describe the feature of central bias, as usually done in [7]. The results demonstrated that participants with different evaluation methodologies have different fixation durations (F $(1, 28) = 4.74$, $p < 0.05$; Fig. 4c) and central bias (F $(1, 28) = 5.18$, $p < 0.05$; Fig. 4e). There is no significant difference, however, in saccade amplitude (F $(1, 28) = 2.32$, $p = 0.14$; Fig. 4d). Actually, when people use speed-driven methodology, they have shorter fixation durations and stronger central bias, compared to those utilizing accuracy-driven methodology.

We made use of the average temporal-spatial entropy plot to understand the temporal evolution of gaze allocation for different evaluation methodologies. We draw the average TSEP of each group of people adopting different evaluation methodologies (the solid line) and the average TSEP of all participants is also shown in Fig. 4b (the broken line). As we can see in Fig. 4b, the average TSEP of the speed-driven methodology group indicates relatively high temporal-spatial entropy value. This means that participants in this group have dispersed gaze allocation in most of the time and make evaluations quickly. Also, the average TSEP of the accuracy-driven methodology group is longer. Entropy is relatively high in the beginning of evaluation process and decreases over time. This shows that participants in this group have long evaluation time and their gaze allocations change from dispersion to concentration. Actually, people adopting speed-driven methodology have higher entropy and more dispersed gaze allocation than those who utilizing accuracy-driven methodology in the process of noise evaluation. Note that these two evaluation methodologies belong to a kind of top-down impact to modulate the eye movement patterns.

Participants No. 10 and No. 5, whose corresponding eye movement data are respectively visualized in Figs. 2 and 3, are two representatives respectively belonging to two people groups dependent upon two different evaluation methodologies. Participant No. 10 relied on speed-driven methodology to make evaluations and had dispersed gaze allocation with strong central bias (see Fig. 2). Participant No. 5 employed accuracy-driven methodology for evaluation, and his gaze allocation was dispersed in the beginning and then became gradually concentrated to some local region far from image center (see Fig. 3).

3.3   Decision-Making Efficiency and Reduced Redundant Information

Decision-Making Efficiency. To assess the performance of noise evaluation, we define the decision-making efficiency for the evaluation, inspired by the efficiency definition of Monte Carlo estimation [14]:

$$Efficiency = \frac{1}{Error \cdot Time}, \tag{3}$$

where $Error$ and $Time$ represent decision error and evaluation time, respectively. Decision-making efficiency values of participants are shown in Fig. 5a, and note that the efficiency of the limit situation is of the value of infinity (yellow point).

Reduced Redundant Information. The process of noise evaluation is described by temporal and spatial fixation distribution involving the information gathered by participants during the whole evaluation. This gathered information can be actually defined by EE. Importantly, noise evaluation can be considered as the processing of extracting the most effective information, which can be essentially characterized by AE, for obtaining the final evaluation result. In the mean time, this evaluation can also be deemed as the processing for reducing the statistical redundancy [8,15]. As a result, In the process of noise evaluation, we define a quantitative measure, so-called Reduced Redundant Information (RRI), by combing EE and AE:

$$RRI = EE - AE. \tag{4}$$

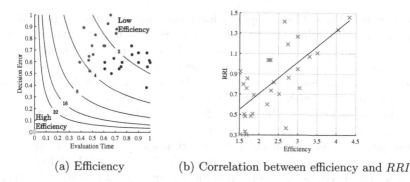

(a) Efficiency   (b) Correlation between efficiency and RRI

Fig. 5. Contour map of decision-making efficiency(a), its correlation with RRI(b). (Color figure online)

RRI can be described as how much ineffective information a participant reduces in the process of noise evaluation, implying the efficiency of evaluation processing.

Correlation Analysis. Because RRI represents a kind of efficiency, we hypothesize that RRI should be a proxy of the decision-making efficiency. To validate this hypothesis, we analyze the correlation between decision-making efficiency and RRI by using the Pearson linear correlation coefficient (PLCC), Spearman rank order correlation coefficient (SROCC) and Kendall rank order correlation coefficient (KROCC). The results of correlation analysis are shown in Table 1 and Fig. 5b. The results demonstrate the significant correlation between decision-making efficiency and RRI. This finding suggests that the RRI may be a proxy of decision-making efficiency.

Table 1. Correlation analysis

	Correlation coefficient	p-value
PLCC	0.71	< 0.0005
SROCC	0.67	< 0.0005
KROCC	0.49	< 0.0005

4 Discussion

In this study, we analyzed the evaluation methodologies and decision-making efficiency in the process of the impulse noise level evaluation. To this end, a well-designed psychophysical experiment is needed to avoid as many interferences as possible. As mentioned above, top-down impacts significantly affect human gaze behaviors. If participants have not ever seen the original image without noise, which helps understand the content, it is hard to guarantee that participants would focus on the evaluation task. In this case, we ask the participants to observe the original image. Also, people basically strive to make good decisions. When time constraint exists, people will tend to use different strategies/methodologies to finish the task [9]. As a result, we use a time constraint when evaluating noise level, which is helpful for investigating the methodologies and efficiency of noise evaluation processing.

In this paper, in terms of both evaluation time and decision error, we identified two top-down methodologies for noise evaluation. Two methodologies have shown clear differences in their corresponding eye movement patterns. As shown in Fig. 4, people employing speed-driven methodology make their evaluations more quickly with shorter fixation duration, compared to those using accuracy-driven methodology. Note that, they may focus on central region of images to get overall perceptions when evaluating the image noise level. In contrast, those who adopting accuracy-driven methodology may be more willing to ensure the accuracy of their answer, which certainly leads to more time consumption. Their gaze allocations would finally gather to a small region, which may far away from image center (see Fig. 3), for focused perceptions. Furthermore, the average TSEP of speed-driven methodology is higher than that of accuracy-driven methodology (see Fig. 4b), which means people adopting speed-driven methodology have higher entropy and gather more information than those who utilizing accuracy-driven methodology during the evaluation processing. People using speed-driven methodology may be willing to gather as much information as possible and make their decision within a short time. In contrast, people adopting accuracy-driven methodology may pay more attention to some local areas. These results demonstrated that the top-down methodologies can modulate the eye movement pattern and give us deep insights into the top-down impacts.

Moreover, we took a further step for understanding the process of noise evaluation. We utilized the temporal-spatial entropy analysis method to obtain the correlation between decision-making efficiency and eye movement data. We defined a measure, the so-called Reduced Redundant Information (RRI), which shows significant correlation with decision-making efficiency. Human vision system employs the reduction of information redundancy to well interact with stimuli [15]. In this case, RRI can be described as the amount of redundant information reduced in the process of noise evaluation. In other word, it reflects the human ability to reduce redundant information for completing the task. The more redundant information is reduced, the stronger the ability a human being has and the higher decision-making efficiency is. Therefore, we speculate that RRI may be a proxy for decision-making efficiency.

Evaluation strategies and decision-making efficiency may reveal different human personalities and abilities. It will help us build more detailed cognitive models and realize more accurate personalized recommendation and services. It should be noticed that our work is to analyze methodologies and efficiency in the process of noise evaluation. We admit that our results may not be substantial for all cases, but it does work for impulse noise level evaluation. More importantly, we believe that our work is instructive and may be suitable for more kinds of decision-making tasks.

5   Conclusion

In this study, we conducted psychophysical eye-tracking experiments and utilized temporal-spatial entropy analysis on eye movement data to deeply understand how and how efficient people do evaluations for impulse noise of image. We obtained two evaluation methodologies, speed-driven and accuracy-driven, based on evaluation time and decision error. Moreover, we proposed Reduced Redundant Information (RRI) to describe how much redundant information a human being reduces in the process of noise evaluation. Importantly, We found that the decision-making efficiency shows significant correlation with RRI in evaluation processing.

In the near future, we will additionally exploit low-level image features, for combining both top-down and bottom-up impacts to gain more insights into the noise evaluation processing. Also, we will discuss the top-down impacts in other real-life decision-making situations, for instance, driving tasks.

References

1. Xu, Q., Li, Y., Guo, Y., Wu, S., Sbert, M.: Random-valued impulse noise removal using adaptive ranked-ordered impulse detector. J. Electron. Imaging **27**(1), 013001 (2018). https://doi.org/10.1117/1.JEI.27.1.013001
2. Zhang, W., Liu, H.: Learning picture quality from visual distraction: psychophysical studies and computational models. Neurocomputing **247**, 183–191 (2017). https://doi.org/10.1016/j.neucom.2017.03.054
3. Holmqvist, K., Nyström, M., Andersson, R., Dewhurst, R., Jarodzka, H., Van de Weijer, J.: Eye Tracking: A Comprehensive Guide to Methods and Measures. OUP, Oxford (2011). ISBN 9780199697083
4. Engelke, U., Zepernick, H.J., Maeder, A.: Visual fixation patterns in subjective quality assessment: the relative impact of image content and structural distortions. In: 2010 International Symposium on Intelligent Signal Processing and Communication Systems (ISPACS), pp. 1–4. IEEE (2010). https://doi.org/10.1109/ispacs.2010.5704603
5. Allard, R., Cavanagh, P.: Different processing strategies underlie voluntary averaging in low and high noise. J. Vision **12**(11), 6–6 (2012). https://doi.org/10.1167/12.11.6
6. Min, X., Zhai, G., Gao, Z., Hu, C.: Influence of compression artifacts on visual attention. In: 2014 IEEE International Conference on Multimedia and Expo (ICME), pp. 1–6. IEEE (2014). https://doi.org/10.1109/icme.2014.6890189
7. Röhrbein, F., Goddard, P., Schneider, M., James, G., Guo, K.: How does image noise affect actual and predicted human gaze allocation in assessing image quality? Vision. Res. **112**, 11–25 (2015). https://doi.org/10.1016/j.visres.2015.03.029
8. Shiferaw, B., Downey, L., Crewther, D.: A review of gaze entropy as a measure of visual scanning efficiency. Neurosci. Biobehav. Rev. **96**, 353–366 (2019). https://doi.org/10.1016/j.neubiorev.2018.12.007

9. Shojaeizadeh, M., Djamasbi, S., Paffenroth, R.C., Trapp, A.C.: Detecting task demand via an eye tracking machine learning system. Decis. Support Syst. **116**, 91–101 (2019). https://doi.org/10.1016/j.dss.2018.10.012

10. Ponomarenko, N., et al.: Image database TID2013: peculiarities, results and perspectives. Sig. Process. Image Commun. **30**, 57–77 (2015). https://doi.org/10.1016/j.image.2014.10.009

11. Shannon, C.E.: A mathematical theory of communication. Bell Syst. Tech. J. **27**(3), 379–423 (1948). https://doi.org/10.1002/j.1538-7305.1948.tb01338.x

12. Feixas, M., Bardera, A., Rigau, J., Xu, Q., Sbert, M.: Information theory tools for image processing. Synth. Lect. Comput. Graph. Animation **6**(1), 1–164 (2014). https://doi.org/10.2200/S00560ED1V01Y201312CGR015

13. Wooding, D.S.: Fixation maps: quantifying eye-movement traces. In: Proceedings of the 2002 Symposium on Eye Tracking Research & Applications, pp. 31–36. ACM (2002). https://doi.org/10.1145/507072.507078

14. Hammersley, J.: Monte Carlo Methods. Springer, London (2013). https://doi.org/10.1007/978-94-009-5819-7

15. Simoncelli, E.P., Olshausen, B.A.: Natural image statistics and neural representation. Annu. Rev. Neurosci. **24**(1), 1193–1216 (2001). https://doi.org/10.1146/annurev.neuro.24.1.1193

IBDNet: Lightweight Network for On-orbit Image Blind Denoising

Ling Li[1,2]([⊠]), Junxing Hu[1,2], Yijun Lin[1,2], Fengge Wu[2], and Junsuo Zhao[2]

[1] University of Chinese Academy of Sciences, Beijing, China
`liling2017@iscas.ac.cn`
[2] Institute of Software Chinese Academy of Sciences (ISCAS), Beijing, China

Abstract. To reduce the data transmission pressure from the satellite to the ground, it is meaningful to process the image directly on the satellite. As the cornerstone of image processing, image denoising exceedingly improves the image quality to contribute to subsequent works. For on-orbit image denoising, we propose an end-to-end trainable image blind denoising network, namely IBDNet. Unlike existing image denoising methods, which either have a large number of parameters or are unable to perform image blind denoising, the proposed network is lightweight due to the residual bottleneck blocks as the main structure. Although our network does not use clean images for training, the experimental results on the public datasets indicate that the blindly denoised image quality of our method can be roughly the same as that of the state-of-the-art denoisers. Furthermore, we deploy the model (513 KB only) on the same equipment as the one on a satellite, which verifies the feasibility of running on the satellite.

Keywords: Image blind denoising · Lightweight ·
Residual bottleneck block

1 Introduction

Remote sensing image processing is always a popular topic, as it can extract large amounts of valuable information. However, not all images captured by the satellite are valuable, for example, some images are severely damaged and can not be restored. So we can process the images on the satellite and only transmit the valuable results after processing to the ground to reduce the transmission pressure.

Image denoising is the basis of other image processing, we conduct on-orbit image denoising research on the TianZhi-1 satellite which is a software-defined satellite. As the first technical verification satellite of the "TianZhi" series, TianZhi-1 is equipped with four reinforced Android smart-phones and has been launched on November 2018. Compared to general image denoising, there are three differences in on-orbit image denoising. One is the lack of clean training

© Springer Nature Switzerland AG 2019
I. V. Tetko et al. (Eds.): ICANN 2019, LNCS 11729, pp. 41–52, 2019.
https://doi.org/10.1007/978-3-030-30508-6_4

data. Imaging on satellites has a high cost and is prone to external environmental disturbances, such as the illumination, atmosphere and cosmic materials. The other is the limited computational capability. Due to limitations in size and weight, it is impossible to equip satellites with computing resources as advanced as those on the ground, in our research, our computing resources is the smartphone equipped on TianZhi-1. The third is the low upload speed. According to our previous records, in the absence of errors, it took about 6 days to upload a 150 KB file to TianZhi-1, so it is meaningless to upload a large model to the satellite.

In this paper, taking into account the situations of TianZhi-1 as above, we design a network that can balance parameters and image denoising quality. We make some modifications on the residual neural network [1] to reduce the parameters of the network without impacting the image denoising performance. Our network has three contributions:

(1) The network is lightweight. This property is an indispensable requirement for on-orbit image denoising. Our proposed network has much fewer parameters than the current excellent image denoising networks (UNet [13] and RED30 [10]). This determines the smaller size and the less floating point operations (FLOPs) of our model, making it possible to upload to TianZhi-1 and run on it.
(2) Clean images are not required. We add noise to both the input image and the target image, make the model trained by noisy-noisy image pairs.
(3) Noisy images are blindly denoised. Neither inputting the noise level nor using a sub-network to estimate the noise level, our model is capable of being adaptable to different noise levels. In other words, our model can directly remove the noise by simply inputting a noisy image of any noise level.

The rest of the paper is organized as follows. Section 2 introduces some related works. Section 3 details our method. And the experiment results are shown in Sect. 4. Finally, Sect. 5 concludes this paper.

2   Related Work

In this section, we briefly introduce previous work on image denoising. From the perspective of image denoising principle, there are three common categories: filter-based, sparse representation and external priori.

Filter-based methods are the most traditional, they denoise noisy images by designing filters. The early filters mainly focus on local filtering, such as local mean filter, local Laplacian filter. NL-means [2] breaks the tradition and promotes the development of non-local filters. Based on this, BM3D [3] combines the spatial and frequency domains to process noisy images. Sparse representation methods utilize sparsity to constrain images to remove noise. They generally have a dictionary learning process, so a long time is consumed for image denoising.

For example, KSVD [4] uses singular value decomposition (SVD) to update the dictionary.

In recent years, many methods based on deep learning have also been applied to image denoising and most of which belong to the external priori category. The general image denoising networks are trained to map the noisy input image to a clean image. The process can be seen as training a regression model by minimizing the empirical risk as follows:

$$\arg\min_{\theta} \sum_i L(F_\theta(I_i^{NI}), I_i) \tag{1}$$

where I_i^{NI} is the noisy input image and I_i is the corresponding clean image, F_θ means the model with parameters θs, and L is the loss function. However, most models can not blindly denoise noisy images, they train a specific noise model for a specific noise level, such as MLP [5], CSF [6] and TNRD [7]. And some improved models handle a wide range of noise levels, such as DnCNN [8], FFDNet [9] and RED-Net [10], but the noise level needs to be input into the network as a priori knowledge when denoising a noisy image. Chen et al. [11] use an extra network to evaluate the image noise level before non-blind denoising, namely GCBD. This structure leads to a complex model with a large number of parameters, insulting a large amount of calculation, which is not suitable for the satellite environment analyzed earlier. It is worth mentioning that the above deep learning models are trained by using clean images as targets. Lehtinen et al. [12] point out image restoration can be implemented by learning from noisy images, as long as some statistical values of the noisy images can minimize Eq. 1. UNet [13] and RED30 are used to support the feasibility of the theory.

Our previous work [14] analyzes in detail some outstanding image denoising methods (both blind and non-blind) in these three categories and experimentally concludes that the BM3D can perform best in image denoising quality. But BM3D is a non-blind denoiser and has a large computations, it consumes about 100 MB memory at denoising a 512×512-pixel image while our model only takes 13.45 MB memory (details in Sect. 4.4), meanwhile, most of the deep neural networks are either not lightweight enough for on-orbit image denoising or can not achieve image blind denoising.

In this paper, we inherit Lehtinen et al. [12] point to study a more lightweight network than UNet and RED30 to achieve the image blind denoising for satellites.

3   Method

The noisy image can be formulated as:

$$I^N = HI + N_n \tag{2}$$

where I represents the clean image, I^N is the corresponding noisy image, H is a linear operator corresponds to the imaging device and N_n is the noise distribution. In our method, we assume the imaging device does not introduce any other

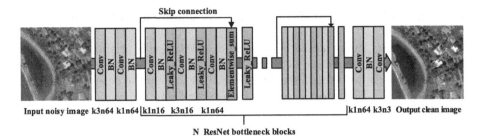

Fig. 1. The architecture of the proposed IBDNet for image blind denoising. The middle part consists of N identical residual bottleneck blocks, and we omit the duplicate blocks. The input is the noisy image without noise priori, and the output is the clean image.

distortions to the image, H reduces to the identity matrix. Since Additive White Gaussian Noise (AWGN) can simulate most of the real noises very well and be used in most image denoising research, N_n refers to AWGN in our research, and the noise level is determined by standard deviation σ in Gaussian function. In this section, we introduce how to make the network lightweight enough to achieve on-orbit image blind denoising.

3.1   Lightweight Image Blind Denoising Architecture

For limited computational capability and low upload speed of the satellite, we propose a lightweight network architecture based on residual bottleneck block [1], namely IBDNet, to perform on-orbit image blind denoising. Figure 1 illustrates the proposed IBDNet architecture, the input is the noisy image and the output is the clean image. The two ends of the network are mainly used to process the input and output of data separately. More specifically, we respectively use a 3×3 convolution layer to accept the noisy image and output the clean image. The accept convolution layer has 64 filters and the output convolution layer has 3 filters (same as the image channel, 1 for gray image and 3 for color image). The two 'Conv k1n64' layers in IBDNet have 64 filters with 1×1 kernel size, which mainly increases the number of non-linear features learned by combining activation functions. The middle part consists of several residual bottleneck blocks as shown in Fig. 2. The depth of the network depends on the value of N which represents the number of residual bottleneck blocks. It is worth mentioning that the size of the input image can be arbitrary because the proposed network is fully convolutional.

In IBDNet, each convolution layer is followed by a batch normalization layer, except the last output convolution layer. We use batch normalization to make the network focus on the relative differences in the images, to accelerate the distinction between noise and real signal. Another powerful choice is to use Leaky ReLU instead of ReLU to prevent some nodes in the network from becoming dead nodes.

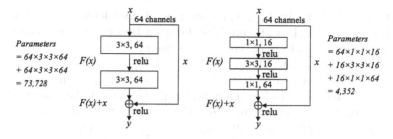

Fig. 2. Conventional residual block (left) and residual bottleneck block (right).

3.2   Parameters Reduction

Image denoising is a pixel-wise prediction process, the network does not need to learn the semantic information of the image. A natural idea is using a lightweight network with fewer parameters to implement the simple image processing task.

The most important structure to make our network be lightweight is the residual bottleneck block in our network. In addition to preventing the network degradation and speeding up training, the main contribution of the residual bottleneck block in IBDNet is to exceedingly reduce the parameters by using 1×1 convolution layers without degrading learning performance. Residual bottleneck block first uses a 1×1 convolution layer to reduce the data channels, then uses a 3×3 convolution layer to process the channel-reduced data, and finally uses a 1×1 convolution layer to restore the data channels. Because the 3×3 convolution layer processes fewer input channels, the residual bottleneck blocks used in IBDNet can greatly decrease the parameters as shown in Fig. 2.

To observe the influence of the channels changing on the network parameters and image denoising quality, we use the conventional residual blocks to replace the residual bottleneck blocks and get another end-to-end blind denoising network, namely IBDNet-c. Table 2 shows the parameters of IBDNet18-c ($N = 18$) are much more than that of IBDNet.

3.3   Learning from Noisy Targets

Limited by the number of clean remote sensing images, it makes sense to exploit noisy images to train a network directly. We follow the basic idea of Noise2Noise [12] to train IBDNet with using noisy-noisy image pairs.

Considering IBDNet maps a pixel to another pixel during image denoising, we choose the pixel-wise mean squared error (MSE) loss to optimize training at each iteration:

$$L_{mse} = \frac{1}{WH} \sum_{x=1}^{W} \sum_{y=1}^{H} (I_{x,y}^{NT} - F_\theta(I^{NI})_{x,y})^2 \qquad (3)$$

where I^{NT} refers to the noisy target image, I^{NI} denotes the noisy input image, W and H are the width and height of the image, and F_θ is our network with parameters θs. Essentially, L_{mse} is the average of pixel-level L_2 loss. For IBD-Net training, using L_2 loss minimization brings a benefit: the prediction keeps unchanged if the original target replaces by some random numbers whose expectation matches the target. That is, if $E\{I^{NT}|I^{NI}\} = I$, where I is the clean image of I^{NI}, IBDNet can be trained by noisy-noisy image pairs, and get the same effect as using noisy-clean pairs training. So, even if the training target image is corrupted by zero-mean noise, the noise level is not necessarily the same as the noisy input image, after training by a large number of noisy-noisy image pairs, IBDNet model can still predict the clean image.

In fact, the L_{mse} does not decrease while training IBDNet, because it can not succeed in transforming one noisy image to another noisy image, and our training goal is not to get a noisy image. Although the loss does not decrease, the network training still can converge fast. Instead of observing the loss decreasing, we choose the average Peak Signal to Noise Ratio (PSNR) of the validation images to determine whether the network training is converged, see Fig. 3.

3.4   Image Blind Denoising

Equation 2 gives two hints to obtain a clean image from the noisy image: one is to learn the noise distribution and then remove it from the noisy image, the other is to learn the clean image directly.

To avoid the impact of noise level changes on model training, we make IBD-Net directly learn the clean signals instead of the noise distributions from the noisy images. Moreover, to enhance the robustness of the model for different noise levels, we make some changes in data training. Considering too high-level noises can seriously damage the image and make it less valuable for research, motivated by [12], we set the AWGN standard deviation $\sigma \in [0, 50]$ to determine the range of our research noise levels. For a clean training image, we add two zero-mean noises with random σ to it separately to form a noisy-noisy image pair. For each epoch, the same clean training image is re-added with a random σ zero-mean noise. Due to the noise level is changed, in the strict sense, the training pairs are different at each epoch, but the clean images are the same. At every iteration, the training image randomly brings a noise level to train the model which strengthens the learning of the network on clean images and increases the network awareness of different level noises. After training, within the range of training noise levels, the model can achieve image blind denoising without giving a noise level priori.

4   Experiments

In this section, we first use noisy-noisy image pairs to conduct experiments on the influence of IBDNet depth on image denoising performance. Then we compare IBDNet with BM3D, UNet and RED30 to verify the image denoising quality. Finally, we apply our lightweight model on the same computation resource on the TianZhi-1 satellite. Specifically, we use a machine with 64 GB RAM, Intel(R)

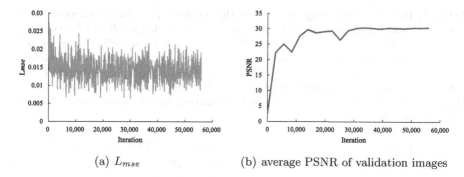

(a) L_{mse} (b) average PSNR of validation images

Fig. 3. Training phase of IBDNet18. L_{mse} does not converge, but the average PSNR of the validation images keeps rising until unchanged.

Xeon(R) E5-2680 @v4 2.40 GHz processor and one NVIDIA TITAN Xp GPU card. And we test the model on an Android smart-phone with 6G RAM, 64G ROM and 8 Snapdragon processors, which is the same as the one equipped on the TianZhi-1 satellite.

4.1 Datasets and Additive White Gaussian Noise

We aim to solve the problem of remote sensing image blind denoising on satellites, so we mainly apply the Inria Aerial Image dataset [22] to our experiments. The dataset has 180 images with size 5000 × 5000-pixel, each image has a 0.3 meters resolution. In order to use the dataset effectively, the original TIF image format is compressed into JPEG format. We extract 4,464 training images with a size of 92 × 92-pixel from the large images and use 416 images with a size of 512 × 512-pixel as the test set (Aerial416). To avoid extreme effects, the average image denoising results of the images in the test set is used to judge the performance of the denoisers. To prove the universality of IBDNet, we also use the DIV2K dataset [23] to train the model and then use it to denoise the well-known dataset BSD100 [24].

We randomize zero-mean AWGN with standard deviation $\sigma \in [0, 50]$ for each training image. Although both the input image and the target image are noisy, their noise levels are not necessarily the same because the σ is randomly assigned. For each image in the test set, we separately add four noise levels ($\sigma = 15, 25, 35$ and 50) of noise to it to form four noisy test images, so one test set can generate four test sets corresponding to four noise levels. We use PSNR and Structural Similarity Index (SSIM) to evaluate the denoised image quality.

4.2 IBDNet Depth Comparison

Both ends of IBDNet architecture shown in Fig. 1 remain unchanged, we focus on the influence of the number (N value) of the residual bottleneck blocks on network performance. After a series of trial experiments, we set $N \in [10, 22]$.

Table 1. IBDNet depth comparison. N is the number of residual bottleneck blocks in the network. PSNR represents the average image denoising results on Aerial416 for each noise level($\sigma = 15, 25, 35, 50$), R1 is the reverse ranking according to the sum of the PSNR for all noise levels, R2 is the ranking based on the parameters(Params) of the network, and ΣR is the sum of R1 and R2. Floating point operations(FLOPs) reflects the amount of computation of the model to denoise a 512×512-pixel image. Model priority (MP) is sorted by ΣR, if two numbers are the same, the model with fewer parameters ranks in front.

N	PSNR					Params		FLOPs(M)	ΣR	MP
	15	25	35	50	R1	VAL	R2			
10	32.56	30.29	28.82	27.31	13	56,323	1	28.92	14	6
11	32.61	30.35	28.87	27.27	12	60,771	2	31.21	14	7
12	32.84	30.49	28.98	27.33	10	65,219	3	33.49	13	2
13	32.89	30.62	29.11	27.47	9	69,667	4	35.77	13	3
14	32.73	30.47	29.10	27.42	11	74,115	5	38.05	16	11
15	32.98	30.61	29.10	27.52	8	78,563	6	40.33	14	8
16	33.06	30.69	29.15	27.51	7	83,011	7	42.61	14	9
17	33.11	30.68	29.13	27.49	6	87,459	8	44.90	14	10
18	**33.13**	**30.77**	**29.28**	**27.73**	**1**	**91,907**	**9**	**47.18**	**10**	**1**
19	33.08	30.71	29.20	27.59	3	96,355	10	49.46	13	4
20	33.13	30.74	29.23	27.69	2	100,803	11	51.74	13	5
21	33.04	30.66	29.15	27.58	5	105,251	12	54.02	17	12
22	33.07	30.68	29.17	27.56	4	109,699	13	56.30	17	13

Because the denoising quality is unsatisfactory when N is too small, on the contrast, if N is too large, the network is so complicated that the NVIDIA TITAN Xp GPU can not bear it, besides, as N increases, the value of PSNR does not increase significantly or even decreases. For each depth, the Aerial training images and Aerial test images (i.e., Aerial416) are used to train and test, respectively. Table 1 illustrates the comparison results. With the increase of N, the parameters and the floating point operations (FLOPs) increase while the PSNR of denoised images is only slightly improved. To find a trade-off between image denoising quality (i.e., PSNR) and parameters (i.e., Params), we propose a simple formula as follows:

$$MP = rank^{\uparrow}_{Params}(rank^{\uparrow}(Params) + rank^{\downarrow}(\sum_{\sigma}(PSNR))) \qquad (4)$$

MP denotes the abbreviation for model priority, the smaller MP value, the higher the priority of the model, $rank^{\uparrow}$ means the ranking from small to large, $rank^{\downarrow}$ means the ranking from large to small, and the subscript $Params$ indicates that if the sum of Params ranking and PSNR ranking is equal, then compare the Params ranking. Specifically, the model with fewer parameters has a

Table 2. Average PSNR(db) and average SSIM(%) on Aerial416 and BSD100. We set four levels ($\sigma = 15, 25, 35, 50$) for zero-mean AWGN.

Method	Params	Metrics	Aerial416				BSD100			
			15	25	35	50	15	25	35	50
IBDNet18(blind, noisy)	**91,907**	PSNR	33.13	30.77	29.28	27.73	32.32	29.92	28.41	26.82
		SSIM	0.91	0.86	0.81	0.75	0.91	0.86	0.81	0.74
IBDNet18(blind, clean)	**91,907**	PSNR	33.22	30.79	29.28	27.69	32.72	30.26	28.67	27.02
		SSIM	0.91	0.86	0.81	0.75	0.91	0.86	0.81	0.74
IBDNet18-c(blind, noisy)	1,340,032	PSNR	33.46	31.02	29.53	28.00	33.26	30.68	29.47	28.01
		SSIM	0.92	0.86	0.82	0.76	0.92	0.87	0.81	0.77
UNet(blind, noisy)	991,203	PSNR	33.01	30.64	29.07	27.37	32.25	29.93	28.40	26.74
		SSIM	0.91	0.85	0.80	0.73	0.91	0.87	0.85	0.76
RED30(blind, noisy)	1,037,507	PSNR	32.34	30.17	28.72	27.16	32.00	29.76	28.23	26.53
		SSIM	0.90	0.85	0.80	0.73	0.92	0.85	0.80	0.73
BM3D(non-blind)	-	PSNR	33.58	30.90	29.18	27.75	33.33	30.51	28.68	27.17
		SSIM	0.94	0.90	0.86	0.82	0.96	0.93	0.90	0.86

higher priority because we want the model to be lightweight, and the model with lower PSNR has a lower priority because we want high PSNR. For the models with different N, we first sum the average PSNR of the four noise levels ($\sigma = 15, 25, 35$ and 50) for each model, then sum their Params ranking and PSNR ranking and rank them by the sum value. The model which has the smallest sum is ranked first and has the highest model priority. If two sum values are equal, the model with fewer parameters ranks in front. Table 1 shows that IBDNet18 ($N = 18$) not only achieves the best PSNR but also has the highest priority.

4.3 Experiments on Noise Removal

By using the same data set as this paper, [14] compares almost 11 outstanding image denoising methods, including non-blind and blind. Its results show that BM3D performs best in traditional methods and UNet and RED30 excel in deep learning methods and can perform blind image denoising. Based on Sect. 4.2 and [14], we further compare IBDNet18 with BM3D, UNet and RED30.

For IBDNet18, we mainly focus on its ability of image blind denoising after training it with noisy-noisy pairs, we also use clean targets to train it to confirm the effect of learning from noisy targets. In Table 2, IBDNet18(blind, clean) is trained by clean targets, while other deep learning methods are trained by noisy targets. Table 2 shows the image denoising average results of these methods on Aerial416 and BSD100. Although the overall image denoising results of IBDNet18-c and IBDNet18 are slightly worse than BM3D, considering the PSNR only, IBDNet18-c is as good as BM3D, and even better when the noise level becomes higher. For IBDNet18(blind, noisy), its performance is better than both UNet and RED30, and is almost equal to IBDNet18(blind, clean), but is slightly worse than IBDNet18-c(blind, noisy), yet its loss is acceptable for lightweight. What is more, we select 2 noisy images from Aerial416 with noisy

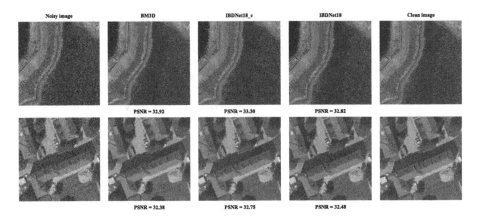

Fig. 4. Example denoised results for images corrupted by AWGN with $\sigma = 25$. Although the average PSNR of BM3D on Aerial416 is better, it does not mean that it has a higher PSNR for each image. IBDNet18-c has a better PSNR than BM3D on the first image, and both IBDNet18-c and IBDNet18 perform better than BM3D on the second image.

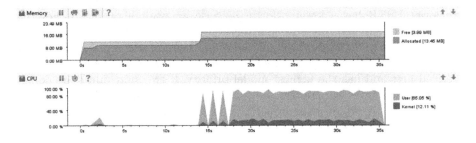

Fig. 5. Performance for image denoising on the same Android smart-phone as the one equipped on TianZhi-1 satellite. At the 14th second, the application starts to denoise a 512×512-pixel image. It costs about 22 s and takes up about 13.45 MB memory during the noise removal.

level $\sigma = 25$ to detail their denoised images in Fig. 4. The figure indicates that even though BM3D has the better average denoised results on Aerial416, it does not mean that it produces better results on every image in Aerial416. For several images, IBDNet18-c and IBDNet18 outperform BM3D.

4.4   Experiment on the TianZhi-1 Satellite Computing Resource

In this section, we pay attention to the time cost and memory consumption of IBDNet18 on image denoising and further deploy it to the Android smart-phone same as the one on TianZhi-1 to blindly denoise the noisy image, the phone is the same as the one equipped on the TianZhi-1 satellite. Before directly deploying the IBDNet18 model to the phone, we first record its image denoising time on

CPUs. By using the same computing resource, the average time IBDNet18 model spends on one image in Aerial416 is 2.70 s, while the BM3D takes 4.68 s.

The size of IBDNet18 model is only 513KB, it is small enough to be transmitted to the TianZhi-1 satellite in an acceptable time (about 20 days), so we further package it into an application and install it into the phone for performance testing. Figure 5 shows that it takes about 22 s to denoise a 512×512-pixel image while consuming 13.45 MB memory on the phone. It shows that our proposed lightweight model is feasible to run on the TianZhi-1 satellite.

5 Conclusion

In this paper, based on the satellite environment, we have proposed a lightweight network architecture for image blind denoising. Residual bottleneck blocks are used to extract clean signals from noisy images and change the channels of the data to reduce parameters required for calculation while processing it. More importantly, we add zero-mean AWGN with random σ to the target image of the training data pair, and use the noisy-noisy pairs to train the model to achieve the effect of automatically recognizing the noise level for the noisy image during denoising. The experimental results show that the image denoising result of our method is almost the same as that of the current excellent methods. What is more, we have successfully deployed our model on the same Android smart-phone equipped on the TianZhi-1 satellite, providing the possibility to blindly denoise image on-orbit.

References

1. He, K., Zhang, X., Ren, S., Sun, J.: Deep residual learning for image recognition. In: Proceedings of the IEEE Conference on Computer Vision and Pattern Recognition, pp. 770–778 (2016). https://doi.org/10.1109/CVPR.2016.90
2. Buades, A., Coll, B., Morel, J.M.: A non-local algorithm for image denoising. In: IEEE Computer Society Conference on Computer Vision and Pattern Recognition, vol. 2, pp. 60–65. IEEE (2005)
3. Dabov, K., Foi, A., Katkovnik, V., Egiazarian, K.: Image denoising by sparse 3-D transform-domain collaborative filtering. IEEE Trans. Image Process. **16**(8), 2080–2095 (2007). https://doi.org/10.1109/TIP.2007.901238
4. Elad, M., Aharon, M.: Image denoising via sparse and redundant representations over learned dictionaries. IEEE Trans. Image Process. **15**(12), 3736–3745 (2006). https://doi.org/10.1109/TIP.2006.881969
5. Burger, H.C., Schuler, C.J., Harmeling, S.: Image denoising: can plain neural networks compete with BM3D? In: IEEE Conference on Computer Vision and Pattern Recognition, pp. 2392–2399. IEEE (2012)
6. Schmidt, U., Roth, S.: Shrinkage fields for effective image restoration. In: Proceedings of the IEEE Conference on Computer Vision and Pattern Recognition, pp. 2774–2781 (2014). https://doi.org/10.1109/CVPR.2014.349
7. Chen, Y., Pock, T.: Trainable nonlinear reaction diffusion: a flexible framework for fast and effective image restoration. IEEE Trans. Pattern Anal. Mach. Intell. **39**(6), 1256–1272 (2017)

8. Zhang, K., Zuo, W., Chen, Y., Meng, D., Zhang, L.: Beyond a Gaussian denoiser: residual learning of deep cnn for image denoising. IEEE Trans. Image Process. **26**(7), 3142–3155 (2017). https://doi.org/10.1109/TIP.2017.2662206

9. Zhang, K., Zuo, W., Zhang, L.: FFDNet: toward a fast and flexible solution for CNN-based image denoising. IEEE Trans. Image Process. **27**(9), 4608–4622 (2018). https://doi.org/10.1109/TIP.2018.2839891

10. Mao, X., Shen, C., Yang, Y.B.: Image restoration using very deep convolutional encoder-decoder networks with symmetric skip connections. In: Advances in Neural Information Processing Systems, pp. 2802–2810 (2016)

11. Chen, J., Chen, J., Chao, H., Yang, M.: Image blind denoising with generative adversarial network based noise modeling. In: Proceedings of the IEEE Conference on Computer Vision and Pattern Recognition, pp. 3155–3164 (2018). https://doi.org/10.1109/CVPR.2018.00333

12. Lehtinen, J., et al.: Noise2noise: learning image restoration without clean data. arXiv preprint arXiv:1803.04189 (2018)

13. Ronneberger, O., Fischer, P., Brox, T.: U-Net: convolutional networks for biomedical image segmentation. In: Navab, N., Hornegger, J., Wells, W.M., Frangi, A.F. (eds.) MICCAI 2015. LNCS, vol. 9351, pp. 234–241. Springer, Cham (2015). https://doi.org/10.1007/978-3-319-24574-4_28

14. Ling, L., Junxing, H., Fengge, W., Junsuo, Z.: A research and strategy of remote sensing image denoising algorithms. arXiv preprint arXiv:1905.10236 (2019)

15. Simonyan, K., Zisserman, A.: Very deep convolutional networks for large-scale image recognition. arXiv preprint arXiv:1409.1556 (2014)

16. LeCun, Y., Bottou, L., Bengio, Y., Haffner, P.: Gradient-based learning applied to document recognition. Proc. IEEE **86**(11), 2278–2324 (1998). https://doi.org/10.1109/5.726791

17. Lin, M., Chen, Q., Yan, S.: Network in network. arXiv preprint arXiv:1312.4400 (2013)

18. Szegedy, C., Liu, W., Jia, Y., et al.: Going deeper with convolutions. In: Proceedings of the IEEE Conference on Computer Vision and Pattern Recognition, pp. 1–9 (2015)

19. Maas, A.L., Hannun, A.Y., Ng, A.Y.: Rectifier nonlinearities improve neural network acoustic models. In: International Conference on Machine Learning, vol. 30, no. 1, p. 3 (2013)

20. Kim, J., Kwon Lee, J., Mu Lee, K.: Deeply-recursive convolutional network for image super-resolution. In: Proceedings of the IEEE Conference on Computer Vision and Pattern Recognition, pp. 1637–1645 (2016). https://doi.org/10.1109/CVPR.2016.181

21. Ioffe, S., Szegedy, C.: Batch normalization: accelerating deep network training by reducing internal covariate shift. arXiv preprint arXiv:1502.03167 (2015)

22. Maggiori, E., Tarabalka, Y., Charpiat, G., Alliez, P.: Can semantic labeling methods generalize to any city? The Inria aerial image labeling benchmark. In: IEEE International Geoscience and Remote Sensing Symposium, pp. 3226–3229. IEEE (2017)

23. Agustsson, E., Timofte, R.: NTIRE 2017 challenge on single image super-resolution: dataset and study. In: Proceedings of the IEEE Conference on Computer Vision and Pattern Recognition Workshops, pp. 126–135 (2017). https://doi.org/10.1109/CVPRW.2017.150

24. Martin, D., Fowlkes, C., Tal, D., Malik, J.: A database of human segmented natural images and its application to evaluating segmentation algorithms and measuring ecological statistics. In: IEEE International Conference on Computer Vision (2001)

Object Detection

Aggregating Rich Deep Semantic Features for Fine-Grained Place Classification

Tingyu Wei[1], Wenxin Hu[1(✉)], Xingjiao Wu[1], Yingbin Zheng[2], Hao Ye[2], Jing Yang[1], and Liang He[1]

[1] East China Normal University, Shanghai, China
wxhu@cc.ecnu.edu.cn
[2] Videt Tech, Shanghai, China

Abstract. This paper proposes a method that aggregates rich deep semantic features for fine-grained place classification. As is known to all, the category of images depends on the objects and text as well as the various semantic regions, hierarchical structure, and spatial layout. However, most recently designed fine-grained classification systems ignored this, the complex multi-level semantic structure of images associated with fine-grained classes has not yet been well explored. Therefore, in this work, our approach composed of two modules: Content Estimator (CNE) and Context Estimator (CXE). CNE generates deep content features by encoding global visual cues of images. CXE obtains rich context features of images, and it consists of three children Estimator: Text Context Estimator (TCE), Object Context Estimator (OCE), and Scene Context Estimator (SCE). When inputting an image into CXE, TCE encodes text cues to identify word-level semantic information, OCE extracts high-dimensional feature then maps it to object semantic information, SCE gains hierarchical structure and spatial layout information by recognizing scene cues. To aggregate rich deep semantic features, we fuse the information about CNE and CXE for fine-grained classification. To the best of our knowledge, this is the first work to leverage the text information from an arbitrary-oriented scene text detector for extracting context information. Moreover, our method explores the fusion of semantic features and demonstrates scene features to give more complementary information with the other cues. Furthermore, the proposed approach achieves state-of-the-art performance on a fine-grained classification dataset, 84.3% on Con-Text.

Keywords: Semantic features · Fine-grained place classification · Scene text detector · Scene features

1 Introduction

In this paper, we focus on the fine-grained classification task, which involves classification of instances within a subordinate category. The challenge of fine-grained classification is that categories can only be discriminated by subtle differences between subordinate-level classes, such as flower types [18] and dog species

© Springer Nature Switzerland AG 2019
I. V. Tetko et al. (Eds.): ICANN 2019, LNCS 11729, pp. 55–67, 2019.
https://doi.org/10.1007/978-3-030-30508-6_5

[15]. Differ from the typical coarse object category recognition which focuses on the low-level visual cue, the fine-grained classification is richer and deeper in semantic feature concerning.

Most existing fine-grained classification methods integrate domain-specific knowledge to solve this problem. As we all know, different species of dog and bird have different appearances in specific parts like nose, ears, and body, etc., and these differences are very useful to distinguish all kinds of species. Thus, [6,15,27,28] added local information or geometrical constraints to distinguish object types with similar appearance. In the task of fine-grained classification of business places, it is obvious that texts on billboards in coffee shops and bakeries of street view are critical cues to classify different categories, due to the rich knowledge that the scene text implies. Hence, [2,9–11] combined text features with visual features to support the classification.

Although previous methods have incorporated text information into visual information to learn feature representations, there are various limitations to these models. For one thing, images are usually associated with multiple semantic labels that text and visual information are inadequate for dealing with relatively complex semantic features. Based on this theory, our fine-grained classification not just depends on the off-the-shelf CNN features or handcraft features to encode the textual and visual information, but also on scene cues and the context of the image. For another, it is challenging to model the text cue to accurately detect text information, including horizontal text and rotated text. Consequently, an approach of multimodal is required to extract rich deep semantic features, which cannot be handled well by the above methods and has not been well studied.

We tackle the above problems by aggregating rich deep semantic context, and the selected features have been shown effective in recognizing image semantics. Our contributions are summarized as follows:

- We propose a novel framework for fine-grained place classification, which aggregates rich deep semantic features. To the best of our knowledge, this is the first work employ arbitrary-oriented scene text detector to obtain text features in the task.
- The experimental results prove that the scene and text cues are critical to place classification, combining them with the object-level features further boost the classification performance. Additionally, all the semantic features are learned by transfer learning which reduces expensive manual labeling.
- We achieve the state-of-the-art fine-grained place classification performance on the Con-text dataset [9].

The rest of the paper is organized as follows: after a review of the existing work in Sect. 2, Sect. 3 describes the construction of aggregate rich deep semantic architecture. Then Sect. 4 shows its effectiveness with experiments. Finally, we conclude our work in Sect. 5.

2   Related Work

Here we briefly explain the related works in three aspects: Fine-grained Classification, Scene Text Detection and Scene Recognition.

2.1   Fine-Grained Classification

Recently, various approaches are proposed to tackle the problem of fine-grained classification in images, such as using semantic, spatial and scale context into their solutions. [5] took the advantages of the fact that the posture of birds is fixed; it is aimed to recognize birds' shape by an ellipse. In [3], a number of pose normalization schemes were studied, the features were computed by applying deep convolutional nets to image patches that were located and normalized by the pose. In [27,28], the feature of particular parts was selected to capture the subtle differences. [28] whole-object and part detectors were learned by performing geometric constraints. Since variances in the pose, scale or rotation usually make the problem more difficult, [27] visual attention was applied to fine-grained classification task.

Furthermore, to categorize business locations, which are more related to this paper, [17] is the earliest paper to distinguish different business places only by applying visual cues. Nevertheless, [2,9–11] hold that it was not enough just to use visual information, so they combined text cues and visual cues for commercial sites. [9–11] advanced a method of extracting text information, which did not directly focus on detecting foreground text regions but aimed to eliminate the background regions by obtaining initial background seeds and then computed background connectivity. [2] embedded word to reconstruct recognized words into text cues, then combined word representations and deep visual features into a globally trainable deep convolutional neural network.

2.2   Scene Text Detection

With the advancements of scene text detection, a large number of novel deep convolutional neural network were introduced in the wild. These techniques allow us to automatically extract accurate scene text features for enhancing fine-grained place classification. In the recent models, there are several popular methods such as CTPN [23], TextBoxes [14], RRPN [16], and EAST [31]. CTPN [23] adopted the LSTM model to predict the text region and generate proposals. TextBoxes [14] considered default boxes for text detection, and then the model combined with the similar manner of general object detection. RRPN [16] took the advantages of text orientation angle information to generate inclined proposals, using the angle information to match the text region in the orientation. EAST [31] predicted rotated box (RBOX) and quadrangle (QUAD) in full images, directly produced text lines by a fully convolutional network (FCN) model, eliminating unnecessary intermediate steps. In this paper, we choose EAST [31] model as part of fine-grained classification architecture to complete text detection.

2.3 Scene Recognition

Scene recognition has a close relationship with object recognition. The objects contained in the scene have a great influence on the category of the scene, while the category of the scene is not only determined by objects, but also determined by semantic area, hierarchy, and spatial layout [24,25,29]. Many computer vision problems are closely related to datasets, which emerged in the field of scenarios over the past decade. The earlier one was Scene15 [13,19] with only a few thousand pictures and 15 categories, where current classifiers are saturating this dataset nearing human performance at 95%. Then it was expanded into two datasets of MIT Indoor [20] and SUN database [26]. MIT Indoor [20] had 67 categories of indoor places. SUN database [26] was composed of 397 categories containing more than 100 images per category, which provided wide coverage of scene categories. The most commonly used scene recognition dataset is Place [30], which contained 365 categories. There are more than 8 million training images and more than 300,000 test images, whose data size is larger than the ImageNet data set. The model obtained from the training of this dataset which is very different from the ImageNet dataset and the datasets are highly complementary. In our method, the Place [30] is adopted to compute scene scores.

3 Rich Deep Semantic Features Aggregation

To fine-grained classification, our approach uses the multimodal features, each pipeline of the multimodal approach maps an image to a feature vector f. Our architecture is composed of two modules: Context Estimator (CXE) and Content Estimator (CNE). They extract context feature f^1 and content feature f^2 of an image, respectively. As for the Context Estimator module construction, three types of feature are learned, and the module consists of three children Estimators: Text Context Estimator (TCE), Object Context Estimator (OCE) and Scene Context Estimator (SCE), as shown in Fig. 1. In the following subsection, we detailedly describe each of them and introduce the method of aggregating.

3.1 Context Features

Text-Level Features. The TCE aims to obtain arbitrary-oriented scene text from images, and the procedure is as follows. The first step is to train an EAST [31] model based on the VGG16 [22] network on the ICDAR2015 dataset [12]. Because scene text datasets have common characters, scene text is learned by transfer learning from the characters of ICDAR2015 dataset. With an image in the dataset of fine-grained classification as input, in this case, the model gains word box proposals of arbitrary orientations by predicting text lines directly. The second step of our method is text recognition, a framework of nearly 90k-way dictionary encoding [8] for the recognition of natural scene text is used for TCE, the network formulates the text recognition as a multi-class classification problem where one word is regarded as a class. [8] considers a dictionary of 88,172

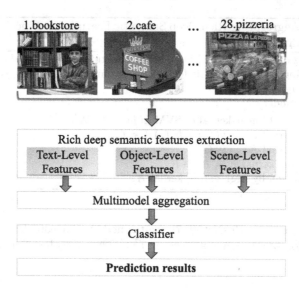

1.bookstore   2.cafe   ...   28.pizzeria

...

Rich deep semantic features extraction

| Text-Level Features | Object-Level Features | Scene-Level Features |

Multimodel aggregation

Classifier

Prediction results

Fig. 1. Overview of Context Estimator for fine-grained place classification. The module consists of three children Estimator: TCE, OCE, and SCE, which extract Text-Level, Object-Level, and Scene-Level Features, respectively.

words, and its model is trained by a network of four convolutional layers and two fully-connected layers. Word box proposals detected by the first step enter the model to generate the probabilities of each word in the dictionary. In the third step, we sum up the corresponding words' probabilities of text proposals in an image, because each proposal represents a detected word in the case. Thus, we obtain a text feature vector $f_t^1 \in \mathbb{R}^{88,172}$. This baseline is denoted as TCE.

Object-Level Features. Similarly, due to the absence of annotation information in the dataset, our OCE is a ResNet50 [7] network pre-trained on millions of ImageNet [21] images which can leverage the object semantic information of images. The utilization of pre-trained ResNet [7] results in deeper features as well as better performance in context estimation, as a result, the output of fully connected (FC) is extracted as the object-level feature vector $f_o^1 \in \mathbb{R}^{1,000}$. This baseline is denoted as OCE.

Scene-Level Features. As we know, both scene and object features in an image have a great significance on the classification, and they affect the classification in different ways. As scene context information captures hierarchical structure and spatial layout information of an image, we believe that aggregating it can achieve better fine-grained classification. To this effect, our method learn scene cues by SCE.

SCE is based on a Place365 model [30] which is a state-of-the-art scene recognition approach. Scene features are obtained from the classification layer

Algorithm 1. Aggregating Rich Deep Semantic Features for Fine-Grained Place Classification Algorithm

Input: Training dataset D with N images, TCE features of training dataset f_t, OCE features of training dataset f_o, SCE features of training dataset f_s, CNE features of training dataset f_2.

Output: SVM model

1: Set the method of linear kernal of SVM $k(f) = X * X'$.
2: Get Context kernal $K_1 = k(f_t^1) + k(f_o^1) + k(f_s^1)$.
3: Get Content kernal $K_2 = k(f_2)$.
4: The aggregating kernal $K = K_1 + K_2$.
5: Train SVM model by aggregating kernal K.

of the model, which is a ResNet50 [7] pre-trained on Place365 [30] dataset. The scene information of an image is a vector $f_s^1 \in \mathbb{R}^{365}$. This baseline is denoted as SCE.

3.2 Content Features

As indispensable semantic information, the content features contain global and local information of an image. CNE aims to transform the input image into a high-dimensional vector, thus deeper content semantic features will be provided. When extracting object-level features by the model, we obtain pre-trained ResNet50 [7] on the ImageNet at the beginning. Then fine-tune the parameters of ResNet50 [7] on our dataset. The optimal parameters could be derived by using SGD with momentum which is set to be 0.9. The network is fine-tuned for 32 epochs. We set the learning rate to be 0.001 initially, and is decreased by a factor of 10 every 8 epochs. At last, accept the last average pooling layer output of the network as the Content Features. The content information of an image is a vector $f_c^2 \in \mathbb{R}^{2,048}$. This baseline is denoted as CNE.

3.3 Multimodal Aggregation

During our research, context and content features provide important and complementary information about the image. To make the best use of the set of high-level semantics features, we obtain comprehensive features by employing kernel fusion as context cues to perform the classification. Before aggregating, the RootSift [1] is provided as an optimizing service of generalization capacity to the above features. The method of aggregating rich deep semantic features is as follows: Assuming that the features are denoted by a matrix X of n-by-f. n is the number of samples, f is the vector of features, and these features are normalized by L2. The final classification result is calculated by highly efficient LIBSVM library [4] with the linear kernel, the kernel matrix K, which is an n-by-n matrix, and can be computed by

$$k(f) = X * X' \tag{1}$$

Table 1. Fine-grained place classification performance on the Con-Text dataset. mAP numbers in the table are reported as relative improvements to previous state-of-the-art methods. The table shows that our method obtains the highest mAP.

Method	mAP%
Textual + Visual (DEEP) [10]	66.2
Textual (full) + Visual (DEEP) [11]	71.0
Textual (TCE) + Object (OCE)	73.7
Context (TCE + OCE + SCE)	**76.5**
Textual + Visual (DEEP-FT) [10]	70.7
Textual + Visual (DEEP-FT) [11]	74.5
Textual (full) + Visual (DEEP-FT-GL) [11]	77.3
Context (TCE + OCE + SCE) + Content (CNE)	**84.3**

Accordingly, we define a fine-grained place classification function as follows:

Firstly, the kernel K_1 is computed from context features, and K_2 is the kernel matrix computed from content features, which are respectively represented as

$$K_1 = k(f_t^1) + k(f_o^1) + k(f_s^1) \tag{2}$$

$$K_2 = k(f_2) \tag{3}$$

Then, the aggregating kernel of context and content features is simply computed by

$$K = K_1 + K_2 \tag{4}$$

Finally, we assume there are a set of class labels $\eta = \{1, ..., C\}$, and C times classification experiments with the binary-class SVMs are performed. Algorithm 1 describes the algorithm.

4 Experiments

We measure our method on the Con-text dataset. The Con-text dataset aims to fine-grained place classification, e.g., Pizzeria, Restaurant, and School, which contains 24,255 images that labeled over 28 classes and divided into three folds. We follow the standard protocol used in previous methods, during which experiments are repeated three times, using one fold as testing and others as training for each time, and the mean performance over the three runs are reported.

Through the experiments to obtain the results, as shown in Table 1, we compare the results of aggregating context and content features as the paper proposed. When the rich deep semantic features are aggregated, we choose a simple kernel addition to fuse these features. In this task, the mean of Average Precision (mAP) of all categories is adopted to evaluate the performance.

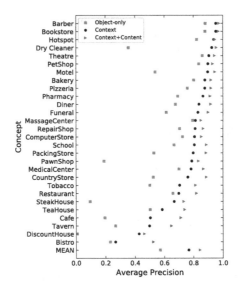

Fig. 2. Fine-grained classification results on each class for Object-Only(OCE), Context, and Context + Content. The Object-only mAP is 57.2%, the proposed multimodal approach improves the Context from 76.7% to 84.3% in mean average precision.

4.1   Results and Comparison

Table 1 compares the results of our method with previously state-of-the-art approaches, using the same experimental setup. The experimental results show that our method obtains the highest mAP. With aggregating Textual (TCE/full) and Object (OCE) cues extracted without fine-tuning, our approach improves with 2.7% and 7.5% over the result obtained in [10] and [11], respectively. This is because we adopt high-level features to obtain deeper semantic information. In Context (TCE + OCE + SCE), using Scene (SCE) in combination with the fusion of textual and object features increases the mean average precision up to 76.5%, which has increased by 2.8%. The difference between our method and others lies in whether to extract scene features or not, and this evidence further indicates that scene cues are helpful to the fine-grained place classification.

By the integration of Content in Context, the model is better than the closely related [10] and [11] in performance. The result gains significant improvements of 13.6% and 7% than their best performance, which shows both Content and Context are important to generate rich deep semantic features. As our crucial information, Content (CNE) exceedingly improves the accuracy - as no such good results can be reached without it.

The classification scores for each category are shown in Fig. 2. There are two kinds of improvements in performance. The first promotion is assembled Context component by adding textual and scene to object cues, and the mAP elevated from 57.2% to 76.7%. The second one is aggregated Content and Context features to lift the result to 83.4%. Through the aggregating, we find that our framework

Table 2. Ablation study for fine-grained classification. mAP numbers in the table reported as the results of only one feature or a combination of two features to quantify the influence of them.

Ablation	mAP%
Text-Only (CTPN) [10]	27.1
Text-Only (TCE)	33.4
Object-Only (VGG)	35.4
Visual-Only (GoogLeNet) [11]	53.3
Object-Only (OCE)	57.2
Scene-Only (SCE)	52.6
Scene (SCE) + Object (OCE)	61.8
Content (CNE)	74.3

provides a higher-level accurate to all categories, about 5% of MassageCenter to 64.3% of PawnShop.

4.2 Ablation Study

Table 2 shows the results of our ablation study, where we calculated the results of only one feature or a combination of two features. The above of experiments contain Textual-only (TCE), Object-only (OCE), Scene-only (SCE), Scene (SCE) +Object (OCE), and Content (CNE) to quantify the influence of them.

Text-Only Features: As mAP is given in Table 2, performance of Textual-Only is 33.4%, which is higher than the CTPN showed in [11] of 6.3% improvement.

Object-Only Features: In the Context, it is clear that object features are the most critical component by far. When computing object cues, a VGG16 model pre-trained on ImageNet as a baseline, which is adopted as the low-level feature for comparison. The table illustrates that ResNet50 is better than VGG16 and GoogLeNet [11] on the dataset. Therefore we employ ResNet50 as our model to extract object features.

Scene-Only Features: The result of the only scene features is 52.6%, which is 19.4% higher than Textual-Only.

Scene + Object Features: We know both text and scene cues can improve the performance, however, which is more valuable in aggregating features for fine-grained place classification? Although the result of Scene-Only is exceeded Textual-Only, the impact of combine scene and object on the result is smaller than that of fusion text and object, as shown in Table 1. By analysis, we find that compared with the relationship between Text-Only and Object-Only, Scene-Only and Object-Only features are more relevant and similar with each other. Thus the integration of these two features does not work as well as Text-Only and Object-Only.

swirl	1.00	motor	.999	cigars	1.00
bakery	.501	street sign	.440	tobacconist	.415
bakery shop	.791	motel	.922	shopfront	.762
pharmacy	1.00	barber	.997	light	.999
grocery	.416	barbershop	.458	laptop	.416
pharmacy	.731	shopfront	.827	office	.574

Fig. 3. Example images from the Con-Text dataset, predictions marked for text, objects and scenes probability of the images by Text Context Estimator, Object Context Estimator, and Scene Context Estimator, respectively.

Content Features: It is clear that the Content (CNE) is full of visual information, which is helpful to the classification and achieves a good result of 74.3% mAP when only computing these cues.

We investigate the predicting confidence of objects, text, and scenes in the images collected from the Con-Text dataset, and the confidence demonstrates these semantic cues that support the study of classification (see example images in Fig. 3).

5   Conclusions

In this paper, we propose a fine-grained classification approach for incorporating content and context information in an image, the approach is to generate rich deep semantic features. This content information feeds the model with powerful visual information to the task, then context information fused with three context features focus on text, objects, and locations recognition of an image. In contrast to the existing methods, this work focuses on generating rich deep semantic features in addition to achieving higher mAP. All the features are generic and effective, the features compensate each other nicely by kernel fusion to learn rich deep semantic information. As a result, we achieve significant improvements over state-of-the-art baselines on the Con-Text dataset.

Acknowledgement. This research is funded by the Science and Technology Commission of Shanghai Municipality (No. 18511103105) and by Xiaoi Research. The computation is performed in ECNU Public Platform for Innovation (001).

References

1. Arandjelović, R., Zisserman, A.: Three things everyone should know to improve object retrieval. In: IEEE Conference on Computer Vision and Pattern Recognition (CVPR), pp. 2911–2918 (2012). https://doi.org/10.1109/cvpr.2012.6248018
2. Bai, X., Yang, M., Lyu, P., Xu, Y., Luo, J.: Integrating scene text and visual appearance for fine-grained image classification. IEEE Access **6**, 66322–66335 (2018). https://doi.org/10.1109/access.2018.2878899
3. Branson, S., Van Horn, G., Belongie, S., Perona, P.: Bird species categorization using pose normalized deep convolutional nets. arXiv preprint arXiv:1406.2952 (2014)
4. Chang, C.C., Lin, C.J.: LIBSVM: a library for support vector machines. ACM Trans. Intell. Syst. Technol. **2**, 27 (2011). https://doi.org/10.1145/1961189.1961199
5. Gavves, E., Fernando, B., Snoek, C.G., Smeulders, A.W., Tuytelaars, T.: Fine-grained categorization by alignments. In: International Conference on Computer Vision (ICCV), pp. 1713–1720 (2013). https://doi.org/10.1109/iccv.2013.215
6. Gavves, E., Fernando, B., Snoek, C.G., Smeulders, A.W., Tuytelaars, T.: Local alignments for fine-grained categorization. Int. J. Comput. Vis. **111**, 191–212 (2015). https://doi.org/10.1007/s11263-014-0741-5
7. He, K., Zhang, X., Ren, S., Sun, J.: Deep residual learning for image recognition. In: IEEE Conference on Computer Vision and Pattern Recognition (CVPR) (2016). https://doi.org/10.1109/cvpr.2016.90
8. Jaderberg, M., Simonyan, K., Vedaldi, A., Zisserman, A.: Synthetic data and artificial neural networks for natural scene text recognition. arXiv Preprint arXiv:1406.2227 (2014)
9. Karaoglu, S., van Gemert, J.C., Gevers, T.: Con-text: text detection using background connectivity for fine-grained object classification. In: ACM International Conference on Multimedia (MM), pp. 757–760 (2013). https://doi.org/10.1145/2502081.2502197
10. Karaoglu, S., Tao, R., van Gemert, J.C., Gevers, T.: Con-text: text detection for fine-grained object classification. IEEE Trans. Image Process. **26**, 3965–3980 (2017). https://doi.org/10.1109/tip.2017.2707805
11. Karaoglu, S., Tao, R., Gevers, T., Smeulders, A.W.: Words matter: scene text for image classification and retrieval. IEEE Trans. Multimedia **19**, 1063–1076 (2017). https://doi.org/10.1109/tmm.2016.2638622
12. Karatzas, D., et al.: ICDAR 2015 competition on robust reading. In: International Conference on Document Analysis and Recognition (ICDAR), pp. 1156–1160 (2015). https://doi.org/10.1109/icdar.2015.7333942
13. Lazebnik, S., Schmid, C., Ponce, J.: Beyond bags of features: spatial pyramid matching for recognizing natural scene categories. In: IEEE Conference on Computer Vision and Pattern Recognition (CVPR), pp. 2169–2178 (2006). https://doi.org/10.1109/cvpr.2006.68
14. Liao, M., Shi, B., Bai, X., Wang, X., Liu, W.: TextBoxes: a fast text detector with a single deep neural network. In: AAAI Conference on Artificial Intelligence (AAAI), pp. 4161–4167 (2017)

15. Liu, J., Kanazawa, A., Jacobs, D., Belhumeur, P.: Dog breed classification using part localization. In: Fitzgibbon, A., Lazebnik, S., Perona, P., Sato, Y., Schmid, C. (eds.) ECCV 2012. LNCS, vol. 7572, pp. 172–185. Springer, Heidelberg (2012). https://doi.org/10.1007/978-3-642-33718-5_13

16. Ma, J., et al.: Arbitrary-oriented scene text detection via rotation proposals. IEEE Trans. Multimedia **20**, 3111–3122 (2018). https://doi.org/10.1109/tmm.2018.2818020

17. Movshovitz-Attias, Y., Yu, Q., Stumpe, M.C., Shet, V., Arnoud, S., Yatziv, L.: Ontological supervision for fine grained classification of street view storefronts. In: IEEE Conference on Computer Vision and Pattern Recognition (CVPR), pp. 1693–1702 (2015). https://doi.org/10.1109/cvpr.2015.7298778

18. Nilsback, M.E., Zisserman, A.: Automated flower classification over a large number of classes. In: Indian Conference on Computer Vision, Graphics and Image Processing (ICVGIP), pp. 722–729 (2008). https://doi.org/10.1109/icvgip.2008.47

19. Oliva, A., Torralba, A.: Modeling the shape of the scene: a holistic representation of the spatial envelope. Int. J. Comput. Vision **42**, 145–175 (2001)

20. Quattoni, A., Torralba, A.: Recognizing indoor scenes. In: IEEE Conference on Computer Vision and Pattern Recognition (CVPR), pp. 413–420 (2009). https://doi.org/10.1109/cvprw.2009.5206537

21. Russakovsky, O., et al.: Imagenet large scale visual recognition challenge. Int. J. Comput. Vision **115**, 211–252 (2015). https://doi.org/10.1007/s11263-015-0816-y

22. Simonyan, K., Zisserman, A.: Very deep convolutional networks for large-scale image recognition. arXiv Preprint arXiv:1409.1556 (2014)

23. Tian, Z., Huang, W., He, T., He, P., Qiao, Y.: Detecting text in natural image with connectionist text proposal network. In: Leibe, B., Matas, J., Sebe, N., Welling, M. (eds.) ECCV 2016. LNCS, vol. 9912, pp. 56–72. Springer, Cham (2016). https://doi.org/10.1007/978-3-319-46484-8_4

24. Torresani, L., Szummer, M., Fitzgibbon, A.: Efficient object category recognition using classemes. In: Daniilidis, K., Maragos, P., Paragios, N. (eds.) ECCV 2010. LNCS, vol. 6311, pp. 776–789. Springer, Heidelberg (2010). https://doi.org/10.1007/978-3-642-15549-9_56

25. Vogel, J., Schiele, B.: Semantic modeling of natural scenes for content-based image retrieval. Int. J. Comput. Vision **72**(2), 133–157 (2007). https://doi.org/10.1007/s11263-006-8614-1

26. Xiao, J., Hays, J., Ehinger, K.A., Oliva, A., Torralba, A.: Sun database: large-scale scene recognition from abbey to zoo. In: IEEE Conference on Computer Vision and Pattern Recognition (CVPR), pp. 3485–3492 (2010). https://doi.org/10.1109/cvpr.2010.5539970

27. Xiao, T., Xu, Y., Yang, K., Zhang, J., Peng, Y., Zhang, Z.: The application of two-level attention models in deep convolutional neural network for fine-grained image classification. In: IEEE Conference on Computer Vision and Pattern Recognition (CVPR), pp. 842–850 (2015). https://doi.org/10.1109/cvpr.2015.7298685

28. Zhang, N., Donahue, J., Girshick, R., Darrell, T.: Part-based R-CNNs for fine-grained category detection. In: Fleet, D., Pajdla, T., Schiele, B., Tuytelaars, T. (eds.) ECCV 2014. LNCS, vol. 8689, pp. 834–849. Springer, Cham (2014). https://doi.org/10.1007/978-3-319-10590-1_54

29. Zheng, Y., Jiang, Y.-G., Xue, X.: Learning hybrid part filters for scene recognition. In: Fitzgibbon, A., Lazebnik, S., Perona, P., Sato, Y., Schmid, C. (eds.) ECCV 2012. LNCS, vol. 7576, pp. 172–185. Springer, Heidelberg (2012). https://doi.org/10.1007/978-3-642-33715-4_13

30. Zhou, B., Lapedriza, A., Khosla, A., Oliva, A., Torralba, A.: Places: a 10 million image database for scene recognition. IEEE Trans. Pattern Anal. Mach. Intell. **40**, 1452–1464 (2017). https://doi.org/10.1109/tpami.2017.2723009
31. Zhou, X., et al.: East: an efficient and accurate scene text detector. In: IEEE Conference on Computer Vision and Pattern Recognition (CVPR), pp. 2642–2651 (2017). https://doi.org/10.1109/cvpr.2017.283

Improving Reliability of Object Detection for Lunar Craters Using Monte Carlo Dropout

Tomoyuki Myojin$^{(\boxtimes)}$ (ID), Shintaro Hashimoto, Kenji Mori, Keisuke Sugawara, and Naoki Ishihama

Japan Aerospace Exploration Agency, 2-1-1 Sengen, Tsukuba, Ibaraki, Japan
{myojin.tomoyuki,hashimoto.shintaro,mori.kenji,
sugawara.keisuke,ishihama.naoki}@jaxa.jp

Abstract. In the task of detecting craters on the lunar surface, some craters were difficult to detect correctly, and a Deep Neural Network (DNN) could not represent the uncertainty of such detection. However, a measure of uncertainty could be expressed as the variance of the prediction by using Monte Carlo Dropout Sampling (MC Dropout). Although MC Dropout has often been applied to fully connected layers in a network in recent studies, many convolutional layers are used to recognize the subtle features of a crater in the crater-detecting network. In this paper, we extended the application of MC Dropout to a network having a number of convolutional layers, and also evaluated the methodology of dropping out the convolutional layers. As a result, in the convolutional neural network, we represent the more correct variance by using filter-based dropout and evaluating the uncertainty for each feature map size. The precision of prediction in lunar crater detection was improved by 2.1% by rejecting a prediction result with high variance as a false positive compared with the variance when predicting the training data.

Keywords: Lunar crater · Object detection · Uncertainty · Monte Carlo Dropout Sampling · Deep learning

1 Introduction

Object detection methods based on a convolutional neural network (CNN) have been widely used in recent years. However, the object prediction of an object detector which trained based on training data is not necessarily correct. One reason for such incorrect results is the uncertainty caused by insufficient training data, inadequate training, and a different distribution between training data and inference data. In object detection, uncertainty leads to a false positive, which means that there are no objects even though CNN predicted one. Moreover, too many false positives in detection will lower the detector's reliability. For example, an autonomous vehicle requires high reliability to brake when detecting an object and not crashing into it. If the object detector predicts an object that

© Springer Nature Switzerland AG 2019
I. V. Tetko et al. (Eds.): ICANN 2019, LNCS 11729, pp. 68–80, 2019.
https://doi.org/10.1007/978-3-030-30508-6_6

is a false positive, the possibility of an accident will increase as the vehicle stops or decelerates unnecessarily. Therefore, it is necessary to eliminate results having high uncertainty by evaluating the uncertainty of the detector's results.

With regard to the evaluation of uncertainty on CNN, methods based on Monte Carlo Dropout Sampling have been studied [2,3]. In terms of object detection methods, uncertainty has been evaluated by such object detection methods as Single Shot Multibox Detector (SSD) [6] and Faster R-CNN [1].

Lunar crater detection is one of the applications affected by uncertainty in object detection. Craters are circular topographical depressions on the surface that were formed by a small meteorite, comet or asteroid colliding with such celestial bodies as the Moon and Mars in the Solar System or elsewhere. We have been developing a method of estimating the location and size of craters in lunar surface images by using the YOLOv3 object detector [7,8] as shown in Fig. 1 [4]. By using the results on a given lunar crater's location and size, we can find a safe area to land the "rover" exploration vehicle and determine a safe course for the rover to follow. However, if the detector predicts a crater even though no crater actually exists, it will take a long time to select a landing point or a driving course. Thus, the reliability of detection such as its precision must be improved as much as possible to achieve a critical mission on the lunar surface.

In this paper, in order to increase the reliability of lunar crater detection using YOLOv3, we aim to eliminate false positives from the detection results by evaluating uncertainty using MC Dropout. YOLOv3 adopts U-Net network architecture capable of capturing objects of various sizes, and which is useful for detecting craters. Therefore, we propose an uncertainty evaluation method for object detection using U-Net network architecture. We also propose a method of estimating suitable criteria for uncertainty using training data. Moreover, in order to overcome processing time, which is a weak point of MC Dropout, we introduce cache architecture to CNN. This paper is organized as follows: Sect. 2 describes

   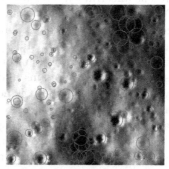

(a) Label data   (b) Prediction data

Fig. 1. Results of lunar crater detection. (a) Yellow circles denote label data. (b) Purple circles denote predictions by the detector. (Color figure online)

the related work. Section 3 explains the architecture of object detection with MC Dropout and a method of evaluating uncertainty. Section 4 presents an evaluation of the methods proposed for lunar crater detection. Section 5 illustrates the evaluation results, which are discussed in Sect. 6. Finally, Sect. 7 presents the conclusion.

2   Related Work

Object detection entails recognizing objects in input images, and predicting the location and class of such objects. Recognition accuracy has recently been improved using deep neural networks. State-of-the-art object detection methods include Faster R-CNN [9], Single Multi-Box Detector (SSD) [5], CraterIDNet [10], and YOLOv3. We have been developing a lunar crater detection system using YOLOv3. YOLOv3 features an up-sampling layer, skip connection of U-Net, and residual network architecture. Due to these features, YOLOv3 can detect objects of various sizes including small craters. Thus, this research utilizes YOLOv3 for object detection.

A Bayesian neural network is one of the methods used for capturing the uncertainty of neural networks. Ordinarily, a neural network learns the parameters of weights and biases, and predicts output using those parameters. In contrast, a Bayesian neural network learns the distribution of weights and biases. Therefore, a Bayesian neural network can predict the distribution of output, which presents uncertainty. Although a Bayesian neural network is useful for evaluating uncertainty, it is difficult to optimize in adapting it to a deep neural network.

In order to solve this problem, recent investigations have demonstrated a method of approximating a Bayesian neural network. Gal proposed approximating a Bayesian neural network by dropout [2,3]. In a deep neural network, a dropout layer that stochastically removes neurons is often used to prevent over-fitting in the training phase. Using dropout in inference, a neural network outputs different values each time for the inference and distribution of outputs that present uncertainty. This method is called Monte Carlo Dropout Sampling (MC Dropout Sampling) and several studies have reported adopting it to object detection. Miller [6] adopted MC Dropout Sampling to SSD and Feng [1] adopted to Faster R-CNN. However, Miller and Feng do not consider feature map size or object size. Thus, whether uncertainty is properly evaluated when detecting objects of various sizes remains unclear. Moreover, Feng adopted dropout only to fully connected layer, and it is not clear how Miller adopt dropout to convolutional layer. Since YOLOv3 does not contain any fully connected layers, it is necessary to evaluate adopting dropout to convolutional layer. Therefore, this paper adopts MC Dropout Sampling to YOLOv3, which can detect objects of various size using U-Net architecture.

3   Object Detection with MC Dropout Sampling

In this section, we explain how to evaluate uncertainty in YOLOv3 using MC Dropout Sampling.

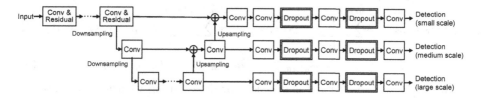

Fig. 2. Network structure based on YOLOv3.

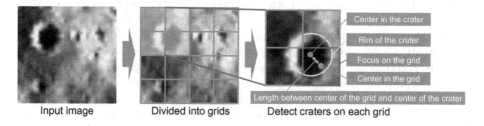

Input image	Divided into grids	Detect craters on each grid

Fig. 3. Mechanism of crater detection by grids.

3.1   Network Architecture

The detecting process of YOLOv3 is described above. YOLOv3 divides an input image into cells of grids and then predicts probability, center of location (x-axis and y-axis), size (width and height), and class of the object in each cell. The network structure of YOLOv3 is that of a fully convolutional neural network, and includes residual network architecture and U-Net structure. There is a total number of 122 layers. The standard YOLOv3 network configuration has three detection layers that detect different scales of an object: small, medium and large. Figure 2 shows our network structure based on YOLOv3.

There is a clear difference between the original YOLOv3 and our YOLOv3. The original YOLOv3 detects a bounding box (x-axis, y-axis, width, height) of an object, although our detector detects a circle (x-axis, y-axis, diameter) that denotes the shape of a lunar crater. Figure 3 shows the mechanism of crater detection. In order to realize the mechanism, the loss function is modified to detect lunar craters as expressed in (1) to (5) below.

$$T_{(i,j)} = if(x_i \cdot grid_x < object_x^j) and (x_i \cdot grid_x + grid_x \geq object_x^j) and$$
$$(y_i \cdot grid_y < object_y^j) and (y_i \cdot grid_y + grid_y \geq object_y^j) then\, 1\, else\, 0. \quad (1)$$

$$Loss_{distance} = \sum_{i=0}^{grid} \sum_{j=0}^{object} T_{(i,j)} \{ (\hat{x}_i - \hat{x}_j)^2 + (\hat{y}_i - \hat{y}_j)^2 \}. \quad (2)$$

$$Loss_{diameter} = \sum_{i=0}^{grid} \sum_{j=0}^{object} T_{(i,j)} (\sqrt{\hat{d}_i} - \sqrt{\hat{d}_j})^2. \quad (3)$$

$$Loss_{existence} = \lambda \sum_{i=0}^{grid} \sum_{j=0}^{object} T_{(i,j)}(\hat{c}_i - c_j)^2 + \sum_{i=0}^{grid} \sum_{j=0}^{object} |T_{(i,j)} - 1|(\hat{c}_i - c_j)^2. \quad (4)$$

$$Loss_{total} = Loss_{distance} + Loss_{diameter} + Loss_{existence}. \quad (5)$$

Equation (1) is a conditional expression for determining whether the center of a crater is included in each grid after the input image is divided into grids. If the center of a crater is included in one grid, "1" is returned; otherwise, "0" is returned. The suffix i indicates each grid, and the suffix j indicates each object. $grid_x$ and $grid_y$ denote the size of each grid, respectively. $object_x$ and $object_y$ denote the center position of each crater, respectively. Equation (2) calculates the estimation error of the center position of a crater included in one grid among the grids, and thus improves the estimation accuracy of crater position relative to the image compressed by CNN. Equation (3) is the prediction error of the crater diameter estimated in each grid. The crater diameters show a large difference in size, and the calculated loss may be too small or too large, thereby hindering any learning. Therefore, in order to reduce the influence due to numerical differences, the square root was calculated to the diameter. Equation (4) calculates the error regarding whether the center position of a crater exists in each grid. The label data is given "1" when a crater exists, and "0" if it does not exist. However, when the number of craters is small compared to the number of grid divisions, there is a tendency in learning where each grid does not contain a crater. Therefore, this research adopted a penalty. Despite the presence of a crater in each grid, a large loss is imposed when estimating that there is no crater. This research adopted penalty $(\lambda) = 2$. Equation (5) then gives the total loss function.

3.2   Dropout Layer

In this research, dropout layers are inserted after the two preceding convolution layers of each detection layer. Unlike the case of a fully connected layer, adopting dropout to a convolution layer is challenging. Adopting simple dropout to the convolution layer results in making a feature map of an image that lacks some pixels, thereby leading to large losses. Therefore, the dropout rate is set to a low value (such as 0.1). Moreover, this research proposes filter-based dropout instead of simple dropout. Instead of applying dropout to each pixel of an image, filter-based dropout applies it on the dropout convolution filter in order to prevent any lacking images. Figure 4 shows an overview of how both the pixel- and filter-based dropout layers work. Figure 5 shows some feature maps (52×52 pixels) extracted from a dropout layer for prediction using a lunar crater image.

3.3   Measuring Uncertainty

The YOLOv3 network in this paper outputs the location (x-axis and y-axis), size (diameter), and probability of objects at three detection layers that have different sizes of feature maps. In other words, the network divides the input

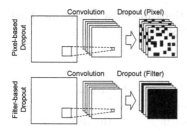

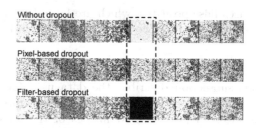

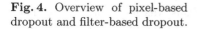

Fig. 4. Overview of pixel-based dropout and filter-based dropout.

Fig. 5. Feature maps without dropout and with dropout by filter and pixel.

image into cells with three kinds of grid sizes (small, medium, large), and the location, size, and probability of the object are output for each cell.

Because the network with MC Dropout Sampling only inferences the number of samplings, the network outputs results for the number of samplings for each cell. For example, if there are C_s small cells, C_m medium cells and C_l large cells, and the number of samplings is N_{mc}, the network outputs the results of $N_{mc} \cdot (C_s + C_m + C_l)$ cells. The average value of each cell is the inference result, and the variance value of each cell represents uncertainty.

The value of variance means the stability of prediction. If an input image used for prediction is similar to an image learned by a model in the training phase, the inference results converge to a certain value and the values of variance become lower. Conversely, if an input image used for prediction is not similar to an image learned by a model in the training phase, the inference results diverge and the values of variance become higher.

3.4   Method of Estimating Allowable Uncertainty

Determining whether a threshold of variance is uncertain poses an important issue. Because a threshold of variance depends on a given model and training data, it should be an appropriate value that represents allowable uncertainty according to the model and training data. We propose a method of determining the threshold based on training data. If an input image included in the training data is predicted, the inference result has low variance.

Let V_{train} be the maximum value of variance when inferring training data and V_{pred} be the variance when inferring target data in the inferring phase. If V_{train} is higher than V_{pred}, the inference is considered to be uncertain. If V_{train} is lower than V_{pred}, the inference is considered to be reliable.

4   Evaluation

In this section, we measure uncertainty as variance in the YOLOv3 network and evaluate how much the reliability of prediction is improved by eliminating inference results with high uncertainty. The elimination of high uncertainty reduces false positives, which are false determinations made by detectors. This is expected to improve the precision of the detection results.

4.1   Lunar Crater Dataset

This subsection describes the data used for evaluation. Our research project predicts the locations and sizes of lunar craters on the lunar surface by object detection. Thus, we used images of the lunar surface to train and evaluate. We have generated the training data and test data. The lunar surface image is 512×512 pixels in size. A size of 104×104 pixels was used for testing. The label data include the diameter and center coordinates of each crater. Label data were provided by humans in recognizing the center position and diameter of each crater. Each value of the label data is normalized by 0 to 1 in the coordinate system, with the origin at the top left of the image. The generated input image is 416×416 pixels in size (as compared to the original size of 104×104 pixels). Rotation (in variations of 0, 90, 180, and 270°), scaling, and gamma value correction were added to increase the number of images randomly clipped from the original image. There was a total number of 3,000 training images.

4.2   Evaluation of Detection

This subsection describes the evaluation method of lunar crater detection. First, let $O = \{X, Y, D, P, C\}$ be a prediction by YOLOv3, where X is the x-axis, Y is the y-axis, D is diameter, P is a probability of existence, and C is a probability of classes. Moreover, let $O_{mean} = \{X_{mean}, Y_{mean}, D_{mean}, P_{mean}, C_{mean}\}$ be the average of each prediction when sampling N times. If P_{mean} is higher than the thresholds of detection, it means that there is an object at the location (X_{mean}, Y_{mean}) with size of D_{mean}. If the overlapped area between the detected object and an object in labeled data is higher than the threshold of truth, the detection is a true positive. The overlapped area as calculated in (6) is called Intersection-over-Union (IoU), where A is the area of detected objects. Equation (7) calculates true positives. Finally, recall is calculated in (8) and precision is calculated in (9), where $Pred_{count}$ is the number of detected objects that are true positives and false positives and $Label_{count}$ is the number of label data.

$$IoU_{(i,j)} = \frac{A_i^{pred} \cap A_j^{label}}{A_i^{pred} \cup A_j^{label}}. \tag{6}$$

$$TP_{count} = \sum_{i=0}^{pred} \sum_{j=0}^{label} \begin{cases} 1 \; if(IoU_{(i,j)}) \geq threshold \\ 0 \; if(IoU_{(i,j)}) < threshold \end{cases}. \tag{7}$$

$$Recall_{count} = \frac{TP_{count}}{Lable_{count}}. \tag{8}$$

$$Precision_{count} = \frac{TP_{count}}{Pred_{count}}. \tag{9}$$

4.3 Evaluation of Uncertainty

This subsection describes the evaluation of uncertainty in lunar crater detection. Let $O_{var} = \{X_{var}, Y_{var}, D_{var}, P_{var}, C_{var}\} = \frac{1}{N}\sum_n^N (O_n - O_{mean})^2$ be the variance of each prediction when sampling N times. This research adopted $N = 100$. If the variance of a predicted detection is higher than the threshold of allowable uncertainty, the detection is likely to be a false positive. Acceptance or rejection of the detection is determined according to (10) below.

$$Judge(O^i) = \begin{cases} Accept \; if \; O_{var}^i \leq V_{train} \\ Reject \; if \; O_{var}^i > V_{train} \end{cases}. \tag{10}$$

However, the detection of high variance is not necessarily a false positive. Therefore, it is necessary to properly evaluate the value of variance. In this paper, the variance was evaluated by the following three methods:

- M1: Separate the variance of the x-axis, y-axis, and diameter, and use a different V_{train} for each detection layer.
- M2: Separate the variance of the x-axis, y-axis, and diameter, and use the same V_{train} for all detection layers.
- M3: Sum the variance of the x-axis, y-axis, and diameter, and use the same V_{train} for all detection layers.

The distribution of variance is presumed to differ depending on the size of the object to be detected. Thus, we evaluate variance for each detection layer. In the same way, we evaluate variance of the x-axis, y-axis, and diameter separately. If the variance of detection is evaluated as being higher, the detection has high uncertainty and is regarded as a false positive. Detecting more false positives without mistakenly rejecting true positives as false positives is a good evaluation method.

5 Results

This section presents the evaluation results. Table 1 lists all the methods showing an improved precision rate and F1 score. The scores in the 'Actual' column were evaluated using the criteria of uncertainty estimated from the training data. The scores in the 'Max' column were evaluated using the criteria of uncertainty that maximizes the scores. In other words, the criteria for the 'Max' column are the maximum values of variance for true positives. All recall rates are retained except for the method that uses a separating axis with filter dropout, and are sufficiently higher than the identification by human at 75% [11]. In the filter dropout group, the method that uses a separating axis and a separating layer improves the precision rate by 2.1 points and F1 score by 1.7 points. In the pixel dropout group, the method that uses a separating axis and a separating layer improves the precision rate by 2.1 points and F1 score by 1.7 points. Although both sets of results are similar, the eliminated false positives differed. Figure 6 shows the detected craters that are judged as false positives and those not judged as false positives. In Fig. 6(a) indicates that the method with filter dropout can

Table 1. Accuracy of crater detection

Dropout type	Separate axis	Separate layer	Recall (Actual/Max)	Precision (Actual/Max)	F1 score (Actual/Max)
Filter	(without MC Dropout)		80.6	45.6	58.2
Filter	Yes	Yes	80.6/80.6	**47.7/49.1**	**59.9/61.0**
Filter	Yes	No	78.6/80.6	46.3/46.9	58.3/59.3
Filter	No	No	80.6/80.6	46.4/47.2	58.9/59.5
Pixel	(without MC Dropout)		80.6	42.8	55.9
Pixel	Yes	Yes	80.6/80.6	**43.9/46.9**	**56.8/59.3**
Pixel	Yes	No	80.6/80.6	**44.9/45.6**	**57.6/58.2**
Pixel	No	No	80.6/80.6	43.0/44.6	56.1/57.4

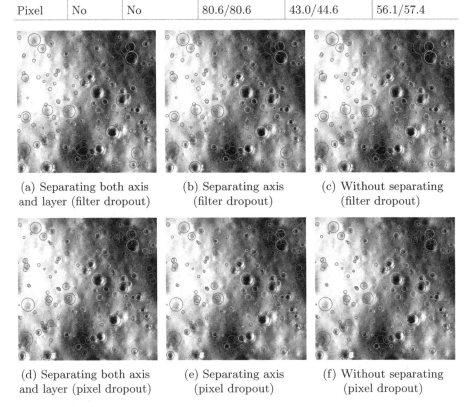

(a) Separating both axis and layer (filter dropout)

(b) Separating axis (filter dropout)

(c) Without separating (filter dropout)

(d) Separating both axis and layer (pixel dropout)

(e) Separating axis (pixel dropout)

(f) Without separating (pixel dropout)

Fig. 6. Results of eliminating false positives of lunar crater detection with dropout. Yellow circles denote label data. Both red and blue circles denote predicted data. Red circles denote eliminated false negatives. The top row shows results obtained by filter based dropout; the bottom row shows results obtained by pixel based dropout. (Color figure online)

eliminate false positives regarding various crater sizes, whereas the method with pixel dropout can only eliminate false positives regarding a small crater size. Therefore, the method with filter dropout is better than pixel dropout.

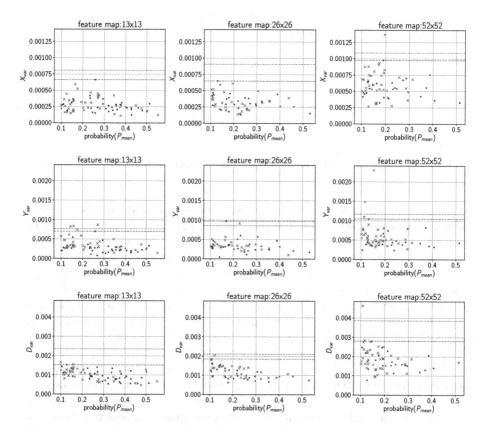

Fig. 7. Variance of results predicted with filter dropout for each axis and layer. The top row shows variance of the x-axis, the middle row shows variance of the y-axis, and the bottom row shows variance of diameter for each detection layer (feature map). Each point represents a detected crater, where circle markers denote correct predictions and crossed markers denote incorrect predictions. Blue dashed lines denote the thresholds of variance estimated for the training data (V_{train}), and green dashed lines denote the thresholds of variance for maximizing the scores. (Color figure online)

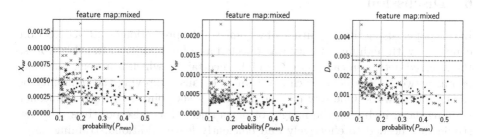

Fig. 8. Variance of results predicted with filter dropout for each axis. (Color figure online)

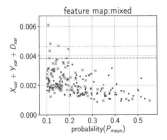

Fig. 9. Variance of results predicted with filter dropout. (Color figure online)

In order to examine how false positives were eliminated, we also analyzed the variance of predicted data. Figures 7, 8 and 9 shows the variance of results predicted with filter dropout. Figure 7 shows variance of the x-axis, y-axis and diameters for each detection layer(feature map). In the same way, Fig. 8 shows variance of the x-axis, y-axis, and diameter in mixed detection layers; Fig. 9 shows variance of the sum of the x-axis, y-axis, and diameter in mixed detection layers. The lines of threshold effectively separate correct predictions from incorrect predictions in Fig. 7 as compared to Figs. 8 and 9. In particular, the distribution of variance differs among the layers. As the size of the feature map gets larger, the values of variance also become higher. Thus, a single threshold for which the sizes of objects are not taken into account cannot effectively separate correct predictions from wrong ones. Moreover, different trends are also seen among the x-axis, y-axis, and diameter. Therefore, it may be useful to separate the x-axis, y-axis, and diameter for evaluating uncertainty. These results suggest that the proposed methods which separate both the axes and layers can effectively detect false positives. Moreover, estimating variance from training data is shown to be effective as the thresholds of variance estimated for the training data (blue dashed lines) and the thresholds of variance for maximizing the scores (green dashed lines) are close enough to separate false positives and true positives.

6   Discussion

In this paper, using the magnitude of variance of the prediction result, a detection candidate with high uncertainty was rejected as a false positive. In other words, the rejected detection candidate has high uncertainty, which is a weak point for neural networks. Reducing such a weakness entails improving the reliability of the neural network. One way to overcome this weak point is to learn additional training data, including the images of parts rejected as false positives. Further studies are needed to effectively and efficiently learn additional training data. The calculation resources pose a common problem in applications using MC Dropout Sampling, and also cannot be ignored in lunar crater detection. With MC Dropout, one hundred samplings are needed simply when the sampling number is 100. In this lunar crater detection when using a GeForce GTX TITAN X GPU, the inference time takes approximately 0.035 s per image, and 3.09 s for one hundred samplings. To address this problem, we implemented a caching mechanism in the network. Because our YOLOv3 network inserts dropout layers only in the two layers just before the YOLOv3 detection layers, the layers before Dropout output the same results each time. Therefore, in order to reduce the calculation time, in the first inference, we cached the results up to the layer before the dropout layers, and then recalculated only after the dropout layers in the second and subsequent samplings. As a result, the calculation time was reduced to 0.972 s even with one hundred samplings, thus marking a reduction to approximately one-third of the previous time required.

7 Conclusion

In order to increase the reliability of lunar crater detection using YOLOv3, in this paper we intended to eliminate false positives from detection results by evaluating uncertainty representing variance when detecting multiple times using MC Dropout. As YOLOv3 has U-Net network architecture that can capture objects of various sizes and is also useful for detecting craters, we proposed a method of evaluating uncertainty for the setting criteria for each object detection layer that captures an object of a different size. Moreover, in order to evaluate uncertainty from various viewpoints, we evaluated uncertainty by separating the location (x-axis, y-axis) and size (diameter) of the object. As a result, it was possible to eliminate more false positives compared with evaluation using mixed detection layers where the location and size are not separated. In addition, we proposed a method of estimating the evaluation criteria for uncertainty based on training data. The estimated criteria was close to the ideal values of variance sufficient to distinguish between false positives and true positives. Finally, our method could improve the precision rate by 2.1 points without adversely affecting the recall rate for lunar crater detection. Moreover, calculation time was reduced to one-third by adopting a cache mechanism into multiple inferences in U-Net network.

References

1. Feng, D., Rosenbaum, L., Dietmayer, K.: Towards safe autonomous driving: capture uncertainty in the deep neural network for lidar 3D vehicle detection. In: 2018 21st International Conference on Intelligent Transportation Systems (ITSC) (2018). https://doi.org/10.1109/itsc.2018.8569814
2. Gal, Y., Ghahramani, Z.: Bayesian convolutional neural networks with Bernoulli approximate variational inference. In: 4th International Conference on Learning Representations (ICLR) Workshop Track (2016)
3. Gal, Y., Ghahramani, Z.: Dropout as a Bayesian approximation: representing model uncertainty in deep learning. In: Proceedings of the 33rd International Conference on International Conference on Machine Learning, ICML 2016, vol. 48, pp. 1050–1059. JMLR.org (2016)

4. Hashimoto, S., Mori, K.: Lunar crater detection based on grid partition using deep learning. In: 2019 IEEE 13th International Symposium on Applied Computational Intelligence and Informatics (SACI) (2019, to appear)
5. Liu, W., et al.: SSD: single shot MultiBox detector. In: Leibe, B., Matas, J., Sebe, N., Welling, M. (eds.) ECCV 2016. LNCS, vol. 9905, pp. 21–37. Springer, Cham (2016). https://doi.org/10.1007/978-3-319-46448-0_2
6. Miller, D., Dayoub, F., Milford, M., Sünderhauf, N.: Evaluating merging strategies for sampling-based uncertainty techniques in object detection (2018). arXiv:1809.06006 [cs.CV]
7. Redmon, J., Divvala, S., Girshick, R., Farhadi, A.: You only look once: unified, real-time object detection. In: 2016 IEEE Conference on Computer Vision and Pattern Recognition (CVPR), pp. 779–788 (2016). https://doi.org/10.1109/CVPR.2016.91
8. Redmon, J., Farhadi, A.: Yolov3: an incremental improvement (2018). arXiv:1804.02767 [cs.CV]
9. Ren, S., He, K., Girshick, R., Sun, J.: Faster R-CNN: towards real-time object detection with region proposal networks. IEEE Trans. Pattern Anal. Mach. Intell. **39**(6), 1137–1149 (2017). https://doi.org/10.1109/TPAMI.2016.2577031
10. Wang, H., Jiang, J., Zhang, G.: CraterIDNet: an end-to-end fully convolutional neural network for crater detection and identification in remotely sensed planetary images. Remote Sens. **10**(7), 1067 (2018). https://doi.org/10.3390/rs10071067
11. Wetzler, P., Honda, R., Enke, B., Merline, W., Chapman, C., Burl, M.: Learning to detect small impact craters. In: 2005 Seventh IEEE Workshops on Applications of Computer Vision (WACV/MOTION 2005), vol. 1. IEEE (2005). https://doi.org/10.1109/acvmot.2005.68

An Improved Convolutional Neural Network for Steganalysis in the Scenario of Reuse of the Stego-Key

Bartosz Czaplewski$^{(\boxtimes)}$ (iD)

Faculty of Electronics, Telecommunications and Informatics,
Gdańsk University of Technology, 11/12 Gabriela Narutowicza Street,
80-233 Gdańsk, Poland
bartosz.czaplewski@eti.pg.edu.pl

Abstract. The topic of this paper is the use of deep learning techniques, more specifically convolutional neural networks, for steganalysis of digital images. The steganalysis scenario of the repeated use of the stego-key is considered. Firstly, a study of the influence of the depth and width of the convolution layers on the effectiveness of classification was conducted. Next, a study on the influence of depth and width of fully connected layers on the effectiveness of classification was conducted. Based on the conclusions from the studies, an improved convolutional neural network was created, which is characterized by the state-of-art level of classification efficiency but containing 20 times less parameters to learn during the training process. Smaller number of learnable parameters results in faster network learning, easier convergence, and smaller memory and computing power requirements. The paper contains description of the current state of art, description of the experimental environment, structures of the studied networks and the results of classification accuracy.

Keywords: Convolutional neural networks · Deep learning ·
Image processing · Steganalysis

1 Introduction

Steganography is a field of science of concealing communications by hiding secret messages within other data, e.g. images. At the sender side, the aim of steganography scheme is to embed a secret message into innocent-looking image called cover image. An image containing hidden message is called a stego image and is usually transmitted through public channel. At the receiver side, the aim of steganography scheme is to extract the hidden message from the received stego image. This paper concerns the steganography by cover modification [1, 2], in which the sender introduces modifications to a cover image in order to hide the secret message.

Steganalysis is a field of science of detecting secret communications carried by steganography schemes. The aim of steganalysis is to detect the presence of a hidden message in a test image by distinguishing between stego and cover images. If a stego image is detected then the secret communication is revealed and the steganography

© Springer Nature Switzerland AG 2019
I. V. Tetko et al. (Eds.): ICANN 2019, LNCS 11729, pp. 81–92, 2019.
https://doi.org/10.1007/978-3-030-30508-6_7

scheme is broken. This paper concerns the passive warden steganalysis [1, 2], in which the communication is observed and analyzed, but not interfered, in order to detect secret messages. Moreover, this paper concerns the blind steganalysis scenario [1, 2], in which a steganalysis algorithm is universal and not designed to detect any specific embedding algorithm.

For more than a decade, the best steganalyzers have been built based on the concept of Rich Model of images with Ensemble Classifier (RM+EC) [3, 4], which firstly obtained a high dimensional feature vector and secondly used a classifier trained on the basis of that feature vector. In recent years, a more frequent topic is the use of deep-learning techniques, more specifically Convolutional Neural Networks (CNN) [5–12], for the same purpose. It turns out that a well-shaped CNN, which provides an empirical and automatic approach, can produce effects comparable to the previously mentioned heuristic and handcrafted two-step approach of RM+EC. What is more, CNN-based steganalyzer allows to unify feature extraction and classification in one uniform algorithm and to reduce the input's dimensionality at the same time.

In this paper, a unique scenario of using the same stego key for embedding has been investigated. This scenario was discussed for the first time in [5] by Pibre *et al.* For this particular scenario, unprecedented effectiveness of detection were obtained. The authors [5] stated that the experimental setup was artificial because the key used for the embedding was always the same which is an unsecure scenario from the steganographic point of view. However, the repeated use of the key in real conditions with the participation of a human factor is not completely unrealistic. On the contrary, if frequent errors in security resulting from a human factor are taken into account, this can take place more often than using a one-time key. For this reason, the scenario is revisited and investigated further.

The contribution of this paper to the field is as follows. Studies on the steganalysis scenario of the reuse of the stego-key, which is usually omitted in the literature, were further investigated and better shape of CNN for that problem was obtained. The influence of the depth and width of the convolution layers on the classification accuracy was investigated. For this purpose, 1536 convolutional neural networks were designed, trained and validated. The effect of depth and width of the fully connected layers on the classification accuracy was investigated. For this purpose, 1860 convolutional neural networks were designed, trained and validated. Finally, an improved network was built, which offers the state-of-art level of accuracy of classification but consists 20 times less parameters to learn during the training process. Smaller number of learnable parameters has many benefits, such as faster network learning, easier convergence and smaller memory and computing power requirements.

The structure of this paper is as follows. In Sect. 2, the related work in the field is listed. The used research methodology is stated in Sect. 3. In Sect. 4, experiments on convolutional layers are presented. In Sect. 5, experiments on fully connected layers are presented. A new improved CNN is presented in Sect. 6. A summary is listed in Sect. 7.

2   Related Work

For the first time, the concept of deep learning aimed for stegoanalysis used auto-encoders and was described in [6] by Tan and Li. The authors pointed out that SRM possesses a similar architecture to CNN. They used a stack of convolutional auto-encoders which formed a CNN. The results showed that initializing a CNN with the mixture of the filters from a trained stack of convolutional auto-encoders and feature pooling layers can give promising results.

Then, the use of a convolutional neural network was published in [7] by Qian *et al.* The authors proposed a model that can automatically learn feature representations with several convolutional layers. The feature extraction and classification steps were unified under a single architecture, which means the guidance of classification can be used during the feature extraction step.

Another use of CNN for stegoanalysis has been presented and examined in [5] by Pibre *et al.* In this scenario steganographer always uses the same embedding key for embedding. The experimental results obtained for a proposed CNN or a Fully Connected Neural Network (FNN) surpassed the RM+EC approach. This very interesting scenario has not yet been sufficiently explored.

First time when the deep learning gave similar results to the RM+EC approach for the general scenario was described in [8] by Xu *et al.* The authors employed CNNs as base learners for ensemble and tested different ensemble strategies. The proposed methodology included a partial recovery of the lost information due to spatial sub-sampling in the pooling layers during feature vectors forming.

The first research concerning JPEG stegoanalysis was presented in [9] by Zeng *et al.* The authors tried to fit CNN to a rich-model feature set through pre-training the network. Moreover, the authors pointed out that the main reason why deep learning frameworks cannot surpass rich-model based frameworks is because training tends to get stuck at local plateaus or to diverge.

The next solution related to the JPEG stegoanalysis was published in [10] by Chen *et al.* The authors proposed an concept of porting JPEG-phase awareness into the CNN in order to increase the accuracy of detection. They introduced the so-called catalyst kernel, which allowed the network to learn kernels more relevant for detection of stego signal introduced by JPEG steganography.

Yet another solution against J-UNIWARD, which is the most secure JPEG steganographic method, has been presented in [11] by Xu. The author verified that both the pooling method and the depth of the CNNs are critical for performance. What is more, the author proved that a 20-layer CNN in general outperforms the most sophisticated feature model-based methods. Yet again, another ensemble of CNNs was presented in that paper.

The most current studies, which outperform the state-of-the-art in terms of error probability, have been presented in [12] by Yedroudj *et al.* The authors presented a CNN which consists of a pre-processing filter bank, a Truncation activation function, five convolutional layers with a batch normalization and scale layers, and a sufficiently sized fully connected layers. However, this work concerns analysis of spatial steganographic systems.

3 Research Methodology

The research has been divided into four stages: 1. Implementation of the reference network [5]. 2. Study on the influence of the depth and width of the convolution layers on the effectiveness of the network. 3. Study on the influence of depth and width of fully connected layers on the effectiveness of the network. 4. Implementation of a new CNN containing improvements in relation to the reference network.

In the first stage, the reference CNN has been implemented as presented here [5].

In the second stage, in order to investigate the influence of the depth and width of the convolution layers, the overall structure of the reference network has been preserved, i.e. two convolutional layers and two fully connected layers, however, experimental CNNs were varied in terms of the shape of the convolutional layers. The fully connected layers of CNNs were fixed. Details are described in Sect. 4. Pre-processing of input images results in faster learning and convergence and increased accuracy of the CNN. Hence, input images were pre-filtered using $F^{(0)}$ kernel, which is a kernel with size of 5×5, defined in [5].

In the third stage, in order to investigate the influence of the depth and width of the fully connected layers, the overall structure of the reference network has been preserved, however, experimental CNNs were varied in terms of the shape of the fully connected layers. The convolutional layers of CNNs were fixed. Details are described in Sect. 5. Input images were pre-filtered using previously mentioned $F^{(0)}$ kernel.

In the final stage, on the basis of the conclusions drawn from previous results, a new improved CNN for the scenario of reusing of the stego-key was proposed, trained and validated. The new proposed network consists of pre-processing filtering, two convolutional layers, one fully connected layer and classification layer. Details are described in Sect. 6. Input images were pre-filtered using $F^{(0)}$ kernel.

In all the stages, the modified BossBase has been used, which originally consisted of 10,000 natural images in greyscale with a size of 512×512. In order to increase the number of images and at the same time reduce processing times, each image was divided into four sub-images, each with a size of 256×256 pixels, thus obtaining a database of 40,000 cover images. In each picture a message was embedded using the S-Uniward steganographic technique with an embedding strength of 0.4 bpp using the same stego key, thus obtaining a database of 40,000 stego images.

In all the stages, for each training process, the database was shuffled and 75% of database was selected for the training, whereas the remaining 25% was selected for validation. The solving algorithm was the stochastic gradient descent with momentum optimizer SGDM. The training parameters were set as follows: momentum was 0.9, initial learn rate was 0.01, learn rate schedule was 'none', learn rate drop factor was 0.1, learn rate drop period was 10, L2 regularization was 0.0001, max epochs was 200, mini-batch size was 128, validation frequency was 234, validation patience was 5, verbose was 1, verbose frequency was 234, weight learn rate factor in convolutional layers was 0.001, bias learn rate factor in convolutional layers was 0.002. The above experimental settings were chosen empirically and the goal was to achieve precise training of over three thousand CNNs in a reasonable time of a few months.

MATLAB 2018a with Deep Learning Toolbox has been used as a programming environment. Nvidia GeForce GTX 1080 Ti graphics card has been used for calculations using CUDA technology.

4 Experiments on Convolutional Layers

In contrast to the reference network, the convolutional layers were parameterized in terms of the number of filters in the first convolution layer $N_1 \in \{8, 16, 24, \ldots 64\}$, the number of filters in the second convolution layer $N_2 \in \{2, 4, 6, \ldots 16\}$, filter size in the first convolution layer $S_1 \times S_1, S_1 \in \{2, 3, 4, \ldots 7\}$, and filter size in the second convolution layer $S_2 \times S_2, S_2 \in \{2, 3, 4, \ldots 5\}$. The first layer has stride equal to 2 vertically and horizontally. The second layer has stride equal to 1 vertically and horizontally. For both convolutional layers, the size of the zero padding was to ensure that the layer output has the same size as the input. Activation functions in both convolutional layers were ReLu functions. After activation functions, there are channel-wise local response normalization layers. Afterwards, the fully connected part is as follows. The first and the second fully connected layer have 1000 neurons and ReLU activation functions. The final classification is done via 2 neurons with softmax function. The structure of the networks in this study is shown in Fig. 1. Taking into consideration all the possible values of parameters N_1, N_2, S_1 and S_2, the total number of trained networks at this stage of the research was 1536. The uninterrupted training and validation of the above 1536 networks of different structures lasted about 24 days.

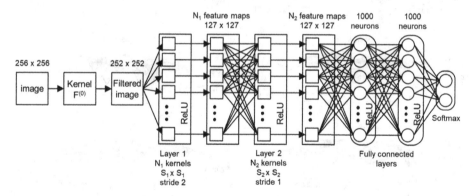

Fig. 1. The structure of the CNNs in the study of the convolutional part.

Resulting accuracy of the classification with the variable parameters of the convolutional layers are shown in Fig. 2. The sample size is 1536. The minimum value from the obtained measurements is 0.8348. The maximum value from the obtained measurements is 0.9487. The mean value of the obtained measurements is 0.9294, and the width of the confidence interval, for the confidence level 0.95, is 0.0017. With such a small width of the confidence interval, it can be concluded that the obtained results are reliable. The variance from the measurements obtained is $2.8806 \cdot 10^{-4}$.

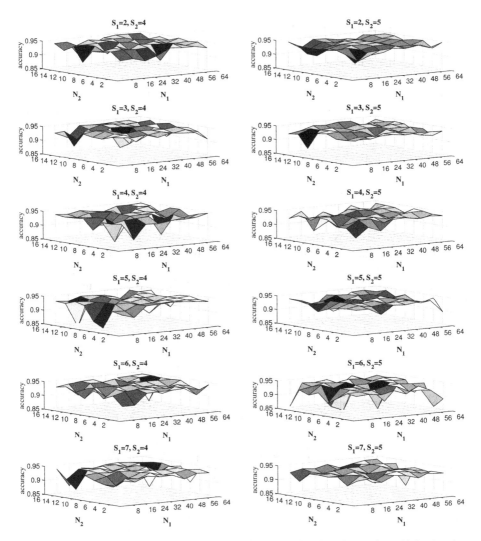

Fig. 2. The results of the accuracy of classifications for the CNNs in which the first convolutional layer has N_1 kernels with size of $S_1 \times S_1$, and the second convolutional layer has N_2 kernels with size of $S_2 \times S_2$.

The obtained results indicate that the depth or width of the convolutional layers in the reference network have a marginal influence on the classification effectiveness. During the tests, it was assumed that even if the shape of the convolutional layers influences the classification, it is disproportionately smaller compared to the influence of the assumed form of fully connected layers in the reference network. Investigating this supposition was the goal of the next stage of research.

5 Experiments on Fully Connected Layers

At the beginning, the convolutional part is as follows. The number of filters in the first convolution layer is 64. The number of filters in the second convolution layer is 16. Filter size in the first convolution layer is 7×7. Filter size in the second convolution layer is 5×5. The first layer has stride equal to 2 vertically and horizontally. The second layer has stride equal to 1 vertically and horizontally. For both convolutional layers, the size of the zero padding was that the layer output has the same size as the input. Activation functions in both convolutional layers were ReLu functions. After activation functions, there are channel-wise local response normalization layers. Afterwards, the fully connected layers were parametrized in terms of the number of layer $N_F \in \{1, 2\}$, the number of neurons in the first fully connected layer $F_1 \in \{5, 10, 15, 20, 25, 30, 35, 40, 45, 50, 75, 100\}$, and the number of neurons in the second fully connected layer $F_2 \in \{5, 10, 15, 20, 25, 30, 35, 40, 45, 50, 75, 100\}$. Activation functions in fully connected layers were ReLu functions. The final classification is done via 2 neurons with softmax function. Structures of the networks in this study are shown in Figs. 3 and 4. Taking into consideration all the possible values of parameters N_F, F_1, and F_2, the number of all possible combinations is 156. In case of $N_F = 1$, training has been repeated 35 times for each F_1. In case of $N_F = 2$, training has been repeated 10 times for each F_1 and F_2. Thus the total number of trained networks at this stage of the research was 1860. The uninterrupted training and validation of the above 1860 networks of different structures lasted about 28 days.

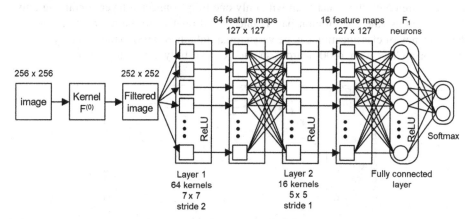

Fig. 3. The structure of the CNNs in the study of the fully connected part with only one fully connected layer.

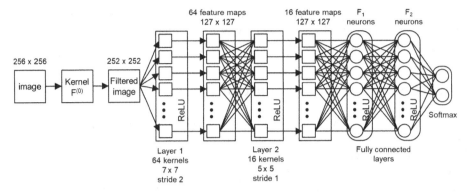

Fig. 4. The structure of the CNNs in the study of the fully connected part with two fully connected layers.

Figure 5 and Table 1 present the results of the classification accuracy in the case of one fully connected layer with the number of neurons from 5 to 100. The chart shows the measured average values and the widths of confidence intervals for the confidence level of 0.95. For values of F1 $\geq$ 40, the average accuracy is ~ 0.93 and the confidence intervals are very narrow, which testify to the reliability of the results. For values of F1 from 5 to 15, the confidence intervals are wider, and this is due to the fact that for such a small number of neurons in the fully connected layer, the algorithm sometimes does not converge to any local extreme and after some trainings the classification accuracy stucked at ~ 0.5.

The obtained results confirm the supposition that the fully connected layers in the reference convolution neural network were decidedly too wide, i.e. they contained relatively too many neurons for the considered problem, and their effect on the classification efficiency was incomparably greater than the effect of convolutional layers. The measurements show that even with only one fully connected layer containing only 30–50 neurons (the convolution part is unchanged relative to the reference network), the efficiency of classification can be very similar (about ~ 0.93) to the accuracy shown in [5] for a CNN with 1000 neurons in each of two fully connected layers.

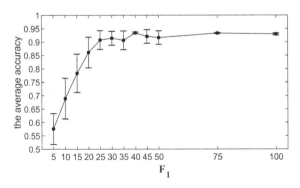

Fig. 5. The average value of classification accuracy with confidence intervals in case of one fully connected layer with F_1 neurons.

Table 1. A statistical analysis of classification accuracy in case of one fully connected layer.

F_1	Mean value	Confidence intervals for the mean ($\alpha = 0.05$)	Variance	Standard deviation
5	0.5755	<0.5176; 0.6334>	0.0284	0.1684
10	0.6888	<0.6128; 0.7648>	0.0490	0.2213
15	0.7835	<0.7120; 0.8550>	0.0433	0.2081
20	0.8613	<0.8039; 0.9187>	0.0279	0.1670
25	0.9078	<0.8724; 0.9432>	0.0106	0.1030
30	0.9143	<0.8882; 0.9405>	0.0058	0.0760
35	0.9065	<0.8714; 0.9417>	0.0105	0.1023
40	0.9345	<0.9312; 0.9377>	9.1959e−05	0.0096
45	0.9210	<0.8955; 0.9466>	0.0055	0.0744
50	0.9167	<0.8912; 0.9422>	0.0055	0.0742
75	0.9332	<0.9312; 0.9352>	3.4785e−05	0.0059
100	0.9298	<0.9260; 0.9336>	1.2155e−04	0.0110

Figure 6 presents the results of the classification accuracy in the case of two fully connected layers with the number of neurons ranged from 5 to 100. It can be observed that this network structure gives high accuracy (~ 0.93) only when both F_1 and F_2 are about 100 neurons. It should be noted that when $F_1 < 75$ and $F_2 < 75$, the networks often had troubles converging. This is due to the small number of interconnections between the first and the second fully connected layer. Optimization of parameters in the fully connected layers with the reference parameters of the convolutional layers led to a situation in which an output of convolutional part cannot be further processed by a reduced number of fully connected neurons. For this reason, in the next phase of research, it was decided to use the structure with only one fully connected layer.

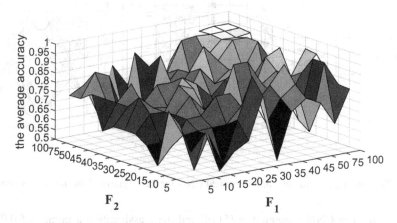

Fig. 6. The average value of classification accuracy in case of two fully connected layers with F_1 and F_2 neurons.

6   Improved Convolutional Neural Network

On the basis of the conclusions drawn from previous results, the structure of a new improved CNN for steganalysis of images in the scenario of reuse of the stego-key was proposed. The new proposed network consists of pre-processing filtering, two convolutional layers, one fully connected layer and classification layer. Input images are pre-filtered using $F^{(0)}$ kernel with size of 5×5, which results in faster learning and convergence and increased accuracy of the CNN.

$$F^{(0)} = \frac{1}{12} \begin{bmatrix} -1 & 2 & -2 & 2 & -1 \\ 2 & -6 & 6 & -6 & 2 \\ -2 & 8 & -12 & 8 & -2 \\ 2 & -6 & 8 & -6 & 2 \\ -1 & 2 & -2 & 2 & -1 \end{bmatrix} \quad (1)$$

The number of filters in the first convolution layer is 32. The number of filters in the second convolution layer is 16. Filter size in the first convolution layer is 5×5. Filter size in the second convolution layer is 5×5. The first layer has stride equal to 2 vertically and horizontally. The second layer has stride equal to 1 vertically and horizontally. For both convolutional layers, the size of the zero padding was to ensure that the layer output has the same size as the input. Activation functions in both convolutional layers were ReLu functions. After activation functions, there are channel-wise local response normalization layers. The fully connected part consists of only one layer. The fully connected layer has 50 neurons and ReLU activation function. The final classification is done via 2 neurons with softmax function. The improved CNN is presented in Fig. 7.

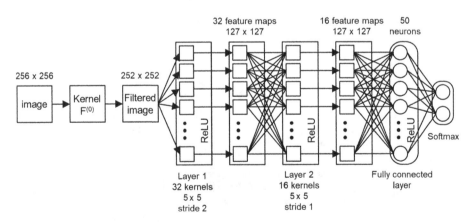

Fig. 7. The structure of the new and improved CNN for the scenario of the reuse of stego-key.

The reference CNN presented in [5] offered the classification accuracy of 0.9357, with 255 048 818 of parameters to be learned. The new proposed CNN offers the classification accuracy of 0.9363, with 12 714 600 of parameters to be learned. In conclusion, a new network was built, that in a given scenario of the stegoanalysis, offers classification accuracy at the same level as the current state of knowledge, but consists of narrower convolutional and fully connected layers. More specifically, the improved CNN contains 20 times less parameters to learn during the training process than the reference CNN which results in faster network learning, easier convergence and smaller memory and computing power requirements.

7 Summary

The research involved the use of convolutional neural networks for steganalysis of images in the scenario of repeated use of the stego-key. The reference point was the only previously published CNN in this scenario of steganalysis. Firstly, a study of the influence of the depth and width of the convolution layers on the effectiveness of classification was conducted (1536 CNNs were trained and validated). Later on, based on the drawn conclusions, a study on the influence of depth and width of fully connected layers on the effectiveness of classification was conducted (1860 CNNs were trained and validated).

The original hypothesis was that parameters of convolutional layers of the reference network have a major impact on the precision of classification. A conclusion on how the different modified parameters of the architectures modify the prediction of the network was the original goal of the research. However, the research showed the contrary. Initial results indicated that the depth or width of the convolutional layers in the reference network have a marginal influence on the classification effectiveness. Further tests showed that even if the shape of the convolutional layers impacts the precision, its influence is disproportionately smaller compared to the influence of the assumed form of fully connected layers. From that point, the alternative hypothesis was assumed and the new goal was to minimize the number of parameters while maintaining the classification precision. Although the experimental findings cannot be generalized to a principle, the results proved that more parameters in CNN do not mean a better network.

Based on the conclusions, a new improved convolutional neural network was created, which is characterized by the state-of-art level of classification accuracy in the considered scenario but containing drastically less parameters to learn. In this way, an improvement to the existing state of knowledge for a particular steganographic scenario has been proposed. Future work will consider detection of steganographic methods operating in the JPEG domain, e.g. J-Uniward.

References

1. Fridrich, J.: Steganography in Digital Media: Principles, Algorithms, and Applications. Cambridge University Press, Cambridge (2010). ISBN 978-0-521-19019-0. https://doi.org/10.1109/msp.2011.941841
2. Czaplewski, B.: Current trends in the field of steganalysis and guidelines for constructions of new steganalysis schemes. Przegląd Telekomunikacyjny + Wiadomości Telekomunikacyjne

[= Telecommun. Rev. + Telecommun. News] **10**, 1121–1125 (2017). https://doi.org/10.15199/59.2017.10.3

3. Fridrich, J., Kodovský, J.: Rich models for steganalysis of digital images. IEEE Trans. Inf. Forensics Security **7**(3), 868–882 (2012). https://doi.org/10.1109/TIFS.2012.2190402

4. He, F., Zhong, S., Chen, K.: An effective ensemble-based classification algorithm for high-dimensional steganalysis. J. Softw. **9**(7), 1833–1840 (2014). https://doi.org/10.4304/jsw.9.7.1833-1840

5. Pibre, L., Pasquet, J., Ienco, D., Chaumont, M.: Deep learning is a good steganalysis tool when embedding key is reused for different images, even if there is a cover source-mismatch. In: Proceedings of Media Watermarking, Security, and Forensics, MWSF 2016, Part of I&ST International Symposium on Electronic Imaging, EI 2016, San Francisco, California, USA, pp. 1–11 (2016). https://doi.org/10.2352/ISSN.2470-1173.2016.8.MWSF-078

6. Tan, S., Li, B.: Stacked convolutional auto-encoders for steganalysis of digital images. In: Proceedings of Signal and Information Processing Association Annual Summit and Conference, APSIPA 2014, Siem Reap, Cambodia, pp. 1–4 (2014). https://doi.org/10.1109/apsipa.2014.7041565

7. Qian, Y., Dong, J., Wang, W., Tan, T.: Deep learning for steganalysis via convolutional neural networks. In: Proceedings of Media Watermarking, Security, and Forensics 2015, MWSF 2015, Part of IS&T/SPIE Annual Symposium on Electronic Imaging, SPIE 2015, San Francisco, California, USA, vol. 9409, pp. 94090J–94090J–10 (2015). https://doi.org/10.1117/12.2083479

8. Xu, G., Wu, H.Z., Shi, Y.Q.: Ensemble of CNNs for steganalysis: an empirical study. In: Proceedings of the 4th ACM Workshop on Information Hiding and Multimedia Security, Vigo, Galicia, Spain, IH&MMSec 2016, pp. 103–107 (2016). https://doi.org/10.1145/2909827.2930798

9. Zeng, J., Tan, S., Li, B., Huang, J.: Pre-training via fitting deep neural network to rich-model features extraction procedure and its effect on deep learning for steganalysis. In: Proceedings of the Media Watermarking, Security, and Forensics 2017, MWSF 2017, Part of IS&T Symposium on Electronic Imaging, EI 2017, Burlingame, California, USA, p. 6 (2017). https://doi.org/10.2352/ISSN.2470-1173.2017.7.MWSF-324

10. Chen, M., Sedighi, V., Boroumand, M., Fridrich, S.: JPEG-phase-aware convolutional neural network for steganalysis of JPEG images. In: Proceedings of the 5th ACM Workshop on Information Hiding and Multimedia Security, Drexel University in Philadelphia, PA, IH&MMSec 2017, pp. 75–84 (2017). https://doi.org/10.1145/3082031.3083248

11. Xu, G.: Deep convolutional neural network to detect JUNIWARD. In: Proceedings of the 5th ACM Workshop on Information Hiding and Multimedia Security, Drexel University in Philadelphia, PA, IH&MMSec 2017, pp. 67–73 (2017). https://doi.org/10.1145/3082031.3083236

12. Yedroudj, M., Comby, F., Chaumont, M.: Yedroudj-Net: an efficient CNN for spatial steganalysis. In: Proceedings of the IEEE International Conference on Acoustics, Speech and Signal Processing, ICASSP 2018, Calgary, Alberta, Canada (2018). https://doi.org/10.1109/icassp.2018.8461438

A New Learning-Based One Shot Detection Framework for Natural Images

Sen Na[ID] and Ruoyu Yan[✉][ID]

Department of Computer Science and Technology, Nanjing University,
Nanjing 210023, China
yangry@nju.edu.cn

Abstract. Nowadays, existing object detection methods based on deep learning usually need vast amounts of training data and cannot deal with unseen classes of objects well. In this paper, we propose a new framework that applies one-shot learning to object detection. During the training period, the network learns an ability from known object classes to compare the similarity of two image parts. For the image of a new category, selective search seeks proposals in the first step. Then the comparison based on traditional feature is used to screen out some inaccurate proposals. Next, our deep learning model can extract features and measure the similarity through feature fusion (which means concatenating the channels of two feature maps in this paper). After these steps, we can obtain a temporary result. Based on this result and some proposals related to it, we refine the proposals through the intersection. Then we conduct second-round detection with new proposals and improve the accuracy. Experiments on different datasets demonstrate that our method is effective and has a certain transferability.

Keywords: One shot · Feature fusion · Second round detection

1 Introduction

From traditional features to deep learning model, great progress has been made in visual recognition tasks. Object detection is one of the important tasks and still in constant exploration. In recent years, although the accuracy and speed of object detection have been improved a lot, those methods usually need a mass of data for the object that will be detected. In practical application, this condition may not always be satisfied. However, with the rise of few-shot and one-shot learning, the classification task which does not require large numbers of samples has achieved initial success.

There are two main categories of methods for object detection, two-stage detection and single-stage detection. The representative network of the former has R-CNN [5], Fast R-CNN [4] and Faster R-CNN [14]. Such methods are more accurate, whereas the speed is slower. On the contrary, single-stage detection, including YOLO [13] and SSD [12], is faster but less accurate. Despite both

© Springer Nature Switzerland AG 2019
I. V. Tetko et al. (Eds.): ICANN 2019, LNCS 11729, pp. 93–104, 2019.
https://doi.org/10.1007/978-3-030-30508-6_8

approaches strive to improve on their shortcomings, using numerous images containing the target object as training data is unavoidable.

In recent years, few-shot and one-shot learning [18] entered our field of vision. Researchers began studying how to use a handful of samples to learn the generalization feature of image. Some are based on meta-learning and some use metric learning. However, they're more focused on the classification tasks. Although the research in [8] is about one-shot detection based on learning, it only considers the easy dataset such as Omniglot. [2] combines multi-model learning and self-paced learning. The research uses only a few labeled images per category, but at the same time, it also uses a large pool of unlabeled images. So it's essentially a semi-supervised task.

To deal with these problems, we propose a new framework by using one-shot learning in the training phase for natural images. For a new unseen class, when knowing only one image of this class, we can detect the location of the object in another picture. This is the purpose of one-shot detection.

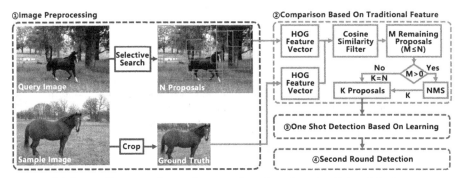

(a) Image Prepocessing and comparison based on traditional feature

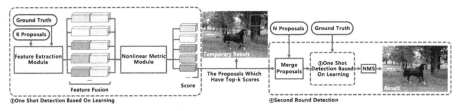

(b) One shot detection based on learning and second-round detection

Fig. 1. Detection Process (Testing framework). (a) is the whole detection process and (b) is a part of (a). In (a) we explain the comparison based on traditional in detail. In (b) one-shot detection based on learning and second-round detection are illustrated clearly.

In the training phase, we train the feature extraction module and the nonlinear metric module. Because the training dataset is completely different from the categories of the testing dataset, what the network learns is the generalization ability. This network is good at generalizing features, but when the network detects very similar objects, this characteristic may lead to poor results thanks to the interference of background. So during the testing phase, after obtaining proposals that are generated by selective search [17], we use the traditional feature to cope with this case. Traditional feature can show the contour features of objects better. If the comparison based on traditional feature gets no result, we use all proposals. Otherwise, the remaining proposals are what we need. Then the remaining proposals of testing image and sample image are sent into the network together to compare the similarity and predict the result. After getting the first round result, we carry out second-round detection according to it and some proposals that overlap with it. The detection process is shown in Fig. 1.

Overall, our main contributions have three parts. Firstly, we apply one-shot learning to object detection and this makes it possible to detect natural images of computer vision datasets. To our best knowledge, this is the first time to combine these two research for natural images in the literature. Secondly, the combination of traditional feature and deep learning model can achieve better results for pictures with different degrees of similarity. Finally, we perform second-round detection. Through taking full advantage of the best result in the first round, our approach gets further improvement. In addition, for different datasets, our method has a certain transferability.

2 Related Work

2.1 Object Detection

Two-stage detection and single-stage detection have their own merits. Two-stage detection has better accuracy due to performing stepwise. The first step of two-stage detection is generating a series of proposals by the algorithm which computes the regional similarity, such as selective search and edge box [21]. This kind of algorithm is suitable for all images and it doesn't need to train. Furthermore, this step can also be made by Region Proposal Network [14] which needs plenty of image data to train. Then the convolutional neural network will classify the proposals and perform the border regression operation. [19] replaces the RPN of Fast R-CNN with anchor refinement module. In the process of continuous development, many networks have made unique contribution such as ROI pooling [4], multi-task loss [4], thinner feature map [11], large separable convolution [11] and so on.

Single-stage detection, which doesn't have the step of proposals generating, is usually faster than two-stage detection. It uses the end-to-end training mode. YOLO divides the image into grids and uses convolutional neural network to directly predict the border coordinates and category confidence of object within the grid. While SSD unites the idea of regression and the anchor box mechanism. It makes full use of the semantic information of different level feature maps to detect object more precisely. [20] uses segmentation module and global activation module to acquire semantics information on the basis of SSD.

However, thanks to the use of mass data, the approaches mentioned above cannot deal with one-shot detection.

2.2   One-Shot Learning

In order to determine if two images belong to the same category, [9] came up with the idea that uses Siamese Neural Network based on one-shot learning. It mainly focuses on the embedding expression of the whole image. Through the same neural network, two images are represented as their respective feature vector. Then a linear classifier will give a score to indicate the likelihood that two pictures are in the same category. Applying this idea to n-way k-shot [16] experiments, it can also deal with the classification problem with a few samples effectively.

As is well-known, the linear classifier is not suitable in many cases, therefore [16] further ameliorated one-shot learning on the basis of Siamese Neural Network. It designs a learnable metric to cope with many different categories. By using the CNN as a nonlinear classifier, which is a learnable metric, the ability of classifying is greatly improved.

Whereas, most research of one-shot learning is applied to classification task at present. It inspires us to study one-shot detection based on learning.

2.3   One-Shot Detection

[1] uses LARK [7] as local descriptor and build the graph laplacian with geodesic affinities. By PCA or LPP [6], the local descriptor can keep more useful components. Since the length and width of the detected object are known in their research, the traditional sliding window is used. Then through the computation of Matrix Cosine Similarity and non-maxima suppression, the final detection result is obtained. Due to the use of the traditional feature (LARK), they detect similar objects better. They pay more attention to in-plane pose variation (scaling and rotation), but class-specific contextual information and viewpoint change problem cannot be solved.

[8] proposed a method that combines siamese network and attention mechanism. They trained the network to compare similarity between different object parts in a weakly supervised manner (They don't know the position of the object, and only ascertain if the image contains the object). This approach cannot use the box bounding information (representing the length, width and position of object), so their detection has to compare the similarity in the unit interval. And their approach can only be used in some easy datasets such as Omniglot. For natural images which are needed to confirm the box bounding, their method is to no avail.

3   Our Method

3.1   Training Framework

In the training period, along the extension line which belongs to the edge of ground truth, we divide the query image into five pieces—one object piece and four background pieces, as shown in Fig. 2. If the edge of the object piece is

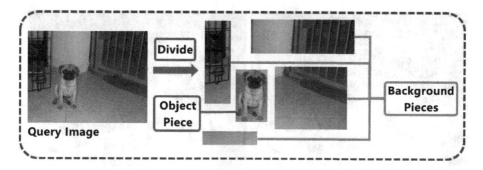

Fig. 2. How to divide the query image

overlapped with the edge of the image, the number of background pieces will be less than five. So we repeat the last background piece until the number of pieces meets five. For the sample picture which is of the same category as the query picture, we only use its ground truth. The ground truth and five pieces of the query picture are sent into the network to train. Through the feature extraction module, each piece gets a 256-channel feature map. Then we fuse the query and sample feature map by concatenating their channels. There are five 512-channel feature maps in total. The purpose of this step is to treat the two feature maps as one more complex feature map. Next, the metric module will evaluate their similarity by scoring the fusion feature from 0 to 1. The real label for the fusion feature of object piece and ground truth is 1, for other 4 fusion feature is 0. That is to say, the more likely the two parts are in the same category, the higher the fusion feature score. We adopt MES loss as our loss function. In Eq. (1), x_i denotes the score, and y_i denotes the real label.

$$L(X, Y) = \sum_{i=1}^{N} (x_i - y_i)^2 \qquad (1)$$

In this paper, we use Alexnet [10] without the last three full connected layers to extract image feature map because of balancing the efficiency and effectiveness. For nonlinear metric module, we use three convolutional blocks and two full connected layers. The first convolutional block consists of a 512-channel 3 * 3 convolution layer, a batch normalization layer and a ReLU activation layer. The second block is the same as the first block except that its number of channels is 256. The third block adds a 2 * 2 max-pooling layer in the basis of the second block. This module learns how to evaluate the similarity by performing regression operation of fusion feature.

3.2 Testing Framework

In the testing period, because the category of query image is unseen, we can't use RPN to generate proposals. Selective search is chosen to use. When we use

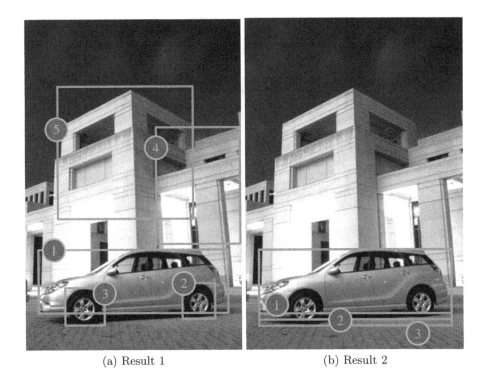

(a) Result 1	(b) Result 2

Fig. 3. Merging proposals. To show the process better, we remove some proposals. (a) is the proposals generated from selective search, and proposal 1 is the best result of the first round detection. (b) is the result of merging proposals.

selective search, we make some configuration changes so that we can achieve a better trade-off between accuracy and efficiency. The first step of selective search is obtaining initial regions by image segmentation [3]. Then it merges these initial regions to form proposals according to the similarity of different aspect. In consideration of the relationship of initial regions and image, we set the threshold value (minimum value) of the size for initial regions according to the size of the image. In this paper, it's 1/400 of the image size. For the final obtained proposals, they are set to different sizes so that they can find the object of a corresponding scale. At first, the threshold value (minimum value) is 1/15 of the image size. However, if the number of obtained proposals cannot meet 5, the object may be small. So the factor will be reduce to 1/50. The rest can be done in the same manner and the factor can be 1/120 or 1/300. If 1/300 still cannot meet requirement, ignore it.

Because our network pay more attention to generalize the feature of object, it has a better tolerance for viewpoint change and different individuals of the same species. At the same time, this tolerance may lead to poor results because of the interference of background for two similar objects. To make up this deficiency, we make use of the comparison of traditional feature to detect more similar

---

Algorithm 1. merge proposals

Input: proposals generated by selective search $\{P_n\}_1^N$,
      the best result of the first round R
Output: merged proposals $\{Q_m\}_1^M$
1 Initialization: n=1,m=1
2 while n $\leq$ N **do**
3   **if** P_n is overlapped with R
4   **then** Q_m = merge$\{P_n,R\}$,m=m+1
5   n=n+1
6 return $\{Q_m\}_1^M$

---

objects. We use the HOG feature vector and compute the cosine similarity of two vectors. This value can compare the similarity of two objects' contour better. If the value is greater than our threshold, we remain the proposal. If the number of remaining proposals isn't 0, we keep some proposals of them by Non-Maximum Suppression. Otherwise, we just use all proposals. The rest process is consistent with the training process. Equations (2) and (3) express our detection process. In Eq. (2), X is the query image and S means the selective search. In Eq. (3), x_n is the proposal generated by $S(X)$ and Y is the sample image. c fuses the feature by concatenating the channels of $g(x_n)$ and $g(Y)$. g means the feature extraction module and f is the nonlinear metric module. K_{top} denotes that it gets the top-k values.

$$\{x_n\}_1^N = S(X) \tag{2}$$

$$R = \underset{1 \leq n \leq N}{K_{top}} \{f(c(g(x_n), g(Y)))\} \tag{3}$$

Through the above steps, the proposals get their own scores. We choose the proposals that have top-k scores as the prediction result of the first round. In order to find the target object more accurately, we conduct second-round detection by using the result of the first round and some proposals which are overlapped with it. As we know, selective search finds proposals through the similarity of color and texture. So in some cases, a whole object may be divided into a few parts and these parts may be in different proposals. These proposals probably overlap with each other. We provided that we have found out a part of object (called as R) in the first round. Then we should merge R and the proposals that is overlapped with R to locate the target precisely. We show our thoughts in Algorithm 1. Merging proposals means that we pick the minimum and maximum value in the vertical and horizontal direction from the coordinates of two rectangles to form a new rectangle. From Fig. 3 we can clearly see that after merging proposals, the boxes become more precise. After second-round detection, we remaining the proposals with top-k scores. Then the final results are obtained by NMS. Because the result of the first round is also in new proposals, in most cases, the detection results will be more accurate.

4   Experiments

Now there isn't any public special dataset and measurement criteria for one-shot detection. In this paper, we choose four datasets to verify the effect of our method. For Pascal VOC 2007, Pascal VOC 2012 and Caltech 101, the criteria of detection is described as follows: if the IoU (Intersection over Union) of detected region and ground truth is more than 0.5, we think it's right. For UIUC CAR, because we will compare the result with [1], we follow their criterion which is described in [15]. In all experimental figures of this paper, the image in the first row is sample image and images in the second row are query images. The yellow box means the ground truth and the red box means our detection result.

Fig. 4. Some examples of Pascal VOC 2007.

Table 1. Result of Pascal VOC.

Datasets	Using second-round detection	Accuracy
VOC2007	No	43.51%
VOC2007	Yes	45.72%
VOC2012	No	45.62%
VOC2012	Yes	47.42%

4.1 Pascal VOC

Pascal VOC, which has 20 categories, is a frequently-used dataset of object detection. We choose the pictures to train and test from datasets following this criteria: each picture has only one object. For Pascal VOC 2007, we use 12 classes to train, 3 classes to validate and 5 classes to test. For Pascal VOC 2012, we use 11 classes to train, 3 classes to validate and 5 classes to test. Because the number of person category in Pascal VOC 2012 is much more than other categories, we remove it. In these two datasets, we set top-3 as top-k in the first round detection and top-1 in second-round. Table 1 shows the result of Pascal VOC 2007 and 2012. To demonstrate the effect of second-round detection, we compare two cases. Figure 4 shows some examples of detection result in VOC2007. If the object to be detected has tiny parts, our proposals may have some deviation. The second image in the second row shows this phenomenon in Fig. 4. If the background is too complicated, our approach probably cannot locate the object. This case is showed in the third picture of the second row in Fig. 4.

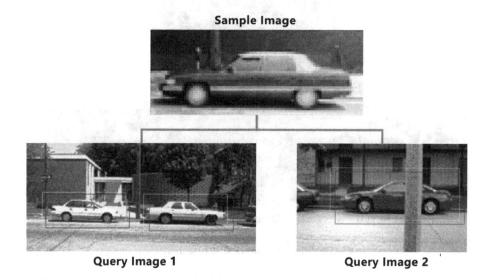

Fig. 5. Some examples of UIUC CAR.

4.2 UIUC CAR

UIUC CAR is a gray-scale image dataset, all of which are the sides of the car. We demonstrate the effectiveness of our method in Table 2 by comparing with the approach in [1], whose research is about one-shot detection with traditional feature. In this part, we use the model trained from Pascal VOC 2012 to detect and this also demonstrates the transferability of our method. In addition, due to the use of sliding window, we don't use selective search and second-round detection in this dataset. We set top-4 as top-k in the detection process. Figure 5 shows two examples of detection result in UIUC CAR. Because [1] focus on visual similarity involving scaling and rotation, their approach is more suitable for this dataset. However, for individual difference and viewpoint change, we are far ahead of them.

Table 2. Result of UIUC CAR.

Methods	CAR (EER [1])
Sujoy [1]	90.76%
Ours	79.38%

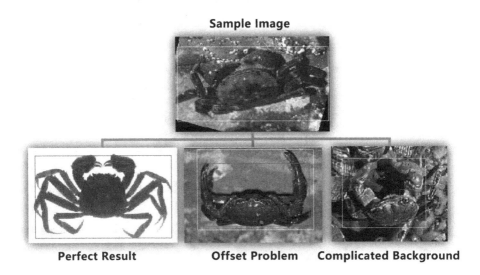

Fig. 6. Some examples of Caltech 101.

4.3   Caltech 101

This is a color dataset, which contains 101 classes of object. For this dataset, we also use the model trained from Pascal VOC 2012 to detect and compare the result with [1]. In this dataset, we set top-3 as top-k in the first round detection and top-1 in second-round. Table 3 shows the result. The characteristic of images in Caltech 101 is similar to Pascal VOC. They both have individual difference and viewpoint change, but Caltech 101 usually has a simpler background. That is the reason why it's accuracy is higher than Pascal VOC. Figure 6 shows some examples of detection result in Caltech 101. In this case, the ability of generalizing feature is important, so our approach achieved much better result than [1].

Table 3. Result of Caltech 101.

Methods	Caltech 101 (Accuracy)
Sujoy [1]	18.50%
Ours	57.25%

5 Conclusion

In this paper, we try our best to deal with one-shot detection based on deep learning for natural images. As a relatively new topic, it has great value to be explored. When information about images of new category is scarce, we make the most of the known information to learn the generalization ability. In our approach, the traditional feature and deep learning model can complement each other's advantages. Then second-round detection can take one step further on the basis of temporary results. The key point of one-shot detection is to learn the generalization ability from existing information, and apply this ability to detect new classes. When there are multiple categories in one picture and each species has multiple inviduals, it will creates more interference on one-shot detection. In the future, we will research this topic, which is a much more difficult issue.

References

1. Biswas, S.K., Milanfar, P.: One shot detection with laplacian object and fast matrix cosine similarity. IEEE Trans. Pattern Anal. Mach. Intell. **38**(3), 546–562 (2016). https://doi.org/10.1109/TPAMI.2015.2453950
2. Dong, X., Zheng, L., Ma, F., Yang, Y., Meng, D.: Few-example object detection with model communication. IEEE Trans. Pattern Anal. Mach. Intell. 1 (2018). https://doi.org/10.1109/TPAMI.2018.2844853
3. Felzenszwalb, P.F., Huttenlocher, D.P.: Efficient graph-based image segmentation. Int. J. Comput. Vision **59**(2), 167–181 (2004). https://doi.org/10.1023/B:VISI.0000022288.19776.77
4. Girshick, R.B.: Fast R-CNN. In: International Conference on Computer Vision, pp. 1440–1448 (2015). https://doi.org/10.1109/ICCV.2015.169
5. Girshick, R.B., Donahue, J., Darrell, T., Malik, J.: Rich feature hierarchies for accurate object detection and semantic segmentation. In: Computer Vision and Pattern Recognition, pp. 580–587 (2014). https://doi.org/10.1109/CVPR.2014.81
6. He, X., Yan, S., Hu, Y., Niyogi, P., Zhang, H.: Face recognition using laplacianfaces. IEEE Trans. Pattern Anal. Mach. Intell. **27**(3), 328–340 (2005). https://doi.org/10.1109/TPAMI.2005.55
7. Hiroyuki, T., Sina, F., Peyman, M.: Kernel regression for image processing and reconstruction. IEEE Trans. Image Process. **16**(2), 349–366 (2007). https://doi.org/10.1109/TIP.2006.888330
8. Keren, G., Schmitt, M., Kehrenberg, T., Schuller, B.: Weakly supervised one-shot detection with attention siamese networks. Stat **1050**, 12 (2018). http://arxiv.org/abs/1801.03329

9. Koch, G., Zemel, R., Salakhutdinov, R.: Siamese neural networks for one-shot image recognition. In: ICML Deep Learning Workshop, vol. 2 (2015). http://www.cs.toronto.edu/~gkoch/files/msc-thesis.pdf
10. Krizhevsky, A., Sutskever, I., Hinton, G.E.: Imagenet classification with deep convolutional neural networks. In: International Conference on Neural Information Processing Systems, pp. 1097–1105 (2012). https://doi.org/10.1145/3065386
11. Li, Z., Peng, C., Yu, G., Zhang, X., Deng, Y., Sun, J.: Light-head R-CNN: in defense of two-stage object detector. arXiv preprint arXiv:1711.07264 (2017). http://arxiv.org/abs/1711.07264
12. Liu, W., et al.: SSD: single shot MultiBox detector. In: Leibe, B., Matas, J., Sebe, N., Welling, M. (eds.) ECCV 2016. LNCS, vol. 9905, pp. 21–37. Springer, Cham (2016). https://doi.org/10.1007/978-3-319-46448-0_2
13. Redmon, J., Divvala, S., Girshick, R., Farhadi, A.: You only look once: unified, real-time object detection. In: Proceedings of the IEEE Conference on Computer Vision and Pattern Recognition, pp. 779–788 (2016). https://doi.org/10.1109/CVPR.2016.91
14. Ren, S., He, K., Girshick, R., Sun, J.: Faster R-CNN: towards real-time object detection with region proposal networks. IEEE Trans. Pattern Anal. Mach. Intell. **39**(6), 1137–1149 (2017). https://doi.org/10.1109/TPAMI.2016.2577031
15. Shivani, A., Aatif, A., Dan, R.: Learning to detect objects in images via a sparse, part-based representation. IEEE Trans. Pattern Anal. Mach. Intell. **26**(11), 1475–1490 (2004). https://doi.org/10.1109/TPAMI.2004.108
16. Sung, F., Yang, Y., Zhang, L., Xiang, T., Torr, P.H.S., Hospedales, T.M.: Learning to compare: relation network for few-shot learning. In: Computer Vision and Pattern Recognition, pp. 1199–1208 (2018). https://doi.org/10.1109/CVPR.2018.00131
17. Uijlings, J.R., Van De Sande, K.E., Gevers, T., Smeulders, A.W.: Selective search for object recognition. Int. J. Comput. Vision **104**(2), 154–171 (2013). https://doi.org/10.1007/s11263-013-0620-5
18. Vinyals, O., Blundell, C., Lillicrap, T.P., Kavukcuoglu, K., Wierstra, D.: Matching networks for one shot learning. In: Neural Information Processing Systems, pp. 3637–3645 (2016). http://papers.nips.cc/paper/6385-matching-networks-for-one-shot-learning
19. Zhang, S., Wen, L., Bian, X., Lei, Z., Li, S.Z.: Single-shot refinement neural network for object detection. In: Proceedings of the IEEE Conference on Computer Vision and Pattern Recognition, pp. 4203–4212 (2018). https://doi.org/10.1109/CVPR.2018.00442
20. Zhang, Z., Qiao, S., Xie, C., Shen, W., Wang, B., Yuille, A.L.: Single-shot object detection with enriched semantics. In: Computer Vision and Pattern Recognition, pp. 5813–5821 (2018). https://doi.org/10.1109/CVPR.2018.00609
21. Zitnick, C.L., Dollár, P.: Edge boxes: locating object proposals from edges. In: Fleet, D., Pajdla, T., Schiele, B., Tuytelaars, T. (eds.) ECCV 2014. LNCS, vol. 8693, pp. 391–405. Springer, Cham (2014). https://doi.org/10.1007/978-3-319-10602-1_26

Dense Receptive Field Network: A Backbone Network for Object Detection

Fei Gao$^{(\boxtimes)}$, Chengguang Yang, Yisu Ge, Shufang Lu, and Qike Shao

College of Computer Science and Technology, Zhejiang University of Technology, HangZhou, China
{feig,yangcg,geyisu,sflu,sqk}@zjut.edu.cn

Abstract. Although training object detectors with ImageNet pre-trained models is very common, the models designed for classification are not suitable enough for detection tasks. So, designing a special backbone network for detection tasks is one of the best solutions. In this paper, a backbone network named Dense Receptive Field Network (DRFNet) is proposed for object detection. DRFNet is based on Darknet-60 (our modified version of Darknet-53) and contains a novel architecture named Dense Receptive Field Block (DenseRFB) module. DenseRFB is a densely connected mode of RFB and can form much denser effective receptive fields, which can greatly improve the feature presentation of DRFNet and keep its fast speed. The proposed DRFNet is firstly tested with ScratchDet for fast evaluation. Moreover, as a pre-trained model on ImageNet, DRFNet is also tested with SSD. All the experiments show that DRFNet is an effective and efficient backbone network for object detection.

Keywords: Real-time object detection · Backbone network · Convolutional neural network

1 Introduction

In recent years, a wave of novel and effective CNN-based methods [1–5] were proposed to boost the development of object detection. However, few works [5–7] focused on the backbone network that is the fundamental component in the CNN-based object detector. Both two-stage methods [2,4,8,9] and one-stage methods [1,3] mainly adopt classification networks as backbone networks. Those pre-trained models may not be suitable enough for detection tasks and have some disadvantages as follows.

First, some improper structures in the classification networks like the down-sampling layer at the beginning will reduce the detection performance. Second, most methods above construct feature pyramids to perform multi-scale detection to solve scale problem, but they should still detect instances in a certain range size at each stage. To improve the detection performance at each stage, it is important to obtain discriminative features. However, the insufficient receptive

© Springer Nature Switzerland AG 2019
I. V. Tetko et al. (Eds.): ICANN 2019, LNCS 11729, pp. 105–118, 2019.
https://doi.org/10.1007/978-3-030-30508-6_9

field distribution of classification networks may prevent the improvement of these multi-scale detectors. As a result, in order to avoid drawbacks mentioned above, it is one of the best ways to design a special backbone network for detection tasks.

In this paper, based on the backbone network Darknet-53 [5], a backbone network named DRFNet(Dense Receptive Field Network) is proposed. At first, Darknet-53 is modified into Darknet60. The modifications are as follows: (1) an additional residual block is inserted into the root stage of Darknet-53 to enhance image information extraction; (2) single downsampling layers are replaced with downsampling residual blocks to make the network easier be optimized and avoid information loss. And then, to obtain DRFNet, Dense Receptive Field Block (DenseRFB), the dense mode of RFB module [10], is proposed and imported into Darknet-60 by replacing several residual blocks in the last three stages. The proposed DenseRFB helps DRFNet generate much denser receptive fields to make features more robust and discriminative for object detection.

For fast evaluation, all the modifications above are tested with ScratchDet [7] to avoid time-consuming phase of ImageNet [11] pre-training. ScratchDet is a scratch-training method by integrating Batch Normalization (BN) [12] into SSD [1]. The experiments results on VOC2007 [13] and MS COCO [14] datasets show the great effect of our modifications, and the proposed backbone network DRFNet has a close performance to Root-ResNet-34 [7] and is about twice faster. Moreover, DRFNet is also trained on the ImageNet and then tested with SSD on MS COCO dataset to further prove its effect as a backbone network.

The main contributions of this paper are summarized as follows: (1) a dense mode of RFB, named DenseRFB, is presented, which can generate much denser receptive fields to make features more robust and discriminative, (2) a new backbone network named DRFNet is investigated through modifying the Darknet-53 and importing DenseRFB into it, which noticeably improves the detection accuracy while maintaining the fast speed.

2 Related Work

2.1 The CNN-Based Detectors

Most of current object detectors are CNN-based methods, which is either two-stage method or one-stage method. Two-stage method is represented by Faster R-CNN [8] families like R-FCN [9], Mask-RCNN [4], and so on. The methods generate lots of proposals at the first stage and then recognize and refine these proposals to get the final results. One-stage detectors reframe object detection as a regression problem, which contains YOLO [5,15], SSD [1] and its various variants like DSSD [16], RetinaNet [3], STDN [17], etc. In contrast to two-stage methods, one-stage detection methods directly predict a certain number of bounding boxes based on the output information from the feature layer, which makes the network much faster. However, because of lacking refinement stage, one-stage method relies much more on the features extracted from the network. To improve the detection performance, the feature enhancement method like

RFBNet [10] is used on the backbone network due to the usage of pre-trained classification models.

2.2 Backbone Networks for Object Detection

Although most detectors use pre-trained models directly, there are still a few backbone networks designed for object detection. Darknet-53 [5] can improve the performance of YOLOv3 while keeping the fast speed. DetNet [6] can maintain high spatial resolution in the deeper layers and enhance the detection performance of detectors. Furthermore, the recently proposed backbone network, Root-ResNet-34 [7], can avoid local information loss by removing downsampling operation at the first stage of the original ResNet [18] and get the state-of-art-performance. However, there are still some problems and limitations in these methods. For example, Darknet-53 utilizes a single convolutional layer instead of the residual block for downsampling, which may be harmful to the network convergence. DetNet still has not removed the drawback of the classification network because it does not change the main structure of ResNet-50. Although Root-ResNet-34 achieves high performance, its speed is limited by the over-used convolutional layers. Therefore, it is essential to explore the efficient and effective backbone network for object detection.

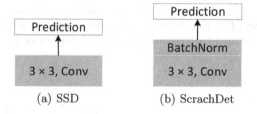

(a) SSD   (b) ScrachDet

Fig. 1. Different types of head subnetworks. (a) SSD: a single 3×3 convolutional layer without BN and ReLU. (b) ScratchDet: additional BN layer after convolutional layer to make the optimization landscape smoother.

3 Method

In this section, ScratchDet and RFB components are revisited and the structures of DRFNet including the modifications on Darknet-53 and the architecture of DenseRFB are described.

3.1 ScratchDet

Our network architecture is designed with the help of ScratchDet [7]. ScratchDet is a one-stage detector that can be trained from scratch while performing as good as using pre-trained models. It adds BN layers into the detection head sub-network of SSD and assumes that BN makes the optimization landscape smoother and the gradient more stable. The comparison between SSD and ScratchDet is shown in Fig. 1(a) and (b). By taking advantage of ScratchDet, the time-consuming training on large-scale ImageNet dataset can be avoided and the network architecture can be directly designed.

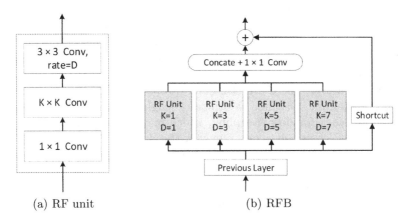

(a) RF unit   (b) RFB

Fig. 2. The architectures of RF Unit, RFB module. (a) RF Unit is the combination structure of standard convolution and dilated convolution. By setting different kernel size K and dilated rate D, RF Unit can form different sizes of effective receptive fields. (b) RFB module is formed by combining multiple branches of RF units to generate multi-scale features.

3.2   Receptive Field Block

Liu et al. [10] proposed the Receptive Field Block (RFB) module, a hand-crafted network architecture, which was developed from Inception-ResNet module [19] and ASPP module [20]. As shown in Fig. 2(a), RFB adopts the so called Receptive Field (RF) units to produce more stable effective RFs [21]. RF unit is a novel combination structure of standard convolutional layers and dilated convolutional layers. By setting different values of K (kernel size for standard convolution) and D (dilated rate for dilated convolution), RF units can form different sizes of effective RFs. These RF units of different effective RFs are parallelly organized in RFB to produce dense effective RFs, as shown in Fig. 2(b). The RFB modules are then attached to the backbone network as branches to generate the robust multi-scale features, which can make the great improvement of performance of VGG-based SSD with the fast inference speed.

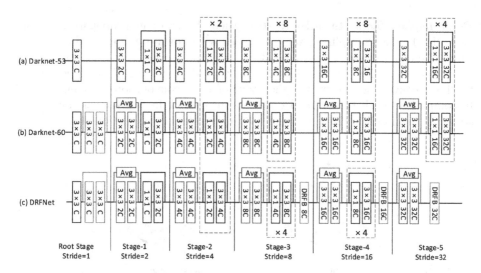

Fig. 3. Illustration of backbone networks. Each rectangle includes Conv, BN and ReLU. C is 32, denoted as the number of feature channels. (a) Darknet-53: original structure proposed in [5]. (b) Darknet-60: additional residual block (green block) and substituted downsampling residual block (blue block). (c) DRFNet: every four residual blocks in the last three stage of Darknet-60 are respectively replaced by DenseRFB (red block). (Color figure online)

3.3   Dense Receptive Field Network

Darknet-53. Darknet-53 [5] is a ResNet-like network, and its architecture is shown in Fig. 3(a). There are four differences between Darknet-53 and ResNet-101. First, Darknet-53 adopts 3×3 convolution operation at the input resolution, which has been proved to exploit more local information from the image [7]. Second, Darknet-53 uses a single 3×3 convolution layer as the downsampling layer. Third, a new type of bottleneck block like that used in DenseNet [22] is used to speed up the inference. Forth, ResNet-101 has {3, 4, 23, 3} building blocks from stage-2 to stage-5 respectively while Darknet-53 has {1, 2, 8, 8, 4} build blocks from stage-1 to stage-5, respectively. As a result, more layers in Stage-3 helps Darknet-53 generating more semantic features for detecting small objects.

Darknet-60. We propose Darknet-60 as shown in Fig. 3(b) which includes two types of modifications to improve the performance of Darknet-53, as follows.

Additional Root Block. Original ResNet adopts a 7×7 convolution layer to extract features from input images. A useful but straightforward scheme is replacing the 7×7 convolutions with three 3×3 convolutions. Moreover, the extensive experiment [7] shows the performance improvement by using plural 3×3 convolutions. So, a residual block in root stage is added and is shown as a green block in Fig. 3(b).

Downsampling Block. In order to strengthen the gradient propagation in the network, the downsampling layer is replaced with downsampling residual block, which is shown as blue blocks in Fig. 3(b). In the projection shortcut path of such residual block, a 2 × 2 average pooling layer with a stride of 2 is added before the 1 × 1 convolution layer, and the stride of 1 × 1 convolution is changed to 1. In comparison with the original downsampling block in ResNet, the improved structure proposed in [23] can avoid information loss in projection shortcuts.

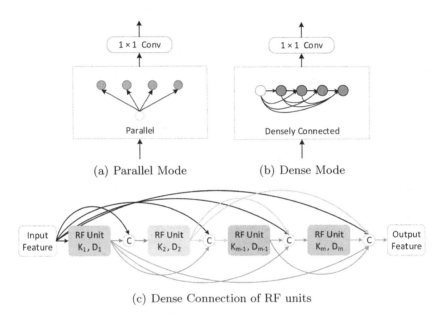

(a) Parallel Mode   (b) Dense Mode

(c) Dense Connection of RF units

Fig. 4. Illustration of the parallel mode and the dense mode. Note that dense mode changes the arrangement of RF units except other structures of RFB. The detail of dense mode is illustrated in (c).

DRFNet. Since each stage of multi-scale detectors should detect a certain range of objects in different sizes, and the suitable effective RF for object size helps network generate discriminative features to detect corresponding objects. It means that the distribution of effective RFs should be dense enough in a certain range, to fit different object sizes in the corresponding scale.

As mentioned in the Sect. 3.2, the arrangement of RF units in RFB module is in parallel mode as shown in Fig. 4(a). This arrangement makes the input information of RF units the same, and the effective RFs are just stacked. The number of effective RF size is equal to the paralleled RF unit number, which means that the RF unit number should be enough to form dense effective RFs. However, it will increase the computation cost.

Motivated by DenseASPP [24], RF units in RFB are rearranged from the parallel mode to the dense mode. The modified structure is named as Dense Receptive Field Block (DenseRFB), as shown in Fig. 4(b). The details in DenseRFB is illustrated like Fig. 4(c). Let's assume that there are totally m RF units, denoted by $\mathbf{RFU}_i()$, where $i \in \{1, 2, ..., m\}$, and the corresponding output of each $\mathbf{RFU}_i()$ is denoted as $\mathbf{y}_i$. The input features and output features are denoted as $\mathbf{x}_{in}$ and $\mathbf{y}_{out}$ respectively, and $\mathbf{y}_{out}$ can be obtained by

$$\mathbf{y}_{out} = \mathbf{x}_{in} + \sum_{i=1}^{m} \mathbf{y}_i \qquad (1)$$

$$\mathbf{y}_i = \begin{cases} \mathbf{RFU}_i(\mathbf{x}_{in}) & , i = 1 \\ \mathbf{RFU}_i(\mathbf{x}_{in} + \sum_{j=1}^{i-1} \mathbf{y}_{i-1}) & , 1 < i \leq m \end{cases} \qquad (2)$$

That is, for each RF unit, the intermediate feature maps of all preceding RF units are used as inputs and its feature maps are used as inputs into all subsequent RF units. In other words, there is an information exchange between each RF unit. As a result, a small number of RF units can form extremely dense RFs in a certain range.

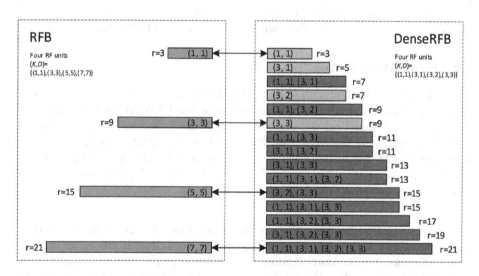

Fig. 5. Illustration of RF pyramids between RFB and DenseRFB. With different K and D settings, both of them has same maximum RF. However DenseRFB produces RF pyramid with much denser distribution in the same range. r beside each strip represents the receptive field size of the corresponding combination.

For example, Fig. 5 illustrates the RF pyramids of RFB and DenseRFB to help readers to understand the dense RF distribution better. The RFB is composed of four RF units, whose values of K and D are (1, 1), (3, 3), (5, 5) and (7, 7), respectively, and the DenseRFB also contains four RF units with smaller K

and D. The number set(s) in each strip represents the combination of different K and D, and the length of each strip represents the RF of each combination. Evidently, dense connections between RF units can compose RF pyramid with much denser scale diversity.

To decrease the inference time of the backbone network, the last four residual blocks in the stage-3, stage-4, and stage-5 of Darknet-60 are replaced with the DenseRFB module. Then, a faster and more powerful backbone network, DRFNet, is obtained.

4 Experiments

4.1 Experiment Setup and Implementation

The experiments are executed on PASCAL VOC and MS COCO datasets that have 20 and 80 object categories, respectively. In PASCAL VOC, a prediction is positive if its Intersection over Union (IoU) with the ground truth is higher than 0.5, while in MS COCO, various IoU thresholds are used for more comprehensive calculation. The metric to evaluate detection performance is the mean Average Precision (mAP). The proposed networks are based on the Pytorch framework. All the models are trained with SGD solver with a weight decay of 0.0005 and a momentum of 0.9 on a machine with NVIDIA GTX TITAN Xp GPUs.

4.2 PASCAL VOC 2007

The PASCAL VOC Object Detection Challenge is a benchmark test for the detection of visual objects. In the experiments on the PASCAL VOC benchmark, all models are trained on the union of 2007 trainval set and 2012 trainval set (16,551 images), and tested on the VOC2007 test set (4,952 images). The batch size is set to 128, the initial learning rate is set to 0.05 and the total number of training epochs is 800. The 'warmup' strategy in [10] is adopted, and the cosine learning rate annealing schedule in [23] is also used.

The Ablation Study. The ablation experiments on VOC 2007 are designed to verify the effects of the network modifications. The results are shown in Table 1. The performance of Darknet-53 based ScratchDet is 79.1%. The second and third rows of Table 1 show that the modifications of the additional root block and the downsampling blocks improve the performance to 79.7% and 79.9%, respectively. Moreover, with both modifications mentioned above, Darknet-60 can achieve 80.3%. The fifth row shows the effect of DenseRFB. DRFnet improves the performance further to 81.0%. In comparison with Root-ResNet-34, DRFNet can get the higher mAP (0.6%).

Table 1. Ablation study on PASCAL VOC 2007 test set. The results are tested with ScratchDet on 300 × 300 input size.

Backbone	mAP(%)	Delta
Darknet-53	79.1	0
Darknet-55 (Root block)	79.7	0.6
Darknet-58 (Bridge Connection)	79.9	0.8
Darknet-60	80.3	1.2
DRFNet	**81.0**	**1.9**
Root-Resnet-34	80.4	1.3

Comparison with Other Methods. Table 2 shows the comparison between our method and the state-of-the-art methods. Using small input size 300 × 300, our method produces 81.0% mAP, which outperforms other one-stage methods with similar input size, e.g. STDN321-DenseNet169 (79.3%, 1.7% higher mAP), DES300VGG16 (79.7%, 1.3% higher mAP), Refine-Det320-VGG16 (80.0%, 1.0% higher mAP) and RFBNet300-VGG16 (80.5%, 0.5% higher mAP). As for speed, the DRFNet-based detector can process the image at 61 FPS, which is faster than most of the one-stage methods such as DSSD321, STDN321, DES300, and RefineDet320.

Table 2. PASCAL VOC 2007 test detection results

One-stage method	Backbone	Input size	mAP (%)	FPS
SSD300 [1]	VGG-16	300 × 300	77.2	120
DSSD321 [16]	ResNet-101	321 × 321	78.6	10
STDN321 [17]	DenseNet-169	321 × 321	79.3	40
DES300 [25]	VGG-16	300 × 300	79.7	30
RefineDet320 [26]	VGG-16	320 × 320	80.0	40
RFBNet300 [10]	VGG-16	300 × 300	80.5	83
ScratchDet300 [7]	**DRFNet**	300 × 300	**81.0**	61

4.3 MS COCO

MS COCO is a large dataset for the competition of image object detection, its evaluation criteria is more complex, including AP_{small}, AP_{medium} and AP_{large}, which is used to evaluate the detection performance for objects of different scales.

To further validate the proposed DRFNet, additional experiments are carried out on the MS COCO dataset, all models are trained on the train set (118,287 images), and tested on the test set (5,000 images). The experiments contain two parts: (1) with the help of ScratchDet, and the comparison experiments with other one-stage methods are presented; (2) as a pre-trained model on ImageNet dataset, DRFNet is tested with large input size on SSD for further comparison.

For the model trained with ScratchDet, the batch size is 128, the total training epoch is 400, and the initial learning rate is set to 0.05. The 'warmup' strategy and the cosine learning rate annealing schedule are used. For the model trained with SSD, the batch size is 32, the total training epoch is 200, and the initial learning rate is set to 0.004. The 'warmup' strategy and the cosine learning rate annealing schedule are also used.

Table 3. MS COCO test detection results.

One-stage method	Backbone	AP	AP_{50}	AP_{75}	AP_s	AP_m	AP_l	FPS
DSSD321 [16]	ResNet-101	28.0	46.1	29.2	7.4	28.1	47.6	9.5
STDN300 [17]	DenseNet-169	28.0	45.6	29.4	7.9	29.7	45.1	38
RefineDet320 [26]	VGG-16	29.4	49.2	31.3	10.0	32.0	44.4	36
RFBNet300 [10]	VGG-16	30.3	49.3	31.8	11.8	31.9	45.9	66
RetinaNet400 [3]	ResNet-50-FPN	30.5	47.8	32.7	11.2	33.8	46.1	16
RetinaNet400 [3]	ResNet-101-FPN	31.9	49.5	34.1	11.6	35.8	48.5	12
SratchDet300 [7]	Root-ResNet-34	32.7	52.0	34.9	13.0	35.6	49.0	25
SratchDet300 [7]	**DRFNet**	32.2	50.4	34.4	**13.2**	**37.2**	48.2	54

The Results on ScratchDet. Table 3 shows the results on the MS COCO test set. DRFNet with similar input size (300×300) outperforms the one-stage methods like DSSD321 (28.0%, 4.2% higher AP), STDN300 (28.0%, 4.2% higher AP), RefineDet320-VGG16 (29.4%, 2.8% higher AP), RFBNet300-VGG (30.3%, 1.9% higher AP). Moreover, our method even gets the higher mAP than both RetinaNet400, while keeping about three or four times FPS.

Comparing with Root-ResNet-34, the proposed DRFNet is slightly worse than Root-ResNet-34 (32.7%, 0.5% lower AP). The reason is that much more convolution operations are used on the feature maps of higher spatial resolution, like adding more residual blocks in early stage (stride = 2, 4, 8). However, it has greatly affected the detection speed on the contrary, which makes the FPS of Root-ResNet-34 is about half of that of DRFNet.

Moreover, the in-depth comparison between DRFNet and Root-ResNet-34 shows that DRFNet get better results in AP_S (13.2% vs 13.0%, 0.2% higher AP) and AP_M (37.2% vs 35.6%, 1.6% higher AP). This proves that the usage of DenseRFB helps our backbone network generate more discriminative features for detecting densely distributed objects.

The Results on SSD. To further evaluate the effect of DRFNet as a backbone network, we adopt it on SSD. The DRFNet is first pre-trained on ImageNet

Table 4. Results on ImageNet ILSVRC 2012.

Model	Top-1	Top-5	FPS
ResNet-101 [18]	77.4	93.7	112
ResNet-152 [18]	78.4	94.1	70
DRFNet	78.5	94.1	143

dataset, and the result is shown in Table 4. Surprisingly, it outforms ResNet-152 and is twice faster. Then DRFNet-based SSD is trained on MS COCO trainval dataset. The result, as shown in Table 5, proves that the DRFNet is an effective backbone network. With the input size of 512×512, the simple DRFNet-based SSD achieve 34.7% mAP, which directly outperforms other one-stage methods in the Table. Moreover, it is good at detecting small and medium objects (18.7%AP_s and 43.2%AP_m respectively), and even better than YOLOv3 (608×608) on detecting small objects (18.7% vs 18.3%, 0.4% higher AP_s). The example of detection results is shown as Fig. 6.

Table 5. MS COCO test detection results (lager input size).

One-stage method	Backbone	AP	AP_{50}	AP_{75}	AP_s	AP_m	AP_l	FPS
STDN513 [17]	DenseNet-169	31.8	51.0	33.6	14.4	36.1	43.4	25
RefineDet512 [26]	VGG-16	33.0	54.5	35.5	16.3	36.3	44	22
YOLOv3 [5]	Darknet-53	33.0	**57.9**	34.4	18.3	35.4	41.9	20
DSSD513 [16]	ResNet-101	33.2	53.3	35.2	13.0	35.4	**51.1**	6
RFBNet512 [10]	VGG-16	33.8	54.2	35.9	16.2	37.1	47.4	**33**
RetinaNet500 [3]	ResNet-101-FPN	34.4	53.1	36.8	14.7	38.5	49.1	11
SSD512 [1]	**DRFNet**	**34.7**	53.2	**37.2**	**18.7**	**43.2**	50.2	29

5   Conclusion

This paper focuses on designing an efficient backbone network that is suitable for detection tasks. DenseRFB that can form denser receptive fields is proposed to generate more discriminative and robust features for object detection. A powerful and efficient backbone network, DRFNet, is obtained through embedding DenseRFB into the modified Darknet-53 for fully reusing the generated features. The experiment results show that the proposed DRFNet can achieve 32.2% mAP at 54 FPS (as the backbone network of ScratchDet with 300×300 input size), 34.7% mAP at 29 FPS (as the backbone network of SSD with 512×512 input size) on MS COCO test dataset. Through the experiments, the proposed backbone network, DRFNet is proved to be effective and efficient.

Fig. 6. Example of object detection results on the MS COCO test set. Each output box is associated with a category label and a score in [0, 1]. A score threshold of 0.4 is used for displaying.

Acknowledgements. This work was being supported by the National Natural Science Foundation of China (Grant No. 61402410), the Zhejiang Provincial Science and Technology Planning Key Project of China (Grant No. 2018C01064), and the Zhejiang Provincial Natural Science Foundation of China (Grant No. LY19F020027, LY18F020029).

References

1. Liu, W., et al.: SSD: single shot MultiBox detector. In: Leibe, B., Matas, J., Sebe, N., Welling, M. (eds.) ECCV 2016. LNCS, vol. 9905, pp. 21–37. Springer, Cham (2016). https://doi.org/10.1007/978-3-319-46448-0_2
2. Lin, T.Y., Dollár, P., Girshick, R., He, K., Hariharan, B., Belongie, S.: Feature pyramid networks for object detection. In: 2017 IEEE Conference on Computer Vision and Pattern Recognition (CVPR), pp. 936–944. IEEE (2017). https://doi.org/10.1109/cvpr.2017.106
3. Lin, T.Y., Goyal, P., Girshick, R., He, K., Dollár, P.: Focal loss for dense object detection. In: 2017 IEEE International Conference on Computer Vision (ICCV), pp. 2999–3007. IEEE (2017). https://doi.org/10.1109/iccv.2017.324
4. He, K., Gkioxari, G., Dollár, P., Girshick, R.: Mask R-CNN. In: 2017 IEEE International Conference on Computer Vision (ICCV), pp. 2980–2988. IEEE (2017). https://doi.org/10.1109/iccv.2017.322
5. Redmon, J., Farhadi, A.: YOLOv3: an incremental improvement. arXiv preprint arXiv:1804.02767 (2018)

6. Li, Z., Peng, C., Yu, G., Zhang, X., Deng, Y., Sun, J.: DetNet: design backbone for object detection. In: Ferrari, V., Hebert, M., Sminchisescu, C., Weiss, Y. (eds.) ECCV 2018. LNCS, vol. 11213, pp. 339–354. Springer, Cham (2018). https://doi.org/10.1007/978-3-030-01240-3_21

7. Zhu, R., et al.: ScratchDet: exploring to train single-shot object detectors from scratch. arXiv preprint arXiv:1810.08425 (2018)

8. Ren, S., et al.: Faster R-CNN: towards real-time object detection with region proposal networks. IEEE Trans. Pattern Anal. Mach. Intell. **39**(6), 1137–1149 (2016). https://doi.org/10.1109/tpami.2016.2577031

9. Dai, J., et al.: R-FCN: object detection via region-based fully convolutional networks. arXiv preprint arXiv:1605.06409 (2016)

10. Liu, S., Huang, D., Wang, Y.: Receptive field block net for accurate and fast object detection. In: Ferrari, V., Hebert, M., Sminchisescu, C., Weiss, Y. (eds.) ECCV 2018. LNCS, vol. 11215, pp. 404–419. Springer, Cham (2018). https://doi.org/10.1007/978-3-030-01252-6_24

11. Deng, J., Dong, W., Socher, R., Li, L.J., Li, K., Fei-Fei, L.: ImageNet: a large-scale hierarchical image database. In: IEEE Conference on Computer Vision and Pattern Recognition, CVPR 2009, pp. 248–255. IEEE (2009) https://doi.org/10.1109/cvprw.2009.5206848

12. Ioffe, S., Szegedy, C.: Batch normalization: accelerating deep network training by reducing internal covariate shift. arXiv preprint arXiv:1502.03167 (2015)

13. Everingham, M., Van Gool, L., Williams, C.K., Winn, J., Zisserman, A.: The pascal visual object classes (VOC) challenge. Int. J. Comput. Vision **88**(2), 303–338 (2010). https://doi.org/10.1007/s11263-009-0275-4

14. Lin, T.-Y., et al.: Microsoft COCO: common objects in context. In: Fleet, D., Pajdla, T., Schiele, B., Tuytelaars, T. (eds.) ECCV 2014. LNCS, vol. 8693, pp. 740–755. Springer, Cham (2014). https://doi.org/10.1007/978-3-319-10602-1_48

15. Redmon, J., Farhadi, A.: YOLO9000: better, faster, stronger. In: 2017 IEEE Conference on Computer Vision and Pattern Recognition (CVPR), pp. 6517–6525. IEEE (2017). https://doi.org/10.1109/cvpr.2017.690

16. Fu, C.Y., Liu, W., Ranga, A., Tyagi, A., Berg, A.C.: DSSD: deconvolutional single shot detector. arXiv preprint arXiv:1701.06659 (2017)

17. Zhou, P., Ni, B., Geng, C., Hu, J., Xu, Y.: Scale-transferrable object detection. In: Proceedings of the IEEE Conference on Computer Vision and Pattern Recognition, pp. 528–537 (2018). https://doi.org/10.1109/cvpr.2018.00062

18. He, K., Zhang, X., Ren, S., Sun, J.: Deep residual learning for image recognition. In: Proceedings of the IEEE Conference on Computer Vision and Pattern Recognition, pp. 770–778 (2016). https://doi.org/10.1109/cvpr.2016.90

19. Szegedy, C., et al.: Inception-v4, inception-ResNet and the impact of residual connections on learning. arXiv preprint arXiv:1602.07261 (2016)

20. Chen, L.C., Papandreou, G., Schroff, F., Adam, H.: Rethinking atrous convolution for semantic image segmentation. arXiv preprint arXiv:1706.05587 (2017)

21. Luo, W., et al.: Understanding the effective receptive field in deep convolutional neural networks. arXiv preprint arXiv:1701.04128 (2017)

22. Huang, G., Liu, Z., van der Maaten, L., Weinberger, K.Q.: Densely connected convolutional networks. In: 2017 IEEE Conference on Computer Vision and Pattern Recognition (CVPR), pp. 2261–2269. IEEE (2017). https://doi.org/10.1109/cvpr.2017.243

23. Xie, J., He, T., Zhang, Z., Zhang, H., Zhang, Z., Li, M.: Bag of tricks for image classification with convolutional neural networks. arXiv preprint arXiv:1812.01187 (2018)

24. Yang, M., Yu, K., Zhang, C., Li, Z., Yang, K.: Denseaspp for semantic segmentation in street scenes. In: Proceedings of the IEEE Conference on Computer Vision and Pattern Recognition, pp. 3684–3692 (2018). https://doi.org/10.1109/cvpr.2018.00388
25. Zhang, Z., Qiao, S., Xie, C., Shen, W., Wang, B., Yuille, A.L.: Single-shot object detection with enriched semantics. In: 2018 IEEE/CVF Conference on Computer Vision and Pattern Recognition. IEEE, June 2018. https://doi.org/10.1109/cvpr.2018.00609
26. Zhang, S., Wen, L., Bian, X., Lei, Z., Li, S.Z.: Single-shot refinement neural network for object detection. In: Proceedings of the IEEE Conference on Computer Vision and Pattern Recognition, pp. 4203–4212 (2018). https://doi.org/10.1109/cvpr.2018.00442

Referring Expression Comprehension via Co-attention and Visual Context

Youming Gao[1], Yi Ji[1], Ting Xu[1], Yunlong Xu[2(✉)], and Chunping Liu[1(✉)]

[1] School of Computer Science and Technology, Soochow University,
SuZhou 215006, China
{ymgao,txu7}@stu.suda.edu.cn, {jiyi,cpliu}@suda.edu.cn
[2] Applied Technical School of Soochow University, SuZhou 215325, China
ylxu@suda.edu.cn

Abstract. As a research hotspot of multimodal media analysis, referring expression comprehension locates the referred object region in an image by mapping a natural language. Though the localizing accuracy of similar objects is often distorted by the presence or absence of supporting objects in the referring expression, we propose a referring expression comprehension method via co-attention and visual context. For lacking supporting objects in referring expression, we propose co-attention to enhance the attention on attributes for the subject module. For existing supporting objects, we introduce visual context to explore the latent link between the candidate object and its supporters. Experiments on three datasets RefCOCO, RefCOCO+, and RefCOCOg, show that our approach outperforms published approaches by a considerable margin.

Keywords: Neural network · Co-attention · Visual context ·
Referring expression comprehension

1 Introduction

Referring expressions are natural language that describe the actual objects in the visual scene [23]. With the development of application requirements such as human-computer interaction and natural language based object detection, referring expression comprehension has tremendous research significance in the field of robotics research and multimodal media analysis [10,21,26].

Referring expression comprehension is usually formalized as selecting the target object with the highest matching score from the candidate object set in an image, given an input referring expression. Most methods can be divided into two categories, based on trained generation models [7,15,16,24] and joint visual-language embedding frameworks [2,11,14,19,23]. The former generates a description based on the CNN-LSTM framework, and matches it with the given referring expression to select the region with the highest similarity. The latter converts the visual features and linguistic features into the common embedding space respectively and calculates the distance between them. And then the

© Springer Nature Switzerland AG 2019
I. V. Tetko et al. (Eds.): ICANN 2019, LNCS 11729, pp. 119–130, 2019.
https://doi.org/10.1007/978-3-030-30508-6_10

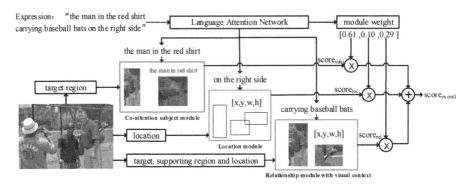

Fig. 1. The architecture of our model. In language attention network, we choose GloVe [17] instead of one hot embedding to generate the word vector. The location module retains the classic structure of MAttNet [23]. The subject module uses co-attention to enhance the module's attention to attribute features. The relationship module improves the visual representation by introducing a visual context. Finally, the overall score is calculated by the weighted sum of three modules. (Color figure online)

region with the smallest distance is chosen as the target. However, most methods only focus on how to mine visual features, such as object features, location features and context features [16, 24], ignoring the correspondence between words in referring expression and visual features in image.

Later, Yu et al. proposes MAttNet model [23] which focusing on different components of the language. But the attention of attribute features in subject module is reduced, and sufficient visual representation of the relationship module is not extracted. Hence the positioning accuracy of similar objects is decreased by these two problems. Human vision has the ability to automatically select prominent areas of the image [3]. Human brain can automatically focus and weight words on the referring expression. In addition, for the understanding of multimodal media information, humans can also use collaborative attention to accurately locate objects in images. Therefore, a referring expression comprehension method combining collaborative attention mechanism(co-attention) and visual context is proposed based on the MAttNet [23]. The overall framework is shown in Fig. 1.

There are three main contributions in this paper:

(1) The co-occurrence description of GloVe embedding [17] to strengthen the discriminability of the words of the referring expression.
(2) Co-attention enhances the subject module's attention on the candidate object attribute features by jointly guide the attention of vision and language, so as to distinguish analogous objects in the image.
(3) Visual context is introduced to get better visual representation by achieving the connection between candidate object and supporting objects.

2   Related Work

The task of referring expression comprehension is about locating the corresponding region of the image whrere matches the given referring expression [23]. The set of candidate regions is generally obtained by the object detection algorithm [5,18]. Each region is scored by matching with the referring expression. The highest score is chosen as the target object. The early models mainly study the representation of visual features, [7,16,24] add contextual features from other regions, [11] adds the candidate object attribute features. Recent models introduce attention mechanism into the referring expression comprehension. [19] proposes a comprehension model by reconstructing the expression using an attention mechanism. [6] uses a soft attention mechanism to decompose the referring expression. [23] learns the correspondence between language and vision through soft attention mechanism, and acquires the spatial attention guided by the referring expression.

Recently, co-attention is proposed in VQA(Visual Question Answering) [13] and applied to various tasks, such as visual reasoning [8], question answering [22], image captioning [12], visual dialog [4], visual explanations [20]. Co-attention solves the problem of "which area to look at" in the visual scene and "what words to read" in the language. In this work, we proposed the combination of visual and linguistic attention based on the alternating co-attention mechanism to strengthen the attention of the subject module on attribute features. As far as we know, it is the first time that co-attention has been introduced into the referring expression comprehension task.

3   Proposed Model

3.1   MAttNet Model

The MAttNet [23] was a modular attention network consisting of four parts: language attention network module, visual subject, location and relationship module. Given a candidate object and a referring expression, the referring expression was firstly mapped to three phrase representations (one for each visual module) and three module weights by language attention network. Then MAttNet matched visual representation and phrase representation of the three visual modules respectively.

Among them, the subject module used phrase representation to guide the spatial attention of the visual representation which combines the C4 features and attribute features of the candidate object. The attribute features are predicted by the fusion of C3 (last convolutional output of 3rd-stage contains high-leve visual cues for category) and C4 (last convolutional output of 4th-stage contains low-level cues for candidate judgment) extracted by res101-mrcn (res101-based Mask R-CNN) model. In location module, visual representation is achieved by fusing the position vector and position offsets with the same-type objects. The relationship module fused the position offsets and C4 features of supporting objects as visual representation. Finally, the total score is computed by weighting the sum of three module scores.

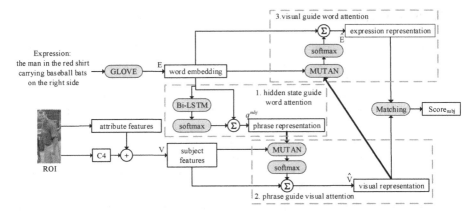

Fig. 2. Overview of the co-attention subject module.

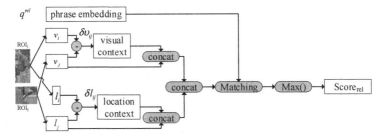

Fig. 3. Illustration of relationship module. v_i and v_j are visual features, l_i and l_j are location features. $j \in \{1, \cdots, N\}$. In the experiment, N is usually set to 5.

3.2 Co-Attention for Subject Module

Co-attention is a novel mechanism that jointly reasons about visual attention and language attention. For example, the three men in the image of Fig. 1 are wearing different colors of clothes. If the model notices the attribute word "red shirt", then the target object is beyond doubt. Therefore, we used co-attention to devote more attention to the attribute features of the candidate object.

First, we used the GloVe [17] embedding to obtain word vector $E = \{u_t\}_{t=1}^{T}$ and achieved the phrase representation q^{subj} with guiding the word attention through the hidden state of bidirectional LSTM. Then, visual features of the candidate object V were concatenated by attribute features and C4 features. The visual and linguistic features were fused by MUTAN [1], and we obtained visual attention a_v based on softmax. The weighted sum of V was the final attribute-enhanced visual representation $\hat{V}$. Afterwards, the way that we got the attribute-enhanced referring expression representation $\hat{E}$ was the same as the previous step. Finally, we used a matching function to calculate the score between $\hat{V}$ and $\hat{E}$. The matching function used MLP (Multilayer Perceptron) and L2 normalization to transform $\hat{V}$ and $\hat{E}$ into a common embedding space,

Algorithm 1. Co-attention Subject Module	Algorithm 2. Relationship Module
Input : $Expression, ROI$	Input : q^{rel}, ROI_i, ROI_j
output : $Score_{subj}$	output : $Score_{rel}$
1 $Subject\_Module(Expression, ROI)$:	1 $Relationship\_Module(Expression, ROI)$:
2 $E = GloVe(Expression)$	2 $v_i, v_j = res101 - mrcn(ROI_i, ROI_j)$
3 $h = Bi - LSTM(E)$	3 $l_i, l_j = encode(ROI_i, ROI_j)$
4 $a = softmax(h)$	4 $\delta_{v_{ij}} = v_i - v_j$
5 $q^{subj} = weighted\_sum(E, a)$	5 $\delta_{l_{ij}} = l_i - l_j$
6 $C3, C4 = res101 - mrcn(ROI)$	
7 $Attribute = attribute\_prediction(C3, C4)$	6 $visual = concat(\delta_{v_{ij}}, v_j)$
8 $V = fusion(C4, Attribute)$	7 $location = concat(\delta_{l_{ij}}, l_j)$
9 $H_v = MUTAN(V, q^{subj})$	8 $v_{ij}^{rel} = concat(visual, location)$
10 $a_v = softmax(H_v)$	
11 $\hat{V} = weighted\_sum(V, a_v)$	9 $Score_{rel} = Max(Matching(q^{rel}, v_{ij}^{rel}))$
12 $H_q = MUTAN(E, \hat{V})$	10 $return\ Score_{rel}$
13 $a_q = softmax(H_q)$	
14 $\hat{E} = weighted\_sum(\hat{V}, a_q)$	
15 $Score_{subj} = Matching(\hat{E}, \hat{V})$	
16 $return\ Score_{subj}$	

and then computed their inner product. The overall framework is shown in Fig. 2 and detailed steps are shown in Algorithm 1.

3.3 Relationship Module Based on Visual Context

The influence of context [2,6] on visual representation has been researched for a long time. Most of the previous methods exploit global or partial images as context input, disregarding the potential connection between the objects in the image. We proposed visual context to enhance the representation of the potential link between the candidate object and the supporting objects. The framework of relationship module is shown in Fig. 3 and detailed steps are shown in Algorithm 2.

Visual feature v in this module was the C4 features extraced from the res101-based Mask R-CNN model. The visual context $\delta_{v_{ij}}$ was obtained from the difference between the candidate object(ROI_i) and each supporting object visual features(ROI_j). $l = \left[\frac{x_1}{W}, \frac{y_1}{H}, \frac{x_2}{W}, \frac{y_2}{H}, \frac{w \cdot h}{W \cdot H}\right]$ encoded the position vector, where x_1, y_1, x_2, y_2 are top-left position and bottom-right position of the object, w, h, W, H are the width and height of the object area and the entire image. Location context $\delta_{l_{ij}}$ was the supporting object position offsets to the candidate object and their area ratio, i.e., $\delta_{l_{ij}} = \left[\frac{[\triangle x_1]_{ij}}{w_i}, \frac{[\triangle y_1]_{ij}}{h_i}, \frac{[\triangle x_2]_{ij}}{w_i}, \frac{[\triangle y_2]_{ij}}{h_i}, \frac{w_j \cdot h_j}{w_i \cdot h_i}\right]$. The final visual representation v_{ij}^{rel} was obtained by the fusion of visual and location features. Lastly, v_{ij}^{rel} and q^{rel} were sent to the matching function for scoring. Lastly, the score of the relationship module was the highest score.

4 Experiments

4.1 Datasets and Evaluation Metrics

We evaluate the referring expression comprehension on RefCOCO [24], Ref-COCO+ [24], and RefCOCOg [15]. Their images are all from MSCOCO [9],

Table 1. Ablation study of our model using different combination of improvement. The results are obtained computing the comprehension accuracies. MAttNet is MAttNet model. v_c represents visual context, co_att represents co-attention.

Models	RefCOCO			RefCOCO+			RefCOCOg	
	val	testA	testB	val	testA	testB	val	test
1 MAttNet	85.71	86.30	83.91	72.23	74.80	66.52	78.91	78.83
2 MAttNet+co_att	85.55	87.02	83.93	73.34	75.90	68.30	79.82	**79.71**
3 MAttNet+v_c	85.76	86.19	84.36	72.93	76.02	68.05	79.70	79.36
4 MAttNet+co_att+v_c	**85.89**	**87.06**	**84.38**	**73.44**	**76.49**	**68.40**	**79.94**	79.43

Table 2. Ablation study of our model on fully-automatic comprehension task using different combination of improvement.

Models	RefCOCO			RefCOCO+			RefCOCOg	
	val	testA	testB	val	testA	testB	val	test
1 MAttNet	76.69	81.67	70.29	66.51	71.31	57.39	67.40	67.80
2 MAttNet+co_att	77.64	81.93	70.62	67.48	72.18	58.42	68.30	68.48
3 MAttNet+v_c	**77.85**	81.81	**70.87**	67.49	71.92	58.64	68.38	68.73
4 MAttNet+co_att+v_c	77.29	**82.06**	70.60	**68.07**	**72.67**	**59.46**	**68.40**	**69.06**

but referring expressions are collected in different ways. Both RefCOCO and RefCOCO+ are collected interactively. RefCOCO has no restrictions on words, but the position words are relatively more. RefCOCO+ prohibits the use of position words, so its referring expression is purely based on the appearance of the object. RefCOCOg is collected in a non-interactive manner. Both RefCOCO and RefCOCO+ divide the test set into multiple people(testA) and multiple objects(testB). Early RefCOCOg is stochastically divided into training set and validation set according to the object in the dataset. Since the test set is not public, the evaluation is generally done on the validation(val*). Most of the current experiments randomly divide the images into train, validation and test. Our experiments on RefCOCOg are conducted in the second division way.

We use accuracy as metric to evaluate all models. Moreover, the relative growth rate(the formula is $(B - A)/A$) is employed to more pronounce the magnitude of the increase in the accuracy of model B relative to model A.

4.2   Ablation Study

In this section, we perform ablation analysis to estimate the contribution of each modification part. We choose MAttNet [23] and use GloVe [17] substitute for one-hot as baseline model. The candidate regions are the ground truth of MSCOCO, and the visual features are extracted using res101-mrcn. As shown in Table 1, both co-attention and visual context achieve certain growth in localizing accuracy, especially on RefCOCO+ and RefCOCOg. Experimental results show that our proposed method does make full use of the attribute and supporting

Table 3. Comparison with state-of-art models on ground-truth MSCOCO regions.

	Models	Feature	RefCOCO			RefCOCO+			RefCOCOg		
			val	testA	testB	val	testA	testB	val*	val	test
1	Mao [15]	vgg16	-	63.15	64.21	-	48.73	42.13	62.14	-	-
2	Varun [16]	vgg16	76.90	75.60	78.00	-	-	-	-	-	68.40
3	Luo [14]	vgg16	-	74.04	73.43	-	60.26	55.03	65.36	-	-
4	Liu [11]	vgg19	-	78.85	78.07	-	61.47	57.22	69.83	-	-
5	Speaker + listener + Reinforcer [25]	vgg16	79.56	78.95	80.22	62.26	64.60	59.62	72.63	71.65	71.92
6	MAttNet [23]	res101-frcn	85.65	85.26	**84.57**	71.01	75.13	66.17	-	78.10	78.12
7	MAttNet [23] (our experiment)	res101-mrcn	85.69	85.93	83.77	72.01	74.59	66.23	-	78.70	78.54
8	MAttNet + co_att + v_c **(ours)**	res101-mrcn	**85.89**	**87.06**	84.38	**73.44**	**76.49**	**68.40**	-	**79.94**	**79.43**

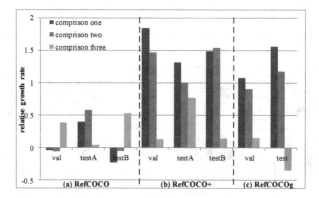

Fig. 4. The comparsion of relative growth rate on three datasets. Comparison one, two, and three respectively corresponds to one, two, and three columns of each dataset in this histogram. Comprison one represents MAttNet+co_att(GloVe) vs MAttNet+co_att(one-hot), comparison two represents MAttNet+co_att+v_c(GloVe) vs MAttNet+co_att+v_c(one-hot), comprison three represents MAttNet+co_att+v_c(GloVe) vs MAttNet+co_att(GloVe).

obejcts. Compared with co-attention and visual context, our full model also achieves certain improvements in localizing accuracy. Experimental results show the excellent fault tolerance of the modular network.

In addition, we analyze the effect of word embedding [17] on referring expression comprehension by three sets of comparative experiments (seen in Fig. 4). Comparison one and Comparison two high relative growth rates reflect that GloVe does bring significant improvements to our model. The comparison three low relative growth rate indicates that the semantic features of the words extracted by GloVe is correctly utilized by co-attention mechanism.

Table 2 shows the experimental results of referring expression comprehension based on automatic detection of objects by Mask R-CNN [5]. Although the overall accuracy has been decreased due to errors in object detection, each module

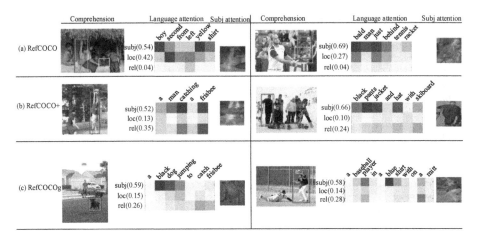

Fig. 5. Examples of our full model (MAttNet+co_att+v_c) in three datasets.

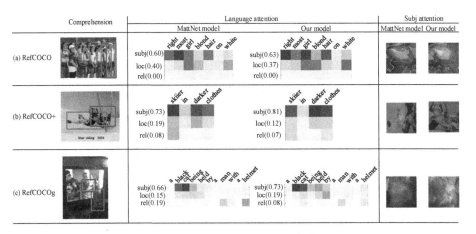

Fig. 6. Part of results from MAttNet and our model (MAttNet+co_att) in three datasets. The language attention is multiplied by module weights. The darker the color, the greater the weight. The blue boxes show our model's prediction and the green boxes are the ground-truth (The green box is scaled down because the prediction overlaps with the ground-truth.). Red boxes show wrong prediction of MAttNet model. (Color figure online)

maintains a certain growth in localizing accuracy. Two experiments of ground truth and fully-automatic comprehension prove the robustness of our model.

4.3   Comparsion with Existed Models

As shown in Table 3, we compare our model with previous six models. The accuracies of models without using the correspondence between words in referring expression and visual features in the image are generally low. The accuracy of

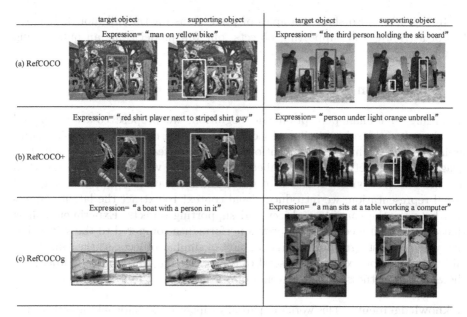

Fig. 7. Part of results from MAttNet model and our model (MAttNet+v_c) in three datasets. In addition to the target object, the yellow boxes show the supporting object of our model's prediction. White boxes show the prediction of MAttNet model. (Color figure online)

MAttNet [23] is increased by modular network. Since the regional visual features of our model are extracted by res101-based Mask R-CNN [5], we apply the same features to re-implement the experiment of MAttNet. Experiments show that our full model is overall on average 1% higher than MAttNet. This proves that our model takes full advantage of attributes and supporting objects, and surpasses the state-of-art.

4.4 Qualitative Analysis

In order to prove the validity of the proposed method, we visualize part of experimental results in Figs. 6 and 7. As shown in RefCOCO+ of Fig. 6, there are two skiers in the image. The MAttNet model is more concerned about "skier" from the language attention, so it cannot determine which person is the target object. Whether it is visual or language, co-attention pays close attention to the attribute features "darker" and predicts the target object correctly.

In Fig. 7, the referring expression is "red shirt player next to striped shirt guy". MAttNet model extracts the inadequate visual representation in relationship module, so it predicts the error person. However, the relationship module with visual context extracts the connection between the candidate object and the supporting objects, enhancing the visual representation. Consequently, our model accurately predicts the target object.

In Fig. 5, we also show examples of predictions for the full model. Regardless of attribute and supporting objects, our full model gains an outstanding performance.

5   Conclusion

According to human perception and cognition, we propose co-attention and visual context to solve similar objects detection in referring expression comprehension. To enhance the attention of attribute features in visual and language, we firstly let the GloVe embedding guide the visual attention, and then use the attended visual features to guide the language attention. To improve visual representation, we introduce visual context to extract the latent connection between the candidate object and supporting objects. Experiments show that co-attention mechanism improves performance compared to the soft attention when we distinguishing a large amount of similiar objects, at the same time, and the visual context is more useful to the positioning of supporting objects. It shows the robustness and effectivenes of our model.

Acknowledgements. This work was partially supported by National Natural Science Foundation of China (NSFC Grant No. 61773272, 61272258, 61301299), Key Laboratory of Symbolic Computation and Knowledge Engineering of Ministry of Education, Jilin University (Grant No. 93K172016K08), Collaborative Innovation Center of Novel Software Technology and Industrialization, and the Priority Academic Program Development of Jiangsu Higher Education Institutions.

References

1. Ben-Younes, H., Cadene, R., Cord, M., Thome, N.: Mutan: multimodal tucker fusion for visual question answering. In: Proceedings of the IEEE International Conference on Computer Vision, vol. 3 (2017). https://doi.org/10.1109/iccv.2017. 285
2. Chen, K., Kovvuri, R., Nevatia, R.: Query-guided regression network with context policy for phrase grounding. In: Proceedings of the IEEE International Conference on Computer Vision (ICCV) (2017). https://doi.org/10.1109/iccv.2017.95
3. Corbetta, M., Shulman, G.L.: Control of goal-directed and stimulus-driven attention in the brain. Nat. Rev. Neurosci. **3**(3), 201 (2002). https://doi.org/10.1038/nrn755
4. Das, A., et al.: Visual dialog. In: Proceedings of the IEEE Conference on Computer Vision and Pattern Recognition, vol. 2 (2017)
5. He, K., Gkioxari, G., Dollár, P., Girshick, R.: Mask R-CNN. In: 2017 IEEE International Conference on Computer Vision (ICCV), pp. 2980–2988. IEEE (2017). https://doi.org/10.1109/iccv.2017.322
6. Hu, R., Rohrbach, M., Andreas, J., Darrell, T., Saenko, K.: Modeling relationships in referential expressions with compositional modular networks. In: CVPR, pp. 4418–4427 (2017). https://doi.org/10.1109/cvpr.2017.470
7. Hu, R., Xu, H., Rohrbach, M., Feng, J., Saenko, K., Darrell, T.: Natural language object retrieval. In: Proceedings of the IEEE Conference on Computer Vision and Pattern Recognition, pp. 4555–4564 (2016). https://doi.org/10.1109/cvpr.2016.493

8. Johnson, J., et al.: Inferring and executing programs for visual reasoning. In: ICCV, pp. 3008–3017 (2017). https://doi.org/10.1109/iccv.2017.325
9. Lin, T.-Y., et al.: Microsoft COCO: common objects in context. In: Fleet, D., Pajdla, T., Schiele, B., Tuytelaars, T. (eds.) ECCV 2014. LNCS, vol. 8693, pp. 740–755. Springer, Cham (2014). https://doi.org/10.1007/978-3-319-10602-1_48
10. Lindh, A., Ross, R.J., Mahalunkar, A., Salton, G., Kelleher, J.D.: Generating diverse and meaningful captions. In: Kůrková, V., Manolopoulos, Y., Hammer, B., Iliadis, L., Maglogiannis, I. (eds.) ICANN 2018. LNCS, vol. 11139, pp. 176–187. Springer, Cham (2018). https://doi.org/10.1007/978-3-030-01418-6_18
11. Liu, J., Wang, L., Yang, M.H., et al.: Referring expression generation and comprehension via attributes. In: Proceedings of CVPR (2017). https://doi.org/10.1109/iccv.2017.520
12. Lu, J., Xiong, C., Parikh, D., Socher, R.: Knowing when to look: adaptive attention via a visual sentinel for image captioning. In: Proceedings of the IEEE Conference on Computer Vision and Pattern Recognition (CVPR), vol. 6, p. 2 (2017). https://doi.org/10.1109/cvpr.2017.345
13. Lu, J., Yang, J., Batra, D., Parikh, D.: Hierarchical question-image co-attention for visual question answering. In: Advances In Neural Information Processing Systems, pp. 289–297 (2016)
14. Luo, R., Shakhnarovich, G.: Comprehension-guided referring expressions. In: Computer Vision and Pattern Recognition (CVPR), vol. 2 (2017). https://doi.org/10.1109/cvpr.2017.333
15. Mao, J., Huang, J., Toshev, A., Camburu, O., Yuille, A.L., Murphy, K.: Generation and comprehension of unambiguous object descriptions. In: Proceedings of the IEEE Conference on Computer Vision and Pattern Recognition, pp. 11–20 (2016). https://doi.org/10.1109/cvpr.2016.9
16. Nagaraja, V.K., Morariu, V.I., Davis, L.S.: Modeling context between objects for referring expression understanding. In: Leibe, B., Matas, J., Sebe, N., Welling, M. (eds.) ECCV 2016. LNCS, vol. 9908, pp. 792–807. Springer, Cham (2016). https://doi.org/10.1007/978-3-319-46493-0_48
17. Pennington, J., Socher, R., Manning, C.: GloVe: global vectors for word representation. In: Proceedings of the 2014 Conference on Empirical Methods in Natural Language Processing (EMNLP), pp. 1532–1543 (2014). https://doi.org/10.3115/v1/d14-1162
18. Ren, S., He, K., Girshick, R., Sun, J.: Faster R-CNN: towards real-time object detection with region proposal networks. In: Advances in Neural Information Processing Systems, pp. 91–99 (2015). https://doi.org/10.1109/tpami.2016.2577031
19. Rohrbach, A., Rohrbach, M., Hu, R., Darrell, T., Schiele, B.: Grounding of textual phrases in images by reconstruction. In: Leibe, B., Matas, J., Sebe, N., Welling, M. (eds.) ECCV 2016. LNCS, vol. 9905, pp. 817–834. Springer, Cham (2016). https://doi.org/10.1007/978-3-319-46448-0_49
20. Selvaraju, R.R., Cogswell, M., Das, A., Vedantam, R., Parikh, D., Batra, D., et al.: Grad-cam: visual explanations from deep networks via gradient-based localization. In: ICCV, pp. 618–626 (2017). https://doi.org/10.1109/iccv.2017.74
21. Wei, W.L., et al: Seethevoice: learning from music to visual storytelling of shots. In: 2018 IEEE International Conference on Multimedia and Expo (ICME), pp. 1–6. IEEE (2018). https://doi.org/10.1109/icme.2018.8486496
22. Xiong, C., Zhong, V., Socher, R.: Dynamic coattention networks for question answering. arXiv preprint arXiv:1611.01604 (2016)
23. Yu, L., et al.: MAttNet: modular attention network for referring expression comprehension. In: CVPR (2018). https://doi.org/10.1109/CVPR.2018.00142

24. Yu, L., Poirson, P., Yang, S., Berg, A.C., Berg, T.L.: Modeling context in referring expressions. In: Leibe, B., Matas, J., Sebe, N., Welling, M. (eds.) ECCV 2016. LNCS, vol. 9906, pp. 69–85. Springer, Cham (2016). https://doi.org/10.1007/978-3-319-46475-6_5
25. Yu, L., Tan, H., Bansal, M., Berg, T.L.: A joint speaker-listener-reinforcer model for referring expressions. In: Computer Vision and Pattern Recognition (CVPR), vol. 2 (2017). https://doi.org/10.1109/cvpr.2017.375
26. Zhang, Y., Gu, Y., Gu, X.: Two-stream convolutional neural network for multimodal matching. In: Kůrková, V., Manolopoulos, Y., Hammer, B., Iliadis, L., Maglogiannis, I. (eds.) ICANN 2018. LNCS, vol. 11139, pp. 14–21. Springer, Cham (2018). https://doi.org/10.1007/978-3-030-01418-6_2

Comparison Between U-Net and U-ReNet Models in OCR Tasks

Brian B. Moser[1,2], Federico Raue[1(✉)], Jörn Hees[1], and Andreas Dengel[1,2]

[1] German Research Center for Artificial Intelligence (DFKI),
Kaiserslautern, Germany
{brian.moser,federico.raue,joern.hees,andreas.dengel}@dfki.de
[2] TU Kaiserslautern, Kaiserslautern, Germany

Abstract. The goal of this paper is explore the benefits of using RNNs instead of using CNNs for image transformation tasks. We are interested in two models for image transformation: U-Net (based on CNNs) and U-ReNet (partially based on CNNs and RNNs). In this work, we propose a novel U-ReNet which is almost entirely RNN based. We compare U-Net, U-ReNet (partially RNN), and our U-ReNet (almost entirely RNN based) in two datasets based on MNIST. The task is to transform text lines of overlapping digits to text lines of separated digits. Our model reaches the best performance in one dataset and comparable results in the other dataset. Additionally, the proposed U-ReNet with RNN upsampling has fewer parameters than U-Net and is more robust to translation transformation.

Keywords: U-ReNet · ReNet · RNN · U-Net · CNN · OCR

1 Introduction

Convolutional layers have been a crucial component for Computer Vision. The current trend is to build deep Convolutional Neural Networks (CNNs), which are a combination of several convolutional operations with different kernel sizes and connections [4,10]. As a result, CNNs increase the number of parameters that are required to optimize. Some examples are GoogLeNet-V1(5M parameters), ResNet-18 (11.7M parameters) and VGG (138M parameters) [7,18,19].

In this work, we are interested in the network capacities of transforming from a source image to a target image. For example, a source image has random noise, whereas the noise is removed in the target image. A common approach for transforming images is U-Net (which has in the original paper around 31M parameters), an encoder-decoder approach [16]. The encoder is downsampling the input space to a feature representation, whereas the decoder is upsampling the feature representation to the wanted target image.

Furthermore, we want to analyze Recurrent Neural Networks (RNNs) in the U-Net architecture because of two reasons: The first one is to exploit global context based on sequential information and the second one is that we want

© Springer Nature Switzerland AG 2019
I. V. Tetko et al. (Eds.): ICANN 2019, LNCS 11729, pp. 131–142, 2019.
https://doi.org/10.1007/978-3-030-30508-6_11

to reduce the number of parameters. In this context, a RNN treats the input elements as sequences and exploits the sequential order as context information. We use ReNet as a core element which uses two bidirectional RNNs as an alternative for CNN and Pooling layers [20]. Two versions of fusion between U-Net and ReNet (U-ReNet) have already been proposed: One for segmentation and another one for speech enhancement [2,21]. Both versions still employ many convolutional operations.

In this paper, we propose a new version of U-ReNet, which has an upsampling module based on ReNet modules and reducing the number of CNN layers. Our version of U-ReNet is evaluated in two OCR tasks, in which the image source is a text line of overlapped digits and the image target is the text line with separated digits. Note that text lines of digits are similar to a panorama view (e.g., image size 32×224). In summary, the contributions of this paper are:

- U-Net failed on one dataset of text lines because the target images also require a translation operation, whereas U-ReNet accomplishes this task well with fewer parameters.
- Upsampling ReNet has a positive effect on the performance of U-ReNet.
- The first layers of our version of U-ReNet is more discriminant than the U-Net architecture.

2   Background

Three components are crucial for understanding our work. The first component is ReNet, which proposes a combination of RNNs as an alternative for Convolutional and Pooling layers. The second component is U-Net, which uses encoder-downsampling and decoder-upsampling approach. The last component is U-ReNet, which is a combination of ReNet and U-Net. The next sections will briefly explain each of these components.

2.1   ReNet

ReNet is an architecture based on Recurrent Neural Networks (RNNs) as an alternative to convolution layers [20]. The idea is to divide the image into patches and run a Bidirectional RNN (Bidi-RNN) through the patches column-wise [17]. Consecutively, another Bidi-RNN runs through the patches row-wise. The combination of both Bidi-RNNs learn the global context of the image. An example of this architecture is shown in Fig. 1.

More formally, let $X \in \mathbb{R}^{w \times h \times c}$ be an input image, where h, w, and c are the width, height and number of channels, respectively. A ReNet layer with a window size of (w_p, h_p) creates a set of non-overlapping and flattened patches $P = \{p_{i,j} \in \mathbb{R}^{w_p \times h_p \times c} \mid i = 0, ..., \frac{w}{w_p} \text{ and } j = 0, ..., \frac{h}{h_p}\}$ of X, where $p_{i,j}$ denotes the (i, j)-th patch of X.

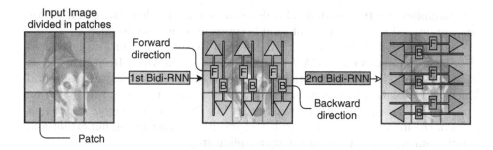

Fig. 1. A single ReNet layer. Initially, it sweeps over the image in the vertical direction and then in the horizontal direction in order to capture the whole image.

Two steps are required for training: First, the input is processed in the vertical direction with a Bidi-RNN, resulting in a new activation map V with elements

$$v_{i,j}^{F} = RNN^{F} \left(p_{i,j}, v_{i,j-1}^{F} \right),$$
$$v_{i,j}^{B} = RNN^{B} \left(p_{i,j}, v_{i,j+1}^{B} \right). \tag{1}$$

The superscripts F and B denote the two directions, forward and backward, of the Bidi-RNN. Second, another Bidi-RNN is processing through the activation map V in a similar manner but in the horizontal direction, creating a new feature map H. The combination of both RNNs produces a feature map H that is generated with respect to the whole image (full context).

Note that if a ReNet layer has d hidden units, then both Bidi-RNNs are using d hidden units. For simplification, the results of the forward and the backward directions of a Bidi-RNN are concatenated. In consequence, V and H have a shape of $\frac{w}{w_p} \times \frac{h}{h_p} \times 2d$.

So far, ReNet has been described only with vanilla RNN. Nonetheless, other RNN architectures can be used such as Gated Recurrent Units (GRUs) [3] or Long Short-Term Memories (LSTMs) [8].

2.2 U-Net and Attention-Based U-Net

The U-Net model is a symmetric encoder-decoder architecture (see Fig. 2) [16]. The encoder, also called contracting path, downsamples the feature map (reducing the spatial size). The decoder, also called expansive path, is upsampling the feature map (increasing the spatial size) back to its original shape.

This approach is inspired by Fully Convolutional Networks (FCNs) [1,13,16]. The idea behind the contracting and expansive path is to keep the number of parameters low and still use the advantages of deep convolutional layers.

The crucial aspect of U-Net and the difference to FCN relies on the different levels between the encoder and decoder. The current feature map is copied and concatenated to the corresponding upsampling step at each level. In other words, levels are the paths between the encoder and decoder, where the results of the downsampling are transported (also denoted in Fig. 2). Thus, there is not only one compressed feature representation between encoder and decoder.

Additionally, U-Nets can be combined with ReNet for exploiting global context. One example is the PiCANet architecture [12], in which ReNet is used as an attention module. The attention concept was originally formulated for Neural Machine Translation to support weighting of an input sentence in the prediction steps of the corresponding target sentence [14]. PiCANet is weighting different areas of the input image to achieve better results by highlighting important and ignoring unimportant parts in the upsampling steps.

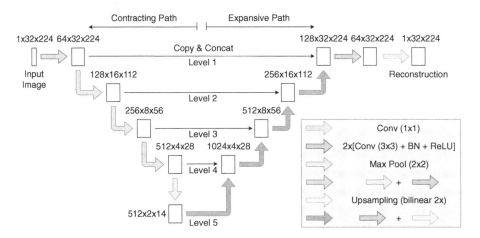

Fig. 2. Overview of the U-Net model that is used in this work. Note that the contracting path (left) are both reducing the activation map size and storing information. The expansive path (right) is increasing the spatial size using the activation map in the contracting path at each level.

3   U-ReNet

There are two architectures similar to our U-ReNet approach. One architecture has been applied to image segmentation and the other architecture has been applied to speech enhancement [2, 6]. The main idea behind U-ReNet was to use ReNet layers as alternatives to convolution layers in the U-Net architecture. An important difference of our approach in comparison to the existing ones is that we propose a U-ReNet with a simple RNN-based upsampling.

The other architectures still used CNN as a crucial feature processing part. The U-ReNet for image segmentation uses ReNet layers only for downsampling (upsampling is realized via transposed convolution) [2]. The other U-ReNet for speech enhancement also uses multiple convolution layers after a ReNet and in addition, it does not downsample the feature space like U-Net (i.e., the spatial size (h, w) is not changing) [6]. Table 1 summarizes the similarities and differences between our U-ReNet model and the other variations of U-ReNet. Furthermore, we introduce a simple Upsampling-ReNet layer for our U-ReNet version.

Table 1. Summary of similarities and differences between existing U-ReNet models and our presented model. Note that our model is based only on RNNs.

Models	Similarities	Differences
U-ReNet for agricultural image segmentation [2]	Use ReNets instead of max pooling	• Deep Convolution layers after ReNets • Transposed Convolution for upsampling
U-ReNet for speech enhancement [6]	Convolutional layer as Bottleneck (as runtime boost instead of feature extraction)	• Different task • No spatial down- and upsampling • Convolution layers after ReNet (not as Bottleneck)

3.1 Upsampling-ReNet

ReNet layers can be used for upsampling, i.e., increasing the spatial size (h, w) of a given input $w \times h \times c$. This allows our model to avoid interpolation or transposed convolution layers. A ReNet layer with window size of $(2, 1)$ is reducing only one dimension (in this case the width) by a factor of 2. Instead of decreasing the width and increasing the channel size c, it is possible to decrease the channel size and to increase the width by permuting the dimensions (see Fig. 3).

However, a window size of $(1, 1)$ and a proper amount of hidden units increases the spatial size without changing the channel size at all. Nevertheless, double sizing the image to $(2h, 2w)$ requires two ReNet layers: One is increasing the width and the other one is increasing the height.

The limitation of this method is that it is not scale invariant with respect to parameter size. E.g., upscaling the width by a factor of 2 needs a hidden dimensionality equal to the width (since ReNet is producing a feature size of $2d$). Thus, it needs more parameters for generating bigger upsamplings.

3.2 Our U-ReNet Model with Upsampling-ReNet

Our U-ReNet model is adapting the structure of the U-Net without max pool and stacked convolution layers. The general idea of the contracting and the expansive path remains the same (see Fig. 4). ReNet layers with window size (2, 2) are replacing the pooling layers and the following two 3×3 convolution layers were replaced by a single ReNet layer with window size (1, 1).

To avoid any transposed convolution operations or other upsampling techniques, Upsampling-ReNets were used. Even though an Upsampling-ReNet layer

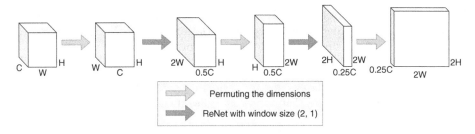

Fig. 3. Example of the upsampling based on ReNet. Two steps are required in this module: permuting dimensions and upsampling ReNet with windows (2,1). Applying the upsampling has an effect of increasing the spatial dimension (i.e. 2W x H - third block from the left) and decreasing the channel dimension (i.e. 0.5C).

is not scale invariant, the total number of parameters is nevertheless smaller than those of the U-Net model above for all the following experiments.

Similar to GoogLeNet, we used "Bottleneck" convolution layers (1×1) to half-size the channels after a ReNet layer [19]. They are used to boost the computation time and not as a main feature extractor. Thus, a ReNet layer with hidden dimensionality of d and "Bottleneck" after it produces a feature map with channel size d instead of $2d$. This was found to be very effective in light of computation time and parameter amount in the experiments. In consequence, the "Bottleneck" layer is combining the results of both directions, i.e., only manipulating the channel dimension.

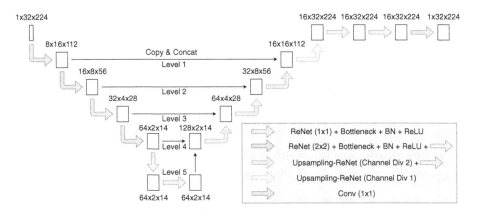

Fig. 4. Our U-ReNet model with Upsampling-ReNet.

4   Experiments

In this work, we want to compare our U-ReNet model against U-Net and the other U-ReNet architectures for evaluating the effects of the Upsampling-ReNet module. Two datasets of sequential data were generated based on MNIST. Also, we have analyzed the differences between the best and worst performance of U-Net with our model.

4.1 Datasets

Two datasets were used for comparison. The difference between both datasets is that one dataset contains similar generated images, but with arbitrary continuous shifting in the horizontal direction. Both consists of 50K train images (10K will be split for validation) for 5-fold Cross-Validation and 10K extra test images for a separate analysis.

OverlappingMNIST (OMNIST). One input image of OMNIST consists of four to eight MNIST images, partially overlapping in the center of the image [11]. The target image is the same sequence of digits without overlapping (see Fig. 5). Since the dataset is handcrafted, no data augmentation was applied. Only normalization of the input was used to have zero mean and unit variance.

shiftedOMNIST. This dataset is generated like OMNIST with the difference that the numbers in the input images are not centered anymore. Basically, it is OMNIST with random horizontal shifting (see Fig. 5). The purpose of this dataset is to test the translational robustness of the models. Therefore, the numbers can be presented between the very left and the very right of the image. The normalization step remains the same as for the OMNIST dataset.

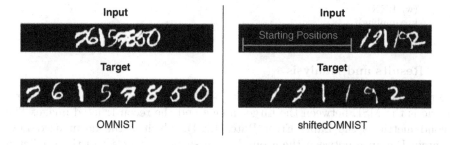

Fig. 5. Example of two images from the OMNIST and shiftedOMNIST dataset. Note that shiftedOMNIST has multiple, continuous starting points in contrast to OMNIST.

4.2 Training

The models were trained to minimize the Mean Squared Error (MSE) between the reconstruction and the desired output. Adam optimizer turned out to be the best optimizer for this task [9]. Early Stopping was used to avoid overfitting. Additionally, a learning rate decay was used every 20 epoch (learning rate was halved) because it was beneficial for both models.

4.3 Model Parameters

The modified U-Net model used in this work is different from the model in the original paper [16]. One of the difference relies on the number of parameters (ca. 20M parameters less) and performance. Another difference is the bi-linear upsampling instead of transposed convolutions and in the midst of the forward pass, the last downsampling is not increasing the feature size (it stays 512).

GRU was used for the ReNet layers in U-ReNet since LSTMs did not improve the performance in a notably way and GRU uses fewer parameters.

Table 2. Average results of MSE and LER between U-Net and U-ReNet. We want to point out that our model reaches similar results to U-Net with less number of parameters. As a result, the upsampling based on RNNs has a positive effect in the model.

Model	Size [M]	OMNIST		shiftedOMNIST	
		MSE	LER [%]	MSE	LER [%]
modified U-Net	13.4	11.3 ± 7.5	5.8 ± 10.0	163.2 ± 69.2	48.5 ± 20.3
original U-Net [16]	31.0	18.5 ± 11.8	6.2 ± 10.2	280.6 ± 83.7	73.2 ± 20.8
PiCANet [12]	47.2	29.0 ± 13.0	7.3 ± 11.1	64.9 ± 22.7	13.7 ± 14.3
Speech U-ReNet [6]	0.1	26.4 ± 16.6	7.6 ± 11.2	104.5 ± 44.7	26.9 ± 19.4
Agri. U-ReNet [2]	0.6	55.8 ± 29.7	8.5 ± 11.9	185.1 ± 65.2	39.5 ± 20.7
Our U-ReNet (w/o RNN-upsampling)	1.0	58.4 ± 25.6	9.4 ± 12.4	158.2 ± 58.5	34.4 ± 19.6
Our U-ReNet (w/ RNN-upsampling)	1.3	13.8 ± 8.8	6.6 ± 10.7	55.6 ± 25.8	13.1 ± 14.2

4.4 Results and Analysis

We reported the average of two metrics (5-fold validation) in Table 2. The first metric is the MSE between the target image and the reconstructed image. The second metric is the Label Error Rate (LER), which is the normalized Levenshtein Distance between the ground-truth sequence labels and the predicted sequence labels. Furthermore, a LSTM network trained with Connectionist Temporal Classification (CTC) [5] on the ground-truth for predicting the labels of the reconstructed image.

In short, our U-ReNet reaches a similar result to U-Net on OMNIST and a far better result on shiftedOMNIST. It can be inferred that the sequential nature of ReNet is better captured by a RNN based upsampling method since using simple upsampling methods, that are not RNN based, failed to create comparable results (see our ReNet without Upsampling-ReNet and Agriculture U-ReNet). The U-ReNet model for speech enhancement shows good performance with respect to its low parameter amount but it does not use spatial reduction and expansion for its computations. PiCANet, the attention-based U-Net, showed an outstanding performance on shiftedOMNIST, which we attribute to its high parameter amount (by far the highest among all observed models) and its attention mapping.

Figure 6 shows the best and worst reconstructions of U-Net and our U-ReNet on the shiftedOMNIST dataset. U-Net can reconstruct digits that are located at the same position in the input and target images. However, it fails to reconstruct digits that also requires a translation operation. For example, the reconstruction of the digit 3 (first column - U-Net) is blurred. This pattern is not found in our U-ReNet. In the following, we will only explore our U-ReNet.

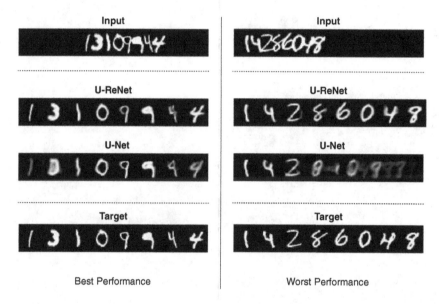

Fig. 6. Examples of the best and worst reconstructions for shiftedOMNIST. U-Net fails to reconstruct digits that are not located at similar positions between the input and target images. This translation might be the cause of the bad performance of U-Net. In contrast, the presented U-ReNet model does not have that problem.

Hence, U-ReNet seems to be more translation robust than U-Net which makes sense because the ReNet layers can learn global context information, which is the result of combining row- and column-wise sequences. There are five paths where information/features are transported between the encoder and the decoder of the network (starting with the copy and concatenation operation after the first downsampling and ending with the output of the encoder). We applied the models (which were trained on shiftedOMNIST) to OMNIST to fix the alignment of the digits in the center. The feature space representations are shown in Fig. 7.

In this case, we have used t-distributed Stochastic Neighbor Embedding (t-SNE) [15]. It can be observed that the models create clusters that correspond clearly to the sequence lengths. The clusters get clearer for U-Net with increasing

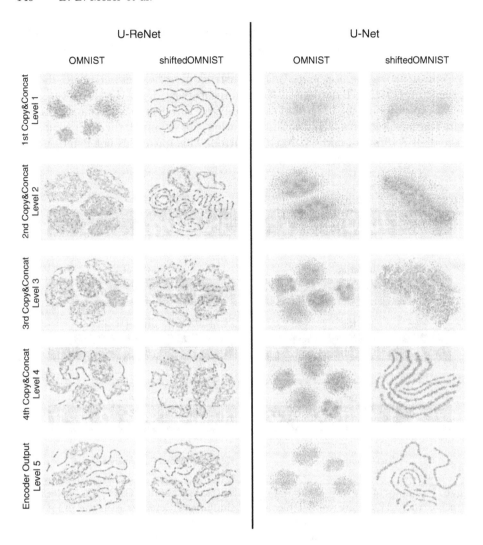

Fig. 7. Feature vector representation space for both models via t-SNE. One dot represents the encoding of one image in one of the five paths between the encoder and decoder. The feature representation of an input image is colored according to the sequence length in the input image (possible range is from four to eight, so five cases in total). U-Net and U-ReNet (trained on shiftedOMNIST) applied on OMNIST show clear clusters that are easily separable. We can clearly observe that U-Net needs more downsampling steps. Applying the models on shiftedOMNIST shows a shifting in the latent space but it is easier to separate the images with different sequence lengths with U-ReNet if you directly compare the centered (OMNIST) and the shifted (shiftedOM-NIST) case for at least the first three levels. After that, U-ReNet seems to encode something different that does not correlate directly to the sequence length.

levels, while U-ReNet shows clusters from the beginning. This clarity of the centered case vanishes if the models are applied on shiftedOMNIST.

Nevertheless, U-ReNet's shifting in the encoding is easier to separate afterward. U-Net's encoding is getting noisy for the shifted version. Moreover, the clusters start to overlap in U-Net for the shifted case, especially in the first downsampling steps. This separability of the encoding space can affect the reconstruction process of the decoder because each upsampling is processing the last upsampling result and the encoding of a lower feature representation (copy and concatenation operation of the same level).

5 Conclusion and Future Work

This work showed a comparison between U-Net and U-ReNet in text lines of digits. One of our findings is that our U-ReNet is more robust to translation in one dimension, which reaches good performance compared to U-Net in terms of the number of parameters. Another finding is related to feature representations. Our U-ReNet is able to recognize the sequence lengths from the first level whereas U-Net learns the sequence lengths from deeper levels. In the future, we are interested in evaluating our model on more difficult transformations, such as from handwritten text to printed text. Additionally, PiCANet reaches good results because of an attention mechanism based on ReNet. With this in mind, we are interested in extending our model in the direction of attention based on RNNs.

Acknowledgement. This work was supported by the BMBF project DeFuseNN (Grant 01IW17002) and the NVIDIA AI Lab (NVAIL) program.

References

1. Badrinarayanan, V., Kendall, A., Cipolla, R.: Segnet: a deep convolutional encoder-decoder architecture for image segmentation. IEEE Trans. Pattern Anal. Mach. Intell. **39**(12), 2481–2495 (2017). https://doi.org/10.1109/tpami.2016.2644615
2. Cereda, S.: A comparison of different neural networks for agricultural image segmentation (2017)
3. Chung, J., Gulcehre, C., Cho, K., Bengio, Y.: Empirical evaluation of gated recurrent neural networks on sequence modeling. In: NIPS 2014 Workshop on Deep Learning, December 2014 (2014)
4. Fukushima, K., Miyake, S.: Neocognitron: a self-organizing neural network model for a mechanism of visual pattern recognition. In: Amari, S., Arbib, M.A. (eds.) Competition and Cooperation in Neural Nets. LNCS, vol. 45, pp. 267–285. Springer, Heidelberg (1982). https://doi.org/10.1007/978-3-642-46466-9_18
5. Graves, A., Fernández, S., Gomez, F., Schmidhuber, J.: Connectionist temporal classification: labelling unsegmented sequence data with recurrent neural networks. In: Proceedings of the 23rd International Conference on Machine Learning, pp. 369–376. ACM (2006). https://doi.org/10.1145/1143844.1143891
6. Grzywalski, T., Drgas, S.: Using recurrences in time and frequency within U-net architecture for speech enhancement, pp. 6970–6974, May 2019. https://doi.org/10.1109/ICASSP.2019.8682830

7. He, K., Zhang, X., Ren, S., Sun, J.: Deep residual learning for image recognition. In: Proceedings of the IEEE Conference on Computer Vision and Pattern Recognition, pp. 770–778 (2016). https://doi.org/10.1109/CVPR.2016.90

8. Hochreiter, S., Schmidhuber, J.: Long short-term memory. Neural Comput. **9**(8), 1735–1780 (1997). https://doi.org/10.1162/neco.1997.9.8.1735

9. Kingma, D.P., Ba, J.: Adam: A method for stochastic optimization (2015)

10. LeCun, Y., et al.: Backpropagation applied to handwritten zip code recognition. Neural Comput. **1**(4), 541–551 (1989). https://doi.org/10.1162/neco.1989.1.4.541

11. LeCun, Y., Cortes, C.: MNIST handwritten digit database (2010). http://yann.lecun.com/exdb/mnist/

12. Liu, N., Han, J., Yang, M.H.: Picanet: learning pixel-wise contextual attention for saliency detection. In: Proceedings of the IEEE Conference on Computer Vision and Pattern Recognition, pp. 3089–3098 (2018). https://doi.org/10.1109/CVPR.2018.00326

13. Long, J., Shelhamer, E., Darrell, T.: Fully convolutional networks for semantic segmentation. In: Proceedings of the IEEE conference on Computer Vision and Pattern Recognition, pp. 3431–3440 (2015). https://doi.org/10.1109/CVPR.2015.7298965

14. Luong, T., Pham, H., Manning, C.D.: Effective approaches to attention-based neural machine translation, pp. 1412–1421, September 2015

15. van der Maaten, L., Hinton, G.: Visualizing data using t-SNE. J. Mach. Learn. Res. **9**(Nov), 2579–2605 (2008)

16. Ronneberger, O., Fischer, P., Brox, T.: U-Net: convolutional networks for biomedical image segmentation. In: Navab, N., Hornegger, J., Wells, W.M., Frangi, A.F. (eds.) MICCAI 2015. LNCS, vol. 9351, pp. 234–241. Springer, Cham (2015). https://doi.org/10.1007/978-3-319-24574-4_28

17. Schuster, M., Paliwal, K.K.: Bidirectional recurrent neural networks. IEEE Trans. Sig. Process. **45**(11), 2673–2681 (1997). https://doi.org/10.1109/78.650093

18. Simonyan, K., Zisserman, A.: Very deep convolutional networks for large-scale image recognition (2015)

19. Szegedy, C., et al.: Going deeper with convolutions. In: Proceedings of the IEEE Conference on Computer Vision and Pattern Recognition, pp. 1–9 (2015). https://doi.org/10.1109/CVPR.2015.7298594

20. Visin, F., Kastner, K., Cho, K., Matteucci, M., Courville, A., Bengio, Y.: Renet: A recurrent neural network based alternative to convolutional networks. arXiv preprint arXiv:1505.00393 (2015)

21. Yan, Z., Zhang, H., Jia, Y., Breuel, T., Yu, Y.: Combining the best of convolutional layers and recurrent layers: A hybrid network for semantic segmentation. arXiv preprint arXiv:1603.04871 (2016)

Severe Convective Weather Classification in Remote Sensing Images by Semantic Segmentation

Ming Yuan[1], Zhilei Chai[2(✉)] [iD], and Wenlai Zhao[3,4]

[1] School of IoT Engineering, Jiangnan University, Wuxi, China
[2] School of IoT Engineering, Jiangnan University,
Engineering Research Center of IoT Applications Ministry of Education, Wuxi, China
zlchai@jiangnan.edu.cn
[3] Tsinghua University, Beijing, China
[4] National Supercomputer Center in Wuxi, Wuxi, China

Abstract. Severe convective weather is a catastrophic weather that can cause great harm to the public. One of the key studies for meteorological practitioners is how to recognize severe convection weather accurately and effectively, and it is also an important issue in government climate risk management. However, most existing methods extract features from satellite data by classifying individual pixels instead of using tightly integrated spatial information, ignoring the fact the clouds are highly dynamic. In this paper, we propose a new classification model, which is based on image segmentation of deep learning. And it uses U-net architecture as the technology platform to identify all weather conditions in the datasets accurately. As heavy rainfall is one of the most frequent and widespread server weather hazards, when the storms come ashore with high speed of wind, it makes the precipitation time longer and causes serious damage in turn. Therefore, we suggest a new evaluation metric to evaluate the performance of detecting heavy rainfall. Compared with existing methods, the model based on Himawari-8 dataset has a better performance. Further, we explore the representations learned by our model in order to better understand this important dataset. The results play a crucial role in the prediction of climate change risks and the formulation of government policies on climate change.

Keywords: Severe convective weather · Segmentation · Evaluation metric

1 Introduction

Since the 21st century, climate change has been one of the major challenges that human beings need to face. The extreme weather caused by climate change posed great potential risk on infrastructure and human health. In recent decades, professional meteorologists have developed numerical weather prediction (NWP)

© Springer Nature Switzerland AG 2019
I. V. Tetko et al. (Eds.): ICANN 2019, LNCS 11729, pp. 143–156, 2019.
https://doi.org/10.1007/978-3-030-30508-6_12

model, which used the meteorological data, such as wind speed, temperature, and air pressure, to identify and predict the extreme weather events. In this work, we make a research on severe convective weather, which is one of the most common types of extreme weather events, and it will cause short-term heavy rainfall, thunderstorm gale, hail, and other catastrophic weather. The existing methods of detecting severe convection weather events are mainly proposed by experts in the field of meteorology, which is based on a wide variety of historical data.

However, the methods are of great value but there are some areas that can be improved. For one hand, there are no accurate definitions and unified evaluation metrics for it. Existing extreme climate events detection and classification all build on human experience, which results in low recognition accuracy of extreme weather events. For another, extreme weather identification based on data analysis involves a huge amount of computation and long analysis time-consuming, which results in a poor real-time performance of traditional methods.

In the past 10 years, deep learning, and specifically convolutional neural network, have developed rapidly. And it also has made groundbreaking achievements in various fields. Recent efforts [1–3] have shown that deep learning can be successfully applied for detection, classification, and prediction of extreme weather patterns. However, there are still several major drawbacks to the current approach. First of all, there is some noise in the datasets in terms of label confusion and incorrect labels, while there is no exhaustive annotation, it is difficult for us to estimate the recall of the labels, and the noise in datasets hurts the performance of the model. Secondly, most existing methods focus on the independent classification of individual pixels, ignoring the dynamic correlation of cloud information. Last but not least, when dealing with meteorological problems with neural network-based methods, it is lacking suitable evaluation metrics to judge the quality of the technology.

To address the above problems, in this paper, we propose an end-to-end deep CNN architecture, which will be used to identify severe convection weather. The major contributions of this paper include:

(1) We propose a model based on CNN method, using the structure of the encoder-decoder, all pixels are classified simultaneously, instead of individually.
(2) We propose a new preprocessing method to eliminate the data redundancy, combining with the characteristics of actual remote sensing data.
(3) We propose a new evaluation metric to measure the performance of this model, which narrows the recognition of the heavy rainfall coverage.

The proposed methods can achieve 91% accuracy in severe convection weather classification problem, 6% higher than existing methods, and 7 times faster than existing methods, so that can support real-time processing of the satellite data. The paper is organized as follows: Sect. 2 discusses the related works on existing ML/DL-based methods proposed for meteorological applications. Sections 3, 4 and 5 introduce the data preprocessing, the proposed

CNN architecture and the customized metrics respectively. Evaluation results are shown in Sect. 6 and Sect. 7 concludes the paper.

2   Related Work

The detection and classification of the short-time severe convection weather is mainly based on Doppler radar and high-resolution remote sensing satellite, which can be used to identify the mesoscale weather systems. The detection of severe convection weather based on Doppler radar mainly analyzes the intensity and position of radar echo, and the radial velocity of particles detected as well, so as to infer the characteristics of large airflow field and wind field structure. Most of the methods based on remote sensing data extract features pixel by pixel, with setting a threshold to determine what types of weather the pixel belongs to [4]. The key point of this method is to choose the most suitable optimum threshold. With the increasing accuracy requirements, the methods with fixed thresholds have been replaced by dynamic threshold methods [5].

With the popularity of deep learning in computer science, many researchers have investigated the methods of deep learning to solve various weather-related problems. In extracting masks of extreme weather patterns, [6] proposed the variants of Tiramisu [7] and the DeepLabv3+ neural network [8], which makes improvements to software frameworks, input pipeline and network training algorithms. This model efficiently scales deep learning on the Piz Daint [9] and Summit system [10]. Yuan and Hu [11] also designed a model of object-based cloud detection with Bag-of-Words (BoW) feature representation. [12] showed their model that can make full use of temporal information and unlabeled data to improve the localization of extreme weather events, by using a multi-channel spatiotemporal CNN architecture for semi-supervised bounding box prediction. [13] suggested the use of multi-layer neural networks, which is based on multi-channel satellite data, and this model was evaluated by using s special linear regression to predict single typhoon coordinates. [14] proposed a Hierarchical Fusion CNN (HFCNN), which takes full use of low-level features and is more applicable to cloud detection task. Compared with the existing applications of deep learning, meteorological data is more difficult to extract features accurately. Besides, there is a unanimous agreement that the current ConvNet revolution is a product of big labeled datasets. In the existing datasets, the labels have been automatically obtained, but the labels are noisy and not exhaustive. These labels have been cleaned by using complex algorithms to increase the precision of labels, but there is still approximately 20% error in precision.

3   Data Preprocessing

3.1   The Data and Label

The climate science community only makes full use of three kinds of global datasets to identify extreme weather events. The first is observation products, whose data sources are mainly remote sensing satellites and meteorological stations. The second is reanalysis data, which is based on observations from various climate models. The last is the variety of data generated by computer simulations of extreme weather. In the field of meteorology, different kinds of weather systems have certain space scale and time scale, and they interweave and interact with each other. The combination of many weather systems constitutes a wide range of weather patterns, forming hemispheric and even global atmospheric circulation, and accurate recognition of severe convective weather are according to the comprehensive and accurate data. Climatologists divide the weather conditions during the severe convective weather cycle into: sunny, storm, cumulonimbus and stratocumulus. Therefore, in this work, we analyze output from the first category because we hope to find out the characteristics of severe convection weather in real data, and the dataset we use comes from Himawari-8 satellite, which is operated by the Japan Meteorological Agency (JMA). Himawari-8 satellite has a dedicated meteorological mission, whereas MTSAT performs both meteorological and aeronautical functions. It can produce images with a resolution down to 500 m and can provide full disk observations every 10 minutes and images of Japan every 2.5 min, which contains 15 channels. And the algorithm is applied to create labels for each pixel when running as well.

3.2   Customized Data Preprocessing Method

In the real world, satellite data is generally incomplete and inconsistent, data preprocessing is needed before model establishment. Since the Himawari-8 satellite officially launched in 2015, the amount of data received is about 8 GB per hour. In 2016, the data received was as large as 300 TB, which is a challenge for storage capacity. In the data preprocessing, mining the relationship between data and labels not only helps solve the problem of data redundancy but also save valuable storage resources. Besides, the data redundancy usually leads to huge matrix calculations, which is unnecessary in the training process, and it is a waste of computing resource. Even with the help of GPU accelerators, it still needs a long running time. Therefore, we decide to fully exploit the correlation between the data, by choosing the Pearson correlation coefficient [15] to measure whether there is a linear relationship between the variables and results. When the correlation coefficient is closer to 1 or −1, it means they have a stronger correlation, and if the correlation coefficient is closer to 0, it means they have a weaker correlation. The coefficient is in the format:

$$r = \frac{N \sum xy - (\sum x \sum y)}{\sqrt{[N \sum x^2 - (\sum x)^2][N \sum y^2 - (\sum y)^2]}} \tag{1}$$

Since the dataset covers 12 months of remote sensing data, and the amount of dataset is up to 3 TB. It is a difficult task to analyze all data directly, so we use a random sampling strategy to select data in order to ensure the objectivity of the method, a total of 1000 images are selected in this work, and the results are shown in Fig. 1. It is obviously that cumulonimbus and storm have a strong linear relationship with infrared radiation and water vapor content, while sunny days are associated only with visible light channels. Therefore, the original data of 15 channels is replaced with 6 far-infrared channel data to detect severe convection weather events as input data (Fig. 2).

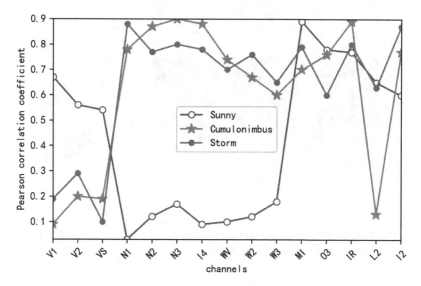

Fig. 1. The image of correlations between data and labels. The larger the coefficient is, the stronger the correlation will be.

4 Model Design

In order to make high-quality spatial classification from multi-channel spectral remote sensing data, we propose a delicate model to detect and classify severe convection weather (SCW-CNN). SCW-CNN is an image segmentation architecture based on U-net [16], due to its remarkable performance in biomedical image segmentation. As illustrated in Fig. 3, the architecture is divided into two parts: encoder and decoder. The encoder reduces the spatial dimension of the pooling layer, and the decoder restores the detail and spatial dimension of the object. The classical symmetrical structure of SCW-CNN is similar to several other CNN image segmentation structures [17,18], in terms of the composition of a sequence of down-sampling layers, followed by another sequence of up-sampling layers. We use the MXNET [19] deep learning framework to implement the SCW-CNN model as a graph of connected convolution layers. By using GPU accelerators, the data processing time is much less than the data generation cycle to avoid redundant operations.

On the left-hand side of Fig. 3, the input for the network is shown. The spatial coverage is 512 * 512 pixels, which matches the size of the selected area,

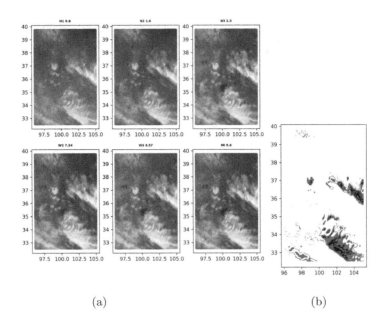

(a)   (b)

Fig. 2. The image of input data and labels. (a) shows the image of 6 far-infrared channel data, (b) shows the image of labels.

and the depth of the input depends on the number of selected channels per scene. To evaluate the influence of the different channel characteristics, either ten or nine infrared channels (IR) and optionally visible light channels are used. However, according to the results of Sect. 3, 6 far-infrared channels were selected for the input data, which are most relevant to the ground truth. Since the central wavelength of channel I is not within the range of the center wavelength, we considered it as an additional bias error to increase the robustness of the model. The sequence of learning blocks, consisting of multiple convolution layers, is shown next to the input layer, and each block has a label (D0-U0) attached. The output size of encoder can refers to Table 1 where the details of the convolution layer blocks is given, and the output size of decoder is the inverse of encoder. Note that the output of the SCW-CNN is a symmetric subset of the input with a size of 512 * 512, since SCW-CNN uses unpadded convolutions. On the right hand-side of Fig. 3, there is a regression operation. The output of the network is a 4-dimensional probability vector, which represents the membership degree of each class. For each pixel, SCW-CNN assigns the class with the highest probability.

The principle of SCW-CNN is similar to that of U-net, but we improve this model for the specific data to some degree. First of all, compared with the classical U-net structure, the copy and crop operations are cancelled. When making 3×3 convolution operation, the unpadded operation is used in order to make the output size consistent with the input size. Because of the uneven distribution of clouds in the picture, and the edge of the image contains important cloud infor-

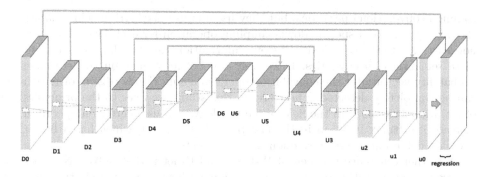

Fig. 3. SCW-CNN architecture used for detecting severe convection weather.

Table 1. The description of each operation in the encoding section.

Operation	Layer type	Output size
Input	Input	$6 \times 512 \times 512$
D0	3×3 conv.Relu	$16 \times 512 \times 512$
D0	3×3 conv.Relu	$16 \times 512 \times 512$
D0	3×3 conv.Relu Stride $= 2$	$16 \times 256 \times 256$
D1	3×3 conv.Relu	$32 \times 256 \times 256$
D1	3×3 conv.Relu	$32 \times 256 \times 256$
D1	3×3 conv.Relu Stride $= 2$	$32 \times 128 \times 128$
D1-Normalization		$32 \times 128 \times 128$
D2	3×3 conv.Relu	$64 \times 128 \times 128$
D2	3×3 conv.Relu	$64 \times 128 \times 128$
D2	3×3 conv.Relu Stride $= 2$	$64 \times 64 \times 64$
D2-Normalization		$64 \times 64 \times 64$
...	...	...
D6	3×3 conv.Relu	$128 \times 4 \times 4$
D6	3×3 conv.Relu	$128 \times 4 \times 4$
D6	3×3 conv.Relu Stride $= 2$	$128 \times 2 \times 2$
D6-Normalization		$128 \times 2 \times 2$

mation, so we need to ensure the integrity of the edge information. Secondly, in the SCW-CNN model, the number of filters is greatly decreased in the convolution operation, which reduces the scale of the network to reduce the running time of training and inference. We also add the operation of batch normalization before block by block to avoid the vanishing gradient problem.

Furthermore, in contrast to the U-net, we perform the operation of downsampling instead of pooling layers in our model. Strided convolutions are common convolution operations, but they use a larger pixel stride. This enables the model to learn a specific down-sampling operation for each layer. Last but not least, due to the complexity of cloud information, and the data has no complete semantic characteristics. If we only use Softmax function to determine probability vector after the convolution operation, only clouds edge information can be completely detected. Therefore, in this study, we refer to the principles of traditional methods in the field of meteorology, and use regression operation instead of softmax function in the last part of the model, which has a better effect on detecting severe convection weather events.

A further difference between SCW-CNN and U-net is that SCW-CNN does not require the operation of data augmentation, such as rotation or elastic deformation of input data to increase the amount of training data. When we use smaller training datasets, the operations of data augmentation are necessary, which can slightly improve the precision of the model. However, it is unnecessary to take this operation in this study, because a great quantity of annotated original satellite images is obtained as large as 10 TB, which is hard to manage on normal hardware.

5   Evaluation Metrics

5.1   Execution Time

For a segmentation system to be useful and actually produce a significant contribution to the field, its performance must be evaluated with rigor. [20] states the evaluation must be performed, and should use standard and well-known metrics to ensure the validity the usefulness of a system. And the most important evaluation metrics will be described to measure the performance of the model. As speed is an important metric since the majority of systems must meet the requirement of real-time, and in computer science, execution time is the time during which a program is running (executing), in contrast to other program lifecycle phases such as compile time, link time and load time. Generally, it is not meaningful to provide the exact time of the methods, because the execution time is extremely dependent on hardware devices and backend implementation, rendering some comparisons pointless. However, if done properly, it can help fellow researchers with providing timings with a thorough description.

5.2   Accuracy

Many evaluation criteria have been used to assess the accuracy of all kinds of technique for semantic segmentation, and most of them are variations on pixel accuracy and IoU. Pixel Accuracy and Mean Intersection over Union are the most common used metrics. Pixel Accuracy is the simplest metric, it just simply computes a radio between the amount of properly classified pixels and total number of them. Mean Intersection over Union is the standard metric for segmentation purposes. It computes a ratio between the intersection and the union of two sets, in our case the ground truth and our predicted segmentation. That radio can be reformulated as the number of the true positives over the sum of true positives, false negatives, and false positives. Since MIoU stands out of crowd as the most used metric, due to its representativeness and simplicity. Therefore, our study decides to use pixel accuracy and MIoU to report our results. The result is shown in Fig. 4.

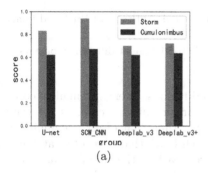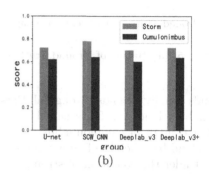

(a)   (b)

Fig. 4. The result of classifying storms and cumulonimbus with different models respectively. (a) shows the result of Pixel Accuracy, (b) shows the result of MIoU.

In Fig. 4, it shows the results of classifying storms and cumulonimbus on U-net model, SCW-CNN model, DeepLabv3 model, and DeepLabv3+ model respectively. With the dataset which was preprocessed, the SCW-CNN model has a great result on detecting storm, the matric of PA reaches 0.943 and MIoU reaches 0.802, which is higher than the result of classification on other models. Besides, the results of cumulonimbus also have an increase with SCW-CNN, and it is 14.3% higher than that on other models. However, we find that the actual accuracy for detecting cumulonimbus is only 70.6%, which is much lower than that of storm detection, and the result of MIoU is only 60%. In order to solve this problem, we carried out a large number of visual analysis of the ground truth and the predicted value. Compared with them, we find that the detection of cumulonimbus which is around the storm is very accurate, but the edge of the cumulonimbus is very blurred, which is often mistakenly divided into stratocumulus, which refer to Fig. 5.

After a series of analysis, we find that the reason is the error of partial labels. In the field of meteorology, the major difference between stratocumulus and cumulonimbus is water vapor content and cloud base height.

Well-developed cumulonimbus clouds are characterized by a flat, anvil-like top (anvil dome), caused by wind shear or inversion near the tropopause. The shelf of the anvil may precede the main cloud's vertical component for many miles, and be accompanied by lightning. Occasionally, rising air parcels surpass the equilibrium level (due to momentum) and form an overshooting top culminating at the maximum parcel level. When vertically developed, this largest of all

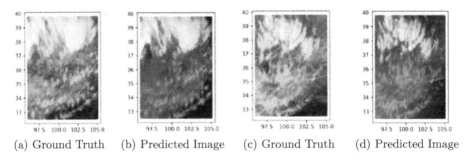

(a) Ground Truth   (b) Predicted Image   (c) Ground Truth   (d) Predicted Image

Fig. 5. Illustration of Ground Truth and Predicted Image at different moments

clouds usually extends through all three cloud regions. Even the smallest cumulonimbus cloud dwarfs its neighbors in comparison. In that case, as the water vapor content of cumulonimbus is much higher than that of stratocumulus, so the cloud base height of cumulonimbus is much lower than that of stratocumulus. Under the condition of strong convective weather, the cumulonimbus with low water vapor content would rapidly rising with the wind, which is caused by storm, and the water content in the cumulonimbus cloud will decrease quickly in the process of rise. When the original cumulonimbus clouds rise to the height of stratocumulus, they will merge with each other.

However, there is a monitoring period difference between infrared channels and visible channels, the infrared monitoring period is 10 min, while visible channel monitoring period is 30 min, which will lead to some deviations. In view of this situation, we cannot fundamentally solve this problem because we cannot correct the error of label completely. Therefore, we need to review the evaluation metric of test again, and find a suitable evaluation metric in this study.

5.3   New Metric to Evaluate Cumulonimbus

Many studies have shown that storm cell is the direct cause of great damage to society during severe convective weather. And in the field of meteorology, the leading area of a squall line is composed primarily of storm cells, and singular regions of an updraft. The updraft rises from ground level to the highest extensions of the troposphere, condensing water and building a dark, ominous cloud to one with a noticeable overshooting top and anvil. Because of the chaotic nature of updrafts and downdrafts, pressure perturbations are important, and it causes heavy rainfall, which refer to Fig. 6.

The heavy rain was concentrated near the storm cells, and we only evaluate the area around the storm cells. Especially, the storm cell is a generally circular area, usually 4 to 6 km in diameter, surrounded by a series of towering thunderstorms that can easily trigger heavy rainfall, and the maximum coverage area of storm cell is nearly $10 \, km^2$. As we know, if the place is away from the coverage of storm cell, the wind speed will be decreased quickly, so does the rainfall, and the rainfall at the edge of the storm can be seen as light rain. So if we select the most suitable safe distance as the radius to ensure security of society, we will can get a safe heavy rainfall detection circle instead of the whole area. Therefore, we only need to narrow the recognition range of the coverage of squall line, and get the damage of the severe convective weather to the greatest extent, instead of worrying about the weather conditions away from the squall line.

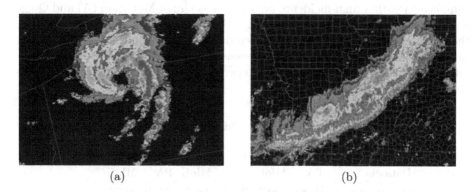

(a)   (b)

Fig. 6. The heat map of severe convective weather, the red area represents squall line, where has the worst weather (Color figure online)

In this study, we propose a more accurate detecting area. As the storm can be accurately identified, and the shape of the storm is nearly round, the maximum and minimum location of storm can also be found in latitude and longitude, as shown in Fig. 7. Therefore, we get the distribution area of heavy rainfall by taking the intersection of the lines of longitude and latitude as the center of the circle, and the safe distance (3 km) as the radius.

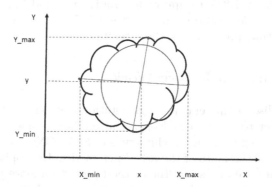

Fig. 7. The distribution map of heavy rainfall in a storm cell. The X and Y coordinates represent longitude and latitude, respectively

6   The Results

In this section, compared with evaluation results with original metrics, we have evaluated the performance of the model to classify cumulonimbus with new evaluation metric we proposed. In this study, in order to verify the strong robustness of the mode, we analyzed the scope of the research area and choosed two severe convective weather high-incidence areas, such as Qilian Mountain (A) and Qinghai Lake (B). These places are in line with the characteristics of rich water vapor, the large temperature difference between day and night. During the evaluation, we showed the results of each single scene, using the SCW-CNN model with different metrics. Then, we evaluate the performance of the model with different metrics on the whole dataset.

Table 2. Statistics for 3 datasets with different metrics to detect cumulonimbus

Datasets	A		B		The whole dataset	
	PA	MIoU	PA	MIoU	PA	MIoU
Original metric	0.784	0.683	0.712	0.623	0.730	0.629
New metric	0.912	0.865	0.892	0.856	0.902	0.850

Table 2 shows the results of cumulonimbus with different evaluation metrics in three datasets. It can be seen from the table that the performance of SCW-CNN model with new metric is better than that with original metric. At last, the running time of the methods is counted. The model loading times are not included in the execution time, SCW-CNN model can run on the platform both CPU and GPU. When SCW-CNN is running on the GPU (V100), it takes an average of 0.15 s and the running time on the CPU is 1.04 s. However, the existing methods takes about 1.89 s to apply the traditional model to all pixels in a scene, which the implementation runs on the CPU, so that SCW-CNN model can support real-time processing of the satellite data.

7   Conclusions and Future Work

In this work, we discuss the semantic segmentation method for classifying severe convection weather patterns in multi-spectral remote sensing datasets. Therefore, we propose a segmentation architecture of SCW-CNN to further improve the performance of the state-of-the-art U-net model. By applying extra constraints to the data preprocessing, the method presents a more powerful ability in feather representation. Besides, we propose a new metric to evaluate the performance of the SCW-CNN model in complex weather conditions, providing a reference for the following application of deep learning in meteorology. The study on the remote sensing dataset covering the most areas of Qinghai province in China and our model performed well in storm segmentation. And heavy rainfall can also be accurately identified within the range of the storm. This successful model can become a pioneer to process numerous climate model monitoring in the field of climate science, greatly avoiding the systematic bias caused by the subjective thresholding method. In future studies, the short - term prediction of severe convection weather will be conducted by deep learning. Alerts will be issued as soon as severe convection weather is detected, and the forecast of severe convection weather will be conveyed to the relevant regions and units concerned promptly. The results play a crucial role in the prediction of climate change risks and the formulation of government policies on climate change.

References

1. Kim, D.H., Ahn, M.H.: Introduction of the in-orbit test and its performance for the first meteorological imager of the Communication, Ocean, and Meteorological Satellite. Atmos. Measur. Tech. **7**(8), 2471–2485 (2014). https://doi.org/10.5194/amt-7-2471-2014
2. Moradi Kordmahalleh, M., Gorji Sefidmazgi, M., Homaifar, A.: A sparse recurrent neural network for trajectory prediction of atlantic hurricanes. In: Proceedings of the 2016 on Genetic and Evolutionary Computation Conference - GECCO 2016. ACM Press (2016). https://doi.org/10.1145/2908812.2908834
3. Tan, C., et al.: FORECAST-CLSTM: a new convolutional LSTM network for cloudage nowcasting. In: 2018 IEEE Visual Communications and Image Processing (VCIP). IEEE, December 2018. https://doi.org/10.1109/vcip.2018.8698733
4. Shi, M., et al.: Cloud detection of remote sensing images by deep learning. In: 2016 IEEE International Geoscience and Remote Sensing Symposium (IGARSS). IEEE, July 2016. https://doi.org/10.1109/igarss.2016.7729176
5. Jedlovec, G.J., Haines, S.L., LaFontaine, F.J.: Spatial and temporal varying thresholds for cloud detection in GOES imagery. IEEE Trans. Geosci. Remote Sens. **46**(6), 1705–1717 (2008). https://doi.org/10.1109/tgrs.2008.916208
6. Kurth, T., et al.: Exascale deep learning for climate analytics. In: SC18: International Conference for High Performance Computing, Networking, Storage and Analysis. IEEE, November 2018. https://doi.org/10.1109/sc.2018.00054
7. Jegou, S., et al.: The one hundred layers tiramisu: fully convolutional densenets for semantic segmentation. In: 2017 IEEE Conference on Computer Vision and Pattern Recognition Workshops (CVPRW). IEEE, July 2017. https://doi.org/10.1109/cvprw.2017.156
8. Kong, H., Fan, L., Zhang, X.: Semantic segmentation with inverted residuals and atrous convolution. In: SAE Technical Paper Series. SAE International, August 2018. https://doi.org/10.4271/2018-01-1635
9. Filipcic, A., et al.: ATLAS computing on CSCS HPC. J. Phys.: Conf. Ser. **664**(9), 092011 (2015). https://doi.org/10.1088/1742-6596/664/9/092011
10. Hines, J.: Stepping up to summit. Comput. Sci. Eng. **20**(2), 78–82 (2018). https://doi.org/10.1109/mcse.2018.021651341
11. Yuan, Y., Hu, X.: Bag-of-words and object-based classification for cloud extraction from satellite imagery. IEEE J. Sel. Topics Appl. Earth Observ. Remote Sens. **8**(8), 4197–4205 (2015). https://doi.org/10.1109/jstars.2015.2431676
12. Racah, E., et al.: Extremeweather: a large-scale climate dataset for semi-supervised detection, localization, and understanding of extreme weather events. In: Advances in Neural Information Processing Systems, pp. 3402–3413 (2017)

13. Hong, S., et al.: GlobeNet: convolutional neural networks for typhoon eye tracking from remote sensing imagery (2017)
14. Liu, H., Zeng, D., Tian, Q.: Super-pixel cloud detection using hierarchical fusion CNN. In: 2018 IEEE Fourth International Conference on Multimedia Big Data (BigMM). IEEE, September 2018. https://doi.org/10.1109/bigmm.2018.8499091
15. Nahler, G.: Pearson correlation coefficient. In: Dictionary of Pharmaceutical Medicine, pp. 132–132. Springer, Vienna (2009). https://doi.org/10.1007/978-3-211-89836-9_1025
16. Ronneberger, O.: Invited talk: U-Net convolutional networks for biomedical image segmentation. Bildverarbeitung für die Medizin 2017. I, p. 3. Springer, Heidelberg (2017). https://doi.org/10.1007/978-3-662-54345-0_3
17. Berger, L., Eoin, H., Cardoso, M.J., Ourselin, S.: An adaptive sampling scheme to efficiently train fully convolutional networks for semantic segmentation. In: Nixon, M., Mahmoodi, S., Zwiggelaar, R. (eds.) MIUA 2018. CCIS, vol. 894, pp. 277–286. Springer, Cham (2018). https://doi.org/10.1007/978-3-319-95921-4_26
18. Badrinarayanan, V., Kendall, A., Cipolla, R.: SegNet: a deep convolutional encoder-decoder architecture for image segmentation. IEEE Trans. Pattern Anal. Mach. Intell. 39(12), 2481–2495 (2017). https://doi.org/10.1109/tpami.2016.2644615
19. Chen, T., et al.: Mxnet: A flexible and efficient machine learning library for heterogeneous distributed systems. arXiv preprint arXiv:1512.01274 (2015)
20. Lateef, F., Ruichek, Y.: Survey on semantic segmentation using deep learning techniques. Neurocomputing 338, 321–348 (2019). https://doi.org/10.1016/j.neucom.2019.02.003

Action Recognition Based on Divide-and-Conquer

Guanghua Tan$^{(\boxtimes)}$ ⓘ, Rui Miao ⓘ, and Yi Xiao ⓘ

Hunan University, Changsha 10532, China
guanghuatan@gmail.com, 12maorea@gmail.com,
yixiao_csee@hnu.edu.cn

Abstract. Recently, deep convolutional neural networks have made great breakthroughs in the field of action recognition. Since sequential video frames have a lot of redundant information, compared with dense sampling, sparse sampling network can also achieve good results. Due to sparse sampling's limitation of access to information, this paper mainly discusses how to further improve the learning ability of the model based on sparse sampling. We proposed a model based on divide-and-conquer, which use a threshold α to determine whether action data require sparse sampling or dense local sampling for learning. Finally, our approach obtains the state-the-of-art performance on the datasets of HMDB51 (72.4%) and UCF101 (95.3%).

Keywords: Action recognition · Divide-and-conquer · Sparse sampling · Dense sampling

1 Introduction

Due to the development of multimedia technology, the number of videos on the network is increasing, and video-based action recognition has drawn a significant amount of attention. Video-based action recognition was applied in many areas, such as security and behavior analysis. Recently, using convolutional neural networks [1], artificial intelligence has made significant progress in the field of image recognition. Video-based action recognition faces more difficulties and challenges than image recognition, including scale variations, viewpoint changes, and so on.

Traditional methods are based on manual extraction of action features, such as Improved Dense Trajectories (IDT) algorithm [2]. It uses the tracking of the frame-by-frame trajectory of one video to extract features and finally classifies the elements to achieve the classification. The limitation of these methods is that they cannot obtain enough useful features, and have a large amount of calculation.

With the development of deep neural networks, considerable progress has been made recently. For example, AlexNet [1] achieved 80% accuracy in ImageNet challenge.

This work is supported by the National Key R&D Program of China (2018YFB0203904), National Natural Science Foundation of China (61602165), Natural Science Foundation of Hunan Province (2018JJ3074), NSFC from PRC (61872137, 61502158), Hunan NSF (2017JJ3042).

I. V. Tetko et al. (Eds.): ICANN 2019, LNCS 11729, pp. 157–167, 2019.
https://doi.org/10.1007/978-3-030-30508-6_13

Convolutional Networks (ConvNets) have witnessed great success in classifying images of objects, scenes, and complex events [3–5, 14]. ConvNets have also been introduced to solve the problem of video-based action recognition [6–9]. Then there is a key observation that consecutive frames of action are highly redundant. Therefore, dense temporal sampling, which usually results in highly similar sampled frames, is unnecessary. Motivated by this observation, a video-level framework, called Temporal Segment Network (TSN) [10] was proposed. This framework extracts short snippets over a long video sequence with a sparse sampling scheme, where the samples distribute uniformly along the temporal dimension. Thereon, a segmental structure is applied to aggregate information from the sampled snippets. Sparse sampling can reduce the amount of training data and speed up the learning process, but its learning effect is weak when faced with similar actions.

This paper mainly tried a divide-and-conquer method. First, the sparse sampling neural network is used, and a threshold α is used to evaluate sparse sampling network's learning effect. At this time, the action data is divided into two categories, one of which can be well studied by sparse sampling, and the second's learning effect is relatively poor through sparse sampling. For the second actions, we will conduct learning based on intensive sampling. Finally, a unified learning effect is obtained.

2   Related Work

Before the neural network is applied, video-based action recognition has been studied for decades. Laptev and Lindeberg [11] proposed spatio-temporal interest points (STIPs) by extending Harris corner detectors to 3D. SIFT and HOG are also extended into SIFT-3D [12] and HOG3D [13] for action recognition. Dollar et al. proposed Cuboids features for behavior recognition [14]. Sadanand and Corso built ActionBank for action recognition [15]. Recently, Wang et al. introduced Improved Dense Trajectories [2] which is currently the state-of-the-art hand-crafted feature. In our model the dense sampling uses IDT algorithms.

Then the neural network was applied frequently in video-based recognition. Karpathy et al. [6] tested ConvNets with deep structures on a large dataset (Sports-1 M). Simonyan et al. [7] designed two-stream ConvNets containing spatial and temporal net by exploiting ImageNet dataset for pre-training and calculating optical flow to explicitly capture motion information. Tran et al. [16] explored 3D ConvNets [17] on the realistic and large-scale video datasets, where they tried to learn both appearance and motion features with 3D convolution operations. Sun et al. [18] proposed a factorized spatio-temporal ConvNets and exploited different ways to decompose 3D convolutional kernels. Diba et al. [19] mainly suggested "Temporal Linear Encoding Layer" to encode the features of different locations in the action video. Zhu et al. [20] identify the Key Volume in the video and use Key Volume to establish the CNN model. Ng et al. [21] used the CNN network to acquire the image features of a single frame, and then passed the output of the CNN through the LSTM in chronological order, thus finally characterizing the video data in spatial and temporal dimensions.

Kezhen et al. [22] started with Kinect data and segmented each human action by temporal regions where the direction of motion is constant, creating a sketch graph that provides a form of qualitative representation of the behavior that is easy to visualize.

3   Framework

3.1   Our Model

The general action data set contains a large amount of video data, such as UCF-101, which includes 101 kinds of behavioral data, and HMDB51, which includes 51 kinds of behavioral data.

For two completely different types of actions, as shown (1) in Fig. 1, they can be distinguished very well by sparse sampling-based neural network because their characteristics are entirely different. Sparse sampling randomly extracts frames from the data set for network's training. On the one hand, it reduces the amount of training data; on the other hand, it can obtain the overall information of actions. However, if these two actions are easily confused, as shown (2) in Fig. 1, the sparse sampling neural network does not perform well enough, which means that sparse sampling cannot obtain enough details to distinguish those actions.

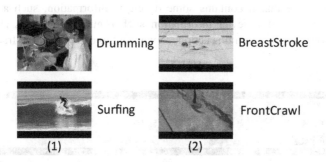

Fig. 1. Different learning strategies are suitable for different action types: sparse sampling is suitable for actions like (1), and dense sampling is suitable for actions like (2).

To this end, we introduced a single frame-based algorithm to compensate for the shortcomings of sparse sampling network, as shown in Fig. 2. When the predicted output of sparse sampling network exceeds a certain threshold, we will use the single frame-based algorithm to learn those actions. The final output consists of two parts: the first part is the output of the sparse sampling neural network, and the second part is the fusion of the sparse sampling neural and the dense sampling algorithm.

Based on dense sampling

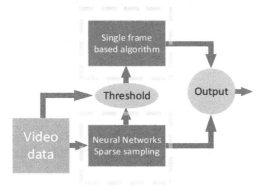

Based on sparse sampling

Fig. 2. The process of our model uses two learning methods: sparse sampling and dense sampling.

3.2 Key Frames Extraction

A large number of frames can be extracted from a single action video, but not every structure is equally important, as shown in Fig. 3, which are extracted from action Diving. We can see that it contains some duplicate information, such as frames of number 66, 87, 140, and irrelevant information, such as number 190,203. Those are not very helpful for model to learn this action, so we want to extract the key frames to train our model.

Fig. 3. Parts of frames in action Diving.

In order to extract the key frames of those actions, we use AdaScan to achieve this. AdaScan learns to pool discriminative and informative frames, while discarding a majority of the non-informative frames in a single temporal scan of the video. It first extracts deep features for each frame in a video and then passes the features to the proposed Adaptive Pooling module, as shown in Fig. 4. For more details about AdaScan, readers can refer to [25].

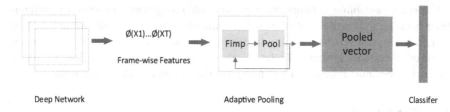

Fig. 4. The process of AdaScan.

Key frames get the importance of each frame, as shown in Fig. 5. In our experiment, frames with importance greater than 0.6 are used as input data in sparse sampling network.

Fig. 5. Predicted discriminative importance for a video.

3.3 Sparse Sampling Network

Since sequential frames are highly redundant, the dense temporal sampling usually results in highly similar sampled frames, which not only causes the training data to be too large but also affects the learning effect. Based on sparse sampling network, we refer to the TSN, as shown in Fig. 6. It extracts short snippets over a long video sequence with a sparse sampling scheme, where the samples distribute uniformly along the temporal dimension, composed of spatial stream ConvNets and temporal stream ConvNets.

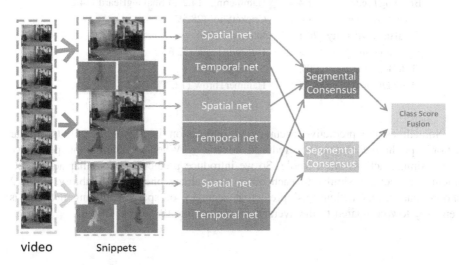

Fig. 6. The process of temporal segment network. Each snippet produces its own preliminary prediction. A consensus among the snippets will be derived finally.

The sparse sampling network has very variable recognition accuracy for different actions because sufficient detail information cannot be obtained. As shown in the (1) of Fig. 1, it is easy for sparse sampling to distinguish what they are with 95% accuracy. But for other actions, as shown in the (2), the recognition accuracy of BreastStroke is only 76.4%, because Frontcrawl has many similar features with BreastStroke.

3.4   Threshold Setting

We set a threshold α for the prediction of sparse sampling network. Let

$$f = (Pmax - Psec)/Pmax \tag{1}$$

where *Pmax* is the maximum classification probability of the prediction result, and *Psec* is the second largest classification probability. When f is less than α, we think that sparse sampling cannot distinguish this action very well, so the prediction result must be merged with the results of the external algorithm. For example, we use the sparse sampling neural network to test the BreastStroke data. The results show that the maximum probability of this action is 76.4% for BreastStroke, and the second probability 23.5% is FrontCrawl. In the test, we take α for 3/4, and the prediction's f is 69% which is less than α, so the prediction must be merged with external algorithm. Table 1 includes all the actions whose f is less than α in UCF-101, and their prediction accuracy, including: BreastStroke, BrushingTeeth, CricketBowling, FieldHockeyPenalty, ShavingBeard, SkateBoarding, ThrowDiscus.

Table 1. Actions whose prediction f is less than threshold α in UCF-101.

Action	Accuracy	Correct classification
BreastStroke	76.4%	FrontCrawl (23.5%)
BrushingTeeth	71.4%	Hammering (14.2%) ShavingBeard (14.2%)
CricketBowling	71.4%	CricketShot (28.5%)
FieldHockeyPenalty	70.1%	Shotput (14%)
ShavingBeard	69.8%	BrushingTeeth (22.6%)
SkateBoarding	80%	Skiing (20%)
ThrowDiscus	77.5%	HammerThrow (12.2%)

Sometimes the predictive accuracy of one action is improved, but its similar action's predictive accuracy is reduced adversely. When evaluating the predictive effect, similar actions are a whole. So we introduce prediction on similar action sets (include all actions similar to each other) to evaluate one model's ability. Table 2 shows that similar action sets' predictive accuracy of sparse sampling network is generally low compared to the average prediction rate (94%) for all data.

Table 2. Sparse sampling network's prediction accuracy of different similar action sets.

Similar action sets	Accuracy
BreastStroke + FrontCrawl	83.1%
BrushingTeeth + ShavingBeard + Hammering	73.1%
CricketBowling + CricketShot	64.7%
FieldHockeyPenalty + Shotput	82.3%
ThrowDiscus + HammerThrow	92.7%

3.5 Dense Sampling Algorithm

Dense sampling algorithm can give sparse sampling more detailed information when f is less than threshold α. For dense sampling, we use a single-frame-based algorithm, referring to the IDT algorithm, as shown in Fig. 7, which can obtain details that cannot be obtained by sparse sampling.

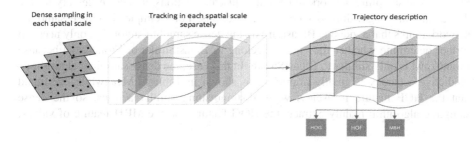

Fig. 7. The entire process of the Improved Dense Trajectories algorithm mainly consists of 3 parts: dense sampling in each spatial scale, tracking in each spatial scale separately, and trajectory description. The extracted features mainly include HOG (Histogram of Oriented Gradient), HOF (Histograms of Oriented Optical Flow), and MBH (Motion Boundary Histograms).

If the dense sampling algorithm is trained with the complete UCF-101 training data which contains 101 different kinds of actions, the result is shown in Table 3. It can be seen that the predictive accuracy of those chosen actions is not as good as the sparse sampling network.

Table 3. Dense sampling's performance on actions chosen by α in sparse sampling.

Action	Dense sampling
BreastStroke	59.2%
BrushingTeeth	66.7%
CricketBowling	61.6%
FieldHockeyPenalty	68.5%
ShavingBeard	67.2%
SkateBoarding	65.4%
ThrowDiscus	70.7%

On different similar action sets, dense sampling's prediction is shown in Table 4. Compared to sparse sampling's result, it is also not good.

Table 4. For different similar actions sets, dense sampling's prediction is showed.

Similar action sets	Dense sampling
BreastStroke + FrontCrawl	67.7%
BrushingTeeth + ShavingBeard + Hammering	58.9%
CricketBowling + CricketShot	66.7%
FieldHockeyPenalty + Shotput	51.5%
ThrowDiscus + HammerThrow	89.1%

4   Performance Analysis

Since sparse sampling network filters out obfuscated actions, it is not necessary for the dense sampling algorithm to recognize all actions. For example, if sparse sampling network thinks that a video is BreastStroke, the dense sampling algorithm only needs to further determine whether the video is belong to BreastStroke or FrontCrawl because FrontCrawl is only similar to BreastStroke. In this case, the dense sampling algorithm's predictive accuracy is greatly improved, as shown in Table 5. Meanwhile, we found that the HOF feature is useless when distinguishing similar actions, so the dense sampling algorithm mainly extracts the HOG feature and the MBH feature of videos.

Table 5. Trained by similar actions merely rather than the whole training data, dense sampling can get the best result.

Action	Dense sampling (similar actions)	Dense sampling (all training data)	Sparse sampling
BreastStroke	96.4%	59.2%	76.4%
BrushingTeeth	72.2%	66.7%	71.4%
CricketBowling	91.8%	61.6%	71.4%
FieldHockeyPenalty	80.4%	68.5%	70.1%
ShavingBeard	83.3%	67.2%	69.8%
SkateBoarding	93.7%	65.4%	80%
ThrowDiscus	86.7%	70.7%	77.5%

For all similar actions sets, dense sampling trained by similar actions merely has better results compared to TSN based on sparse sampling and IDT based on dense sampling, as shown in Table 6.

Table 6. Accuracy comparison for our model and sparse sampling and dense sampling.

Similar action sets	Our model	Sparse sampling	Dense sampling
BreastStroke + FrontCrawl	84.3%	83.1%	67.7%
BrushingTeeth + ShavingBeard+ Hammering	78.2%	73.1%	58.9%
CricketBowling + CricketShot	83.3%	64.7%	66.7%
FieldHockeyPenalty + Shotput	89.4%	82.3%	51.5%
ThrowDiscus + HammerThrow	91.6%	92.7%	89.1%

In UCF-101, for different α, the final classification accuracy is shown in Fig. 8, and α finally gets 3/4.

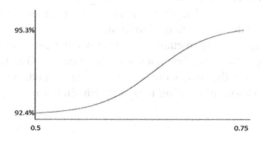

Fig. 8. Different α's results. Our model's α gets 3/4 finally.

Table 7 shows the final results of our model in UCF-101 and HMDB51, and we com-pared it with other methods.

Table 7. Comparing our model with other methods.

Framework	UCF-101	HMDB51
Our model	95.3%	72.4%
TSN	94.2%	69.4%
IDT	85.9%	57.2%
CO2FI + ASYN + IDT [23]	95.2%	72.6%
NOASSOM + IDT [24]	93.8%	69.3%
GRP + IDT	92.3%	67.0%
AdaScan + IDT	91.3%	61.0%
ST-VLMPF	93.6%	69.5%
LSTM	93.6%	66.2%

5 Conclusion

In this paper, we present the idea of divide-and-conquer and finally fuse the sparse sampling and dense sampling to better understanding action. Benefit from previous research, we use sparse sampling to get a big picture and use dense sampling to get details of action. Using sparse sampling to distinguish between similar actions can obtain preliminary prediction while greatly reducing the number of calculations in dense sampling. The following is the process of using the whole model: Firstly, training sparse sampling network with complete data. Secondly, sparse sampling network filters out similar actions set according to the f of each action and threshold α, and then training dense sampling algorithm with similar actions set merely. In order to predict actions, test data first enters sparse sampling network to obtain preliminary prediction result. If sparse sampling's prediction belongs to selected similar actions set, it needs to enter dense sampling model to get accurate prediction result. Otherwise, sparse sampling's prediction is the final output. The final output incorporates the prediction of sparse sampling network and dense sampling algorithm.

Compared to deep learning, methods based on manual extraction of features have limitations. This paper has two directions for improvement. One is to use recurrent neural network instead of the artificial feature extraction method, and the other is to try to use the human skeleton information to distinguish similar behaviors.

References

1. Krizhevsky, A., Sutskever, I., Hinton, G.E.: ImageNet classification with deep convolutional neural networks. In: International Conference on Neural Information Processing Systems, pp. 1097–1105 (2012). https://doi.org/10.1145/3065386
2. Wang, H., Schmid, C.: Action recognition with improved trajectories. In: IEEE International Conference on Computer Vision, pp. 3551–3558. IEEE (2014). https://doi.org/10.1109/iccv. 2013.441
3. Simonyan, K., Zisserman, A.: Very deep convolutional networks for large-scale image recognition. Comput. Sci. (2014)
4. Szegedy, C., Liu, W., Jia, Y., et al.: Going deeper with convolutions. In: Computer Vision and Pattern Recognition, pp. 1–9 (2014). https://doi.org/10.1109/cvpr.2015.7298594
5. Xiong, Y., Zhu, K., Lin, D., et al.: Recognize complex events from static images by fusing deep channels. In: Computer Vision and Pattern Recognition, pp. 1600–1609. IEEE (2015). https://doi.org/10.1109/cvpr.2015.7298768
6. Karpathy, A., Toderici, G., Shetty, S., Leung, T., Sukthankar, R., Fei-Fei, L.: Large-scale video classification with convolutional neural networks. In: Computer Vision and Pattern Recognition, pp. 1723–1732 (2014). https://doi.org/10.1109/cvpr.2014.223
7. Simonyan, K., Zisserman, A.: Two-stream convolutional networks for action recognition in videos. Comput. Linguis. **1**(4), 568–576 (2014). https://doi.org/10.1002/14651858. CD001941.pub3
8. Du, T., Bourdev, L., Fergus, R., et al.: Learning spatio-temporal features with 3D convolutional networks. In: International Conference on Computer Vision, pp. 4489–4497. IEEE (2014). https://doi.org/10.1109/iccv.2015.510

9. Zhang, B., Wang, L., Wang, Z., et al.: Real-time action recognition with enhanced motion vector CNNs. In: Computer Vision and Pattern Recognition, pp. 2718–2726 (2016). https://doi.org/10.1109/cvpr.2016.297

10. Wang, L., et al.: Temporal segment networks: towards good practices for deep action recognition. In: Leibe, B., Matas, J., Sebe, N., Welling, M. (eds.) ECCV 2016. LNCS, vol. 9912, pp. 20–36. Springer, Cham (2016). https://doi.org/10.1007/978-3-319-46484-8_2

11. Laptev, I.: On space-time interest points. Int. J. Comput. Vis. **64**(2–3), 107–123 (2005). https://doi.org/10.1007/s11263-005-1838-7

12. Scovanner, P.: 3-dimensional sift descriptor and its application to action recognition. In: ACM Multimedia (2007). https://doi.org/10.1145/1291233.1291311

13. Kläser, A., Marszałek, M., Schmid, C.: A spatio-temporal descriptor based on 3D-gradients. In: The British Machine Vision Conference (2008)

14. Dollar, P., Rabaud, V., Cottrell, G., et al.: Behavior recognition via sparse spatio-temporal features. In: IEEE International Workshop on Visual Surveillance and Performance Evaluation of Tracking and Surveillance (2005). https://doi.org/10.1109/vspets.2005.1570899

15. Sadanand, S., Corso, J.J.: Action bank: a high-level representation of activity in video. In: Computer Vision & Pattern Recognition (2012). https://doi.org/10.1109/cvpr.2012.6247806

16. Tran, D., Bourdev, L.D., Fergus, R., Torresani, L., Paluri, M.: Learning spatiotemporal features with 3D convolutional networks. In: International Conference on Computer Vision, pp. 4489–4497 (2015). https://doi.org/10.1109/iccv.2015.510

17. Xu, W., Xu, W., Yang, M., et al.: 3D convolutional neural networks for human action recognition. IEEE Trans. Pattern Anal. Mach. Intell. **35**(1), 221–231 (2012). https://doi.org/10.1109/tpami.2012.59

18. Sun, L., Jia, K., Yeung, D.Y., et al.: Human action recognition using factorized spatio-temporal convolutional networks. In: International Conference on Computer Vision, pp. 4597–4605 (2015). https://doi.org/10.1109/iccv.2015.522

19. Diba, A., Sharma, V., Gool, L.V.: Deep temporal linear encoding networks. In: Computer Vision and Pattern Recognition pp. 2329–2338 (2016). https://doi.org/10.1109/cvpr.2017.168

20. Zhu, W., Hu, J., Sun, G., et al.: A key volume mining deep framework for action recognition. In: Computer Vision and Pattern Recognition, pp. 1991–1999. IEEE (2016). https://doi.org/10.1109/cvpr.2016.219

21. Ng, Y.H., Hausknecht, M., Vijayanarasimhan, S., et al.: Beyond short snippets: deep networks for video classification. In: Computer Vision and Pattern Recognition (2015). https://doi.org/10.1109/cvpr.2015.7299101

22. Chen, K., Forbus, K.: Action recognition from skeleton data via analogical generalization over qualitative representations. In: AAAI Conference on Artificial Intelligence (2016)

23. Lin, W., Mi, Y., Wu, J., et al.: Action recognition with coarse-to-fine deep feature integration and asynchronous fusion. In: AAAI Conference on Artificial Intelligence (2017)

24. Du, Y., Yuan, C., Hu, W., et al.: Hierarchical nonlinear orthogonal adaptive-subspace self-organizing map based feature extraction for human action recognition. In: AAAI Conference on Artificial Intelligence (2018)

25. Kar, A., Rai, N., Sikka, K., et al.: AdaScan: adaptive scan pooling in deep convolutional neural networks for human action recognition in videos. In: Computer Vision and Pattern Recognition (2016). https://doi.org/10.1109/cvpr.2017.604

An Adaptive Feature Channel Weighting Scheme for Correlation Tracking

Zhen Zhang[ID], Chao Wang[ID], and Xiqun Lu[(✉)][ID]

College of Computer Science and Technology, Zhejiang University, Yuquan Campus,
Hangzhou 310027, China
{21721207,21721206,xqlu}@zju.edu.cn

Abstract. In most of Discriminative Correlation Filter (DCF) based trackers, they used a fixed weight for each feature channel for all incoming frames. However, in the experiment, we find that different features have pros and cons under different scenarios. In this paper, we propose to couple the response of a DCF based tracker with the weights of different feature channels to strengthen their positive effects while weaken their negative effects simultaneously. This coupling is achieved by an adaptive feature channel weighting scheme. The tracking is formulated as a two-stage optimization problem: the tracker is learned using the alternative direction method of multipliers (ADMM) and the weights of feature channels are adaptively adjusted by a least-square estimation. We integrate the adaptive feature channel weighting scheme into two state-of-the-art handcrafted DCF based trackers, and evaluate them on two benchmarks: OTB2013 and VOT2016, respectively. The experimental results demonstrate its accuracy and efficiency when compared with some state-of-the-art handcrafted DCF based trackers.

Keywords: Visual tracking · DCF based tracker · Coupling ·
Adaptive feature weighting · Least-square estimation

1 Introduction

Despite visual object tracking has been intensively studied in past decades, visual object tracking still remains a challenging problem due to two factors: one is that only very limited information about the target is available because generally only a single example of the target is given in the first input frame. Moreover, the given example of the target is usually with lower spatial resolution, and the appearance of the target is prone to have diverse variations during tracking because of deformation, occlusion, rotation, illumination change, and so on. The other challenge is the real-time requirement because timely response is essential to many applications, such as human computer interaction, visual surveillance, and robotics.

Recently, Discriminative Correlation Filter (DCF) based trackers [4,10,15] attracted wide attention due to their superior computation and fair robustness

© Springer Nature Switzerland AG 2019
I. V. Tetko et al. (Eds.): ICANN 2019, LNCS 11729, pp. 168–183, 2019.
https://doi.org/10.1007/978-3-030-30508-6_14

to the photometric and geometric variations of the target. To cope with the variety of variations of the target during the tracking, some research work tried to use multi-dimensional features [10,15], to integrate deep features [3,11,23], to employ adaptive scale estimation schemes [9,21], nonlinear kernel [19], and to reduce the boundary effects brought by circularly shifted examples of the target [14,16,24], and so on. Whereas other research work is to integrate multiple independently running trackers based on different types of features, such as the Parallel Tracking and Verifying (PTAV) [13], which consists of two asynchronously but cooperatively working trackers: a DCF based real-time tracker and a deep features based verifier. To leverage the complementary properties of deep and shallow features, the Multi-Cue Correlation filter based Tracker (MCCT) [28] tried to fuse the outputs of the multiple trackers running in parallel.

In Fig. 1, we illustrate the performances of Histogram of Oriented Gradient (HOG) [6] and Colornames (CN) [27] features within one of the state-of-the-art trackers—Efficient Convolution Operators (ECO) [7] under some challenging tracking scenarios: "background clutter", "fast motion", "deformation", and "occlusion", respectively. The precision plots and the success plots in Fig. 1 show that different challenging scenarios prefer different features.

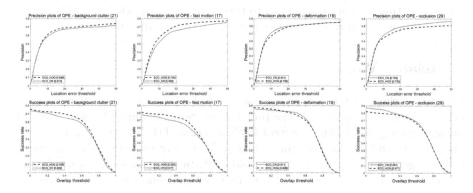

Fig. 1. The precision plots and the success plots of the ECO tracker [7] with HOG and CN features on the OTB2013 dataset [29], respectively, under the "background clutter", "fast motion", "deformation" and "occlusion" scenarios (the number of video sequences in each scenario set is given in parenthesis).

1.1 Motivation

Although feature-level fusion methods [1,3,23] have been used or extended to boost the performance, the redundancy among features may bring the overfitting of tracker to the existing samples and add extra computational load to the tracker. So far, as we know that no one consider coupling the response of DCF based trackers with the weights of feature channels directly. In this paper, we propose an adaptive feature weighting scheme for visual tracking which can explicitly learn the weight of each feature channel for each incoming frame through a least-square estimation. We integrate the adaptive feature weighting scheme into two state-of-the-art handcrafted DCF based trackers—Background-Aware Correlation Filters (BACF) [14] and Channel and Spatial Reliability DCF (CSRDCF) [22]. We evaluate the two trackers with the adaptive feature weighting scheme on two benchmarks: Object Tracking Benchmark (OTB2013) [29] and Visual Object Tracking (VOT2016) [20], and we find that the adaptive feature weighting scheme can outperform the feature-level fusion methods [1] and the decision-level fusion of the outputs of multiple trackers [28].

1.2 Contributions

The main contribution of this paper is three-fold. First, we propose an adaptive feature weighting scheme to exploit the strengths of different feature channels under different scenarios, while keeping the tracker compact at the same time. Secondly, we formulate the tracking as a two-stage optimization problem: the tracker or the appearance model is learned using the alternative direction method of multipliers (ADMM) [5], while the weights of feature channels are adaptively adjusted by a least-square estimation, alternatively. Thirdly, we integrate the adaptive feature weighting scheme into two state-of-the-art DCF based trackers, and the experimental results demonstrate its accuracy and efficiency.

2 Related Work

A typical tracking system consists of three crucial components: (1) an appearance model, which will discriminate the target from the surrounding background, (2) a search strategy for finding the most likely location of the target in the currently input frame, and (3) an updating strategy for timely capturing the variations of the target during the tracking to avoid drift. In this paper, we do not intend to review the references about all the three components, but just focus on the strategies of feature channel selection, the feature-level fusion and the decision-level fusion of the outputs of multiple trackers, and spatial reliability analysis of feature channels.

In order to improve the discriminative ability of the appearance model, the simplest way is to integrate different types of features directly into a tracker, such as [2,10,15]. In order to learn a robust appearance model, the Multiple Instance Learning (MIL) tracker [1] used labeled bags of training samples in which the label of each instance is unknown to reduce the negative affect caused by the slight accuracies produced by the tracker. Under the situation of occlusion, even the state-of-the-art trackers do not know how to handle it. To reduce the influence of the contaminated samples on the appearance model, when the target was occluded, the SRDCFdecon filter [8] tried to select previous "clean" training samples online to update the correlation filter.

The advantages of deep features are their ability to encode high-level semantic information, which is invariant to complex appearance changes and background clutter, but deep features are unfavorable for the target with low resolution. Whereas the low-level features can provide higher spatial resolution, which is crucial in accurate target localization, but they are very sensitive to the appearance variations and background clutter. To fuse the deep features and low-level features can boost the performance to some degree [23]. Gundogdu et al. [18] proposed to learn good deep features during the tracking. Due to the inherent scarcity of training data in tracking, the data hungry of learning deep features is prone to be over-fitting. Furthermore, the high dimensionality of deep features will cause an increasing in the computational complexity. Therefore, fusing different types of features is still an open problem.

Other research work tried to handle the diversity of the appearance model by fusing the outputs of multiple trackers at the decision-level [13,25,28]. The PTAV [13] was built on two trackers: one is a real-time tracker based on hand-crafted features, and the other is a tracker based on deep features. The two trackers run asynchronously and cooperatively with an efficient communication mechanism. The MCCT [28] used different combinations of features on multiple light-weighted trackers, such as the Kernelized Correlation Filter (KCF) [19]. Though all the trackers in the MCCT [28] run in parallel, the MCCT used deep features on each tracker, so the detection rate is slow down for about 1/10 of the speed of the KCF which only used handcrafted features [19].

Because the target region may include samples from the background, the CSRDCF filter [22] tried to learn a spatial reliability map by a graph-based segmentation technique, In the CSRDCF filter [22], the channel reliability is to take the magnitude of the maximum response and the ratio between the maximum response and the second maximum response into consideration. The DRT [26] proposed some similar ideas as the CSRDCF filter [22] to take different parts in the target region to have different reliability weights.

The redundancy of feature channels is a two-side sword. Although it may induce over-fitting sometimes, it can help to tell the target from the clutter background. The key difference between the proposed approach and the above mentioned approaches is that we recognize different features may have different effects under different scenarios, and we adaptively select the weight for each feature channel for each incoming frame to strengthen its advantages but to weaken its disadvantages simultaneously.

3   Adaptive Feature Channel Weighting Scheme

In this section, before we introduce the adaptive feature channel weighting scheme, and integrate it into two state-of-the-art trackers: the BACF [14] and the CSRDCF [22], we briefly review the principle of DCF based trackers.

3.1   The Principle of DCF Based Trackers

The Minimum Output Sum of Squared Error (MOSSE) correlation filter [4] can be expressed as a ridge regression problem in the spatial domain:

$$E(\mathbf{h}) = \frac{1}{2} \left\| \mathbf{y} - \sum_{k=1}^{K} \mathbf{C}_k \mathbf{h}_k \right\|_2^2 + \frac{\lambda}{2} \|\mathbf{h}\|_2^2 \tag{1}$$

where $\mathbf{y}$ is the desired response for the input $\mathbf{x} \in R^D$ and λ is a regularization term. Bolme et al. advocated the use of a 2D Gaussian with small variance (2–3 pixels) for $\mathbf{y}$ centered at the location of the target. K is the number of feature channels. Each row in $\mathbf{C}_k$ represents a cyclic shift for the kth input feature channel $\mathbf{x}_k$, so $\mathbf{C}_k$ is a circulant matrix:

$$\mathbf{C}_k = \begin{bmatrix} \mathbf{x}_k(1) \ \mathbf{x}_k(2) \ \cdots \ \ \mathbf{x}_k(D) \\ \mathbf{x}_k(D) \ \mathbf{x}_k(1) \ \cdots \ \mathbf{x}_k(D-1) \\ \vdots \quad \vdots \quad \ddots \quad \vdots \\ \mathbf{x}_k(2) \ \mathbf{x}_k(3) \ \cdots \quad \mathbf{x}_k(1) \end{bmatrix}_{D \times D} \tag{2}$$

It is well-known that any circular matrix can be diagonalized by the Discrete Fourier Transform (DFT) matrix $\mathbf{F}$ [17]. So $\mathbf{F}^H \mathbf{C}_k \mathbf{F} = diag(\hat{\mathbf{x}}_k(1), \cdots, \hat{\mathbf{x}}_k(D))$, where $\hat{\mathbf{x}}_k(i), (i = 1, 2, \cdots, D)$ are the Fourier coefficients of the input channel $\mathbf{x}_k$. According to the Parseval Theorem, we can express Eq. 1 in the frequency domain:

$$E(\hat{\mathbf{h}}) = \frac{1}{2} \left\| \hat{\mathbf{y}} - \sum_{k=1}^{K} diag(\hat{\mathbf{x}}_k(i))^* \hat{\mathbf{h}}_k \right\|_2^2 + \frac{\lambda}{2} \left\| \hat{\mathbf{h}} \right\|_2^2 \tag{3}$$

where $\hat{\mathbf{h}} = \left(\hat{\mathbf{h}}_1^T \cdots \hat{\mathbf{h}}_K^T \right)^T$ is a KD dimensional super-vector of the Fourier transforms of each channel of the correlation filter $\mathbf{h}$, and the superscript $*$ denotes the conjugate. If let $\hat{\mathbf{X}} = \left(diag(\hat{\mathbf{x}}_1)^* \cdots diag(\hat{\mathbf{x}}_K)^* \right)_{D \times KD}$, the correlation filter $\mathbf{h}$ can be solved in the frequency domain

$$\hat{\mathbf{h}} = (\lambda \mathbf{I} + \hat{\mathbf{X}}^T \hat{\mathbf{X}})^{-1} (\hat{\mathbf{X}}^T \hat{\mathbf{y}}) \tag{4}$$

The computational complexity of solving this equation is $O(K^3 D^3)$, and it is too high for real-time applications. Fortunately, $\hat{\mathbf{X}}$ is sparse banded and the jth element of each correlation response is dependent only on the K values of $V(\hat{\mathbf{h}}(j))$ and $V(\hat{\mathbf{x}}(j))$, where V is a concatenation operator that returns a $K \times 1$ vector when it is applied on the jth element of a K-channel vectors, i.e. $V(\hat{\mathbf{h}}(j)) = \left(conj(\hat{\mathbf{h}}_1(j)) \cdots conj(\hat{\mathbf{h}}_k(j)) \right)^T$. Therefore, an efficient solution of Eq. 4 can be found by solving D independent $K \times K$ linear systems:

$$V(\hat{\mathbf{h}}(j)) = (\lambda \mathbf{I} + V(\hat{\mathbf{x}}(j)) V(\hat{\mathbf{x}}(j))^T)^{-1} (V(\hat{\mathbf{x}}(j)) \hat{\mathbf{y}}(j)) \tag{5}$$

where $\hat{\mathbf{y}}(j)$ is the jth Fourier coefficient of the desired output $\mathbf{y}$.

By exploiting the circulant structure, we can compute all the responses simultaneously and efficiently in the Fourier domain. The vector with all responses at all positions of the image patch $\mathbf{z}$ in the frequency domain is given by:

$$\hat{\mathbf{r}} = \sum_{k=1}^{K} \hat{\mathbf{h}}_k \odot \hat{\mathbf{z}}_k \tag{6}$$

where $\hat{\mathbf{h}}_k$ and $\hat{\mathbf{z}}_k$ are the DFT of the kth channel of the learned correlation filter $\mathbf{h}$ and image patch $\mathbf{z}$, and $\odot$ denotes the Hadamard product. The image patch $\mathbf{z}$ is extracted from the region centered at the previously detected target. The position with the maximal response is the currently estimated center of the target.

3.2   Adaptive Feature Channel Weighting Scheme

Since different features have different effects under different scenarios, here we assign different weights to different feature channels under different scenarios, and constraint the weights not stray away from their initial weights too much. The Eq. 1 now becomes:

$$E(\mathbf{h}) = \frac{1}{2} \left\| \mathbf{y} - \sum_{k=1}^{K} \alpha_k \mathbf{C}_k \mathbf{h}_k \right\|_2^2 + \frac{\lambda_1}{2} \|\mathbf{h}\|_2^2 + \frac{\lambda_2}{2} \left\| \boldsymbol{\alpha} - \boldsymbol{\alpha}^{(0)} \right\|_2^2$$
$$s.t. \quad \alpha_k \geq 0 \quad (k = 1, \cdots, K) \tag{7}$$

where α_k is the weight of the kth feature channel, λ_1 and λ_2 are the regularization factors. $\boldsymbol{\alpha}$ is a K dimensional vector ($\boldsymbol{\alpha} = (\alpha_1, \cdots, \alpha_K)^T$) and $\boldsymbol{\alpha}^{(0)}$ is the initial weight vector.

To solve Eq. 7, we optimize it in a two-stage alternatively. In the first stage, we employ the Alternating Direction Methods of Multipliers (ADMM) [5] to optimize the correlation filter $\mathbf{h}$ and some auxiliary variables iteratively. In the second stage, based on the learned correlation filter $\mathbf{h}$ and the auxiliary variables, we use the least square method to estimate the weights of feature channels directly. The two processes are optimized alternatively for a fixed times.

Suppose we have obtained the current estimation of the correlation filter $\mathbf{h}$, now only the first term and the last term in the objective function of Eq. 7 are related to the weight vector $\boldsymbol{\alpha}$, we can rewrite it in the frequency domain as

$$E(\boldsymbol{\alpha}) = \frac{1}{2} \left\| \hat{\mathbf{y}} - \hat{\mathbf{X}} \mathbf{A} \hat{\mathbf{h}} \right\|_2^2 + \frac{\lambda_2}{2} \left\| \boldsymbol{\alpha} - \boldsymbol{\alpha}^{(0)} \right\|_2^2$$
$$s.t. \quad \alpha_k \geq 0 \quad (k = 1, \cdots, K) \tag{8}$$

where $\mathbf{A}$ is a diagonal block matrix with diagonal blocks of $\alpha_k \mathbf{I}(k = 1, 2, \cdots, K)$ on its diagonal, and $\mathbf{I}$ is an identity matrix. Because the weight α_k only affects the kth channel, we can rewrite the diagonal block matrix $\mathbf{A}$ in Eq. 8 as its vector form $\boldsymbol{\alpha}$:

$$E(\boldsymbol{\alpha}) = \frac{1}{2} \sum_{j=1}^{D} (\hat{\mathbf{y}}(j) - \hat{\mathbf{r}}(j)^T \boldsymbol{\alpha})^2 + \frac{\lambda_2}{2} \left\| \boldsymbol{\alpha} - \boldsymbol{\alpha}^{(0)} \right\|_2^2$$
$$s.t. \quad \alpha_k \geq 0 \quad (k = 1, \cdots, K) \tag{9}$$

where $\hat{\mathbf{r}}(j)$ is a K dimensional vector containing the jth element of the responses of all input channels. Since $\hat{\mathbf{r}}(j)^T \alpha \hat{\mathbf{r}}(j) = \hat{\mathbf{r}}(j)\hat{\mathbf{r}}(j)^T \alpha$, and the each weight α_k in α should be no less than zero, we can have the close-form solution of α:

$$\alpha = \max\{0, (\sum_{j=1}^{D} \hat{\mathbf{r}}(j)\hat{\mathbf{r}}(j)^T + \lambda_2 \mathbf{I})^{-1}(\sum_{j=1}^{D} \hat{\mathbf{y}}(j)\hat{\mathbf{r}}(j) + \lambda_2 \alpha^{(0)})\} \qquad (10)$$

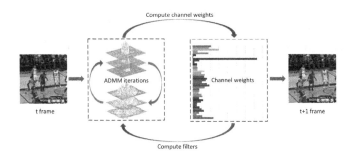

Fig. 2. The adaptive feature channel weighting scheme.

Since the weights $\alpha_k (k = 1, \cdots, K)$ are real, in the implementation Eq. 10 is computed in the spatial domain. Figure 2 illustrates how the weights of different feature channels are changing adaptively during the tracking.

3.3   The AW-BACF Tracker and the AW-CSRDCF Tracker

In this section, we integrate the adaptive feature channel weighting scheme into two state-of-the-art DCF-based trackers: the BACF [14] and the CSRDCF [22].

The AW-BACF Tracker. In order to alleviate the boundary effect caused by circularly shifted patches, Galoogahi et al. introduced a $D \times T$ binary selection mask $\mathbf{P}$ in [14] where T is the spatial size of training samples and D is the spatial size of the correlation filter (here T is much larger than D). This binary selection mask $\mathbf{P}$ allows the surrounding background to form virtual negative samples at the learning stage. The objective function of the BACF tracker is

$$E(\mathbf{h}) = \frac{1}{2}\left\|\mathbf{y} - \sum_{k=1}^{K} \mathbf{C}_k \mathbf{P}^T \mathbf{h}_k\right\|_2^2 + \frac{\lambda}{2}\|\mathbf{h}\|_2^2 \qquad (11)$$

where the transpose of $\mathbf{P}$ acts like a zero-padding operator, $\mathbf{y} \in \mathbf{R}^T$, and $\mathbf{h}_k \in \mathbf{R}^D, (k = 1, \cdots, K)$. The $\mathbf{C}_k$ is a circulant matrix formed by applying the circular shift operator on a training sample but now its size is $T \times T$. Since the binary matrix $\mathbf{P}$ prohibits a close-form solution of Eq. 11, they introduced an auxiliary variable $\hat{\mathbf{g}} = \sqrt{T}(\mathbf{I}_k \otimes \mathbf{FP}^T)\mathbf{h}$ (where $\otimes$ indicates the Kronecker product) and employed an Alternating Direction Methods of Multipliers (ADMM) [5] to learn the correlation filter $\mathbf{h}$ in the spatial domain, and to optimize the auxiliary variable $\hat{\mathbf{g}}$ in the frequency domain, alternatively.

To integrate the adaptive feature channel weighting scheme into the BACF tracker, we have the AW-BACF tracker, and its objective function becomes:

$$E(\mathbf{h}) = \frac{1}{2}\left\| \mathbf{y} - \sum_{k=1}^{K} \alpha_k \mathbf{C}_k \mathbf{P}^T \mathbf{h}_k \right\|_2^2 + \frac{\lambda_2}{2}\|\mathbf{h}\|_2^2 + \frac{\lambda_2}{2}\left\| \alpha - \alpha^{(0)} \right\|_2^2 \quad (12)$$

We use a two-stage optimization process to learn the correlation filter $\mathbf{h}$ and the weight vector α, alternatively. The detail of learning the correlation filter $\mathbf{h}$ please refers to [14]. The adaptive adjustment of the weights of feature channels for each incoming frame please refers to Sect. 3.2. The $\hat{\mathbf{r}}(j)$ in Eq. 9 and Eq. 10 has the form $\hat{\mathbf{r}}(j) = (\hat{\mathbf{g}}_1(j)\hat{\mathbf{x}}_1(j) \cdots \hat{\mathbf{g}}_K(j)\hat{\mathbf{x}}_K(j))^T$.

The AW-CSRDCF Tracker. The CSRDCF tracker [22] tried to address the boundary effect caused by circularly shifted patches in a very similar way as the BACF tracker [14] did, but the important difference between the CSRDCF tracker [22] and the BACF tracker [14] is that the binary selection mask $\mathbf{P}$ in the BACF tracker is with regular form: the central small rectangular is with "1"s, and the surrounding part is with "0"s, whereas the spatial reliability map $\mathbf{m}$ in the CSRDCF tracker constructed by a graphic model can be irregularly shaped. As in the BACF tracker, the constraint $\mathbf{h} = \mathbf{m} \odot \mathbf{h}$ prohibits a close-form solution of the correlation filter $\mathbf{h}$ also. So they introduced a dual variable $\mathbf{h}_c$ and the constraint $\mathbf{h}_c - \mathbf{m} \odot \mathbf{h} \equiv 0$, and this also leads an augmented Lagrangian problem. For the details of learning, please refer to [22].

In CSRDCF tracker [22], each feature channel is weighed by its channel reliability score $w_k = 1 - \min(\rho_{max2}/\rho_{max1}, 0.5)$, and ρ_{max2}/ρ_{max1} is the ratio between the second and first major mode in the kth response channel. In the AW-CSRDCF Tracker, we replace the channel reliability score with the adaptive feature channel weighting scheme (Sect. 3.2), and get a new AW-CSRDCF tracker, where $\hat{\mathbf{r}}(j)$ in Eqs. 9 and 10 has the form of $(\hat{\mathbf{h}}_{c1}(j)\hat{\mathbf{x}}_1(j) \cdots \hat{\mathbf{h}}_{cK}(j)\hat{\mathbf{x}}_K(j))^T$.

4 Experimental Results

This section presents an experimental evaluation of the proposed adaptive feature weighting scheme. In Sect. 4.1, we discuss implementation details. In Sect. 4.2, we give a baseline comparison of the AW-BACF tracker and the AW-CSRDCF tracker with their original versions, respectively. In Sects. 4.3 and 4.4, we compare the two new trackers with some state-of-the-art trackers on two benchmarks: OTB2013 [29], and VOT2016 [20], individually. In Sect. 4.5, we compare some tracking results of the AW-BACF tracker and the AW-CSRDCF tracker with their original versions, and one tracker based on decision-level fusion [28], visually.

4.1   Implementation Details

The original version of the BACF tracker [14] used the HOG features [6]. Now, we integrate the CN features [10] into the BACF tracker. In the evaluation, we found that if we adopted the adaptive scale estimation scheme proposed by Li and Zhu [21], the estimated scale of the target would become smaller and smaller with time going, so we turn to learn a separate 1-D scale correlation filter as done in [9] to overcome this problem. All the corresponding parameters are set as the BACF [14] and the DSST [9]. The regularization factor λ_2 in Eq. 12 is set as 0.008. For efficiency, we run the two-stage optimization process only for one time. The initial weights for all feature channels are set to 1. The original version of the CSRDCF [22] already used the HOG [6] and CN [10], we only replace the channel reliability score with the adaptive feature channel weighting scheme (Sect. 3.3). The regularization factor λ_2 in Eq. 12 for the AW-CSRDCF is set as 6. The rest parameters are set as the CSRDCF tracker [22].

Our tracker is implemented in MATLAB 2017b on a computer with an Intel i5-6300HQ 2.3 GHz CPU and 8 GB RAM.

4.2   Baseline Comparison

Since the AW-BACF tracker is built on the BACF [14], we have several different versions of the BACF: the BACF with the scale estimation scheme [9] (BACF_dsst_HOG), the BACF_dsst_HOG_CN with additional CN features, and the proposed AW-BACF tracker. We tested them on the OTB2013 dataset [29]. To illustrate the results clearly, we present the success plots and the precision plots of two attributes: "scale variation" and "occlusion" in Fig. 3. The CSRDCF tracker [22] already used the HOG and CN features, so here we only compare the performances of the CSRDCF tracker and the new AW-CSRDCF tracker on the OTB2013 dataset [29]. Due to the space limitation, we present the precision plots and the success plots of these two trackers on two attributes subsets: "low resolution" and "deformation" in Fig. 4. We can see that the adaptive feature weighting scheme does bring a large margin improvement over their original versions and the simple feature combination scheme.

4.3   OTB2013 Dataset

For fair comparison, we validate the BACF with the proposed adaptive feature weighting scheme in a comprehensive comparison with 9 state-of-the-art trackers: MIL [1], KCF [19], DSST [9], SRDCF [12], SRDCFdecon [8], BACF [14], Staple [2], MCCT-H [28] and CSRDCF [22]. All these trackers use handcrafted features. In Fig. 5, we record the overall precision plots and the overall success plots on the OTB2013 dataset [29] of the 10 trackers including ours, respectively. Though the proposed adaptive feature weighting scheme does help to improve the performance of the CSRDCF tracker [22], the performance of the AW-CSRDCF tracker is not as good as that of the BACF [14], so we will not show the plots of the AW-CSRDCF tracker in Fig. 5. From these results, we can

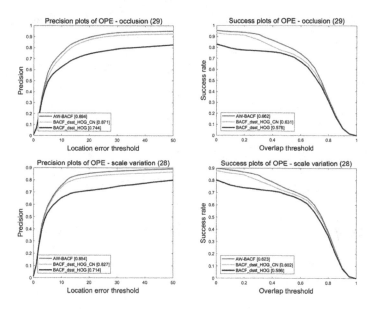

Fig. 3. The precision plots and success plots of the three variants of the BACF tracker of the "scale variation" and "occlusion" subsets of the OTB2013 dataset [29]. In the legend, the DP at a threshold of 20 pixels and area-under-curve (AUC) are reported in the left and right figures, respectively.

see that even without the deep features, the AW-BACF tracker can achieve the distance precision (DP) score of 89%, which is ranking no.1 among the 10 trackers. Our DP score is very close to 91.4% of the MCCT [28], but in the MCCT tracker, the deep features were used. In addition, the proposed tracker is just a single tracker, while the MCCT was based on multiple trackers.

Table 1. The accuracy (Acc.), robustness (failure rate is abbreviated as FR), EAO and frame per second (fps) of the 8 state-of-the-art trackers on the VOT2016 [20]. The first and second highest values are highlighted by red and blue, respectively.

	AW-BACF	CSRDCF	SRDCF	BACF	KCF	DSST	Staple	MCCT-H
Acc	0.55	0.51	0.53	0.55	0.48	0.53	0.54	0.56
FR	22	16	28	36	38	45	23	21
EAO	0.31	0.34	0.25	0.22	0.19	0.18	0.29	0.30
FPS	27	13	5	30	172	24	80	16

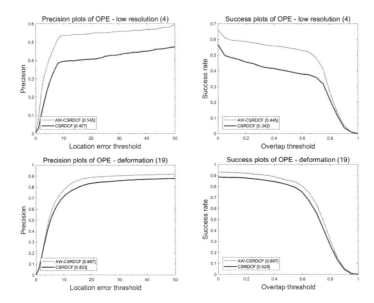

Fig. 4. The precision plots and success plots of the CSRDCF tracker and the AW-CSRDCF tracker of "low resolution" and "deformation" subsets of the OTB2013 dataset [29].

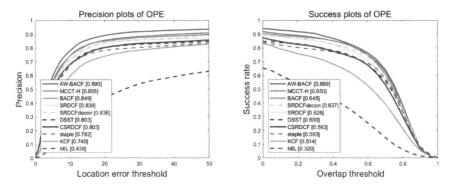

Fig. 5. The overall precision plots and the overall success plots of the 10 trackers on the OTB2013 dataset [29]. In the legend, the DP at a threshold of 20 pixels and area-under-curve (AUC) are reported in the left and right figures, respectively.

4.4 VOT2016 Dataset

Figure 6 shows the ranking results in terms of expected average overlap (EAO) in VOT2016 [20]. In this evaluation, the AW-BACF tracker ranks in the 2nd place, but the speed is 2 times faster than that of the CSRDCF tracker [22]. In order to show the results clearly, in Table 1, we list the detail results of our approach and the other 7 trackers ranked on the top in VOT2016 [20].

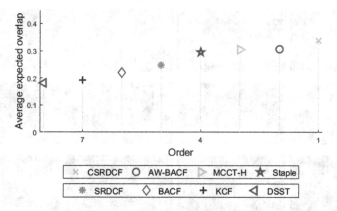

Fig. 6. Expected Average Overlap (EAO) graph with trackers ranked from right to left evaluated on VOT2016 [20].

4.5   Visual Comparison

Here, we compare the tracking results of different trackers visually. For clarity, we only compare the visual tracking results of the AW-BACF tracker and the AW-CSRDCF tracker, and those of their original versions: the BACF tracker [14] and the CSRDCF tracker [22], and those of the MCCT tracker [28]. In Fig. 7, results on different rows are extracted from different sequences. We use different color rectangles to represent the outputs of different trackers. These sequences have different attributes: Illumination Variation (IV), Scale Variation (SV), Occlusion (OCC), Motion Blur (MB), Deformation (DEF), Fast Motion (FM), In-Plane Rotation (IPR), Out-of-Plane Rotation (OPR), Out-of-View (OV), Background Clutter (BC), and Low Resolution (LR). Each sequence has several different attributes, for example, the "soccer" sequence (on the 1st row) is with IV, SV, OCC, MB, FM, IPR, OPR, and BC, while the "skating" sequence (on the 2nd row) has IV, SV, OCC, DEF, OPR, and BC attributes. From these results, the AW-BACF tracker has the highly consistent performance under different challenges. It always locks on the target tightly. The CSRDCF filter [22] tried to select the "clean" training samples online, but it is still very sensitive to occlusion, and scale variations. Though the AW-CSRDCF tracker helps to handle "occlusion" to some degree, it fails to capture the target when it is moving fast, such as the results of the "dragon-baby" on the 4th row. The MCCT-H tracker [28] will give biased outputs under scale variation and large illumination variations.

Fig. 7. Visual comparison of the tracking results of the BACF tracker [14], the AW-BACF tracker, the CSRDCF tracker [22], the AW-CSRDCF tracker, and the MCCT-H tracker [28]. (Color figure online)

5   Conclusions

As we know that different features play different roles under different scenarios. Under some challenge scenarios, handcrafted features can have better performance than deep features. Based on these observations, in this paper, we proposed an adaptive feature weighting scheme, and integrate it into two state-of-the-art DCF based trackers. We evaluated the two new DCF based trackers on two benchmarks: OTB2013 and VOT2016, and compared them with some state-of-the-art handcraft DCF based trackers. On the OTB2013 dataset, the AW-BACF tracker ranks the No.1 among 10 trackers. The AW-CSRDCF tracker is not as good as the BACF tracker [14], but it is better than its original version: the CSRDCF tracker [22]. Although the VOT2016 benchmark adopts different metrics to evaluate the performance of trackers, the AW-BACF tracker is overall ranked on the top among the 10 trackers if we take the accuracy, robustness and time efficiency into consideration.

Acknowledgement. This work was supported by the National Research Foundation of Zhejiang Province, China (LY16F020009).

References

1. Babenko, B., Yang, M., Belongie, S.: Robust object tracking with online multiple instance learning. IEEE Trans. Pattern Anal. Mach. Intell. **33**(8), 1619–1632 (2011). https://doi.org/10.1109/TPAMI.2010.226
2. Bertinetto, L., Valmadre, J., Golodetz, S., Miksik, O., Torr, P.H.S.: Staple: complementary learners for real-time tracking. In: 2016 IEEE Conference on Computer Vision and Pattern Recognition (CVPR), pp. 1401–1409, June 2016. https://doi.org/10.1109/CVPR.2016.156
3. Bhat, G., Johnander, J., Danelljan, M., Khan, F.S., Felsberg, M.: Unveiling the power of deep tracking. In: Ferrari, V., Hebert, M., Sminchisescu, C., Weiss, Y. (eds.) ECCV 2018. LNCS, vol. 11206, pp. 493–509. Springer, Cham (2018). https://doi.org/10.1007/978-3-030-01216-8_30
4. Bolme, D.S., Beveridge, J.R., Draper, B.A., Lui, Y.M.: Visual object tracking using adaptive correlation filters. In: 2010 IEEE Computer Society Conference on Computer Vision and Pattern Recognition, pp. 2544–2550, June 2010. https://doi.org/10.1109/CVPR.2010.5539960
5. Boyd, S., Parikh, N., Chu, E., Peleato, B., Eckstein, J.: Distributed Optimization and Statistical Learning via the Alternating Direction Method of Multipliers. Now (2011). https://doi.org/10.1561/2200000016
6. Dalal, N., Triggs, B.: Histograms of oriented gradients for human detection. In: 2005 IEEE Computer Society Conference on Computer Vision and Pattern Recognition (CVPR 2005), vol. 1, pp. 886–893, June 2005. https://doi.org/10.1109/CVPR.2005.177
7. Danelljan, M., Bhat, G., Khan, F.S., Felsberg, M.: Eco: efficient convolution operators for tracking. In: 2017 IEEE Conference on Computer Vision and Pattern Recognition (CVPR), pp. 6931–6939, July 2017. https://doi.org/10.1109/CVPR.2017.733
8. Danelljan, M., Häger, G., Khan, F.S., Felsberg, M.: Adaptive decontamination of the training set: a unified formulation for discriminative visual tracking. In: 2016 IEEE Conference on Computer Vision and Pattern Recognition (CVPR), pp. 1430–1438, June 2016. https://doi.org/10.1109/CVPR.2016.159
9. Danelljan, M., Häger, G., Khan, F.S., Felsberg, M.: Discriminative scale space tracking. IEEE Trans. Pattern Anal. Mach. Intell. **39**(8), 1561–1575 (2017). https://doi.org/10.1109/TPAMI.2016.2609928

10. Danelljan, M., Khan, F.S., Felsberg, M., van der Weijer, J.: Adaptive color attributes for real-time visual tracking. In: 2014 IEEE Conference on Computer Vision and Pattern Recognition, pp. 1090–1097, June 2014. https://doi.org/10.1109/CVPR.2014.143

11. Danelljan, M., Bhat, G., Gladh, S., Khan, F.S., Felsberg, M.: Deep motion and appearance cues for visual tracking. Pattern Recogn. Lett. **124**, 74–81 (2019). https://doi.org/10.1016/j.patrec.2018.03.009

12. Danelljan, M., Häger, G., Khan, F.S., Felsberg, M.: Learning spatially regularized correlation filters for visual tracking. In: 2015 IEEE International Conference on Computer Vision (ICCV), pp. 4310–4318 (2015). https://doi.org/10.1109/ICCV.2015.490

13. Fan, H., Ling, H.: Parallel tracking and verifying: a framework for real-time and high accuracy visual tracking. In: 2017 IEEE International Conference on Computer Vision (ICCV), pp. 5487–5495, October 2017. https://doi.org/10.1109/ICCV.2017.585

14. Galoogahi, H.K., Fagg, A., Lucey, S.: Learning background-aware correlation filters for visual tracking. In: 2017 IEEE International Conference on Computer Vision (ICCV), pp. 1144–1152, October 2017. https://doi.org/10.1109/ICCV.2017.129

15. Galoogahi, H.K., Sim, T., Lucey, S.: Multi-channel correlation filters. In: 2013 IEEE International Conference on Computer Vision, pp. 3072–3079, December 2013. https://doi.org/10.1109/ICCV.2013.381

16. Galoogahi, H.K., Sim, T., Lucey, S.: Correlation filters with limited boundaries. In: 2015 IEEE Conference on Computer Vision and Pattern Recognition (CVPR), pp. 4630–4638, June 2015. https://doi.org/10.1109/CVPR.2015.7299094

17. Gray, R.M.: Toeplitz and circulant matrices: a review. Found. Trends® Commun. Inf. Theory **2**(3), 155–239 (2006). https://doi.org/10.1561/0100000006

18. Gundogdu, E., Alatan, A.A.: Good features to correlate for visual tracking. IEEE Trans. Image Process. **27**(5), 2526–2540 (2018). https://doi.org/10.1109/TIP.2018.2806280

19. Henriques, J.F., Caseiro, R., Martins, P., Batista, J.: High-speed tracking with kernelized correlation filters. IEEE Trans. Pattern Anal. Mach. Intell. **37**(3), 583–596 (2015). https://doi.org/10.1109/TPAMI.2014.2345390

20. Kristan, M., et al.: A novel performance evaluation methodology for single-target trackers. IEEE Trans. Pattern Anal. Mach. Intell. **38**(11), 2137–2155 (2016). https://doi.org/10.1109/TPAMI.2016.2516982

21. Li, Y., Zhu, J.: A scale adaptive kernel correlation filter tracker with feature integration. In: Agapito, L., Bronstein, M.M., Rother, C. (eds.) ECCV 2014. LNCS, vol. 8926, pp. 254–265. Springer, Cham (2015). https://doi.org/10.1007/978-3-319-16181-5_18

22. Lukežic, A., Vojír, T., Zajc, L.C., Matas, J., Kristan, M.: Discriminative correlation filter with channel and spatial reliability. In: 2017 IEEE Conference on Computer Vision and Pattern Recognition (CVPR), pp. 4847–4856, July 2017. https://doi.org/10.1109/CVPR.2017.515

23. Ma, C., Huang, J., Yang, X., Yang, M.: Hierarchical convolutional features for visual tracking. In: 2015 IEEE International Conference on Computer Vision (ICCV), pp. 3074–3082, December 2015. https://doi.org/10.1109/ICCV.2015.352

24. Mueller, M., Smith, N., Ghanem, B.: Context-aware correlation filter tracking. In: 2017 IEEE Conference on Computer Vision and Pattern Recognition (CVPR), pp. 1387–1395, July 2017. https://doi.org/10.1109/CVPR.2017.152

25. Rapuru, M.K., Kakanuru, S., Venugopal, P.M., Mishra, D., Subrahmanyam, G.R.K.S.: Correlation-based tracker-level fusion for robust visual tracking. IEEE Trans. Image Process. **26**(10), 4832–4842 (2017). https://doi.org/10.1109/TIP. 2017.2699791
26. Sun, C., Wang, D., Lu, H., Yang, M.: Correlation tracking via joint discrimination and reliability learning. In: 2018 IEEE/CVF Conference on Computer Vision and Pattern Recognition, pp. 489–497, June 2018. https://doi.org/10.1109/CVPR. 2018.00058
27. van de Weijer, J., Schmid, C., Verbeek, J., Larlus, D.: Learning color names for real-world applications. IEEE Trans. Image Process. **18**(7), 1512–1523 (2009). https:// doi.org/10.1109/TIP.2009.2019809
28. Wang, N., Zhou, W., Tian, Q., Hong, R., Wang, M., Li, H.: Multi-cue correlation filters for robust visual tracking. In: 2018 IEEE/CVF Conference on Computer Vision and Pattern Recognition, pp. 4844–4853, June 2018. https://doi.org/10. 1109/CVPR.2018.00509
29. Wu, Y., Lim, J., Yang, M.: Online object tracking: a benchmark. In: 2013 IEEE Conference on Computer Vision and Pattern Recognition, pp. 2411–2418, June 2013. https://doi.org/10.1109/CVPR.2013.312

In-Silico Staining from Bright-Field and Fluorescent Images Using Deep Learning

Dominik Jens Elias Waibel[1,2]👁, Ulf Tiemann[3]👁, Valerio Lupperger[1,2]👁,
Henrik Semb[3(✉)]👁, and Carsten Marr[1(✉)]👁

[1] Institute of Computational Biology, Helmholtz Zentrum Munich,
German Research Center for Environmental Health, Neuherberg, Germany
`Carsten.Marr@helmholtz-muenchen.de`
[2] School of Life Sciences Weihenstephan, Technical University of Munich,
Munich, Germany
[3] Novo Nordisk Foundation Center for Stem Cell Biology - DanStem,
University of Copenhagen, Copenhagen, Denmark
`Semb@sund.ku.dk`

Abstract. Fluorescent markers are commonly used to characterize single cells and to uncover molecular properties. Unfortunately, fluorescent staining is laborious and costly, it damages tissue and suffers from inconsistencies. Recently deep learning approaches have been successfully applied to predict fluorescent markers from bright-field images [1–3]. These approaches can save costs and time and speed up the classification of tissue properties. However, it is currently not clear how different image channels can be meaningfully combined to improve prediction accuracy. Thus, we investigated the benefits of multi channel input for predicting a specific transcription factor antibody staining.

Our image dataset consists of three channels: bright-field, fluorescent GFP reporter and transcription factor antibody staining. Fluorescent GFP is constantly expressed in the genetically modified cells from a particular differentiation step onwards. The cells are additionally stained with a specific transcription factor antibody that marks a subtype of GFP positive cells. For data acquisition we used a Leica SP8 and a Zeiss LSM780 microscope with 20x objectives.

We trained a deep neural network, a modified U-Net [4], to predict the transcription factor antibody staining from bright-field and GFP channels. To this end, we trained on 2432 three-dimensional images containing roughly 7600 single cells and compared the accuracy for prediction of the transcription factor antibody staining using bright-field only, GFP only, and both channels together on a test-set of 576 images with approximately 1800 single cells. The same training- and test-set was used for all experiments (Fig. 1).

The prediction error, measured as the mean relative pixel-wise error over the test-set, was calculated to 61% for prediction from bright-field, 55% for prediction from GFP and 51% for prediction both bright-field and GFP images. The median pixel-wise Pearson correlation coefficient, increases from 0.12 for prediction from bright-field channels to 0.17 for

I. V. Tetko et al. (Eds.): ICANN 2019, LNCS 11729, pp. 184–186, 2019.
https://doi.org/10.1007/978-3-030-30508-6_15

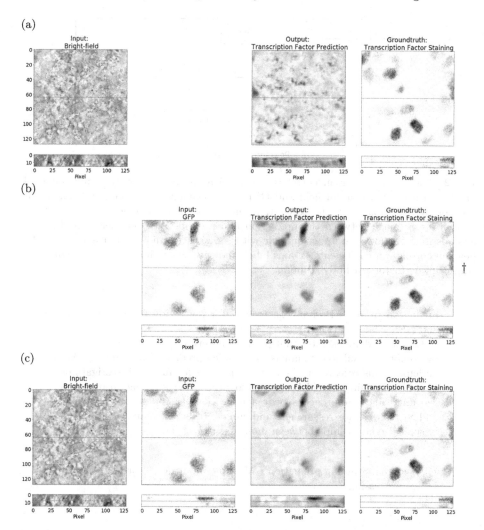

Fig. 1. Multi channel input from bright-field and GFP images leads to a higher performance when predicting transcription factor antibody staining as compared to using bright-field or GFP channels. The columns are (a) prediction from the bright-field channel, (b) prediction from the GFP channel, (c) prediction from both bright-field and GFP channel. The z-direction of the three dimensional images is displayed below each image with the grey line indicating where the section above was taken.

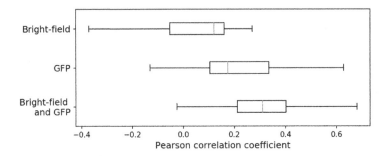

Fig. 2. The median pearson correlation coefficient is highest for the multi channel prediction using both bright-field and GFP. The pearson coefficient is calculated for each of the 576 images in the test-set. It measures correlation between the 262144 pixel in each image between the prediction and ground-truth channels. The boxplot extends from the lower to upper quartile with the whiskers indicating the range of the pearson correlation coefficients. Y-axis labels indicate the staining used to predict the transcription factor antibody staining.

prediction from GFP channels, to 0.31 for prediction from bright-field and GFP channels (Fig. 2).

Our work demonstrates that prediction performance can be increased by combining multiple channels for in-silico prediction of stainings. We anticipate this research to be a starting point for further investigations on which stainings could be predicted from other stainings using deep learning. These approaches bear a huge potential in saving laborious and costly work for researchers and clinical technicians and could reveal biological relationships between fluorescent markers.

Keywords: Staining prediction · Multiple input deep learning · Image processing

References

1. Christiansen, E.M., et al.: In silico labeling: predicting fluorescent labels in unlabeled images. Cell **173**(3), 792–803.e19 (2018). https://doi.org/10.1016/j.cell.2018.03.040
2. Ounkomol, C., Seshamani, S., Maleckar, M.M., Collman, F., Johnson, G.R.: Label-free prediction of three-dimensional fluorescence images from transmitted-light microscopy. Nature Methods **15**(11), 917–920 (2018). https://doi.org/10.1038/s41592-018-0111-2
3. Rivenson, Y., et al.: Virtual histological staining of unlabelled tissue-autofluorescence images via deep learning. Nat. Biomed. Eng. 1 (2019). https://doi.org/10.1038/s41551-019-0362-y
4. Ronneberger, O., Fischer, P., Brox, T.: UNet Convolutional Networks for Biomedical Image Segmentation. arXiv:1505.04597 [cs], May 2015. https://doi.org/10.1007/978-3-319-24574-4_28

Image Segmentation

A Lightweight Neural Network for Hard Exudate Segmentation of Fundus Image

Song Guo[1], Tao Li[1], Kai Wang[1,2], Chan Zhang[1], and Hong Kang[1,3]

[1] College of Computer Science, Nankai University, Tianjin, China
kanghong@nankai.edu.cn
[2] KLMDASR, Tianjin, China
[3] Beijing Shanggong Medical Technology Co. Ltd., Beijing, China

Abstract. Fundus image is an important indicator for diagnosing diabetic retinopathy (DR), which is a leading cause of blindness in adults. Moreover, hard exudate, a special kind of lesion in the fundus image, is treated as the basis to evaluate the severity level of DR. Therefore, it is crucial to segment hard exudate exactly. However, the segmentation results of existing deep learning-based segmentation methods are rather coarse due to successive pooling operations. In this paper, we propose a lightweight segmentation network with only one down-sampling operation and $1.9M$ parameters. Further, we propose a two-stage training algorithm to train our network from scratch. We conduct experiments on the IDRiD and e-ophtha EX datasets. Experimental results show that our network achieves superior performance with the fewest parameters and the fastest speed compared with baseline methods on the IDRiD dataset. Specially, with 1/20 parameters and 1/3 inference time, our method is over 10% higher than DeepLab v3+ in terms of F1-score on the IDRiD dataset. The source code of LWENet is available at https://github.com/guomugong/LWENet.

Keywords: Hard exudate segmentation · Fundus image · Diabetic retinopathy · Neural network

1 Introduction

Diabetic retinopathy (DR) has been the leading causes of blindness in working-age individuals. It is estimated by the World Diabetes Foundation that there will be 438 million people get DR by 2030 [21]. However, early interventions and DR screening are essential to prevent vision loss [6]. Analyzing fundus retinal image is the most popular method for DR screening with the advantages of low cost, painless, non-invasive, etc. Moreover, the presence and size of hard exudate (EX) in fundus images are the main indicator to diagnose the severity of DR. Therefore, it is crucial to development an automated tool for hard exudate detection.

Deep learning skills, specially deep convolutional neural networks (DCNN), have produced impressive performance improvements compared with traditional

© Springer Nature Switzerland AG 2019
I. V. Tetko et al. (Eds.): ICANN 2019, LNCS 11729, pp. 189–199, 2019.
https://doi.org/10.1007/978-3-030-30508-6_16

methods in computer vision tasks [10, 19, 22] and medical image analysis [6, 20]. DCNN learns much rich feature representation by stacking multiple convolutional operations and non-linear transformations together. However, in the traditional methods, the feature representation is human-designed. Hard exudate detection can be viewed as a segmentation task in computer vision. And, in the past few years, there are several literature on designing DCNN for hard exudate segmentation. Such as, Mo et al. proposed a Fully Convolutional Residual Network (FCRN) that fuses multi-level feature to segment hard exudate [14]. FCRN uses ResNet-50 [10] as a backbone, and it is pre-trained on ImageNet dataset [3]. Tan. et al. designed a patch-based classification network to detect hard exudate and other two kinds of lesions [20]. Obviously, this kind of patch-based method needs to split fundus image into a huge number of patches, and each patch needs to be fed into the network to get its prediction. This procedure always corresponds to large time cost. Guo et al. designed an image-level multi-lesion segmentation network, and their model can segment four kinds of fundus lesions simultaneously [7]. Among these methods, segmentation network shows superior performance compared with classification network in terms of speed and accuracy on hard exudate segmentation task.

In order to achieve good performance, most of the segmentation models finetune their networks pre-trained on ImageNet. This transfer procedure has two advantages. First, there are numerous state-of-the-art semantic segmentation models and classification models available online. It is convenient to use them for hard exudate segmentation with only minor modification. Second, fine-tuning can alleviate the over-fitting problem since the number of fundus images (several ten to several hundred) is limited. However, there are also critical limitations when adopting the pre-trained networks in hard exudate segmentation: (1) Domain mismatch [9]. The source domain (ImageNet) has a huge mismatch to the target domain (fundus image). (2) Limited structure design space [17]. The backbones of state-of-the-art semantic segmentation models, such as DeepLab v3+ [1] and FCN [16] are all from ImageNet-based classification network either VGGNet [18] or ResNet [10]. Therefore, there is little flexibility to adjust the network structures. (3) Large amount of parameters. Either VGGNet or ResNet has a large amount of parameters and requires a lot of computing resources, which make it difficult to deploy a hard exudate segmentation model to a resource-constrained device.

Our work is motivated by the following two questions. First, is it possible to design a lightweight hard exudate segmentation network rather than a patch-based classification network from scratch considering both performance and the number of parameters? Second, how to train such a segmentation network with limited fundus images with pixel-level annotations. To achieve this goal, we propose a *LightWeight hard Exudate segmentation Network* (LWENet) with $1.9M$ parameters, so that it is possible to deploy LWENet to embedded devices, such as smart phone and handheld medical devices.

LWENet is composed of three parts: multi-scale feature fusion module, context information encoder module and segmentation map generation module.

Since there are too few fundus images with pixel-annotations which makes it easy to over-fitting, we propose a two-stage training algorithm which making full use of DR screening images. The details will be introduced in Sect. 2.2. We conduct experiments on two publicly available datasets, i.e., IDRiD and e-ophtha EX dataset. They all provide pixel-level annotations of EX. On one hand, experimental results on the IDRiD dataset show pre-training on DR screening dataset leads to higher performance compared with training from scratch. This observation shows the effectiveness of the two-stage training algorithm. On the other hand, our network achieves the highest F1-score, recall and precision with the fewest parameters and the fastest speed compared with baseline models on the IDRiD dataset. Specially, compared with DeepLab v3+, our LWENet achieves the highest F1-score with $1/20$ parameters and 3 times faster speed on the IDRiD dataset. On the e-ophtha EX dataset, the F1-score of our LWENet is more than $6\%/8\%$ higher than that of FCRN and DeepLab v3+, but lower than HED.

To summarize, our main contributions of this work are as follows.

- We present LWENet, a lightweight network with $1.9M$ parameters for EX segmentation. We only down-sample resolution $2\times$ to refine the segmentation results. In addition, we use multi-scale feature fusion modules to enlarge receptive field and decrease parameters.
- Due to the limited fundus images with pixel-level annotations (<100), we propose a two-stage training algorithm to train LWENet. Experimental results on the IDRiD dataset show the effectiveness of this training algorithm.
- We conduct experiments on two publicly available datasets. Experimental results show, compared with three baseline models, LWENet achieves the highest F1-score with the fewest parameters and the faster speed on the IDRiD dataset.

The remainder of this paper is organized as follows. Details of LWENet and the training algorithm are described in Sect. 2. Experiments and analysis are given in Sect. 3. Discussion and Conclusions are drawn in Sect. 4.

2   LWENet

In this section, we first introduce our LWENet and its components. Then we describe the training algorithms and settings.

2.1   Network Architecture

LWENet forms the traditional semantic segmentation framework which consists of an encoder part and a decoder part. The encoder part is composed of a multi-scale feature encoder, a context information encoder, several convolutional operations and one pooling operation. In addition, the segmentation map generation module can be treated as a decoder. The overall architecture of LWENet is shown in Fig. 1 and its main modules are shown in Fig. 2. Each part of LWENet is described as below.

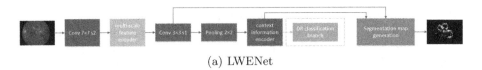

(a) LWENet

Fig. 1. Overview of LWENet. In LWENet, the multi-scale feature encoder consists of three successive multi-scale feature modules (Fig. 2(a)), and the context information encoder consists of two successive context information modules (Fig. 2(c)). The segmentation map generation module and DR classification branch are shown in Fig. 2(b) and (d), respectively.

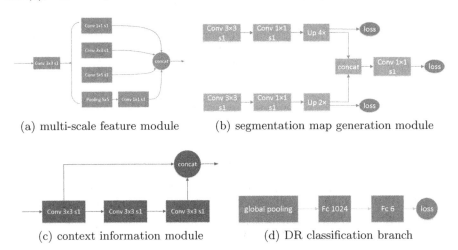

(a) multi-scale feature module   (b) segmentation map generation module

(c) context information module   (d) DR classification branch

Fig. 2. Main modules of LWENet.

- Multi-scale feature module. Inspired by inception module proposed in GoogLeNet [19], we propose the multi-scale feature module for feature learning, as can be seen in Fig. 2(a). On one hand, we use a single convolutional operation before four parallel convolutions for feature map reduction rather than four 1×1 kernels in the inception. On the other hand, we use a convolution with kernel size 3×3 for enlarging receptive field, since larger receptive field is important for small lesion recognition. Too small receptive field may lead to serious misclassification. In addition, this module is repeated 3 times to constitute the multi-scale feature encoder. Moreover, to decrease parameters, the number of kernels in each multi-scale feature module is non-increasing.
- Context information module. Similar to dense connection [11], we use the shortcut connection to alleviate vanishing-gradient problem and more effective use of features. This module consists of three convolutional operations each with 3×3 kernel 128 channels. The output of the first and the third convolution are concatenated to get the output of this module. This module is repeated 2 times to form the context information encoder.

- Segmentation map generation module. This part is used for generating segmentation probability maps, as can be seen in Fig. 2(b). A convolutional operation with kernel size 3×3 is performed for vertical feature extraction. Then, a convolution with kernel size 1×1 is used for feature map reduction, and this procedure outputs one feature map. An up-scaling or de-convolutional operation restores the feature map to the same size as the input image, so that we get two segmentation results at different scales. At last, we use concatenation and convolution operations to fuse the above two segmentation results together to form the output of LWENet.
- DR classification branch. This part is designed for pre-training on DR screening dataset, and consists of a global max pooling and two fully connected layers, as can be seen in Fig. 2(d). The first fully connected layer contains 1024 hidden neurons and the second one is connected to a classifier.

2.2 Training Algorithm

Here, we use LWENet-encoder to denote the encoder part of LWENet. To train the LWENet for EX segmentation, we use a two-stage training algorithm. In the first stage, we add the DR classification branch to LWENet-encoder. We train this net on DDR DR screening dataset [13] for 260,000 iterations with a learning rate 0.001, momentum 0.9 and weight decay 0.0002. The weights were initialized using xavier method [5]. After the first stage, the DR screening accuracy on the validation set is around 0.76. In the second stage, the parameters of the LWENet-encoder were initialized using parameters learned in the first stage. Then, we add the segmentation map generation module to LWENet-encoder to construct LWENet. We train LWENet using weighted sigmoid cross entropy loss [22] on two EX datasets, since the distribution of EX pixels and background pixels is highly imbalanced (around 1/100). We set the learning rate, momentum, weight decay and maximum iterations to $1e-8$, 0.9, 0.0005 and 160,000, respectively. The learning rate decreases by a factor of 10 after 100,000 iterations. Note that there exists three losses in total, and they are optimized simultaneously.

3 Experiments

3.1 Datasets

We use DDR to pre-train LWENet and then evaluate our method over two publicly available datasets, i.e., IDRiD and e-ophtha EX dataset.

DDR is a publicly available dataset for diabetic retinopathy screening [13]. It contains 13,673 fundus images for DR screening task, and the images were collected from 147 hospitals, covering 23 provinces in China. All images have been desensitized for common use. In our experiments, we use the training set (6835 images) of DDR for pre-training LWENet.

The IDRiD (Indian Diabetic Retinopathy Image Dataset) [15] consists of 81 images, each of which has a resolution of 4288×2848, and pixel-level annotations of hard exudate is provided. All 81 images have EX. The partition of training set and testing set are provided, with 54 images for training and the remaining 27 images to test.

The e-ophtha EX dataset [2] contains 82 retinal images, of which 47 images with hard exudate. In addition, the resolution of these images ranges from 1440×960 to 2544×1696 pixels. In our experiments, we adopted five-fold cross validation to evaluate the performance of all models, since there is no explicit partition of training set and testing set.

3.2   Baseline Segmentation Models

We compare LWENet with HED [22], FCRN [14] and DeepLab v3+ [1]. FCRN was designed specially for hard exudate segmentation. It forms the traditional encoder-decoder framework. It uses ResNet-50 for feature learning (encoder) and a proposed multi-level feature fusion method for generating segmentation results (decoder). It shows state-of-the-art performance in hard exudate segmentation. HED was originally designed for edge detection, however in recent studies, it shows competitive performance compared with FCRN in EX segmentation [8]. So, we use HED as one of our baseline models. HED uses VGGNet for feature learning and a weight fusion layer is used for generating edge probability map. Moreover, deep supervision is adopted to alleviate gradient vanish problem in HED. Besides HED and FCRN, we also compare our model with DeepLab v3+ which is the state-of-the-art semantic segmentation model on PASCAL VOC dataset [4].

3.3   Evaluation Metrics

In hard exudate segmentation, each pixel belongs to hard exudate or background (non-exudate). By comparing the segmentation result with ground truth, we adopted three metrics to evaluate the segmentation results, including recall (RE), precision (PR) and F1-score. F1-score is an important metric, since it is high if and only if both RE and PR are high. RE, PR and F1-score are defined as.

$$RE = \frac{TP}{TP + FN} \tag{1}$$

$$PR = \frac{TP}{TP + FP} \tag{2}$$

$$F1\text{-}score = \frac{2 \times RE \times PR}{RE + PR} \tag{3}$$

The number of true positives (TP), false positives (FP) and false negatives (FN) can be calculated pixel-by-pixel. TPs are hard exudate pixels classified correctly, FPs are background pixels mis-classified as hard exudate pixels and FNs are hard exudate pixels mis-classified as background pixels.

3.4   Implementation Details

Data Preprocessing and Augmentation. To train the classification branch of LWENet, we adopted data augmentation methods on DDR DR screening training set. First, we cropped out all backgrounds and resized the images to 224×224. Then, we applied a resampling strategy to all classes in the training set so that the number of images in each category is roughly the same. At last, 200,000 training images were obtained through data augmentation methods, including stretching, rotation, translation, etc.

To train the LWENet for EX segmentation, we resized the images from IDRiD and e-ophtha EX datasets to 1440×960. We used various transformation methods[1] to generate more training samples. After augmentation, there are 3456 and 328 training images on the IDRiD and e-ophtha EX datasets, respectively. Moreover, we use the same amount of training data for training LWENet and the other three baseline models.

Running Environment. We implemented LWENet using an open source convolution neural network framework *caffe* [12]. The running environment is a workstation equipped with NVIDIA GTX 1080ti GPUs and 128G RAM. In addition, we use MATLAB R2015b and python for data augmentation and the calculation of evaluation metrics.

3.5   Results

Parameters Analysis. The number of learnable parameters (weights and biases) is shown in the $4th$ column of Table 1. Our LWENet contains only $1.9M$ parameters. As a comparison, DeepLab v3+ has more than $40M$ parameters. HED has more than $14M$ parameters, and FCRN has nearly $22M$ parameters. And we can observe from the $7th$ column of Table 1 that our LWENet achieves the highest F1-score with the fewest parameters on the IDRiD dataset. Specially, our LWENet uses only 1/20 parameters to DeepLab v3+, but achieves more than 10% points improvement in terms of F1-score. Meanwhile, our network uses only 1/7 parameters to HED, 1/11 to FCRN, and obtains more than 3% and 14% improvement.

Moreover, we can observe from Table 2 that on the e-ophtha EX dataset, our LWENet achieves more than 8% improvement compared with FCRN and DeepLab v3+ in terms of PR. Although HED gets the highest F1-score, it contains 7 times the parameters of our LWENet. Fewer parameters make LWENet possible for employing to embedded devices.

Speed Analysis. The inference speed is shown in the $5th$ column of Table 1. With 1440×960 input, our LWENet can process a fundus image in 99 ms (11.1 fps) on a single GTX 1080ti GPU. As a comparison, HED runs at 169 ms

---

[1] https://github.com/aleju/imgaug.

Table 1. Comparison of LWENet and baseline models (fps was measured with input size 1440×960).

Model	Pre-train	Backbone	#Params(M)	Speed(fps)	F1-score	
					IDRiD	e-ophtha EX
HED [22]	ImageNet	VGGNet	≈14.3	5.9	0.7514	**0.5336**
FCRN [14]	ImageNet	ResNet-50	≈22.5	7.1	0.6412	0.4326
DeepLab v3+ [1]	Pascal VOC	Xception_65	≈41.3	3.5	0.6784	0.4162
LWENet	DDR	-	≈1.9	**11.1**	**0.7815**	0.4960

Table 2. Statistical results of baseline models and our LWENet over IDRiD and e-ophtha EX datasets (best results are shown in bold)

Model	IDRiD			e-ophtha EX		
	RE	PR	F1-score	RE	PR	F1-score
HED [22]	0.7618	0.7414	0.7515	**0.5727**	**0.5049**	**0.5336**
FCRN [14]	0.6862	0.6018	0.6412	0.5073	0.3807	0.4326
DeepLab v3+ [1]	0.7012	0.6571	0.6784	0.4395	0.3969	0.4162
LWENet	**0.7803**	**0.7826**	**0.7815**	0.5147	0.4812	0.4960

(5.9 fps) for VGGNet. FCRN runs at 141 ms (7.1 fps) for ResNet-50. DeepLab v3+ runs at 286 ms (3.5 fps) for Xception_65. Specially, our LWENet runs about 3 times faster than DeepLab v3+, and the F1-score is over 10% higher on IDRiD dataset. Faster speeds make our model runs more efficiently.

Results of Pre-training. To show the effectiveness of proposed two-stage training algorithm, we trained LWENet for EX segmentation from scratch on the IDRiD dataset. For fair comparison, we use the same amount of training images on both cases. The comparison results are shown in Table 3. We can observe that pre-training on the DR screening dataset leads to over 7% improvement in terms of all three metrics. We conclude that pre-training is indeed important for EX segmentation due to limited images with pixel-level annotations.

Table 3. Comparison results between training LWENet from scratch and proposed a two-stage training algorithm on the IDRiD dataset.

Model	RE	PR	F1-score
LWENet (without pre-training)	0.6984	0.7044	0.6968
LWENet (pre-training on DDR)	**0.7803**	**0.7826**	**0.7815**

Visualization. We binarized the segmentation probability maps using threshold 0.5, and the binary maps of LWENet and baseline models are shown in Fig. 3. We can observe that the segmentation results of LWENet is very fine, and it can

segment very small EX pixels due to there exists only one down-sampling operation in LWENet. For HED and FCRN, the segmentation results are very coarse,
and small EX areas join together. DeepLab v3+ missed many EX areas on both
datasets.

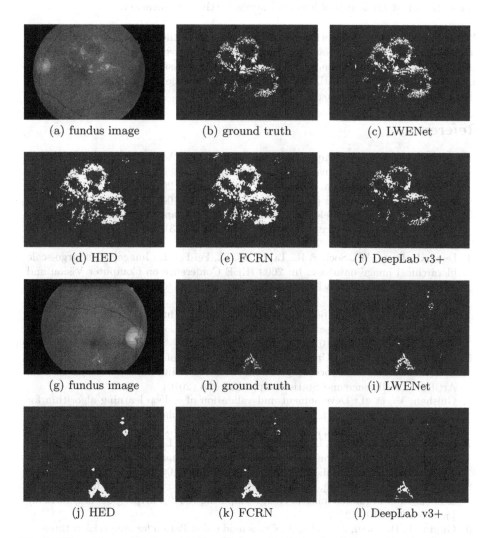

Fig. 3. Binary segmentation results. The results from the first row to the last row
corresponds to the IDRiD and e-ophtha EX datasets, respectively.

4   Discussion and Conclusion

In this paper, we present LWENet for hard exudate segmentation. LWENet
achieves the highest F1-score with the fewest parameters and the fastest speed
on the IDRiD dataset. Moreover, the segmentation results of LWENet are much

fine compared with baseline models, since we only down-sampled resolution 2×. Besides, we conduct experiments to show the effectiveness of pre-training on DR screening dataset. However, in spite of progress made, segmentation network stills produces false positives and false negatives (see Table 2). And we believe this is the most critical problem and needs further exploration.

Acknowledgment. This work is partially supported by the National Natural Science Foundation (61872200), the National Key Research and Development Program of China (2016YFC0400709), the Science and Technology Commission of Tianjin Binhai New Area (BHXQKJXM-PT-ZJSHJ-2017005), the Natural Science Foundation of Tianjin (18YFYZCG00060) and Nankai University (91922299).

References

1. Chen, L.-C., Zhu, Y., Papandreou, G., Schroff, F., Adam, H.: Encoder-decoder with atrous separable convolution for semantic image segmentation. In: Ferrari, V., Hebert, M., Sminchisescu, C., Weiss, Y. (eds.) ECCV 2018. LNCS, vol. 11211, pp. 833–851. Springer, Cham (2018). https://doi.org/10.1007/978-3-030-01234-2_49
2. Decencière, E., et al.: TeleOphta: machine learning and image processing methods for teleophthalmology. Irbm **34**(2), 196–203 (2013). https://doi.org/10.1016/j.irbm.2013.01.010
3. Deng, J., Dong, W., Socher, R., Li, L., Li, K., Fei-Fei, L.: ImageNet: a large-scale hierarchical image database. In: 2009 IEEE Conference on Computer Vision and Pattern Recognition (CVPR), pp. 248–255, June 2009. https://doi.org/10.1109/CVPR.2009.5206848
4. Everingham, M., Van Gool, L., Williams, C.K.I., Winn, J., Zisserman, A.: The Pascal visual object classes (VOC) challenge. Int. J. Comput. Vis. **88**(2), 303–338 (2010). https://doi.org/10.1007/s11263-009-0275-4
5. Glorot, X., Bengio, Y.: Understanding the difficulty of training deep feedforward neural networks. In: Proceedings of the Thirteenth International Conference on Artificial Intelligence and Statistics, pp. 249–256 (2010)
6. Gulshan, V., et al.: Development and validation of a deep learning algorithm for detection of diabetic retinopathy in retinal fundus photographs. Jama **316**(22), 2402–2410 (2016). https://doi.org/10.1001/jama.2016.17216
7. Guo, S., Li, T., Kang, H., Li, N., Zhang, Y., Wang, K.: L-Seg: an end-to-end unified framework for multi-lesion segmentation of fundus images. Neurocomputing **349**, 52–63 (2019). https://doi.org/10.1016/j.neucom.2019.04.019
8. Guo, S., Wang, K., Kang, H., Liu, T., Gao, Y., Li, T.: Bin loss for hard exudates segmentation in fundus images. Neurocomputing (2019). https://doi.org/10.1016/j.neucom.2018.10.103
9. Gupta, S., Hoffman, J., Malik, J.: Cross modal distillation for supervision transfer. In: 2016 IEEE Conference on Computer Vision and Pattern Recognition (CVPR), pp. 2827–2836, June 2016. https://doi.org/10.1109/CVPR.2016.309
10. He, K., Zhang, X., Ren, S., Sun, J.: Deep residual learning for image recognition. In: 2016 IEEE Conference on Computer Vision and Pattern Recognition (CVPR), pp. 770–778, June 2016. https://doi.org/10.1109/CVPR.2016.90
11. Huang, G., Liu, Z., van der Maaten, L., Weinberger, K.Q.: Densely connected convolutional networks. In: 2017 IEEE Conference on Computer Vision and Pattern Recognition (CVPR), pp. 2261–2269, July 2017. https://doi.org/10.1109/CVPR.2017.243

12. Jia, Y., et al.: Caffe: convolutional architecture for fast feature embedding. In: Proceedings of the 22nd ACM International Conference on Multimedia, MM 2014, pp. 675–678. ACM, New York (2014). https://doi.org/10.1145/2647868.2654889

13. Li, T., Gao, Y., Wang, K., Guo, S., Liu, H., Kang, H.: Diagnostic assessment of deep learning algorithms for diabetic retinopathy screening. Inf. Sci. **501**, 511–522 (2019). https://doi.org/10.1016/j.ins.2019.06.011

14. Mo, J., Zhang, L., Feng, Y.: Exudate-based diabetic macular edema recognition in retinal images using cascaded deep residual networks. Neurocomputing **290**, 161–171 (2018). https://doi.org/10.1016/j.neucom.2018.02.035

15. Porwal, P., et al.: Indian diabetic retinopathy image dataset (IDRiD): A database for diabetic retinopathy screening research. Data **3**(3), 25 (2018). https://doi.org/10.3390/data3030025, http://www.mdpi.com/2306-5729/3/3/25

16. Shelhamer, E., Long, J., Darrell, T.: Fully convolutional networks for semantic segmentation. IEEE Trans. Pattern Anal. Mach. Intell. **39**(4), 640–651 (2017). https://doi.org/10.1109/TPAMI.2016.2572683

17. Shen, Z., Liu, Z., Li, J., Jiang, Y., Chen, Y., Xue, X.: DSOD: learning deeply supervised object detectors from scratch. In: 2017 IEEE International Conference on Computer Vision (ICCV), pp. 1937–1945, October 2017. https://doi.org/10.1109/ICCV.2017.212

18. Simonyan, K., Zisserman, A.: Very deep convolutional networks for large-scale image recognition. CoRR abs/1409.1556 (2014). http://arxiv.org/abs/1409.1556

19. Szegedy, C., et al.: Going deeper with convolutions. In: 2015 IEEE Conference on Computer Vision and Pattern Recognition (CVPR), pp. 1–9, June 2015. https://doi.org/10.1109/CVPR.2015.7298594

20. Tan, J.H., et al.: Automated segmentation of exudates, haemorrhages, microaneurysms using single convolutional neural network. Inf. Sci. **420**, 66–76 (2017). https://doi.org/10.1016/j.ins.2017.08.050

21. Wild, S., Roglic, G., Green, A., Sicree, R., King, H.: Global prevalence of diabetes: estimates for the year 2000 and projections for 2030. Diabetes Care **27**(5), 1047–1053 (2004). https://doi.org/10.2337/diacare.27.5.1047

22. Xie, S., Tu, Z.: Holistically-nested edge detection. Int. J. Comput. Vis. **125**(1), 3–18 (2017). https://doi.org/10.1007/s11263-017-1004-z

Attentional Residual Dense Factorized Network for Real-Time Semantic Segmentation

Lulu Yang[1,2(✉)], Long Lan[2,3(✉)], Xiang Zhang[2,3(✉)], Xuhui Huang[4], and Zhigang Luo[1,2(✉)]

[1] Science and Technology on Parallel and Distributed Laboratory, NUDT, Changsha 410073, Hunan, People's Republic of China
[2] College of Computer, NUDT, Changsha 410073, Hunan, People's Republic of China
windychanchan@163.com, zgluo@nudt.edu.cn
[3] State Key Laboratory of High Performance Computing, NUDT, Changsha 410073, Hunan, People's Republic of China
{long.lan,zhangxiang08}@nudt.edu.cn
[4] Department of Computer Science, NUDT, Changsha 410073, Hunan, People's Republic of China

Abstract. Semantic segmentation is a pixel-level image dense labeling task and plays a core role in autonomous driving. In this regard, how to balance between precision and speed is a frequently-studied issue. In this paper, we propose an alternative attentional residual dense factorized network (AttRDFNet) to address this issue. Specifically, we design a residual dense factorized convolution block (RDFB), which reaps the benefits of low-level and high-level layer-wise features through dense connection to boost segmentation precision whilst enjoying efficient computation by factorizing large convolution kernel into the product of two smaller kernels. This reduces computational burdens and makes real time become possible. To further leverage layer-wise features, we explore the graininess-aware channel and spatial attention modules to model different levels of salient features of interest. As a result, AttRDFNet can run with the inputs of the resolution 512×1024 at the speed of 55.6 frames per second on a single Titan X GPU with solid 68.5% Mean IOU on the test set of Cityscapes. Experiments on the Cityscapes dataset show that AttRDFNet has real-time inference whilst achieving competitive precision against well-behaved counterparts.

Keywords: Real-time semantic segmentation · Attention module · Residual dense factorized convolution block

1 Introduction

Semantic segmentation is in efforts to assign each pixel of an image a class label, e.g., *car* or *road*. Despite much progress in this regard, it is still a challenging task for the sake of difficulty in balancing between precision and efficiency.

© Springer Nature Switzerland AG 2019
I. V. Tetko et al. (Eds.): ICANN 2019, LNCS 11729, pp. 200–212, 2019.
https://doi.org/10.1007/978-3-030-30508-6_17

With advance of deep learning, accurate semantic segmentation models emerge quickly and dominate most traditional counterparts. In seminal studies, Seg-Net [1] and FCN [17] are two representative methods which treat VGG16 [24] as the backbone in an encoder-decoder framework. Currently, DeepLabv3+ [6] explores a new encoder-decoder architecture, which employs DeepLabv3 [5] as a powerful encoder module and a simple yet effective decoder module. However, it sacrifices efficiency. Efficiency matters in semantic segmentation. For instance, ENet [19] is the first high-efficiency method for semantic segmentation by taking a smaller downsampled substitute of the raw image as the inputs of deep networks. ESPNet [18] designs an efficient spatial pyramid module that considers a point-wise convolution operation to reduce the parameters. Unluckily, ESPNet degrades in precision. Several recent efforts struggle to balance precision and efficiency. Among them, ERFNet [21] designs an efficient factorized convolution residual layer composed of residual skip connections and factorized convolution [14,19,25]. ContextNet [20] explores the factorized convolution, network compression and pyramid representation in a unified network and produces competitive semantic segmentation precision in real time with low memory footprint. Although these methods have achieved proper trade-offs both precision and efficiency, there is still much room to improve.

In this paper, we propose an attentional residual dense factorized network (AttRDFNet), which provides alternative promising compromise way to balance precision and efficiency. Particularly, we equip AttRDFNet with three basic modules, i.e., residual dense factorized block (RDFB), graininess-aware channel attentional module (GCAM) and graininess-aware spatial attentional module (GSAM). To our best knowledge, [29] firstly proposed the residual dense network (RDN) based on residual dense block (RDB) for image super-resolution. However, previous work did not apply RDB for semantic segmentation. Furthermore, RDB of RDN contains dense connected layers and local feature fusion with residual connections, while our RDFB devises efficient dense blocks with factorized convolution as the basic component of a residual block. In RDFB, all the 3×3 kernels are factorized with two smaller convolutional kernels, i.e., 3×1 followed by 1×3. In a nutshell, dense connections collect rich layer-wise features, skip connections facilitate training the block and factorized convolution can reduce the number of parameters with similar accuracy to standard convolution. Besides, to keep satisfactory precision, GCAM exploits high-level features as guidance of low-level features to select localization detail and GSAM fuses rich layer-wise features to construct attention map as guidance of low-level features to highlight salient areas. It is non-trivial to realize AttRDFNet because it is not easy to organize existing advanced tactics in a novel way. In summary, our network is an efficient light-weight architecture that effectively performs semantic segmentation. We evaluate AttRDFNet on Cityscapes [8] and Camvid [2] datasets to show the promising of AttRDFNet compared with several well-behaved approaches.

2   Proposed Model

2.1   Network Architecture

We visually outline our network architecture in Fig. 1, where five types of the modules are involved. The 'Down' denotes the downsampling with 2× pixels and the 'Upsample' denotes upsampling. Inspired by [19] and [21], the raw image first goes through two downsampling operations and becomes the smaller image with 1/4 size. Downsampling the raw image not only reduces the computational cost but also enlarges the receptive field of deeper layer. Although downsampling could reduce the pixel precision, it is tolerable that the network only performs three downsampling operations, where the 3 × 3 convolution with stride 2 and max-pooling operation are simultaneously performed in two-stream way and then both outputs are concatenated. RDFB is the compound of residual and dense blocks, which is a special residual block because the net branch consists of several dense blocks. To meet real time, we factorize large kernels such as 3 × 3 two cascade layers with a 3 × 1 convolutional kernel followed by a 1 × 3 convolutional kernel. This induces fewer parameters. Then we term our block as residual dense factorized convolutional block. Besides, to enlarge the receptive field of the convolution, we also substitute efficient dilated convolution into general convolution. This avoids repeating the downsampling to reduce the size of feature maps. More details will be given in next section.

To infer the final segmentation map, the network output should share the same size with the raw image. As we downsample the input several times, it is necessary to use the upsampling to restore the size of the output. In many state-of-the-art methods, a decoder is often used for this purpose. In most methods [1, 17], the decoders greatly dominate the overall computation cost. To effectively support the upsampling, we design two light-weight attention modules including GCAM and GSAM to integrate different grainness features.

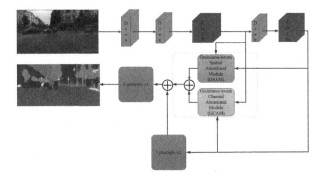

Fig. 1. An overview of AttRDFNet. Components of network architecture: three down-sampling block used for reducing the size of feature maps, graininess-aware spatial attention module (GSAM) and graininess-aware channel attention module (GCAM). GSAM and GCAM explore different levels of salient features of interest.

2.2   Residual Dense Factorized Convolutional Block (RDFB)

In Fig. 2(b), RDFB consists of dense connection, residual learning and factorized convolution. In RDFB, the inputs of each layer consist of the features of all the previous layers via the concatenation, thus each convolution layer can access previous layers and deliver multi-scale semantic information. As a result, the network will become compact and narrow. As in [12,13], the last output of a dense block depends on the features of all the previous layers. Formally, given the lth layer of a dense block to be the output layer, the corresponding output feature x_l is the nonlinear transformation of the feature maps from all its preceding layers, i.e.,

$$x_l = H_l\left([x_0, x_1, \ldots, x_{l-1}]\right) \tag{1}$$

where $[x_0, x_1, \ldots, x_{l-1}]$ refers to the concatenation operation, and H_l is a composite function of consecutive operations: Conv 3×1-ReLU [16]-Conv 1×3-ReLU-BN. As in Fig. 2 (a), for efficiency, we apply the factorized convolution for RDFB. The factorized convolution is to factorize a $n \times n$ convolution filter into two asymmetric $n \times 1$ and $1 \times n$ convolution filters. Following the expression of atrous convolution, we have the following factorized convolution formulation:

$$y_{ij} = \sum_{u=1}^{m} W_u \left[\sum_{v=1}^{n} W_v X_{i-u+1, j-v+1} + b^V \right] + b^h \tag{2}$$

where $x_{i-u+1, j-v+1}$ is a 2D image, W_v and W_u are two 1D kernels, and both b^V and b^h are the bias. [21,25] shows that (2) can greatly reduce computational cost whilst keeping similar precision, as compared to standard convolution. Note that ReLU is inserted between $n \times 1$ and $1 \times n$ convolutions to improve learning ability.

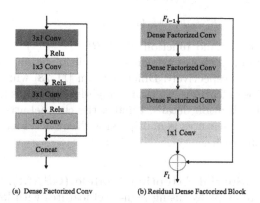

(a) Dense Factorized Conv   (b) Residual Dense Factorized Block

Fig. 2. (a) Dense Factorized Conv, consists of two 3×3 factorized convolution. (b) Residual Dense Factorized Block consists of dense factorized convolutions.

2.3   Attention Module

To model different levels of salient features of interest, we propose two simple and effective attention modules: GCAM and GSAM. Unlike DANet [9], which uses the expansive matrix multiply operation to calculate the attention map, our computational cost is negligible. As one knows, high-level features contain category information, while low-level features have texture information and contour of objects, which are conducive to semantic segmentation. Thus, we use the high-level features to guide the low-level features to select the localization details by GCAM. Through GSAM, we exploit low-level features and high-level features to construct the attention map, which guides low-level features to focus on regions of interest. Finally, in terms of our empirical studies, we combine two attention modules with the addition operation since this way is effective.

Graininess-aware Channel Attention Module (GCAM). As high-level features with abundant category information can extract detailed information. We build a GCAM, which uses the high-level features to attend the low-level ones to select categorical semantics.

The structure of GCAM is illustrated in Fig. 3(a). First, to aggregate the feature maps in each channel, we take the global pooling on the high-level features to generate the global context descriptor F_c. This descriptor encodes global context information. Then, we use a 1×1 convolution with batch normalization (BN) followed by the nonlinear activation function to calculate the weights that guide low-level features from the global descriptor F_c. To save parameter overhead, we choose to use the convolution operations instead of fully connected operations to learn the attentive weights. In short, the ultimate channel attention is computed by:

$$
\begin{aligned}
M_c\left(F_h\right) &= \sigma\left(BN\left(f^{1\times 1}\left(AvgPool\left(F_h\right)\right)\right)\right) \\
&= \sigma\left(BN\left(W * F_c\right)\right)
\end{aligned}
\tag{3}
$$

$$
F_c' = F_l \cdot M_c\left(F_h\right)
\tag{4}
$$

where σ denotes the sigmoid function, $W \in R^{1\times 1\times C\times C}$, $f^{1\times 1}$ represents 1×1 convolution operation, $\cdot$ denotes element-wise multiplication and $*$ denotes the convolution operation respectively. Different from [11,28] which explores inter-channel relationships of features, we exploit high-level features to guide low-level features to select localization details. Finally, the channel attention vector calculated from high-level features is multiplied with low-level features to produce channel attention map F_c'.

Graininess-aware Spatial Attention Module (GSAM). GSAM still considers spatial feature maps by fusing high-level features with low-level features. Different from the graininess-aware channel attention, the graininess-aware spatial attention mainly focuses on position information. For instance, in [7,27,28], spatial attention is used to highlight which pixels of the interest.

As in Fig. 3(b), we utilize low-level features and high-level features to calculate attention map. We first operate the global pooling on high-level features to

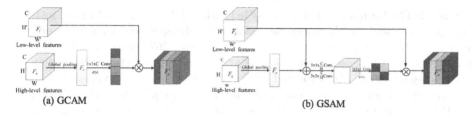

(a) GCAM   (b) GSAM

Fig. 3. The structure of graininess-aware channel attentional module (GCAM) and graininess-aware spatial attentional module (GSAM). Note that $\otimes$ represents element-wise multiplication, $\oplus$ represents element-wise summation and σ denotes sigmoid function.

produce the vector F_c, then use the 1×1 convolution to integrate and compress feature maps to a specific size. The fused feature maps are added to both F_c and the low-level features. Thereafter, a 3×3 convolution operation is applied to capture contextual information. Finally, the feature map is mapped into the spatial map of the size with $R^{1 \times W \times H}$ by 1×1 convolution. Thus, the resultant spatial attention is yielded as follows:

$$M_s\left(F_l, F_h\right) = \sigma\left(f^{1 \times 1}\left(f^{3 \times 3}\left(f^{1 \times 1}\left(AvgPool\left(F_h\right) + F_l\right)\right)\right)\right) \quad (5)$$

$$F_s' = F_l \cdot M_s\left(F_l, F_h\right) \quad (6)$$

where $f^{1 \times 1}$ denotes 1×1 convolution operation and $f^{3 \times 3}$ denotes 3×3 convolution operation. There are two 1×1 convolutions for channel compression. The intermediate 3×3 convolution is applied to aggregate contextual information. Finally, the spatial attention vector calculated from high-level and low-level features is multiplied with low-level features to produce spatial attention map F_s'.

3   Experiments

We conduct experiments to demonstrate the efficacy of the proposed network. We evaluate the performance results on Cityscapes dataset [8] and also report the accuracy and speed of the Cityscapes dataset and the accuracy of the Camvid [2] dataset as compared to the well-established counterparts.

Cityscapes: Cityscapes Dataset provides an image segmentation dataset in a driverless environment. It contains 50 scenes with different combinations of backgrounds and seasons, and provides 5,000 finely annotated images with 20 classes including the ignored class. This dataset is divided into training, validation and testing sets with 2,975, 500 and 1,525 images, respectively. All the images have a high resolution of 2048 × 1024. Besides, it also provides another coarsely annotated 20,000 images. In experiments, we merely utilize fine annotations to train our network.

Camvid: The Cambridge-driving Labeled Video Database (CamVid) is the first collection of videos with object class semantic labels, which has a total of 701 images with 11 semantic categories. Among them, 367 images are treated as training set, 101 images as validation set and 233 as testing set. The resolution of these images is 960×720, captured from a set of high resolution video sequences.

Our experiments are implemented with Pytorch equipped with CUDA and CUDNN as backbends. We first use the Adam optimizer [15] to train the model with a momentum of 0.9, using L2 regularization to avoid overfitting with a weight decay of $1e - 4$. Then we replace the Adam optimizer with SGD to train the model. We used a poly learning strategy, the initial learning rate is multiplied by $\left(1 - \frac{iter}{max\_iters}\right)^{power}$ after each iteration. Since training samples are few, we consider standard data augmentation techniques in experiments. To train the network, we define the segmentation loss as the cross-entropy loss function as follows:

$$L = - \sum_{h,w} \sum_{c \in C} Y^{(h,w,c)} \log(P^{(h,w,c)}) \tag{7}$$

where Y is the ground truth annotations for images and P is the predicted segmentation maps.

Following [4, 19, 20], we also use mean intersection-over-union (mIoU) to evaluate our model, which indicates the ratio of the intersection and union of the ground truth set and predicted segmentation set.

3.1 Ablation Study

This section studies the efficacy of two components of our network, including the structure of RDFB and the attention modules. We evaluate them on the validation set of Cityscapes.

Ablation for RDFB Structure: Two blocks involved in the experiments are the candidates for semantic segmentation. To choose the proper block, we conduct experiments to validate their advantages. The efficacy of the other blocks related to dense or residual networks are left in the comparisons of the baselines. As shown in Fig. 4, we exchange the summation and concatenation. Meanwhile, we also remove the 1×1 convolution layer. We call the variant dense residual factorized convolution (DRFB). We compare RDFB and DRFB at the same time cost. The comparisons are shown in Table 1, RDFB outperforms DRFB by 2.6% gain. This result demonstrates the advantage of RDFB over DRFB.

Table 1. Comparison of RDFB and DRFB in precision and time.

Blocks	Mean IoU (%)	Mean Class Acc (%)	Time (ms)
RDFB	70.6	82.7	18
DRFB	68.0	79.7	18

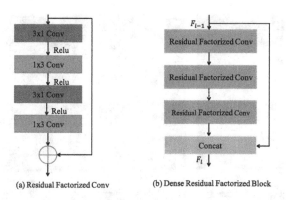

Fig. 4. A revised RDFB structure: the summation and concatenation are exchanged for ablation study.

Ablation for Attention Modules: Many the state-of-the-art semantic segmentation methods [1,10,17,22] mostly adopt the concatenation or summation operations to fuse high-level features and low-level features for multi-granularity feature aggregation. However, our fusion mechanism is better than the above mentioned methods in our network. For simultaneous effective fusion and efficient computation, we propose GCAM and GSAM to respectively fuse multi-granularity features by employing both high-level and low-level features to attend the low-level features for preserving semantic details. We experimentally verify the performance of the GCAM and GSAM. Experimental results are shown in Table 2. Compared with hybrid method, only employing GCAM yields a result of 69% in Mean IoU, which brings 1.6% drop. Meanwhile, employing GSAM independently underperforms the results by 2.1% drop. When we use the hybrid method, i.e., GCAM+GSAM, in the network, experimental results show that the hybrid module gains great benefits to segmentation. The comparison of such modules can be visualized in Fig. 5.

Table 2. Ablation study on Cityscapes validation set.

Model	Road	Sidewalk	Building	Wall	Fence	Pole	Traffic light	Traffic sign	Vegetation	Terrain	Sky	Person	Rider	Car	Truck	Bus	Train	Motorcycle	Bicycle	mIoU(%)
GCAM	97.0	78.0	89.4	55.2	51.5	53.1	57.3	66.6	90.4	59.7	92.7	70.9	51.7	91.0	59.1	72.7	59.1	49.6	66.5	69.0
GSAM	96.8	77.5	89.2	53.1	49.3	52.5	57.4	66.5	90.0	58.5	92.6	71.7	49.9	91.2	61.1	74.6	58.1	45.3	66.0	68.5
GCAM+GSAM	97.0	78.7	90.1	57.4	54.0	56.1	59.0	69.0	90.6	59.8	92.7	72.6	52.8	91.5	64.7	74.8	60.6	52.4	68.5	70.6

3.2 Comparison with the Baselines

We compare our network with several well-established real-time segmentation networks including SegNet [1], ENet [19], ERFNet [21], SQ [26], Deeplab [3], ESPNet [18] and ContextNet [20] on two benchmarks including Camvid and Cityscapes.

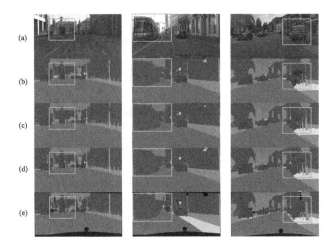

Fig. 5. Visualization results on Cityscapes validation set. From top to bottom, (a) Input, (b) GCAM, (c) GSAM, (d) hybrid attention module, and (e) ground truth.

Camvid: We first compare our network with several existing segmentation networks on the Camvid testing dataset. Our network is not pre-trained on ImageNet [23] beforehand. We only compare the accuracy of such compared methods and the corresponding classification accuracy per category. The compared results are listed in Table 3. Table 3 shows that our network achieves competitive results with the compared networks with significant gains in some categories. Especially, for the bicyclist, our network improves the performance greatly compared with the compared counterparts.

Table 3. Results on the Camvid test set, n/a means no result is given

Model	Building	Tree	Sky	Car	Sign	Road	Pedestrian	Fence	Pole	Sidewalk	Bicyclist	mIoU (%)
SegNet-Basic* [1]	75.0	84.6	91.2	82.7	36.9	93.3	55.0	47.5	44.8	74.1	16.0	n/a
SegNet*	88.8	87.3	92.4	82.1	20.5	97.2	57.1	49.3	27.5	84.4	30.7	55.6
ENet [19]	74.7	77.8	95.1	82.4	51.0	95.1	67.2	51.7	35.4	86.7	34.1	51.3
Ours	80.4	74.8	91.9	79.8	40.0	93.3	56.1	35.5	35.7	80.1	**55.2**	65.6

Cityscapes: We also conduct experiments on the Cityscapes test dataset and report the precision and speed of all the compared networks. Table 4 shows that our network with proper parameters achieves a good balance between performance and efficiency. Our network achieves 68.5% mIoU, which outperforms most of the existing methods in accuracy that run in real time, such as ENet [19] and ESPNet [18]. Our network can run on a single GPU card with a speed of 55.6 FPS and still meets the real-time demands. ContextNet [20] has a similar run-time but achieves 66.1% mIoU. DeepLabv3+ [6] achieves 82.1% mIoU, but

Table 4. Comparison of the accuracy and speed of different methods on the Cityscapes test set, we evaluate on NVIDIA Titan X GPU with 1024×512 resolution input, n/a means no corresponding result is given. (Methods with * are pre-trained on ImageNet)

Model	Class mIoU(%)	Class iIoU(%)	Category IoU(%)	Category iIoU(%)	FPS
SegNet* [1]	56.1	34.2	79.8	66.4	n/a
SQ* [26]	59.8	32.3	84.3	66.0	n/a
DeepLabv3+* [6]	82.1	62.4	92.0	81.9	n/a
FCN-8s* [17]	65.3	41.7	85.7	70.1	n/a
Deeplab* [3]	63.1	34.5	81.2	58.7	0.3
ERFNet [21]	68.0	40.4	86.5	70.4	41.7
ContextNet [20]	66.1	36.8	82.8	64.3	65.5
ENet [19]	58.3	34.4	80.4	64.0	76.9
ESPNet* [18]	60.3	31.8	82.2	63.1	112.9
Ours	68.5	40.0	86.0	70.4	55.6

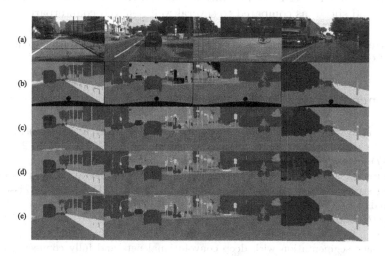

Fig. 6. Some segmentation examples of the compared methods on Cityscapes validation dataset. From top to bottom, (a) input, (b) ground truth, (c) ENet [19], (d) ERFNet [21] and (e) AttRDFNet.

is considerably slower than our network. As in Fig. 6, we visualize several exemplar images and the corresponding segmentation results respectively inferred by (d) ERFNet [21], (c) ENet and (e) our AttRFDNet compared to (b) the ground truth. The exemplar images are from the Cityscapes validation set. By comparing the visualization results, we find that our network yields qualitative results for vehicle category, even at far distances and small vehicle. Although ENet and ERFNet can accurately predict the car, they cannot segment buses and trucks very well. As stated above, our network is relatively well-balanced in speed and performance. Note that our network does not involve any post-processing and achieves 68.5% mIoU on the Cityscapes testing set with 55.6 FPS on a single NVIDIA Titan X GPU card for an image of the resolution $1,024 \times 512$.

4   Conclusion

This paper proposes an attentional residual dense factorized network (AttRDFNet) for real-time semantic segmentation, which consists of residual dense factorized convolution block (RDFB), graininess-aware channel attentional module (GCAM) and graininess-aware spatial attentional module (GSAM). RDFB treats the dense blocks equipped with efficient factorized convolution as the basic component of a residual block to collect rich layer-wise features. Besides, both GCAM and GSAM can be integrated with any real-time segmentation architecture and model different levels of salient features to boost the performance without sacrificing efficiency. Experiments on Camvid and Cityscapes demonstrate that AttRDFNet provides an alternative promising compromise of precision and speed, as compared to several well-behaved counterparts.

Acknowledgments. This work was supported by the National Natural Science Foundation of China [61806213, 61702134, U1435222].

References

1. Badrinarayanan, V., Kendall, A., Cipolla, R.: SegNet: a deep convolutional encoder-decoder architecture for image segmentation. TPAMI **39**(12), 2481–2495 (2017). https://doi.org/10.1109/TPAMI.2016.2644615
2. Brostow, G.J., Shotton, J., Fauqueur, J., Cipolla, R.: Segmentation and recognition using structure from motion point clouds. In: Forsyth, D., Torr, P., Zisserman, A. (eds.) ECCV 2008. LNCS, vol. 5302, pp. 44–57. Springer, Heidelberg (2008). https://doi.org/10.1007/978-3-540-88682-2_5
3. Chen, L.C., Papandreou, G., Kokkinos, I., Murphy, K., Yuille, A.L.: Semantic image segmentation with deep convolutional nets and fully connected CRFs. arXiv:1412.7062 (2014). https://doi.org/10.1080/17476938708814211
4. Chen, L.C., Papandreou, G., Kokkinos, I., Murphy, K., Yuille, A.L.: DeepLab: semantic image segmentation with deep convolutional nets, atrous convolution, and fully connected CRFs. TPAMI **40**(4), 834–848 (2017). https://doi.org/10.1109/TPAMI.2017.2699184
5. Chen, L.C., Papandreou, G., Schroff, F., Adam, H.: Rethinking atrous convolution for semantic image segmentation. arXiv:1706.05587 (2017)
6. Chen, L.-C., Zhu, Y., Papandreou, G., Schroff, F., Adam, H.: Encoder-decoder with atrous separable convolution for semantic image segmentation. In: Ferrari, V., Hebert, M., Sminchisescu, C., Weiss, Y. (eds.) ECCV 2018. LNCS, vol. 11211, pp. 833–851. Springer, Cham (2018). https://doi.org/10.1007/978-3-030-01234-2_49
7. Chen, L., et al.: SCA-CNN: spatial and channel-wise attention in convolutional networks for image captioning. In: CVPR, pp. 5659–5667 (2017). https://doi.org/10.1109/CVPR.2017.667

8. Cordts, M., et al.: The cityscapes dataset for semantic urban scene understanding. In: CVPR, pp. 3213–3223 (2016). https://doi.org/10.1109/CVPR.2016.350

9. Fu, J., Liu, J., Tian, H., Fang, Z., Lu, H.: Dual attention network for scene segmentation, pp. 3146–3154 (2019)

10. Gamal, M., Siam, M., Abdel-Razek, M.: ShuffleSeg: Real-time semantic segmentation network. arXiv:1803.03816 (2018)

11. Hu, J., Shen, L., Sun, G.: Squeeze-and-excitation networks. In: CVPR, pp. 7132–7141 (2018). https://doi.org/10.1109/CVPR.2018.00745

12. Huang, G., Liu, Z., Van Der Maaten, L., Weinberger, K.Q.: Densely connected convolutional networks. In: CVPR, pp. 4700–4708 (2017). https://doi.org/10.1109/CVPR.2017.243

13. Jégou, S., Drozdzal, M., Vazquez, D., Romero, A., Bengio, Y.: The one hundred layers tiramisu: fully convolutional densenets for semantic segmentation. In: CVPR Workshop, pp. 1175–1183 (2017). https://doi.org/10.1109/CVPRW.2017.156

14. Jin, J., Dundar, A., Culurciello, E.: Flattened convolutional neural networks for feedforward acceleration. arXiv:1412.5474 (2014)

15. Kingma, D.P., Ba, J.: Adam: A method for stochastic optimization. arXiv preprint arXiv:1412.6980 (2014)

16. Krizhevsky, A., Sutskever, I., Hinton, G.E.: Imagenet classification with deep convolutional neural networks. In: NIPS, pp. 1097–1105 (2012). https://doi.org/10.1145/3065386

17. Long, J., Shelhamer, E., Darrell, T.: Fully convolutional networks for semantic segmentation. In: CVPR, pp. 3431–3440 (2015). https://doi.org/10.1109/CVPR.2015.7298965

18. Mehta, S., Rastegari, M., Caspi, A., Shapiro, L., Hajishirzi, H.: ESPNet: efficient spatial pyramid of dilated convolutions for semantic segmentation. In: Ferrari, V., Hebert, M., Sminchisescu, C., Weiss, Y. (eds.) ECCV 2018. LNCS, vol. 11214, pp. 561–580. Springer, Cham (2018). https://doi.org/10.1007/978-3-030-01249-6_34

19. Paszke, A., Chaurasia, A., Kim, S., Culurciello, E.: ENet: A deep neural network architecture for real-time semantic segmentation. arXiv:1606.02147 (2016)

20. Poudel, R.P., Bonde, U., Liwicki, S., Zach, C.: ContextNet: Exploring context and detail for semantic segmentation in real-time. arXiv:1805.04554 (2018)

21. Romera, E., Alvarez, J.M., Bergasa, L.M., Arroyo, R.: ERFNet: efficient residual factorized convnet for real-time semantic segmentation. TITS **19**(1), 263–272 (2018). https://doi.org/10.1109/TITS.2017.2750080

22. Ronneberger, O., Fischer, P., Brox, T.: U-Net: convolutional networks for biomedical image segmentation. In: Navab, N., Hornegger, J., Wells, W.M., Frangi, A.F. (eds.) MICCAI 2015. LNCS, vol. 9351, pp. 234–241. Springer, Cham (2015). https://doi.org/10.1007/978-3-319-24574-4_28

23. Russakovsky, O., et al.: Imagenet large scale visual recognition challenge. IJCV **115**(3), 211–252 (2015). https://doi.org/10.1007/s11263-015-0816-y

24. Simonyan, K., Zisserman, A.: Very deep convolutional networks for large-scale image recognition. arXiv:1409.1556 (2014)

25. Szegedy, C., Vanhoucke, V., Ioffe, S., Shlens, J., Wojna, Z.: Rethinking the inception architecture for computer vision. In: CVPR, pp. 2818–2826 (2016). https://doi.org/10.1109/CVPR.2016.308

26. Treml, M., et al.: Speeding up semantic segmentation for autonomous driving. In: NIPS Workshop, vol. 2, p. 7 (2016)

27. Wang, X., Girshick, R., Gupta, A., He, K.: Non-local neural networks. In: CVPR, pp. 7794–7803 (2018). https://doi.org/10.1109/CVPR.2018.00813

28. Woo, S., Park, J., Lee, J.-Y., Kweon, I.S.: CBAM: convolutional block attention module. In: Ferrari, V., Hebert, M., Sminchisescu, C., Weiss, Y. (eds.) ECCV 2018. LNCS, vol. 11211, pp. 3–19. Springer, Cham (2018). https://doi.org/10.1007/978-3-030-01234-2_1
29. Zhang, Y., Tian, Y., Kong, Y., Zhong, B., Fu, Y.: Residual dense network for image super-resolution. In: CVPR, pp. 2472–2481 (2018). https://doi.org/10.1109/CVPR.2018.00262

Random Drop Loss for Tiny Object Segmentation: Application to Lesion Segmentation in Fundus Images

Song Guo[1], Tao Li[1], Chan Zhang[1], Ning Li[1], Hong Kang[1,2], and Kai Wang[1,3](✉)

[1] College of Computer Science, Nankai University, Tianjin, China
wangk@nankai.edu.cn
[2] Beijing Shanggong Medical Technology Co. Ltd., Beijing, China
[3] KLMDASR, Tianjin, China

Abstract. Convolutional neural network (CNN), has achieved state-of-the-art performance in computer vision tasks. The segmentation of dense objects has been fully studies, but the research is insufficient on tiny objects segmentation which is very common in medical images. For instance, the proportion of lesions or tumors can be as low as 0.1%, which can easily lead to misclassification. In this paper, we propose a random drop loss function to improve the segmentation performance of tiny lesions on medical image analysis task by dropping negative samples randomly according to their classification difficulty. In addition, we designed three drop functions to map the classification difficulty to drop probability with the principle that easy negative samples are dropped with high probabilities and hard samples are retained with high probabilities. In this manner, not only can the sorting process existing in Top-k BCE loss be avoided, but CNN can also learn better discriminative features, thereby reducing misclassification. We evaluated our method on the task of segmentation of microaneurysms and hemorrhages in color fundus images. Experimental results show that our method outperforms other methods in terms of segmentation performance and computational cost. The source code of our method is available at https://github.com/guomugong/randomdrop.

Keywords: Tiny object segmentation · Cross entropy loss · Random drop · Class imbalance · Fundus lesion segmentation

1 Introduction

Convolutional neural network (CNN), as a deep learning model, has achieved state-of-the-art performance in many computer vision tasks, such as image classification [5,6], object detection [11,13] and semantic segmentation [1,12]. In recent years, semantic segmentation methods based on deep learning have been well studied, and achieved remarkable performance. As far as we know, most

© Springer Nature Switzerland AG 2019
I. V. Tetko et al. (Eds.): ICANN 2019, LNCS 11729, pp. 213–224, 2019.
https://doi.org/10.1007/978-3-030-30508-6_18

existing models are concentrated on objects of normal size, such as animals and vehicles [2], and the segmentation of tiny objects has not been fully studied. However, the segmentation of small objects is also very important in certain areas, such as medical image analysis where identifying tiny lesions or tumors is critical to clinical diagnosis.

Recent works on fundus lesion segmentation shown that CNN achieves good performance [9,14]. However, there always exists class imbalance in fundus lesion segmentation, for instance, the proportion of lesions in the fundus image can be as low as 0.1%. This extreme class imbalance will make the traditional cross entropy loss function fails to work, since it is easy to classify all pixels into background pixels and achieves meaningless 99.9% accuracy. An intuitive solution to this class imbalance is assigning different weights to different categories, this type of method is called class balanced cross entropy (BCE) loss function [16], where pixels with a small proportion are given high weights, and pixels with a high proportion are given low weights. However, this solution does not consider easy/hard negative samples, all negatives are treated equally. As a result, in BCE loss, negative samples tend to misclassified as positive ones since the weighted loss for misclassifying a background pixel is much smaller than that for misclassifying a positive one. Lin et al. proposed *Focal Loss* [8] to emphasize hard-to-classify samples in object detection. In Focal Loss, different pixels are given different weights according to the difficulty level. Easy samples are given low weights, so the model can focus training on hard negatives. Different from Focal Loss, Guo. et al. proposed a Top-k balanced cross entropy (Top-k BCE) loss function [4], where only the top-k negative pixels with high losses are selected during each iteration, and the remaining easy negative samples are dropped. This method forces the model to focus on hard-to-classify samples, but a time-consuming sorting process is required.

In this paper, we propose a random drop loss function to improve the segmentation performance of tiny objects by dropping negative samples randomly according to their classification difficulty. Easy negative samples are dropped with high probabilities and hard negative samples are dropped with low probabilities. Further, three drop functions with different computational cost and drop strength are designed to convert the level of difficulty to the drop probability. In this random dropping manner, an explicit time-consuming sorting procedure can be avoided, which means a significant amount of training time can be saved compared to Top-k BCE. Moreover, once easy samples are dropped, the CNN only needs to consider these hard negative samples during each iteration, forcing the model to learn much discriminative features to distinguish them. As a result, less misclassification obtained. We evaluate our method to segment tiny objects in fundus lesion segmentation task. We employ experiments on a publicly available fundus image datasets - IDRiD [10]. We conducted two sets of experiments, microaneurysms (MA) segmentation and hemorrhages (HE) segmentation, since both MA and HE are very small, and it is very easy to classify non-lesion pixels as lesion pixels, as can be seen in Fig. 1. Even for humans, accurate identification of MA and HE is very difficult. The proposed method is compared with

BCE, Focal Loss and Top-k BCE. Experimental results show that our method achieves the highest AUC (area under the Precision-Recall curve) on all two segmentation tasks compared with other methods. Specially, compared with BCE, our method leads to 7.86%/15.76% improvement of AUC on two segmentation tasks. Moreover, compared with Top-k BCE, the speed of our method's forward propagation has increased by nearly 100%, and the forward time of the baseline model has been reduced by more than 30% (305.78 ms reduced to 190.95 ms).

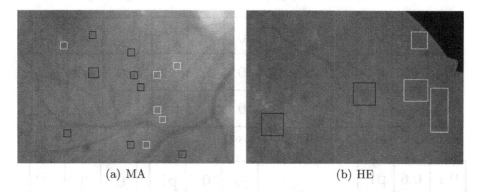

(a) MA   (b) HE

Fig. 1. Examples of MA and HE. Inside the black box is a certain lesion (MA is marked in (a) and HE is marked in (b)), and in the white box is something highly similar to that kind of lesion.

In summary, the main contributions of our work are as follows.

- We present a random drop loss function for tiny lesion segmentation by drop negative samples randomly according to their difficulty in classification.
- We design three drop functions based on their drop strength and computational cost.
- We conducted experiments on two kinds of lesion segmentation tasks to evaluate our method, and experimental results show our method shows superior performance than other three methods in terms of segmentation performance and computational cost.

The remainder of this paper is organized as follows. Section 2 provides a detailed description of the proposed method. Experimental settings and results are described in Sect. 3. The conclusion is drawn in Sect. 4.

2   Random Drop Loss

Random Drop Loss is designed to address the tiny object segmentation scenario in which there is an extreme class imbalance between negative samples and positive samples (e.g., 1000:1). This class imbalance leads to misclassification and poor training efficiency. In this section, we introduce *Random Drop Loss* starting from the Balanced Cross Entropy (BCE) loss. And we only consider binary classification problem in our work for simplicity.

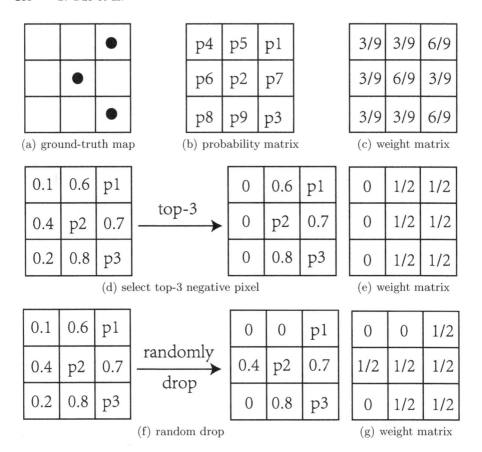

Fig. 2. (a) Ground-truth map for positive and negative samples. Three solid black dots represent positive samples, and the rest six blank parts denote negative samples. (b) Probability matrix for BCE. Each element is obtained by sigmoid operation, and represents the probability being positive samples. (c) Weight matrix for BCE. The weights for positive and negative samples are 6/9 and 3/9, respectively. (d) Changes in the probability matrix after selecting top 3 negative samples. p1, p2 and p3 denote positive samples. And, the activation probabilities for negative samples are given. Low probability corresponds to high loss, so that p5, p7, p9 are selected. (e) Weight matrix for top-3 BCE. There are three positive samples and three negative samples, so the weights of both positive and negative samples are 1/2. Zero means that the corresponding sample contributes zero to the loss. (f) Changes in the probability matrix after using random drop method. p4, p5 and p8 are dropped, and p6, p7 and p9 are retained. (g) Weight matrix for random drop loss.

2.1   Balanced Cross Entropy

In Balanced Cross Entropy Loss, a weight factor is introduced to balance positive/negative samples. It is defined follows.

$$L_{BCE}(p, y) = -\beta \sum_{y_j=1} \log p_j - (1 - \beta) \sum_{y_j=0} \log (1 - p_j) \qquad (1)$$

where y_j denotes the category of the jth sample, p_j denotes the probability of the jth sample belongs to a positive sample, and β denotes weight factor. β can be defined as the proportion of negative samples in all samples or be treated as a hyperparameter.

In the BCE loss, the first term sums the losses of all positive samples and the second term sums the losses of all negative samples. We could also regard the BCE loss as dot product of the loss matrix and the weight matrix, as can be seen in Fig. 2(a)–(c). Loss matrix can be computed directly by the probability matrix. For positive samples, a high activation probability corresponds to a low loss. Also, for negative samples, a high activation probability corresponds to a high loss. From the perspective of matrix, different cross-entropy-based losses differ in the weight matrix. For example, traditional cross-entropy loss corresponds to a weight matrix with all elements 1. It is easy to see that BCE loss doesn't distinguish easy and hard negative samples since they have the same weight (Fig. 2(c)). This method is considered as an experimental baseline for our proposed method.

2.2   Random Drop Loss Definition

BCE introduces a weight factor to balance negative and positive samples. However, this method does not consider easy/hard negative samples, and all negative samples are treated equally. This can lead to misclassification problem, since the weighted loss for misclassifying a background pixel is much smaller than that for misclassifying a positive one.

In Top-k BCE, only top-k negative samples with high loss are retained, and other samples are dropped, as can be observed in Fig. 2(d) and (e). However, this method has a drawback that a time-consuming sorting procedure is required. This method is also considered as an experimental baseline for our proposed method.

We propose the random drop loss to address above-mentioned problems. We drop easy-to-classify samples at random according to their difficulty level in classification, thereby no sorting procedure is required and hard-to-classify samples are kept in high probabilities. The random drop loss is defined as:

$$L_{drop}(p, y) = -\beta \sum_{y_j=1} \log p_j - (1 - \beta) \sum_{y_j=0} \mathbb{1}(p_j) \log (1 - p_j) \qquad (2)$$

where y_j denotes the category of the jth sample, p_j denotes the activation probability of the jth sample, β denotes weight factor, and $\mathbb{1}(p_j)$ is an indicator function to specify a negative sample is dropped or not, and is defined below.

$$\mathbb{1}(p_j) = \begin{cases} 0 & r < p_{drop}(p_j) \\ 1 & otherwise \end{cases} \tag{3}$$

where r is a random number between 0 and 1, and $p_{drop}(\cdot)$ represents random drop function which computes the drop probability for a given negative sample with activation probability p_j. Details about random drop function will be introduced later.

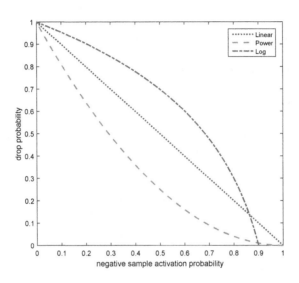

Fig. 3. Function figures of three drop functions.

A simple example for the random drop loss is shown in Fig. 2(f) and (g). Three positive samples (marked red) are all kept, and three of the six negative samples are retained after random drop. Then, the weight matrix is calculated. For dropped samples, they contribute zero to loss so that their weights are placed at zero. For negative samples, their weights equal $1/2$ $(3/6)$, that is the number of positive samples divided by the sum of positive samples and retained negative samples.

2.3 Random Drop Function

We designed three different drop functions, including linear function, power function and log function, according to their drop strength. The formulas are shown in Eqs. 4–6, and the function figures are shown in Fig. 3.

$$p_{drop}(p_j) = 1.0 - p_j; \tag{4}$$

$$p_{drop}(p_j) = (1.0 - p_j)^2; \tag{5}$$

$$p_{drop}(p_j) = 1.0 + \log(1.0 - p_j); \tag{6}$$

where p_j represents the activation probability for a negative sample, and it also corresponds to an element in the probability matrix (Fig. 2(f)).

We can observe from Fig. 3 that negative samples with high activation probability are dropped with low probability. Generally speaking, log function has the biggest drop strength and linear function has the smallest drop strength, since log function takes the highest drop probability among three functions when the activation probability is the same. Meanwhile, the bigger the drop strength, the smaller the expected number negative samples retained. Considering computational cost, linear function costs the least and log function costs the most. Note that if there is a function that always maps activation probability to a low drop probability, then our method is close to BCE loss. In Sect. 3 we will compare the performance of above three functions on lesion segmentation tasks.

3   Experiments and Results

3.1   Materials

We evaluate our proposed method on the IDRiD (Indian Diabetic Retinopathy Image Dataset) [10]. IDRiD provides pixel-annotations for four kinds of fundus lesions. As well, it provides an explicit partition of training set and test set, providing conditions for a fair comparison.

There are a total of 81 fundus images in the dataset, including 54 training images and 27 test images, each of which has a resolution of 4288×2848 (width $\times$ height). In terms of pixels, the proportion of microaneurysms is the lowest among the four lesions, as low as 0.1%, and the proportion of hemorrhages is the highest among the four lesions, as high as 1.01%. Therefore, we evaluate our method on microaneurysms and hemorrhages segmentation to show that our method can work well on different levels of class imbalance.

3.2   Segmentation Model

Holistically-Nested Edge Detection (HED) [16] was proposed for edge detection, and Guo. et al. have shown HED behaves well in fundus lesion segmentation [3]. So that we use HED as our segmentation model, but with some modifications. HED contains five side-output layers with different receptive fields, and each side-output layer can be used to extract vertical direction features. Then, the weight-fusion layer is used to fuse the outputs of side-output layers. In our experiments, we only use four side-output layers, since small lesion points cannot respond at a high level. Moreover, the weight-fusion layer only fuses the output of the second, third and fourth side-output layers, since the output of the first side-output layer contains too much noise.

3.3   Training Data Preparation and Augmentation

The resolution of training images is too large to fit them into GPU memory, therefore, we resize each image and its ground-truth to 1440×960

(width × height) before training. Moreover, we use various transformations to augment the training set, including rotation by an angel of 90, 180 and 270, flipping horizontally and vertically. As a result, the training set was augmented by a factor of 5, and there are 324 training images in total.

3.4 Training Details

The training and testing procedures of segmentation model run on a workstation equipped with two Intel Xeon E5-2620 CPUs, three NVIDIA GTX 1080ti GPUs and 128G RAM.

We implement the baseline model using the *Caffe* framework [7], and for fair comparison, we implement a CPU version for BCE loss, Focal loss, Top-k BCE loss and random drop loss. We set the weight factor equals 0.99 and focusing parameter equals 1 in Focal Loss. And, we use quicksort [15] to select the top 20% negative samples in Top-k BCE loss.

For training segmentation model, we perform SGD with a batch size of 1, a momentum of 0.9, and a weight decay of 0.0005. We adopt a polynomial decay strategy for learning rate. The power and max iterations are set to 0.9 and 100k, respectively. The initial learning rate for MA segmentation is equals 1e-7, and it is set to 1e-8 for HE segmentation. In addition, instead of feeding the entire fundus image into model, we use a random clipping method to crop a patch with size 800 × 800 as input to save GPU memory and to accelerate computation.

3.5 Evaluation Metrics

We adopt four metrics to evaluate the segmentation results, including precision (Pr), recall (Re), F1-score and the area under the Precision-Recall Curve (AUC). F1-score is the harmonic mean of precision and recall. They are defined as below.

$$Pr = \frac{TP}{TP + FP}, \quad Re = \frac{TP}{TP + FN}, \quad F1\text{-score} = \frac{2 \cdot Pr \cdot Re}{Pr + Re} \tag{7}$$

TP is the number of correctly classified lesion pixels, FP is the number of background pixels misclassified as lesion pixels, and FN is the number of lesion pixels misclassified as background pixels.

3.6 Results

Segmentation Performance. Since the segmentation results are probability maps, we select the equilibrium point of Precision-Recall curve to calculate Pr, Re and F1-score. The statistical results of four evaluation metrics are summarized in Table 1.

We can observe from Table 1 that our method achieves the highest AUC score on microaneurysms and hemorrhages segmentation tasks compared with the other three methods. Specially, compared with BCE loss, our method leads to sufficient improvement (7.86%/15.76%) of AUC of two segmentation tasks,

Table 1. Experimental results over microaneurysms and hemorrhages segmentation tasks (best results shown in bold).

Method	Microaneurysms				Hemorrhages			
	Pr	Re	F1-score	AUC	Pr	Re	F1-score	AUC
BCE [16]	0.4776	0.4730	0.4753	0.3299	0.5145	0.5123	0.5134	0.4828
Top-k BCE [4]	0.4987	0.5013	0.5000	0.4702	**0.5562**	**0.5579**	**0.5570**	0.5606
Focal Loss [8]	0.4799	0.4844	0.4821	0.4540	0.5504	0.5470	0.5487	0.5466
Our method (Log)	0.5066	0.5035	0.5051	**0.4875**	0.5485	0.5450	0.5468	**0.5614**
Our method (Power)	**0.5072**	**0.5060**	**0.5066**	0.4838	0.5500	0.5517	0.5508	0.5461
Our method (Linear)	0.5024	0.5063	0.5043	0.4855	0.5458	0.5429	0.5443	0.5526

verifying the effectiveness of our method. Moreover, our method shows superior performance over Focal Loss in terms of all metrics on MA segmentation.

We could also observe from Table 1 that our method works well with all three drop functions, and there is not much difference among them. In addition, we found that log drop function achieves the highest AUC among all three drop functions. Recall Fig. 3, log drop function drops a negative sample with a higher probability compared with other two drop functions. Thus, the expected number of samples retained in log drop function is the smallest, as a result, segmentation model has to find much discriminative features to fit these negative samples. For different tasks, we can select different drop function or design task-specify one to achieve better performance, which shows the flexibility of our method.

Computational Cost Analysis. To show the advantage of our method in computational cost, we summarize the time of the segmentation model and the time of one loss layer in Table 2. The forward time and backward time measured in the table is the average of 100 iterations, and the time is measured by the tool provided by *Caffe*.

As can be seen from Table 2, our method has obvious advantages in speed compared with Top-k BCE. Specially for linear drop function, the speed of forward propagation of our methods has increased by nearly 100% (59.13 ms

Table 2. Comparison of forward time and backward time for different methods (best results shown in bold).

Method	Forward time		Backward time	
	Model	Loss layer	Model	Loss layer
Top-k BCE [4]	305.78 ms	59.13 ms	264.92 ms	1.98 ms
Our method (Log)	278.73 ms	52.07 ms	262.88 ms	1.41 ms
Our method (Power)	199.36 ms	32.42 ms	263.15 ms	1.49 ms
Our method (Linear)	**190.95 ms**	**30.47 ms**	**262.31 ms**	**1.39 ms**

reduced to 30.47 ms), and the forward time of the segmentation model has been reduced by more than 30% (305.78 ms reduced to 190.95 ms). Similar improvements can also be observed for other two drop functions.

Visualization of Segmentation Results. The segmentation probability maps of MA and HE are shown in Figs. 4 and 5, respectively. We can observe BCE and

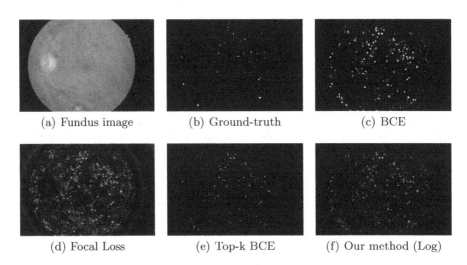

(a) Fundus image   (b) Ground-truth   (c) BCE

(d) Focal Loss   (e) Top-k BCE   (f) Our method (Log)

Fig. 4. Visualization of MA segmentation probability maps. (a) A fundus image from test set. (b) Expert annotated ground-truth. (c)–(f) Segmentation results of different methods.

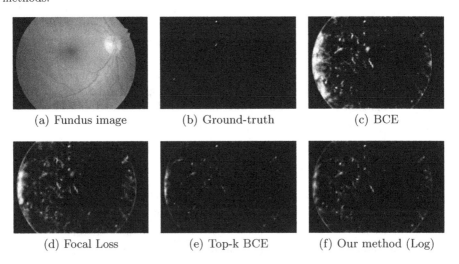

(a) Fundus image   (b) Ground-truth   (c) BCE

(d) Focal Loss   (e) Top-k BCE   (f) Our method (Log)

Fig. 5. Visualization of HE segmentation probability maps. (a) A fundus image from test set. (b) Expert annotated ground-truth. (c)–(f) Segmentation results of different methods.

Focal Loss give high probability to a large part of hard negative samples (Fig. 5). It is especially serious for BCE, since it does not distinguish easy/hard negative samples. For Top-k BCE and our method, segmentation results look less noisy, which means our method can alleviate misclassification in some certain.

4   Conclusion

This paper focuses on the segmentation of tiny objects, where extreme class imbalance always exists, as a result, it is easy to classify background pixels to lesion pixels. To overcome this problem, we propose a random drop loss function in which negative samples are dropped randomly according to the classification difficulty. In addition, we also designed three kinds of drop functions to map the difficulty of classification to drop probability. In this random dropping approach, the model is forced to learn how to distinguish these hard samples thereby reducing misclassification. We evaluated our method on fundus MA and HE segmentation tasks. Experimental results show our method shows advantages in both segmentation performance and computational cost.

Acknowledgment. This work is partially supported by the National Natural Science Foundation (61872200), the National Key Research and Development Program of China (2016YFC0400709), the Science and Technology Commission of Tianjin Binhai New Area (BHXQKJXM-PT-ZJSHJ-2017005), the Natural Science Foundation of Tianjin (18YFYZCG00060) and Nankai University (91922299).

References

1. Chen, L.-C., Zhu, Y., Papandreou, G., Schroff, F., Adam, H.: Encoder-decoder with atrous separable convolution for semantic image segmentation. In: Ferrari, V., Hebert, M., Sminchisescu, C., Weiss, Y. (eds.) ECCV 2018. LNCS, vol. 11211, pp. 833–851. Springer, Cham (2018). https://doi.org/10.1007/978-3-030-01234-2_49
2. Everingham, M., Van Gool, L., Williams, C.K.I., Winn, J., Zisserman, A.: The Pascal visual object classes (VOC) challenge. Int. J. Comput. Vis. **88**(2), 303–338 (2010). https://doi.org/10.1007/s11263-009-0275-4
3. Guo, S., Li, T., Kang, H., Li, N., Zhang, Y., Wang, K.: L-Seg: an end-to-end unified framework for multi-lesion segmentation of fundus images. Neurocomputing **349**, 52–63 (2019). https://doi.org/10.1016/j.neucom.2019.04.019
4. Guo, S., Wang, K., Kang, H., Liu, T., Gao, Y., Li, T.: Bin loss for hard exudates segmentation in fundus images. Neurocomputing (2019). https://doi.org/10.1016/j.neucom.2018.10.103
5. He, K., Zhang, X., Ren, S., Sun, J.: Deep residual learning for image recognition. In: 2016 IEEE Conference on Computer Vision and Pattern Recognition (CVPR), pp. 770–778 (2016). https://doi.org/10.1109/CVPR.2016.90
6. Huang, G., Liu, Z., van der Maaten, L., Weinberger, K.Q.: Densely connected convolutional networks. In: 2017 IEEE Conference on Computer Vision and Pattern Recognition (CVPR), pp. 2261–2269 (2017). https://doi.org/10.1109/CVPR.2017.243

7. Jia, Y., et al.: Caffe: convolutional architecture for fast feature embedding. In: Proceedings of the 22nd ACM International Conference on Multimedia, pp. 675–678 (2014). https://doi.org/10.1145/2647868.2654889

8. Lin, T.Y., Goyal, P., Girshick, R., He, K., Dollar, P.: Focal loss for dense object detection. IEEE Trans. Pattern Anal. Mach. Intell. **PP**(99), 2999–3007 (2017). https://doi.org/10.1109/TPAMI.2018.2858826

9. Mo, J., Zhang, L., Feng, Y.: Exudate-based diabetic macular edema recognition in retinal images using cascaded deep residual networks. Neurocomputing **290**, 161–171 (2018). https://doi.org/10.1016/j.neucom.2018.02.035

10. Porwal, P., et al.: Indian diabetic retinopathy image dataset (IDRiD): a database for diabetic retinopathy screening research. Data 3(3) (2018). https://doi.org/10.3390/data3030025

11. Ren, S., He, K., Girshick, R., Sun, J.: Faster R-CNN: towards real-time object detection with region proposal networks. IEEE Trans. Pattern Anal. Mach. Intell. **39**(6), 1137–1149 (2017). https://doi.org/10.1109/TPAMI.2016.2577031

12. Shelhamer, E., Long, J., Darrell, T.: Fully convolutional networks for semantic segmentation. IEEE Trans. Pattern Anal. Mach. Intell. **39**(4), 640–651 (2017). https://doi.org/10.1109/TPAMI.2016.2572683

13. Shen, Z., Liu, Z., Li, J., Jiang, Y., Chen, Y., Xue, X.: DSOD: learning deeply supervised object detectors from scratch. In: 2017 IEEE International Conference on Computer Vision (ICCV), pp. 1937–1945 (2017). https://doi.org/10.1109/ICCV.2017.212

14. Tan, J.H., et al.: Automated segmentation of exudates, haemorrhages, microaneurysms using single convolutional neural network. Inf. Sci. **420**, 66–76 (2017). https://doi.org/10.1016/j.ins.2017.08.050

15. Wilkes, M.V.: The art of computer programming, volume 3, sorting and searching. Comput. J. **17**(4), 324–324 (1998). https://doi.org/10.1093/comjnl/17.4.324

16. Xie, S., Tu, Z.: Holistically-nested edge detection. Int. J. Comput. Vis. **125**(1), 3–18 (2017). https://doi.org/10.1007/s11263-017-1004-z

Flow2Seg: Motion-Aided Semantic Segmentation

Xiangtai Li[1], Jiangang Bai[1], Kuiyuan Yang[2], and Yunhai Tong[1(✉)]

[1] Key Laboratory of Machine Perception, MOE, School of EECS, Peking University,
Beijing, China
{lxtpku,pku_bjg,yhtong}@pku.edu.cn
[2] DeepMotion, Beijing, China
kuiyuanyang@deepmotion.ai

Abstract. Motion is an important clue for segmentation. In this paper, we leverage motion information densely represented by optical flow to assist the semantic segmentation task. Specifically, our framework takes both image and optical flow as input, where image goes through a state-of-the-art deep network and optical flow goes through a relatively shallow network, and results from both paths are fused together in a residual manner. Unlike image, optical flow is weakly related to semantics but can separate different objects according motion consistency, which motivates us to use relatively shallow network to process optical flow to avoid overfitting and keep spatial information. In our experiment on Cityscapes, we find that optical flow improves image-based segmentation on object boundaries especially on small thin objects. Aided by motion, we achieve comparable results with state-of-the-art methods.

Keywords: Optical flow · Flow2Seg · Semantic segmentation

1 Introduction

Semantic segmentation is a fundamental task in computer vision, which aims to predict a semantic category for each pixel in an image. Such comprehensive image understanding is valuable for many vision-based applications such as autonomous driving, remote sensing, human-computer interaction and virtual reality.

In the deep learning era, semantic segmentation has made steady progress after the introducing of Fully Convolutional Networks (FCNs) [24]. However, most existing methods only take a static image as input and ignores the rich motion information in image sequences.

Motion is an important clue for segmentation task and can separate different objects apart based their different motion patterns, which is complementary to static patterns in an image. Motivated by this, we propose to add one path network named Flow2Seg by taking optical flow as input, in addition to the image path modeled by a state-of-the-art network. Figure 1 presents our basic

© Springer Nature Switzerland AG 2019
I. V. Tetko et al. (Eds.): ICANN 2019, LNCS 11729, pp. 225–237, 2019.
https://doi.org/10.1007/978-3-030-30508-6_19

idea. We use flownet [14] to extract optical flow between video frames and use FCN [24] to learn semantic segmentation map directly from optical flow. Considering optical flow is weakly related to semantics and contains lots of noises, we use relatively shallow network to process optical flow to avoid overfitting and keep spatial information, the design is also empirically verified through ablation study. On the widely used semantic segmentation benchmark Cityscapes [6], Flow2Seg improves the image-based baseline significantly and achieves comparable performance with state-of-the-arts methods. Notably, Flow2Seg improves segmentation of object boundaries, which is crucial for real-world tasks which require to know precise object boundary.

In summary, we propose to use motion information for semantic segmentation task via specifically design network. By combining the new designed motion path with the single frame path modeled by a state-of-the-method segmentation network, we achieve better performance. To best of our knowledge, we are the first to use network to learn semantic segmentation map directly from optical flow input. Our main contribution can be listed in two points:

1. We propose a novel and light module Flow2Seg for directly mapping optical flow into segmentation map. Combined with image segmentation model, we achieve considerable improvement compared with PSP-net [42] baseline on Cityscapes dataset [6]. When training with coarse data, our method achieves 81.4% mIoU which is the top performance compared with other video semantic segmentation methods.
2. We explore the usage of FCNs for learning semantic segmentation map directly from optical flow. Optical flow itself contain little appearance information and we show shallow network can learn better segmentation result than deep models. In addition, we try different optical flow prediction methods, and find that optical flow predicted FlowNet2 [14] contains more detailed information and achieves better results than others.

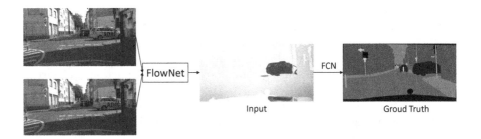

Fig. 1. Overview of the Flow2Seg path. Two consecutive frames are used to estimated the optical flow, then the optical flow is fed into a FCN for semantic segmentation.

2   Related Work

In this section, we briefly review recent works for advancing semantic segmentation from three directions, i.e., context modeling, multi-level feature fusion and using temporal information.

Contextual information is modeled to gather information from larger receptive field. ParseNet [23] utilizes global pooling to encode contextual information, and PSPNet [42] uses spatial pyramid pooling to aggregate multi-scale contextual information. Deeplab series [2–4] develop atrous spatial pyramid pooling (ASPP) to capture multi-scale contextual information by dilated convolutional layers with different dilation rates. Instead of parallelly aggregation as PSPNet and Deeplab, Yang et al. [36] and Bilinski et al. [1] follow the idea of dense connection [13] to encode contextual information in a dense way. In [27], factorized large filters are directly used to increase the receptive field size for context modeling. In PSANet [43], contextual information is collected from all positions according the similarities defined in a projected feature space.

In addition to contextual information, high-resolution features are also important for high-resolution prediction demanded in semantic segmentation. Accordingly, multi-level feature fusion becomes a common way to use both high-level/low-resolution and low-level/high-resolution features. U-Net [28] adds skip connections between the encoder and decoder to reuse low level features, [41] improves U-Net by fusing high-level features into low-level features. DeepLabV3+ [5] improves the decoder of previous version by combing low-level features. In [21], Conv-LSTM [34] is proposed to fuse features between layers bidirectionally. Some works fuse different modalities for better performance. PAD-Net [35] is proposed to use gates to fuse multi-modal features trained from multiple auxiliary tasks. Le et at. [19] combines optical flow and surface normals to learn joint multimodal features. Different from their approach, our method uses label map to supervise the optical flow learning process and fuse into the image path in a residual way.

Sequential frames contain more information than a signal frame, thus temporal modeling is also a promising direction. Fayyaz et al. [9] apply a spatial-temporal LSTM on per-frame CNN features. Nilsson et al. [25] proposed spatio-temporal transformer gated recurrent units (STGRU) to propagate semantic labels bidirectionally towards center frame using optical flow. Jin et al. [16] proposed to learn discriminative features by predicting future frames and combine both the predicted results and current features to parse a frame. Gadde et al. [11] proposed to combine the features wrapped from previous frames with flows and those from the current frames to predict the final results. However, all these methods model temporal motion in an implicit way. For example, Netwarp [11] and STGRU [25] use optical flow to warp features for temporal consistency. One drawback of those method is that they use optical flow to warp feature from previous or future frames and if we suppose the optical flow is accurate, the warped feature is directly matched with current feature and no extra information is added. Our methods focus on learning segmentation maps directly from the raw optical flow inputs and bring motion information as extra guidance.

3   Proposed Method

In this section, we describe our proposed framework in detail. The overall network architecture is shown in Fig. 2, which consists of three parts: two independent fully convolutional networks with RGB image and optical flow as input respectively, and one fusion module to learn a joint representation for final segmentation output, the whole network is trained end-to-end with one final loss together with several auxiliary losses.

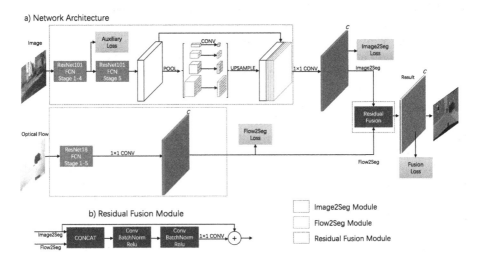

Fig. 2. (a) Network Architecture. It contains three different parts: Image2Seg Module, Flow2Seg Module and Residual Fusion Module. (b) Residual Fusion Module. C denotes the number of categories. Best view it in color.

3.1   Flow2Seg Module

Learning semantic information from optical flow using deep network is first proposed in using a two-stream network [30]. However, unlike video action recognition tasks, pixel-level semantic understanding task needs labeling each pixel rather than only one label for the whole image or optical flow. Thus we adopt fully convolutional network [24] as the feature extractor for the motion stream. In our work, we use off-the-shelf methods for optical flow estimation, in our ablation study we found FlowNet2 [14] is more suitable for our task since it can generate sharp object boundaries and generalize well for both small and large motions. Unlike very deep networks those used to extract features for image, relatively shallow ResNet18 is used to process optical flow. To take two channels of optical flow as input for a ImageNet [29] pre-trained ResNet18, we average the weights of the first convolutional layer along the channel dimension to initialize two-channel input ResNet18. In addition, dilated convolution with dilation rate 2 and 4 are used in stage4 and stage5 to increase the receptive field size while keeping the spatial resolution. The output stride of this network is 8.

Like context modeling for image segmentation, three different context modeling modules are tried after the backbone, including ASPP [4], DenseASPP [36] and pyramid pooling [42], but without observed performance improvement in Flow2Seg. This can be explained that optical flow contains weak semantics and contextual information is not helpful as on image, which is also the reason to choose a relatively shallow network as the backbone. The output of Flow2seg module is a segmentation map with C channels, where C represents the numbers of categories.

3.2   Image2Seg Module

Image2Seg Module maps the input RGB image to semantic segmentation map. Image2Seg module can be any existing FCN architectures [24]. We choose the previous state-of-the-art model PSPNet [42] as our Image2Seg Module. In particular, we use the pretrained ResNet101 [12] with the same dilated strategy as our backbone to extract the feature map. The final feature map size is 1/8 of the input image resolution. On top of the feature map, pyramid pooling module [42] is utilized to incorporate contextual information of multiple levels. Following [42], four average pooling operations with sizes of 1×1, 2×2, 3×3, 6×6 are applied which are represented by different colors in the blue box of Fig. 2. Those context features are upsampled to keep the same size with the original feature map by bilinear interpolation, which are further concatenated with the original feature. Then, 1×1 convolution is employed to reduce the feature dimension and fuse the multi-scale context information. Finally, 1×1 convolution is performed on the fused feature map to predict the pixel-level segmentation map. With the same setting as PSPNet [42], auxiliary loss is added after the fourth stage to ease optimization.

3.3   Residual Fusion Module

Flow2Seg and Image2Seg generate two semantic maps with C channels in Fig. 2 based on two different input modalities, where one is dynamic and the other is static. Though Flow2Seg and Image2Seg are complementary, simply fusing by adding or concatenating their outputs cannot obtain better results since Flow2Seg performs much worse results than Image2Seg. To dig out the useful part in Flow2Seg while discards the useless part, we design a lightweight residual fusion module as illustrated in Fig. 2. Both output maps from Flow2Seg and Image2Seg are concatenated together followed by two blocks consist of convolution and batch normalization [15], and a residual fused semantic map is generated with 1×1 convolution, which is further added to the semantic map generated by Image2Seg for final segmentation. The residual fusion module can refine the weakness part in Image2Seg and leave well segmented part unaffected.

The output of residual fusion module with fused segmentation maps is the final results of our system.

3.4 Loss Function

As illustrated in Fig. 2, the whole network is learned in an end-to-end manner driven by four loss functions defined on four predictions inside the network. In summary, the total loss is defined as:

$$\mathcal{L} = \mathcal{L}_{Image2Seg} + \mathcal{L}_{Fusion} + \alpha * \mathcal{L}_{Flow2Seg} + \beta * \mathcal{L}_{Aux} \tag{1}$$

where $\mathcal{L}_{Image2Seg}$ represents the cross entropy loss between image input results and the ground truth, $\mathcal{L}_{Flow2Seg}$ denotes the cross entropy loss between optical flow input results and the ground truth, $\mathcal{L}_{Aux}$ denotes the auxiliary loss which are used for easy optimization [42,43] and $\mathcal{L}_{fusion}$ denotes the cross entropy loss between final fusion results and the ground truth, we set $\alpha = 0.2$ and $\beta = 0.4$ respectively in our experiment.

4 Experiments

4.1 Datasets

We evaluate the proposed method on Cityscapes [6] which is a standard benchmark for semantic urban scene understanding. It contains 5000 fine pixel-level annotated images, which are divided into 2975, 500, and 1525 images for training, validation and testing, respectively. It also provides 20000 coarsely annotated images. Each finely annotated frame is sampled from the 20th frame of a 30-frame video clip in the dataset, giving in total 180 K frames. The previous frame(19th frame) of these images are used for optical flow calculation in our experiment. 30 classes are annotated and 19 of them are used for pixel-level semantic labeling task. Images are high resolution with the same size of 1024×2048. Standard performance metric mean Intersection over Union (mIoU) is used for evaluation on both validation set and test set, where labels of test set are not given and predicted results are submitted to server for evaluation.

4.2 Implementation Details

Our implementation is based on PyTorch [26], and uses ResNet series as the backbone. In particular, we use ResNet101 as the backbone of Image2Seg and ResNet18 as the backbone of Flow2Seg. We set weight decay to 1e-4, and use Adam [18] as optimizer. We adopt "poly" learning rate scheduling policy, where initial learning rate is set to 2e-5 and decayed by $(1 - \frac{epoch}{max\_epoch})^{power}$ with $power = 0.9$. Synchronized batch normalization [39] is used for better mean and variance estimation due the limited number of images can be hosted in each GPU. We choose crop size of 832×832 for image input and 1024×1024 for optical flow input. We employ about 100 K training iterations with mini-batch size of 8.

Table 1. Ablation study with different optical flow inputs, architecture is FCN with ResNet18.

Method	mIoU(%)
FlowNetS	35.6
FlowNet2	**39.6**
PWC	36.3
GF-flow	25.4

As a common practice to avoid overfitting, data augmentation including random horizontal flipping, random cropping, random color jittering within the range of $[-10, 10]$, and random scaling in the range of $[0.5, 2]$ are used during training and we do these operations for both image and optical flow input. Note for final result submission, we first train the Flow2Seg and Image2Seg independently, then jointly finetune the trained models together with fusion module.

4.3 Experiments on Cityscapes

In this set of experiments except the last experiment, only the 2975 fine annotated images with corresponding optical flows are used for training, and evaluation results on the validation set are reported using single scale prediction. The optical flow is calculated between current frame and previous frame. For the last experiment, we also use coarse data to boost our model as well as for fair comparison with other video semantic segmentation methods.

Ablation Study on Input Optical Flow. We first explore four different methods for optical flow estimation: FlowNetS [10], FlowNet2 [14], PWC [31], and GF-flow [8]. Note that first three are generated by trained network. The result is reported in Table 1, FlowNet2 is slightly better than others because it contains more detailed information on object boundaries and more consistent motion on both large and small objects.

Ablation Study on Architecture of Flow2Seg Module. We also explore the different network architectures for Flow2Seg and report the results in Table 2. We first choose different backbone networks from ResNet series, and find that increasing the depth of network decreases the performance. Then we also add context modeling module [4,36,42] on the top of ResNet18, and find no performance improvement, which demonstrates that optical flow contains limited semantics and without requiring deep and large contextual modeling.

Comparison with PSPNet Baseline. We re-implement PSPNet on Cityscapes and achieve similar performance with mIoU of 77.8% which are used as our strong baseline model. We use weights of PSPNet to initialize our

Table 2. Ablation study architecture of Flow2Seg Module. Optical flow is generated from FlowNet2. First three rows use different network backbone while last three rows use different context modeling methods.

Method	mIoU(%)
ResNet18-FCN	**39.6**
ResNet50-FCN	37.4
ResNet101-FCN	35.4
ResNet18 + ASPP	39.4
ResNet18 + DenseASPP	39.3
ResNet18 + PSP	38.2

Table 3. Comparison experiments with baseline on Cityscapes validation set

Method	mIoU(%)
ResNet101-FCN	75.3
ResNet101 + PSP	77.8
ResNet101 + PSP + Flow2Seg	79.7 (1.9 ↑)

Image2Seg module. Then we add our Flow2Seg module together with residual fusion module and we train three components together. Finally we get a significant improvement of 1.9% with mIoU of 79.7%, Table 3 summarizes the results. Figure 3 visually compares the segmentation results of PSPNet and our method. We observed that our method improves the object boundaries especially small and thin objects mostly. For example, in the second row of Fig. 3, our method can find missing pole in the scene shown in yellow boxes and in the third and fourth rows of Fig. 3, our method can handle in-consistent of moving car shown in yellow boxes.

Comparison with State-of-the-Art Image Semantic Segmentation Methods. We first show the comparison between our proposed method and current state-of-the-art image semantic segmentation methods (illustrated in Table 4). Firstly, we train our method only using the train-fine dataset, and achieve better performance than PSPNet [42] and PSANet [43] on the test set. We improve baseline PSPNet [42] by around 1% point. Secondly, we further fine-tune the model with both train-fine and val-fine datasets and get a better performance. Following the same setting as [42], multi-scale sliding-window crop test is used for fair comparison. Detailed per-class results on test set are reported in Table 5. In particular, our method gets superior performance in small objects like "pole","traffic light" and "traffic sign" shown in Table 5 which is consistent with our observation in Fig. 3.

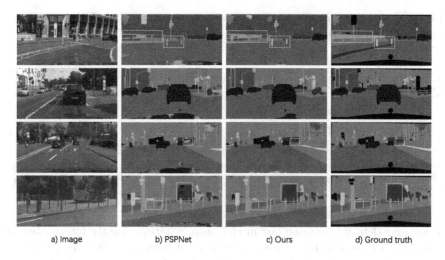

a) Image   b) PSPNet   c) Ours   d) Ground truth

Fig. 3. Comparison of segmentation results of PSPNet and our results on Cityscapes validation set. Our method refines small objects on boarder and generate more consistent results inside objects. Best viewed in color.

Table 4. State-of-the-art comparison experiments on Cityscapes test set. †means training with only the train-fine dataset. ‡means training with both the train-fine and val-fine datasets. Note that our methods also use optical flow extracted from previous frame.

Method	Backbone	mIoU(%)
PSPNet [42]†	ResNet101	78.4
PSANet [43]†	ResNet101	78.6
Ours †	ResNet101	**79.4**
RefineNet [22]‡	ResNet101	73.6
SAC [40]‡	ResNet101	78.1
DUC-HDC [32]‡	ResNet101	77.6
AAF [17]‡	ResNet101	79.1
BiSeNet [37]‡	ResNet101	78.9
PSANet [43]‡	ResNet101	80.1
DFN [38]‡	ResNet101	79.3
DSSPN [20]‡	ResNet101	77.8
Ours‡	ResNet101	**80.4**

Comparison with Other Video Semantic Segmentation Methods. We further compare our method with other video semantic segmentation methods. For fair comparison, we also use coarse data to boost our model accuracy. We start with trained model on fine dataset and then we use both coarse and fine data to train Image2Seg model for 20 epoch and we fix Flow2Seg path during the

Table 5. Per-category results on Cityscapes test set. Note that all the models are trained with only fine-data. Our method outperforms existing approaches on 12 out of 19 categories.

Method	road	swalk	build.	wall	fence	pole	tlight	sign	veg.	terrain	sky	person	rider	car	truck	bus	train	mbike	bike	mIoU
FCN [24]	97.4	78.4	89.2	34.9	44.2	47.4	60.1	65.0	91.4	69.3	93.9	77.1	51.4	92.6	35.3	48.6	46.5	51.6	66.8	65.3
DeepLabv2 [3]	97.9	81.3	90.3	48.8	47.4	49.6	57.9	67.3	91.9	69.4	94.2	79.8	59.8	93.7	56.5	67.5	57.5	57.7	68.8	70.4
RefineNet [22]	98.2	83.3	91.3	47.8	50.4	56.1	66.9	71.3	92.3	70.3	94.8	80.9	63.3	94.5	64.6	76.1	64.3	62.2	69.9	73.6
DSSPN [20]	-	-	-	-	-	-	-	-	-	-	-	-	-	-	-	-	-	-	-	77.8
SAC [40]	98.6	86.5	93.1	56.3	59.5	65.1	72.9	78.2	93.5	72.6	95.6	85.9	70.8	95.9	71.2	78.6	66.2	67.7	76.0	78.1
GCN [27]	-	-	-	-	-	-	-	-	-	-	-	-	-	-	-	-	-	-	-	76.9
DUC-HDC [32]	98.5	85.5	92.8	**58.6**	55.5	65.0	73.5	77.8	93.2	72.0	95.2	84.8	68.5	95.4	70.9	78.7	68.7	65.9	73.8	77.6
ResNet38 [33]	98.5	85.7	93.0	55.5	59.1	67.1	74.8	78.7	**93.7**	72.6	**95.5**	86.6	69.2	95.7	64.5	78.8	74.1	**69.0**	76.7	78.4
AAF [17]	98.5	85.6	93.0	53.8	58.9	65.9	75.0	78.4	**93.7**	72.4	95.6	86.4	70.5	95.9	73.9	82.7	76.9	68.7	76.4	79.1
SegModel [7]	**98.6**	**86.4**	92.8	52.4	59.7	59.6	72.5	78.3	93.3	**72.8**	95.5	85.4	70.1	95.6	75.4	84.1	75.1	68.7	75.0	78.5
DFN [38]	-	-	-	-	-	-	-	-	-	-	-	-	-	-	-	-	-	-	-	79.3
BiSeNet [37]	-	-	-	-	-	-	-	-	-	-	-	-	-	-	-	-	-	-	-	78.9
PSANet [43]	-	-	-	-	-	-	-	-	-	-	-	-	-	-	-	-	-	-	-	80.1
Ours	98.5	85.8	**93.3**	57.6	**63.1**	**68.7**	**76.1**	**80.3**	93.6	72.3	95.4	**87.0**	**72.2**	**96.1**	**75.4**	**88.2**	**77.8**	68.8	**76.4**	**80.4**

training and then we finetune our model on fine dataset jointly for another 15 epoch. Also, we use multi-scale inference when submitting to test server. Finally, we achieve 81.4 %mIoU which is the state-of-the art result compared with other video semantic segmentation methods. The results are shown in Table 6. Our method perform better than those [11,16] using flow to warp features which indicates effectiveness of direct motion information.

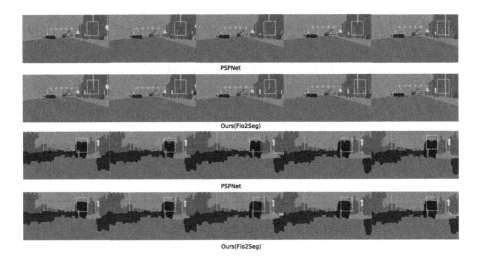

Fig. 4. More comparison of segmentation results of PSPNet and our results on Cityscapes video sequences. First two rows show our method handles missing small objects on successive frames while the last two rows show our method can remove ambiguities of the same object. Both are shown in red boxes. Best view in color and zoom in.

More Visible Results on Video Sequence. To further prove effectiveness and generality of our method, we show our method results on Cityscapes video clips in Fig. 4. We extract optical flow between each frame pair and take both flows and images as inputs. Compared with baseline PSPNet, our method can find missing objects like poles and eliminate ambiguities in the same truck. Since Flow2Seg is a lightweight module with ResNet18 as feature extractor, our method only costs a little extra computation cost compared with PSPNet but leads to better performance.

Table 6. Video semantic segmentation comparison experiments on Cityscapes test set. All the methods use both coarse and fine data.

Method	Backbone	Use optical flow	mIoU(%)
Netwarp [11]	ResNet101	Yes	80.5
STGRU [25]	ResNet101	Yes	80.2
VSPFL [16]	ResNet101	No	79.3
Ours	ResNet101	Yes	**81.4**

5   Conclusion

In this paper, Flow2Seg is proposed to use motion information to improve image semantic segmentation. By exploring this module with different optical flows processed by networks with different depths, we achieve comparable results on Cityscapes benchmark. In particular, we find the motion information provided by optical flow can enhance segmentation on object boundaries and small things in the scene. Our method is especially suitable for video semantic segmentation where both successive optical flows and image frames can be used as inputs. We will consider adding multi-frame optical flows into our module as the future work.

References

1. Bilinski, P., Prisacariu, V.: Dense decoder shortcut connections for single-pass semantic segmentation. In: CVPR (2018)
2. Chen, L.C., Papandreou, G., Kokkinos, I., Murphy, K., Yuille, A.L.: Semantic image segmentation with deep convolutional nets and fully connected CRFs. ICLR (2015)
3. Chen, L.C., Papandreou, G., Kokkinos, I., Murphy, K., Yuille, A.L.: DeepLab: semantic image segmentation with deep convolutional nets, atrous convolution, and fully connected CRFs. PAMI (2018)
4. Chen, L.C., Papandreou, G., Schroff, F., Adam, H.: Rethinking atrous convolution for semantic image segmentation. arXiv preprint arXiv:1706.05587 (2017)
5. Chen, L.-C., Zhu, Y., Papandreou, G., Schroff, F., Adam, H.: Encoder-decoder with atrous separable convolution for semantic image segmentation. In: Ferrari, V., Hebert, M., Sminchisescu, C., Weiss, Y. (eds.) ECCV 2018. LNCS, vol. 11211, pp. 833–851. Springer, Cham (2018). https://doi.org/10.1007/978-3-030-01234-2_49

6. Cordts, M., et al.: The cityscapes dataset for semantic urban scene understanding. In: CVPR (2016)
7. Shen, F., Gan, R., Yan, S., Zeng, G.: Semantic segmentation via structured patch prediction, context CRF and guidance CRF. In: CVPR (2017)
8. Farnebäck, G.: Two-frame motion estimation based on polynomial expansion. In: Bigun, J., Gustavsson, T. (eds.) SCIA 2003. LNCS, vol. 2749, pp. 363–370. Springer, Heidelberg (2003). https://doi.org/10.1007/3-540-45103-X_50
9. Fayyaz, M., Saffar, M.H., Sabokrou, M., Fathy, M., Klette, R., Huang, F.: STFCN: spatio-temporal FCN for semantic video segmentation. arXiv preprint arXiv:1608.05971 (2016)
10. Fischer, P., et al.: FlowNet: learning optical flow with convolutional networks. arXiv preprint arXiv:1504.06852 (2015)
11. Gadde, R., Jampani, V., Gehler, P.V.: Semantic video CNNs through representation warping. In: ICCV (2017)
12. He, K., Zhang, X., Ren, S., Sun, J.: Deep residual learning for image recognition. In: CVPR (2016)
13. Huang, G., Liu, Z., van der Maaten, L., Weinberger, K.Q.: Densely connected convolutional networks. In: CVPR (2017)
14. Ilg, E., Mayer, N., Saikia, T., Keuper, M., Dosovitskiy, A., Brox, T.: FlowNet 2.0: evolution of optical flow estimation with deep networks. In: CVPR (2017)
15. Ioffe, S., Szegedy, C.: Batch normalization: accelerating deep network training by reducing internal covariate shift. arXiv preprint arXiv:1502.03167 (2015)
16. Jin, X., et al.: Video scene parsing with predictive feature learning. In: ICCV (2017)
17. Ke, T.-W., Hwang, J.-J., Liu, Z., Yu, S.X.: Adaptive affinity fields for semantic segmentation. In: Ferrari, V., Hebert, M., Sminchisescu, C., Weiss, Y. (eds.) ECCV 2018. LNCS, vol. 11205, pp. 605–621. Springer, Cham (2018). https://doi.org/10. 1007/978-3-030-01246-5_36
18. Kingma, D.P., Ba, J.: Adam: a method for stochastic optimization. arXiv preprint arXiv:1412.6980 (2014)
19. Le, H.A., Baslamisli, A.S., Mensink, T., Gevers, T.: Three for one and one for three: flow, segmentation, and surface normals. arXiv preprint arXiv:1807.07473 (2018)
20. Liang, X., Zhou, H., Xing, E.: Dynamic-structured semantic propagation network. In: CVPR (2018)
21. Lin, D., Ji, Y., Lischinski, D., Cohen-Or, D., Huang, H.: Multi-scale context intertwining for semantic segmentation. In: Ferrari, V., Hebert, M., Sminchisescu, C., Weiss, Y. (eds.) ECCV 2018. LNCS, vol. 11207, pp. 622–638. Springer, Cham (2018). https://doi.org/10.1007/978-3-030-01219-9_37
22. Lin, G., Milan, A., Shen, C., Reid, I.D.: RefineNet: multi-path refinement networks for high-resolution semantic segmentation. In: CVPR (2017)
23. Liu, W., Rabinovich, A., Berg, A.C.: ParseNet: looking wider to see better. arXiv preprint arXiv:1506.04579 (2015)
24. Long, J., Shelhamer, E., Darrell, T.: Fully convolutional networks for semantic segmentation. In: CVPR (2015)
25. Nilsson, D., Sminchisescu, C.: Semantic video segmentation by gated recurrent flow propagation. In: CVPR (2018)
26. Paszke, A., et al.: Automatic differentiation in pytorch. In: NIPS-W (2017)
27. Peng, C., Zhang, X., Yu, G., Luo, G., Sun, J.: Large kernel matters – improve semantic segmentation by global convolutional network. In: CVPR (2017)

28. Ronneberger, O., Fischer, P., Brox, T.: U-net: convolutional networks for biomedical image segmentation. In: Navab, N., Hornegger, J., Wells, W.M., Frangi, A.F. (eds.) MICCAI 2015. LNCS, vol. 9351, pp. 234–241. Springer, Cham (2015). https://doi.org/10.1007/978-3-319-24574-4_28

29. Russakovsky, O., et al.: Imagenet large scale visual recognition challenge. IJCV **115**(3), 211–252 (2015)

30. Simonyan, K., Zisserman, A.: Two-stream convolutional networks for action recognition in videos. In: Advances in Neural Information Processing Systems, pp. 568–576 (2014)

31. Sun, D., Yang, X., Liu, M.Y., Kautz, J.: PWC-net: CNNs for optical flow using pyramid, warping, and cost volume. In: CVPR (2018)

32. Wang, P., et al.: Understanding convolution for semantic segmentation. In: WACV (2018)

33. Wu, Z., Shen, C., van den Hengel, A.: Wider or deeper: revisiting the resnet model for visual recognition. arXiv preprint arXiv:1611.10080 (2016)

34. Xingjian, S., Chen, Z., Wang, H., Yeung, D.Y., Wong, W.K., Woo, W.C.: Convolutional LSTM network: a machine learning approach for precipitation nowcasting. In: NIPS (2015)

35. Xu, D., Ouyang, W., Wang, X., Sebe, N.: PAD-net: multi-tasks guided prediction-and-distillation network for simultaneous depth estimation and scene parsing. In: CVPR (2018)

36. Yang, M., Yu, K., Zhang, C., Li, Z., Yang, K.: Denseaspp for semantic segmentation in street scenes. In: CVPR (2018)

37. Yu, C., Wang, J., Peng, C., Gao, C., Yu, G., Sang, N.: BiSeNet: bilateral segmentation network for real-time semantic segmentation. In: Ferrari, V., Hebert, M., Sminchisescu, C., Weiss, Y. (eds.) ECCV 2018. LNCS, vol. 11217, pp. 334–349. Springer, Cham (2018). https://doi.org/10.1007/978-3-030-01261-8_20

38. Yu, C., Wang, J., Peng, C., Gao, C., Yu, G., Sang, N.: Learning a discriminative feature network for semantic segmentation. In: CVPR (2018)

39. Zhang, H., et al.: Context encoding for semantic segmentation. In: CVPR (2018)

40. Zhang, R., Tang, S., Zhang, Y., Li, J., Yan, S.: Scale-adaptive convolutions for scene parsing. In: ICCV (2017)

41. Zhang, Z., Zhang, X., Peng, C., Xue, X., Sun, J.: ExFuse: enhancing feature fusion for semantic segmentation. In: Ferrari, V., Hebert, M., Sminchisescu, C., Weiss, Y. (eds.) ECCV 2018. LNCS, vol. 11214, pp. 273–288. Springer, Cham (2018). https://doi.org/10.1007/978-3-030-01249-6_17

42. Zhao, H., Shi, J., Qi, X., Wang, X., Jia, J.: Pyramid scene parsing network. In: CVPR (2017)

43. Zhao, H., et al.: PSANet: point-wise spatial attention network for scene parsing. In: Ferrari, V., Hebert, M., Sminchisescu, C., Weiss, Y. (eds.) ECCV 2018. LNCS, vol. 11213, pp. 270–286. Springer, Cham (2018). https://doi.org/10.1007/978-3-030-01240-3_17

COCO_TS Dataset: Pixel–Level Annotations Based on Weak Supervision for Scene Text Segmentation

Simone Bonechi$^{(\boxtimes)}$ ⓘ, Paolo Andreini ⓘ, Monica Bianchini ⓘ,
and Franco Scarselli ⓘ

DIISM, University of Siena, Via Roma 56, Siena, Italy
`simone.bonechi@unisi.it`

Abstract. The absence of large scale datasets with pixel–level supervisions is a significant obstacle for the training of deep convolutional networks for scene text segmentation. For this reason, synthetic data generation is normally employed to enlarge the training dataset. Nonetheless, synthetic data cannot reproduce the complexity and variability of natural images. In this paper, a weakly supervised learning approach is used to reduce the shift between training on real and synthetic data. Pixel–level supervisions for a text detection dataset (i.e. where only bounding–box annotations are available) are generated. In particular, the COCO–Text–Segmentation (COCO_TS) dataset, which provides pixel–level supervisions for the COCO–Text dataset, is created and released. The generated annotations are used to train a deep convolutional neural network for semantic segmentation. Experiments show that the proposed dataset can be used instead of synthetic data, allowing us to use only a fraction of the training samples and significantly improving the performances.

Keywords: Scene text segmentation · Weakly supervised learning · Bounding–box supervision · Convolutional Neural Networks

1 Introduction

Scene text segmentation is an important and challenging step in the extraction of textual information in natural images. It aims at making dense predictions in order to detect, for each pixel of an image, the presence of text. Convolutional Neural Networks (CNNs) are the state of the art in many computer vision tasks, including scene text segmentation. Nonetheless, their training is usually based on large sets of fully supervised data. To the best of our knowledge, only two public datasets are available for scene text segmentation, i.e. ICDAR–2013 [1] and Total–Text [2], that anyway contain a number of pixel–level annotated images barely sufficient to train a deep segmentation network. A solution to this problem

---

S. Bonechi and P. Andreini—Equal Contribution.

© Springer Nature Switzerland AG 2019
I. V. Tetko et al. (Eds.): ICANN 2019, LNCS 11729, pp. 238–250, 2019.
https://doi.org/10.1007/978-3-030-30508-6_20

has been proposed in [3], where a pixel–level supervision is produced employing the synthetic image generator introduced by [4]. However, unfortunately, there is no guarantee that a network trained on synthetic data will generalize to real images. This usually depends on the quality of the generated data (i.e. how much they are similar to real images), since the domain–shift may affect the generalization capability of the model.

In this paper, we propose to employ weak supervisions to improve the performances on real data. Indeed, a lot of datasets for text localization, in which the supervision is given by bounding–boxes around the text, are available (f.i. COCO text [5], ICDAR–2013 [1], ICDAR–2015 [6], and MLT [7]). In fact, obtaining this type of annotations is easier than providing a full pixel–level supervision, despite being less accurate. Inspired by [8], we adopt a training procedure that exploits these weak annotations. Specifically, the training procedure consists of two distinct steps.

1. A background–foreground network is trained on a large dataset of synthetically generated images with full pixel–level supervision. The purpose of this network is to recognize text within a bounding–box.
2. A scene text segmentation network is trained on a text localization dataset, in which the pixel–level supervision is obtained exploiting the output of the background–foreground network.

The logic behind this approach is that training a segmentation network focused on a bounding–box is a simpler task than using the entire image. In fact, inside a bounding–box, the text dimension is known (directly related to the box dimensions) and the background (i.e. non textual objects) variability is reduced. Moreover, the box annotation gives a precise information on the text position, since each pixel which is not included in a box does not represent text. Therefore, we exploit weak annotations to produce accurate pixel–level supervisions for a dataset of real images, which allows to reduce the domain–shift between synthetic and real data. In particular, employing the background–foreground network, the COCO–Text–Segmentation (COCO_TS) dataset, which contains pixel–level segmentation supervisions for the COCO–Text dataset [5], has been generated. COCO_TS is now publicly available[1] to foster reproducibility and to promote future research in scene text segmentation.

A series of experiments was conducted to evaluate the effectiveness of the proposed dataset compared to the use of synthetic data, as previously proposed in literature. The obtained results suggest that, using the COCO_TS dataset, a deep convolutional segmentation network can be trained more efficiently than using synthetic data, employing only a fraction of the learning set. Moreover, it is worth noting that the proposed procedure, used for COCO–Text, can be applied to generate pixel–level supervisions for any text localization dataset annotated at the bounding–box level.

The paper is organized as follows. In Sect. 2 related works are briefly reviewed. In Sect. 3 the COCO_TS generation procedure is described. Section 4 reports the

---

[1] http://clem.diism.unisi.it/~coco_ts/.

experimental setup and the results obtained in scene text segmentation on the ICDAR–2013 and Total–Text datasets. Finally, some conclusions are drawn in Sect. 5.

2   Related Works

The proposed method is related to four main research topics, namely synthetic data generation, bounding–boxes for semantic segmentation, semantic segmentation with CNNs, and scene text segmentation, whose literature is reviewed in the following.

Synthetic Data Generation. Synthetic datasets are a cheap and scalable alternative to the human ground–truth supervision in machine learning. Recently, several papers reported on the use of synthetic data to face a variety of different problems. Large collections of synthetic images of driving scenes in urban environments were generated in [10], synthetic indoor scenes have been exploited by [9], while artificial images of Petri plates were created in [11]. In text analysis, [12] proposed the use of synthetic data for text spotting, localization and recognition. An improved synthetic data generator for text localization in natural images was proposed by [4]. This synthetic data generator engine has been modified in [3] to extract pixel–wise segmentation annotations. Similarly to [3], in this work, the engine proposed in [4] was used for scene text segmentation.

Bounding–Boxes for Semantic Segmentation. In order to reduce the data labeling efforts, weakly supervised approaches aim at learning from weak annotations, such as image–level tags, partial labels, bounding–boxes, etc. Bounding–box supervision was used to aid semantic segmentation in [13], where the core idea is that to iterate between automatically generating region proposals and training convolutional networks. Similarly, in [14], an Expectation–Maximization algorithm was used to iteratively update the training supervision. Instead, in [15], a GrabCut–like algorithm is employed to generate training labels from bounding boxes. Finally, more related to this work, in [8], the segmentation supervision for a semantic segmentation network is directly produced from bounding–box annotations, exploiting a deep CNN.

Semantic Segmentation with CNNs. Image semantic segmentation aims at inferring the class of each pixel of an image. Recent semantic segmentation algorithms often convert existing CNN architectures, designed for image classification, to fully convolutional networks [16]. Generally, these networks have an encoder–decoder structure. Moreover, the level of details required by semantic segmentation inspired the use of dilated convolution to enlarge the receptive field without decreasing the resolution [17]. Besides, different solutions have been proposed to deal with the presence of objects at different scales. The Pyramid Scene Parsing Network (PSPNet) [18] applies a pyramid of pooling to collect contextual information at different scales. Instead, Deeplab [19] employs atrous spatial pyramid pooling, which consists of parallel dilated convolutions with different rates.

Scene Text Segmentation. Document image segmentation has a long history and was originally based on thresholding approaches (local, global or adaptive) [20–22]. The application of these methods to scene text segmentation is quite challenging, due to the high variability of conditions that can be found in natural images. To face this variability, in [23], low level features are used to identify the seed points of texts and backgrounds and then to segment the text using semi–supervised learning. In [24], the binarization of scene text has been formulated as a Markov Random Field model optimization problem, where the optimal binarization is obtained iteratively with Graph Cuts. To improve the segmentation performance, a multilevel maximally stable extremal region approach, applied together with a text candidate selection algorithm based on hand–extracted text–specific features, has been presented in [25]. Finally, in [3], a CNN approach to scene text segmentation is described, which employs three stages for extraction, refinement and classification.

3   Materials and Methods

In the following, a general overview of the proposed method is provided. The sets of data involved in the creation of the COCO_TS dataset are introduced in Sect. 3.1. Section 3.2 describes the weakly supervised approach used to generate COCO_TS and finally, in Sect. 3.3, the COCO_TS dataset is used to train a deep segmentation network.

3.1   Datasets

Synthetic Dataset. In this work, the same generation process proposed by [4] has been employed to create a large set of synthetic scene text images. The engine renders synthetic text to existing background images, accounting for the local three dimensional scene geometry. A synthetic dataset of about 800000 images was generated following this procedure. From this set of images, about 1000000 image crops have been extracted. Specifically, for each word, a bounding–box is defined and enlarged by a factor of 0.3, and then the image is cropped around the bounding–box. These bounding boxes have been used to train the background–foreground network described in Sect. 3.2.

COCO–Text. The COCO–2014 dataset [26], firstly released by Microsoft Corporation, collects instance–level fully annotated images of natural scenes. COCO–Text [5] is based on COCO–2014 and contains a total of 63686 images, split in 43686 training, 10000 validation, 10000 test images, supervised at the bounding–box level for text localization. Differently from other scene text datasets, the COCO–2014 dataset was not collected specifically for the extraction of textual information, hence some of its images do not contain text. Therefore, for the generation of the proposed COCO_TS dataset, a subset of 14690 images have been selected from COCO–Text, each one at least including a bounding–box labeled as legible, machine printed, and written in English.

ICDAR–2013. The ICDAR–2013 [1] dataset collects a training and a test set containing 229 and 233 images, respectively. The images are extracted from ICDAR–2011 [27], after the removal of duplicated images and with some revisited ground–truth annotations. The scene text segmentation challenge in the ICDAR–2015 competition [6] was based on the same datasets as ICDAR–2013.

Total–Text. Total–Text [2] is a scene text dataset which collects 1255 training images and 300 test images with a pixel–level supervision. Differently from ICDAR–2013, where texts have always a horizontal appearance, this dataset contains images with texts showing highly diversified orientations.

3.2   COCO_TS Dataset

Collecting supervised images for scene text segmentation is costly and time consuming. In fact, only few datasets with a reduced number of images are available. Instead, numerous datasets provide bounding–box level annotations for text detection. In this paper, we introduce the COCO_TS dataset, which provides 14690 pixel–level supervisions for the COCO–Text images. The supervision is obtained from the available bounding–boxes of the COCO–Text dataset exploiting a weakly supervised algorithm. The supervision generation procedure is explained in the following and summarized in Fig. 1.

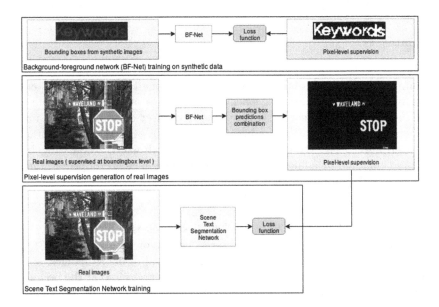

Fig. 1. Scheme of the supervision generation procedure. Steps 1. to 3. are sketched starting from the top.

Supervision Generation of COCO_TS

The supervision generation consists of three different steps.

1. A background–foreground network is trained on synthetic data to extract text from bounding–boxes.
2. The background–foreground network is employed to generate pixel–level supervisions for real images of the COCO_TS dataset.
3. A scene text segmentation network is trained on the real images with the generated supervisions.

Background–Foreground Network. A deep neural network is trained to segment the text inside a bounding–box, thus separating the background from the foreground. The rationale beneath the proposed approach is that realizing a background–foreground segmentation, constrained to a bounding–box, is significantly simpler than producing the segmentation of the whole image. For this reason, we suppose that even if trained on synthetic data, the background–foreground network can effectively be used to segment text in bounding boxes extracted from real images. To train the background–foreground network, pixel–level supervisions of a significant number of bounding–boxes is required. The 1000000 bounding–box crops extracted from the synthetic dataset have been used to this purpose.

Pixel–Level Supervision Generation. After the training phase, the background–foreground network is applied on the bounding–boxes extracted from the COCO–Text dataset. For each image, the pixel–level supervision is obtained combining the probability maps (calculated by the background–foreground network) for all the bounding–boxes inside the image. It can happen that a region belongs to more than one bounding box at the same time (f.i., two written texts close to each other could have overlapping bounding–boxes) and, in this case, the prediction with the highest foreground probability value is considered. The final pixel–wise annotation $l(x, y)$, at position (x, y), is obtained employing two fixed thresholds, th_1 and th_2, on the probability maps $prob(x, y)$:

$$l(x, y) = \begin{cases} background & \text{if} \quad prob(x, y) < th_1 \\ foreground & \text{if} \quad prob(x, y) > th_2 \\ uncertain & \text{otherwise} \end{cases} \tag{1}$$

The two thresholds th_1 and th_2 have been fixed to 0.3 and 0.7, respectively, based on a grid search approach. If $prob(x, y) \in (th_1, th_2)$, then (x, y) is labeled as uncertain. To provide a significant pixel–level supervision, bounding–boxes that are not labeled as legible, machine printed and written in English have been added to the uncertainty region. The insertion in the generated supervision of this uncertainty region proves to be effective, avoiding the gradient propagation in regions where text could be potentially misclassified with the background. This procedure has been used to extract the COCO_TS dataset. Some examples of the obtained supervisions are reported in Fig. 2.

Fig. 2. The original images and the generated supervisions, on the top and at the bottom, respectively. The background is colored in black, the foreground in red, and the uncertainty region in yellow. (Color figure online)

3.3 Scene Text Segmentation

The COCO_TS dataset is used to train a deep segmentation network (bottom of Fig. 1) for scene text segmentation of both the ICDAR–2013 and Total–Text datasets. The effects obtained by the use of the COCO_TS dataset, as an alternative to synthetic data, will be described in the next section.

4   Experiments

In the following, our experimental setup is shown. In particular, Sect. 4.1 and Sect. 4.2 introduce the segmentation network and define the implementation details used in our experimental setup. In Sect. 4.3, the generated annotations for the COCO_TS dataset are evaluated, whereas Sect. 4.4 assesses the insertion of the COCO_TS dataset during the training of a scene text segmentation network.

4.1   PSPNet

All the experiments are carried out with the PSPNet architecture [18], originally designed for semantic segmentation of natural images. This model, like most of the other semantic segmentation networks, takes an image as input and produces a per–pixel prediction. The PSPNet is a deep convolutional neural network, built on the ResNet model for image classification. To enlarge the receptive field of the neural network, a set of dilated convolutions replaces standard convolutions in the ResNet part of the network. The ResNet encoder produces a set of feature maps and a pyramid pooling module is used to gather context information. Finally, an upsample layer transforms, by bilinear interpolation, the low–dimension feature maps to the resolution of the original image. A convolutional layer produces the final per–pixel prediction. In this work, to better handle the presence of thin text and similarly to [3], we modified the network structure adding a two level convolutional decoder.

4.2   Implementation Details

The PSPNet architectures, used both for the background–foreground network and for scene text segmentation, are implemented in TensorFlow. Due to computational issues, in this work, the PSPNet based on the ResNet50 model is used as the CNN encoder. The experiments are realized based on the training procedure explained in the following. As far as the background–foreground network is considered, the image crops are resized so that the min side dimension is equal to 185, while maintaining the original aspect–ratio. Random crops of 185×185 are used during training. Instead, for the scene text segmentation network, the input images have not been resized, and random crops of 281×281 are extracted for training. A multi–scale approach is employed during training and test. In the evaluation phase, a sliding window strategy is used for both the networks. The Adam optimizer [28], with a learning rate of 10^{-4}, has been used to train the network. The experimentation was carried out in a Debian environment, with a single NVIDIA GeForce GTX 1080 Ti GPU.

4.3   Evaluation of the Supervision Generation Procedure

The quality of the generation procedure cannot be assessed on COCO–Text, due to the absence of pixel–level targets. Therefore, we used the ICDAR–2013 dataset for which ground–truth labels are available. Following the procedure described in Sect. 3.2, the segmentation annotations for the ICDAR–2013 test set have been extracted and compared to the original ground–truth. The results, measured using the pixel–level precision, recall and F1 score, are reported in Table 1. For this analysis, the uncertainty region has been considered as text. A qualitative evaluation of the generated supervision for the COCO_TS dataset is reported in Fig. 2.

Table 1. Results of the annotation generation approach on the ICDAR–2013 test set.

	Precision	Recall	F1 Score
Proposed approach	89.10%	70.74%	78.87%

4.4   Scene Text Segmentation Evaluation

Due to the inherent difficulties in collecting large sets of pixel–level supervised images, only few public datasets are available for scene text segmentation. To face this problem, in [3], synthetic data generation has been employed. Nevertheless, due to the domain–shift, there is no guarantee that a network trained on synthetic data would generalize well also to real images. The COCO_TS dataset actually contains real images and, therefore, we expect that, when used for network training, the domain–shift can be reduced. To test this hypothesis, the PSPNet is used for scene text segmentation and evaluated on the ICDAR–2013 and Total–Text test sets, that provides pixel–level annotations. In particular, the following experimental setups have been compared:

– **Synth:** The training relies only on the synthetically generated images;
– **Synth + COCO_TS:** The network is pre–trained on the synthetic dataset and fine–tuned on the COCO_TS images;
– **COCO_TS:** The network is trained only on the COCO_TS dataset.

The influence of fine–tuning on the ICDAR–2013 and Total–Text datasets was also evaluated. The results, measured using the pixel–level precision, recall and F1 score, are reported in Table 2a and b, respectively. It is worth noting that training the network using the COCO_TS dataset is more effective than using synthetic images. Specifically, employing the proposed dataset, the F1 Score is improved of 10.17% and 31.40% on ICDAR–2013 and Total–Text, respectively. These results are quite surprising and prove that the proposed dataset substantially increases the network performance, reducing the domain–shift from synthetic to real images. If the network is fine–tuned on ICDAR–2013 and

Table 2. Scene text segmentation performances using synthetic data and/or the proposed COCO_TS dataset. The notation "+ Dataset" indicates that a fine–tune procedure has been carried out on "Dataset". The last column reports the relative increment, with and without fine–tuning, compared to the use of synthetic data only.

	Precision	Recall	F1 Score	
Synth	73.19%	55.67%	63.23%	–
Synth + COCO_TS	77.80%	70.14%	**73.77%**	**+10.54%**
COCO_TS	78.86%	68.66%	73.40%	+10.17%
Synth + ICDAR–2013	81.12%	78.33%	79.70%	–
Synth + COCO_TS + ICDAR–2013	80.08%	79.53%	80.15%	+0.45%
COCO_TS + ICDAR–2013	81.68%	79.16%	**80.40%**	**+0.70%**

(a) Results on the ICDAR–2013 test set

	Precision	Recall	F1 Score	
Synth	55.76%	22.87%	32.43%	–
Synth + COCO_TS	72.71%	54.49%	62.29%	+29.86%
COCO_TS	72.83%	56.81%	**63.83%**	**+31.40%**
Synth + Total Text	84.97%	65.52%	73.98%	–
Synth + COCO_TS + Total Text	84.65%	66.93%	74.75%	+0.77%
COCO_TS + Total Text	84.31%	68.03%	**75.30%**	**+1.32%**

(b) Results on the Total–Text test set

Total–Text, the relative difference between the use of synthetic images and the COCO_TS dataset is reduced, but still remains significant. Specifically, the F1 Score is improved by 0.70% on ICDAR–2013 and 1.32% on Total–Text. Fur-

(a)   (b)   (c)   (d)   (e)

Fig. 3. Results on the ICDAR–2013 test set. In (a) the original image, in (b), (c) and (d) the segmentation obtained with Synth, Synth+COCO_TS and COCO_TS setups, respectively. The ground–truth supervision is reported in (e).

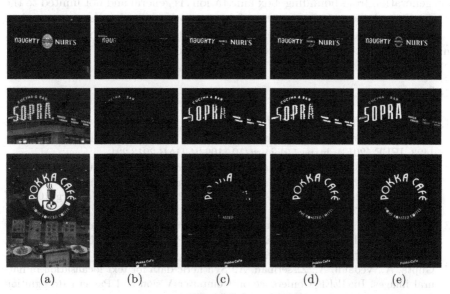

(a)   (b)   (c)   (d)   (e)

Fig. 4. Results on the Total–Text test set. In (a) the original image, in (b), (c) and (d) the segmentation obtained with Synth, Synth+COCO_TS and COCO_TS setups, respectively. The ground–truth supervision is reported in (e).

thermore, it can be observed that using only COCO_TS provides comparable results as training the network with both the synthetic and the proposed dataset. Therefore, the two datasets are not complementary and, in fact, the proposed COCO_TS is a valid alternative to synthetic data generation for scene text segmentation. Indeed, the use of real images increases the sample efficiency, allowing to substantially reduce the number of samples needed for training. In particular, the COCO_TS dataset contains 14690 samples that are less than 1/50 of the synthetic dataset cardinality. Some qualitative output results of the scene text segmentation network are shown in Figs. 3 and 4.

5   Conclusions

In this paper, a weakly supervised learning approach has been used to generate pixel–level supervisions for scene text segmentation. Exploiting the proposed approach, the COCO_TS dataset, which contains the segmentation ground–truth for a subset of the COCO–Text dataset, has been automatically generated. Unlike previous approaches based on synthetic images, a convolutional neural network is trained on real images from the COCO_TS dataset for scene text segmentation, showing a very significant improvement in the generalization on both the ICDAR–2013 and Total–Text datasets, although with only a fraction of the samples. To foster further research on scene text segmentation, the COCO_TS dataset has been released. Interestingly, our procedure for pixel–level supervision generation from bounding–box annotations is general and not limited to the COCO–Text dataset. It is a matter of future work to employ the same method to extract pixel–level supervisions for different text localization problems (f.i., on multilingual scene text datasets, such as MLT [7]).

References

1. Karatzas, D., et al.: ICDAR 2013 robust reading competition. In: 2013 12th International Conference on Document Analysis and Recognition (ICDAR), pp. 1484–1493. IEEE (2013). https://doi.org/10.1109/ICDAR.2013.221
2. Ch'ng, C.K., Chan, C.S.: Total-text: a comprehensive dataset for scene text detection and recognition. In: 14th IAPR International Conference on Document Analysis and Recognition (ICDAR), pp. 935–942 (2017). https://doi.org/10.1109/ICDAR.2017.157
3. Tang, Y., Wu, X.: Scene text detection and segmentation based on cascaded convolution neural networks. IEEE Trans. Image Process. 26(3), 1509–1520 (2017). https://doi.org/10.1109/TIP.2017.2656474
4. Gupta, A., Vedaldi, A., Zisserman, A.: Synthetic data for text localisation in natural images. In: IEEE Conference on Computer Vision and Pattern Recognition (2016). https://doi.org/10.1109/CVPR.2016.254
5. Veit, A., Matera, T., Neumann, L., Matas, J., Belongie, S.: Coco-text: Dataset and benchmark for text detection and recognition in natural images. arXiv preprint arXiv:1601.07140 (2016). http://vision.cornell.edu/se3/wp-content/uploads/2016/01/1601.07140v1.pdf

6. Karatzas, D., et al.: ICDAR 2015 competition on robust reading. In: 2015 13th International Conference on Document Analysis and Recognition (ICDAR), pp. 1156–1160. IEEE (2015). https://doi.org/10.1109/ICDAR

7. RRC-MLT: Mlt: Competition on multi-lingual scene text detection and script identification. http://rrc.cvc.uab.es/?ch=8&com=introduction

8. Bonechi, S., Andreini, P., Bianchini, M., Scarselli, F.: Generating bounding box supervision for semantic segmentation with deep learning. In: Pancioni, L., Schwenker, F., Trentin, E. (eds.) ANNPR 2018. LNCS (LNAI), vol. 11081, pp. 190–200. Springer, Cham (2018). https://doi.org/10.1007/978-3-319-99978-4_15

9. Handa, A., Patraucean, V., Badrinarayanan, V., Stent, S., Cipolla, R.: Synthcam3d: Semantic understanding with synthetic indoor scenes. arXiv preprint arXiv:1505.00171 (2015). https://doi.org/10.17863/CAM.26487

10. Ros, G., Sellart, L., Materzynska, J., Vazquez, D., Lopez, A.M.: The synthia dataset: a large collection of synthetic images for semantic segmentation of urban scenes. In: Proceedings of the IEEE Conference on Computer Vision and Pattern Recognition, pp. 3234–3243 (2016). https://doi.org/10.1109/CVPR.2016.352

11. Andreini, P., Bonechi, S., Bianchini, M., Mecocci, A., Scarselli, F.: A deep learning approach to bacterial colony segmentation. In: Kůrková, V., Manolopoulos, Y., Hammer, B., Iliadis, L., Maglogiannis, I. (eds.) ICANN 2018. LNCS, vol. 11141, pp. 522–533. Springer, Cham (2018). https://doi.org/10.1007/978-3-030-01424-7_51

12. Jaderberg, M., Simonyan, K., Vedaldi, A., Zisserman, A.: Reading text in the wild with convolutional neural networks. Int. J. Comput. Vis. **116**(1), 1–20 (2016). https://doi.org/10.1007/s11263-015-0823-z

13. Dai, J., He, K., Sun, J.: Boxsup: exploiting bounding boxes to supervise convolutional networks for semantic segmentation. In: Proceedings of the IEEE International Conference on Computer Vision, pp. 1635–1643 (2015). https://doi.org/10.1109/ICCV.2015.191

14. Papandreou, G., Chen, L., Murphy, K.P., Yuille, A.L.: Weakly-and semi-supervised learning of a deep convolutional network for semantic image segmentation. In: 2015 IEEE International Conference on Computer Vision (ICCV), pp. 1742–1750. https://doi.org/10.1109/ICCV.2015.203

15. Khoreva, A., Benenson, R., Hosang, J., Hein, M., Schiele, B.: Simple does it: weakly supervised instance and semantic segmentation. In: Proceedings of the IEEE Conference on Computer Vision and Pattern Recognition, pp. 876–885 (2017). https://doi.org/10.1109/CVPR.2017.181

16. Long, J., Shelhamer, E., Darrell, T.: Fully convolutional networks for semantic segmentation. In: Proceedings of the IEEE Conference on Computer Vision and Pattern Recognition, pp. 3431–3440 (2015). https://doi.org/10.1109/CVPR.2015.7298965

17. Papandreou, G., Kokkinos, I., Savalle, P.A.: Untangling local and global deformations in deep convolutional networks for image classification and sliding window detection. arXiv preprint arXiv:1412.0296 (2014)

18. Zhao, H., Shi, J., Qi, X., Wang, X., Jia, J.: Pyramid scene parsing network. In: 2017 IEEE Conference on Computer Vision and Pattern Recognition (CVPR), pp. 6230–6239 (2017). https://doi.org/10.1109/CVPR.2017.660

19. Chen, L.C., Papandreou, G., Kokkinos, I., Murphy, K., Yuille, A.L.: Deeplab: semantic image segmentation with deep convolutional nets, atrous convolution, and fully connected CRFs. IEEE Trans. Pattern Anal. Mach. Intell. **40**(4), 834–848 (2017). https://doi.org/10.1109/TPAMI.2017.2699184

20. Otsu, N.: A threshold selection method from gray-level histograms. IEEE Trans. Syst. Man Cybern. **9**(1), 62–66 (1979). https://doi.org/10.1109/TSMC.1979.4310076
21. Su, B., Lu, S., Tan, C.L.: Binarization of historical document images using the local maximum and minimum. In: Proceedings of the 9th IAPR International Workshop on Document Analysis Systems, pp. 159–166. ACM (2010). https://doi.org/10.1016/j.patcog.2005.09.010
22. Howe, N.R.: A Laplacian energy for document binarization. In: 2011 International Conference on Document Analysis and Recognition (ICDAR), pp. 6–10. IEEE (2011). https://doi.org/10.1109/ICDAR.2011.11
23. Bai, B., Yin, F., Liu, C.L.: A seed-based segmentation method for scene text extraction. In: 2014 11th IAPR International Workshop on Document Analysis Systems (DAS), pp. 262–266. IEEE (2014). https://doi.org/10.1109/DAS.2014.34
24. Mishra, A., Alahari, K., Jawahar, C.: An MRF model for binarization of natural scene text. In: ICDAR-International Conference on Document Analysis and Recognition. IEEE (2011). https://doi.org/10.1109/ICDAR.2011.12
25. Tian, S., Lu, S., Su, B., Tan, C.L.: Scene text segmentation with multi-level maximally stable extremal regions. In: 2014 22nd International Conference on Pattern Recognition (ICPR), pp. 2703–2708. IEEE (2014). https://doi.org/10.1109/ICPR.2014.467
26. Lin, T.-Y., et al.: Microsoft COCO: common objects in context. In: Fleet, D., Pajdla, T., Schiele, B., Tuytelaars, T. (eds.) ECCV 2014. LNCS, vol. 8693, pp. 740–755. Springer, Cham (2014). https://doi.org/10.1007/978-3-319-10602-1_48
27. Shahab, A., Shafait, F., Dengel, A.: ICDAR 2011 robust reading competition challenge 2: reading text in scene images. In: 2011 International Conference on Document Analysis and Recognition (ICDAR), pp. 1491–1496. IEEE (2011). https://doi.org/10.1109/ICDAR.2011.296
28. Kingma, D.P., Ba, J.: Adam: A method for stochastic optimization. arXiv preprint arXiv:1412.6980 (2014)

Occluded Object Recognition

Learning Deep Structured Multi-scale Features for Crisp and Object Occlusion Edge Detection

Zihao Dong[1] , Ruixun Zhang[2], and Xiuli Shao[1]([⊠])

[1] College of Computer Science, Nankai University, Tian Jin, China
1120170132@mail.nankai.edu.cn, shaoxl@nankai.edu.cn
[2] MIT Laboratory for Financial Engineering, Cambridge, MA, USA
zhangruixun@gmail.com

Abstract. The key challenge for edge detection is that predicted edges are thick and need Non-Maximum Suppression to post-process to obtain crisp edges. In addition, object occlusion edge detection is an important research problem in computer vision. To increase the crispness and accuracy of occlusion relationships effectively, we propose a novel method of edge detection called MSDF (Multi Scale Decode and Fusion) based on deep structured multi-scale features to generate crisp salient edges in this paper. The decoder layer of MSDF can fuse the adjacent-scale features and increase the affinity between the features. We also propose a novel loss function to solve the class imbalance in object occlusion edge detection and a two streams learning framework to predict edge and occlusion orientation. Extensive experiments on BSDS500 dataset and the larger NYUD dataset show that the effectiveness of the proposed model and of the overall hierarchical framework. We also surpass the state of the art on the BSDS ownership dataset in occlusion edge detection.

Keywords: Crisp edge · Occlusion relationship ·
Multi Scale Decode and Fusion · Occlusion edge detection

1 Introduction

Edge detection aims on extracting the salient edge or getting the relationship between foreground and background from the input image with complex background accurately. Convolutional Neural Networks (CNNs) have become a recent trend to improve the state of varieties of methods and the performance of training models.

CNN is no longer dependent on the manual design of researchers for learning image features unlike traditional methods. Though training large quantities of image data, it tends to get general features such as intensity, depth, and texture. These features are usually used to get a classifier by supervised learning of edge detection, and the classifier will predict the edge and non-edge pixels. But edge detection is still a very challenging problem and remains unsolved due to

© Springer Nature Switzerland AG 2019
I. V. Tetko et al. (Eds.): ICANN 2019, LNCS 11729, pp. 253–266, 2019.
https://doi.org/10.1007/978-3-030-30508-6_21

(a)   (b)   (c)   (d)

Fig. 1. The crispness comparison from the BSDS500 dataset between our method MSDF and the other two methods. (a) Is the input image. (b) Is the predicted result of HED [18]. (c) Is the predicted result of RCF [7]. (d) Is the predicted result of MSDF. They do not apply post-processing.

the facts that: (1) The prediction of many CNN-based methods is much thicker than the ground truth, although predicted edge can be obtained in the thinning post-processing way, the quality of CNN-based model prediction need to be improved. (2) Object occlusion boundary detection [15,16] is an important distinction between foreground and background, but it relies on having precise object boundary.

This paper mainly has two parts. The first one is to propose a new edge detection method called MSDF (Multi Scale Decode and Fusion) based on learning multi-scale features. MSDF can extract the edge features of 5 scales in VGG-16 network [14] using a novel bottom-up decoder architecture, learn high-resolution feature map with rich semantic information and predict crisp results without postprocessing. In feature encoder part, a new fusion strategy for adjacent scales is proposed which has a refinement module with a *Resnet* block [14] and *subpixel* [12] up-sampling layer. Figure 1 shows three examples from HED (Holistically-nested Edge Detection) detector [18], RCF (Richer Convolutional Features) detector [7] and MSDF detector, we can find the crispness of MSDF is better than the other two methods, which generate the crisp edge map that closed to Ground Truth. Finally, in order to solve the class imbalance, a novel loss function is defined though adding modulating factors of focal loss to HED cross entropy loss, then we use weighted summation method between our loss function and HED cross entropy loss function, and final loss [6] function is achieved.

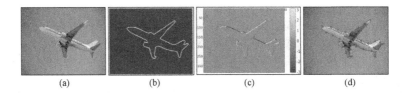

(a)   (b)   (c)   (d)

Fig. 2. An example image and its ground truth in the PIOD dataset. (a) Is the input image. (b) Is the annotated edge map. (c) Is the annotated occlusion orientation map. (d) Is the notation of occlusion edge by red arrows, the left side of each arrow is the salient object. (Color figure online)

The second one is using MSDF model to achieve occlusion object edge detection. Our proposed network can share convolutional features to predict object edge and occlusion orientation, which can be seen as the process of two streams learning. Figure 2 is an example in the Pascal Instance Occlusion Dataset (PIOD) [16], which defines a occlusion relationships to distinguish background and salient object. As mentioned in [16], the left side of the arrows is foreground.

The remainder of this paper is structured as follows. In Sect. 2, the related work is introduced in edge detection and occlusion boundary detection. Section 3 describes the overall framework of the proposed method. Section 4 introduces the occlusion boundary detection structure based on MSDF. Section 5 presents the experiment and application. Section 6 concludes this paper.

2   Related Work

This paper focuses on edge detection in images with complex background and occlusion boundary detection. Typically, some traditional methods focus on extracting local cues of brightness, colors, gradients and textures, or other manually designed features. As for the local edge feature detectors, Arbelaez et al. [1] combine multi-scale local brightness, color and texture cues into a globalization framework using spectral clustering to detect salient edge. Dollar et al. [2] present structured edge detector SE to construct a structured decision tree for edge detection, where PCA is used to achieve data dimensionality reduction and the random forest is used to capture the structured information.

In recent years, CNN-based method began to be applied and achieve impressive performance in the edge detection. Shen et al. [11] use k-means clustering method to classify image patches and multi-class shape patches is extracted through a 6-layer CNN network, then structured random forest is used to further classify the edge to obtain more discriminative features. Xie and Tu [18] propose a deep learning model combining full convolutional network (FCN) [8] and deeply supervised nets [5] to detect edges. Based on the deep learning model of [18], some methods focus on improving the network structure to generate better features for performing the pixel-wise prediction, such as RCF [7] and CED [17], other methods add some useful components to achieve better accuracy, such as Deep Boundary [4] and COB [9].

To estimate the occlusion relationships on edge detection, DOC builded a deep convolutional network on the FCN literature, it adapted HED network to perform occlusion boundary and orientation two tasks separately, its another contribution is creating a dataset called the PASCAL instance occlusion dataset (PIOD) and achieved a state-of-the-art performance. Similar to DOC [16], DOOBNet [15] proposed an encoder-decoder architecture [19] with skip connection and dilated convolutional layer, it is a deep end-to-end multitask network including occlusion boundary and orientation, a novel loss function called *AttentionLoss* is used to solve class imbalance problem.

3   MSDF Model

3.1   Network Architecture

Overview. The overall network architecture of the proposed MSDF model is illustrated in Fig. 3. The MSDF model leverages a bottom-up decoded pathway to complete the fusion of multi-layer features. It consists of two sub-networks: (1) a VGG-16 sub-net that extracts top-down multi-scale features, (2) a decoder sub-net to decode bottom-up feature information. Each branch produces different edge maps at different layers of this network, such as VGG-16 convolutional layer (1–5). In the decoder sub-net, each fine module fuses a bottom-up feature map from its bottom layer with a top-down feature map from the convolutional layer in VGG-16 network. We average 1×1 convolutional layer behind the last decoder layer them to generate the final edge map.

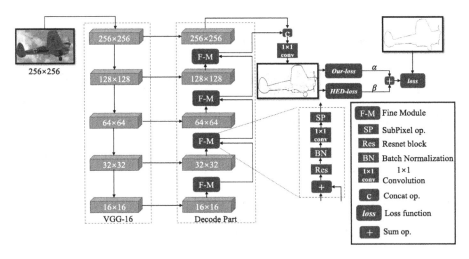

Fig. 3. Architecture of the proposed multi-scale deep learning MSDF model. (Color figure online)

Top-Down Scale Feature Extraction. The top-down architecture is based on that of FCN. In Fig. 3, we extract side features from each scale from VGG-16, respectively $conv1\_2$, $conv2\_2$, $conv3\_3$, $conv4\_3$ and $conv5\_3$, which will be the input scale features of decoder sub-net. The number inside the blue cubes is the size of output feature map.

Bottom-Up Decoder Sub-net. The modules of decoder are associated with each side conv-layer in VGG-16 Net. Each fine module of this sub-net up-samples the map by a factor $(2\times)$ and fuses with the output of left side layers in Fig. 3.

For bottom to up pathway, the number convolutional layer is set to 1024 for the bottom layer, this value is reduced by 2 times from bottom layer to top layer. For example, the first conv-layer on the top of the bottom layer will have 256 feature channels, the second and third bottom-up module will have 128 and 64 feature channels respectively. We add the *Resnet* block and batch normalization in the fine module, which can extract more refined features and prevent over-fitting of training result. In this sub-net, up-sampling and fusion is important for better resolution and affinity of prediction edges.

Up-Sample of Decoder Sub-net. In order to improve the image resolution after up-sampling, the *subpixel* method is used to perform standard convolution processing on the low-scale features, which can generate a feature map of $r^2 \times c$ feature channels with the same resolution through a standard convolutional operation.

Fusion Method of Decoder Sub-net. In the decoder sub-net of MSDF model, the number of feature channels of different scales is not the same, splicing two feature matrices directly will lead to lost some low-dimensional features. Therefore, this paper reduces the dimensions of high-scale features by increasing the number of convolutional layers, which generates the same number of channels as low-scale features. In Fig. 3, we add some fine modules such as convolutional layers and PS operation above to realize the fuse between two different feature maps.

3.2 Learning and Deployment

The image edge detection problem can be expressed as a general mathematical form. This paper uses X_n to represent the image in data layer, which is generally transformed into a multidimensional matrix, Y_n denotes the set of edge feature pixels of the Ground Truth $Y_n = \{y_j^{(n)}, j = 1, ..., |X_n|\}$ Where $|X_n|$ represents the number of pixels in the image n. $P(y_j = 1|X_n)$ is defined to represent the probability of predicted pixel labeled by annotator. A threshold μ is defined here (the paper sets μ to 0.5). When $P(y_j = 1|X_n)$ is greater than 0 and less than μ, the pixel is controversial and should not be considered. The image training data will be represented as $S = \{(X_n, Y_n), n = 1, 2, ..., N\}$, where N is the number of training images.

We compute the loss functions of the top-down architecture and the decoder sub-net at every pixel with respect to the Ground Truth pixel label as:
When $P(y_j = 1|X_n) \geq \mu$,

$$l_{side}(W, X_n) = -\beta \sum_{j \in y^+} \log P(y_j = 1|X_n, W)$$

$$-(1-\beta) \sum_{j \in y^-} \log P(y_j = 0|X_n, W)$$

$$(1)$$

where W denotes all the parameters that will be learned in MSDF model.

When $0 < P(y_j = 1|X_n) < \mu$, $l_{side}(W, X_n) = 0$.

In which

$$\beta = \frac{0.9 \cdot |Y_-|}{|Y_-| + |Y_+|}; 1 - \beta = \frac{|Y_+|}{|Y_-| + |Y_+|} \tag{2}$$

Y_+ denote positive sample set and Y_- is negative sample set. 0.9 is set to balance positive and negative samples.

In the experimental process, we found that the single using of the above loss function l_{side} would lead to over-learning problem, which is caused by class imbalance of positive (edge) and negative (non-edge) samples. From the perspective of pixel level, we can see that the distribution of edge/non-edge is heavily unbalanced in Fig. 6: 90% of ground truth is non-edge. However, they are commonly used in large false negative or false positive examples bi-classification and multi-classification problems. So we refer to the design idea of focal loss and literature [10], two modulation factors $\alpha^{(1-P)^{\gamma}}$ and $\alpha^{P^{\gamma}}$ are added to the l_{side} loss function, which is defined as follow:

We express $P(y_j = 1|X_n)$ as P, when $P \geq \mu$,

$$l_{weight}(W, X_n) = -\alpha^{P^{\gamma}} \beta \sum_{j \in y^+} \log P$$
$$-\alpha^{(1-P)^{\gamma}} (1 - \beta) \sum_{j \in y^-} \log (1 - P) \tag{3}$$

when $0 < P < \mu$, $l_{weight}(W, X_n) = 0$.

The total loss function of the multi-scale edge detection model is the weighted sum of l_{side} and l_{weight}, the value of W will be learned and updated during the training process. Therefore, our improved loss function can be formulated as:

$$l_{fuse}(W, X_n) = \sum_{j=1}^{M} a l^j_{side}(W, X_n) + b l^j_{weight}(W, X_n) \tag{4}$$

where M is the number of training images, a (here is set to 0.4) and b (here is set to 0.6) are set to balance two different loss function.

4   Occlusion Boundary Detection

The purpose of edge detection is to obtain the location of salient object accurately, in order to apply MSDF model to the object orientation scene, we experimented the performance of MSDF on occlusion boundary detection. As in [15], we use two steams structure to compute convolutional features respectively, including object boundary (the above-mentioned) and occlusion orientation to indicate the occlusion relationship using the left rule in Fig. 2.

In this section, our goal is mainly to compute the occlusion orientation map corresponding to boundary map, which can be seen as a problem of multi-task learning. To perform occlusion orientation estimation, we use θ to specify the tangent of the boundary predicted by MSDF and adapt the l_{smooth} loss function as defined in [15], $f(\theta_j, \overline{\theta}_j)$ denotes the difference between the predicted and ground truth orientation (θ_j and $\overline{\theta}_j$), which is to penalize the wrong predicted occlusion orientation values. The multi-task loss function can be defined as:

$$l(W, X_n) = \sum_{j=1}^{M} l_{fuse}^j(W, X_n) + \lambda \sum_{j=1}^{M} l_{smooth}^j(f(\theta_j, \overline{\theta}_j)) \qquad (5)$$

where the weighted value λ is set to 0.5.

If $\theta_j > \pi, \overline{\theta}_j > 0$ or $\theta_j < -\pi, \overline{\theta}_j < 0$,

$$f(\theta_j, \overline{\theta}_j) = \theta_j + \overline{\theta}_j. \qquad (6)$$

otherwise,

$$f(\theta_j, \overline{\theta}_j) = \theta_j - \overline{\theta}_j. \qquad (7)$$

x is assumed to be an independent variable, the occlusion orientation loss l_{smooth} can be defined as:

$$l_{smooth}(x) = \begin{cases} 0.5(\sigma x)^2, & if \ |x| < 1. \\ |x| - 0.5/\sigma^2, & otherwise. \end{cases} \qquad (8)$$

where σ adjusts the l_{smooth} loss contribution curve, θ_j is the predicted occlusion orientation which is defined $\theta_j \in (-\pi, \pi]$.

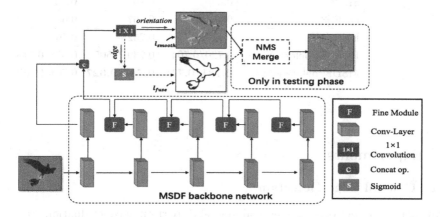

Fig. 4. Network architecture of occlusion boundary detection based on MSDF model.

In Fig. 4, after concatenation layer of MSDF, in parallel with the object boundary detection sub-net for pixel-wise classification, we output the feature of convolutional layer (1×1) for occlusion orientation estimation. The dotted lines indicate that the two models are trained respectively. When MSDF model training, the ground truth includes a binary edge map and occlusion orientation map (Y, O), l_{fuse} need to be computed for every pixel, but l_{smooth} only exists when the pixel belongs to the edge. In test phase, to combine the crisp edge, we perform non-maximum suppression (NMS) on the edge map, then we can obtain the occlusion orientation for each edge pixel. Similar to [16], we adjust the orientation estimation to ensure that neighboring pixels on the curve have similar orientations.

Table 1. Comparative results against state-of-the-art edge detection methods performance on BSDS500 and NYUD+RGB dataset, including without post-processing and with NMS. '/-' refers to training before NMS.

DataSet	Methods	ODS	OIS	AP
BSDS500	gpb+spb+ucm [1]	0.726	0.760	0.727
	SE [2]	0.739	0.759	0.792
	OEF [3]	0.739	0.761	0.720
	DeepContour [11]	0.757	0.776	0.790
	HED [18]/before NMS	0.788/0.761	0.807/0.778	0.840/0.660
	RCF (VOC) [7]/-	**0.806**/**0.773**	**0.823**/0.789	-/-
	MSDF(with l_{side})	0.791	0.805	0.793
	MSDF(with l_{weight})	0.789	0.804	0.795
	MSDF(with l_{fuse})/-	0.795/**0.773**	0.813/**0.790**	**0.842**/**0.695**
NYUD+RGB	gpb+spb+ucm [1]	0.631	0.661	0.562
	SE [2]	0.695	0.708	**0.719**
	OEF [3]	0.651	0.667	0.653
	HED [18]	0.717	0.732	0.704
	RCF [7]/before NMS	0.720/0.704	0.739/0.505	0.578/0.518
	MSDF/before NMS	**0.731**/**0.716**	**0.745**/**0.627**	0.701/**0.605**

5   Experiments

5.1   General Edge Detection

Dataset. We perform model training and performance evaluation on the BSDS500 [1] and NYUD [13] datasets. BSDS500 is a dataset widely used in image segmentation and edge detection. It is composed of 200 training images, 100 verification images, and 200 test images. We rotate and resize 200 training pictures and 100 verification pictures to expand the size of the training set, and use 200 test pictures as performance evaluation. The NYUD dataset consists of 1449 images containing three parts: RGB, Depth, and acceleration data. In order to facilitate the model training, we divide the NYUD dataset into two parts of

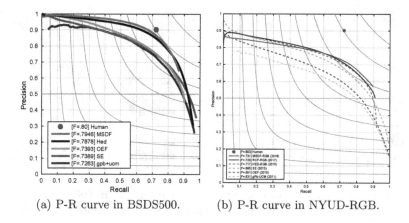

(a) P-R curve in BSDS500.   (b) P-R curve in NYUD-RGB.

Fig. 5. The evaluation results on BSDS500 dataset and NYUD+RGB dataset.

RGB and HHA. We found that the training of MSDF model on HHA part is unstable which makes it difficult to draw any conclusion, so only RGB part is selected.

Implementation Details. Our MSDF model uses caffe as backend with a single NVIDIA GTX1070 GPU. In this MSDF model, we initialize the conv-layers of encoder subnet with Gaussian random distribution with fixed mean (0.0) and variance (0.01), the other hyper parameters include the initial learning rate ($5e-7$), $30k$ training iterations. In l_{weight} loss function, α is set to 2 and γ is 0.5, which is about 2% higher than other settings in ODS. When NYUD-RGB dataset evaluation, we increase localization tolerance from 0.0075 to 0.011 [7]. Finally, we use SGD for optimization.

Evaluation Metrics. The evaluation metrics used here are P/R (precision/recall) curves, ODS (optimal dataset scale), OIS (optimal image scale), AP (average precision), and F-measure parameters for predicting edge matching result. ODS divides the fixed parameters of all images. OIS selects the optimal segmentation parameters for each image, and F-measure is calculated by the precision and recall:

$$F\text{-}measure = \frac{2 \times precision \times recall}{precision + recall} \tag{9}$$

Comparisons Against Other Methods. Our model is compared to other edge detection methods in Table 1. The following observations can be made: (1) An ablation study is performed for BSDS500 dataset to confirm the advantage of our fuse loss function. MSDF(with l_{fuse}), which adapts l_{fuse} loss function for

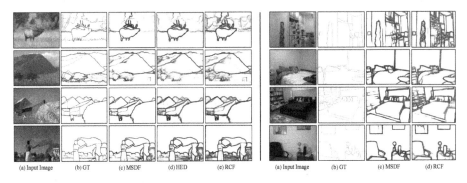

Fig. 6. Some examples of state-of-the-art comparisons on BSDS500 (left 4 input images) and NYUD-RGB (right 4 input images). No postprocessing is applied.

training MSDF model, is higher 0.4% than l_{side} and 0.7% than l_{weight}. (2) Without post-processing (using NMS) before evaluation, our method outperforms all compared models in BSDS500 dataset (ODS f-score of 0.773) and NYUD-RGB dataset (ODS f-score of 0.716), which proves that our method predicts more crisp edge than most of start-of-the-art edge detectors. (3) After the post-processing method such as NMS, RCF training with extra PASCAL VOC context data achieves the best performance of ODS f-score of 0.806 in BSDS500 dataset. Without extra training data, our method already outperforms other edge detection models in BSDS500 (ODS f-score of 0.795) dataset and NYUD dataset (ODS f-score of 0.731). (4) In Fig. 5, the precision-recall curves of our methods are also higher than other methods of comparison.

Table 2. Comparative results against state-of-the-art object boundary detection methods performance on BSDS ownership data, including with NMS and without post-processing. DOC+HED and MSDF model are trained from extra BSDS500 dataset. An ablation study is performed to confirm the superiority of proposed l_{fuse} loss function. '/-' refers to training before NMS.

Methods	ODS	OIS	AP
SRF-OCC	0.511	0.544	0.442
DOC+HED (BSDS500) [16]/-	0.655/0.454	0.683/0.484	0.635/0.415
DOOBNET (VGG16) [15]/-	0.600/0.573	0.617/0.576	0.476/0.463
MSDF(l_{side}, l_{smooth})/-	0.618/0.580	0.638/0.597	0.340/0.326
MSDF(l_{fuse}, l_{smooth})/-	0.626/0.592	0.652/0.600	0.550/0.372
MSDF(BSDS500)(l_{fuse}, l_{smooth})/-	**0.693/0.601**	**0.717/0.611**	**0.655/0.532**

Table 3. Comparative results against state-of-the-art orientation detection methods performance.

Methods	ODS	OIS	AP
SRF-OCC	0.419	0.448	0.337
DOC+HED (BSDS500) [16]	0.564	0.588	0.509
DOOBNET (VGG16) [15]	0.508	0.523	0.382
MSDF(l_{side}, l_{smooth})	0.543	0.559	0.272
MSDF(l_{fuse}, l_{smooth})	0.546	0.565	0.444
MSDF(BSDS500)(l_{fuse}, l_{smooth})	**0.594**	**0.615**	**0.525**

Qualitative Results. Example edge detection results of the proposed model are shown in Fig. 6. The results suggest that the model is more robust over different kinds of images. It can be seen that MSDF model can improve global resolution and crispness of the image edges without any post-processing. Our edge detection method is fairly close to the annotated edge of Ground Truth, especially the edges detected in the fourth row of BSDS500 dataset.

5.2 Occlusion Boundary Detection

Dataset. Many occlusion boundary detection methods usually use additional datasets to improve their performance, the small size of BSDS ownership makes it challenging to train, it only contains 100 training images and 100 test images from BSDS300 dataset, which can verify the robustness of our proposed model. We augment the BSDS ownership by rotating each image to 0,90,180,270 different angles 8 times.

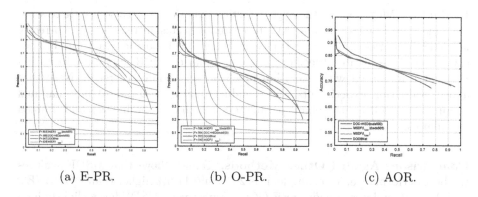

(a) E-PR.   (b) O-PR.   (c) AOR.

Fig. 7. Quantitative comparison on BSDS ownership data. (a) Is edge detection PR curve. (b) Is orientation PR curve. (c) Is occlusion AOR curve. MSDF model is trained from the BSDS ownership and extra data of BSDS500 dataset respectively.

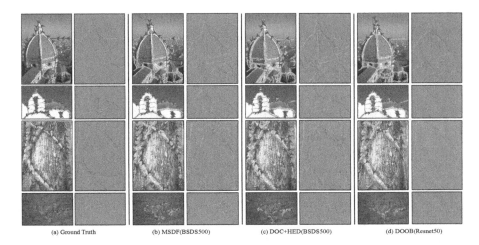

Fig. 8. Example results and comparison on BSDS ownership dataset. Ground Truth (columns 1–2): Visualization using "left" rule with arrows (see Fig. 1), and object occlusion boundaries ("cyan" pixels are correctly labeled boundaries, "green" pixels are false negative boundaries, and orange pixels are false positive boundaries). (Color figure online)

Implementation Details. During model training, we train the model of computing orientation and object salient edge respectively as Fig. 4. These two deep model hyper-parameters include mini-batch size (1), learning rate (1e−6), iterations (10000; divide learning rate by 10 after 2000 iterations), and sigma (3) in l_{smooth} loss function. The edge loss function is the same as the first part of this experiment.

Evaluation Metrics. As the edge detection experience, we also use three standard measures: ODS, OIS and AP. To evaluate occlusion relations on correctly labeled boundaries, AOR curve is measured with occlusion accuracy and boundary recall. To evaluate object occlusion boundaries, OPR curve is orientation P-R curve measured with occlusion precision and boundary recall. Note that above evaluation experiments were conducted after a standard non-maximal suppression (NMS) with default parameters, which can obtain crisp and thinned boundaries.

Comparisons Against Other Methods. Table 2 shows that MSDF achieves the best performance, for example, it is 2.6% and 11.5% higher than DOOBNET with VGG16 architecture and SRF-OCC, respectively. MSDF has a slightly high ODS as using l_{fuse} loss instead of l_{side} loss. We also employ the extra training data from BSDS500 dataset, which can further improve ODS, OIS and AP to 0.693, 0.717 and 0.655. Without NMS before evaluation, our method also outperform all compared models. Orientation detection results are shown in Table 3 and

Fig. 7(b), MSDF (ODS = 0.540) is lower than DOOBNET with Resnet50 (ODS = 0.555) but has a higher AOR curve. After trained from BSDS500 dataset, it achieves the best performance in compared methods.

Qualitative Results. Example occlusion boundary detection results of compared methods are shown in Fig. 8, illustrating that our MSDF model can recover better semantic boundaries. We compared the performance of MSDF, DOC+HED and DOOBNet with Resnet50 architecture. From some test results, DOC+HED model recover some internal occlusion boundaries that are not labeled correct, such as the surroundings of the running leopard, the inner texture of the first image, DOOB model may have lost some key boundaries information, such as edge features of tree branch in the third figure, MSDF model can alleviate the above two problems, although it also learns a few false inner boundaries in some cases.

6   Conclusion

This paper proposes a new CNN structure MSDF to predict object edge and occlusion orientation based on learning multi-scale features. The architecture mainly includes the top-down scale feature extraction and the new proposed decoder sub-net, the decoder sub-net shows a new method for feature fusion in different scales and how to balance the fusion and up-sampling to carry out edge detection. Finally, the paper uses a new loss function to address the positive/negative class imbalance. Our method can produce high-quality and high-resolution edge very efficiently, this makes it promising to be used for image segmentation and another high-level task.

References

1. Arbelaez, P., Maire, M., Fowlkes, C., Malik, J.: Contour detection and hierarchical image segmentation. IEEE Trans. Pattern Anal. Mach. Intell. **33**(5), 898–916 (2011). https://doi.org/10.1109/TPAMI.2010.161
2. Dollár, P., Zitnick, C.L.: Fast edge detection using structured forests. IEEE Trans. Pattern Anal. Mach. Intell. **37**(8), 1558–1570 (2015). https://doi.org/10.1109/TPAMI.2014.2377715
3. Hallman, S., Fowlkes, C.C.: Oriented edge forests for boundary detection. In: Proceedings of the IEEE Conference on Computer Vision and Pattern Recognition, pp. 1732–1740 (2015). https://doi.org/10.1109/CVPR.2015.7298782
4. Kokkinos, I.: Pushing the boundaries of boundary detection using deep learning (2015). arXiv preprint arXiv:1511.07386
5. Lee, C.Y., Xie, S., Gallagher, P., Zhang, Z., Tu, Z.: Deeply-supervised nets. In: Artificial Intelligence and Statistics, pp. 562–570 (2015)
6. Lin, T.Y., Goyal, P., Girshick, R., He, K., Dollár, P.: Focal loss for dense object detection. IEEE Trans. Pattern Anal. Mach. Intell. (2018). https://doi.org/10.1109/TPAMI.2018.2858826

7. Liu, Y., Cheng, M.M., Hu, X., Wang, K., Bai, X.: Richer convolutional features for edge detection. In: 2017 IEEE Conference on Computer Vision and Pattern Recognition (CVPR), pp. 5872–5881. IEEE (2017). https://doi.org/10.1109/CVPR.2017.622

8. Long, J., Shelhamer, E., Darrell, T.: Fully convolutional networks for semantic segmentation. In: Proceedings of the IEEE Conference on Computer Vision and Pattern Recognition, pp. 3431–3440 (2015). https://doi.org/10.1109/CVPR.2015.7298965

9. Maninis, K.K., Pont-Tuset, J., Arbeláez, P., Van Gool, L.: Convolutional oriented boundaries: from image segmentation to high-level tasks. IEEE Trans. Pattern Anal. Mach. Intell. 40(4), 819–833 (2018). https://doi.org/10.1109/TPAMI.2017.2700300

10. Milletari, F., Navab, N., Ahmadi, S.A.: V-net: fully convolutional neural networks for volumetric medical image segmentation. In: 2016 Fourth International Conference on 3D Vision (3DV), pp. 565–571. IEEE (2016). https://doi.org/10.1109/3DV.2016.79

11. Shen, W., Wang, X., Wang, Y., Bai, X., Zhang, Z.: DeepContour: a deep convolutional feature learned by positive-sharing loss for contour detection. In: Proceedings of the IEEE Conference on Computer Vision and Pattern Recognition, pp. 3982–3991 (2015). https://doi.org/10.1109/CVPR.2015.7299024

12. Shi, W., et al.: Real-time single image and video super-resolution using an efficient sub-pixel convolutional neural network. In: Proceedings of the IEEE Conference on Computer Vision and Pattern Recognition, pp. 1874–1883 (2016). https://doi.org/10.1109/CVPR.2016.207

13. Silberman, N., Hoiem, D., Kohli, P., Fergus, R.: Indoor segmentation and support inference from RGBD images. In: Fitzgibbon, A., Lazebnik, S., Perona, P., Sato, Y., Schmid, C. (eds.) ECCV 2012. LNCS, vol. 7576, pp. 746–760. Springer, Heidelberg (2012). https://doi.org/10.1007/978-3-642-33715-4_54

14. Simonyan, K., Zisserman, A.: Very deep convolutional networks for large-scale image recognition (2014). arXiv preprint arXiv:1409.1556

15. Wang, G., Liang, X., Li, F.W.: DOOBNet: deep object occlusion boundary detection from an image (2018). arXiv preprint arXiv:1806.03772. https://doi.org/10.1007/978-3-030-20876-9_43

16. Wang, P., Yuille, A.: DOC: Deep OCclusion estimation from a single image. In: Leibe, B., Matas, J., Sebe, N., Welling, M. (eds.) ECCV 2016. LNCS, vol. 9905, pp. 545–561. Springer, Cham (2016). https://doi.org/10.1007/978-3-319-46448-0_33

17. Wang, Y., Zhao, X., Huang, K.: Deep crisp boundaries. In: Proceedings of the IEEE Conference on Computer Vision and Pattern Recognition, pp. 3892–3900 (2017). https://doi.org/10.1109/CVPR.2017.187

18. Xie, S., Tu, Z.: Holistically-nested edge detection. In: Proceedings of the IEEE International Conference on Computer Vision, pp. 1395–1403 (2015). https://doi.org/10.1109/ICCV.2015.164

19. Yang, J., Price, B., Cohen, S., Lee, H., Yang, M.H.: Object contour detection with a fully convolutional encoder-decoder network. In: Proceedings of the IEEE Conference on Computer Vision and Pattern Recognition, pp. 193–202 (2016). https://doi.org/10.1109/CVPR.2016.28

Graph-Boosted Attentive Network for Semantic Body Parsing

Tinghuai Wang[1]($\boxtimes$)(iD) and Huiling Wang[2]

[1] Nokia Technologies, Espoo, Finland
wang.tinghuai@gmail.com
[2] Tampere University, Tampere, Finland

Abstract. Human body parsing remains a challenging problem in natural scenes due to multi-instance and inter-part semantic confusions as well as occlusions. This paper proposes a novel approach to decomposing multiple human bodies into semantic part regions in unconstrained environments. Specifically we propose a convolutional neural network (CNN) architecture which comprises of novel semantic and contour attention mechanisms across feature hierarchy to resolve the semantic ambiguities and boundary localization issues related to semantic body parsing. We further propose to encode estimated pose as higher-level contextual information which is combined with local semantic cues in a novel graphical model in a principled manner. In this proposed model, the lower-level semantic cues can be recursively updated by propagating higher-level contextual information from estimated pose and vice versa across the graph, so as to alleviate erroneous pose information and pixel level predictions. We further propose an optimization technique to efficiently derive the solutions. Our proposed method achieves the state-of-art results on the challenging Pascal Person-Part dataset.

1 Introduction

Human semantic part segmentation, *i.e.* assigning pixels with semantic class labels corresponding to the belonging human body parts, is a fundamental task in computer vision which provides richer structural representation for higher-level tasks such as video surveillance [15,21,24,25,33], person identification [12,17,22], image/video retrieval [8,9,36,39], fine-grained recognition [28,29,32,42], image editing [34,35] and artistic rendering [13,30,31].

Significant progress has been made recently on human part segmentation [4,5,11,16,18,27,37,38] due to the advancement of deep neural networks and availability of large scale dataset with body part annotations [7]. However, there are several limitations of the existing methods which lead to failures in parsing unusual pose or interacting multi-person body parts in natural scenes. Those methods either take a bottom-up semantic segmentation approach relying on pixel-level training [4,5,11,18,37], or top-down approach incorporating person level recognition [16], segmentation [27] or pose skeleton [38] into the unary potentials of a CRF framework.

I. V. Tetko et al. (Eds.): ICANN 2019, LNCS 11729, pp. 267–280, 2019.
https://doi.org/10.1007/978-3-030-30508-6_22

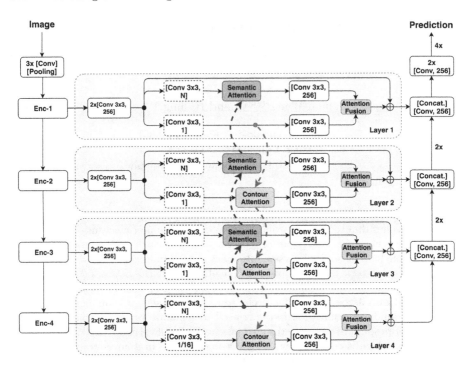

Fig. 1. Illustration of the proposed network architecture. (Color figure online)

The bottom-up approaches lack overall human structure and configuration information, and thus usually produce erroneous predictions when limbs intertwined, or bodies partially occluded. Some of the top-down approaches complement the bottom-up methods with object level information to constrain the pixel labeling, whereas the object level detection or segmentation suffer from multi-person scenes where people are overlapping or in unusual non-pedestrian-like body poses. As a well studied representation of people, [38] directly uses the estimated pose skeleton as part score map which, however, suffers from early commitment—if the pose estimation fails there is no recourse to recovery.

To thoroughly exploit higher-level human configuration information in a principled manner, we propose a novel graphical model to jointly model and infer the human body parsing problem in totally unconstrained scene scenarios, where there are large variations of people in scale, location, occlusion, and pose. Our approach is able to systematically integrate the top-down part configuration information and bottom-up semantic cues into a unified model.

The key contributions of this work are as follows.

- We propose a novel architecture to overcome the fundamental obstacles to FCN based semantic body parsing, i.e., semantic ambiguity and boundary localization.

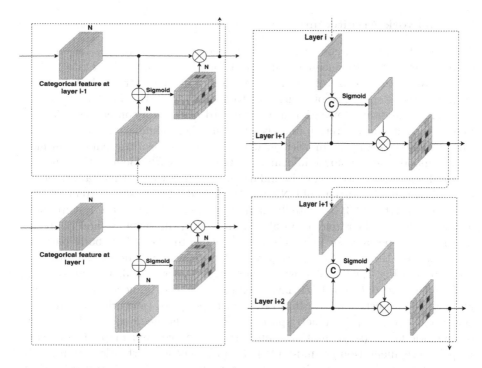

Fig. 2. Illustration of the proposed semantic attention module (left) and contour attention module (right).

- We propose a novel graphical model which integrates higher-level human configuration information with local semantic cues in a principled manner.
- The proposed graphical model is able to recursively estimate the part configuration cues from local semantic cues and vice versa. In this manner, long-range intrinsic structure facilitates propagation of local semantic cues across higher-level body configuration.
- We develop an optimization technique to simultaneously estimate the proposed two quadratic cost functions which are supplementary to each other in the proposed graph.

2 Our Approach

Given a $H \times W \times 3$ input image I, our goal is to output a pixel-wise part segmentation map. We start by designing and training a network to predict a stack of initial probability maps $H \times W \times N$ where $N = P + 1$ and P is the number of semantic part classes with one background class.

2.1 Network Architecture

The overall network architecture is illustrated in Fig. 1, which is an encoder-decoder network. The encoder consists of four blocks, i.e., Enc-i (i = 1, 2, 3, 4), according to the size of the feature maps. Encoder extracts feature maps with decreasing spatial resolutions (due to pooling and strided convolution) and increasing semantic information in the forward pass. As a consequence, feature maps from early layers retain fine visual details, i.e., boundary related information, and little semantic knowledge, whilst the coarse feature maps from later layers embody rich semantic information. One can clearly identify the semantic gap and uneven distribution of boundary information within this feature hierarchy. Albeit these limitations of CNN have been addressed to some extent via skip connections [2, 6, 20, 23], repeatedly merging and transforming the feature maps across the feature hierarchy inevitably dilutes both the semantic and boundary information especially for fine-grained regions or objects such as body parts.

To address the above issues, we propose a novel attentive decoder network, as illustrated in Fig. 1, which consists of four layers (Layer 1, 2, 3, 4) corresponding to four encoder outputs. Each layer comprises of two branches, i.e., semantic and contour branches, to transform the feature maps to categorical (N-channel) space and contour (1-channel) space enabled by the deep supervision [14,26] of semantic labels (segmentation ground-truth) and contour maps (Canny edge map from segmentation ground-truth). Two *element-wise* attention modules are proposed to process categorical and contour feature maps respectively. Each attention module is also connected across (illustrated as red and blue dashed arrows in Fig. 1) the feature hierarchy to propagate consistent semantic and contour information in opposite directions respectively.

Semantic attention module, as illustrated in Fig. 2 (left), takes N-channel categorical feature maps from current layer (Layer i) and the N-channel processed feature map from later layer (Layer i + 1) as inputs, and computes element-wise attention weights (S_c) by applying an element-wise sigmoid function on the summed feature maps, and weighs the feature map F_c via $F_c' = S_c \odot F_c$. As a result the feature map of current layer is semantically enhanced by the feature map from later layer in categorical feature space. Similarly, contour attention module, as illustrated in Fig. 2 (right), takes 1-channel contour feature maps from current layer (Layer i) and the 1-channel processed contour feature map from earlier layer (Layer i − 1) as inputs, and computes element-wise attention weights (S_b) by applying an element-wise sigmoid function on the concatenated feature maps, and weighs the feature map F_b via $F_b' = S_b \odot F_b$. As a result the contour feature of current layer is enhanced by earlier layer which has much stronger boundary information. Note, our attention mechanism is element-wise attention which is different from the channel-wise attention model proposed by [41]. Our element-wise attention model suits better for semantic segmentation which is a dense prediction problem. Overall, there are consistent semantic and contour information flows across the CNN feature hierarchy which are missing in the state-of-the-art architectures. Feature maps from semantic and contour branches are summed in the *attention fusion* module at each layer.

2.2 Pose as Context

In order to generate the initial person configuration, we employ Deeper-Cut [10], which addresses the multi-person scenario explicitly using integer linear programming, to extract human skeleton map. We put forward a notion of using geodesic distance to encode the contextual information of people location and body part configuration. We employ superpixel maps [1] rather than pixels to exploit pose context leveraging perceptually meaningful and coherent lower-level features. Specifically, we generate multi-layer superpixels with different granularities to encode the pose context at multiple scales. In each superpixel map, we compute the geodesic distance from all superpixels w.r.t. the set of superpixels associated with each skeleton line (corresponding to pose parameters Θ_p). The geodesic distance $d(y_i, \Theta_p)$ between superpixel y_i and skeleton line Θ_p is defined as the smallest integral of a weight function over all paths from y_i to the set of superpixels Ω_p associated with Θ_p. Formally, $d_{geo}(y_i, \Theta_p)$ is computed as

$$d_{geo}(y_i, \Theta_p) = \min_{y_j \in \Omega_p} d(y_i, y_j)$$

where

$$d(y_i, y_j) = \min_{C_{y_i, y_j}} \int_0^1 |W \cdot \dot{C}_{y_i, y_j}(s)| ds,$$

where $C_{y_i, y_j}(s)$ is a path connecting the superpixels y_i, y_j (for $s = 0$ and $s = 1$ respectively). The weights W are set the gradient of the average CIE Lab color of superpixels, i.e. $W = \nabla \bar{c}$ with $\bar{c}$ as the average color of superpixels. If a superpixel is outside the desired part, its geodesic distance is large since all the possible pathway to the skeleton line cross the boundaries with higher gradient value (edges) and spatial distance. Based on the geodesic distance, the likelihood that semantic part Θ_p occurs at superpixel y_i can be computed as

$$p(y_i | \Theta_p) = \exp(-\beta d_{geo}^2(y_i, \Theta_p))$$

where β is a parameter which controls the decay of likelihood w.r.t. geodesic distance.

2.3 Graphical Model

The computed superpixel based part confidence maps serve as the higher-level contexts of body configurations. Our goal is to combine this contextual information with the bottom-up predictions in a principled manner. To this end, we propose a novel graphical model to provide a unified framework for this task.

We construct an undirected graph $G = (V, E)$ with pixels and superpixels as nodes $V = \{X, Y\}$ respectively. Denoted as $E = \{E_{XY}, E_{XX}, E_{YY}\}$, we define the edges as links between pairs of graph nodes. The existence of edges is determined based on the spatial adjacency in the graph as follows.

Pose-Pixel Edge E_{XY}. The connections between each superpixel and its constituent pixels are added as pose-pixel edges. Superpixels comprise of higher-level cues of human body configuration, as well as perceptually meaningful and coherent features. The weight w_{im}^{XY} on edge $e_{im}^{XY} \in E^{XY}$ between pixel x_i and superpixel y_m is defined as $w_{im}^{XY} = [x_i \in y_m] \cdot e^{-(1-\mathbf{Pr}(x_i|y_m))}$, where $[\cdot]$ is the indicator function, and $\mathbf{Pr}(x_i|y_m)$ is the likelihood of observing x_i given the probability density function (PDF) of superpixel y_m. We estimate the probability density of superpixel via the fast kernel density estimation [40] on CIE Lab color. These pose-pixel edges transfer the person level multi-scale contextual cues into the pixels, whilst each superpixel can incorporate the complementary semantic information from local pixel.

Pixel Edge E_{XX}. All spatially adjacent (8-way connectivity neighborhood assumed) pixels are connected to form pixel edges E_{XX}. Weight of an edge $e_{ij}^{XX} \in E_{XX}$ is defined to reflect both the local appearance similarity and spatial distance as follows. Let $\mathcal{N}_i$ be the set of pixels in the spatial neighborhood of x_i, we define $w_{ij}^{XX} = [x_j \in \mathcal{N}_i] \cdot e^{-d^c(x_i, x_j)}$, where $d^c(x_i, x_j)$ indicates the color distance between x_i and x_j which is defined as $d^c(i,j) = \frac{||c_i - c_j||^2}{2 < ||c_i - c_j||^2 >}$, where $< \cdot >$ indicates expectation.

Superpixel Edge E_{YY}. All spatially adjacent superpixels are connected to form superpixel edges E_{YY}. Weight of an edge $e_{mn}^{YY} \in E_{YY}$ is defined to reflect both the local appearance similarity and spatial distance as follows. Let $\mathcal{N}_m^s$ be the set of superpixels in the spatial neighborhood of y_m.

$$w_{mn}^{YY} = [y_n \in \mathcal{N}_m^s] \cdot e^{-\chi^2(h_m, h_n)d^s(y_m, y_n)}$$

where $\chi^2(h_m, h_n)$ is the χ^2 distance between L_1-normalized CIE Lab color histograms h_m, h_n of superpixels y_m and y_n respectively, and $d^s(y_m, y_n)$ indicates the spatial distance between y_m and y_n.

2.4 Cost Functions

We define two novel quadratic cost functions to facilitate the joint inference of likelihoods for pixels and superpixels respectively, harnessing the complementary contextual information to each other.

We infer the pixel likelihoods $\mathbf{U}_l$ by incorporating the superpixel likelihoods $\mathbf{V}_l$ as higher-level context cues in a principled manner. By characterizing the relationship between all nodes in the graph, the quadratic cost function J_l^X of pixel likelihoods $\mathbf{U}_l$ with respect to a label l is as follows. Let the diagonal element of node degree matrix $D^X = \text{diag}([d_1^X, \ldots, d_{N_X}^X])$ be defined as $d_i^X = \sum_{j=1}^{N_X} w_{ij}^{XX}$.

$$\begin{aligned}
J_l^X &= J_{l,U}^X + J_{l,P}^X + J_{l,C}^X \\
&= \sum_{i=1}^{N_X} \lambda^X d_i^X (u_{il} - \tilde{u}_{il})^2 + \sum_{i,j=1}^{N_X} w_{ij}^{XX}(u_{il} - u_{jl})^2 \\
&\quad + \sum_{i=1}^{N_X} \pi d_i^X (u_{il} - \bar{u}_{il})^2
\end{aligned} \tag{1}$$

where λ and π are parameters. The pixel probability $\tilde{u}_{il}$ is the initial likelihood with respect to label l from the trained network. The estimated likelihood $\bar{u}_{il}$ of pixel x_i from superpixel likelihood $v_{ml} \in \mathbf{V}_l$ is define as the weighted average of its corresponding superpixels from multi-layer superpixel maps,

$$\bar{u}_{il} = \sum_{m=1}^{N_Y} p_{im}^{XY} v_{ml}, \tag{2}$$

where

$$p_{im}^{XY} = \frac{w_{im}^{XY}}{\sum_{m=1}^{N_Y} w_{im}^{XY}}. \tag{3}$$

In this cost function, $J_{l,U}^X$ and $J_{l,P}^X$ are the fitting constraint and smoothness constraint respectively, while $J_{l,C}^X$ is the contextual constraint.

$J_{l,U}^X$ encourages pixels to have the initial likelihood, which is controlled by λ^X measuring how much the inferred likelihood should agree with the initial likelihood. $J_{l,P}^X$ promotes the continuity of inferred likelihood among adjacent nodes lying in a close vicinity in the feature space. $J_{l,C}^X$ facilitates the inference of each pixel to be aware of higher-level context information. The intuition is that superpixel confidence map encodes richer semantics and intrinsic information of person parts and configuration, which can be propagated to its constituent pixels during inference.

In order to solve (1), the superpixel likelihoods $\mathbf{V}_l$ are also required to be estimated by referring to the pixel likelihoods $\mathbf{U}_l$ in graph G. Similar to (1), the cost function J_l^Y of superpixels likelihoods $\mathbf{V}_l$ is defined as follows. Let the diagonal element of node degree matrix $D^Y = \mathrm{diag}([d_1^Y, \ldots, d_{N_Y}^Y])$ be defined as $d_m^Y = \sum_{n=1}^{N_Y} w_{mn}^{YY}$,

$$\begin{aligned} J_l^Y &= J_{l,U}^Y + J_{l,P}^Y + J_{l,C}^Y \\ &= \sum_{m=1}^{N_Y} \lambda^Y d_m^Y (v_{ml} - \tilde{v}_{ml})^2 + \sum_{m,n=1}^{N_Y} w_{mn}^{YY}(v_{ml} - v_{nl})^2 \\ &\quad + \sum_{m=1}^{N_Y} \psi d_m^Y (v_{ml} - \bar{v}_{ml})^2 \end{aligned} \tag{4}$$

where λ^Y and ψ are parameters, $\tilde{v}_{ml}$ is the initial likelihood of superpixels m given label l from the geodesic distance of skeleton notion, and the estimated likelihood $\bar{v}_{ml}$ of the superpixels y_m is defined by incorporating local semantic cues, i.e., pixel likelihoods $\mathbf{U}_l$. $\bar{v}_{ml}$ is computed as the weighted average of its constituent pixel likelihoods:

$$\bar{v}_{ml} = \sum_{i=1}^{N_X} p_{mi}^{YX} u_{il}, $$

where

$$p_{mi}^{YX} = \frac{w_{mi}^{YX}}{\sum_{i=1}^{N_X} w_{mi}^{YX}}. \tag{5}$$

Similarly, (4) consists of three terms, i.e., $J_{l,U}^Y$, $J_{l,P}^Y$ and $J_{l,C}^Y$. $J_{l,U}^Y$ is the fitting constraint that encourages each superpixel to have its initial likelihood. $J_{l,P}^Y$ is the smoothness constraint which promotes label continuity among superpixels to preserve the configuration of person pose. The third term $J_{l,C}^Y$ is the contextual constraint which collects local semantic cues in a bottom-up manner to refine the superpixel likelihood $\mathbf{V}_l$ using pixel likelihoods $\mathbf{U}_l$, since it can not guarantee that the estimated pose is always correct and the superpixel might carry erroneous contextual information.

2.5   Convex Optimization

Two cost functions $\mathbf{U}_l$ and $\mathbf{V}_l$ should be minimized simultaneously since they are complementary to each other. We reformulate these functions as matrix forms with respect to the likelihoods $\mathbf{U}_l = [u_{il}]_{N_X \times 1}$ and $\mathbf{V}_l = [v_{ml}]_{N_Y \times 1}$ from the initial likelihoods $\tilde{\mathbf{U}}_l = [\tilde{u}_{il}]_{N_X \times 1}$ and $\tilde{\mathbf{V}}_l = [\tilde{v}_{ml}]_{N_Y \times 1}$ respectively,

$$
\begin{aligned}
J_l^X =&(\mathbf{U}_l - \tilde{\mathbf{U}}_l)^T \mathbf{D}^X \mathbf{\Lambda}^X (\mathbf{U}_l - \tilde{\mathbf{U}}_l) + \mathbf{U}_l^T (\mathbf{D}^X - \mathbf{W}^X)\mathbf{U}_l \\
&+ \pi(\mathbf{U}_l - \mathbf{P}^{XY}\mathbf{V}_l)^T D^X (\mathbf{U}_l - \mathbf{P}^{XY}\mathbf{V}_l)
\end{aligned}
\tag{6}
$$

$$
\begin{aligned}
J_l^Y =&(\mathbf{V}_l - \tilde{\mathbf{V}}_l)^T \mathbf{D}^Y \mathbf{\Lambda}^Y (\mathbf{V}_l - \tilde{\mathbf{V}}_l) + \mathbf{V}_l^T (\mathbf{D}^Y - \mathbf{W}^Y)\mathbf{V}_l \\
&+ \psi(\mathbf{V}_l - \mathbf{P}^{YX}\mathbf{U}_l)^T D^Y (\mathbf{V}_l - \mathbf{P}^{YX}\mathbf{U}_l)
\end{aligned}
\tag{7}
$$

where $\mathbf{W}^X = [w_{ij}^{XX}]_{N_X \times N_X}$ and $\mathbf{W}^Y = [w_{mn}^{YY}]_{N_Y \times N_Y}$. The contextual dependencies between pixels and their corresponding superpixels in graph G are formulated by $\mathbf{P}^{XY} = [p_{im}^{XY}]_{N_X \times N_Y}$ and $\mathbf{P}^{YX} = [p_{mi}^{YX}]_{N_Y \times N_X}$. The diagonal elements of $N_X \times N_X$ matrix $\mathbf{\Lambda}^X = \text{diag}([\lambda^X, \cdots, \lambda^X])$ and $N_Y \times N_Y$ matrix $\mathbf{\Lambda}^Y = \text{diag}([\lambda^Y, \cdots, \lambda^Y])$ are the parameter λ^X and λ^X respectively.

By differentiating J_l^X and J_l^Y with respect to $\mathbf{U}_l$ and $\mathbf{V}_l$ respectively, we have

$$
\begin{aligned}
\frac{\partial J_l^X}{\partial \mathbf{U}_l} =& \mathbf{U}_l(\mathbf{I}^X - \mathbf{P}^X) + \mathbf{\Lambda}^X (\mathbf{U}_l - \tilde{\mathbf{U}}_l) \\
&+ \pi(\mathbf{U}_l - \mathbf{P}^{XY}\mathbf{V}_l) = 0
\end{aligned}
\tag{8}
$$

$$
\begin{aligned}
\frac{\partial J_l^Y}{\partial \mathbf{V}_l} =& \mathbf{V}_l(\mathbf{I}^Y - \mathbf{P}^Y) + \mathbf{\Lambda}^Y (\mathbf{V}_l - \tilde{\mathbf{V}}_l) \\
&+ \psi(\mathbf{V}_l - \mathbf{P}^{YX}\mathbf{U}_l) = 0
\end{aligned}
\tag{9}
$$

where $\mathbf{P}^X = \mathbf{D}^{X^{-1}}\mathbf{W}^X$ (or $\mathbf{P}^Y = \mathbf{D}^{Y^{-1}}\mathbf{W}^Y$), and $\mathbf{I}^X$ (or $\mathbf{I}^Y$) is identify matrix.

By denoting all likelihoods as $\mathbf{Z}_l = [\mathbf{U}_l; \mathbf{V}_l]$ and initial likelihoods as $\tilde{\mathbf{Z}}_l = [\tilde{\mathbf{U}}_l; \tilde{\mathbf{V}}_l]$, (8) and (9) can be jointly transformed into

$$
(\mathbf{I} - (\mathbf{I} - \Gamma)\Pi)\mathbf{Z}_l = \Gamma\tilde{\mathbf{Z}},
\tag{10}
$$

where

$$
\Pi = \begin{bmatrix} \frac{\mathbf{P}^X}{1+\pi} & \frac{\pi \mathbf{P}^{XY}}{1+\pi} \\ \frac{\psi \mathbf{P}^{YX}}{1+\psi} & \frac{\mathbf{P}^Y}{1+\psi} \end{bmatrix},
\tag{11}
$$

Table 1. Quantitatively segmentation results on Pascal Person-Part dataset

Method	Head	Torso	U-arms	L-arms	U-legs	L-legs	Background	Avg.
DeepLab-LargeFOV [3]	78.09	54.02	37.29	36.85	33.73	29.61	92.85	51.78
HAZN [37]	80.79	59.11	43.05	42.76	38.99	34.46	93.59	56.11
Attention [5]	-	-	-	-	-	-	-	56.39
LG-LSTM [19]	82.72	60.99	45.40	47.76	42.33	37.96	88.63	57.97
Graph LSTM [18]	82.69	62.68	46.88	47.71	45.66	40.93	94.59	60.16
DeepLab v2 [4]	-	-	-	-	-	-	-	58.90
JPS (final, CRF) [38]	85.50	67.87	54.72	54.30	48.25	44.76	95.32	64.39
PCNet-126 [43]	86.81	69.06	55.35	55.27	50.21	48.54	96.07	65.90
Our model (w/o graph)	89.19	74.88	55.98	60.76	50.76	41.45	95.12	66.87
Our model (final)	90.84	75.85	56.18	64.86	52.86	43.52	95.75	**68.55**

and

$$\Gamma = \begin{bmatrix} \frac{\Lambda^X}{(1+\pi)\mathbf{I}+\Lambda^X} & \\ & \frac{\Lambda^Y}{(1+\psi)\mathbf{I}+\Lambda^Y} \end{bmatrix}. \tag{12}$$

Denoting

$$\mathbf{B} = \mathbf{I} - (\mathbf{I} - \Gamma)\Pi, \tag{13}$$

(10) can be solved by a sparse matrix inversion

$$\mathbf{Z}_l = \mathbf{B}^{-1}\Gamma\tilde{\mathbf{Z}}. \tag{14}$$

2.6 Semantic Part Labeling

Posterior probabilities of each pixel with respect to part label l can then be computed following Bayes rule

$$p(l|x_i) = \frac{p(x_i|l)p(l)}{\sum_{l'=1}^{L} p(x_i|l')p(l')} = \frac{u_{il}}{\sum_{l'=1}^{L} u_{il'}} \tag{15}$$

where an uniform prior probability $p(l)$ is assumed.

Each pixel is finally assigned with the label corresponding to the class with the *maximum a posterior* probability, which constitutes to the semantic person part segmentation,

$$\hat{l}_i = \underset{l}{\mathrm{argmax}}\, p(l|x_i) \tag{16}$$

3 Experiments

We evaluate our proposed approach on the Pascal Person-Part dataset [7] which is a subset from the PASCAL VOC 2010 dataset, containing 1716 training images, and 1817 test images. This dataset contains multiple person per image

Input   Result   Ground-truth   Input   Result   Ground-truth

Fig. 3. Qualitative results of our algorithm on Pascal Person-Part dataset.

in unconstrained poses and challenging natural environments with detailed person part annotations (head, torso, upper/lower arms and upper/lower legs) and one background class. The segmentation results are evaluated in terms of mean Intersection-over-Union (mIOU) averaged across classes. We adopt ResNet-101 pretrained on ImageNet as encoder.

As shown in Table 1, we compare our model with 7 state-of-the-art methods, *i.e.* DeepLab-LargeFOV [3], HAZN [37], Attention [5], LG-LSTM [19], Graph LSTM [18], DeepLab v2 [4] and JPS [38]. Our proposed approach obtains the performance of 68.55%, which outperforms all the compared methods. Our approach improves the segmentation accuracy in all parts with considerable margins. Comparing with DeepLab v2 which also uses ResNet-101 as encoder, our architecture significantly improves the accuracy by 7.97%, which demonstrates the capability of our network in dealing with fine-grained body parts. As ablation study, we evaluate our architecture in comparison to a baseline network without semantic and contour attention modules. The result shows that incorporating semantic attention module improves the performance by 2.43%. We further observe a performance improvement of 1.36% by introducing the contour attention module. Our architecture outperfoms the state-of-the-art end-to-end body parsing network PCNet-126 [43] by 1%.

All top-down approaches, *i.e.* JPS and ours, significantly surpass bottom-up approaches DeepLab-LargeFOV (w/o CRF), HAZN, Attention, LG-LSTM, Graph LSTM and DeepLab-v2 (w/o CRF) with large margins. Bottom-up approaches normally rely on pixel level training and inference without explicitly taking into account of person part configuration, and thus they are error-prone to unusual human poses, as well as scenes where people are overlapping and interacting. This comparison confirms the benefits of incorporating person-level information in resolving the ambiguity of various parts in challenging situations.

Our method outperforms the best competing method JPS [38] by 4.16%. Note we do not use any CRF for post processing. JPS takes a similar top-down approach as our method, however it directly utilizes skeletons from estimated pose as confidence map to improve the part segmentation which is sensitive to erroneous person pose estimations. Our approach is able to systematically integrate the higher-level part configuration information and local semantic cues into a graphical model, which recursively estimates both to propagate long-range intrinsic structure to facilitate local semantic labeling against spurious pose context and pixel level predictions.

More qualitative evaluations on Pascal Person-Part dataset are provided in Fig. 3. Specifically, for multi-person highly overlapping instances (*e.g.* rows 1 and 6), our method can resolve the inter-person occlusions, relieve the local inter-part confusions (*e.g.* lifted lower arms in row 1), recover the parts for small scale human instances (*e.g.* right images of rows 6 and 7) and exclude regions occluded from non-person object (*e.g.* row 5).

4   Conclusion

We have proposed a network architecture which comprises of novel semantic and contour attention mechanisms to resolve the semantic ambiguities and boundary localization issues related to fine-grained body parsing problem. We further proposed a novel graphical model to tackle the multi-person semantic part segmentation problem in challenging natural scenes. This model is able to combine person level configuration information with the pixel level semantic cues in a unified framework, where the lower-level semantic cues can be recursively estimated by propagating higher-level contextual information from estimated pose and vice versa, across the proposed graph. We further proposed an optimization technique to efficiently estimate the cost functions. The experiments confirmed the significantly improved robustness and accuracy over the state-of-the-art approaches on challenging Pascal Person-Part dataset.

References

1. Achanta, R., Shaji, A., Smith, K., Lucchi, A., Fua, P., Süsstrunk, S.: Slic superpixels compared to state-of-the-art superpixel methods. IEEE Trans. Pattern Anal. Mach. Intell. **34**(11), 2274–2282 (2012)
2. Badrinarayanan, V., Kendall, A., Cipolla, R.: Segnet: a deep convolutional encoder-decoder architecture for image segmentation. arXiv preprint arXiv:1511.00561 (2015)
3. Chen, L., Papandreou, G., Kokkinos, I., Murphy, K., Yuille, A.L.: Semantic image segmentation with deep convolutional nets and fully connected CRFs. CoRR abs/1412.7062 (2014)
4. Chen, L.C., Papandreou, G., Kokkinos, I., Murphy, K., Yuille, A.L.: Deeplab: semantic image segmentation with deep convolutional nets, atrous convolution, and fully connected CRFs. arXiv preprint arXiv:1606.00915 (2016)
5. Chen, L.C., Yang, Y., Wang, J., Xu, W., Yuille, A.L.: Attention to scale: scale-aware semantic image segmentation. In: CVPR, pp. 3640–3649 (2016)
6. Chen, L.C., Zhu, Y., Papandreou, G., Schroff, F., Adam, H.: Encoder-decoder with atrous separable convolution for semantic image segmentation. arXiv preprint arXiv:1802.02611 (2018)
7. Chen, X., Mottaghi, R., Liu, X., Fidler, S., Urtasun, R., Yuille, A.: Detect what you can: detecting and representing objects using holistic models and body parts. In: CVPR, pp. 1971–1978 (2014)
8. Hu, R., James, S., Wang, T., Collomosse, J.: Markov random fields for sketch based video retrieval. In: Proceedings of the 3rd ACM Conference on International Conference on Multimedia Retrieval, pp. 279–286. ACM (2013)
9. Hu, R., Wang, T., Collomosse, J.P.: A bag-of-regions approach to sketch-based image retrieval. In: ICIP, pp. 3661–3664 (2011)
10. Insafutdinov, E., Pishchulin, L., Andres, B., Andriluka, M., Schiele, B.: DeeperCut: a deeper, stronger, and faster multi-person pose estimation model. In: Leibe, B., Matas, J., Sebe, N., Welling, M. (eds.) ECCV 2016. LNCS, vol. 9910, pp. 34–50. Springer, Cham (2016). https://doi.org/10.1007/978-3-319-46466-4_3
11. Jiang, H., Grauman, K.: Detangling people: individuating multiple close people and their body parts via region assembly. arXiv preprint arXiv:1604.03880 (2016)
12. Kalayeh, M.M., Basaran, E., Gökmen, M., Kamasak, M.E., Shah, M.: Human semantic parsing for person re-identification. In: Proceedings of the IEEE Conference on Computer Vision and Pattern Recognition, pp. 1062–1071 (2018)
13. Kyprianidis, J.E., Collomosse, J., Wang, T., Isenberg, T.: State of the "art": a taxonomy of artistic stylization techniques for images and video. IEEE Trans. Visual Comput. Graph. **19**(5), 866–885 (2012)
14. Lee, C.Y., Xie, S., Gallagher, P., Zhang, Z., Tu, Z.: Deeply-supervised nets. In: Artificial Intelligence and Statistics, pp. 562–570 (2015)
15. Li, D., Chen, X., Zhang, Z., Huang, K.: Pose guided deep model for pedestrian attribute recognition in surveillance scenarios. In: 2018 IEEE International Conference on Multimedia and Expo (ICME), pp. 1–6. IEEE (2018)

16. Li, Q., Arnab, A., Torr, P.H.: Holistic, instance-level human parsing. arXiv preprint arXiv:1709.03612 (2017)
17. Li, S., Bak, S., Carr, P., Wang, X.: Diversity regularized spatiotemporal attention for video-based person re-identification. In: Proceedings of the IEEE Conference on Computer Vision and Pattern Recognition, pp. 369–378 (2018)
18. Liang, X., Shen, X., Feng, J., Lin, L., Yan, S.: Semantic object parsing with graph LSTM. In: Leibe, B., Matas, J., Sebe, N., Welling, M. (eds.) ECCV 2016. LNCS, vol. 9905, pp. 125–143. Springer, Cham (2016). https://doi.org/10.1007/978-3-319-46448-0_8
19. Liang, X., Shen, X., Xiang, D., Feng, J., Lin, L., Yan, S.: Semantic object parsing with local-global long short-term memory. In: CVPR, pp. 3185–3193 (2016)
20. Long, J., Shelhamer, E., Darrell, T.: Fully convolutional networks for semantic segmentation. In: CVPR, pp. 3431–3440 (2015)
21. Luo, P., Wang, X., Tang, X.: Pedestrian parsing via deep decompositional network. In: ICCV, pp. 2648–2655 (2013)
22. Ma, L., Yang, X., Xu, Y., Zhu, J.: Human identification using body prior and generalized EMD. In: ICIP, pp. 1441–1444. IEEE (2011)
23. Ronneberger, O., Fischer, P., Brox, T.: U-net: convolutional networks for biomedical image segmentation. In: Navab, N., Hornegger, J., Wells, W.M., Frangi, A.F. (eds.) MICCAI 2015. LNCS, vol. 9351, pp. 234–241. Springer, Cham (2015). https://doi.org/10.1007/978-3-319-24574-4_28
24. Wang, H., Raiko, T., Lensu, L., Wang, T., Karhunen, J.: Semi-supervised domain adaptation for weakly labeled semantic video object segmentation. In: Lai, S.-H., Lepetit, V., Nishino, K., Sato, Y. (eds.) ACCV 2016. LNCS, vol. 10111, pp. 163–179. Springer, Cham (2017). https://doi.org/10.1007/978-3-319-54181-5_11
25. Wang, H., Wang, T., Chen, K., Kämäräinen, J.K.: Cross-granularity graph inference for semantic video object segmentation. In: IJCAI, pp. 4544–4550 (2017)
26. Wang, L., Lee, C.Y., Tu, Z., Lazebnik, S.: Training deeper convolutional networks with deep supervision. arXiv preprint arXiv:1505.02496 (2015)
27. Wang, P., Shen, X., Lin, Z., Cohen, S., Price, B., Yuille, A.L.: Joint object and part segmentation using deep learned potentials. In: ICCV, pp. 1573–1581 (2015)
28. Wang, T., Collomosse, J., Hu, R., Slatter, D., Greig, D., Cheatle, P.: Stylized ambient displays of digital media collections. Comput. Graph. 35(1), 54–66 (2011)
29. Wang, T., Collomosse, J., Slatter, D., Cheatle, P., Greig, D.: Video stylization for digital ambient displays of home movies. In: Proceedings of the 8th International Symposium on Non-Photorealistic Animation and Rendering, pp. 137–146. ACM (2010)
30. Wang, T., Collomosse, J.P., Hunter, A., Greig, D.: Learnable stroke models for example-based portrait painting. In: BMVC (2013)
31. Wang, T., Han, B., Collomosse, J.P.: Touchcut: fast image and video segmentation using single-touch interaction. Comput. Vis. Image Underst. 120, 14–30 (2014)
32. Wang, T., Wang, H.: Graph transduction learning of object proposals for video object segmentation. In: Cremers, D., Reid, I., Saito, H., Yang, M.-H. (eds.) ACCV 2014. LNCS, vol. 9006, pp. 553–568. Springer, Cham (2015). https://doi.org/10.1007/978-3-319-16817-3_36
33. Wang, T., Wang, H.: Non-parametric contextual relationship learning for semantic video object segmentation. In: Vera-Rodriguez, R., Fierrez, J., Morales, A. (eds.) CIARP 2018. LNCS, vol. 11401, pp. 325–333. Springer, Cham (2019). https://doi.org/10.1007/978-3-030-13469-3_38
34. Wang, T., Wang, H., Fan, L.: Robust interactive image segmentation with weak supervision for mobile touch screen devices. In: ICME, pp. 1–6 (2015)

35. Wang, T., Wang, H., Fan, L.: A weakly supervised geodesic level set framework for interactive image segmentation. Neurocomputing **168**, 55–64 (2015)

36. Wei, L., Zhang, S., Yao, H., Gao, W., Tian, Q.: GLAD: global-local-alignment descriptor for pedestrian retrieval. In: Proceedings of the 25th ACM International Conference on Multimedia, pp. 420–428. ACM (2017)

37. Xia, F., Wang, P., Chen, L.-C., Yuille, A.L.: Zoom better to see clearer: human and object parsing with hierarchical auto-zoom net. In: Leibe, B., Matas, J., Sebe, N., Welling, M. (eds.) ECCV 2016. LNCS, vol. 9909, pp. 648–663. Springer, Cham (2016). https://doi.org/10.1007/978-3-319-46454-1_39

38. Xia, F., Wang, P., Chen, X., Yuille, A.: Joint multi-person pose estimation and semantic part segmentation. arXiv preprint arXiv:1708.03383 (2017)

39. Yamaguchi, K., Kiapour, M.H., Ortiz, L.E., Berg, T.L.: Retrieving similar styles to parse clothing. IEEE Trans. Pattern Anal. Mach. Intell. **37**(5), 1028–1040 (2015)

40. Yang, C., Duraiswami, R., Gumerov, N.A., Davis, L.: Improved fast gauss transform and efficient kernel density estimation. In: ICCV, p. 464 (2003)

41. Yu, C., Wang, J., Peng, C., Gao, C., Yu, G., Sang, N.: Learning a discriminative feature network for semantic segmentation. arXiv preprint arXiv:1804.09337 (2018)

42. Zhang, N., Donahue, J., Girshick, R., Darrell, T.: Part-based R-CNNs for fine-grained category detection. In: Fleet, D., Pajdla, T., Schiele, B., Tuytelaars, T. (eds.) ECCV 2014. LNCS, vol. 8689, pp. 834–849. Springer, Cham (2014). https://doi.org/10.1007/978-3-319-10590-1_54

43. Zhu, B., Chen, Y., Tang, M., Wang, J.: Progressive cognitive human parsing. In: AAAI, pp. 7607–7614 (2018)

A Global-Local Architecture Constrained by Multiple Attributes for Person Re-identification

Chao Liu and Hongyang Quan[(✉)]

School of Computer Science and Software Engineering,
East China Normal University, Shanghai, China
51174500106@stu.ecnu.edu.cn, hyquan@sei.ecnu.edu.cn

Abstract. Person re-identification (person re-ID) is often considered as a sub-problem of image retrieval, which aims to match pedestrians under non-overlapping cameras. In this work, we present a novel global and local network structure integrating pedestrian identities with multiple attributes to improve the performance of person re-ID. The proposed framework consists of three modules: shared one, global one and local one. The shared module based on pre-trained residual network extracts low-level and mid-level features. And the global module guided by identification loss learns high-level semantic feature representations. To achieve accurate localization of local attribute features, we propose a multi-attributes partitioning learning method and consider pedestrian attributes as supervised information of the local module. Meanwhile, we employ whole-to-part spatial transformer networks (STNs) to achieve coarse-to-fine meaningful feature locations. By applying a multi-task learning strategy, we design various objective functions including identification and multiple attributes classification losses for training our model. The experimental results on several challenging datasets show our method significantly improves person re-ID performance and surpasses most of the state-of-the-art methods. Specifically, our model achieves 87.49% of the attribute recognition accuracy on Market1501 dataset.

Keywords: Person re-ID · Global and local ·
Multi-attributes partitioning learning · Whole-to-part STNs ·
Multi-task learning

1 Introduction

Person re-ID, originating from object tracking across the cameras, aims to solve the problem of pedestrian matching whether pedestrians under different cameras belong to the same identity. The main challenges for person re-ID come from low-resolution images, huge variation in person postures, occlusion between pedestrians and other objects as well as illumination. Nevertheless, these challenges have brought difficulties to person re-ID tasks, and thus it is necessary to develop an effective algorithm model to explore the technology of person re-ID.

© Springer Nature Switzerland AG 2019
I. V. Tetko et al. (Eds.): ICANN 2019, LNCS 11729, pp. 281–293, 2019.
https://doi.org/10.1007/978-3-030-30508-6_23

In recent years, the prosperity of convolutional neural networks (CNN) promotes the rapid development of the performance of person re-ID. Most of the existing methods solve person re-ID by constructing effective CNN models that have powerful representations. Massive studies [9,15,16] have shown that local features augment the discriminative capability of the model and are less affected by the problems of unrelated background and partial occlusion. In [9], the strategy of joint learning learned pedestrian local features and global features by using multi-classification loss simultaneously. A network named Part-based Convolutional Baseline (PCB) is proposed in [15] and this study adopted a uniform partitioning strategy to extract part-level features. However, a simple uniform segmentation strategy may result in a situation where some regions contain only insignificant background information.

Some studies including [11–14] introduced pedestrian attributes into their proposed model. In theory, attributes as high semantic features can provide key auxiliary information that has contributed to making the model better pay more attention to discriminative local features. Our method is to classify pedestrian attributes according to corresponding parts of the body and we propose a strategy of multi-attributes partition learning in our re-ID model. For satisfying accurate location of local features, we perform horizontal region segmentation to extract desired regions containing different level attributes.

Our main contributions are summarized as follows: (1) We develop a novel global-local network structure constrained by multiple attributes. (2) To alleviate background information, we introduce whole-to-part STNs [7] to make our model focus more on pedestrian information and extract more robust and meaningful features. (3) Guided by the strategy of multi-attributes partition learning, a local network structure is used to capture accurate attribute information. As shown in Fig. 1, different color boxes represent different pedestrian body areas, which have corresponding pedestrian attributes. Furthermore, experiments show that our proposed method can improve the performance of person re-ID.

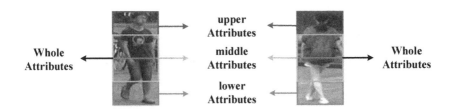

Fig. 1. Sample images contain some visual attributes, and different regions are represented by different attributes. And whole attributes, such as gender, can be reflected in the whole pedestrian. (Color figure online)

2   Related Work

2.1   Hand-Crafted Systems for Person re-ID

Several traditional methods including [3,8,10], solved person re-ID by extracting hand-crafted features such as color histogram, and SIFT descriptor. Farenzena et al. [3] extracted three complementary features for dealing with occlusion, pose, viewpoint and illumination. Koestinger et al. [8] introduced "KISSME" based on scalability and Mahalanobis metric learning model to learn a distance metric from equivalence constraints. Liao et al. [10] proposed an effective feature representation called Local Maximal Occurrence (LOMO) and developed cross-view metric learning (XQDA) based on KISSME Revisit and Bayesian Face.

2.2   Deep Learning for Person re-ID

Compared with hand-crafted methods, deep learning based methods are shown more powerful representation in person re-ID task.

Deep Metric Learning. These approaches usually take two or three images as an input of a model. Representative studies include [1,2,6,18]. Ahmed et al. [1] introduced a novel layer that calculated cross-input neighborhood differences between the mid-level feature of paired images. In [2], triplet loss is proposed for the first time in re-ID tasks. However, the proposed triplet loss method limited the generalization ability of the network. To address this problem, Hermans et al. [6] proposed an online batch hard sample mining strategy.

Deep Representation Learning. Representation learning are shown in [4,11,19,23]. Xiao et al. [19] developed Domain Guided Dropout (DGD) algorithm, which learned robust feature representation from multi data domain in person re-ID datasets. Pedestrian alignment network (PAN) is introduced in [23], which learned discriminative embedding and achieve pedestrian alignment without extra annotations. Lin et al. [11] proposed an attribute recognition network based on CNN that not only learned feature but also predicted pedestrian attributes.

Local Feature Learning. Local feature extraction methods had proven effective in [9,15–17,20]. For instance, Wei et al. [17] proposed Global-Local-Alignment Descriptor (GLAD) which extract robust human local features to solve human pose variation and misalignment of detected images. Sun et al. [15] proposed a uniform partition strategy and used Refined Part Pooling (RPP) to align the segmentation parts which correct within-part inconsistency. Wang et al. [16] based on PCB developed Multiple Granularities Network (MGN) for learning discriminative pedestrian feature.

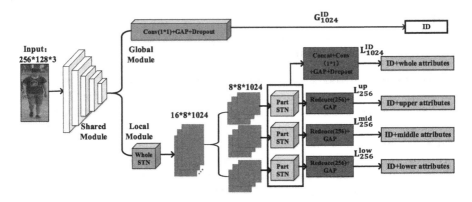

Fig. 2. Overall architecture of our proposed method. It mainly contains three modules. Firstly, the shared module is based on modified ResNet-101 (remove max-pooling and fully connected layers). And we feed ResNet101-4 and ResNet101-5 feature maps into our local and global modules, respectively. Secondly, the global module is trained with identification (ID) loss. Finally, the local module is responsible for learning multi-attributes features and predict multiple pedestrian attributes. Meanwhile, attributes are classified accurately into four categories including whole, upper, middle and lower parts. GAP denotes global average pooling.

3   Proposed Method

In this section, we give a detailed description of our proposed approach. The overall structure of our model is illustrated in Fig. 2. It is essentially an end-to-end network structure that learns discriminative pedestrian features and consists of three modules. The shared module is based on pre-trained ResNet-101 [5], the global module represents pedestrian global features, and the local module extracts local meaningful features and predicts multiple attributes.

3.1   Shared Module

We deliberately adopt ResNet-101 as our basic feature extractor, as it yields competitive person re-ID performance. The first layer of the ResNet-101 has a series of operations that include convolution, batch normalization, ReLU activation, and max pooling. The following layers contain four residual blocks, and we define these blocks as ResNet101-i, i = 2, 3, 4, 5. Concretely, we use the feature extractor to transform raw pixels into convolutional feature maps whilst to capture low-level and mid-level visual information of pedestrians. After ResNet101-5 and ResNet101-4 feature maps are computed for input images, they are feed into global and local modules respectively, which improves the correlation and complementarity between two modules. Further, we argue that sharing low-level and mid-level features facilitates the high-level feature relationship between the global and local modules, also decreases training parameters of our model.

3.2   Global Module

This module learns global spatial information of pedestrian for the whole image and extracts more abstract semantic features for discriminating person. After forward propagation of our pre-trained ResNet-101 network, output feature maps are $8 \times 4 \times 2048$, therefore we select 2048 channels of feature maps as the input of this module. Then they are passed through a 1×1 (1024 channels) convolution layer, followed by a global average pooling (GAP) layer to summarize into a 1024-dimensional vector. As a result, we get a 1024-dimensional global feature as a global representation that increases the speed of the retrieval task. To prevelnt overfitting and improve the generalization ability of the model, we use Dropout of 0.5. Finally, after Batch Normalization, we add a softmax layer to map the 1024-dimensional vector to K probabilities. In Market1501 dataset [21], training set has $K = 751$ identities, and K is 702 in DukeMTMC-reID dataset [22].

3.3   Local Module for Multi-attributes Recognition

The global module only learns global information of pedestrians, and meanwhile, the global feature is more affected by partial occlusion, complex background, and non-rigid deformations of pedestrians. Due to the drawback of the global feature, it is essential to find the local meaningful regions in pedestrian images. And pedestrian attributes, as significant local features, are beneficial to identify different pedestrians. In order to accurately locate pedestrian attributes at different levels, we design an effective local framework including four sub-networks that can predict different level pedestrian attributes. And through the strategy of multi-attributes partition learning, more important pedestrian features are captured.

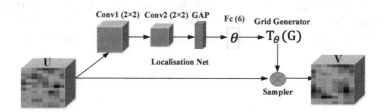

Fig. 3. The structure of STN module.

In order to keep more pedestrian feature information, we adopt feature maps of ResNet101-4 as the input of the local module. In the meantime, we introduce a whole STN acted on ResNet101-4 feature maps to locate foreground information and alleviate background influence. Through the weak supervision of pedestrian identity loss, the whole STN can achieve the overall rough transformation which is beneficial to achieving rough pedestrian location. Figure 3 represents our improved STN and shows the structure parameters of our localization network. Concretely, we discard two fully connected layers and add two convolution layers, GAP, and a fully connected layer. Fully connection layer outputs transformation parameters θ, which is used to realize the transformation of feature maps.

The effect of the whole STN mentioned above is to remove background information interference, so that we implement horizontal partitioning strategy to ensure that each part contains less irrelevant background information. With the usage of horizontal partitioning strategy, we can obtain three uniform parts and integrate these parts to obtain whole attributes features. From top to bottom, each part covers overlapping information whilst each contains different pedestrian body correspondingly. Subsequently, three parts are fed into different subnetworks for extracting different level pedestrian attributes.

Likewise, we apply three part STNs, working for attributes at different levels, which force the local module to learn different level attributes features effectively. Three overlapping parts share the same structure of part STN but have different training parameters. For predicting multiple pedestrian attributes accurately, we introduce local multi-attributes as major supervision. Simultaneously, each region also adds pedestrian identification information, which can be complementary to pedestrian attributes. Further, this module with part STNs encourages the local network to focus more on local information about pedestrians and achieve more accurate feature locations. To get an entire spatial feature for predicting whole attributes, we fuse three overlapping parts that are passed through part STNs into whole features. After a series of operations including dimensionality reduction, GAP, and Dropout, we obtain a 1024-dimensional vector.

3.4 Loss Function

Our model outputs ID classification and the prediction of pedestrian attributes, so the Cross-Entropy loss function is utilized to train this model in the initial stage. Loss functions of the global and local modules are formulated as:

$$L_{global} = L_{global\text{-}ID} = -\sum_{k=1}^{K} log(p(k))q(k), \tag{1}$$

$$L_{local} = \lambda * \frac{1}{M} \sum_{i}^{M} L_{local\text{-}ID} + \frac{1}{N} \sum_{i}^{N} L_{local\text{-}attributes}, \tag{2}$$

where $q(y) = 1$ when y is the ground-truth label, $L_{global\text{-}ID}$ and $L_{local\text{-}ID}$ are the Cross-Entropy loss of pedestrian identification, and $L_{local\text{-}attributes}$ is a binary classification loss. As Fig. 2 shows, the local module has four branches, so we set M to 4. We choose 7 remarkable pedestrian attributes, so N is 7.

The whole model combining the global module with the local module is trained with identification and multiple attributes losses. So final loss function is written as follows:

$$L_{total} = \lambda * L_{global} + L_{local}, \tag{3}$$

where parameter λ is a hyper parameter, which measures the contribution between ID loss and local multiple attributes loss. Our experiment prove that $\lambda = 2$ is best.

Recently, triplet loss has been widely used in reID tasks. In the fine-tuning stage, we also use batch hard triplet loss, similar to [6]. These features including G_{1024}^{ID} and L_{1024}^{ID} (Fig. 2) are concatenated for training with triplet loss to enhance the performance of reID task. The triplet loss is as follows:

$$L_{triplet} = -\sum_{i=1}^{P}\sum_{a=1}^{K}[\beta + \max_{p=1...K}||F_a^{(i)} - F_p^{(i)}||_2 - \min_{\substack{j=1...P \\ n=1...K \\ j \neq i}}||F_a^{(i)} - F_n^{(j)}||_2]_+, \quad (4)$$

where $F_a^{(i)}$, $F_p^{(i)}$, $F_n^{(j)}$ are features of anchor, positive and negative samples respectively, and β is margin hyperparameter. We set β to 1.0 in our paper.

4   Experiment

4.1   Datasets

Market1501 is a large person re-ID dataset, which contains 12936 training images with 751 identities, 19732 gallery images with another 750 identities and 3368 query images captured by 6 cameras. The dataset contains pedestrian attribute annotations, such as whether to carry a backpack or not, and whether to wear a hat or not. And in this dataset, we select 7 attributes that look remarkable in visual. In the evaluation phase, we use two types of evaluation: Single Query and Multi Query.

DukeMTMC-reID is another challenging pedestrian dataset and is a subset of the DukeMTMC dataset. In contrast to Market1501, it contains more training images that have 16522 training images of 702 identities, 17661 gallery images of 702 identities and 2228 query images collected by 8 cameras. The challenge of this dataset is severe occlusion.

Evaluation Metrics. In this paper, we use Rank-k ($k = 1, 5, 10$) and mean average precision (mAP) to evaluate our proposed method. Rank-k stands for the probability of hitting in the first K pictures. For each probe, if K images do not contain the pedestrian category of this probe, Rank-$k = 0$. And if K images contain N ($\leq K$) pictures of this, Rank-$k = N/K$.

4.2   Data Augmented

For two pedestrian datasets, all images are resized to 256×128, which keeps image proportion distribution and prevent geometric distortion. We adopt data augment strategies such as random horizontal flipping, random brightness change and so on. In order to speed up the training process, we normalize pixel values

Fig. 4. Sample images of Random Erasing in Market1501 dataset

of mini-batch images the same interval ($pixel \in \{-1, 1\}$), which makes our input conform to a uniform distribution.

Random Erasing [24] is a data augment method. Our approach is to select one or more specific areas of the processed image and give random pixel values to these specific areas. And the area does not exceed the height and width of a processed image. Figure 4 shows some results of Random Erasing. In our Experiments, the ratio between erased areas and original image is $s \in \{0.02, 0.20\}$.

4.3   Model Learning and Implementation Details

The entire training process is based on the PyTorch framework. Network parameters are optimized by stochastic gradient descent (SGD). For extracting accurate low-level and mid-level pedestrian features, we train a basic ResNet101 model on Market1501 dataset in pre-trained step. In the training phase, we use L_{total} in Eq. (3) to train our overall model. The batch size is set to 32. We set the number of epochs to 200. At the beginning of the training step, we initialize the learning rate to 0.01, dropped to 0.001 after 50 epochs, In order to ensure a steady decline in loss lately, learning rate drops to 0.0001 at the last 100 epochs. In the fine-tuning stage, we fix the training parameters of modified ResNet-101 and add triplet loss in Eq. (4) to train our model until convergence.

During the evaluation stage, we obtain 2816-dimensional feature vectors as our finally pedestrian features. For each probe, we compute the Euclidean distance between each probe and all images of the gallery.

4.4   Evaluation of Our Method

We compare our proposed model with several deep learning and hand-crafted feature re-ID models. Results on two datasets are shown in Table 1. It is obvious that our method outperforms most of the existing methods. For the Market1501, we obtain **Rank-1 = 94.8%, mAP = 85.5%** (without triplet). And we achieve **Rank-1 = 86.5%, mAP = 76.1%** (without triplet) on DukeMTMC-reID.

Similar to APR [11] and Sun et al. [14], our model also employs a multi-task learning strategy, together with the attribute loss function. From Table 1, we can see that our results (without triplet) are better than APR network which also adds multiple attributes loss to the objective functions. Compared to it, Rank-1 increase by 10.51%, and mAP yield a remarkably increase of 20.83%

Table 1. Experimental results on Market1501 and DukeMTMC-reID datasets

Market1501	Rank-1	mAP	DukeMTMC-reID	Rank-1	mAP
LOMO+XQDA [10]	43.79	22.22	LOMO+XQDA [10]	30.75	17.04
ACRN [13]	83.61	62.60	ACRN [13]	72.58	51.6
APR [11]	84.29	64.67	APR [11]	70.69	51.88
JLML [9]	85.1	65.5	JLML [9]	–	–
Alignment (GAN) [23]	86.67	69.33	Alignment (GAN) [23]	71.59	51.5
Sun et al. [14]	87.05	70.12	Sun et al. [14]	80.57	66.68
PCB+RPP [15]	93.8	81.6	PCB+RPP [15]	83.3	69.2
MGN [16]	**95.7**	86.9	MGN [16]	88.7	78.4
Ours	94.8	85.5	Ours	86.5	76.1
Ours + Triplet [6]	95.2	**87.1**	Ours + Triplet [6]	**88.9**	**78.9**

on Market1501 dataset. And Rank-1 and mAP increase by 15.81% and 24.22% by a large margin on DukeMTMC-reID. We apply three part STNs to each segmentation feature maps which can locate and extract meaningful attributes features. It can be seen that our results of Rank-1 and mAP are superior to Alignment (GAN) [23], which some background information is cropped with STN.

Some methods including JLML [9] and PCB [15] adopted horizontal segmentation strategy. We compare our experimental results with these methods. For instance, PCB achieved competitive performance among above existing methods. Comparing with PCB model, Rank-1 and mAP increase by 1.0% and 3.9%. On DukeMTMC-reID dataset, Rank-1 and mAP rise by 3.2% and 6.9%.

Table 2. Single query and multi query on Market1501 dataset

Methods	Single query		Multi query	
	Rank-1	mAP	Rank-1	mAP
Deep Transfer [4]	83.7	65.6	89.6	73.8
Triplet [6]	84.92	69.14	90.53	76.42
Alignment (GAN) [23]	86.67	69.33	90.88	76.32
MGN [16]	**95.7**	86.9	**96.9**	90.7
Ours	94.8	85.5	95.6	88.7
Ours+Triplet [6]	95.2	**87.1**	96.1	**91.1**

By building complex multi-granularities model, MGN [16] achieved high performance. When we use the batch hard triplet loss [6] that MGN [16] also use this triplet loss, the ratio of mAP improve slightly on Market1501 dataset, and the accuracy of Rank-1 has increased only marginally on another dataset.

Further, we compare Single Query and Multi Query results on the Market1501 dataset. Single Query uses a single probe image for retrieving from the gallery. Nevertheless, for Multi Query, a query feature is calculated by the average of all relevant pedestrian features that have the same identity and camera. From Table 2, we can see that the performance of Multi Query is better than Single Query. Both Rank-1 and mAP also improve step by step. In the meantime, our result is better than most of the existing methods.

Table 3. Results of different components (whole-to-part STNs and Attributes) on Market1501 dataset, where G and L denote Global and Local module respectively.

Network structure	Rank-1	mAP
Shared + G	88.1	69.5
Shared + G + L (NoSTN + Attributes)	90.2	78.2
Shared + G + L (STN + NoAttributes)	91.4	79.8
Shared + G + L (STN + Attributes)	94.8	85.5
Shared + G + L (STN + Attributes) + Triplet	**95.2**	**87.1**

4.5   Further Analysis of Our Effective Model

In order to prove the feasibility of our proposed method, we have designed extensive experiments to explore the impact of adding different components to the local module. The results are shown in Table 3. When the overall network only contains shared (ResNet-101) and global module, Rank-1, and mAP are lowest. Through adding whole-to-part STNs, the rates of Rank-1 and mAP have improved significantly. In order to make whole-to-part STNs pay more attention to local multi-attributes information effectively, we add pedestrian attributes as supervision information for different segmentation parts. Table 3 shows that adding attributes has a significant improvement. As a result, we conclude that whole-to-part STNs are complementary to attribute classification learning and promote extractions of attribute features at different levels.

Table 4. Recognition accuracy of seven visual attributes on Market1501 dataset.

Method	Hair	Hat	Backpack	Bag	Clothes	Handbag	Gender	Mean
APR [11]	83.65	97.13	82.79	75.07	91.46	88.98	86.45	86.50
Sun et al. [14]	78.26	97.06	**85.46**	67.28	84.79	88.40	**88.94**	84.31
Ours	**86.62**	**97.75**	81.89	**75.59**	**92.86**	**89.85**	87.92	**87.49**

Further, we evaluate the effect of multiple-attributes learning on Market1501 dataset. As shown in Table 4, we have obtained competitive attribute recognition

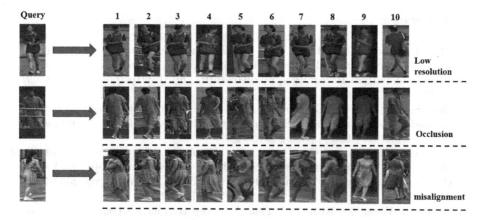

Fig. 5. The visualization results in person retrieval and red bounding box denote false match. (Color figure online)

accuracy and our proposed method outperforms existing methods. Consequently, the integration of multi-attributes learning introduces some degree of complementary information and improves the representation ability of our model.

4.6   Visual Results

For each probe, we visualize the top ten images in the gallery. Figure 5 shows the single-query person re-ID results. It can be seen that there is a good match for the following situation that includes low-resolution, occluded, and misaligned images. For the last row, although the result contains mismatching images that are not the same person, the first five images are successfully matched. This clearly demonstrates the effectiveness of our method against the low-resolution images, occlusion, and misalignment with a person bounding box.

5   Conclusion

Pedestrian attributes are crucial for the study of person re-ID. In this paper, we propose an end-to-end network architecture, which can be capable of expressing robust and discriminative pedestrian features. Whole-to-part STNs make our model concentrate on global and local meaningful features. Multi-attributes partition learning is acted on local convolutional features, which further enables our model to extract effective and distinguishable pedestrian attribute features. And, visual results show that our approach is better for dealing with the problem of partial occlusion and misalignment. Finally, experimental results on two existing datasets with attribute annotations demonstrate the feasibility of our method and are better than most of the state-of-the-art methods. In the future, we will continue to explore the connection between multiple attributes.

References

1. Ahmed, E., Jones, M., Marks, T.K.: An improved deep learning architecture for person re-identification. In: Proceedings of the IEEE Conference on Computer Vision and Pattern Recognition, pp. 3908–3916 (2015). https://doi.org/10.1109/CVPR.2015.7299016

2. Ding, S., Lin, L., Wang, G., Chao, H.: Deep feature learning with relative distance comparison for person re-identification. Pattern Recogn. **48**(10), 2993–3003 (2015). https://doi.org/10.1016/j.patcog.2015.04.005

3. Farenzena, M., Bazzani, L., Perina, A., Murino, V., Cristani, M.: Person re-identification by symmetry-driven accumulation of local features. In: 2010 IEEE Conference on Computer Vision and Pattern Recognition (CVPR), pp. 2360–2367. IEEE (2010). https://doi.org/10.1109/CVPR.2010.5539926

4. Geng, M., Wang, Y., Xiang, T., Tian, Y.: Deep transfer learning for person re-identification. arXiv preprint arXiv:1611.05244 (2016)

5. He, K., Zhang, X., Ren, S., Sun, J.: Deep residual learning for image recognition. In: Proceedings of the IEEE conference on computer vision and pattern recognition, pp. 770–778 (2016). https://doi.org/10.1109/CVPR.2016.90

6. Hermans, A., Beyer, L., Leibe, B.: In defense of the triplet loss for person re-identification. arXiv preprint arXiv:1703.07737 (2017)

7. Jaderberg, M., Simonyan, K., Zisserman, A., et al.: Spatial transformer networks. In: Advances in Neural Information Processing Systems, pp. 2017–2025 (2015)

8. Koestinger, M., Hirzer, M., Wohlhart, P., Roth, P.M., Bischof, H.: Large scale metric learning from equivalence constraints. In: 2012 IEEE Conference on Computer Vision and Pattern Recognition (CVPR), pp. 2288–2295. IEEE (2012)

9. Li, W., Zhu, X., Gong, S.: Person re-identification by deep joint learning of multi-loss classification, pp. 2194–2200 (2017). https://doi.org/10.24963/ijcai.2017/305

10. Liao, S., Hu, Y., Zhu, X., Li, S.Z.: Person re-identification by local maximal occurrence representation and metric learning. In: Proceedings of the IEEE Conference on Computer Vision and Pattern Recognition, pp. 2197–2206 (2015). https://doi.org/10.1109/CVPR.2015.7298832

11. Lin, Y., Zheng, L., Zheng, Z., Wu, Y., Yang, Y.: Improving person re-identification by attribute and identity learning. arXiv preprint arXiv:1703.07220 (2017)

12. Matsukawa, T., Suzuki, E.: Person re-identification using cnn features learned from combination of attributes. In: International Conference on Pattern Recognition, pp. 2428–2433 (2016). https://doi.org/10.1109/ICPR.2016.7900000

13. Schumann, A., Stiefelhagen, R.: Person re-identification by deep learning attribute-complementary information. In: Proceedings of the IEEE Conference on Computer Vision and Pattern Recognition Workshops, pp. 20–28 (2017)

14. Sun, C., Jiang, N., Zhang, L., Wang, Y., Wu, W., Zhou, Z.: Unified framework for joint attribute classification and person re-identification. In: Kůrková, V., Manolopoulos, Y., Hammer, B., Iliadis, L., Maglogiannis, I. (eds.) ICANN 2018. LNCS, vol. 11139, pp. 637–647. Springer, Cham (2018). https://doi.org/10.1007/978-3-030-01418-6_63

15. Sun, Y., Zheng, L., Yang, Y., Tian, Q., Wang, S.: Beyond part models: person retrieval with refined part pooling (and a strong convolutional baseline), pp. 501–518 (2018). https://doi.org/10.1007/978-3-030-01225-0_30

16. Wang, G., Yuan, Y., Chen, X., Li, J., Zhou, X.: Learning discriminative features with multiple granularities for person re-identification. In: 2018 ACM Multimedia Conference on Multimedia Conference, pp. 274–282. ACM (2018)

17. Wei, L., Zhang, S., Yao, H., Gao, W., Tian, Q.: Glad: global-local-alignment descriptor for pedestrian retrieval. In: Proceedings of the 2017 ACM on Multimedia Conference, pp. 420–428. ACM (2017). https://doi.org/10.1145/3123266.3123279

18. Xiao, Q., Luo, H., Zhang, C.: Margin sample mining loss: a deep learning based method for person re-identification. arXiv preprint arXiv:1710.00478 (2017)

19. Xiao, T., Li, H., Ouyang, W., Wang, X.: Learning deep feature representations with domain guided dropout for person re-identification. In: Proceedings of the IEEE Conference on Computer Vision and Pattern Recognition, pp. 1249–1258 (2016). https://doi.org/10.1109/CVPR.2016.140

20. Zhang, X., et al.: AlignedReID: surpassing human-level performance in person re-identification. arXiv preprint arXiv:1711.08184 (2017)

21. Zheng, L., Shen, L., Tian, L., Wang, S., Wang, J., Tian, Q.: Scalable person re-identification: a benchmark. In: Proceedings of the IEEE International Conference on Computer Vision, pp. 1116–1124 (2015). https://doi.org/10.1109/ICCV.2015.133

22. Zheng, Z., Zheng, L., Yang, Y.: Unlabeled samples generated by GAN improve the person re-identification baseline in vitro. In: IEEE International Conference on Computer Vision, pp. 3774–3782 (2017). https://doi.org/10.1109/ICCV.2017.405

23. Zheng, Z., Zheng, L., Yang, Y.: Pedestrian alignment network for large-scale person re-identification. IEEE Trans. Circuits Syst. Video Technol. (2018)

24. Zhong, Z., Zheng, L., Kang, G., Li, S., Yang, Y.: Random erasing data augmentation. arXiv preprint arXiv:1708.04896 (2017)

Recurrent Connections Aid Occluded Object Recognition by Discounting Occluders

Markus Roland Ernst[1,2]([⊠]) [ID], Jochen Triesch[1,2] [ID], and Thomas Burwick[1,2] [ID]

[1] Frankfurt Institute for Advanced Studies,
Ruth-Moufang-Straße 1, 60438 Frankfurt am Main, Germany
{mernst,triesch,burwick}@fias.uni-frankfurt.de
[2] Goethe-Universität Frankfurt,
Max-von-Laue-Straße 1, 60438 Frankfurt am Main, Germany

Abstract. Recurrent connections in the visual cortex are thought to aid object recognition when part of the stimulus is occluded. Here we investigate if and how recurrent connections in artificial neural networks similarly aid object recognition. We systematically test and compare architectures comprised of bottom-up (B), lateral (L) and top-down (T) connections. Performance is evaluated on a novel stereoscopic occluded object recognition dataset. The task consists of recognizing one target digit occluded by multiple occluder digits in a pseudo-3D environment. We find that recurrent models perform significantly better than their feedforward counterparts, which were matched in parametric complexity. Furthermore, we analyze how the network's representation of the stimuli evolves over time due to recurrent connections. We show that the recurrent connections tend to move the network's representation of an occluded digit towards its un-occluded version. Our results suggest that both the brain and artificial neural networks can exploit recurrent connectivity to aid occluded object recognition.

Keywords: Object recognition · Occlusion · Recurrent neural networks

1 Introduction

Given the rapidness of invariant object recognition in primates [9,25], the process is assumed to be mostly feedforward [5]. This assumption has been corroborated by the recent success of feedforward neural networks in computer vision [12,13] and led to modelling of the primate visual system using such networks [19,21]. However, both anatomical and functional evidence suggest that recurrent connections do indeed influence object recognition. Densities of feedforward

This work was supported by the European Union's Horizon 2020 research and innovation programme under grant agreement № 713010 (GOAL-Robots, Goal-based Open-ended Autonomous Learning Robots).

© Springer Nature Switzerland AG 2019
I. V. Tetko et al. (Eds.): ICANN 2019, LNCS 11729, pp. 294–305, 2019.
https://doi.org/10.1007/978-3-030-30508-6_24

and recurrent connections in the ventral visual pathway are comparable in magnitude [7,23] and electrophysiological experiments have demonstrated that the processing of object information unfolds over time, beyond what would normally be attributed to a feedforward process [3,4]. In particular, recognition of degraded or occluded objects produces delayed behavioral and neural responses [10,24] believed to be caused by competitive processing due to lateral recurrent connections [1].

Other evidence suggests that recurrent top-down connections can fill in missing information in partially occluded images [18]. Additionally, recurrent convolutional neural networks have been shown to improve classification performance on occluded stimuli [15,22]. However, the stimuli used in previous research did hardly resemble an authentic natural environment. The world humans live in and interact with is inherently 3D and occlusion consists of more than just masking one stimulus with another. Rather, it is highly dependent on viewing angle, and primates perceive it stereoscopically with two eyes. Unlike previous simulations and experimental work, where part of the input image was deleted or masked in two dimensions [18,22,24,26], we set out to test the effects of occlusion in a more natural environment. Thus, we extended the generative model for occluded stimuli presented in [22] to account for 3D perspective and stereo vision.

We test and compare a range of different recurrent convolutional neural network architectures, assuming the naming scheme of [15,22]. Bottom-up (B) and top-down (T) connections correspond to processing information from lower and higher regions in the ventral visual hierarchy, and lateral (L) connections process information within a region.

To investigate whether recurrent networks outperform feedforward models in a more naturalistic setting, the different architectures were tasked with classifying objects under varying levels of occlusion. The accuracy or error rate reflects the degree to which the networks learn to recognize the target, and how well they cope with occlusion. Additionally we train and test all networks on stereoscopic image data to quantify the benefit of binocular vision. Finally we explore how recurrent connections shape the probability distribution over possible outcomes and we analyze the internal representation of the occluded stimuli. We conduct a geometrical analysis of activations in the final hidden layer and visualize the evolution of the internal representation in time using t-distributed stochastic neighbor embedding (t-SNE) [16]. Our results demonstrate significant performance advantages of recurrent networks and reveal how recurrence helps to discount the effect of occluders.

2   Methods

2.1   Stereo-Digits Dataset

We investigate the effects of occlusion using a novel stereoscopic image data set. Inspired by the generative image model for occlusion stimuli in [22], we focus on digit recognition. Our stereo-digits dataset is meant to bridge the gap between the somewhat artificial task of recognizing computer rendered digits and the natural task of recognizing partially occluded objects. Contrary to past studies, occlusion is generated by overlapping the target stimulus with other digit instances in a pseudo-3D environment.

All images of the stereo-digits dataset contain digits of the same font and color. Occlusion is generated by overlaying digits on top of each other as shown in Fig. 1A. The target object, i.e. the hindmost digit, is centered in the middle of the square canvas. Additional digits are then sequentially placed on top of the target object. These occluding objects remain fixed along the y-axis as if standing on a surface 5 cm below the viewer. The x-coordinate is drawn from a uniform distribution. The font size of the digits was scaled to give the impression of objects with 20 cm height placed at different depths. We assumed a distance of 50 cm from the target object to the viewer, and 10 cm less for every added object. The level of occlusion can be controlled by varying the number of occluder objects, which increases the difficulty of the task. Images for the left and right eye were taken given an interocular distance of 6.8 cm. Each dataset (2, 3, 4 occluders) consists of 100,000 randomly generated images for training and 10,000 images for testing. The images were rendered at a resolution of 512×512 and then downsampled to 32×32.

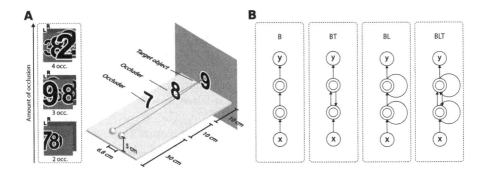

Fig. 1. The used stimuli and network models. (A) The centered target object is occluded by 2–4 digits arranged in a 3D-fashion. (B) A sketch of the four network architectures named after their connection properties. B stands for bottom-up, L for lateral and T for top-down connections.

2.2   Network Models

Four basic network models were compared as shown in Fig. 1B: Bottom-up connection only (B), bottom-up and top-down connections (BT), bottom-up and lateral connections (BL), and bottom-up, lateral, and top-down connections (BLT). As lateral and top-down connections introduce cycles into the computational graph, these models represent recurrent neural networks and allow for information to be retained within a layer or to flow back into earlier layers.

Each model consists of an input layer, two hidden recurrent layers and an output layer. Both bottom-up and lateral connections are implemented as convolutional layers [14] with a stride of 1×1. After convolution the activations go through a 2×2 maxpooling layer with a stride of 2×2. The top-down connections are implemented as a transposed convolution [27] with output stride 2×2 to match the input size of the convolutional layer that came before it. Each of the recurrent network models is unrolled and trained for four time steps by backpropagation [20]. When measuring accuracy, the output at the final unrolled time step available for the particular architecture is used. To compensate for the fact that recurrent network models have more learnable parameters than their non-recurrent counterparts, we introduce two additional feedforward models B-F and B-K. B-F is a feedforward model where the number of convolutional filters or kernels in the hidden layers is increased from 32 to 64. B-K has an increased convolutional kernel size of 5×5 compared to 3×3 of the standard B model. As a larger kernel effectively increases the number of connections that each unit has, B-K is a more appropriate model for control. B-F on the other hand alters the representational power of the model by adding more feature maps. The number of learnable parameters for each of the models can be found in Table 1.

Table 1. Number of learnable parameters for all models and input channels.

	B	B-F	B-K	BT	BL	BLT
Kernel size	3×3	3×3	5×5	3×3	3×3	3×3
Hidden layer units	32	64	32	32	32	32
Image channels	Number of learnable parameters					
1	9,898	38,218	26,794	19,146	28,394	37,642
2	10,186	38,794	27,594	19,434	28,682	37,930

Layers. After the stimulus enters the network, its activations pass two hidden convolutional layers. The inputs to these layer are denoted by $\mathbf{h}_{i,j}^{(t,l)}$. This formulation represents the vectorized input of a patch centered on location (i, j) in layer l computed at time step t across all feature maps indexed by k. Assuming this notation the input stimulus presented to the network becomes $\mathbf{h}_{i,j}^{(t,0)}$. The activation z of a hidden recurrent layer can then be written as

$$z_{i,j,k}^{(t,l)} = \left(\mathbf{w}_k^{(l)B}\right)^{\top} \mathbf{h}_{i,j}^{(t,l-1)} + \left(\mathbf{w}_k^{(l)L}\right)^{\top} \mathbf{h}_{i,j}^{(t-1,l)} + \left(\mathbf{w}_k^{(l)T}\right)^{\top} \mathbf{h}_{i,j}^{(t-1,l+1)}, \quad (1)$$

where $\mathbf{w}_k^{(l)\cdot}$ is the vectorized form of the convolutional kernel at feature map k in layer l for bottom-up (B), lateral (L), and top-down (T) connections, respectively. These kernels become only active for architectures using the particular connection and are otherwise zero. Note that the lateral and top-down connections depend on values one time step earlier, so the inputs are defined to be a vector of zeroes for $t = 0$ where there would be no previous time step. Top-down connections are only present between the two hidden layers (Fig. 1B).

Following the flow of information, the $z_{i,j,k}^{(t,l)}$ of the hidden layers are then batch-normalized [8]. This technique normalizes an activation z using the mean $\mu_\mathcal{B}$ and standard deviation $\sigma_\mathcal{B}$ over a mini-batch of activations $\mathcal{B}$ and adds multiplicative and additive noise.

$$\text{BN}_{\gamma,\beta}(z_{i,j,k}^{(t,l)}) = \gamma_k^{(l)} \cdot \frac{z_{i,j,k}^{(t,l)} - \mu_\mathcal{B}}{\sigma_\mathcal{B}} + \beta_k^{(l)}, \tag{2}$$

where γ and β are additional learnable parameters.

The output then is passed to rectified linear units (ReLU, σ_z)

$$\sigma_z\left(z_{i,j,k}^{(t,l)}\right) = \max\left(0, z_{i,j,k}^{(t,l)}\right) \tag{3}$$

and goes through local response normalization (LRN, ω)

$$\omega(a_{i,j,k}^{(t,l)}) = a_{i,j,k}^{(t,l)} \left(c + \alpha \sum_{k'=\max(0,k-\frac{n}{2})}^{\min(n-1,k+\frac{n}{2})} \left(a_{i,j,k'}^{(t,l)}\right)^2\right)^{-\beta}, \tag{4}$$

with $n = 5$, $c = 1$, $\alpha = 10^{-4}$ and $\beta = 0.5$. Similar in justification to maxpooling, LRN implements a form of lateral inhibition by inducing competition for large activities amongst outputs computed using different kernels [12]. Finally the output $h_{i,j,k}^{(t,l)}$ for each hidden layer can be written as:

$$h_{i,j,k}^{(t,l)} = \omega\left(\sigma_z\left(\text{BN}_{\gamma,\beta}\left(z_{i,j,k}^{(t,l)}\right)\right)\right). \tag{5}$$

After the second hidden layer the information flows through a fully-connected segment with ten output units and softmax activation, defined as:

$$\text{softmax}(\mathbf{a})_i = \frac{\exp(a_i)}{\sum_j \exp(a_j)}. \tag{6}$$

The resulting network output can be interpreted as the probability distribution over the ten classes.

Learning. The labels to be predicted by the network are encoded as one-hot vectors. To make the networks' output $\hat{\mathbf{y}}^{(\tau)}$ match the target $\mathbf{y}$ we use the cross-entropy cost-function summed across all τ time steps and all N output units:

$$J(\hat{\mathbf{y}}^{(\tau)}, \mathbf{y}) = -\sum_{t=0}^{\tau}\sum_{i=0}^{N} y_i \cdot \log \hat{y}_i^{(t)} + (1 - y_i) \cdot \log(1 - \hat{y}_i^{(t)}). \tag{7}$$

The Adam algorithm [11] with an initial learning rate of $\eta = 0.003$ was used to perform gradient descent. Unless stated otherwise training occurred for 25 epochs with mini-batches of size 400.

2.3   Model Performance Metrics and Evaluation Techniques

The different models were evaluated in terms of classification accuracy averaged across the test set. Test performances were compared with each other using pairwise McNemar's tests [17] as suggested in [6]. This technique does not require repeated training and therefore poses a computationally efficient method to evaluate a variety of different models. As multiple comparisons increase the chance of false positives a Bonferroni-type correction procedure was employed to control the false discovery rate (FDR) at 0.05 [2].

3   Results

3.1   Performance Evaluation

Networks were trained on datasets combining all three occlusion levels to evaluate the benefit of feedback connections. Training lasted twenty-five epochs. Figure 2 depicts the classification error $E_{cl} = (1 - \text{accuracy})$ for the models trained with monocular (A) and stereoscopic (B) input.

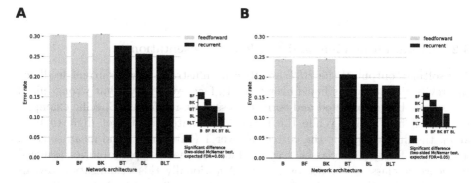

Fig. 2. Performance comparison of different network architectures. Error bars indicate the standard error based on five repetitions of the training and testing procedure. Matrices depict results of pairwise McNemar tests, black squares indicating significant differences at $p < 0.05$. (A) Monocular input. (B) Stereoscopic input.

Our results reveal that recurrent architectures perform consistently better than feedforward networks of approximately equal complexity. Notably, $B\text{-}K$ performs significantly worse than $B\text{-}F$ questioning the benefits of the increased kernel size, $\chi^2(1, N = 30{,}000) = 46.29, p < .01$. Significant differences (FDR = 0.05) can be attested for all combinations except $(B, B\text{-}K)$, $\chi^2(1, N = 30{,}000) = 1.69, p = .13$ and (BL, BLT), $\chi^2(1, N = 30{,}000) = 0.94, p = .26$. The lower left 3×3 square, highlighted by a white line, indicates that all pair-wise tests between feedforward and recurrent models show a significant advantage of the recurrent architectures. The relative differences in error-rate between feedforward and recurrent models are increased for the stereoscopic case.

When trained separately on the three datasets, we observe almost the same patterns while the error-rates grow with the number of occluders as expected (see Table 2). The *BLT* model produces the lowest error-rates for each data set.

Table 2. Error-rates for all model architectures, standard error based on five independent training runs. 2, 3, 4 occ. runs were trained for 100 ep., batchsize 100. Best performance per dataset is highlighted in bold.

Channels	Occ.	B	B-F	B-K	BT	BL	BLT
1 (mono)	2	$.134 \pm .004$	$.123 \pm .003$	$.143 \pm .002$	$.109 \pm .003$	$.103 \pm .003$	$\mathbf{.095 \pm .002}$
	3	$.330 \pm .005$	$.337 \pm .004$	$.359 \pm .004$	$.293 \pm .003$	$.282 \pm .005$	$\mathbf{.280 \pm .003}$
	4	$.512 \pm .005$	$.519 \pm .005$	$.546 \pm .005$	$.477 \pm .003$	$.463 \pm .005$	$\mathbf{.455 \pm .006}$
	all	$.304 \pm .001$	$.284 \pm .001$	$.306 \pm .002$	$.277 \pm .001$	$.257 \pm .001$	$\mathbf{.253 \pm .000}$
2 (stereo)	2	$.095 \pm .003$	$.078 \pm .003$	$.094 \pm .003$	$.069 \pm .003$	$.059 \pm .002$	$\mathbf{.056 \pm .002}$
	3	$.267 \pm .006$	$.279 \pm .003$	$.287 \pm .004$	$.217 \pm .004$	$.199 \pm .003$	$\mathbf{.189 \pm .003}$
	4	$.455 \pm .006$	$.472 \pm .004$	$.482 \pm .005$	$.395 \pm .003$	$.373 \pm .003$	$\mathbf{.361 \pm .003}$
	all	$.244 \pm .000$	$.230 \pm .000$	$.245 \pm .001$	$.207 \pm .001$	$.184 \pm .000$	$\mathbf{.180 \pm .001}$

3.2   Evolution in Time and Hidden Representation

The softmax output of the *BLT* architecture illustrates how recurrent feedback can revise the network's belief over time. In fact, we observe that wrong initial guesses are being corrected and correct guesses are reinforced. Specific examples are shown in Fig. 3A: While the network estimates the target digit to be 6 at t_0, the final output is the correct answer 1 (left panel). The mean softmax activations for specific classes, Fig. 3B, indicate that the probabilities assigned to incorrect classes decrease over time. Additionally this visualization reveals systematic visual similarities that the network has discovered between digits 2 and 7 and digits 4 and 1.

To better understand how recurrent connections contribute to the performance gains, we consider the activation patterns $\mathbf{a}^{(t)}$ from the last hidden layer of the network for every time step t. We visualize the corresponding high-dimensional space using t-SNE [16], see Fig. 4. The black lines represent the activations caused by un-occluded stimuli evolving in time, henceforth called time-trajectories. The colored scatter-plots illustrate the activations corresponding to occluded stimuli of different classes at different time steps.

Interestingly, the t-SNE visualization reveals the internal representation at the first time step to be more intermingled where arguably very similar stimuli across classes are placed close to each other. At later time steps, however, the representation becomes well-separated and classes have seemingly no overlap. As seen in Fig. 4A, the representation of the un-occluded stimuli moves towards a corresponding class-cluster at t_3. The first time step accounts for most of the distance travelled, followed by fine adjustments at t_2 and t_3, see detailed view

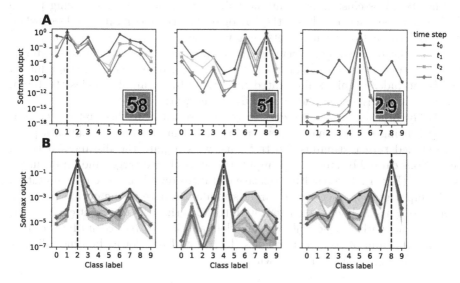

Fig. 3. Softmax output of *BLT*. (A) Specific stimuli (1, 8, 5) illustrating the effect of recurrent feedback. (B) Mean softmax output over all test stimuli of specific classes (2, 4, 8). Shaded areas correspond to standard error.

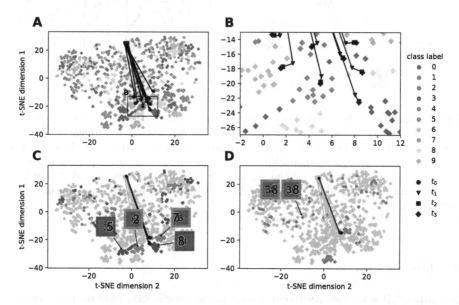

Fig. 4. t-SNE depiction of the network's representation of un-occluded stimuli (black) evolving in time. Time trajectories are shown as black lines, the colors represent clusters of different classes. See text for details. (Color figure online)

in Fig. 4B. Class-clusters at t_3 are actually cluster pairs, corresponding to the occluders appearing mainly on the left or on the right (Fig. 4C). Indeed, when we tested the network with digits that were occluded from one side only, this structure disappeared and every digit was represented by just a single cluster at t_3. Activation patterns that do not fall close to a cluster tend to be dominated by the occluders. This is illustrated in Fig. 4D by a sample of class 9 (blue), shown in high resolution and as seen by the network.

We hypothesize that the recurrent connections help to discount the occluders by keeping the internal representation of the input close to that of a pure, un-occluded target stimulus. To test this, we compare the distances between activations caused by stereo-digit input, the un-occluded target and un-occluded occluders (Fig. 5). The resulting relative distances reveal that the representation of the input grows closer to the target stimulus relative to the occluder stimuli over time. This finding is consistent with the idea that the recurrent connections allow the network to discount the occluders and is also backed up by the finding that the sum of recurrent weights (lateral and top-down) becomes slightly negative during training (not shown).

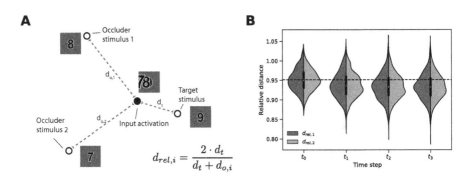

Fig. 5. Analysis of the internal representation of occluded stimuli shows discounting of occluders due to recurrent processing. (A) We define a relative distance measure to quantify if the activation of a stimulus is relatively closer to the un-occluded target compared to the occluder stimuli. Values below one indicate relative proximity to the target. (B) Violin plot displays the relative distances to occluder 1 and 2 at different time steps for stimuli occluded from the left. Dashed line represents mean of the distribution at t_0.

4   Discussion

We studied if and how recurrent connections benefit occluded object recognition. Similar to [22], but for a more realistic dataset we found that recurrent models significantly outperformed their non-recurrent counterparts for a near-equal amount of learnable parameters. Of the feedforward ensemble B-F performed best on the given task suggesting that additional convolutional filters are more helpful than larger filters. Contrary to the findings in [22] *B-K* did not perform better than the standard *B* model. The reported advantage of larger receptive fields might be linked to stimuli, where certain irregularities of the occluders only become obvious at larger scales. Of the recurrent network ensemble *BT* performed worst, suggesting that lateral connections are particularly important. As information has to pass through a convolution, maxpooling and back through a deconvolution instead of being directly transferred within the same layer, information may suffer in quality. In contrast, the *BL* model takes advantage of the lateral shortcuts to pass information through time without utilizing more abstract features. The combination of both models (*BLT*) performs best in all runs.

As previous work has shown, similar recurrent architectures also outperform parameter matched control models when no occlusion is present [15]. This is corroborated by studies that have investigated how object information is unfolding over time in the brain [3]. Therefore, some level of recurrent connectivity in artificial neural networks might be beneficial even for standard object recognition tasks.

The significant performance gains for stereoscopic input can be explained by the fact that the additional input channel introduces a new perspective of the scene, thus giving the network more information about the occluded target. Qualitatively, the results of the statistical network comparisons resemble the ones obtained for monocular stimuli. Interestingly, however, the performance difference between recurrent and feedforward models was substantially higher for stereoscopic stimuli. The on average slightly negative weights of the recurrent connections might contribute to inhibiting or discounting occluders. With the networks dynamics being determined by the ReLU activation function a slight bias towards inhibitory weights might also be key to keep activations centered around the non-linearity.

For recurrent architectures, the probability distribution over possible outcomes has been shown to evolve with time. For challenging stimuli the recurrent dynamics are able to revise the best guess for the target. In line with [18,26], we hypothesized that some of the missing information from occluded regions of the input image is recovered over time by the recurrent connections. The evolution of the output and our qualitative t-SNE analysis supports this hypothesis: At the first time step representations are more intermingled and spread out. Visually very similar stimuli across classes are represented close to each other. At later time steps the representation has evolved in such a way that the classes are well-separated.

The visualization revealed that the recurrent network distinguishes which side of the target stimulus is occluded. This is indicated by the representation of one digit being separated into two well-separated clusters. We conjecture that the network learns the left and right half of the un-occluded stimulus and therefore is able to ignore distractors on the opposing sides. The fragmentation nevertheless allows for high accuracy classification by the final readout layer, since the subsequent fully connected layer is able to classify correctly as long as the activation patterns remain linearly separable.

Investigating the internal representation we could also show that activations of occluded stimuli over time are grouped together with the activation caused by the un-occluded target stimulus relative to the un-occluded occluder digits. The representation being closer to the un-occluded target hints at the recurrent connections playing an important role in discounting the occluders.

In conclusion, recurrent convolutional neural networks have been shown to outperform feedforward networks at occluded object recognition. Building on previous work where parts of the target object were deleted [18] or occluded [22] we could show that the same performance advantages exist for a more realistic 3D occlusion scenario with stereoscopic input. In fact, the advantages were even greater for the more realistic stereoscopic input compared to monocular input. Furthermore, our analysis revealed how recurrent connections revise the network's output over time, sometimes correcting an incorrect initial output after the first feedforward pass through the network. Future work should investigate whether these advantages generalize to larger and more complex network architectures than we considered in this work. Given the better performance and greater biological plausibility of recurrent network architectures, they deserve more detailed study.

References

1. Adesnik, H., Scanziani, M.: Lateral competition for cortical space by layer-specific horizontal circuits. Nature **464**(7292), 1155 (2010). https://doi.org/10.1038/nature08935
2. Benjamini, Y., Hochberg, Y.: Controlling the false discovery rate: a practical and powerful approach to multiple testing. J. Royal Stat. Soc. Ser. B (Methodol.) **57**(1), 289–300 (1995). https://doi.org/10.1111/j.2517-6161.1995.tb02031.x
3. Brincat, S.L., Connor, C.E.: Dynamic shape synthesis in posterior inferotemporal cortex. Neuron **49**(1), 17–24 (2006). https://doi.org/10.1016/j.neuron.2005.11.026
4. Cichy, R.M., Pantazis, D., Oliva, A.: Resolving human object recognition in space and time. Nat. Neurosci. **17**(3), 455 (2014). https://doi.org/10.1038/nn.3635
5. DiCarlo, J.J., Zoccolan, D., Rust, N.C.: How does the brain solve visual object recognition? Neuron **73**(3), 415–434 (2012). https://doi.org/10.1016/j.neuron.2012.01.010
6. Dietterich, T.G.: Approximate statistical tests for comparing supervised classification learning algorithms. Neural Comput. **10**(7), 1895–1923 (1998). https://doi.org/10.1162/089976698300017197
7. Felleman, D.J., Van Essen, D.C.: Distributed hierarchical processing in the primate cerebral cortex. Cereb. Cortex **1**(1), 1–47 (1991). https://doi.org/10.1093/cercor/1.1.1
8. Ioffe, S., Szegedy, C.: Batch normalization: accelerating deep network training by reducing internal covariate shift. In: International Conference on Machine Learning, pp. 448–456 (2015)
9. Isik, L., Meyers, E.M., Leibo, J.Z., Poggio, T.: The dynamics of invariant object recognition in the human visual system. J. Neurophysiol. **111**(1), 91–102 (2014). https://doi.org/10.1152/jn.00394.2013

10. Johnson, J.S., Olshausen, B.A.: The recognition of partially visible natural objects in the presence and absence of their occluders. Vision. Res. **45**(25), 3262–3276 (2005). https://doi.org/10.1016/j.visres.2005.06.007
11. Kingma, D.P., Ba, J.L.: Adam: a method for stochastic optimization. In: Proceedings of the 3rd International Conference on Learning Representations (2014)
12. Krizhevsky, A., Sutskever, I., Hinton, G.E.: Imagenet classification with deep convolutional neural networks. In: Advances in Neural Information Processing Systems, pp. 1097–1105 (2012)
13. LeCun, Y., Bengio, Y., Hinton, G.: Deep learning. Nature **521**(7553), 436 (2015). https://doi.org/10.1038/nature14539
14. LeCun, Y., Bottou, L., Bengio, Y., Haffner, P.: Gradient-based learning applied to document recognition. Proc. IEEE **86**(11), 2278–2324 (1998). https://doi.org/10.1109/5.726791
15. Liang, M., Hu, X.: Recurrent convolutional neural network for object recognition. In: The IEEE Conference on Computer Vision and Pattern Recognition (CVPR), pp. 3367–3375 (2015)
16. Maaten, L.V.D., Hinton, G.: Visualizing data using t-SNE. J. Mach. Learn. Res. **9**(Nov), 2579–2605 (2008)
17. McNemar, Q.: Note on the sampling error of the difference between correlated proportions or percentages. Psychometrika **12**(2), 153–157 (1947). https://doi.org/10.1007/BF02295996
18. O'Reilly, R.C., Wyatte, D., Herd, S., Mingus, B., Jilk, D.J.: Recurrent processing during object recognition. Front. Psychol. **4**, 124 (2013). https://doi.org/10.3389/fpsyg.2013.00124
19. Riesenhuber, M., Poggio, T.: Hierarchical models of object recognition in cortex. Nat. Neurosci. **2**(11), 1019–1025 (1999). https://doi.org/10.1038/14819
20. Rumelhart, D.E., Hinton, G.E., Williams, R.J.: Learning representations by back-propagating errors. Nature **323**(6088), 533 (1986). https://doi.org/10.1038/323533a0
21. Serre, T., Oliva, A., Poggio, T.: A feedforward architecture accounts for rapidcategorization. Proc. Natl. Acad. Sci. **104**(15), 6424–6429 (2007). https://doi.org/10.1073/pnas.0700622104
22. Spoerer, C.J., McClure, P., Kriegeskorte, N.: Recurrent convolutional neural networks: a better model of biological object recognition. Front. Psychol. **8**, 1551 (2017). https://doi.org/10.3389/fpsyg.2017.01551
23. Sporns, O., Zwi, J.D.: The small world of the cerebral cortex. Neuroinformatics **2**(2), 145–162 (2004). https://doi.org/10.1385/NI:2:2:145
24. Tang, H., et al.: Spatiotemporal dynamics underlying object completion in human ventral visual cortex. Neuron **83**(3), 736–748 (2014). https://doi.org/10.1016/j.neuron.2014.06.017
25. Thorpe, S., Fize, D., Marlot, C.: Speed of processing in the human visual system. Nature **381**(6582), 520–522 (1996). https://doi.org/10.1038/381520a0
26. Wyatte, D., Curran, T., O'Reilly, R.: The limits of feedforward vision: recurrent processing promotes robust object recognition when objects are degraded. J. Cogn. Neurosci. **24**(11), 2248–2261 (2012). https://doi.org/10.1162/jocn_a_00282
27. Zeiler, M.D., Krishnan, D., Taylor, G.W., Fergus, R.: Deconvolutional networks. In: 2010 IEEE Computer Society Conference on Computer Vision and Pattern Recognition (CVPR), pp. 2528–2535. IEEE (2010). https://doi.org/10.1109/CVPR.2010.5539957

Learning Relational-Structural Networks for Robust Face Alignment

Congcong Zhu[1], Xing Wang[1], Suping Wu[1,2(✉)], and Zhenhua Yu[1,2]

[1] School of Information Engineering, Ningxia University, Yinchuan 750021, China
{cczhu_nxu,wx_nxu}@163.com, {pswuu,zhyu}@nxu.edu.cn
[2] Collaborative Innovation Center for Cloud Computing and Big Data Applications
of Ningxia, Yinchuan 750021, China

Abstract. Unconstrained face alignment usually undergoes extreme deformations and severe occlusions, which likely gives rise to biased shape prediction. Most existing methods simply exploit shape structure by directly concatenating all landmarks, which leads to losses of facial details in extreme deformation regions. In this paper, we propose a relational-structural networks (RSN) approach to learn both local and global feature representation for robust face alignment. To achieve this goal, we built a structural branch network to disentangle the local geometric relationship among neighboring facial sub-regions. Moreover, we develop a reinforcement learning approach to reason the robust iterative process. Our RSN generates three candidate shapes. Then a Q-net evaluates three candidate shapes by a reward function, which select the best shape to re-initialize network input to alleviate the local optimization problem of cascade regression methods. Authentic experimental results indicate that our approach consistently outperforms the most state-of-the-art methods on widely evaluated challenging datasets.

Keywords: Face alignment · Structured learning ·
Relational network · Reinforcement learning

1 Introduction

Face alignment aims to localize multiple facial landmarks from a given facial image. Recently, efforts have been made to face alignment such as [1–5]. For example, Timothy *et al.* [3] used an appearance model to reconstruct the face and estimate the facial shape, which misses the facial details in complex scenes due to large head poses and occlusion. Georgios *et al.* [5] employed linear regressor, where features employed are hand-crafted and thus require strong prior knowledge. George, Xiong *et al.* [1,4] modeled the face alignment as a cascaded

This work was supported in part by the National Science Foundation of China under Grant 61662059, in part by the Research and Innovation Foundation of First class Universities in Western China under Grant ZKZD2017005.

I. V. Tetko et al. (Eds.): ICANN 2019, LNCS 11729, pp. 306–316, 2019.
https://doi.org/10.1007/978-3-030-30508-6_25

regression process, which adjusts the initial shape to the final shape in a coarse-to-fine manner. These methods impose the shape constraint by jointly regressing over all the points. However, such a coarse constraint cannot be applied to fine prediction of extreme deformed regions. Fan *et al.* [6] proposed to jointly capture global and local features for facial expression recognition by cropping image, which ignores the structural information and the relation of sub-regions. Deng *et al.* [7] proposed the approach based on heat map, which lacks shape constraints leading to the losses of the continuity and integrity of the face shape in the case of occlusion and facial mutilation. Liu *et al.* [8] proposed reasoning-decision networks, which employs the reinforcement learning to reason optimal iteration process. Unfortunately, these methods hardly handle the regions of extreme deformation.

In order to better solve the problem of large poses and self-occlusions, 3D face fitting methods [2,9] have been considered, which aim to fit a 3D morphable model (3DMM) to a 2D image. These methods are retrorse processes and require high quality images. This means that low quality image e.g., severe occlusion can not reconstruct the fine facial model. In addition, these methods of introducing 3D model would consume more computing resources and labeling costs.

To deeply mine the facial structural relation for enhancing the feature representation, we model the shape constraint as a two-order structural relation. From the point of physiological view, the face is divided into different sub-regions. The strong dependence among points in each sub-region is modeled as a first-order structural relation and the position constraint in different sub-regions of the face is modeled as a second-order structural relation. Moreover, we introduce a Q-net based on deep reinforcement learning to evaluate the quality of the candidate shapes. The main contributions of our work are summarized as follows:

(1) In this paper, a relational-structural network is proposed to disentangle the feature representation, which captures both local and global constraint relations to enhance the feature representation and carefully regress landmarks of extreme deformation.

(2) We employ deep reinforcement learning to globally optimize the procedure of learning the alignment error function. We introduce a Q-net to evaluate the quality of the candidate shapes via alignment error, which is used to re-initialize the network input. To achieve this, we design a cumulative reward function to reason the optimal iteration process, which serves to optimize the inferring gradient descent.

2   Relational-Structural Networks

Our basic idea of this paper is to capture both global and local constraint relation of the facial landmarks, in parallel to reason a sequence of efficient iterations. In this section, we describe constraint relation of the facial landmarks, network architecture and optimization strategy.

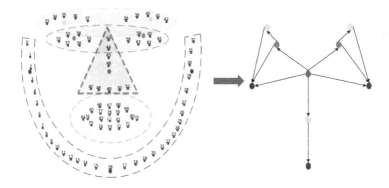

Fig. 1. As can be seen from the left figure, the points in the same sub-region have a strong mutual constraint relation in physiological structure, which is modeled as a first-order structural relation to enhance local feature representation. The structural relation between sub-regions guarantees facial integrity and robustness from the physiological perspective, which is modeled as a second-order structural relationship, as shown on the right.

2.1 Structural Constraint

The facial landmarks physically have a strong mutual constraint relation, we conduct hierarchical modeling for the structural constraint. From the physiological point of view, the face is divided into multiple sub-regions to construct constraint relation, as illustrated in Fig. 1. There is a strong mutual constraint relation among points in each sub-region on physical location. We define this strong constraint relation as the first-order constraint relation and formulate it as:

$$G \to F_{region} \to P_{region} = \{p_1, p_2, \cdots p_n\} \tag{1}$$

where G denotes global feature representation extracted by CNN, F_{region} denotes sub-regional feature disentangled by branch network. P_{region} and n denote a collection of landmarks in a sub-region and the number of points respectively. Our sub-network can capture this constraint relation among physiologically adjacent points in the same sub-region. There are important regional dependencies among the sub-regions, which affects the layout of facial landmarks. We physiologically follow this structural shape dependencies to establish structural relations among sub-regions, which is described in Sect. 2.2.

This fine hierarchical constraint model capture more detailed structural relation. Our method improves the rough joint constraint that makes it difficult to predict the points in extreme deformation of the facial sub-regions.

2.2 Structural Network Module

We construct a relational-structural network to disentangle feature representation for learning constraint relation, which produces a local constraint shape,

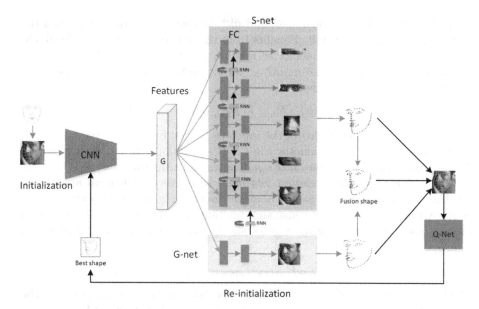

Fig. 2. A graphical representation of our network. Our S-net disentangles the feature representation to subtly predict the facial landmarks in each sub-region. Inside each sub-region, subtle shape constraint is imposed by jointly predicting all the points. The nose, which is physiologically central and has little occlusion and deformation, is placed at the center of the structured network. The G-net captures global shape constraints and share constraint information to S-net. Meanwhile, structural relation are carefully learned by Recurrent Neural Networks (RNN) and we mean structural constraint shape and global constraint shape to generate fusion shape. The Q-net evaluates the quality of the three shapes according to appearance features. Finally, we use the cumulative reward as the evaluation criteria to select the optimal shape and re-initialize the network input.

a global constraint shape, and a fusion shape as candidate shape. Finally, the Markov decision process is used to reason iteration procedure. Our network is shown in Fig. 2. The structural branch network (in Fig. 2 S-net)) consists of five branch networks that are used to subtly disentangle the feature representation for predicting points of each sub-region. The Recurrent Neural Network (RNN) is widely applicable in face alignment and existing works such as MDM [1], which employs a RNN to impose a memory constraint on the descent directions. In the cascade regression methods, the initial shape is gradually adjusted to the final position, which means that learning the constraints between face regions is a gradual process. We use the RNN to impose a gradual constraint on the relation evolution among facial sub-regions, which memorizes the evolution process of the constraint relation to prevent constraints between regions from being divorced from reality. The RNN is formulated as:

$$h^t = \sigma \left(U x^t + W h^{t-1} + b \right) \tag{2}$$

where U and W denote weights, x^t and h^{t-1} denote the current input and the output of $i - 1$th hidden unit. Benefits from the above advantages of the RNN, we employ it to learn and memorize relation features. We take the structural constraint of the nose on the mouth as an example, which can rewrites (2) as the tth iteration constraint feature:

$$f_m^t = \sigma \left(W_m^r \left(F_{nose} \oplus F_{full} \oplus f_m^{t-1} \right) + b_m^r \right) \tag{3}$$

where W_m^r denotes the weights of the input-to-hidden fully connected layers and b_m^r denotes the bias, f_m^{t-1} denotes the $t - 1$th iteration relation feature and $\oplus$ denotes concatenation operation, F_{full} denotes global features learned by G-net (in Fig. 2 gray box). Our relation features can capture both local and global constraint relations. In particular, because the chin region includes the contour of the whole face, it has a constraint relation with the other sub-regions in various poses. Therefore, other regions jointly learn a structural feature, which is formulated as:

$$f_c^t = \sigma \left(W_c^r \left(concat \left(F_{nose}, F_{mouth}, F_{eyes}, F_{brows}, F_{full} \right) \oplus f_c^{t-1} \right) + b_c^r \right) \tag{4}$$

where $concat$ denotes joint concatenation operation. Our branch network of the S-net utilizes the cascading manner to avoid the negative effects of likely occurring extreme deformation regions on other sub-regions. F is the output of the first FC layer and different fs is concatenated into the global feature representations G as the input of multiple branch networks of the S-net.

The outputs of S-net and G-net are fused as a fusion shape and the three shapes are evaluated Q-value by Q-net to select the best shape re-initializing the network input. Our Q-value is designed as a cumulative reward, which helps to optimize regression procedures and infer gradient descents.

2.3   Optimization

Following the MDP process, we design the Q-net network based on the Actor-Critic framework to select the best shape. Our architecture defines an agent to interact with the MDP by an action space, a state space, a state transition function, a reward function, and a policy to select actions.

Action: The action is defined as a selection operation on three shapes, aiming at selecting the best shape to re-initialize the network input.
State: The state is defined as the set of facial features information observed based on shape, which is locally cropped directly from the raw facial image via the shape-indexed manner.
State Transitions: We define a MDP state transition as a transition of appearance features caused by the iterative process.
Reward: The reward function r reflects the shape quality and is designed to measure the misalignment descent by the normalized point-to-point distance, which is defined as follows:

$$r = sign \left(m^* - m \right) = \begin{cases} 1, & m^* - m > 0 \\ 0, & m^* - m = 0 \\ -1, & m^* - m > 0 \end{cases}, m = \frac{\sum_i^N \| \boldsymbol{p}_i - \boldsymbol{p}_i^* \|}{N \cdot \zeta} \tag{5}$$

where m denotes the normalized point-to-point distance of current shape, m^* denotes distance before re-initializing the network input. Moreover, p_i denotes the position of predicted points, p_i^* denotes the position of groundtruths and ζ denotes normalized factor.

Let p_i^t denote the fused shape of the t-th iteration and p_i^* denote the i-th groundtruths, N represents the number of training samples. Our network is optimized by following loss function:

$$minJ = \sum_{t}^{T} \sum_{i}^{N} \left\| p_i^t - p_i^* \right\|_2^2 \tag{6}$$

Reinforcement Learning. Reinforcement learning stage aims to update the parameters of Q-net so that it can predict $Q(s,a)$ of each shape. Following the Q-learning algorithm, which chooses an action according to the current highest $Q(s,a)$ estimated by Q-function. Q-learning iteratively updates $Q(s,a)$ using the Bellman as follows:

$$Q(s,a) = r + \gamma maxQ(s',a') \tag{7}$$

where s and a are the current state and action, γ and $maxQ(s',a')$ represent the discount factor and future maximum benefit. In order to enable Q-net to accurately predict $Q(s,a)$, we let Q-net approximate Q-function and minimize following loss to update all parameters:

$$L = \mathbb{E}\left[Q\left(s^i, a^i\right) - \left(r^i + \gamma maxQ\left(s^{i+1}, a^{i+1}\right)\right) \right]^2 \tag{8}$$

where i represents the i-th iteration, which is a hyper-parameter and works best when set to 4.

3 Experiments

In this section, we presented the wildly used benchmarking datasets, evaluation protocols, and evaluation settings. Especially, we used outer-eye-corner distance as the normalizing factor and evaluated our method using standard normalized landmarks mean error, cumulative errors distribution (CED) curve.

3.1 Datasets

We evaluated our RSN approach on the widely used 300-W [11] (68-landmarks) and 3D Menpo static [12] (84-landmarks)[1] face alignment datasets compared with existing state-of-the-art methods. Note that 3D Menpo static includes two parts: 300-W and Menpo challenges. These annotated face images are collected from completely unconstrained conditions, which exhibit large variations in pose, expression, illumination, etc. The 3D Menpo static is fitted with 3DMM to all

---

[1] https://ibug.doc.ic.ac.uk/resources/1st-3d-face-tracking-wild-competition/.

Table 1. Comparisons of averaged errors of our proposed RSN with the state-of-the-arts (68 landmarks). From the results, we see that our proposed RSN achieves very compelling performance on Challenging set. The w/o RL indicates that reinforcement learning is not used.

Methods	Challenging set	Common set	Full set
SDM	15.40	5.57	8.35
CFSS	9.98	4.73	5.76
PIFA	9.88	5.43	6.30
R-DSSD	8.60	4.80	5.54
3DDFA	9.60	4.70	5.98
MDM	8.67	3.74	4.78
TSR	7.56	4.36	4.99
SBR	7.58	3.28	4.10
RSN (w/o RL)	**6.68**	**3.31**	**3.97**
RSN	**6.55**	**3.28**	**3.92**

Table 2. Comparisons of averaged errors of our proposed RSN with the state-of-the-arts (84 landmarks). We see that our RSN consistently obtains higher performance than the state-of-the-arts and even outperforms previous methods by a large margin on challenging set with a large number of self-occlusion samples.

Methods	Challenging set	Common set	Full set
PIFA	10.41	5.66	6.59
3DDFA	10.20	4.63	5.72
MDM	10.45	4.11	5.35
MHCH	8.39	3.94	4.81
RSN (w/o RL)	**7.01**	**3.53**	**4.21**
RSN	**6.86**	**3.48**	**4.12**

the images provided by the 300-W and Menpo challenges. For images 3D Menpo static provides the x, y coordinates in the image space that correspond to the projections of a 3D model of the face and x, y, z coordinates of the landmarks in the model space. To be fair, we only used the 300-W part of the 3D Menpo static and did not introduce the label information of the model space. We utilized the training sets of LFPW (2000), HELEN (811) and AFW (337) to train our model. Then we evaluated our method on the 224-image LFPW testing set, the 330-image HELEN testing set, as well as the 135-image IBUG, accordingly. We also investigated our approach by following another wildly used evaluation setting [1,9,10,15]: using the LFPW and HELEN testing set as Common set (554), the 135-image IBUG dataset as Challenging set (135), and the union of them as Full set (689).

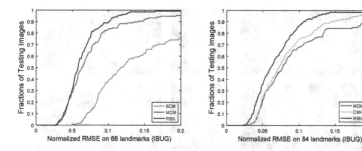

Fig. 3. The comparison of CED curves on the IBUG that was used as a Challenging set and includes 135 hard samples. These results indicate the robustness of our RSN to hard samples including large poses, divers expressions, partial occlusions and self-occlusions. Note that the results of the SDM [4] use the open source pre-training model directly, and we directly execute the open source codes to evaluate the performance of the MDM [1]. We provide web sites for these open source models in footnotes 2 and 3.

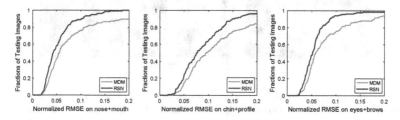

Fig. 4. Comparison CED curves against MDM [1] with global shape constraints on the IBUG (84 landmarks). As can be seen from comparisons, Our method achieves very compelling performance in the prediction of three sub-regions. This proves that our method achieves to reason meaningful structured relation to reinforce feature representation.

3.2   Implementation Details

Our network topology consists of three convolutional layers for the feature extraction. Each layer employs 32 filters with a kernel of 3×3. Meanwhile, each convolutional layer is followed by a 2×2 max-pooling. Each branch network consists of two FC layers to disentangle representation and one RNN hidden unit to memorize relation features. Moreover, we trained our RSN networks for 30k iterations with the following parameters: learning rate 0.001, weight decay 0.1 and batch size 50.

3.3   Results and Analysis

Comparisons with State-of-the-Art Methods. We compared our approach against the state-of-the-art methods on 300-W and 300-W part of the 3D Menpo static face. The mean error is shown in Tables 1 and 2, it can be seen that our RSN consistently obtains higher performance than the state-of-the-arts and even

(a) 68 landmarks

(b) 84 landmarks

Fig. 5. Representative results of the comparisons of predicted landmarks and groundtruths on IBUG. In the two pictures above, the first row indicates the predicted results and the second row indicates the groundtruths. From second image of (a), we can see that our method even overcomes groundtruths on the right profile. From the last image of (b), we can see that our method achieves very fine results on left eye.

outperforms previous methods by a large margin. Moreover, we observe that our method achieves the best perform among all of the state-of-the-art methods and exceeds even the recent SBR by 13% (68 landmarks) and 18% (84 landmarks) on Challenging subset. This fully shows that our RSN approach overcomes the lager pose problem. In Fig. 3, we provided comparison CED curves against the state-of-the-art methods of MDM [1][2], SDM [4][3] and CMHM [7]. From these curves, we can see that our method is more stable and accurate, and can better solve the challenging problem of face alignment.

Investigation of Structural Network Module. To demonstrate that our network can capture both global and local structural relationships, we redesigned a set of experiments based on face components. Figure 4 shows the CED comparisons of our RSN versus MDM on these divided facial components. These curves indicate our RSN is more robust on each sub-regions. In Fig. 5, we give some

---

[2] https://github.com/trigeorgis/mdm.
[3] https://github.com/tntrung/sdm_face_alignment.

examples of alignment results comparing with groundtruths, which demonstrates a very clear and unambiguous detection even under extreme poses, exaggerate expressions or occlusions. These fully prove that our model has a good ability to reason structural shape.

4   Conclusion

We have proposed a relational-structural network to disentangle feature representation for robust face alignment, which captures both local and global constraints on facial sub-regions. We have introduced the reinforcement learning to optimize regression procedures and infer gradient descents. The experimental results have demonstrated the robust results of our approach.

References

1. George, T., Patrick, S., Mihalis, A.N., Epameinondas, A.: Mnemonic descent method: a recurrent process applied for end-to-end face alignment. In: 2016 IEEE Conference on Computer Vision and Pattern Recognition (CVPR), pp. 4177–4187. IEEE (2016)
2. Shi, H.: Face alignment across large poses: a 3D solution. In: 2016 IEEE Conference on Computer Vision and Pattern Recognition (CVPR), pp. 146–155. IEEE (2016)
3. Timothy, F.C., Gareth, J.E., Christopher, J.T.: Active appearance models. IEEE Trans. Pattern Anal. Mach. Intell. **23**(6), 681–685 (2001)
4. Xiong, X., De la Torre, F.: Supervised descent method and its applications to face alignment. In: 2013 IEEE Conference on Computer Vision and Pattern Recognition (CVPR), pp. 532–539. IEEE (2013)
5. Georgios, T.: Project-out cascaded regression with an application to face alignment. In: 2015 IEEE Conference on Computer Vision and Pattern Recognition (CVPR), pp. 532–539. IEEE (2015)
6. Fan, Y., Lam, J.C.K., Li, V.O.K.: Multi-region ensemble convolutional neural network for facial expression recognition. In: Kůrková, V., Manolopoulos, Y., Hammer, B., Iliadis, L., Maglogiannis, I. (eds.) ICANN 2018. LNCS, vol. 11139, pp. 84–94. Springer, Cham (2018). https://doi.org/10.1007/978-3-030-01418-6_9
7. Deng, J., Zhou, Y., Cheng, S.: Cascade multi-view hourglass model for robust 3D face alignment. In: 2018 IEEE Conference on Automatic Face and Gesture Recognition (FG), pp. 339–403. IEEE (2018)
8. Hao, L., Lu, J., Guo, M., Wu, S.: Learning reasoning-decision networks for robust face alignment. IEEE Trans. Pattern Anal. Mach. Intell. (2018)
9. Jourabloo, A., Liu, X.: Pose-invariant face alignment via CNN-based dense 3D model fitting. Int. J. Comput. Vis. **124**(2), 187–203 (2017)
10. Hao, L., Lu, J., Feng, J., Zhou, J.: Learning deep sharable and structural detectors for face alignment. IEEE Trans. Image Process **26**(4), 1666–1678 (2017)
11. Sagonas, C., Tzimiropoulos, G., Zafeiriou, S.: 300 faces in-the-wild challenge: the first facial landmark localization challenge. In: International Conference on Computer Vision Workshops (ICCVW) (2013)
12. Stefanos, Z., Grigorios, C., Anastasios, R., Evangelos, V., Jiankang, D., George, T.: The 3D menpo facial landmark tracking challenge. In: Computer Vision and Pattern Recognition (CVPR) (2018)

13. Zhu, S., Li, C., Change Loy, C.: Face alignment by coarse-to-fine shape searching. In: 2015 IEEE Conference on Computer Vision and Pattern Recognition (CVPR), pp. 4998–5006. IEEE (2015)

14. Lv, J., Shao, X., Xing, J., Cheng, C., Zhou, X.: A deep regression architecture with two-stage re-initialization for high performance facial landmark detection. In: 2017 IEEE Conference on Computer Vision and Pattern Recognition (CVPR), pp. 3691–3700. IEEE (2017)

15. Dong, X.: Supervision-by registration: an unsupervised approach to improve the precision of facial landmark detectors. In: 2018 IEEE Conference on Computer Vision and Pattern Recognition (CVPR), pp. 360–368. IEEE (2018)

Gesture Recognition

An Efficient 3D-NAS Method for Video-Based Gesture Recognition

Ziheng Guo[1], Yang Chen[1(✉)], Wei Huang[2], and Junhao Zhang[2]

[1] Southeast University, Nanjing 210096, China
zhguo94@foxmail.com, chenyang.list@seu.edu.cn
[2] 2012 Lab, Shanghai Huawei Technologies Co., Ltd., Shanghai 200120, China
{huangwei49,zhangjunhao6}@huawei.com

Abstract. 3D convolutional neural network (3DCNN) is a powerful and effective model utilizing spatial-temporal features, especially for gesture recognition. Unfortunately, so many parameters are modified in 3DCNN that lots of researchers choose 2DCNN or hybrid models, but these models are designed manually. In this paper, we propose a framework to automatically construct a model based on 3DCNN by network architecture search (NAS) [1]. In our method called 3DNAS, a 3D teacher network is trained from scratch as a pre-trained model to accelerate the convergence of the child networks. Then series of child networks with various architectures are generated randomly and each is trained under the direction of converted teacher model. Finally, the controller predicts a network architecture according to the rewards of all the child networks. We evaluate our method on a video-based gesture recognition dataset 20BN-Jester dataset v1 [2] and the result shows our approach is superiority against prior methods both in efficiency and accuracy.

Keywords: Gesture recognition · 3D convolutional neural networks · Networks architecture search

1 Introduction

Gesture recognition is one of the most significant approaches to human-computer interaction. Because it is a very natural way to communicate without any touchable devices like touch screen, mouse and keyboard. An excellent gesture recognition algorithm cannot only recognize static gestures but also dynamic gestures. So video-based gesture recognition is more and more popular in this area and is widely applied in many scenes, such as virtual reality and intelligent cabin, etc.

In the beginning, researchers focused on local spatial-temporal features. For example, HOG3D [3] and SIFT3D [4] are proposed as effective representations based on gradients and points information, but they miss the global connection between pixels. After Improved Dense Trajectory Feature (IDTF) [5] is proposed, it becomes the state-of-the-art hand-crafted features. Great progress has been made in recent years with the rapid development of deep neural networks. Two stream convolutional network is proposed to deal with the video, one stream is for appearance features and the other is for optical flow. It's unavoidable for 2DCNN methods to integrate features

I. V. Tetko et al. (Eds.): ICANN 2019, LNCS 11729, pp. 319–329, 2019.
https://doi.org/10.1007/978-3-030-30508-6_26

extracted from frames. Encoding methods like FV encoding [6] and VLAD [7] are embedded as a layer to combine the features of multi-frames. TSN [8], TRN [9] and TPRN [10] focus on frame sampling and integrating the sparse features to obtain the video level presentation. However, 3DCNN can directly take a clip of stacked frames as input and learn spatial-temporal features by 3D convolution layers.

3D-ResNet [11], I3D [12] and C3D [13] are all conversions of 2DCNN architecture. Although 3DCNN has a lot of benefits, the heavy computation burden limits its development. One reason is that 3DCNN fills in over-fitting easily on a small dataset. While 2DCNN has been evolved to NASNet [1], a lot of researchers still design basic 3DCNN by hand.

In this paper, we propose a method of constructing a 3DCNN by NAS. In order to accelerate the speed of convergence of child networks, we use a pre-trained network as a teacher model and kernel conversion is carried out before training. Secondly, four basic 3D blocks are proposed learned from the bottleneck of ResNet [14]. Reinforcement learning based NAS makes it possible to feedback the complexity of the child network as the reward. As different action recognition tasks have different temporal dependence, NAS can find the best architecture on the target task.

2   Related Work

Video Level Presentation. Whether it is a traditional algorithm or deep learning algorithm, they all deal with the individual frame or a short clip of a few frames. To model the long term of a video with several hundreds of frames, TSN divides the whole video into several segments and chooses one clip from each of them, then it can achieve video level representation by averaging over the segments. TSN is a clear but efficient temporal sampling method utilizing sparse clips to represent the whole video. TRN is an improvement of TSN, and it considers the temporal relationship between clips. TRN enables temporal relational reasoning in neural networks by fully connected layers at multiple time scales.

3DCNN. After C3D [13] is used on action recognition, many network structures have been proposed based on 3D convolution. Pseudo-3D Residual Networks (P3D) [15] splits $3 \times 3 \times 3$ convolutions into $1 \times 3 \times 3$ convolutional filters on the spatial domain (equivalent to 2D CNN) plus $3 \times 1 \times 1$ convolutions to construct temporal connections on adjacent feature maps in time. In that way, P3D employs a deeper network with 199 layers. ECO [16] proposes a network that combines the former layers of a 2D network and the deeper layers of a 3D network serially. MFNET [17] finds another way to reduce the model size by proposing a Multi-Fiber Unit, which is realized by group convolution. Because 3DCNN over-fits easily on a small video dataset, I3D [12] proposes a method that they use InceptionV1 pre-trained on ImageNet and then expand the 2D kernels to 3D ones. Designing a 3DCNN is difficult because there are more kernel size options. Xie et al. [18] has discussed what layers should we make 3D, what layers can be 2D and does this depend on the nature of the dataset and task. Finding a good network architecture is what NAS aims to do. Until now, there is quite a few research about neural architecture search for 3DCNN.

NAS. CNN is widely accepted as the strongest representation of images, the results on ImageNet are constantly being refreshed as the rapid development of deep learning. At the latest leaderboard of ImageNet, some classic networks like ResNet, Inception series are still at the forefront, but the best model is not handcrafted but generated by neural architecture search (NAS). NAS is based on the observation that the structure and connectivity of a neural network can be typically specified by a string. It is, therefore, possible to use a recurrent network – the controller – to generate such string. By training a lot of child networks to get rewards, then using the rewards to train a controller which learns networks designing rules. Efficient Neural Architecture Search (ENAS) [19] accelerates the search process through weight sharing between child networks, greatly improving network search efficiency.

In Sect. 3, we describe the framework of the whole searching in Sect. 3.1, and then the detailed designing of the child network is introduced in Sect. 3.2. At last, we will discuss the reward in Sect. 3.3. The experiment is shown in Sect. 4 and we make a conclusion in the final section.

3   Method

3.1   Framework

For a neural network, it usually consists of a variety of modules connected with each other. The structure and connectivity of a neural network can be typically specified by a string. The definition of the string is one of the core problems in NAS. In our paper, the child networks are fixed in length and variable in 3D convolutional kernel size. So every child network is encoded into a fixed length sequence, each element in the sequence represents a pre-defined type of cell. As shown in Fig. 1, at each iteration, the RNN controller takes an action to generate a sequence, then the mapped child network will be trained on the training dataset based on a global pre-trained model. The pre-trained model is trained before the search process and play the role of teacher. It has

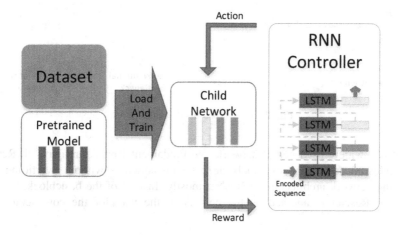

Fig. 1. The framework of the search process

fixed architecture but child networks have various architectures, so before loading the teacher model, it will be converted. The reward is designed according to the evaluation metric on validation dataset to update the controller.

The RNN controller contains an LSTM cell, taking the encoded sequence of child network as input. Every predicted element is carried out by a softmax classifier and then fed into the next time step as input. Every child network will be evaluated on the dataset and feedback its reward R_k. The parameters of the controller are then optimized in order to maximize the expected reward of the proposed architectures. Since the reward is non-differentiable, we follow the policy gradient method of NAS [1] to iteratively update the parameters θ_c in the controller. The empirical approximation formula is:

$$\nabla_{\theta_c} J(\theta_c) = \frac{1}{m} \sum\nolimits_{k=1}^{m} \sum\nolimits_{t=1}^{T} \nabla_{\theta_c} \log P(a_t|a_{(t-1):1}; \theta_c) R_k \tag{1}$$

where m is the number of different architectures that the controller samples in one batch and T is the number of hyperparameters our controller has to predict to design a neural network architecture. After a number of iterations, the controller can reach the convergence and the final predicted network will be trained from scratch to get its exact accuracy.

3.2   3D Child Networks

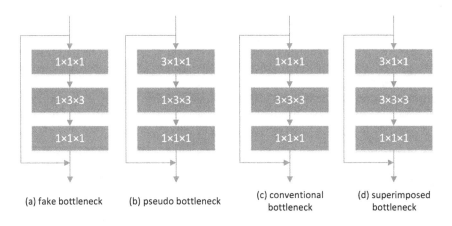

Fig. 2. Four types of 3D bottlenecks

ResNet is a widely used neural network, the fundamental breakthrough with ResNet was it allowed us to train extremely deep neural networks without overfitting. We follow the network architecture of ResNet mostly. Instead of the basicblock, the bottleneck in ResNet is adopted as the cell along the way for the consideration of additional computing burden of 3D convolution, four different types of the 3D bottleneck is designed from the original one, including fake 3D bottleneck, pseudo 3D bottleneck, conventional 3D bottleneck and superimposed 3D bottleneck, which are shown in Fig. 2. They can represent the different levels of how much 3D the bottleneck is. The 2D bottleneck of official ResNet is constructed by a 1×1 convolutional layer, a 3×3 convolutional layer, and a 1×1 convolutional layer. We make the first two convolutional layers optionally 3D. The fake 3D bottleneck contains no temporal convolution and it is an equivalent of 2D bottleneck actually. A pseudo 3D bottleneck is formed by a $3 \times 1 \times 1$ convolution followed by a $1 \times 3 \times 3$ convolution, which can be seen as a decomposition of a complete $3 \times 3 \times 3$ convolution. From another perspective, it's a simulation of 3D by 1D plus 2D. A standard 3D convolution is used in the conventional 3D bottleneck. The superimposed 3D bottleneck is a heavy 3D module as it combines a pseudo one and a conventional one.

For each child network, the first convolution is $7 \times 7 \times 7$. For four cells each contains 2 bottlenecks, bottlenecks in the same cell have identical types, optional in fake bottleneck, pseudo bottleneck, and conventional bottleneck. So it can be called as 3DResNet-20 and the search space is identified with a scale of 3^4, which is a limited one.

Aimed to accelerate the training of child network, a pre-trained model is loaded before training, which is a network with all superimposed 3D bottlenecks. All child networks vary in the temporal dimension of 3D convolutional kernels. The kernel conversion is done by flattening the mismatched convolutional kernels, $3 \times 3 \times 3$ kernels or $3 \times 1 \times 1$ kernels are averaged on the temporal dimension to get $1 \times 3 \times 3$ kernels or $1 \times 1 \times 1$ kernels. Contrary to I3D which loads a 2D pretrained model and expands the kernels, child networks are initialized from a 3D teacher network with more 3D kernels.

3.3   Reward

The controller learns by taking actions and getting rewards, so the higher reward increases the scale of gradients to optimize the controller during the updating procedure. In order to evaluate the complexity of the model, our method adds the regular term in reward function, containing the accuracy on validation dataset. We use computational complexity (FLOPs) to represent the scale of networks and add it to the reward to keep a balance between performance and efficiency.

The formula (2) of reward is shown below:

$$R_k = \alpha(Accuracy_k - Accuracy_{k-1}) - \beta \frac{FLOPs_k - FLOPs_{min}}{FLOPs_{max} - FLOPs_{min}} \tag{2}$$

The reward is composed of two parts, one is the accuracy of the child network on validation dataset and the other is the FLOPs of the child network. $Accuracy_k$ is the accuracy of current child network and $Accuracy_{k-1}$ is the accuracy of previous child network. Subtraction is done to reduce the variance. $FLOPs_k$ is the FLOPs of current child network, it is normalized by the maximum FLOPs $FLOPs_{max}$ and the minimum FLOPs $FLOPs_{min}$ of all the child networks in search space. α and β are hyperparameters that rescale the values and play the role as impact factors.

4 Experiments and Results

The experiments are on densely-labeled videos, 20BN-JESTER dataset [2]. This dataset records humans performing pre-defined hand gestures in front of a laptop camera or webcam, and includes 27 kinds of gestures which can be divided into three parts, 3 static gestures like 'Thumb up', 22 dynamic gestures like 'Swiping left' and 'turning hand counter-clockwise', and 2 in the other class. There are 118562 videos in training set, 14787 videos in validation set and 14743 videos in test set. Every sample contains 12 to 70 frames, extracted in 12 fps from the raw data. This dataset is persuasive in gesture recognition area. Our training experiments are based on 4T V100 GPUs, batch size is 64.

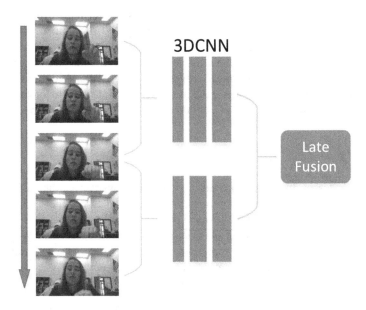

Fig. 3. Temporal Window Clip Pooling

In our experiment, a clip of constant 32 frames is input to the 3D networks. Temporal Window Clip Pooling (TWCP) is employed to cover the whole video during evaluation, which is shown in Fig. 3. For a video sample with N frames, window clip number is the rounding up of N divided by 32 and all window clips are evenly distributed across frames. If a sample has less than 32 frames, it will be padded to 32 frames with the last frame. With M window clips, we use average fusion. For training, one window clip is employed from a random start point. For evaluation single window clip is employed from the first frame as default.

Before training, we normalize the data. The frames are padded to square with constant zero value. Then they are resized to 118×118 pixels. Because a random crop is performed during training and center crop during evaluation, the input is finally sized of 112×112 pixels.

Firstly, four typical networks including Fake, Pseudo, Conventional and Superimposed with all the same bottlenecks are evaluated, whose detailed architectures are shown in Table 1. We use stochastic gradient descent (SGD) with standard categorical cross-entropy loss. Weight decay is $1e^{-6}$ and momentum is 0.9. The initial learning rate is 0.05 and after 15 epochs is reduced with a factor of 0.1 every 5 epochs. The total epoch number is 40.

For child network training, to finetune the network after loading the pre-trained model, the learning rate is 0.001 and it will be trained for 4 epochs. For random exploration, we search about 40 child networks, and RNN predicts a final network with a pseudo-pseudo-conventional-conventional architecture. As the child networks are only trained for 4 epochs, the predicted network is eventually trained from scratch without any pre-trained model, following the setting of four basic networks. The reward hypermeter of α and β is 0.1 and $1e^{-5}$.

Table 1. The architecture of child networks

Stage	Fake	Pseudo	Conventional	Superimposed	Ours
Conv_1	1×7^2	7×7^2	7×7^2	7×7^2	7×7^2
			Maxpooling		
Conv_2	$\begin{bmatrix} 1\times1^2 \\ 1\times3^2 \\ 1\times1^2 \end{bmatrix} \times 2$	$\begin{bmatrix} 3\times1^2 \\ 1\times3^2 \\ 1\times1^2 \end{bmatrix} \times 2$	$\begin{bmatrix} 1\times1^2 \\ 3\times3^2 \\ 1\times1^2 \end{bmatrix} \times 2$	$\begin{bmatrix} 3\times1^2 \\ 3\times3^2 \\ 1\times1^2 \end{bmatrix} \times 2$	$\begin{bmatrix} 3\times1^2 \\ 1\times3^2 \\ 1\times1^2 \end{bmatrix} \times 2$
Conv_3	$\begin{bmatrix} 1\times1^2 \\ 1\times3^2 \\ 1\times1^2 \end{bmatrix} \times 2$	$\begin{bmatrix} 3\times1^2 \\ 1\times3^2 \\ 1\times1^2 \end{bmatrix} \times 2$	$\begin{bmatrix} 1\times1^2 \\ 3\times3^2 \\ 1\times1^2 \end{bmatrix} \times 2$	$\begin{bmatrix} 3\times1^2 \\ 3\times3^2 \\ 1\times1^2 \end{bmatrix} \times 2$	$\begin{bmatrix} 3\times1^2 \\ 1\times3^2 \\ 1\times1^2 \end{bmatrix} \times 2$
Conv_4	$\begin{bmatrix} 1\times1^2 \\ 1\times3^2 \\ 1\times1^2 \end{bmatrix} \times 2$	$\begin{bmatrix} 3\times1^2 \\ 1\times3^2 \\ 1\times1^2 \end{bmatrix} \times 2$	$\begin{bmatrix} 1\times1^2 \\ 3\times3^2 \\ 1\times1^2 \end{bmatrix} \times 2$	$\begin{bmatrix} 3\times1^2 \\ 3\times3^2 \\ 1\times1^2 \end{bmatrix} \times 2$	$\begin{bmatrix} 1\times1^2 \\ 3\times3^2 \\ 1\times1^2 \end{bmatrix} \times 2$
Conv_5	$\begin{bmatrix} 1\times1^2 \\ 1\times3^2 \\ 1\times1^2 \end{bmatrix} \times 2$	$\begin{bmatrix} 3\times1^2 \\ 1\times3^2 \\ 1\times1^2 \end{bmatrix} \times 2$	$\begin{bmatrix} 1\times1^2 \\ 3\times3^2 \\ 1\times1^2 \end{bmatrix} \times 2$	$\begin{bmatrix} 3\times1^2 \\ 3\times3^2 \\ 1\times1^2 \end{bmatrix} \times 2$	$\begin{bmatrix} 1\times1^2 \\ 3\times3^2 \\ 1\times1^2 \end{bmatrix} \times 2$
			Average pooling, Fc		

Table 2. Accuracy on the validation set of Jester datasets. *The results are the accuracy on the test set. Use 3D means whether the method contains 3D convolution and Temporal Consideration means whether the method can model temporal relation.

Method	Use 3D	Temporal consideration	GFLOPs	Accuracy
TSN			–	85.41
TRN		√	–	93.70
TPRN		√	–	95.40
C3D*	√	√	77.19	92.78
ECO*	√	√	–	93.82
Fake			20.87	77.02
Pseudo	√	√	27.92	95.08
Conventional	√	√	33.82	95.29
Superimposed	√	√	40.87	95.51
Superimposed + TCWP	√	√	40.87	**95.63**
Ours	√	√	30.64	95.32
Ours + TCWP	√	√	30.64	**95.44**

In order to evaluate our algorithm, we compare the most famous and popular methods such as TSN, TRN, TPRN, C3D, ECO as well as four typical networks in Table 2. Methods without temporal consideration perform much worse than others, which illustrates the urgent importance of temporal consideration for gesture recognition. For the four typical networks, more 3D kernels lead to more performance as well as more FLOPs. However, our predicted network breaks up the rule, its FLOPs is between that of Pseudo and Conventional but it has higher accuracy than Conventional. The architecture of our predicted network is shown in Table 1, former two bottlenecks are pseudo ones and deeper two are conventional ones. With TCWP, multiple clips with late fusion can cover the whole video sample and help our methods to reach higher accuracy. It is clear that our method has a great promotion and the accuracy is 95.63% and 95.44%. Moreover, all of the procedure for constructing a network is automatic.

To show more clearly, we rearrange all results of child networks in ascending order of accuracy in Fig. 4. We encode cells with the fake, pseudo and conventional bottlenecks as 0, 1 and 2. So each cell corresponds to a number, the red line represents 3D-index, which is the sum of four cell numbers. The histogram represents the accuracy of the networks. The trends of the two are consistent, which tells the importance of temporal convolution. However, the wave of the 3D-index also demonstrates that under the situation with the same 3D-index, the structure order and combination can largely influence the performance. That's the point our predicted network performs even better than an architecture with more 3D kernels.

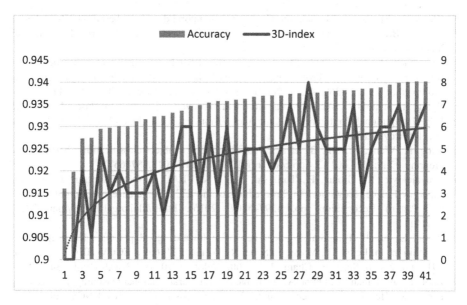

Fig. 4. The accuracy and 3D-index

5   Conclusion

Recognition of human gesture severely depends on the temporal information, 3DCNN turns out to perform much better than 2DCNN with or without the temporal fusion. 3DCNN can efficiently model the temporal relation but will increase the calculation cost, the method we propose can search an efficient 3DCNN to meet the real-time requirement of gesture recognition and achieve a state-of-the-art result on Jester dataset. Limited by computing resource, we only search within a small search space on the cell level, a further search can be done on bottleneck level. A channel search can also be important for reducing calculation. In addition, some rules can be got for 3DCNN designing, all 2D architecture will greatly lower the performance but only a few 3D layers addition can bring great improvement. When the performance of methods based on single image tends to saturation, video analysis will be the next breakthrough. Videos have a larger amount of data but inter-frame information has a lot of redundancy, which raises a big challenge for feature extraction. Temporal data is more common and this paper can be helpful to deal with it.

References

1. Zoph, B., Le, Q.V.: Neural architecture search with reinforcement learning (2016). arXiv preprint arXiv:1611.01578
2. TwentyBN: jester dataset: a hand gesture dataset (2017). https://www.twentybn.com/datasets/jester

3. Klaser, A., Marszałek, M., Schmid, C.: A spatio-temporal descriptor based on 3D-gradients. In: 19th British Machine Vision Conference, BMVC 2008, vol. 275, pp. 1–10. British Machine Vision Association (2008)

4. Scovanner, P., Ali, S., Shah, M.: A 3-dimensional SIFT descriptor and its application to action recognition. In: Proceedings of the 15th ACM International Conference on Multimedia, pp. 357–360. ACM (2007). https://doi.org/10.1145/1291233.1291311

5. Wang, H., Schmid, C.: Action recognition with improved trajectories. In: Proceedings of the IEEE International Conference on Computer Vision, pp. 3551–3558 (2013). https://doi.org/10.1109/iccv.2013.441

6. Tang, P., Wang, X., Shi, B., et al.: Deep fishernet for object classification (2016). arXiv preprint arXiv:1608.00182. https://doi.org/10.1109/tnnls.2018.2874657

7. Arandjelovic, R., Gronat, P., Torii, A., et al.: NetVLAD: CNN architecture for weakly supervised place recognition. In: Proceedings of the IEEE Conference on Computer Vision and Pattern Recognition, pp. 5297–5307 (2016). https://doi.org/10.1109/tpami.2017.2711011

8. Wang, L., et al.: Temporal segment networks: towards good practices for deep action recognition. In: Leibe, B., Matas, J., Sebe, N., Welling, M. (eds.) ECCV 2016. LNCS, vol. 9912, pp. 20–36. Springer, Cham (2016). https://doi.org/10.1007/978-3-319-46484-8_2

9. Zhou, B., Andonian, A., Oliva, A., Torralba, A.: Temporal relational reasoning in videos. In: Ferrari, V., Hebert, M., Sminchisescu, C., Weiss, Y. (eds.) ECCV 2018. LNCS, vol. 11205, pp. 831–846. Springer, Cham (2018). https://doi.org/10.1007/978-3-030-01246-5_49

10. Yang, K., Li, R., Qiao, P., et al.: Temporal pyramid relation network for video-based gesture recognition. In: 2018 25th IEEE International Conference on Image Processing (ICIP), pp. 3104–3108. IEEE (2018)

11. Hara, K., Kataoka, H., Satoh, Y.: Can spatiotemporal 3D CNNs retrace the history of 2D CNNs and imagenet? In: Proceedings of the IEEE Conference on Computer Vision and Pattern Recognition, pp. 6546–6555 (2018)

12. Carreira, J., Zisserman, A.: Quo vadis, action recognition? A new model and the kinetics dataset. In: Proceedings of the IEEE Conference on Computer Vision and Pattern Recognition, pp. 6299–6308 (2017). https://doi.org/10.1109/cvpr.2017.502

13. Tran, D., Bourdev, L., Fergus, R., et al.: Learning spatiotemporal features with 3D convolutional networks. In: Proceedings of the IEEE International Conference on Computer Vision, pp. 4489–4497 (2015). https://doi.org/10.1109/iccv.2015.510

14. He, K., Zhang, X., Ren, S., et al.: Deep residual learning for image recognition. In: Proceedings of the IEEE Conference on Computer Vision and Pattern Recognition, pp. 770–778 (2016). https://doi.org/10.1109/cvpr.2016.90

15. Qiu, Z., Yao, T., Mei, T.: Learning spatio-temporal representation with pseudo-3D residual networks. In: Proceedings of the IEEE International Conference on Computer Vision, pp. 5533–5541 (2017). https://doi.org/10.1109/iccv.2017.590

16. Zolfaghari, M., Singh, K., Brox, T.: ECO: efficient convolutional network for online video understanding. In: Ferrari, V., Hebert, M., Sminchisescu, C., Weiss, Y. (eds.) ECCV 2018. LNCS, vol. 11206, pp. 713–730. Springer, Cham (2018). https://doi.org/10.1007/978-3-030-01216-8_43

17. Chen, Y., Kalantidis, Y., Li, J., Yan, S., Feng, J.: Multi-fiber networks for video recognition. In: Ferrari, V., Hebert, M., Sminchisescu, C., Weiss, Y. (eds.) ECCV 2018. LNCS, vol. 11205, pp. 364–380. Springer, Cham (2018). https://doi.org/10.1007/978-3-030-01246-5_22

18. Xie, S., Sun, C., Huang, J., Tu, Z., Murphy, K.: Rethinking spatiotemporal feature learning: speed-accuracy trade-offs in video classification. In: Ferrari, V., Hebert, M., Sminchisescu, C., Weiss, Y. (eds.) ECCV 2018. LNCS, vol. 11219, pp. 318–335. Springer, Cham (2018). https://doi.org/10.1007/978-3-030-01267-0_19

19. Pham, H., Guan, M.Y., Zoph, B., et al.: Efficient neural architecture search via parameter sharing (2018). arXiv preprint arXiv:1802.03268
20. Simonyan, K., Zisserman, A.: Two-stream convolutional networks for action recognition in videos. In: Advances in Neural Information Processing Systems, pp. 568–576 (2014). https://doi.org/10.1002/14651858.cd001941.pub3
21. Diba, A., Sharma, V., Van Gool, L.: Deep temporal linear encoding networks. In: Proceedings of the IEEE Conference on Computer Vision and Pattern Recognition, pp. 2329–2338 (2017). https://doi.org/10.1109/cvpr.2017.168
22. Li, Y., Miao, Q., Tian, K., et al.: Large-scale gesture recognition with a fusion of RGB-D data based on the C3D model. In: 2016 23rd International Conference on Pattern Recognition (ICPR). IEEE (2016). https://doi.org/10.1109/icpr.2016.7899602

Robustness of Deep LSTM Networks in Freehand Gesture Recognition

Monika Schak[(✉)] and Alexander Gepperth

Fulda University of Applied Sciences, 36037 Fulda, Germany
{monika.schak,alexander.gepperth}@cs.hs-fulda.de

Abstract. We present an analysis of the robustness of deep LSTM networks for freehand gesture recognition against temporal shifts of the performed gesture w.r.t. the "temporal receptive field". Such shifts inevitably occur when not only the gesture type but also its onset needs to be determined from sensor data, and it is imperative that recognizers be as invariant as possible to this effect which we term *gesture onset variability*. Based on a real-world hand gesture classification task we find that LSTM networks are very sensitive to this type of variability, which we confirm by creating a synthetic sequence classification task of similar dimensionality. Lastly, we show that including gesture onset variability in the training data by a simple data augmentation strategy leads to a high robustness against all tested effects, so we conclude that LSTM networks can be considered good candidates for real-time and real-world gesture recognition.

Keywords: LSTM · Hand gestures · 3D sensors

1 Introduction

This article is in the context of freehand gesture recognition using 3D sensors and Long Short-Term Memory (LSTM) networks. We present a case study on the robustness properties of such a system, notably w.r.t. delays and variations in gesture onset. Such effects play a strong role in real-world applications, such as systems that allow the user to interact using dynamic freehand gestures, for example within the scope of 3D object manipulation or augmented reality. In this context, the time at which gestures are initiated is not known and therefore the system needs to be able to not only recognize the gesture itself but also its onset. This is, in some ways, analogous to visual object detection problems where the identity as well as the location of an object needs to be estimated.

In that regard, it is very important to investigate to what extent popular sequence recognizers like LSTM networks are capable of handling onset variations of the gestures (sequences) they are trained to recognize. This article investigates, first of all, the "native" robustness of LSTM networks to such variations and then goes on to specifically train LSTM networks to be robust to such variations by including them into the training data. As in visual object

© Springer Nature Switzerland AG 2019
I. V. Tetko et al. (Eds.): ICANN 2019, LNCS 11729, pp. 330–343, 2019.
https://doi.org/10.1007/978-3-030-30508-6_27

recognition data augmentation is used by simply generating new training data that contain the undesirable variations from existing samples and training new classifiers from these transformed data. We investigate several possible types of onset variations and show what effect training LSTM classifiers with those variations included has on classification accuracy.

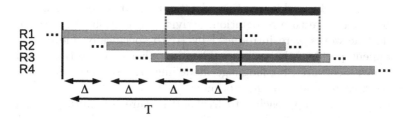

Fig. 1. Overview of the "shifted recognizer" architecture used to recognize freehand gestures. Exemplarily, we show an architecture using 4 recognizers that are shifted w.r.t. each other by a time interval of $\Delta = T/4$ frames. The temporal receptive fields (TRFs) of each recognizer are indicated by blue bars, and each recognizer is run in a continuous loop. A freehand gesture, indicated by a red bar, will usually fall into the TRF of exactly one recognizer which will then hopefully report this, thus giving both gesture type and gesture onset, the accuracy of the latter being principally determined by Δ. (Color figure online)

2   Our Approach

For addressing the issue of recognizing gestures that can start at any given moment in time we propose a solution analogous to object detection where N identical gesture recognizers are run in a continuous loop in parallel. Recognizers are trained to recognize gestures of fixed length T which determines their *temporal receptive field* (TRF). Each recognizer is reset after a full TRF and each receives the same frames from a 3D sensor. However, each recognizer is delayed by $\Delta = \frac{T}{N}$ frames w.r.t. the other recognizers so if enough recognizers are run in parallel it can be hoped that a gesture of length $\tau < T$ will fall fully into the TRF of a single recognizer which will then report it. This approach, which is visualized in Fig. 1 (where the gesture falls into the TRF of recognizer R3), suffers from some obvious problems:

- In general, gesture onset will not coincide with the first frame of the recognizer's TRF.
- If gestures are performed without breaks between them there will be appended or prepended frames to each elementary gesture, coming from other gestures in a recognizers TRF.

This raises the question of how well a LSTM network is able to deal with different onsets consisting of either random frames or frames containing parts of other gestures. Here is where our work comes in.

3   Related Work: RNNs and Dynamic Hand Gesture Recognition

Recurrent Neural Networks (RNNs) are primarily used because of their ability to remember the past activities or inputs and then produce an output that takes past inputs and states into consideration. Due to this specific property of RNNs they are used in fields which involve temporal dependencies over several time steps, such as gesture recognition, activity recognition or speech recognition. LSTM networks were introduced by [7] to specifically address the vanishing gradient problem that was complicating efficient RNN training. LSTM networks have been used for language modelling [12], sequence generation [4], speech recognition [6] and image captioning [8].

There are various approaches to freehand gesture recognition with LSTM networks (of course, this kind of recognition task can also be performed without LSTMs, e.g., [1,3,9,11,20]). Especially in visually defined problems where camera images are analyzed, several authors employ LSTM networks as the top layer of a Convolutional Neural Network (CNN), which performs the basic image transformations that are required for sufficient invariance and robustness [13,14,18]. The precise way of setting up the CNN and coupling CNN and LSTM can of course vary considerably. In case of multiple input streams (e.g., camera and 3D sensors), the underlying CNN architecture can become considerably more complex and offers more design choices, yet many authors still let LSTM recognizers operate on the top layer activities of a (possibly hybrid) CNN architecture, e.g., in [19]. Explicit extensions to the basic deep LSTM model are proposed in [21] in the form of a convolutional LSTM architecture.

4   Methods and Data

We use two datasets in this study: a real-world freehand gesture dataset that we recorded ourselves and a synthetic one constructed from the well-known visual MNIST benchmark [10]. Our own freehand gesture dataset is introduced because we find that using a single ToF-sensor to capture hand gestures for interacting with a device (for example mobile devices or vehicles) allows for more freedom and increased expressiveness [17]. The synthetic dataset is introduced because the real-world gesture dataset is relatively small and we wish to exclude that results are due to overfitting. Table 1 gives an overview over the properties of each dataset.

4.1   Freehand Gesture Dataset

Data Acquisition. Data is collected from a DepthSense ToF sensor at a resolution of 320×160 pixels. Depth thresholding removes most of the irrelevant background information, leaving only hand and arm voxels. Principal-Component Analysis (PCA) is utilized to crop most of the negligible arm parts. The remaining part of the point cloud carries the relevant information, i.e. the shape of the

Table 1. Properties of the two datasets used in this study. The real-world hand gesture dataset is relatively small, which is why we decided to complement it by a large-scale sequence classification dataset constructed from the MNIST classification benchmark. Sequences in both datasets have a length of 40 frames and the frame dimensionalities in both datasets are comparable (625 vs. 784). Both datasets consist of equally distributed classes.

Dataset	Training samples	Test samples	Frames	Dimensions	Classes	Class distrib.
MNIST sequences	20.000	5.000	40	784	4	Balanced
3D hand gestures	320	80	40	625	4	Balanced

hand. We record four different hand gesture types from ten different people for our database: close hand, open hand, pinch-in and pinch-out. The latter gestures are performed by closing/opening two fingers. For recording a single dynamic gesture, 40 consecutive snapshots are taken from the sensor and cropped by the aforementioned procedure. We recorded ten gesture samples per person and gesture type, giving a total of 400 gestures or 100 per gesture type (class). As 40 frames per gesture are present, this sums up to a total of 16,000 sensor frames (point clouds). Figure 2 shows the color-coded snapshot of one of the recorded hand postures.

Fig. 2. Individual point clouds (frames) from the freehand gesture dataset after cropping from the front (left) and side view (right) during a grabbing motion. Point clouds such as these are further processed to form a 625-dimensional feature vector before being presented to the LSTM-based gesture recognizer. (Color figure online)

Data Pre-processing. From each frame represented by a point cloud, we extract a descriptor of fixed size (regardless of the size of the point cloud) that can be fed to the deep LSTM recognizers [16,17]. Such descriptors need to describe the phenomenology of hand, palm and fingers in a precise manner, while remaining computationally feasible. In this contribution, we decided on a representation that is largely based on surface normals. First, these normals are computed for all points. Then, we repeatedly (5000 times) select two random points and compute their point feature histogram (PFH) descriptor [2,15] which yields four numbers based on the distance and the relative orientation of the surface normals. Each of the four numbers is coarsely quantized into five bins, giving a total of 625 discrete possibilities and a histogram over all 5000 realizations is taken. These 625-dimensional histograms, each describing a single point cloud, form the individual frames of the sequences we use for training and testing deep LSTM recognizers.

Dataset Creation. The set of 400 recorded gesture samples can be described by a three-dimensional tensor G, indexed by sequence index $0 \leq i < 400$, frame index $0 \leq j < 40$ and histogram index $0 \leq h < 625$. A single histogram entry accesses as G_{ijh}. The available gesture samples are split into training and test samples for the LSTM recognizers, the train to test ratio being 80/20.

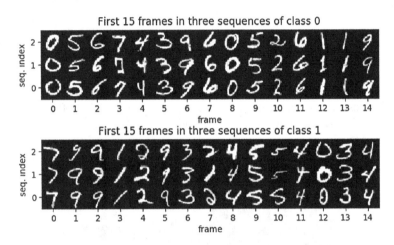

Fig. 3. Six sample sequences from the synthetic MNIST-based dataset. Three sequences (above) come from class 0 and three sequences (below) come from class 1. Classes 3 and 4 are not shown. Please note that sequences from the synthetic dataset have a length of 40 frames, but only the first 15 frames are shown due to space constraints.

4.2   Synthetic Dataset

The synthetic dataset is created to be largely analogous in structure to the freehand gesture dataset, having the same number of frames per sequence and a similar dimensionality per frame. However, due to the synthetic nature of this dataset, we can generate a larger amount of samples with very little effort. The construction is straightforward: we generate four 40-element sequence templates (as shown in Fig. 3). The sequences equate to concatenated frames from a video. Each sequence template is described by the vectors s_0 to s_3, where each position j in all vectors contains integers that indicate a randomly drawn MNIST class: $s_{ij} \in [0, 9]$. For each sequence template s_k we generate 25,000 sequences of $0 \leq j < 40$ frames each, each frame j being represented by a (flattened) randomly drawn MNIST sample of class s_{kj}. Thus, the synthetic data can be represented by a three-dimensional tensor accessed by sequence index $0 \leq i < 25,000$, frame index $0 \leq j < 40$ and image index $0 \leq h < 28 \times 28$. Again, a train/test split of 80/20 is performed subsequently.

4.3   Deep LSTM for Recognition

In our model for dealing with the video frames sequentially, we use a deep RNN with LSTM model neurons. The LSTM term for neuron is "memory cell" and the term for hidden layer is "memory block". A single memory cell at time t has a dynamic state or activity c_t, whereas the vector of all activities in a memory block is denoted c_t.

Any change to the cell state is done with the help of gates: input gate i_t and forget gate f_t, each gate having a value between 0 and 1. The input gate determines how much of the input is forwarded and the forget gate determines how much of the cell's previous state to retain. Output to subsequent layers, denoted h_t, is generated via a simple transfer function (termed output gate).

The LSTM model equations for computing activations h_t of a single LSTM layer read as follows:

$$i_t = \sigma \left(W_{xi} x_t + W_{hi} h_{t-1} + W_{ci} c_{t-1} + b_i \right) \tag{1}$$

$$f_t = \sigma \left(W_{xf} x_t + W_{hf} h_{t-1} + W_{cf} c_{t-1} + b_f \right) \tag{2}$$

$$c_t = f_t c_{t-1} + i_t \tanh \left(W_{xc} x_t + W_{hc} h_{t-1} + b_c \right) \tag{3}$$

$$o_t = \sigma \left(W_{xo} x_t + W_{ho} h_{t-1} + W_{co} c_t + b_o \right) \tag{4}$$

$$h_t = o_t \tanh(c_t) \tag{5}$$

Equation 1 describes the calculation of the input gate. The output of the input gate is a value between 0 and 1. Equation 2 refers to the calculation of the forget gate. The output of the forget gate also is a value between 0 and 1. Equation 3 describes the calculation of the new cell state, replacing the old one. Equation 4 refers to the calculation of the output gate. The output of the output gate is a value between 0 and 1. Equation 5 refers to the calculation of the hidden state or the output of the memory block, which is the input for the next memory block. Due to the tanh function it can output a value between -1 and 1.

We use a standard deep LSTM architecture with linear softmax readout layer and cross-entropy loss function as outlined in [5]. Number and size of memory blocks, which are all set to have the same number of memory cells, are denoted (L, S). The final output of the LSTM network is produced by applying a linear regression readout layer that transforms the states h_t of the last hidden layer into class membership estimates, using the standard softmax non-linearity leading to positive, normalized class membership estimates.

4.4   TensorFlow Implementation

We use the TensorFlow (v1.11) implementation of a Recurrent Neural Network with multiple LSTM cells under Python (v3.6) - mainly the classes *MultiRNN-Cell* and *LSTMCell*, which allow to create networks of stacked LSTM cells. We always use the Adam optimizer included in TensorFlow for performing gradient descent as well as a linear softmax readout layer and cross-entropy loss function.

5   Experiments

For our experiments we use a deep LSTM architecture consisting of three hidden layers with ten LSTM cells each $(L, S) = (3, 10)$, a fixed learning rate of $\epsilon = 0.001$ and a training to test data ratio of $80/20$. During a test phase we varied the learning rate in the range of $\epsilon \in [0.0001, 0.1]$ and the amount of layers and cells in the range of $L \in [1, 10]$ and $S \in [5, 50]$ and used the learning rate, amount of hidden layers and LSTM cells for our architecture that performed best on the test sets. Our architecture has a TRF of $T = 60$ frames. Since the gestures in our database have a length of 40 frames, they can be offset by 20 frames at most. Parameters like learning rate, number of hidden layers and amount of LSTM cells per hidden layer need to be chosen depending on the test and training data since in general the quality of the results can depend on the parameters.

At first, we describe two preliminary experiments to test our network and databases, then we continue with four experiments about the robustness of LSTM networks.

5.1   Preliminary Experiment: Ahead-of-Time Classification

Recurrent neural networks are able to estimate a class before the end of the sequence they are currently classifying. For the use of LSTM networks in real-world scenarios this ability can be very helpful because the network does not have to wait until the end of the sequence to classify it. Therefore, we test the classification accuracy for our 40-frame sequences after $0 < n \leq 40$ frames.

As can be seen in Fig. 4, the classification accuracy is only slightly below its maximum value even for small n. This shows that our network is able to obtain a high accuracy very early in the process of classifying a sequence. Hence, an action can be performed according to the "guessed" classification output before the whole gesture is processed. This allows for faster response times and offers a significant advantage in comparison to having to wait for the whole sequence to be processed. As expected, the results for the artificial dataset are as high as all previous work using MNIST. This is a well-known fact since MNIST is a very easy-to-solve benchmark even when considering only image classification instead of sequences as we do here.

5.2   Preliminary Experiment: Feasibility of the Database

The reason for this experiment is to test if our database of hand gestures is big enough. We use two different strategies to split our data into train and test sets: The first strategy randomly chooses 20% of samples from the whole database as a test set and uses the rest for training. This strategy is only used for our experiment to show that overfitting is a problem here. As required by machine

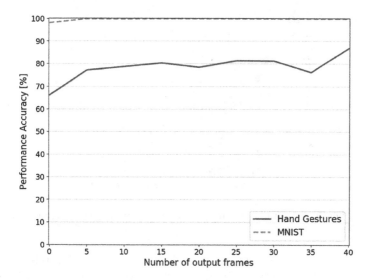

Fig. 4. Classification accuracy depending on the output frame used to generate the gesture classification.

learning theory, data used for training and testing need to be independent and identically distributed.

The second strategy chooses all the gestures from eight people for training and all gestures from the remaining two people for testing, achieving the same 80/20 split as before. As Fig. 5 shows, there is a significant difference in accuracy between the two strategies. Since different people perform the same gesture quite differently the differences between the training and the test set of the second strategy are too big to achieve better results. A bigger database with gestures from substantially more people would be required to decrease this overfitting behavior and train the network well enough to generalize the classification for gestures from unfamiliar people. Comparing the results from our own database to the artificial image dataset proves this point: The experiments with MNIST data shows overall better results.

In a real-life scenario, the system usually would be trained with gestures from different people than the ones using the trained system later on. Therefore, more training data is needed for real-world applications.

5.3   Dependency of LSTM Networks on Previous States and Results

To asses whether our network needs to be reset after a TRF traversal, we concatenate two randomly picked gestures and feed them to our trained network. Accuracy is measured for the classification of the second gesture after 80 frames. For this experiment, the TRF of our network is extended to 80 frames instead of the usual 60 frames.

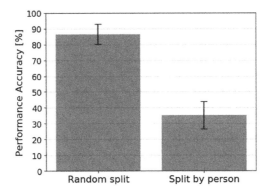

Fig. 5. Classification accuracy depending on the strategy used to split the database into test and training sets.

Figure 6 shows that the network depends on a clean state for well recognizing a gesture since the memory of the first gesture strongly affects the classification of the second gesture and therefore leads to a very low classification accuracy. Thus, we can conclude that the LSTM network has to be reset at the start of every TRF to ensure a correct classification.

5.4 Fixed Noisy or Clean Gesture Onsets

In this experiment, we investigate the robustness of our LSTM network to gesture shifts (onset variability) of a fixed number of frames. For this, we create new test samples from our dataset that consist of 60 frames and contain the actual 40-frame gesture starting at frame n. Hence, the gesture being fed to the trained network consists of three parts which total 60 frames: $x_1 x_2 x_3$ with $0 \le |x_1| \le 20$, x_2 being the actual gesture with $|x_2| = 40$ and $|x_3| = 60 - |x_1| - |x_2|$. Both parts x_1 and x_3 either are initialized to zero-frames or random frames picked from the database.

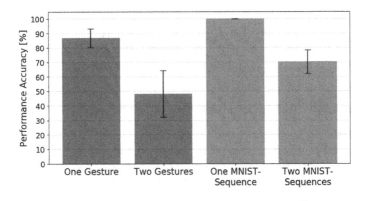

Fig. 6. Classification accuracy whether only one gesture (left) is classified or the second of two concatenated gestures is classified (right).

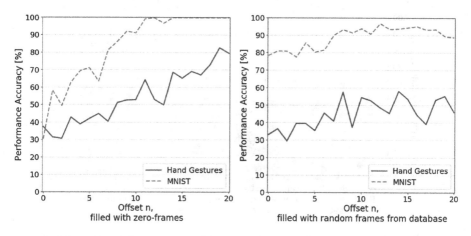

Fig. 7. Classification accuracy for a fixed clean (left) or noisy (right) gesture onset of n frames.

The results in Fig. 7 show that our network can hardly handle any amount of random frames prior or after an actual hand gesture. In contrast to this, it is possible for our network to work decently with fixed-time gesture onsets filled with zero-frames but zero-frames after the actual gesture considerably influence the accuracy.

For the MNIST dataset the results are similar. Zero-frames after the actual sequence strongly influence the accuracy while zero-frames before the sequence hardly do. The effect of random frames prior or after an MNIST sequence is lower than for hand gestures but still visible.

5.5   Random Noisy or Clean Gesture Onsets

Unlike the last experiment where we used a fixed gesture onset, we now embed each test sample into a new 60-frame sample at a random point in time. The samples are initialized either to zero or to random frames from the database. According to the last experiment, each gesture being fed to the trained network also consists of three parts which total 60 frames: $x_1x_2x_3$ with $0 \leq |x_1| \leq 20$ with a random length $|x_1|$ for each gesture, x_2 being the actual gesture with $|x_2| = 40$ and $|x_3| = 60 - |x_1| - |x_2|$.

As can be seen in Fig. 8, choosing a random onset for each gesture leads to a notably decreased accuracy. Since the trained network is the same as for the setting in the last experiment (cf. Sect. 5.4), the results for the random gesture onset correspond to the average results from our experiments with a fixed gesture onset.

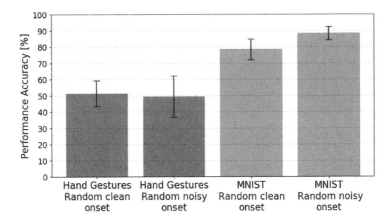

Fig. 8. Classification accuracy for a clean (left) or noisy (right) gesture onset of a random amount of frames.

5.6 Random Clean Gesture Onset Included in Training and Testing

As the last three experiments show, our network has difficulties handling gestures that do not start right at the beginning of the TRF but are padded with additional frames. A possible solution to this is to train the network in such a way that allows it to learn to ignore padding around the actual gestures. To show the effects of this, we train our network with 60 frame gestures, compound as described for the last two experiments: a random amount of zero-frames between 0 and 20 before the actual gesture and then filled up with zero-frames afterwards.

Figure 9 combines the results from multiple experiments: The accuracy shown on the left is the result of a network trained and tested with just the gestures and without any padding (cf. Sect. 5.2). This is the baseline of how good the accuracy can be without any additional frames distracting from the gesture. The accuracy shown in the middle is the result of a network trained with just the gestures and tested on gestures with a clean random onset (cf. Sect. 5.5). And the accuracy on the right is the result on a network trained and tested on gestures with a clean random onset.

As can be seen, the accuracy can be considerably increased by training the network with padded gestures. Then, our network is able to ignore zero-frames before and after the actual gesture to some extent. The effect can be improved by training the network with more variations of the same gesture instead of just one random padding for each gesture as done in our experiment.

6   Discussion and Conclusion

This article investigates robustness properties of LSTMs in the context of sequence classification in general and hand gesture recognition in particular. Our main findings are twofold:

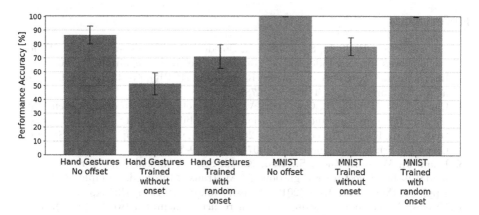

Fig. 9. Classification accuracy for gestures with no padding at all (left) and for gestures with a clean random onset - trained with just the gestures (mid) or with a clean random onset (right).

LSTMs Are Vulnerable to Sequence Onset Variability. First of all, LSTM networks are very sensitive to variability in sequence onset (of which gesture onset is a special case). This has not been empirically studied before, which is why we consider these insights highly relevant for applied settings. The generality and credibility of our results comes from using two sequence learning tasks that derive from very different domains for this investigation.

Robustness Can Be Achieved by Data Augmentation. Secondly, we find that LSTMs can be made very robust against sequence onset variability if this variability is incorporated into the training data by data augmentation strategies. This is particularly straightforward for sequences as the type of variability can be reduced to the maximal delay of sequence onset that a LSTM recognizer should be able to process, which mainly depends on the number of parallel recognizers we can run, see Fig. 1. In other words, we need to first think about robustness properties and then actively include them in the training data.

Conclusion and Future Work. We find the problem of real-world LSTM sequence recognition to be remarkably analogous to training visual sliding-window object detectors, where similar data augmentation strategies must be employed to make detectors robust against small shifts in object position. Data augmentation works for LSTM networks which have, after all, a dynamic internal structure which is potentially much more complex than that of feed-forward CNN models. Further investigations on real-world gesture and activity recognition can build on this insight in order to implement robust real-world sequence recognition. In addition, a comparison to other sequence classification models should be done to further investigate the applicability of the proposed system.

References

1. Camgoz, N.C., Hadfield, S., Koller, O., Bowden, R.: Using convolutional 3D neural networks for user-independent continuous gesture recognition. In: 2016 23rd International Conference on Pattern Recognition (ICPR), pp. 49–54. IEEE (2016). https://doi.org/10.1109/ICPR.2016.7899606
2. Caron, L.-C., Filliat, D., Gepperth, A.: Neural network fusion of color, depth and location for object instance recognition on a mobile robot. In: Agapito, L., Bronstein, M.M., Rother, C. (eds.) ECCV 2014. LNCS, vol. 8927, pp. 791–805. Springer, Cham (2015). https://doi.org/10.1007/978-3-319-16199-0_55
3. Duan, J., Wan, J., Zhou, S., Guo, X., Li, S.Z.: A unified framework for multimodal isolated gesture recognition. ACM Trans. Multimed. Comput. Commun. Appl. (TOMM) 14(1s), 21 (2018). https://doi.org/10.1145/3131343
4. Graves, A.: Generating sequences with recurrent neural networks (2013). arXiv preprint arXiv:1308.0850
5. Graves, A., Jaitly, N.: Towards end-to-end speech recognition with recurrent neural networks. In: International Conference on Machine Learning, pp. 1764–1772 (2014). https://doi.org/10.1186/s13636-018-0141-9
6. Graves, A., Mohamed, A.R., Hinton, G.: Speech recognition with deep recurrent neural networks. In: 2013 IEEE International Conference on Acoustics, Speech and Signal Processing, pp. 6645–6649. IEEE (2013). https://doi.org/10.1109/ICASSP.2013.6638947
7. Hochreiter, S.: The vanishing gradient problem during learning recurrent neural nets and problem solutions. Int. J. Uncertain. Fuzziness Knowl. Based Syst. 6(02), 107–116 (1998). https://doi.org/10.1142/S0218488598000094
8. Karpathy, A., Fei-Fei, L.: Deep visual-semantic alignments for generating image descriptions. In: Proceedings of the IEEE Conference on Computer Vision and Pattern Recognition, pp. 3128–3137 (2015). https://doi.org/10.1109/TPAMI.2016.2598339
9. Lea, C., Flynn, M.D., Vidal, R., Reiter, A., Hager, G.D.: Temporal convolutional networks for action segmentation and detection. In: Proceedings - 30th IEEE Conference on Computer Vision and Pattern Recognition, CVPR 2017, vol. January 2017, pp. 1003–1012. Institute of Electrical and Electronics Engineers Inc., November 2017. https://doi.org/10.1109/CVPR.2017.113
10. Lecun, Y., Bottou, L., Bengio, Y., Haffner, P.: Gradient-based learning applied to document recognition. Proc. IEEE 86, 2278–2324 (1998)
11. Miao, Q., et al.: Multimodal gesture recognition based on the ResC3D network. In: Proceedings of the IEEE International Conference on Computer Vision, pp. 3047–3055 (2017). https://doi.org/10.1109/ICCVW.2017.360
12. Mikolov, T., Karafiát, M., Burget, L., Cernocký, J., Khudanpur, S.: Recurrent neural network based language model. In: 11th Annual Conference of the International Speech Communication Association, INTERSPEECH 2010, Makuhari, Chiba, Japan, 26–30 September 2010, pp. 1045–1048 (2010). http://www.isca-speech.org/archive/interspeech_2010/i10_1045.html
13. Nguyen, A., Kanoulas, D., Muratore, L., Caldwell, D.G., Tsagarakis, N.G.: Translating videos to commands for robotic manipulation with deep recurrent neural networks. In: 2018 IEEE International Conference on Robotics and Automation (ICRA), pp. 1–9. IEEE (2018). https://doi.org/10.1109/ICRA.2018.8460857
14. Ordóñez, F., Roggen, D.: Deep convolutional and LSTM recurrent neural networks for multimodal wearable activity recognition. Sensors 16(1), 115 (2016). https://doi.org/10.3390/s16010115

15. Rusu, R.B., Blodow, N., Marton, Z.C., Beetz, M.: Aligning point cloud views using persistent feature histograms. In: 2008 IEEE/RSJ International Conference on Intelligent Robots and Systems, pp. 3384–3391. IEEE (2008). https://doi.org/10.1109/IROS.2008.4650967

16. Sachara, F., Kopinski, T., Gepperth, A., Handmann, U.: Free-hand gesture recognition with 3D-CNNs for in-car infotainment control in real-time. In: 2017 IEEE 20th International Conference on Intelligent Transportation Systems (ITSC), pp. 959–964, October 2017. https://doi.org/10.1109/ITSC.2017.8317684

17. Sarkar, A., Gepperth, A., Handmann, U., Kopinski, T.: Dynamic hand gesture recognition for mobile systems using deep LSTM. In: Horain, P., Achard, C., Mallem, M. (eds.) IHCI 2017. LNCS, vol. 10688, pp. 19–31. Springer, Cham (2017). https://doi.org/10.1007/978-3-319-72038-8_3

18. Tsironi, E., Barros, P., Wermter, S.: Gesture recognition with a convolutional long short-term memory recurrent neural network. In: Proceedings of the European Symposium on Artificial Neural Networks Computational Intelligence and Machine Learning (ESANN), pp. 213–218 (2016)

19. Wu, J., Ishwar, P., Konrad, J.: Two-stream CNNs for gesture-based verification and identification: learning user style. In: Proceedings of the IEEE Conference on Computer Vision and Pattern Recognition Workshops, pp. 42–50 (2016). https://doi.org/10.1109/CVPRW.2016.21

20. Zhu, G., Zhang, L., Shen, P., Song, J.: Multimodal gesture recognition using 3-D convolution and convolutional LSTM. IEEE Access 5, 4517–4524 (2017). https://doi.org/10.1109/ACCESS.2017.2684186

21. Zhu, G., Zhang, L., Mei, L., Shao, J., Song, J., Shen, P.: Large-scale isolated gesture recognition using pyramidal 3D convolutional networks. In: 2016 23rd International Conference on Pattern Recognition (ICPR), pp. 19–24. IEEE (2016). https://doi.org/10.1109/ICPR.2016.7899601

Saliency Detection

Delving into the Impact of Saliency Detector: A GeminiNet for Accurate Saliency Detection

Tao Zheng, Bo Li$^{(\boxtimes)}$, Delu Zeng, and Zhiheng Zhou

South China University of Technology, Guangzhou, China
eezhengtao@mail.scut.edu.cn, {leebo,dlzeng,zhouzh}@scut.edu.cn

Abstract. Although plenty of saliency detection methods based on CNNs have shown impressive performance, we observe that these methods adopt single-scale convolutional layers as saliency detectors after extracting features to predict saliency maps, which will cause serious missed detection especially those targets having small scales, irregular shapes and sporadic locations in complex scenario of multi-target graphs. In addition, the edges of salient objects predicted by these methods are often confused with their background, causing these partial regions to be very blurred. In order to deal with these issues, we delved into the impact of diverse unified detectors based on convolutional layers and nearest neighbor optimization on saliency detection. It was found that (1) the flattened design contributes to the improvement of accuracy, but due to the inherent characteristics of convolutional layers, it is not the effective way to solve the problems; (2) Nearest neighbor optimization is beneficial to remove background regions from salient objects and restore the missing sections while refining their boundaries, yielding a more reliable final prediction. With the progress of these studies, we built a GeminiNet for accurate saliency detection. Quantitative and qualitative experiments on six benchmark datasets demonstrate that our proposed GeminiNet performs favorably against the state-of-the-art methods under different evaluation metrics.

Keywords: Deep learning · Convolutional neural network · Image segmentation

1 Introduction

Saliency detection aims to localize the most visually conspicuous and distinctive regions that attract human attention in patterns, which commonly serves as the first step to a variety of computer vision applications including scene classification [13], visual tracking [2] and action recognition [1].

Although plenty of preceding state-of-the-art methods [5,6,11,21,23] based on deep convolutional neural networks (CNNs) have shown impressive performance for saliency detection, their accuracies are still far away from satisfactory.

© Springer Nature Switzerland AG 2019
I. V. Tetko et al. (Eds.): ICANN 2019, LNCS 11729, pp. 347–359, 2019.
https://doi.org/10.1007/978-3-030-30508-6_28

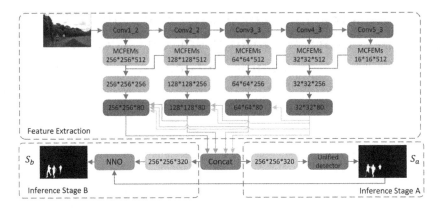

Fig. 1. Architecture of the proposed GeminiNet. For convenience, ReLU activation function and up-sample function are not shown in this diagram. MCFEM [21] is used to obtain abundant multi-scale features. The gray NNO block represents nearest neighbor optimization while Concat denotes cross-channel concatenation. The complete inference process including two stages. Firstly, we adopt a unified detector to predict a coarse saliency map in Stage A. Secondly, nearest neighbor optimization is used to refined the preceding map, yielding a more reliable final prediction in Stage B.

We observed the saliency maps predicted by these methods and found that in the single-target images, the above methods can almost locate the position of salient objects; for the multi-target images, serious missed detection especially those targets having small scales, irregular shapes and sporadic locations in complex scenario will occur. In addition, the edges of salient objects predicted by these methods are often confused with their background, causing these partial regions to be very blurred. These findings drove us to focus our research on the detection of small targets and the recovery of sharp boundaries. Even if these areas are small, they will help much for the quantitative evaluation.

Including the methods mentioned above, many methods [8,9] use single-scale convolutional layers as the final detectors after extracting features to predict saliency maps, which is not robust enough to detect diverse salient targets in complex scenario and will result in the lack of generalization capabilities. Assuming that a deep learning model has extracted rich multi-scale semantic convolutional features, how to construct or select a saliency detector becomes a crucial task at the moment. Actually, several attempts have been performed to extract convolutional features such as Inception [15], ASPP [4] and their variants [16,19], but none of the previous methods attempted to use these structures as saliency detectors at the end of network. However, through a large number of comparative experiments, we found that the structure of saliency detector plays an important role in the effect of neural network. This discovery provoked us to wonder what kind of unified detectors' structure contributes to the improvement of accuracy.

Table 1. The performance between different unified detectors under the metrics of maximum F-measure and MAE on six datasets.

Variable	HKU		OMRON		PASCAL		ECSSD		DUTS-TE		SOD	
	F_{max}	MAE	F_{max}	MAE	F_{max}	MAE	F_{max}	MAE	F_{max}	MAE	F_{max}	MAE
1 × 1 kernel	0.924	0.037	0.798	0.060	0.867	0.077	0.933	0.044	0.855	0.048	0.864	0.108
Inception v3	0.929	0.033	0.800	0.060	0.873	0.074	0.937	0.038	0.866	0.045	0.868	0.106
ASPP	0.930	0.034	0.809	0.059	0.872	0.077	0.938	0.043	0.867	0.045	0.867	0.105
denseASPP	0.928	0.035	0.803	0.060	0.871	0.078	0.937	0.046	0.865	0.045	0.867	0.105
C-ASPP	0.931	0.031	0.811	0.055	0.881	0.068	0.940	0.037	0.874	0.042	0.870	0.102

Some attempts have been performed to optimize the boundaries of salient objects. Previous methods use conditional random field (CRF) [7] which can avoid the problem of label bias by global normalization as post-processing instrument. Although CRF encourages similar pixels to assign the same label and pixels with larger differences assign different labels, its effect on multi-target detection of complex scenes is minimal. Some researches [3,12] attempt to optimize the loss function to obtain relatively exquisite boundary. Different from these methods, Zeng *et al.* [20] learn a nearest neighbor classifier to refine saliency maps generated by other existing methods, showing great potential in saliency detection. But the source of its improvement isn't clear. So we delved into the impact of nearest neighbor optimization to find where the most improvement comes from.

In this paper, to deal with the issues mentioned above and further improve accuracy, we delved into the impact of diverse unified detectors based on convolutional layers and nearest neighbor optimization on saliency detection. Plenty of comparative experiments illustrate that (1) the flattened design contributes to the improvement of accuracy, but due to the inherent characteristics of convolution layers, it is not the effective way to solve the problems; (2) Nearest neighbor optimization is beneficial to remove background regions from salient objects and restore the missing sections while refining their boundaries, yielding a more reliable final prediction. With the progress of these studies, we built a GeminiNet for accurate saliency detection. Quantitative and qualitative experiments on six benchmark datasets demonstrate that our proposed GeminiNet performs favorably against the state-of-the-art methods under different evaluation metrics.

2 Unified Detectors Based on Convolution

To explore the impact of diverse unified detectors on network performance, we simply built the network shown in Fig. 1, then adopted simple 1 × 1 convolution kernel and different multi-branch modules such as Inception v3 [16], ASPP [4] and denseASPP [19] in Stage A to predict a coarse saliency map. Excessive dilated rate will introduce remotely unrelated pixels' impact, so we additionally adjusted the dilated rates in ASPP (dilated rates were set to 1, 3, 5, 7) to build a contracted ASPP dubbed C-ASPP. Table 1 illustrates the performance between different unified detectors under the metrics of maximum F-measure and MAE on six datasets, which shows that the flattened design (C-ASPP) contributes to the improvement of accuracy.

However, due to the inherent characteristics of convolutional layers, the flattened design is not the effective way to solve the issues mentioned at the beginning. It can be explained in two aspects.

(a) Decision-making mechanism: Relying on fixed convolution kernel weights to achieve non-linear mapping leads to serious missed detection and blurred edges. The original intention of convolution kernel is to achieve weight sharing when extracting features. However, when it is used as a detector for pixel-level prediction tasks, its simple mechanism is insufficient to detect various salient objects especially those having small scales, irregular shapes and sporadic locations in complex scenario of multi-target graphs. In addition, when a pixel to be detected is located in an area where the internal features' gradient is not conductive such as the edges of salient objects, convolution will cause 0–1 gradation and instability in the corresponding region of generated grayscale image. This is the reason why the objects' edge generated by unified detector is blurred. Apart from that, when a network encounters other patterns especially those differ greatly from the training set, the saliency of pixels will be misjudged because convolution kernel weights are based on the empirical knowledge of training set, eventually leading to missed detection of salient objects.

(b) Lack of spatial correlation caused by local contrast: Convolutional layers adopt sliding window to share kernel weights, so the entire decision process is based on local contrast. This operation will result in a lack of spatial correlation between different parts of same salient object that are far away, especially those tiny parts such as the limbs and corners of animals. Therefore, the segmentation of salient objects often has a local area missing. If a detector can predict results from global contrast or spatial correlation is introduced into the process of inference, as long as part of a salient object is correctly segmented, the remaining ones can be segmented too regardless of their distances. In addition, saliency detection is an image-specific task. Labels should be assigned to pixels depending on image context rather than local contrast.

3   Details of Nearest Neighbor Optimization

First of all, we show the formulas of NNO for saliency detection in detail. Given an initial coarse saliency prediction S_a and its feature space h, the average feature value of pixels in foreground and background are calculated respectively,

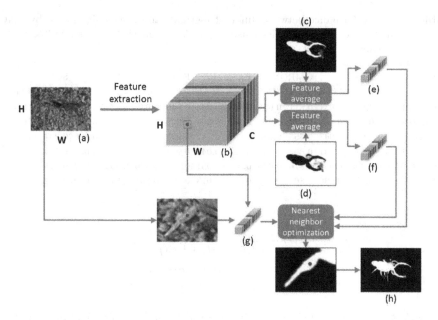

Fig. 2. Visualization of nearest neighbor optimization. The red solid circle represents a pixel to be detected. (a) Input image. (b) Feature space. (c) Foreground region. (d) Background region. (e) Foreground anchor. (f) Background anchor. (g) Feature vector of a pixel to be detected. (h) Refined saliency map. It should be noticed that c = 255-d, and both of them belong to the initial coarse saliency map. (Color figure online)

obtaining two vectors as anchors. This process is performed by:

$$f_+ = \frac{1}{|S_a^+|} \sum_{i \in S_a^+} h^i,$$

$$f_- = \frac{1}{|S_a^-|} \sum_{i \in S_a^-} h^i, \tag{1}$$

where S_a^+ denotes the foreground regions, and S_a^- denotes the background regions, $S_a = S_a^+ \cup S_a^-$. h^i represents the feature vector corresponding to a pixel located in the saliency regions or the background. f_+ denotes the foreground anchor and f_- denotes the background anchor. The probability of the i-th pixel belonging to salient region and non-salient region can be given by the softmax over its Euclidean distance to the anchors, obtaining a final refined prediction S_b. These processes are performed as follows (Fig. 2):

$$dist_i^+ = \|h^i - f_+\|,$$

$$dist_i^- = \|h^i - f_-\| \tag{2}$$

Table 2. The performance between different methods and their refined ones by NNO under the metrics of maximum F-measure and MAE on six datasets. Suffix "++" denotes refinement by NNO.

Variable	HKU		OMRON		PASCAL		ECSSD		DUTS-TE		SOD	
	F_{max}	MAE	F_{max}	MAE	F_{max}	MAE	F_{max}	MAE	F_{max}	MAE	F_{max}	MAE
C-ASPP	0.931	0.031	0.811	0.055	0.881	0.068	0.940	0.037	0.874	0.042	0.870	0.102
GBMPM	0.920	0.038	0.774	0.063	0.862	0.076	0.928	0.044	0.850	0.049	0.851	0.106
NLDF	0.902	0.048	0.753	0.080	0.845	0.112	0.905	0.063	0.812	0.066	0.837	0.123
C-ASPP++	0.933	0.031	0.893	0.043	0.927	0.045	0.944	0.036	0.939	0.024	0.929	0.063
GBMPM++	0.926	0.034	0.876	0.049	0.919	0.051	0.939	0.040	0.934	0.027	0.923	0.074
NLDF++	0.924	0.036	0.869	0.057	0.906	0.073	0.924	0.051	0.913	0.039	0.914	0.079

$$P_b(l_i = 1|\theta) = \frac{exp(-dist_i^+)}{exp(-dist_i^+) + exp(-dist_i^-)},$$

$$P_b(l_i = 0|\theta) = \frac{exp(-dist_i^-)}{exp(-dist_i^+) + exp(-dist_i^-)} \tag{3}$$

where $dist_i^+$ and $dist_i^-$ denote the Euclidean distance of each pixel and the two anchors separately, $P_b(l_i = 1|\theta)$ and $P_b(l_i = 0|\theta)$ represent the label probability of the i-th pixel in S_b. When a pixel is close to the foreground anchor, it indicates that the pixel is likely to belong to the salient object, otherwise it belongs to the background region. Compared to unified detectors, NNO is global contrast and relies on feature similarity calculation based on distance metric.

(1) Feature similarity calculation based on distance metric. NNO is not derived based on convolution kernels' nonlinear mapping. It is a non-parametric decision-making mechanism, so it can greatly reduce the interference of data distribution between pictures and between datasets to improve the generalization ability. Since NNO calculates the feature distance of each pixel and anchors when optimizing a coarse prediction, a pixel is independent of its neighbors in the process of inference. As long as the pixel's vector in feature space can encode the correct information and is close to its corresponding anchor, it can be correctly labeled, so NNO can recover the missed objects and obtain relatively exquisite objects' boundaries.

(2) Global contrast. For each picture to be detected, its anchors are generated by feature averaging from the global perspective of the initial coarse saliency map. In this way, the foreground anchor encodes the central feature of salient regions, while the background anchor encodes the central feature of background regions. Then the saliency value that should be assigned is determined by the similarity between the pixel to be detected and the anchors. Therefore, NNO is based on global contrast rather than local contrast. This decision-making mechanism is also more in line with the characteristics of saliency detection: Saliency detection is an image-specific task, labels should be assigned to pixels depending on the image context.

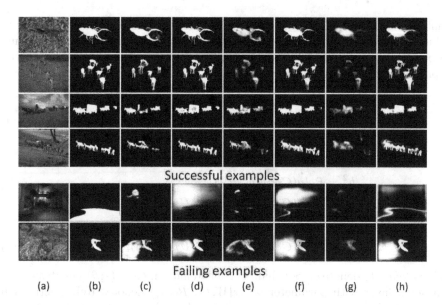

Successful examples

Failing examples

(a)   (b)   (c)   (d)   (e)   (f)   (g)   (h)

Fig. 3. Visualization of successful examples and failing examples. From left to right: (a) input image, (b) ground truth, (c) C-ASPP, (d) C-ASPP+NNO, (e) GBMPM, (f) GBMPM+NNO, (g) NLDF, (h) NLDF+NNO.

In order to better demonstrate the effect of NNO, we use the results predicted by C-ASPP, GBMPM [21] and NLDF [12] as coarse saliency maps then optimize them using the NNO of Stage B in our proposed GeminiNet. Table 2 illustrates the performance between different methods and their refined ones under the metrics of maximum F-measure and MAE on six datasets. By comparing the data in Table 2, it can be found that (1) NNO can greatly improve the accuracy. (2) The better the coarse prediction, the better the refined one. Figure 3 lists some successful examples and failing examples, which shows that NNO is beneficial to remove background regions from salient objects and restore the missing sections while refining their boundaries, yielding a more reliable final prediction. In addition, these examples illustrate that if a coarse prediction is terrible, the corresponding refined one will not get any improvement.

4 Overview of Network Architecture

The proposed GeminiNet is built on the pre-trained VGG16 [14] which has been widely used as feature extraction backbone in many deep learning models due to its simplicity and good generalization properties. We discard all the fully connected layers and remove the last pooling layer. Each input image is resized to 256×256. In order to obtain multi-scale contextual features, we stack two MCFEMs after each side output layer, obtaining $f_i^c, i = 1, 2, 3, 4, 5$.

For the sake of taking full advantage of multi-context information extracted from different side output layers, the two adjacent features f_i^c and f_{i+1}^c are combined by cross-channel concatenation, followed by a convolutional layer to reduce channel size, then we add short connections [6] between shallower and deeper side outputs. All convolutional layers adopt kernel size 3×3. These series of processes can be performed as below:

$$h_i^0 = Concat(f_i^c, Up(f_{i+1}^c)), i = 1, 2, 3, 4$$
$$h_i^1 = Relu(Conv(h_i^0; \theta_i^1)), i = 1, 2, 3, 4 \tag{4}$$

and

$$h_4^2 = Relu(Conv(h_4^1; \theta_4^2)),$$
$$h_3^2 = Relu(Conv(Concat(h_3^1, Up(h_4^2)); \theta_3^2)),$$
$$h_2^2 = Relu(Conv(Concat(h_2^1, Up(h_{3\sim4}^2)); \theta_2^2)),$$
$$h_1^2 = Relu(Conv(Concat(h_1^1, Up(h_{2\sim4}^2)); \theta_1^2)), \tag{5}$$

where $Concat()$ denotes cross-channel concatenation; $Conv(*; \theta)$ denotes a convolutional layer with parameter $\theta = \{W, b\}$; $Relu()$ denotes ReLU activation function; $Up()$ is an up-sample operation to adapt the size of lower level feature map. In practice, we adopt bilinear interpolation as up-sample function. h_j^i represents the convolutional feature of the j-th branch in the i-th layer. We resize h_i^2 to input image and combine them by cross-channel concatenation that can incorporate coarse semantic and fine details at the meantime. We adopt convolution with kernel size 1×1 in Stage A and Stage B respectively to reduce the gap between different ranges in h_i^2, obtaining h_a and h_b.

The process of inference consists of two detachable stages. In Stage A, we append a unified detector after h_a to predict a coarse saliency map S_a. In Stage B, we take h_b and S_a as input, then adopt nearest neighbor optimization to refine S_a, yielding a more reliable final prediction S_b.

Now we have obtained a coarse prediction S_a with its refined result S_b. Cross entropy (CE) is adopted to optimize the proposed network. For S_a and S_b, the loss functions are written as followed:

$$L_{CE1} = -\frac{1}{N \times |\Omega|} \sum_{n=1}^{N} \sum_{i=1}^{|\Omega|} \sum_{y=0}^{1} 1\{l_i^n = y\} ln P_a(l_i^n = y|\theta),$$

$$L_{CE2} = -\frac{1}{N \times |\Omega|} \sum_{n=1}^{N} \sum_{i=1}^{|\Omega|} \sum_{y=0}^{1} 1\{l_i^n = y\} ln P_b(l_i^n = y|\theta), \tag{6}$$

where $1\{\}$ denotes indicator function; N denotes the batch size; $y = 1$ denotes salient pixel and $y = 0$ denotes non-salient pixel; Ω is the pixel domain of the image; $P_a(l_i^n = 1|\theta)$ and $P_a(l_i^n = 0|\theta)$ represent the label probability of the i-th pixel in S_a while $P_b(l_i^n = 1|\theta)$ and $P_b(l_i^n = 0|\theta)$ represent the label probability of the i-th pixel in S_b. L_{CE1} and L_{CE2} denote the cross entropy of S_a and S_b respectively.

Table 3. The performance comparison of different methods under the metrics of maximum F-measure and MAE. The top results are highlighted in red, green, and blue, respectively.

Methods	HKU		OMRON		PASCAL		ECSSD		DUTS-TE		SOD	
	F_{max}	MAE	F_{max}	MAE	F_{max}	MAE	F_{max}	MAE	F_{max}	MAE	F_{max}	MAE
Ours	0.933	0.031	0.893	0.043	0.927	0.045	0.944	0.036	0.939	0.024	0.929	0.063
PiCANet	0.921	0.042	0.794	0.068	0.880	0.088	0.931	0.047	0.851	0.054	0.855	0.108
GBMPM	0.920	0.038	0.774	0.063	0.862	0.076	0.928	0.044	0.850	0.049	0.851	0.106
Amulet	0.896	0.052	0.743	0.098	0.858	0.103	0.915	0.059	0.778	0.085	0.808	0.145
DCL	0.885	0.137	0.739	0.157	0.823	0.189	0.901	0.075	0.782	0.150	0.825	0.198
DHS	0.902	0.054	0.758	0.072	0.841	0.111	0.907	0.060	0.829	0.065	0.827	0.133
DSS	0.911	0.040	0.771	0.066	0.846	0.112	0.916	0.053	0.825	0.057	0.846	0.126
ELD	0.839	0.074	0.720	0.088	0.773	0.123	0.867	0.079	0.738	0.093	0.760	0.154
NLDF	0.902	0.048	0.753	0.080	0.845	0.112	0.905	0.063	0.812	0.066	0.837	0.123
RFCN	0.898	0.080	0.738	0.095	0.850	0.132	0.898	0.095	0.783	0.090	0.807	0.166
SRM	0.906	0.046	0.769	0.069	0.847	0.085	0.917	0.054	0.827	0.059	0.845	0.132
UCF	0.886	0.074	0.735	0.132	0.846	0.128	0.911	0.078	0.771	0.117	0.803	0.169

5 Experiments

5.1 Experimental Setup

Datasets. In order to better compare the performance between different methods, six benchmark datasets are selected for evaluation, including HKU-IS, ECSSD, PASCAL-S, DUT-OMRON, DUTS-TEST and SOD. ECSSD contains 1000 images in diverse scenes while DUT-OMRON includes 5168 images in complex scenario. PASCAL-S consists of 850 images which contains different salient objects with cluttered surrounding. HKU-IS consists of 4447 images with diverse foreground regions in low-contrast appearance. DUTS consists of DUTS-TRAIN and DUTS-TEST. DUTS-TRAIN has 10553 images and DUTS-TEST has 5019 images, both of which contain salient objects with different scales, irregular shapes and sporadic locations. SOD includes 300 images that have diverse salient objects in natural scene.

Evaluation Metrics. We adopt three metrics including Precision-Recall (PR) curves, Maximum F-measure and Mean Absolute Error (MAE) to evaluate the performance between different methods. In the classification task, the precision value is the ratio of ground truth pixels in the predicted salient region while the recall value is the ratio of the predicted saliency pixels in the ground truth area. We threshold the predicted map and compare it with the ground truth to draw the PR curves. F-measure which is computed the relationship between precision and recall at different thresholds with an adjustable coefficient β represents the overall performance:

$$F_\beta = \frac{(1 + \beta^2) \times Precision \times Recall}{\beta^2 \times Precision + Recall} \tag{7}$$

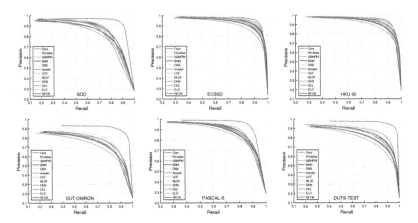

Fig. 4. The PR curves of the proposed GeminiNet and 11 state-of-the-art methods on six datasets.

where β^2 is set to 0.3 as suggested in previous work. Maximum F-measure can well reflect the performance, so it is adopted as one of the evaluation index. Moreover, the mean absolute error (MAE) is calculated to compute the average absolute per-pixel difference between predicted map and the corresponding ground truth. The formula of MAE is defined as below:

$$MAE = \frac{1}{W \times H} \sum_{x=1}^{W} \sum_{y=1}^{H} |S(x,y) - G(x,y)|. \tag{8}$$

$S(x,y)$ and $G(x,y)$ represent the predicted and actual value of the pixel at (x,y).

Implementation Details. In GeminiNet, the parameters of the first 13 convolutional layers are initialized by pre-trained VGG16 net, while the weights of other convolutional layers are initialized by using truncated normal method. We utilize the DUTS-TRAIN dataset to train GeminiNet. In the training phase, both of L_{CE1} and L_{CE2} use ground truth as label. We use Adam with an initial learning rate at 1e−6 and set the batch size N to 1. We augment the training set by horizontal flipping and vertical flipping. We do not use the validation set. The two loss functions were optimized asynchronously. After L_{CE1} converges, L_{CE2} is optimized. Their model parameters while converging are saved separately. The overall training process takes about 28 h and converges after 16 epochs. A NVIDIA TITAN X (Pascal) GPU is used for training and testing.

5.2   Performance Comparison

Performance Comparison Between Different Unified Detectors. Table 1 illustrates the performance between different unified detectors under the metrics of maximum F-measure and MAE on six datasets, which shows that the flattened design (C-ASPP) contributes to the improvement of accuracy.

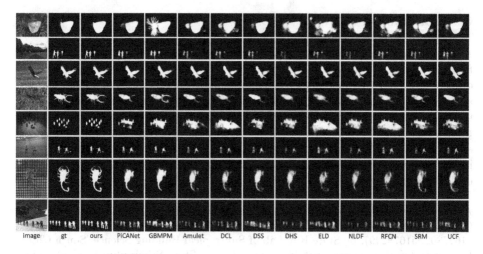

Fig. 5. Visual examples of the proposed GeminiNet and 11 state-of-the-art algorithms.

Performance Comparison Between Different Methods and Their Refined Ones by NNO. Table 2 illustrates the performance between different methods and their refined ones by NNO under the metrics of maximum F-measure and MAE on six datasets, which shows that (1) NNO can greatly improve the accuracy. (2) The better the coarse prediction, the better the refined one. Figure 3 lists some successful examples and failing examples, which shows that NNO is beneficial to remove background regions from salient objects and restore the missing sections while refining their boundaries, yielding a more reliable final prediction. In addition, these examples illustrate that if a coarse prediction is terrible, the corresponding refined one will not get any improvement.

Performance Comparison with State-of-the-Art. We perform comparison of the proposed GeminiNet (adopting C-ASPP as unified detector in Stage A) and 11 state-of-the-art methods that contains PiCANet [11], Amulet [22], GBMPM [21], DCL [9], DHS [10], DSS [6], ELD [8], NLDF [12], RFCN [17], SRM [18], UCF [23] on six datasets. For the sake of achieving fair performance comparison, predicted saliency map of different algorithms are provided from official website or generated by running available codes. Table 3 illustrates the performance of different methods under the metrics of maximum F-measure and MAE. We can observe that our proposed network achieves the best results among six datasets. Figure 4 shows that the PR curves of the proposed algorithm perform better than other methods on six datasets. Some predicted saliency maps randomly selected from testing set are showed in Fig. 5. It can be observed that our GeminiNet can accurately detect salient objects with distinct boundary even if their appearances are similar to background. In addition, the GeminiNet is also robust for images with multiple salient objects in complex scenario.

6 Conclusion

Adopting single-scale convolutional layers as saliency detectors after extracting features to predict saliency maps will cause serious missed detection and blurred objects' boundaries especially those targets having small scales, irregular shapes and sporadic locations in complex scenario of multi-target graphs. We delved into the impact of diverse unified detectors and nearest neighbor optimization, then built a GeminiNet for accurate saliency detection. Quantitative and qualitative experiments on six benchmark datasets demonstrate that our proposed GeminiNet performs favorably against the state-of-the-art methods under different evaluation metrics.

Acknowledgments. This research was supported by National Key R&D Program of China (No. 2017YFC0806000), by National Natural Science Foundation of China (No. 11627802, 51678249), by State Key Lab of Subtropical Building Science, South China University Of Technology (2018ZB33), and by the State Scholarship Fund of China Scholarship Council (201806155022).

References

1. Abdulmunem, A., Lai, Y.K., Sun, X.: Saliency guided local and global descriptors for effective action recognition. Comput. Visual Media **2**(1), 97–106 (2016). https://doi.org/10.1007/s41095-016-0033-9
2. Borji, A., Frintrop, S., Sihite, D.N., Itti, L.: Adaptive object tracking by learning background context. In: 2012 IEEE Computer Society Conference on Computer Vision and Pattern Recognition Workshops (CVPRW), pp. 23–30. IEEE (2012). https://doi.org/10.1109/cvprw.2012.6239191
3. Cai, S., Huang, J., Zeng, D., Ding, X., Paisley, J.: MEnet: a metric expression network for salient object segmentation. arXiv preprint arXiv:1805.05638 (2018). https://doi.org/10.24963/ijcai.2018/83
4. Chen, L.C., Papandreou, G., Kokkinos, I., Murphy, K., Yuille, A.L.: DeepLab: semantic image segmentation with deep convolutional nets, atrous convolution, and fully connected CRFs. IEEE Trans. Pattern Anal. Mach. Intell. **40**(4), 834–848 (2018). https://doi.org/10.1109/tpami.2017.2699184
5. He, S., Jiao, J., Zhang, X., Han, G., Lau, R.W.: Delving into salient object subitizing and detection. In: Proceedings of the IEEE International Conference on Computer Vision, pp. 1059–1067 (2017). https://doi.org/10.1109/iccv.2017.120
6. Hou, Q., Cheng, M.M., Hu, X., Borji, A., Tu, Z., Torr, P.: Deeply supervised salient object detection with short connections. In: 2017 IEEE Conference on Computer Vision and Pattern Recognition (CVPR), pp. 5300–5309. IEEE (2017). https://doi.org/10.1109/cvpr.2017.563
7. Krähenbühl, P., Koltun, V.: Efficient inference in fully connected CRFs with Gaussian edge potentials. In: Advances in Neural Information Processing Systems, pp. 109–117 (2011)
8. Lee, G., Tai, Y.W., Kim, J.: Deep saliency with encoded low level distance map and high level features. In: Proceedings of the IEEE Conference on Computer Vision and Pattern Recognition, pp. 660–668 (2016). https://doi.org/10.1109/cvpr.2016.78

9. Li, G., Yu, Y.: Deep contrast learning for salient object detection. In: Proceedings of the IEEE Conference on Computer Vision and Pattern Recognition, pp. 478–487 (2016). https://doi.org/10.1109/cvpr.2016.58

10. Liu, N., Han, J.: DHSNet: deep hierarchical saliency network for salient object detection. In: Proceedings of the IEEE Conference on Computer Vision and Pattern Recognition, pp. 678–686 (2016). https://doi.org/10.1109/cvpr.2016.80

11. Liu, N., Han, J., Yang, M.H.: PiCANet: learning pixel-wise contextual attention for saliency detection. In: Proceedings of the IEEE Conference on Computer Vision and Pattern Recognition, pp. 3089–3098 (2018). https://doi.org/10.1109/cvpr.2018.00326

12. Luo, Z., Mishra, A.K., Achkar, A., Eichel, J.A., Li, S., Jodoin, P.M.: Non-local deep features for salient object detection. In: CVPR, vol. 2, p. 7 (2017). https://doi.org/10.1109/cvpr.2017.698

13. Ren, Z., Gao, S., Chia, L.T., Tsang, I.W.H.: Region-based saliency detection and its application in object recognition. IEEE Trans. Circuits Syst. Video Technol. 24(5), 769–779 (2014). https://doi.org/10.1109/tcsvt.2013.2280096

14. Simonyan, K., Zisserman, A.: Very deep convolutional networks for large-scale image recognition. arXiv preprint arXiv:1409.1556 (2014)

15. Szegedy, C., et al.: Going deeper with convolutions. In: Proceedings of the IEEE Conference on Computer Vision and Pattern Recognition, pp. 1–9 (2015). https://doi.org/10.1109/cvpr.2015.7298594

16. Szegedy, C., Vanhoucke, V., Ioffe, S., Shlens, J., Wojna, Z.: Rethinking the inception architecture for computer vision. In: Proceedings of the IEEE Conference on Computer Vision and Pattern Recognition, pp. 2818–2826 (2016). https://doi.org/10.1109/cvpr.2016.308

17. Wang, L., Wang, L., Lu, H., Zhang, P., Ruan, X.: Salient object detection with recurrent fully convolutional networks. IEEE Trans. Pattern Anal. Mach. Intell. (2018). https://doi.org/10.1109/tpami.2018.2846598

18. Wang, T., Borji, A., Zhang, L., Zhang, P., Lu, H.: A stagewise refinement model for detecting salient objects in images. In: Proceedings of the IEEE International Conference on Computer Vision, pp. 4019–4028 (2017). https://doi.org/10.1109/iccv.2017.433

19. Yang, M., Yu, K., Zhang, C., Li, Z., Yang, K.: DenseASPP for semantic segmentation in street scenes. In: Proceedings of the IEEE Conference on Computer Vision and Pattern Recognition, pp. 3684–3692 (2018). https://doi.org/10.1109/cvpr.2018.00388

20. Zeng, Y., Lu, H., Zhang, L., Feng, M., Borji, A.: Learning to promote saliency detectors. In: Proceedings of the IEEE Conference on Computer Vision and Pattern Recognition, pp. 1644–1653 (2018). https://doi.org/10.1109/cvpr.2018.00177

21. Zhang, L., Dai, J., Lu, H., He, Y., Wang, G.: A bi-directional message passing model for salient object detection. In: Proceedings of the IEEE Conference on Computer Vision and Pattern Recognition, pp. 1741–1750 (2018). https://doi.org/10.1109/cvpr.2018.00187

22. Zhang, P., Wang, D., Lu, H., Wang, H., Ruan, X.: Amulet: aggregating multi-level convolutional features for salient object detection. In: Proceedings of the IEEE International Conference on Computer Vision, pp. 202–211 (2017). https://doi.org/10.1109/iccv.2017.31

23. Zhang, P., Wang, D., Lu, H., Wang, H., Yin, B.: Learning uncertain convolutional features for accurate saliency detection. In: 2017 IEEE International Conference on Computer Vision (ICCV), pp. 212–221. IEEE (2017). https://doi.org/10.1109/iccv.2017.32

FCN Salient Object Detection Using Region Cropping

Yikai Hua and Xiaodong Gu$^{(\boxtimes)}$

Department of Electronic Engineering, Fudan University,
Shanghai 200433, China
xdgu@fudan.edu.cn

Abstract. An important issue in salient object detection is how to improve the result of saliency map for the reason that it is the basis of many subsequent operations in computer vision. In this paper, we propose a region-based salient object detection model using fully convolutional neural network (FCN) with traditional visual saliency method. We introduce the region cropping and jumping operation into FCN network for a more target-oriented feature extraction, which is a low-level cue based processing. It processes the training images into patches of various sizes and makes these patches jump to convolutional layers with corresponding depths as their input data in training. This operation can preserve the main structure of objects while decrease the background redundancy. In the meantime, it also takes into account topological property, which emphasizes the topological integrity of objects. Experimental results on four datasets show that the proposed model performs effectively on salient object detection compared with other ten approaches, including state-of-the-art ones.

Keywords: Salient object detection · Fully convolutional neural network · Region cropping

1 Introduction

The purpose of salient object detection is to discover the regions of interest of an image automatically and accurately, which conforms to human visual perception. Due to the aim of salient object detection, it has been used in a wide range of computer vision applications such as object motion tracking, object recognition, semantic segmentation and so on. A main target of research in salient object detection is to design various models to compute saliency maps effectively.

Since Itti proposed the visual saliency algorithm [1] for simulating visual attention mechanism of human vision, many work [2–9] had contributed to the research of salient object detection. [2] used intensity and color features to achieve a state-of-the-art performance on several datasets. [3, 4] calculated the saliency map which made use of the information of contour, shape and spatial context. In [5, 6], visual saliency approaches were proposed based on the phase spectrum analysis of images. And on the foundation of phase spectrum theory, [7] introduced topological property into salient

© Springer Nature Switzerland AG 2019
I. V. Tetko et al. (Eds.): ICANN 2019, LNCS 11729, pp. 360–370, 2019.
https://doi.org/10.1007/978-3-030-30508-6_29

object detection, which showed that topological property played an important role in visual perception.

Though traditional salient object detection methods had achieved great results, the effectiveness of these approaches were still restricted with the limitation of the number of model parameters. Moreover, with the rapid increase of the amount of the image data and the improvement of computing performance recent years, researchers intend to take a data-driven strategy and design learning-based computational models in order to get much more accurate salient results. [8] presented a model named ResNet adopting a residual learning framework to make the network deeper than those used previously. In [9], a multi-task FCN model was proposed for salient object detection and image segmentation, using the segmentation task to improve the behavior of salient object detection.

The multi-task model in [9] achieves good saliency performance. But sometimes the segmentation results may not be the salient object, which in this case the topological property of salient object is not manifest enough. In order to emphasize the topological integrity of the whole salient object as well as inspired by the connection way of ResNet, we proposed a region-based FCN model combined region cropping operation with FCN [10] network for image saliency detection. In this model, the training images are first processed by the proposed region cropping operation, which crops the training images into patches with various size containing salient objects and then jumps these patches to different convolutional layers of the network to learn a dense saliency representation. The region cropping operation is on the foundation of a conventional saliency method, which makes our model take the advantage of low-level visual cues. This training mode allows patches with various size to jump to corresponding convolutional layers to train the network directly, which can preserve the main structure of salient objects and thereby guiding target-oriented feature mining.

The rest part of this paper is organized as follows: Sect. 2 gives a thorough description of the proposed model. In Sect. 3, the experimental results and related analysis are discussed. Finally, Sect. 4 makes a brief summary of this paper.

2 Proposed Model

2.1 Overview

The training process of our proposed salient object detection model mainly consists of two parts: (1) the region cropping operation of the training images in order to obtain patches of salient objects as the input data of the saliency model; and (2) the FCN based network for semantic feature extraction and saliency map representation. For (1), we perform the region cropping operation for the purpose of discovering the general salient object location and then cropping the images, which decreases the redundant background information and stresses the topological property of salient object. For (2), based on the size of image patches after cropping, they jump to convolutional layers of different depths respectively as inputs for training the FCN saliency model. Figure 1 shows the main architecture of our proposed saliency model. A detailed description of the two components of our model is presented in the following subsections.

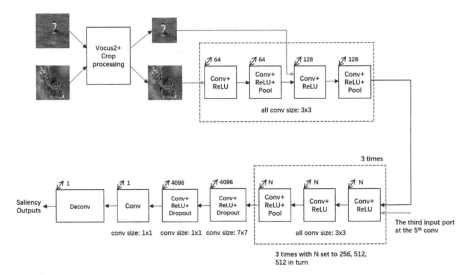

Fig. 1. The architecture of the region-based FCN model for visual saliency. (Color figure online)

2.2 Region Cropping

In salient object detection, both low-level features and high-level features are critical to obtain a saliency map with accurate prediction. Existing researches have proved the effectiveness of deep learning based model in salient object detection, for that the CNNs have powerful performance in image feature mining, while researchers also notice that the performance of CNNs depends more on the high-level semantic features which may lead the model confused about those salient objects with weak semantics. To improve the behavior of CNNs on discovering the salient objects with weak semantics, we combine the region cropping operation into the FCN network. This region cropping mainly relies on a conventional saliency detection method guided by low-level cues, which can crop images into patches with various size. This operation to the training images emphasizes the salient regions in a low-level visual perspective and decrease the background redundancy in the meantime.

Figure 2 shows how the proposed region cropping operation processes the training images. We first apply a conventional method to obtain the saliency maps of the training images. Since the saliency expressions from the conventional method are not as precise as the deep learning models with obvious background interference, we perform a binary operation to the saliency maps, generating binary maps as the masks for the subsequent cropping operation. Finally, we combine the binary masks and original images to crop the training images into various sizes, whose distinguishing features are that salient regions hold predominant area and the background scene is decreased. In this region cropping operation, we adopt the Vocus2 [2] method as our conventional saliency method. This Vocus2 method is an improved method based on the saliency model proposed by Itti [1], which uses low-level cues, including the intensity and color features, to generate the final saliency maps.

Due to the processed image patches jump to different convolutional layers to train the network, it is important to determine the cropping size of images in order to get appropriate patches, whose size match the input size of convolutional layers. In the region cropping operation, we set a series of sliding windows as the same size of the input size of these layers. We move the sliding windows on the binary mask and search for the minimum window which can contain the whole mask in the binary map. Images are then cropped into patches according to the position of sliding windows. Moreover, as the area of sliding window is usually a bit larger than that of the mask in the binary map, it is also more likely to contain some edge information of salient object, which is unrecognized by the conventional method.

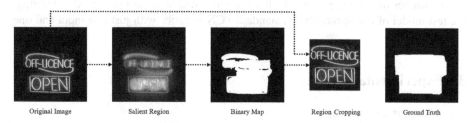

| Original Image | Salient Region | Binary Map | Region Cropping | Ground Truth |

Fig. 2. Pipeline of the region cropping operation in our approach.

2.3 The Region-Based FCN Model

Fully convolutional neural network (FCN) was first put forward by Long [10] for the task of image semantic segmentation, which has been used in many other computer vision missions for the advantage that the FCN model can output pixel-accurate result with the same size as the input image. As the main architecture illustrated in Fig. 1, we adopt the FCN network to extract features and generate a pixel-wise saliency representation. The first 13 convolutional layers, whose kernel size are all 3×3, are used to extract features, which are initialized from the VGG-16 network. The next three convolutional layers can be regarded as saliency extraction layer followed by a dropout layer for relieving the over-fitting problem. At the end on the network, a deconvolution layer is set to learn an up-sampling function for obtaining a salient object detection representation with full resolution. In the training phase, the cross entropy loss is adopted to train the network, and the stochastic gradient descent (SGD) method is used to minimize the above loss function and optimize the network.

The main highlight of the proposed model is that the training images jump to convolutional layers of different depths as their inputs respectively to train the model, judged by their different size of the images. In this way, the cropped image patches which outstand the topological integrity of the whole salient target can directly jump to the convolutional layers with corresponding semantic levels, which leads the network to focus more attention on target-oriented feature mining. Specially, it can be noticed that there are three optional input ports (the red arrows in Fig. 1) in our network for the adaptation of the introduction of region cropping operation. Since the ratio of images, whose area of salient regions are smaller than the input size of the 8th convolutional layer in Fig. 1, is very small, we set three optional input ports for region cropping at the 1st, 3rd, 5th convolutional layers in the experiments.

In practice, in order to input the training images to the intermediate convolutional layers, it is necessary to match the size and channels between image patches and the inputs of corresponding convolutional layers. For the former problem, we adopt the thought of sliding windows to properly enlarge the area of the binary mask to match the size of convolutional layers' inputs, which has been detailed introduced in Subsect. 2.2. For the latter problem, before sending images into the network, we adopt an additional 1×1 convolutional layer to match the channels with the inputs of convolutional layers, the parameters of which are also updated in the training phase. More specifically, these extra convolutional layers play the role of matching channels of image patches in training phase, which are not included in the test phase. After training, the test model of our approach is a standard FCN network with just one input and one output.

3   Experimental Results

3.1   Experiment Settings

In order to evaluate the effectiveness of our proposed model on salient object detection, we set a series of experiments on four benchmark datasets, including MSRA10K [11], ECSSD [12], SED2 [13] and PASCAL-S [14]. The common characteristic of these four datasets is that their visual saliency ground truth are all pixel-wise labelled, which is conducive to measure the relevant metrics accurately. In more detail, the MSRA10K contains 10000 images from MSRA dataset, which are mainly characterized with simple and smooth background. ECSSD is an expanded version of Complex Scene Saliency Dataset (CSSD) [12], whose semantically meaningful composition of images are much more complex than the MSRA10K dataset. SED2 is a multi-objective saliency dataset, usually having two salient object in one image. PASCAL-S dataset is derived from the PASCAL VOC dataset [15] with complex scenes which is challenging for the visual saliency evaluation.

In the experiments, we train and test our model on a desktop computer, under the conditions of Intel Core i7-6700K CPU (4.00 GHz) and NVIDIA GeForce GTX1080 Ti GPU. The region cropping module is implemented in MATLAB and the deep neural network is based on the Caffe framework. The convolutional layers are initialized from the VGG-16 network and the other new added layers are initialized randomly. We randomly pick 5000 images from the MSRA10K dataset as our training set to train our model with a step learning strategy, of which the basic learning rate, step size and gamma are 10^{-8}, 10000 and 0.1 respectively. It takes about 10 h to train the model under the above conditions with 100000 iterations in total.

3.2   Evaluation Metrics

In the experiments, we adopt three metrics to quantitatively evaluate the performance of these visual saliency detection approaches, including precision and recall (P-R) curve, F-measure and mean absolute error (MAE). Specifically, the P-R curve reflects the approach's performance of discovering the salient object by utilizing binary processing to the saliency map which adopts different threshold ranging from 0 to 255 and thereby calculate the corresponding precision and recall values. The precision and recall sometimes appear contradictory situations, therefore F-measure is used to provide a comprehensive result which combines precision and recall as follow:

$$F_\alpha = \frac{(1 + \alpha^2) Precision \times Recall}{\alpha^2 \times Precision + Recall}. \tag{1}$$

In our experiments, α^2 is set to 0.3 for all test conditions. Precisely, maximum F-measure (F_{max}) is the maximum F-measure value calculated from the P-R curve, while average F-measure (F_{avg}) uses the adaptive threshold for saliency map binarization.

In addition, MAE is associated with the average pixel-wise error between the saliency map and ground truth, which is defined as:

$$MAE = \frac{1}{W \times H} \sum_{x=1}^{W} \sum_{y=1}^{H} |S(x, y) - GT(x, y)|. \tag{2}$$

3.3   Performance Comparison

In our experiments, the proposed approach is compared with several other state-of-the-art methods qualitatively and quantitatively, including DeepSaliency [9], DRFI [16], DSR [17], RBD [18], GMR [19], MC [20], GC [21], RC [22], HC [22], and FT [23].

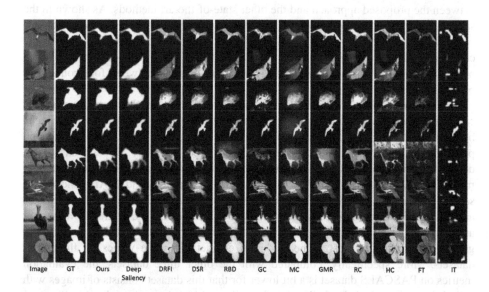

Fig. 3. Qualitative saliency results comparison between different approaches on several sample images with ground truth (GT).

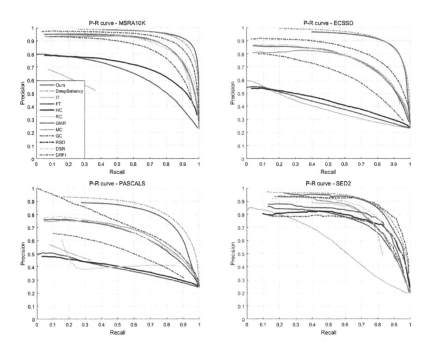

Fig. 4. Precision-recall curves of the proposed approach and other saliency methods on 4 benchmark datasets.

Figure 3 gives an intuitive illustration of the qualitative performance comparison between the proposed approach and the other state-of-the-art methods. As shown in the saliency map results provided from Fig. 3, our proposed approach is able to achieve competitive saliency detection results compared with other methods. Even in some challenging sample images, such as in the third and fifth rows, our approach still performs well in complicated situation which the contrast between foreground and background is low.

For a quantitative comparison between all these approaches, the corresponding P-R curves of these above-mentioned methods on four datasets are displayed in Fig. 4. It can be observed clearly that our proposed approach can obtain a better saliency detection performance than other methods in most cases. More precisely, Table 1 shows the detailed salient object detection performance of these approaches on three evaluation metrics, including maximum F-measure, average F-measure and MAE. The metric scores of compared methods are cited from [9] if available, while the other metric scores are obtained by running the corresponding open source codes. The results show that our approach achieves a favorable performance against other state-of-the-art methods in general, obtaining the best or near-optimal evaluation metric values on these four datasets. More specifically, compared with the other three datasets, the evaluation metrics on PASCALS dataset is a bit lower for that this dataset consists of images with complex scenes, which is challenging for salient object detection task while the proposed model still achieves competitive results compared with other models.

Table 1. Quantitatively comparison between our proposed approach and other methods on four datasets, involving 3 evaluation metrics (maximum F-measure, average F-measure and MAE).

MSRA10K		Ours	DRFI	DSR	RBD	GC	MC
	F_{max}	**0.9193**	0.8825	0.8398	0.8612	0.8021	0.8528
	F_{avg}	**0.8902**	0.7644	0.7767	0.7762	0.7398	0.7434
	MAE	0.0342	0.0493	**0.0251**	0.0252	0.0436	0.0600
		Deep saliency	GMR	RC	HC	FT	
	F_{max}	0.9109	0.8546	0.8523	0.6908	0.6433	
	F_{avg}	0.8592	0.7768	0.7699	0.6118	0.4307	
	MAE	0.0314	0.0371	0.0544	0.1103	0.0796	
ECSSD		Ours	DRFI	DSR	RBD	GC	MC
	F_{max}	**0.8848**	0.7390	0.6987	0.7163	0.6240	0.7037
	F_{avg}	**0.8424**	0.6884	0.6539	0.6219	0.5535	0.6549
	MAE	**0.0378**	0.1841	0.2127	0.1478	0.2382	0.2055
		Deep saliency	GMR	RC	HC	FT	
	F_{max}	0.8095	0.7012	0.7381	0.4564	0.4493	
	F_{avg}	0.7589	0.6498	0.6771	0.3978	0.3785	
	MAE	0.1601	0.2040	0.1506	0.2756	0.2859	
PASCALS		Ours	DRFI	DSR	RBD	GC	MC
	F_{max}	0.7889	0.7307	0.6782	0.6566	0.6384	0.7097
	F_{avg}	**0.7588**	0.6487	0.6172	0.5974	0.4151	0.6304
	MAE	**0.0491**	0.2351	0.2565	0.0635	0.2655	0.2385
		Deep saliency	GMR	RC	HC	FT	
	F_{max}	**0.8182**	0.6893	0.4589	0.4256	0.4837	
	F_{avg}	0.7310	0.6156	0.3617	0.3618	0.3707	
	MAE	0.1695	0.2464	0.1587	0.2133	0.3297	
SED2		Ours	DRFI	DSR	RBD	GC	MC
	F_{max}	0.8539	0.8386	0.7890	0.8583	0.7337	0.7710
	F_{avg}	**0.8075**	0.7479	0.7301	0.8040	0.6648	0.7293
	MAE	**0.0273**	0.1228	0.1452	0.1039	0.1800	0.1512
		Deep saliency	GMR	RC	HC	FT	
	F_{max}	**0.8634**	0.7670	0.7949	0.7508	0.7104	
	F_{avg}	0.7778	0.7334	0.7467	0.6626	0.6324	
	MAE	0.1074	0.1567	0.1099	0.1384	0.1901	

3.4 Contribution of Region Cropping Operation

In order to prove the effectiveness of our region cropping operation which crops the images into patches and jumps to different convolutional layers based on their sizes for training, we compare the saliency performance of our entire salient object detection model with a normal FCN network of the same depth on four datasets. In the experiment, we random select the same 5000 images in MSRA10K dataset as training set for both models while the rest images in MSRA10K dataset with other three datasets are used to test their saliency performance.

The detailed saliency performance comparison of the two models on four datasets is displayed in Table 2. The results of F-measure and MAE shows the improvement brought by the proposed model in the overall performance of salient object detection task. Specifically, after the introduction of region cropping operation, the F_{avg} on four datasets are improved by 1.71%, 1.43%, 4.62%, 5.28% respectively, which reveals the effectiveness of the proposed saliency model when facing with different kinds of images.

Table 2. Comparison of experimental results between the model with region cropping operation ('Cropping') and one without region cropping operation ('No-cropping').

		MSRA10K	ECSSD	PASCALS	SED2
Cropping	F_{max}	**0.9193**	**0.8848**	0.7889	**0.8539**
	F_{avg}	**0.8902**	**0.8424**	**0.7588**	**0.8075**
	MAE	0.0342	**0.0378**	**0.0491**	**0.0273**
No-cropping	F_{max}	0.9071	0.8674	**0.7899**	0.8523
	F_{avg}	0.8752	0.8305	0.7253	0.7670
	MAE	**0.0311**	0.0579	0.0849	0.0647

4 Conclusion

Salient object detection aims to capture a more accurate region of salient objects represented by a pixel-wise prediction. In this paper, we propose a region-based FCN model for salient object detection in order to obtain a more precise saliency representation. We design a region cropping operation for FCN network, which is a low-level cues dependent module, to address target-oriented feature mining during the training of FCN network. The region cropping operation crops the training images into patches with various sizes and makes them jump to different convolutional layers with matched semantic levels for efficient feature extraction. In addition, this region cropping operation also emphasizes the importance of topological property of salient object in visual saliency. The experimental results on four datasets show that our proposed approach achieves a competitive performance against other state-of-the-art methods on salient object detection. Contrast experiments on four datasets reveals the effectiveness of the region cropping operation, which improves the saliency performance of FCN network when dealing with different types of images.

Acknowledgments. This work was supported in part by National Natural Science Foundation of China under grant 61771145 and 61371148.

References

1. Itti, L., Koch, C., Niebur, E.: A model of saliency-based visual attention for rapid scene analysis. IEEE Trans. Pattern Anal. Mach. Intell. **20**(11), 1254–1259 (1998)
2. Frintrop, S., Werner, T., Garcia, G.M.: Traditional saliency reloaded: a good old model in new shape. In: 28th IEEE Conference on Computer Vision and Pattern Recognition, Boston, pp. 82–90. IEEE Press (2015)
3. Wei, Y., Wen, F., Zhu, W., Sun, J.: Geodesic saliency using background priors. In: Fitzgibbon, A., Lazebnik, S., Perona, P., Sato, Y., Schmid, C. (eds.) ECCV 2012. LNCS, vol. 7574, pp. 29–42. Springer, Heidelberg (2012). https://doi.org/10.1007/978-3-642-33712-3_3
4. Jiang, H., Wang, J., Yuan, Z., Liu, T., Zheng, N., Li, S.: Automatic salient object segmentation based on context and shape prior. In: 22nd British Machine Vision Conference, Dundee. BMVA Press (2011)
5. Guo, C., Ma, Q., Zhang, L.: Spatio-temporal saliency detection using phase spectrum of quaternion fourier transform. In: 21st IEEE Conference on Computer Vision and Pattern Recognition, Anchorage, pp. 1–8. IEEE Press (2008)
6. Schauerte, B., Stiefelhagen, R.: Quaternion-based spectral saliency detection for eye fixation prediction. In: Fitzgibbon, A., Lazebnik, S., Perona, P., Sato, Y., Schmid, C. (eds.) ECCV 2012. LNCS, pp. 116–129. Springer, Heidelberg (2012). https://doi.org/10.1007/978-3-642-33709-3_9
7. Gu, X., Fang, Y., Wang, Y.: Attention selection using global topological properties based on pulse coupled neural network. Comput. Vis. Image Underst. **117**(10), 1400–1411 (2013)
8. He, K., Zhang, X., Ren, S., Sun, J.: Deep residual learning for image recognition. In: 29th IEEE Conference on Computer Vision and Pattern Recognition, Las Vegas, pp. 770–778. IEEE Press (2016)
9. Li, X., Zhao, L., Wei, L., Yang, M.H.: DeepSaliency: multi-task deep neural network model for salient object detection. IEEE Trans. Image Process. **25**(8), 3919–3930 (2016)
10. Long, J., Shelhamer, E., Darrell, T.: Fully convolutional networks for semantic segmentation. In: 28th IEEE Conference on Computer Vision and Pattern Recognition, Boston, pp. 3431–3440. IEEE Press (2015)
11. Liu, T., Sun, J., Zheng, N., Tang, X., Shum, H.: Learning to detect a salient object. In: 20th IEEE Conference on Computer Vision and Pattern Recognition, Minneapolis, pp. 353–367. IEEE Press (2007)
12. Yan, Q., Xu, L., Shi, J., Jia, J.: Hierarchical saliency detection. In: 26th IEEE Conference on Computer Vision and Pattern Recognition, Portland, pp. 1155–1162. IEEE Press (2013)
13. Alpert, S., Galun, M., Basri, R., Brandt, A.: Image segmentation by probabilistic bottom-up aggregation and cue integration. IEEE Trans. Pattern Anal. Mach. Intell. **34**(2), 315–327 (2012)
14. Li, Y., Hou, X., Koch, C., Rehg, J.M., Yuille, A.L.: The secrets of salient object segmentation. In: 27th IEEE Conference on Computer Vision and Pattern Recognition, Columbus, pp. 280–287. IEEE Press (2014)
15. Everingham, M., Van Gool, L., Williams, C.K., Winn, I.J., Zisserman, A.: The Pascal Visual Object Classes (VOC) challenge. Int. J. Comput. Vis. **88**(2), 303–338 (2009)
16. Jiang, H., Wang, J., Yuan, Z., Wu, Y., Zheng, N., Li, S.: Salient object detection: a discriminative regional feature integration approach. In: 26th IEEE Conference on Computer Vision and Pattern Recognition, Portland, pp. 2083–2090. IEEE Press (2013)

17. Li, X., Lu, H., Zhang, L., Xiang, R., Yang, M.H.: Saliency detection via dense and sparse reconstruction. In: 26th IEEE Conference on Computer Vision and Pattern Recognition, Portland, pp. 2976–2983. IEEE Press (2013)

18. Zhu, W., Liang, S., Wei, Y., Sun, J.: Saliency optimization from robust background detection. In: 27th IEEE Conference on Computer Vision and Pattern Recognition, Columbus, pp. 2814–2821. IEEE Press (2014)

19. Yang, C., Zhang, L., Lu, H., Ruan, X., Yang, M.H.: Saliency detection via graph-based manifold ranking. In: 26th IEEE Conference on Computer Vision and Pattern Recognition, Portland, pp. 3166–3173. IEEE Press (2013)

20. Jiang, B., Zhang, L., Lu, H., Yang, C., Yang, M.H.: Saliency detection via absorbing Markov chain. In: 14th IEEE International Conference on Computer Vision, Sydney, pp. 1665–1672. IEEE Press (2013)

21. Cheng, M.M., Warrell, J., Lin, W.Y., Zheng, S., Vineet, V., Crook, N.: Efficient salient region detection with soft image abstraction. In: 14th IEEE International Conference on Computer Vision, Sydney, pp. 1529–1536. IEEE Press (2013)

22. Cheng, M.M., Zhang, G.X., Mitra, N.J., Huang, X., Hu, S.M.: Global contrast based salient region detection. IEEE Trans. Pattern Anal. Mach. Intell. 37(3), 409–416 (2011)

23. Achanta, R., Hemami, S., Estrada, F., Susstrunk, S.: Frequency-tuned salient region detection. In: 22th IEEE Conference on Computer Vision and Pattern Recognition, Miami, pp. 1597–1604. IEEE Press (2009)

Object-Level Salience Detection
by Progressively Enhanced Network

Wang Yuan[1(✉)], Haichuan Song[1(✉)], Xin Tan[2], Chengwei Chen[1],
Shouhong Ding[3], and Lizhuang Ma[1,2]

[1] East China Normal University, Shanghai, China
51184501076@stu.ecnu.edu.cn, hcsong@sei.ecnu.edu.cn
[2] Shanghai Jiao Tong University, Shanghai, China
[3] Tencent, Shanghai, China

Abstract. Saliency detection plays an important role in computer vision area. However, most of the previous works focus on detecting the salient regions, rather than the objects, which is more reasonable in many practical applications. In this paper, a framework is proposed for detecting the salient objects in input images. This framework is composed of two main components: (1) progressively enhanced network (PEN) for amplifying the specified layers of the network and merging the global context simultaneously; (2) object-level boundary extraction module (OBEM) for extracting the complete boundary of the salient object. Experiments and comparisons show that the proposed framework achieves state-of-the-art results. Especially on many challenging datasets, our method performs much better than other methods.

Keywords: Progressively enhanced network · Object-level boundary extract · Saliency detection · Global context

1 Introduction

Given an input image and extracting the most salient object are vital in computer vision. This is also known as saliency detection. Moreover, it is also a fundamental operation in many other computer vision tasks, such as semantic segmentation [1], image classification [2], object tracking [3], person re-identification [4], etc.

According to human perception, objects that are well positioned, with bright colors and regular shapes attract more attention in an image. Inspired by this empirical knowledge, traditional methods [5–7] was initially carried out to deal with it. However, these kinds of methods usually get results with blurred boundaries, and incomplete or redundant object segmentation, due to the use of low-level, hand-crafted features.

This work was supported by Pudong NewArea Science and Technology Development Fund (PKJ2018-Y46), the Science and Technology Commission of Shanghai Municipality Program (No. 18D1205903), the National Social Science Foundation of China (No. 18ZD22), and Multidisciplinary Project of Shanghai Jiao Tong University. It was also partially supported by the joint project of Tencent YouTu and East China Normal University.

© Springer Nature Switzerland AG 2019
I. V. Tetko et al. (Eds.): ICANN 2019, LNCS 11729, pp. 371–382, 2019.
https://doi.org/10.1007/978-3-030-30508-6_30

Fully Convolutional Neural Networks (FCNs) is a powerful tool in computer vision. With the development of FCNs, many methods have been proposed based on it, which improved the quality of results a lot [8–10]. However, in many cases, the boundary is still blurred or even incomplete, as shown in Fig. 1. Because most of the previous work aim to extract the most salient regions, rather than salient objects. This gets worse when the difference between foreground and background are inconspicuous (the target person head and the background in Fig. 1), while the target object consists of several parts with significant differences (the head and the white shirt of the target person in Fig. 1). According to previous methods, it is easy to detect the white shirt is salient, but it's tricky to distinguish the head from the background, and group the head and shirt as a whole. So their maps are always incomplete. Therefore, object-level detection is more reasonable and important in saliency detection.

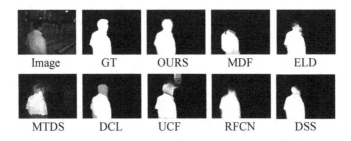

Fig. 1. Result maps of different methods. From top left to bottom right: Input image, Ground Truth, our result, MDF [8], ELD [9], MTDS [12], DCL [10], UCF [13], RFCN [14], DSS [16]. The results of previous methods are either blurred or incomplete.

In this paper, a novel FCN network is proposed to perform object-level saliency detection, which is able to detect the object completely and efficiently, with clear boundaries. Our main contributions are summarized as follows:

- A novel FCN network structure: progressively enhanced network (PEN) is proposed. PEN amplifies the function of the specified layers of the network, and merges the global context simultaneously. In salient detection task, it is applied to integration prospects, and separate them from the background.
- An object-level boundary extraction module (OBEM) is proposed, which is trained to detect the boundaries of objects. OBEM is able to extract both semantics and textures features. So our maps have both accurate position and clear boundary.
- Compared with previous methods, the proposed framework is lightweight, in terms time-saving in both training and testing process. Experiments and comparisons show that our framework performs better compared with other state-of-the-art methods, especially on the most challenging datasets.

The rest of the paper is organized as follows. Section 2 introduces the related work. Section 3 will introduce our framework in detail. Experiments and comparisons will be introduced in Sect. 4. And Sect. 5 will summarize our work.

2 Related Work

Different from traditional methods, many methods directly use convolutional neural networks (CNN) to extract salient features, which improve the results a lot. Li et al. [8] extract multi-scale deep features (MDF) for detecting visual saliency, focusing on pixel-level saliency. Lee et al. [9] generate the saliency maps with both high and low level features fused (ELD). However, the result maps derived by CNN based methods are always not clear-cut, some of which are even too blurred to recognize what the object is. Since 2017, saliency detection methods based on FCNs become the main solution. Li et al. [12] proposed a multi-task deep neural network model (MTDS) based on a fully convolutional network. Li [9] proposed a deep network composed of two components, one is the pixel-level fully convolutional stream, the other is the segment-wise spatial pooling stream (DCL). It indicates that semantic information is important in saliency detection. Zhang et al. [13] and Wang et al. [14] both proposed to reuse high-level information, named UCF and RFCN, but they did not take advantage of shallow layers' features. Cheng et al. [16] proposed an effective network called DSS with short connections between every layer of VGG [17]. Compared with their work, we not only make full use of the maps but also reuse the structure of different layers before getting result maps. So our network has a stronger feature representation ability.

3 Object-Level Saliency Detection

In this section, we will introduce our method in detail. There are two main components in our method: (1) a novel FCN network structure (PEN), which is designed to amplify the specified layer of the network; (2) an encapsulation module OBEM, which is embedded in our PEN net, to extract complete boundary of the saliency object.

3.1 Progressively Enhanced Network

Different layers in CNN have different responsibilities. In the task of saliency detection, we want to make it clear which layers locate the object, which layers identify the foreground and background from the raw image, and which layers distinguish the boundary of the object. Therefore, we designed a pre-experiment to make it clear, in which the feature maps of each layer in FCN are dumped out for visualization, as shown in Fig. 2. Note that, in order to make the changes of image more visible, the maps we used for illustration are from our final complete framework, where PEN and OBEM have been integrated.

Image   Con1-2   Con2-2   Con3-3   Con4-3   Con5-3

Fig. 2. Function of different layers. From left to right: the input image, the output maps of the convolution layers 1–2, 2–2, 3–3, 4–3 and 5–3 of PEN showed in Fig. 3.

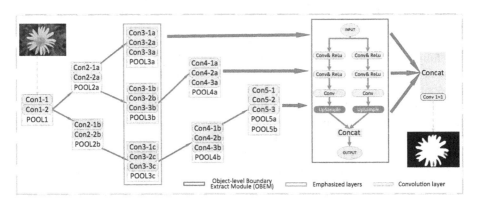

Fig. 3. The main architecture of progressively enhanced network (PEN) with object-level boundary extraction module (OBEM) embedded. OBEM marked with blue box will be detailed in Sect. 3.2. The others will be proposed in Sect. 3.1. (Color figure online)

As illustrated in Fig. 2, low-level layers focus on the textures of the image, including the boundary features, while the output maps of deep layers contain more semantic features, and location information. Then we could infer that the middle layers of FCN are responsible for converting texture features into object features. As mention in Sect. 1, we expect to detect the complete object. So we think middle layers should be amplified to gather more object-level information. At the same time, if we gather different layers' maps, we can obtain more precise boundary features and salient features. Guided by this idea, we design a novel network structure, PEN.

As illustrated in Fig. 3, the network structure of PEN is like a diamond. The branch in the bottom comes from VGG16 [17], where we remove the fully connected layers. The middle column in orange box are the layers whose function we want to amplify. Note that, the OBEM in blue box can be neglected here, and we will explain it later in this section.

In order to use one layer's maps multiple times, Cheng et al. [16] designed DSS net with short connection. However, they only drew on the merits of the maps. In this paper, we design PEN not only focus on the benefits of the maps but also amplify the function of specific layers before getting maps We repeat the middle layer in parallel for several times. The conclusion has been drawn that this network has two properties as follows.

First, we repeat the middle layers and its context in a gradual manner. It means that we not only repeat the middle layers, but also repeat its father layers and child layers. It makes the network like a diamond. We declare that this strategy is not only meaningful for our network, but also useful for any detection network. Designed in this way, the network can enhance the function of converting texture features into object features.

As a comparison, we also implemented another two methods. The first one only repeat the middle layers three times. The results show it has little effect. The second one repeat all layers three times. It achieved almost the same effect as our network, but its parameters are more than twice of ours. So it is much slower. The proposed structure is capable of corresponding different context parameters with different branches. Different branches train their respective parameters separately. Because when we train our network, there are loss layers after all of POOL3, POOL4 and POOL5a.

$$Loss(\Phi) = \sum_{M_i} M_i logP(M_i = 1|G; \Phi) + \sum_{M_i} (1 - M_i)logP(M_i = 0|G; \Phi) \qquad (1)$$

where Φ is the collection of all parameters' weights, and we denote the saliency map as $M_i = \{M_i, i = 1, \ldots\ldots, |M_i|\}$.

Second, our final result incorporates multiple levels of features by the concatenation layer at the end of the network. In this way, we gained not only the texture features from shallow layers but also the semantics features from deep layers. So the result has both precise position and clearly object-level segmentation. It could be formulated as:

$$F_{final} = Concat(F_3, F_4, F_5) \qquad (2)$$

where F_{final} means the final result of our network, F_3, F_4, F_5 is the maps out of OBEM coming from POOL3, POOL4, POOL5a separately.

The proposed network has nine convolutional layer groups. Each group has 2 to 3 convolutional layers, where kernel size = 3, pad = 1. Connection relationship between them are shown in Fig. 3. At the same time, each group has 1 to 2 max pooling layers, where stride = 2, kernel size = 2.

3.2 Object-Level Boundary Extraction Module

OBEM is a simple network and can be considered as an independent module. It is designed to detect the complete edges of objects. As showed in Fig. 4, it consists of two main branches. When we train this model, the first branch's ground truth use highlight to represent salient objects, while the other branch's ground truth only contains the boundary information.

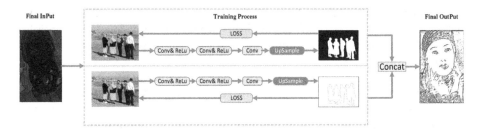

Fig. 4. The architecture of OBEM and its effect in the final result.

In order to get a more accurate and complete boundary feature, besides traditional ground truth, we also use another ground truth which only keep salient objects' boundaries. As showed in Fig. 4, by using this method, the network can not only make the boundaries clearer, but also locate the object according to the extended trend of the boundaries. Its ability to extract boundaries is quite powerful.

The network structure of OBEM is simple, so the convolution filters of the first two convolution layers are large, where kernel size = 7, pad = 3.

It should be noted that, the two branches will be aggregated together in the complete framework, and the weights trained in this step will be used to fine-tune our final framework as the pre-trained model.

4   Experiments

In this section, we evaluate of our framework by comparing with other state-of-the-art methods on five open source datasets.

4.1   Datasets

In order to make a fair comparison with the previous methods, all the data used in our experiments are from the following five open source datasets. DUT [11] is a challenging dataset for many methods, which contains 5168 pairs of images in complex situations. Our method performs much better than other methods on DUT. ECSSD [19] and PACSCAL [20] are small, and only contain 1000 and 851 pairs of images. HKU [15] is also a big dataset has 4446 pairs of images, many of which have more than one salient objects, so it is also quite challenging. MSRA-B [18] contains 5000 pairs of images, and most of the previous methods are trained on this dataset. For a fair comparison with other methods, in training process, we only use images coming from MSRA-B like most of other methods. In order to evaluate the performance of the proposed method on MSRA-B, we even use only 2500 pairs of images to train, and the others to test.

4.2   Evaluation Metrics

In order to evaluate the methods in a quantitative way, we use three metrics including precision-recall (PR) curves, maximum F-measure and mean absolute error (MAE).

As for PR curves, we first convert the result maps into binary images according to a changing threshold within the range of [0, 255]. As the threshold changes, we get multiple pairs of precision and recall values.

Maximum F-measure is defined as:

$$F_\omega = \frac{(1+\omega^2) \times precision \times recall}{\omega^2 \times precision + recall} \tag{3}$$

In order to make a fair comparison with other methods, ω^2 is set to 0.3, same as [5, 6, 10].

For mean absolute error (MAE), it is calculated according to the following formula:

$$MAE = \frac{1}{W \times H} \sum_{x=1}^{W} \sum_{y=1}^{H} |\bar{S}(x,y) - \bar{G}(x,y)| \tag{4}$$

where $\bar{S}$ and $\bar{G}$ denote the saliency map and the ground truth, W and H denote the width and height of the image.

4.3 Implementation Details

We use CAFFE [21], an open source deep learning framework, to train our network. In order to compare with other methods in a quantitative way, PEN is also fine-tuned based on the pre-trained VGG16 [17]. At the same time, OBEM is initialized with Gaussian distribution and is trained as Fig. 4. After that, we embed OBEM with its weights into the PEN becoming the final framework like Fig. 3. Then we trained the final framework as a whole. The hyper-parameters are as follows, base learning rate is set to 10^{-7}, learning policy is "step", stepsize is 12000, momentum is set to 0.9, weight_decay is set to 0.0005 and max iteration is 48000. Note that, we repeated the above training process for 3 times, each of which takes 8 h. So totally about 24 h were spent for training. Each training process is trained based on the weights of previous process.

Our network is trained on an Intel Core computer with an i9-7900 CPU and a single NVIDIA GTX 1080Ti GPU. Our final framework is end-to-end, when we train the network, we use the raw images from datasets directly as the input, and the output of our network is the salience detection maps without other process.

4.4 Comparison with Other Methods

We compare our proposed method with 11 other latest state-of-the-art methods, including 7 deep learning methods: MDF [8], ELD [9], RFCN [14], DCL [10], UCF [13], ASMO+ [24], AGRN [25], and 4 classic algorithms: DRFI [6], RBD [5], MB+ [22], BL [23]. For fair comparison, we use either the saliency maps or the implementations of these methods provided by the authors.

Table 1. Comparison of maxF (the higher the better) and MAE (the lower the better) of other methods in recent years. The best two results are shown in bold and italic.

Method	Evaluation									
	DUT		ECSSD		PACSCAL		HKU		MSRA-B	
	maxF	MAE	maxF	MAE	maxF	MAE	maxF	MAE	maxF	MAE
DRFI [6]	0.664	0.150	0.786	0.164	0.690	0.281	0.783	0.143	0.855	0.119
RBD [5]	0.630	0.141	0.716	0.171	0.655	0.273	0.726	0.141	0.751	0.117
MB+ [22]	0.624	0.168	0.739	0.171	0.677	0.191	0.733	0.149	–	–
BL [23]	0.580	0.240	0.755	0.217	0.659	0.318	0.723	0.206	–	–
MDF [8]	0.694	0.092	0.831	0.105	0.764	0.142	0.861	0.129	0.885	0.104
ELD [9]	0.705	0.091	0.868	0.079	0.771	0.121	0.881	0.063	0.914	*0.042*
RFCN [14]	0.738	0.095	0.898	0.095	**0.832**	0.118	0.888	0.08	**0.926**	0.062
DCL [10]	*0.756*	0.086	0.901	0.075	0.81	0.115	*0.892*	0.055	0.916	0.047
UCF [13]	0.730	0.120	*0.903*	0.069	0.818	0.116	0.888	0.061	–	–
ASMO+ [24]	0.732	0.100	0.845	0.112	0.758	0.154	0.855	0.088	0.896	0.068
AGRN [25]	0.711	*0.072*	0.891	*0.064*	0.803	**0.092**	0.886	**0.048**	–	–
OURS	**0.818**	**0.051**	**0.913**	**0.060**	*0.829*	*0.106*	**0.905**	*0.050*	*0.919*	**0.042**

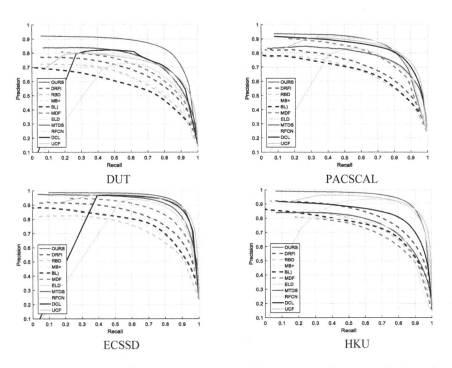

Fig. 5. The performance of PR curves comparing with other state-of-the-art methods on four datasets

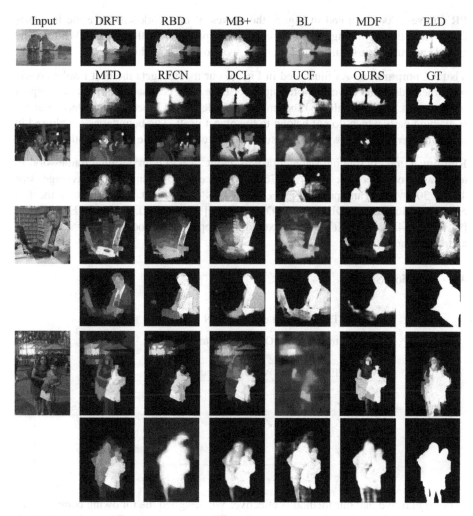

Fig. 6. Visual comparison with other methods. The order of each group is the same as the first group. Our results are most close to ground truth. Other methods cannot detect objects completely or detect unrelated regions..

Max F-Measure. Our results are much higher than most of other state-of-the-art methods according to Table 1. Especially on the dataset DUT, our method is not only the highest, but also is 6% better than the second-best method. Note that DUT has many challenging images in which it is really tricky to identify the boundaries of objects. This means our method is much better at object-level salient detection, compared with other methods.

MAE. MAE is used to calculate the mean error between feature map and ground-truth. So lower MAE means better performance. As shown in Table 1, our method is the best on all five datasets, compared with other methods.

PR Curves. As illustrated in Fig. 5, the curves of our work still have the best performers. At the beginning of the PR curves, our precision is the highest. While at the end of the curves, it is still better than the most of other methods.

Visual Comparison. As illustrated in Fig. 6, our method gets the best results. While other methods either have low precisions, or have low recalls. For objects in complex backgrounds, it is difficult for other methods to detect the objects completely, without containing parts which do not belong to the object itself. The boundaries are blurred in most of other methods, while our results are the closest to the ground-truth.

Running Time. In training stage, it take us about 24 h to train our final framework. In test stage, our network takes 67.76 s to process 1000 images of average size 400×300 without any pre/post-processing (0.068 s, 15 FPS). It is faster than most of existed methods like MDF (8 s) [8], DCL (1.5 s) [10], UCF (0.14 s) [13], ELD (0.5 s) [9], RFCN (4.6 s) [14]. It's easy to extend the proposed method and apply it to videos and other real-time task.

4.5   Ablation Studies

Table 2. The effect of PEN and OBEM.

Architecture			OBEM's pre-trained weights			DUT
VGG	PEN	OBEM	Without	Fixed	Adjustable	maxF
✓						0.704
	✓					0.790
	✓	✓	✓			0.786
	✓	✓		✓		0.804
	✓	✓			✓	0.818

In order to prove that our method is effective. We designed the following comparisons. First, we directly use VGG to get a baseline. Then we train our PEN without OBEM. We also embed OBEM in PEN without its pre-trained weights. After that we embed OBEM in PEN with its weights trained in Subsect. 3.2 fixed. Finally, we train the complete framework including PEN and OBEM. The results are shown in Table 2.

We could see that PEN is very effective compared with the baseline. It increased the maxF value by nearly 9%. As for OBEM, the results show that it is useless to integrate this module directly without training process in Subsection 3.2. At the same time, it is difficult to theoretically prove whether the pre-trained weights should participate in the final training. So we tested both of them. As shown in this experiment, the adjustable weights version gets a better result.

5 Conclusion

In order to obtain a better detection of the salient objects, rather than the regions, a novel framework is proposed in this paper. It consists of two main components: PEN and OBEM. By amplifying the specified layers from FCNs, and merging the global context at the same time, PEN is able to separate the objects from the background effectively, even in complex cases. OBEM on the other hand is able to detect the objects with more precise boundaries. Experiments results show that the complete framework with PEN and OBEM have better performance than other methods, especially when the raw image is complicated on semantics.

References

1. Wei, Y., et al.: STC: a simple to complex framework for weakly-supervised semantic segmentation. IEEE TPAMI **39**, 2314–2320 (2016)
2. Yu, Y., Wu, R., Wang, W.: SCaLE: supervised and cascaded Laplacian Eigenmaps for visual object recognition based on nearest neighbors. In: CVPR, pp. 867–874 (2013)
3. Mahadevan, V., Vasconcelos, N.: Biologically inspired object tracking using center-surround saliency mechanisms. IEEE TPAMI **35**(3), 541–554 (2013)
4. Zhao, R., Ouyang, W., Wang, X.: Unsupervised salience learning for person re-identification. In: CVPR, pp. 3586–3593 (2013)
5. Zhu, W., Liang, S., Wei, Y., Sun, J.: Saliency optimization from robust background detection. In: CVPR, pp. 2814–2821 (2014)
6. Jiang, H., Wang, J., Yuan, Z., Wu, Y.: Salient object detection: a discriminative regional feature integration approach. In: CVPR, pp. 2083–2090 (2013)
7. Xie, Y., Lu, H., Yang, M.-H.: Bayesian saliency via low and mid level cues. IEEE TIP **22**(5), 1689–1698 (2013)
8. Li, G., Yu, Y.: Visual saliency based on multiscale deep features. In: CVPR, pp. 5455–5463 (2015)
9. Lee, G., Tai, Y.W., Kim, J.: Deep saliency with encoded low level distance map and high level features. In: CVPR, pp. 660–668 (2016)
10. Li, G., Yu, Y.: Deep contrast learning for salient object detection. In: CVPR, pp. 478–487 (2016)
11. Yang, C., Zhang, L., Lu, H., Xiang, R., Yang, M.H.: Saliency detection via graph based manifold ranking. In: CVPR, pp. 3166–3173 (2013)
12. Li, X., et al.: Deepsaliency: multi-task deep neural network model for salient object detection. IEEE Trans. Image Process. **25**(8), 3919 (2016)
13. Zhang, P., Wang, D., Lu, H., Wang, H., Yin, B.: Learning uncertain convolutional features for accurate saliency detection. In: ICCV (2017)
14. Wang, L., Wang, L., Lu, H., Zhang, P., Ruan, X.: Saliency detection with recurrent fully convolutional networks. In: Leibe, B., Matas, J., Sebe, N., Welling, M. (eds.) ECCV 2016. LNCS, vol. 9908, pp. 825–841. Springer, Cham (2016). https://doi.org/10.1007/978-3-319-46493-0_50
15. Zhao, R., Ouyang, W., Li, H., Wang, X.: Saliency detection by multi-context deep learning. In: CVPR, pp. 1265–1274 (2015)
16. Hou, Q., Cheng, M.M., Hu, X., Borji, A., Tu, Z., Torr, P.: Deeply supervised salient object detection with short connections. IEEE Trans. Pattern Anal. Mach. Intell. **PP**(99), 1 (2016)

17. Simonyan, K., Zisserman, A.: Very deep convolutional networks for large-scale image recognition. Computer Science (2014)
18. Cheng, M.M., Mitra, N.J., Huang, X., Torr, P.H.S., Hu, S.M.: Global contrast based salient region detection. In: CVPR, pp. 409–416 (2011)
19. Yan, Q., Xu, L., Shi, J., Jia, J.: Hierarchical saliency detection. In: CVPR, pp. 1155–1162 (2013)
20. Li, Y., Hou, X., Koch, C., Rehg, J.M., Yuille, A.L.: The secrets of salient object segmentation. In: CVPR, pp. 280–287 (2014)
21. Jia, Y., et al.: Caffe: convolutional architecture for fast feature embedding. In: ACM MM, pp. 675–678 (2014)
22. Zhang, J., Sclaroff, S., Lin, Z., Shen, X., Price, B., Mech, R.: Minimum barrier salient object detection at 80 FPS. In: ICCV, pp. 1404–1412 (2015)
23. Tong, N., Lu, H., Xiang, R., Yang, M.H.: Salient object detection via bootstrap learning. In: CVPR, pp. 1884–1892 (2015)
24. Li, G., Xie, Y., Lin, L.: Weakly supervised salient object detection using image labels. In: AAAI (2018)
25. Zhang, X., Wang, T., Qi, J., Lu, H., Wang, G.: Progressive attention guided recurrent network for salient object detection. In: CVPR, pp. 714–722 (2018)

Perception

Action Unit Assisted Facial Expression Recognition

Fangjun Wang[✉] and Liping Shen

SEIEE, Shanghai Jiao Tong University, Shanghai, China
{dizaiyoufang,lpshen}@sjtu.edu.cn

Abstract. Facial expression recognition is vital to many intelligent applications such as human-computer interaction and social networks. For machines, learning to classify six basic human expressions (anger, disgust, fear, happiness, sadness and surprise) is still a big challenge. This paper proposed a convolutional neural network based on AlexNet combining a Bayesian network. Besides traditional features, the relationships between facial action units (AU) and expressions are captured. Firstly, a convolutional neural network to extract features from images is constructed. Then, a Bayesian network is established to learn the dependencies of AUs and expressions from joint probabilities and conditional probabilities. Finally, ensemble learning is used to combine the features of expressions, AUs and dependencies between the two. Our experiments on popular datasets show that the proposed method performs well compared with latest approaches.

Keywords: Facial expression recognition · Ensemble learning · Facial action unit

1 Introduction

Facial expressions are vital signaling systems of human emotions. Li and Jain [1] describe it as the facial changes in reaction to a person's moods or the circumstance. Nowadays, a great deal of applications have sprung up based on facial expression recognition, such as interaction games [2] and neuromarketing [3].

It is still a challenge to recognize facial expressions for machines. There are many limitations in this field, for example, frontal face or controlled environments. On the other hand, features of different expressions may be very close and hard to classify. For one person, different expressions may vary widely. But for different people, different expressions may look similar. Rifai et al. [4] pointed out that features of sadness expression of one person may be far away from sadness of the other person, while sometimes can be close to fear of the other person.

The facial action coding system (FACS) [5] uses action units (AUs) to describe facial expressions. Different parts of facial muscles result in 44 different AUs. Motivated by the thoughts that an expression may consist of several AUs, we use AUs to support facial expression recognition.

© Springer Nature Switzerland AG 2019
I. V. Tetko et al. (Eds.): ICANN 2019, LNCS 11729, pp. 385–396, 2019.
https://doi.org/10.1007/978-3-030-30508-6_31

In recent years, the popularity of convolutional neural networks (CNNs) [6,7] also promotes the development of facial expression recognition [8,9]. In this paper, we propose a method based on CNN and Bayesian network (Fig. 1). The rest of this paper is arranged as follows. Literature review is provided in Sect. 2. Then Sect. 3 gives details of our recognition model structure. Experiments and results are introduced in Sect. 4. Finally Sect. 5 makes the conclusion.

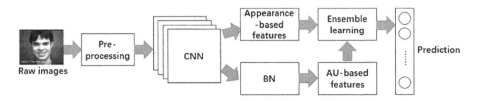

Fig. 1. Overview of the proposed model: pre-processing, CNN, Bayesian network (BN) and ensemble learning

2   Related Work

Automatic facial expression recognition (AFER) has been an active research topic since the important works of Izard [10] and Ekman [11,12] in 1970s. Great advances are achieved in the past few years, thanks to development of AI, especially deep learning algorithms. Lopes et al. [13] divided facial expression recognition systems into two main categories: static image based and dynamic image sequence based. The difference is whether temporal information is used. Meguid and Levine [14] proposed a random forest classifier to recognize facial expressions in videos. Other video-based approaches capture temporal features as well [9,15].

There are mainly two ways to extract facial data, appearance-based and geometric feature-based methods. Appearance-based approaches directly extract features from images. Lopes et al. [13] proposed a combination of CNN and specific image pre-processing steps, including synthetic sample generation, rotation, cropping, down-sampling and intensity normalization, which implies us the impact of pre-processing. Ding et al. [17] presented FaceNet2ExpNet, using two stages, pre-training stage and second stage, by appending fully-connected layers to the pre-trained convolutional layers. This has inspired us to narrow down the overfitting problems via transfer learning. On the other hand, local binary patterns (LBP) extractor and AU-based approaches are two typical geometric feature-based methods. Shan et al. [18] combined and compared classical machine learning techniques, for instance, support vector machine (SVM), using LBP extractors. AU-based approaches firstly detect AUs before decoding specific expression from them. Tian et al. [19] built a AU detection model using facial landmarks and analyze expressions. Tong et al. [20] conducted a dynamic Bayesian network to capture the relationships of AUs and expressions. Liu et al. [21] proposed a deep architecture, AU-inspired Deep Networks (AUDN), which is composed of three sequential modules: MAP representation, feature grouping and group-wise learning. These methods indicate that AU-based features are worthy of study during feature extraction.

However, few of the previous methods pays enough attention to incorporation of appearance-based and geometric-based features. Liu et al. [16] proposed a boosted deep belief network (BDBN) to combine several weak classifiers and each classifier is to classify one expression, which inspired us that ensemble learning may be used at the final stage. In this paper, the proposed method captures both appearance-based and geometric-based (AU) features.

3   Proposed Method

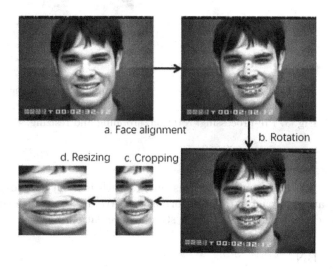

Fig. 2. Preprocessing pipeline.

A CNN structure along with a Bayesian network is proposed, and it combines features directly extracted from images with AUs detected features. The whole structure of our method is shown in Fig. 1. It consists of pre-processing, CNN+Bayesian network and ensemble learning. They will be introduced respectively in the following subsections.

3.1   Pre-processing

As is shown is Fig. 2, the pre-processing has five steps: face alignment, rotation, cropping, resizing and normalization.

Face Alignment and Rotation. In the real world, the faces in the image are usually slanting. Firstly the facial landmarks are used to compute the angle between eye center line and horizontal line if landmarks are provided in given datasets such as RAF dataset. Otherwise the face alignment method [22] is used to detect the facial landmarks (Fig. 2a). Then images are rotated with the angle (Fig. 3(a)).

Cropping and Resizing. We define the distance between two eye centers α (Fig. 3(b)). And we crop 0.65α above the eyes and 1.6α below, i.e., size of the cropped image is $1.2\alpha \times 2.25\alpha$. Next we resize the cropped image into 224×224 (Fig. 2 d).

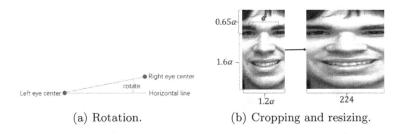

(a) Rotation.   (b) Cropping and resizing.

Fig. 3. Pre-processing: rotation, cropping and resizing.

Normalization. This step transforms images with intensity values into standard ones to avoid impact of different brightness. We use the transform function in pytorch package with mean 0.5 and standard deviation 0.5.

3.2 CNN+BN

This structure is used to automatically generate feature maps and preliminarily give predictions of AUs and expressions. Two kinds of CNN model are used during experiments. AlexNet [23] has five convolutional layers, three pooling layers and three fully connected layers in total. VGG-16 [24] is deeper and has 13 convolutional layers. Due to efficiency, deeper structures are time-consuming and not adopted.

Sigmoid cross entropy loss is used in the CNN model. The loss function can be described as:

$$Loss(Y,\hat{Y}) = -\frac{1}{N_{AU} + N_E} \sum_{i=0}^{N_{AU}+N_E} [Y_i log \hat{Y}_i + (1 - Y_i) log(1 - \hat{Y}_i)] \quad (1)$$

In Eq. (1), Y_i is ground truth and $Y_i \in \{0, 1\}$. $\hat{Y}_i$ is the prediction results of Y_i, and $\hat{Y}_i \in [0, 1]$. So the prediction is the probability of the object.

Table 1. Dependencies among CK+ database*

λ_{ij}	AU1	AU2	AU4	AU5	AU6	AU7	AU12	AU15	AU17	AU25
AU1	/	0.754	/	/	/	/	/	/	/	0.777
AU2	1.0	/	/	0.796	0	0	/	/	/	0.918
AU4	/	/	/	/	/	/	/	/	0.744	/
AU5	0.913	0.848	/	/	/	/	/	/	/	0.924
AU6	/	0	/	/	/	/	0.705	0	/	0.737
AU7	/	0	0.785	/	/	/	/	/	/	/
AU12	/	/	/	/	0.893	/	/	0	/	0.96
AU15	0.759	/	0.724	/	0	/	0	/	0.931	/
AU17	/	/	0.826	/	/	/	/	/	/	/
AU25	/	/	/	/	/	/	/	/	/	/
Anger	0	0	0.889	/	/	0.711	/	/	0.867	0
Disgust	/	0	/	0	/	/	/	/	/	/
Fear	0.88	/	0.84	/	/	/	/	0	/	0.92
Happiness	0	0	0	0	0.957	/	0.971	0	0	0.971
Sadness	0.929	/	0.821	0	0	/	0	0.821	0.964	0
Surprise	0.976	0.976	/	0.843	0	0	/	/	0	0.988

*The values indicate the co-current rate (only $\lambda_{ij} > 0.7$ or $\lambda_{ij} = 0$ listed).

The dependencies among CK+ database [25] are quantified, shown in Table 1, where 10 AU types that have more than 90 samples in the database are chosen. λ_{ij} is computed using conditional probabilities [26]:

$$\lambda_{ij} = P(j|i) = \frac{P(j)}{P(j,i)} \tag{2}$$

$P(j|i)$ is the probability that j happens, given label i happens. And $P(j,i)$ is the probability that label j and i co-occur. To indicate positive and negative probabilities, we only list values that are bigger than 0.7 or equal to 0, while the others are not list in the table.

Observing Table 1, we can find two kinds of relations: positive and negative. For example, λ_{12} is 1.00, which shows AU1 is always coexistent with AU2. While λ_{26} is 0, indicates that AU2 never co-occurs with AU6.

AU types and relationships with expressions are shown in Table 2. As can be seen, expressions are quite related to AU types.

To capture the dependencies among AUs and expressions, a Bayesian network (BN) model is built. It is a directed acyclic graph (DAG) $G = (V, E)$, where $V = \{x_i\}_{i=1}^{n+1}$ represents a collection of $n + 1$ nodes and E denotes a collection of edges. The nodes indicate n AUs and expression, and edges indicate relations (positive and negative). Now we can learn from the data D using maximum likelihood estimation (MLE). The learnt model has a conditional probability

Table 2. AU names and relationships with expressions.

AU	Name	AU	Name	Expression	AU description
1	Inner Brow Raiser	12	Lip Corner Puller	Angry	4,5,7,23,24
2	Outer Brow Raiser	14	Dimpler	Disgust	9,10
4	Brow Lowerer	15	Lip Corner Depressor	Fear	1,2,4,5,7
5	Upper Lip Raiser	17	Chin Raiser	Happy	6,12
6	Cheek Raiser	23	Lip Tightener	Sadness	1,4,15
7	Lid Tightener	24	Lip Pressor	Surprise	1,2,5
10	Upper Lip Raiser	25	Lips Part	Contempt*	12,14

*Only CK+ dataset has contempt expression.

table (CPT) at every node. Then given evidence of some nodes, we can infer the probability of expression nodes from the model.

What if AU labels are not provided for some datasets? Fortunately, transfer learning from large size AU datasets can be conducted. A deep CNN model which is inspired from [27] is trained on BP4D [28] to make prediction on new datasets. AU amount of BP4D is sufficient for training CNN, and 12 kinds of AU in Table 2 have more than 20000 samples each.

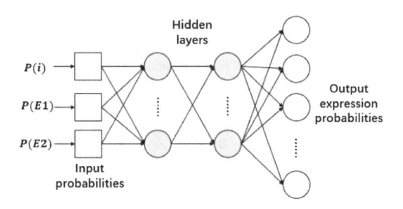

Fig. 4. Ensemble learning perceptron.

3.3 Ensemble Learning

There are usually two kinds of ensemble learning approaches: boosting (AdaBoost [29]) and bagging [30]. Stacking [31] is one of the most famous bagging methods and adopted in our work. Researches [32,33] indicate that using primary model output class probabilities as input of secondary classifiers performs well. Class probabilities are obtained after CNN+BN, so that stacking can be conducted.

Using CNN structure, AU and expression features are obtained as probabilities, denoted as $P(i) \in (0,1)^{n_i}$ and $P(E_1) \in (0,1)^{n_e}$. And BN extracts expression features as probabilities $P(E_2) \in (0,1)^{n_e}$. A three-layered perceptron (two hidden layers) is used as secondary classifier for ensemble learning (shown in Fig. 4). Softmax cross entropy loss is used as loss function during this period.

Cross-validation (CV) is adopted to get a training set for secondary classifier and to reduce the risk of overfitting during training. Denote original training set D, and for a k-fold CV, D is divided into k subsets of similar sizes $D_1, D_2, ..., D_k$. Denote D_j and $\overline{D}_j = D \backslash D_j$ the j-th validation and training sets. The primary model is trained on $\overline{D}_j$, and gives predictions on D_j, denoted as $h_j(D_j)$. After every fold $D' = D' \cup h_j(D_j)$, where D' is the training set for secondary classifier. The parameters of perceptron are kept after this CV training process.

4   Experiments

4.1   Experiment Description

Datasets: Five datasets are used during experiments (Table 3).

Table 3. Datasets.

Database	Used samples	Conditions	Labels	Partition(train/test)
CK+ [25]	327 images	Lab	AU and expression	10-fold CV
JAFFE [34]	213 images	Lab	Expression	10-fold CV
BP4D [28]	146157 images	Lab	AU	All for AU training
RAF [35]	15339 images	Web	Expression	12271/3068
FER2013 [36]	35887 images	Web	Expression	28709/7178

There are several reasons why these datasets are chosen. Firstly, these datasets contain images from laboratory condition to real-world and from small size to large. Secondly, BP4D dataset is chosen because it has good AU labels and can be used to train a model thus predict AU of other datasets. Thirdly, cross datasets experiments can be conducted over them.

Metrics: Confusion matrix and accuracy are used to evaluate the performance. In a confusion matrix, each row of the matrix represents the instances in a predicted class while each column represents the instances in an actual class. The accuracy is defined as:

$$acc = \frac{n_r}{n_t} \times 100\% \tag{3}$$

where n_r is the number of right prediction and n_t is the total number of test samples.

Experiment Settings: For CK+ dataset, A 10-fold cross validation is adopted to ensure subjects are mutually exclusive in train/val sets. And for RAF dataset and FER2013 dataset, the training and testing size are the same as the publishers. Our experiments are conducted on the pytorch platform. The adam optimizer [37] was used with the initial learning rate 0.0001, and total epoch 200. And the learning rate decay strategy is used (every 50 epochs) with decay rate 0.9.

4.2   Experiment Results

Results on CK+: Table 4 is the comparison with other methods on CK+. The bracketed and bold numbers are the best accuracies, while the bold numbers are the second best. The proposed method get the second place using binary classifier method. As it can be seen, the proposed method achieves competitive results on CK+ database. The binary classifier approach is used to improve recognizing individual emotions, especially those with low accuracy. Classifiers are trained separately for different emotions, which means classifiers have more chance to hit the truth.

CK+ dataset is relatively small and deep learning method performs better on larger size database. So as can be seen in Table 4, LBP+SVM is a traditional method that aims at LBP features. Method of [13] concentrated on coping with few data, and the CNN structure has only two convolutional layers.

Table 4. Performance of different methods on CK+.

No.	Method	Accuracy(%)	Binary Accuracy(%)
1	Gu et al. [38]	91.51	-
2	Zhong et al. [39]	93.30	-
3	AUDN [21]	93.70	-
4	BDBN [16]	-	96.70
5	**Proposed**	94.35	**97.13**
6	LBP+SVM [18]	**95.10**	-
7	Lopes et al. [13]	**[96.76]**	**[98.92]**

Results on RAF: Table 5 shows the performance of different methods on RAF. In the RAF database test protocol, the ultimate metric is the mean accuracy rather than the accuracy due to imbalanced distribution in expressions. Several conclusions can be made from the results. Firstly, the proposed method performs well classifying angry, happy and surprise, with accuracy of about 73.46%, 90.01%, 81.16%, respectively. Secondly, VGG-16 performs better than Alex. This is probably due to the large amount of data. Thirdly, our method outperforms the baseline of RAF, reaches average accuracy of about 75.52%.

Table 5. Performance of different methods on RAF(%).

Method	Angry	Disgust	Fear	Happy	Sad	Surprise	Neutral	Average
AlexNet+mSVM [35]	58.64	21.87	39.19	86.16	60.88	62.31	60.15	55.60
AlexNet+LDA [35]	43.83	27.50	37.84	75.78	39.33	61.70	48.53	47.79
VGG+mSVM [35]	68.52	27.50	35.13	85.32	64.85	66.32	59.88	58.22
VGG+LDA [35]	66.05	25.00	37.84	73.08	51.46	53.49	47.21	50.59
DLP-CNN+LDA [35]	77.51	55.41	52.50	90.21	73.64	74.07	73.53	70.98
Our method (Alex)	70.81	50.58	63.51	88.78	73.64	75.23	74.97	71.07
VGG-FACE	82.19	56.62	55.41	86.38	79.52	83.93	71.18	73.60
DLP-CNN+mSVM [35]	71.60	52.15	62.16	92.83	80.13	81.16	80.29	74.20
Our method (VGG-16)	73.46	54.5	69.74	90.01	79.92	81.16	79.82	**75.52**

Results on FER2013: FER2013 database has about 35887 images with 48×48 pixel arrays. Due to the small picture size, FER2013 is still challenging and recognition accuracy of human is around 65% ± 5%. Performance on FER2013 is shown in Table 6. Our method performs nearly the best, with accuracy of 70.24%. The major drawbacks of our model on FER2013 is owing to the small image size, because finding landmarks during pre-processing on these images is not accurate enough relatively.

Table 6. Performance on FER2013(%).

Team	Public test	Private test
Devries et al. [40]	/	67.21
Radu+Marius+Cristi [41]	67.316	67.483
Maxim Milakov	68.15	68.82
Unsupervised	69.07	69.27
Our method (VGG-16)	69.10	70.24
RBM DLSVM [42]	69.77	71.16
Guo et al. [43]	/	**71.33**

Cross Database Comparison: During cross database experiments, all of images from one database is used to train the model, and images from the other for testing. Table 7 illustrates the performance of cross database training. As can be seen, our method has good generalization from CK+ to JAFFE. Furthermore, accuracy from RAF to CK+ is larger than the contrary. This could imply that, to some extent, large and wild database has better capacity of generalization.

Table 7. Cross database performance*.

Train	Test	Method	Accuracy(%)
CK+	JAFFE	Lopes et al. [13]	38.80
CK+	JAFFE	Gu et al. [38]	55.87
CK+	JAFFE	Our method	**59.60**
RAF	CK+	Our method	63.00
CK+	RAF	Our method	39.89

*6 classes due to CK+ has contempt expression.

5   Conclusion and Future Work

In this work, we present a AU-assisted facial expression recognition method, which mainly consists of three steps: pre-processing for better input images, CNN+BN for capturing features from images and a stacking perceptron for ensemble learning. Experiments on popular datasets and cross datasets perform well. In summary, our contributions are: (1) combination of CNN and Bayesian network to capture not only appearance-based features, but also AU features; (2) using transfer learning during AU prediction; (3) ensemble learning for training secondary classifier.

There are many future directions to be explored. For example, the existing model can be strengthened for the challenging, uncontrolled environment, non-frontal face. Also, we can turn to dynamic images and take the temporal features into consideration.

Acknowledgement. The work was supported by the Key Program for International S&T Cooperation Project of China (No. 2016YFE0129500).

References

1. Jain, A.K., Li, S.Z.: Handbook of Face Recognition. Springer, New York (2011). https://doi.org/10.1007/978-0-85729-932-1
2. Sawyer, R., Smith, A., Rowe, J., et al.: Enhancing student models in game-based learning with facial expression recognition. In: Proceedings of the 25th Conference on User Modeling, Adaptation and Personalization, pp. 192–201. ACM (2017)
3. Cuesta, U., Martnez-Martnez, L., Nino, J.I.: A case study in neuromarketing: analysis of the influence of music on advertising effectivenes through eye-tracking, facial emotion and GSR. Eur. J. Soc. Sci. Educ. Res. 5(2), 84–92 (2018)
4. Rifai, S., Bengio, Y., Courville, A., Vincent, P., Mirza, M.: Disentangling factors of variation for facial expression recognition. In: Fitzgibbon, A., Lazebnik, S., Perona, P., Sato, Y., Schmid, C. (eds.) ECCV 2012. LNCS, vol. 7577, pp. 808–822. Springer, Heidelberg (2012). https://doi.org/10.1007/978-3-642-33783-3_58
5. Ekman, P., Friesen, W.: Facial Action Coding System: A Technique for the Measurement of Facial Movement. Consulting Psychologists, San Francisco (1978)
6. LeCun, Y., Bottou, L., Bengio, Y., et al.: Gradient-based learning applied to document recognition. Proc. IEEE **86**(11), 2278–2324 (1998)

7. Ciresan, D.C., Meier, U., Masci, J., et al.: Flexible, high performance convolutional neural networks for image classification. In: IJCAI Proceedings-International Joint Conference on Artificial Intelligence, vol. 22, no. 1, p. 1237 (2011)

8. Song, I., Kim, H.J., Jeon, P.B.: Deep learning for real-time robust facial expression recognition on a smartphone. In: 2014 IEEE International Conference on Consumer Electronics (ICCE), pp. 564–567. IEEE (2014)

9. Byeon, Y.H., Kwak, K.C.: Facial expression recognition using 3D convolutional neural network. Int. J. Adv. Comput. Sci. Appl. 5(12) (2014)

10. Izard, C.E.: The face of emotion (1971)

11. Ekman, P.: Universals and cultural differences in facial expressions of emotion. In: Nebraska Symposium on Motivation. University of Nebraska Press (1971)

12. Ekman, P., Oster, H.: Facial expressions of emotion. Ann. Rev. Psychol. 30(1), 527–554 (1979)

13. Lopes, A.T., de Aguiar, E., De Souza, A.F., et al.: Facial expression recognition with convolutional neural networks: coping with few data and the training sample order. Pattern Recognit. 61, 610–628 (2017)

14. El Meguid, M.K.A., Levine, M.D.: Fully automated recognition of spontaneous facial expressions in videos using random forest classifiers. IEEE Trans. Affect. Comput. 5(2), 141–154 (2014)

15. Fan, X., Tjahjadi, T.: A spatial-temporal framework based on histogram of gradients and optical flow for facial expression recognition in video sequences. Pattern Recognit. 48(11), 3407–3416 (2015)

16. Liu, P., Han, S., Meng, Z., et al.: Facial expression recognition via a boosted deep belief network. In: Proceedings of the IEEE Conference on Computer Vision and Pattern Recognition, pp. 1805–1812 (2014)

17. Ding, H., Zhou, S.K., Chellappa, R.: Facenet2expnet: regularizing a deep face recognition net for expression recognition. In: 2017 12th IEEE International Conference on Automatic Face & Gesture Recognition (FG 2017), pp. 118–126. IEEE (2017)

18. Shan, C., Gong, S., McOwan, P.W.: Facial expression recognition based on local binary patterns: a comprehensive study. Image Vis. Comput. 27(6), 803–816 (2009)

19. Tian, Y.I., Kanade, T., Cohn, J.F.: Recognizing action units for facial expression analysis. IEEE Trans. Pattern Anal. Mach. Intell. 23(2), 97–115 (2001)

20. Tong, Y., Liao, W., Ji, Q.: Facial action unit recognition by exploiting their dynamic and semantic relationships. IEEE Trans. Pattern Anal. Mach. Intell. 29(10), 1683–1699 (2007)

21. Liu, M., Li, S., Shan, S., et al.: Au-inspired deep networks for facial expression feature learning. Neurocomputing 159, 126–136 (2015)

22. Bulat, A., Tzimiropoulos, G.: How far are we from solving the 2D & 3D face alignment problem? (and a dataset of 230,000 3D facial landmarks). In: International Conference on Computer Vision, vol. 1, no. 2, p. 4 (2017)

23. Krizhevsky, A., Sutskever, I., Hinton, G.E.: Imagenet classification with deep convolutional neural networks. In: Advances in Neural Information Processing Systems, pp. 1097–1105 (2012)

24. Simonyan, K., Zisserman, A.: Very deep convolutional networks for large-scale image recognition. arXiv preprint arXiv:1409.1556 (2014)

25. Lucey, P., Cohn, J.F., Kanade, T., et al.: The extended Cohn-Kanade dataset (CK+): a complete dataset for action unit and emotion-specified expression. In: 2010 IEEE Computer Society Conference on Computer Vision and Pattern Recognition Workshops (CVPRW), pp. 94–101. IEEE (2010)

26. Wang, S., Gan, Q., Ji, Q.: Expression-assisted facial action unit recognition under incomplete au annotation. Pattern Recognit. **61**, 78–91 (2017)
27. Hu, Q., Jiang, F., Mei, C., et al.: CCT: a cross-concat and temporal neural network for multi-label action unit detection. In: 2018 IEEE International Conference on Multimedia and Expo (ICME), pp. 1–6. IEEE (2018)
28. Zhang, X., Yin, L., Cohn, J.F., et al.: A high-resolution spontaneous 3D dynamic facial expression database. In: 2013 10th IEEE International Conference and Workshops on Automatic Face and Gesture Recognition (FG), pp. 1–6. IEEE (2013)
29. Freund, Y., Schapire, R.E.: A decision-theoretic generalization of on-line learning and an application to boosting. J. Comput. Syst. Sci. **55**(1), 119–139 (1997)
30. Breiman, L.: Bagging predictors. Mach. Learn. **24**(2), 123–140 (1996)
31. Breiman, L.: Stacked regressions. Mach. Learn. **24**(1), 49–64 (1996)
32. Seewald, A.K.: Exploring the parameter state space of stacking. In: 2002 IEEE International Conference on Data Mining, Proceedings, pp. 685–688. IEEE (2002)
33. Sill, J., Takcs, G., Mackey, L., et al.: Feature-weighted linear stacking. arXiv preprint arXiv:0911.0460 (2009)
34. Lyons, M.J., Akamatsu, S., Kamachi, M., et al.: The Japanese female facial expression (JAFFE) database. In: Proceedings of Third International Conference on Automatic Face and Gesture Recognition, pp. 14–16 (1998)
35. Li, S., Deng, W., Du, J.P.: Reliable crowdsourcing and deep locality-preserving learning for expression recognition in the wild. In: Proceedings of the IEEE Conference on Computer Vision and Pattern Recognition, pp. 2852–2861 (2017)
36. Goodfellow, I.J., et al.: Challenges in representation learning: a report on three machine learning contests. In: Lee, M., Hirose, A., Hou, Z.-G., Kil, R.M. (eds.) ICONIP 2013. LNCS, vol. 8228, pp. 117–124. Springer, Heidelberg (2013). https://doi.org/10.1007/978-3-642-42051-1_16
37. Kingma, D.P., Ba, J.: Adam: a method for stochastic optimization. arXiv preprint arXiv:1412.6980 (2014)
38. Gu, W., Xiang, C., Venkatesh, Y.V., et al.: Facial expression recognition using radial encoding of local Gabor features and classifier synthesis. Pattern Recognit. **45**(1), 80–91 (2012)
39. Zhong, L., Liu, Q., Yang, P., et al.: Learning active facial patches for expression analysis. In: 2012 IEEE Conference on Computer Vision and Pattern Recognition (CVPR), pp. 2562–2569. IEEE (2012)
40. Devries, T., Biswaranjan, K., Taylor, G.W.: Multi-task learning of facial landmarks and expression. In: 2014 Canadian Conference on Computer and Robot Vision, pp. 98–103. IEEE (2014)
41. Ionescu, R.T., Popescu, M., Grozea, C.: Local learning to improve bag of visual words model for facial expression recognition. In: Workshop on Challenges in Representation Learning, ICML (2013)
42. Tang, Y.: Deep learning using linear support vector machines. arXiv preprint arXiv:1306.0239 (2013)
43. Guo, Y., Tao, D., Yu, J., et al.: Deep neural networks with relativity learning for facial expression recognition. In: 2016 IEEE International Conference on Multimedia & Expo Workshops (ICMEW), pp. 1–6. IEEE (2016)

Discriminative Feature Learning Using Two-Stage Training Strategy for Facial Expression Recognition

Lei Gan[1], Yuexian Zou[1,2(✉)], and Can Zhang[1]

[1] ADSPLAB, School of ECE, Peking University, Shenzhen, China
{ganlei,zouyx,zhangcan}@pku.edu.cn
[2] Peng Cheng Laboratory,Shenzhen, China

Abstract. Although deep convolutional neural networks (CNNs) have achieved the state-of-the-arts for facial expression recognition (FER), FER is still challenging due to two aspects: class imbalance and hard expression examples. However, most existing FER methods recognize facial expression images by training the CNN models with cross-entropy (CE) loss in a single stage, which have limited capability to deal with these problems because each expression example is assigned equal weight of loss. Inspired by the recently proposed focal loss which reduces the relative loss for those well-classified expression examples and pay more attention to those misclassified ones, we can mitigate these problems by introducing the focal loss into the existing FER system when facing imbalanced data or hard expression examples. Considering that the focal loss allows the network to further extract discriminative features based on the learned feature-separating capability, we present a two-stage training strategy utilizing CE loss in the first stage and focal loss in the second stage to boost the FER performance. Extensive experiments have been conducted on two well-known FER datasets called CK+ and Oulu-CASIA. We gain improvements compared with the common one-stage training strategy and achieve the state-of-the-art results on the datasets in terms of average classification accuracy, which demonstrate the effectiveness of our proposed two-stage training strategy.

Keywords: Convolutional neural networks ·
Facial expression recognition · Two-stage training strategy ·
Discriminative feature learning

1 Introduction

Recently, facial expression recognition (FER) has received increasing attention [1,5,10–12] due to its wide range of applications among health care, social interaction, human-computer-interaction systems, and etc. Essentially, FER is a multi-class classification problem, which aims at classifying expression images as one of several basic expression labels, i.e., anger, disgust, fear, happiness, sadness,

© Springer Nature Switzerland AG 2019
I. V. Tetko et al. (Eds.): ICANN 2019, LNCS 11729, pp. 397–408, 2019.
https://doi.org/10.1007/978-3-030-30508-6_32

Fig. 1. Illustration of class imbalance and easy/hard expression examples. The pie chart (left) shows the class imbalance problem, i.e., different expressions account for different proportion. The picture (right) indicates the hard expression examples problem. The easy expression example can be obviously recognized as happiness expression. In comparison, the hard expression example is too ambiguous to be directly recognized.

surprise, which are first defined in [2] and have been universally adopted to represent facial expressions.

There are two problems existing in the field of FER including class imbalance and hard expression examples, as illustrated in Fig. 1. On the one hand, the imbalance problem exists because some expressions show frequently, such as *happiness*, meanwhile, some expressions rarely display, such as *anger*. On the other hand, people sometimes display some subtle expressions which are usually too ambiguous to be correctly recognized. For example, the *disgust* and *sadness* expressions can be mixed with each other because they display similarly sometimes. The two problems limit the performance of the FER system.

In this paper, we attempt to mitigate these problems by exploiting the recently proposed focal loss [8] and presenting a two-stage training strategy using CE loss in the first stage and focal loss in the second stage. The focal loss contains two hyper-parameters α and γ, targeting at the class imbalance and hard expression examples problems, respectively. Besides, the learned model after the first training stage can be utilized to further explore discriminative features in the learning process.

2   Related Work

Recently, many studies have been conducted to recognize facial expression from raw images. In [15], a two-stage fine-tuning method follows a transfer learning approaches. Based on a network pre-trained on the ImageNet [7] dataset, it trains on a larger FER dataset in the first stage and then narrows down to train on a smaller FER dataset in the second stage. In [14], three inception convolutional structures are constructed in order to classify the registered facial images into several expression labels, indicating the effectiveness of the inception layers for the FER problem.

In [12], both contrastive loss and softmax loss are jointly utilized to learn features for FER, which aims at developing effective feature representations for identity-invariant FER by balancing the distribution of intra- and inter- class variations.

However, most of the previous methods fail to either incorporate the previously learned information or pay attention to the class imbalance and hard expression examples problems. In this paper, we delicate to investigating the potential improvements using the two-stage training strategy, utilizing the CE loss in the first stage and the focal loss in the second stage.

3 Our Approach

We apply a deep learning method to recognize facial expression. Specifically, We adopt the popular inception-v3 [18] convolutional neural network as our basic network architecture due to its good balance between accuracy and efficiency on many image classification tasks. Most one-stage training strategies apply CE loss already achieve competitive results. Our aim is to further extract discriminative features by focusing on the class imbalance and hard expression examples problems. Thus, we exploit a recently proposed focal loss subsequently and propose a two-stage training strategy utilizing the cross-entropy (CE) loss in the first stage and the focal loss in the second stage.

3.1 CE Loss

Most existing CNN-based FER methods train the model using cross-entropy (CE) loss, which perform reasonably well on the FER task in terms of the average classification accuracy. However, it actually has limited capability to tackle the class imbalance and hard expression examples problems because each training example is assigned equal weight of loss. The cross-entropy (CE) loss is defined in (1) as follows:

$$Loss_1 = -\sum_{i=1}^{c} y_i log(\tilde{y}_i) \tag{1}$$

where y_i is the i-th value of the ground truth label, and $\tilde{y}_i$ is the i-th output value of the softmax of the network. c is the total number of expression classes. The $\tilde{y}_i$ is defined as (2) using logit values of the network:

$$\tilde{y}_i = \sigma(l_i) \tag{2}$$

where l_i is the i-th logit value of the network, and the $\sigma(\cdot)$ is a softmax activation function.

3.2 Focal Loss

Focal loss was first proposed in [8] by reshaping the CE loss. Specifically, it introduces a weighting factor α and a focusing parameter γ to the cross-entropy loss, as formulated in (3):

$$Loss_2 = -\alpha \sum_{i=1}^{c} (1 - \tilde{y}_i)^\gamma y_i log(\tilde{y}_i) \tag{3}$$

where $\alpha \in [0, 1]$ and $\gamma \geq 0$ are two hyper-parameters. α is used to balance the importance among imbalanced examples, and γ is used to differentiate between easy and hard expression examples. The y_i and $\tilde{y}_i$ are of the same meanings as in the CE loss. Final decision $\tilde{o}$ is obtained in (4) using the softmax output of the network:

$$\tilde{o} = arg \max_i \tilde{y}_i \tag{4}$$

We introduce the focal loss to the existing FER system in order to mitigate the class imbalance and hard expression examples problems.

3.3   Two-Stage Training Strategy

Considering that the focal loss can help the network to further extract discriminative features based on the learned feature-separating capability, we propose a two-stage training strategy aiming at mitigating the class imbalance and hard expression examples problems. Since most existing deep learning-based FER methods have performed reasonably well training in a single stage, our training strategy utilizes CE loss in the first stage and focal loss in the second stage in order to boost the FER performance.

For the class imbalance problem, the hyper-parameter α balances the importance of the examples in different categories. In this way, the total loss will not be dominated by those categories which have the number advantage. For the hard expression examples problem, the focusing hyper-parameter γ adjusts the rate of reducing the relative loss for those well-classified examples and concentrates more on those misclassified examples.

For further illustrate the effectiveness of our proposed two-stage training stage, we also perform extensive ablation study in §4.4 to give enough evidence.

4   Experiments and Analysis

We conduct extensive experiments in a supervised training manner on two well-known FER datasets: CK+ [13] and Oulu-CASIA [20], and compare our two-stage training strategy with other state-of-the-art algorithms for FER. Details of each dataset are tabulated in Table 1. The AN, CO, DI, FE, HA, SA, SU are short for Anger, Contempt, Disgust, Fear, Happiness, Sadness and Surprise, respectively. Some images from each dataset are also listed in Fig. 2.

Table 1. The number of images for each expression in the datasets

	AN	CO	DI	FE	HA	SA	SU	All
CK+	135	54	177	75	147	84	249	981
Oulu-CASIA	240	-	240	240	240	240	240	1440

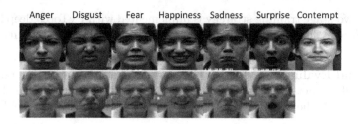

Fig. 2. Cropped facial expression images from the CK+ (1st row) and Oulu-CASIA dataset (2nd row). From the left to the right column, the displaying expressions are anger, disgust, fear, happiness, sadness, surprise and contempt, respectively.

4.1 Implementation Details

Preprocessing. After detecting and cropping face from a raw image by applying the MTCNN [19] module, we perform various data augmentation techniques to obtain more training data for each epoch and make our trained model more robust. In the training session, each image processed after the MTCNN module is first resized to 299 × 299, then horizontally flipped with a probability of 0.5, flipped in the vertical direction with a probability of 0.5, and randomly rotated by 10°. In the testing phase, the processed image after MTCNN module is resized and cropped at the center into size 299 × 299.

Initialization. The weights of convolutional layers are initialized from the adopted Inception-v3 model pre-trained on ImageNet [7]. The weights of the last fully-connected layer in each training stage are randomly initialized using Gaussian distribution $\mathcal{N}(\mu, \sigma^2)$. We set the value of μ and σ to 0 and 0.001, respectively. The output neuron number of the last fully-connected layer is modified as the total number of expression classes.

Training Setup. The network is trained with a mini-batch size of 32 images using back-propagation method and Stochastic Gradient Descent (SGD) optimization algorithm in a supervised training manner. The momentum is 0.9. Also, the dropout method is used for reducing the over-fitting problem, and the dropout ratio is set to 0.5. The weight decay is also used for regularization with a factor of 0.001.

Following the previous work [5,10], a 10-fold subject-independent cross validation protocol is adopted for evaluation in all the experiments in order to avoid the same subject existing in both the training and testing data. Nine subsets are used for training while the remaining subset is used for validation. In the first training stage, the whole network is trained for 80 epochs in total with an initial learning rate of 0.01. In the second training stage, the network is further trained starting from the best model in the first stage, and the training stops at the 80th epoch. The learning rate in this stage is set as 0.01 at first and decay 10× after 60-th epoch. All the settings are the same in the experiments. Our proposed two-stage training strategy is implemented with PyTorch deep learning framework on a single NVIDIA GeForce GTX 1080 GPU with 8 GB memory.

Testing and Evaluation Metric. Given a raw image in the testing phase, the network will predict the final expression label of it. we adopt average classification accuracy as the evaluation metric, which is widely used in the field of FER research.

4.2 Experiments on the CK+ Dataset

Dataset Description. The Extended Cohn-Kanade Dataset (CK+) [13] is a widely used dataset for facial expression recognition. It contains 118 subjects with 327 facial expression sequences in total, ranging from 18 to 30 years old. Each image sequence is annotated with one discrete expression label out of seven expressions, including six basic facial expressions (anger, disgust, fear, happiness, sadness, surprise) and one non-basic expression (contempt). In this dataset, each image sequence begins with a neutral expression and gradually reaches a peak expression at the last frame. The same as [10], we construct our image-based CK+ dataset by extracting the last three frames from each image sequence. Finally, the image-based CK+ dataset consists of 981 images with the resolution of 640×490. This dataset is divided into ten subject-independent subsets by sampling subject ID in ascending order with a step size of 10.

Class Imbalance Problem. From Table 1, we can learn that the class imbalance problem seriously exists in the CK+ dataset, in other words, images number varies among different expression classes. Clearly, the three expressions with least images are contempt, fear and sadness, respectively. In the experiments, the hyper-parameters of α and γ are experimentally set as 0.25 and 0 respectively on this dataset.

Results. The confusion matrix comparisons on the CK+ dataset are reported in Fig. 3. It compares the confusion matrix of the baseline (left) using the CE loss and our two-stage training strategy (right) using the CE loss in the first stage and the focal loss in the second stage. From the results reported from Fig. 3, we observe that the contempt expression is the most difficult one to be classified if we train the network with only the CE loss, because it has the least training data and the network with only the CE loss has limited ability to tackle the class imbalance problem. In contrast, after further training the whole network driven by the focal loss, the network acquires enhanced feature-discriminating capability by consequently paying attention to the expressions with less training images. Clearly, it can be observed from the right confusion matrix in Fig. 3 that the contempt expression is further perfectly classified with an accuracy increase of 5.6%. Besides, for the fear and sadness expressions which account for the second least and third least proportion of all the dataset, the

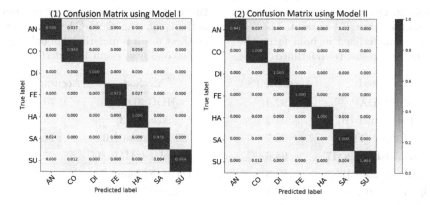

Fig. 3. Confusion matrix of our two-stage training strategy on the CK+ dataset in the first stage (left) and in the second stage (right). The darker the color is, the higher the accuracy reaches. The x-labels and y-labels stand for prediction results and ground truth, respectively. (Color figure online)

classification accuracy of them increase 2.7% and 2.4%, respectively, verifying that our proposed two-stage training strategy is able to learn more discriminative features by mitigating the class imbalance problem. As for the classification accuracy of the anger expression, which has a decrease of 0.7% after the second stage, we speculate that there may be some underlying factors that undermine the system performance, and we will discuss it later in our future work.

The overall accuracy of 10-fold cross validation on the CK+ dataset is shown in Table 2[1]. The best result is underlined in boldface and the second best result is marked with an underline. As shown in Table 2, although the CNN model with only the CE loss perform reasonably well compared with most FER methods, our two-stage training strategy can boost its performance by mitigating the class imbalance problem.

4.3 Experiments on the Oulu-CASIA Dataset

Dataset Description. Oulu-CASIA dataset [20] is a more challenging benchmark dataset for facial expression recognition. It contains 480 image sequences in total, including 80 subjects between 23 and 58 years old. Each image sequence has one of the six basic expression labels: anger, disgust, fear, happiness, sadness and surprise. It is captured by a VIS camera under three different illumination conditions: Strong, Dark and Weak. Similar to the CK+ dataset, each image sequence in this dataset starts from neutral expression to peak expression in the last few frames. Following the previous work in [1,5], we only use the image sequences captured under normal illumination. Then we construct the image-based Oulu-CASIA dataset with the resolution of 320×320 by collecting the

---

[1] For fair comparison, we compare our method with other state-of-the-arts which also use the SGD optimization algorithm.

Table 2. Overall accuracy of different methods on the CK+ dataset. The best result is underlined in bold face. The second best result is underlined.

Method	Accuracy (%)
3DCNN-DAP [9]	92.4
STM-Explet [10]	94.2
BDBN [11]	96.7
Exemplar-HMMs [17]	94.6
DTAGN(Joint) [5]	<u>97.3</u>
2B(N+M)Softmax [12]	97.1
Baseline	98.2
Ours (two stage)	<u>**98.8**</u>

Table 3. Overall accuracy of different methods on the Oulu-CASIA dataset. The best result is underlined in bold face. The second best result is underlined.

Method	Accuracy (%)
HOG 3D [6]	70.6
Atlases [3]	75.5
STM-Explet [10]	74.6
Exemplar-HMMs [17]	75.6
DTAGN(Joint) [5]	81.5
ExprGAN [1]	<u>84.7</u>
Baseline	87.7
Ours (two stage)	<u>**88.3**</u>

last three frames of each sequence and obtain 1440 images in total at last. Then we split the dataset into ten subject-independent groups by sampling subject ID with a step size of 8.

Hard Expression Examples Problem. The Oulu-CASIA dataset is challenging because it contains some hard expression examples that are too ambiguous to be recognized. Some hard expression examples in the Oulu-CASIA dataset are listed below in Fig. 4. In the experiments, the hyper-parameters of α and γ are experimentally set as 0 and 0.5 respectively on this dataset.

Fig. 4. Some hard expression examples. Images in the green, yellow and gray boxes are actually surprise, sadness and disgust expressions, respectively. (Color figure online)

Results. Detailed confusion matrix comparisons on the Oulu-CASIA dataset are presented in Fig. 5. It also compares the confusion matrix of the baseline (left) using the CE loss and our two-stage training strategy (right) using the CE loss in the first stage and the focal loss in the second stage. It is proved that our two-stage training strategy has the ability to distinguish the features extracted from

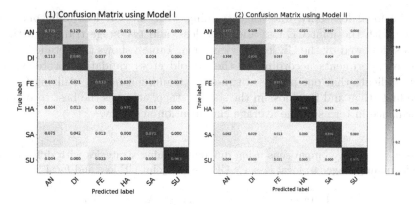

Fig. 5. Confusion matrix of our two-stage training strategy on the Oulu-CASIA dataset in the first stage (left) and in the second stage (right). The darker the color is, the higher the accuracy reaches. The x-labels and y-labels stand for prediction results and ground truth, respectively. (Color figure online)

hard expression examples. For example, the classification accuracy of sadness expression is 87.1% using only the CE loss in the first training stage, and it has a gain of 2.5% when further training using the focal loss in the second stage. Besides, for the surprise expression, our training strategy also gains an increase of 1.2%. Since there are few hard expression examples in the happy and fear expressions after analyzing this dataset, there is little improvements in terms of the classification accuracy of these expressions. For the classification of the anger expression which has a decrease of 0.4% after the second stage, we will investigate the potential influence in our future work.

The overall accuracy of 10-fold cross validation on the Oulu-CASIA dataset is shown in Table 3. The best result is underlined in boldface and the second best result is marked with an underline. Obviously, our two-stage training strategy has some advantages over the common one-stage training method using only the CE loss in terms of the overall classification accuracy.

4.4 Ablation Study

We conducted ablation study to explore and identify the best training strategy for the facial expression recognition (FER) task. Extensive experiments have been conducted on the CK+ and Oulu-CASIA datasets and we drew the conclusion that our proposed two-stage training strategy, utilizing the cross-entropy (CE) loss in the first stage and the focal loss in the second stage, is the best training strategy. Additionally, Our proposed training strategy also works well in other CNN models.

Training Strategy. To explore the best training strategy for the FER task, we conducted five different experiments on each dataset including one-stage training with the focal loss only, one-stage training with the CE loss only, one-stage training with the joint CE loss and focal loss, and two-stage training with the focal loss followed by the CE loss or vice versa. Table 4 shows the detailed results of these experiments according to the 10-fold cross validation protocol. The results indicate that our proposed two-stage training strategy, utilizing CE loss in the first stage and focal loss in the second stage, achieves the best recognition performance in terms of the average classification accuracy.

Table 4. Accuracy comparisons using different training strategies with different loss in each training stage. ●: focal loss, ○: CE loss, ◑: joint CE loss and focal loss.

Dataset	1st stage	2nd stage	Accuracy (%)
CK+	●	✗	98.0
	○	✗	98.2
	◑	✗	97.8
	●	○	98.5
	○	●	**98.8**
Oulu-CASIA	●	✗	88.0
	○	✗	87.7
	◑	✗	87.1
	●	○	85.1
	○	●	**88.3**

Network Architecture. To further illustrate the effectiveness of our proposed two-stage training strategy, we conducted more experiments using two different CNN models, including the VGG-Face [16] and the Resnet-18 [4]. Detailed experimental results are shown in Table 5. It is observed that our proposed two-stage training strategy performs better than the one-stage training using only

Table 5. Accuracy comparisons using the VGG-Face and Resnet-18 network architecture with different loss in each training stage. ●: focal loss, ○: CE loss.

Network	Dataset	1st stage	2nd stage	Accuracy (%)
VGG-Face	CK+	○	✗	94.6
		○	●	97.2
	Oulu-CASIA	○	✗	83.3
		○	●	83.7
Resnet-18	CK+	○	✗	98.4
		○	●	98.6
	Oulu-CASIA	○	✗	87.8
		○	●	88.3

the CE loss in terms of average classification accuracy. Besides, the effectiveness of two-stage training strategy is independent of the CNN model we used.

5 Conclusion

In this paper, we introduce the focal loss to the existing FER system and propose a two-stage training strategy to recognize facial expression from raw images. Specifically, we utilize the cross-entropy (CE) loss in the first stage and the focal loss in the second stage. Due to the fact that the focal loss contains a weighting factor α and a focusing parameter γ, so the network is able to mitigate the class imbalance and hard expression examples problems. Extensive experiments on the CK+ and Oulu-CASIA datasets show that our proposed two-stage training strategy achieves improved performance compared with one-stage training with only the CE loss. Additionally, our proposed training strategy also works well in other CNN models. We believe this work will provide a new perspective in capturing discriminative features for FER using the two-stage training strategy.

Acknowledgment. This paper was partially supported by Shenzhen Science & Technology Fundamental Research Programs. (No: JCYJ20170306165153653) and National Engineering Laboratory for Video Technology - Shenzhen Division, Shenzhen Municipal Development and Reform Commission (Disciplinary Development Program for Data Science and Intelligent Computing). Special acknowledgements are given to Aoto-PKUSZ Joint Lab for its support.

References

1. Ding, H., Sricharan, K., Chellappa, R.: Exprgan: facial expression editing with controllable expression intensity. In: Thirty-Second AAAI Conference on Artificial Intelligence (2018)
2. Ekman, P., Friesen, W.V.: Constants across cultures in the face and emotion. J. Pers. Soc. Psychol. **17**(2), 124 (1971)
3. Guo, Y., Zhao, G., Pietikäinen, M.: Dynamic facial expression recognition using longitudinal facial expression atlases. In: Fitzgibbon, A., Lazebnik, S., Perona, P., Sato, Y., Schmid, C. (eds.) ECCV 2012. LNCS, pp. 631–644. Springer, Heidelberg (2012). https://doi.org/10.1007/978-3-642-33709-3_45
4. He, K., Zhang, X., Ren, S., Sun, J.: Deep residual learning for image recognition. In: Proceedings of the IEEE Conference on Computer Vision and Pattern Recognition, pp. 770–778 (2016)
5. Jung, H., Lee, S., Yim, J., Park, S., Kim, J.: Joint fine-tuning in deep neural networks for facial expression recognition. In: Proceedings of the IEEE International Conference on Computer Vision, pp. 2983–2991 (2015)
6. Klaser, A., Marszałek, M., Schmid, C.: A spatio-temporal descriptor based on 3D-gradients. In: BMVC 2008–19th British Machine Vision Conference, pp. 275–1. British Machine Vision Association (2008)
7. Krizhevsky, A., Sutskever, I., Hinton, G.E.: Imagenet classification with deep convolutional neural networks. In: Advances in Neural Information Processing Systems, pp. 1097–1105 (2012)

8. Lin, T.Y., Goyal, P., Girshick, R., He, K., Dollár, P.: Focal loss for dense object detection. In: Proceedings of the IEEE International Conference on Computer Vision, pp. 2980–2988 (2017)
9. Liu, M., Li, S., Shan, S., Wang, R., Chen, X.: Deeply learning deformable facial action parts model for dynamic expression analysis. In: Cremers, D., Reid, I., Saito, H., Yang, M.-H. (eds.) ACCV 2014. LNCS, vol. 9006, pp. 143–157. Springer, Cham (2015). https://doi.org/10.1007/978-3-319-16817-3_10
10. Liu, M., Shan, S., Wang, R., Chen, X.: Learning expressionlets on spatio-temporal manifold for dynamic facial expression recognition. In: Proceedings of the IEEE Conference on Computer Vision and Pattern Recognition, pp. 1749–1756 (2014)
11. Liu, P., Han, S., Meng, Z., Tong, Y.: Facial expression recognition via a boosted deep belief network. In: Proceedings of the IEEE Conference on Computer Vision and Pattern Recognition, pp. 1805–1812 (2014)
12. Liu, X., Vijaya Kumar, B., You, J., Jia, P.: Adaptive deep metric learning for identity-aware facial expression recognition. In: Proceedings of the IEEE Conference on Computer Vision and Pattern Recognition Workshops, pp. 20–29 (2017)
13. Lucey, P., Cohn, J.F., Kanade, T., Saragih, J., Ambadar, Z., Matthews, I.: The extended cohn-kanade dataset (ck+): A complete dataset for action unit and emotion-specified expression. In: 2010 IEEE Computer Society Conference on Computer Vision and Pattern Recognition-Workshops, pp. 94–101. IEEE (2010)
14. Mollahosseini, A., Chan, D., Mahoor, M.H.: Going deeper in facial expression recognition using deep neural networks. In: 2016 IEEE Winter Conference on Applications of Computer Vision (WACV), pp. 1–10. IEEE (2016)
15. Ng, H.W., Nguyen, V.D., Vonikakis, V., Winkler, S.: Deep learning for emotion recognition on small datasets using transfer learning. In: Proceedings of the 2015 ACM on International Conference on Multimodal Interaction, pp. 443–449. ACM (2015)
16. Parkhi, O.M., Vedaldi, A., Zisserman, A., et al.: Deep face recognition. In: Bmvc, vol. 1, p. 6 (2015)
17. Sikka, K., Dhall, A., Bartlett, M.: Exemplar hidden Markov models for classification of facial expressions in videos. In: Proceedings of the IEEE Conference on Computer Vision and Pattern Recognition Workshops, pp. 18–25 (2015)
18. Szegedy, C., et al.: Going deeper with convolutions. In: Proceedings of the IEEE Conference on Computer Vision and Pattern Recognition, pp. 1–9 (2015)
19. Zhang, K., Zhang, Z., Li, Z., Qiao, Y.: Joint face detection and alignment using multitask cascaded convolutional networks. IEEE Sig. Process. Lett. 23(10), 1499–1503 (2016)
20. Zhao, G., Huang, X., Taini, M., Li, S.Z., Pietikäinen, M.: Facial expression recognition from near-infrared videos. Image Vis. Comput. 29(9), 607–619 (2011)

Action Units Classification Using ClusWiSARD

Leopoldo A. D. Lusquino Filho[1]($\boxtimes$)(iD), Gabriel P. Guarisa[1],
Luiz F. R. Oliveira[1], Aluizio Lima Filho[1], Felipe M. G. França[1],
and Priscila M. V. Lima[1,2]

[1] PESC/COPPE, Universidade Federal do Rio de Janeiro, Rio de Janeiro, RJ, Brazil
{lusquino,lfdeoliveira,aluizio,felipe}@cos.ufrj.br,
gabrielguarisa@gmail.com, priscilamvl@gmail.com
[2] NCE, Universidade Federal do Rio de Janeiro, Rio de Janeiro, RJ, Brazil

Abstract. This paper presents the use of WiSARD and ClusWiSARD weightless neural networks models for the classification of the contraction and extension of *Action Units*, the facial muscles involved in emotive expressions. This is a complex problem due to the large number of very similar classes, and because it is a multi-label classification task, where the positive expression of one class can modify the response of the others. WiSARD and ClusWiSARD solutions are proposed and validated using the CK+ dataset, producing responses with accuracy of 89.66%. Some of the major works in the field are cited here, but a proper comparison is not possible due to a lack of appropriate information about such solutions, such as the subset of classes used and the time of training/testing. The contribution of this paper is in the pioneering use of weightless neural networks in an AUs classification task, in the unpublished application of the WiSARD and ClusWiSARD models in multi-label tasks and in the new unsupervised expansion of ClusWiSARD proposed here.

Keywords: Action units · WiSARD · ClusWISARD · Weightless neural network

1 Introduction

Ekman and Friesen [10] cataloged a set of muscles known as *Action Units* (AUs) – which would be responsible for all facial expressiveness – while attempting to obtain a set of universal emotions present in any human. The automatic identification of these AUs has been developed since the mid-1990s and has several applications: forensics, psychological treatment, physical therapy support and advertising feedback, among others. AUs have also been used in the development of adaptive digital avatars [4].

This work was partially supported by CAPES, CNPq, FAPERJ and FINEP, Brazilian research agencies.

I. V. Tetko et al. (Eds.): ICANN 2019, LNCS 11729, pp. 409–420, 2019.
https://doi.org/10.1007/978-3-030-30508-6_33

Some of the great difficulties in automatic detection of AUs are the large number of classes and the wide variety of forms how AUs express themselves, besides the fact that they usually manifest together, making this a hard multi-label task. In this way, the approaches that are emerging in the literature usually involve complex techniques of computer vision and machine learning, with high computational cost and long learning time. This work presents an alternative that solves that problem by using weightless neural networks (WANNs), which are characterized by their simplicity of implementation and online learning. The weightless solutions presented here are validated in the CK+ dataset, which presents 30 classes of AUs.

This paper is organized as follows: Sect. 2 presents the concept of AUs and their many classifications. Section 3 introduces the two types of WANNs used in this work and explains the approaches used in order to reduce the multi-label problem classification of AUs in acceptable single-label problems for WANNs. In Sect. 4, the experiments are performed using supervised and semi-supervised datasets. Although a description of state-of-the-art works and other relevant solutions with their main characteristics is provided, unfortunately a complete comparison with them is not possible due to lack of information on which classes are used by them and their performance in relation to training time and test. Section 5 concludes the text, highlighting the contribution of this work in providing multi-label solutions for the weightless neural models, while offering a simpler and faster solution for the AU classification.

2   Action Units

The study of human expressions has been developed through scientific analysis since the second half of the 19th century but, due to the lack of objectivity in defining parameters to categorize such expressions, this research was unable to be properly developed until the end of the 1970s, when Ekman and Friesen finally proposed the use of facial muscles as the physiological element, totally independent of cultural context, to support a taxonomy of the face. From there they developed the Facial Action Coding System (FACS) [10], a descriptive code of facial expressions, whose basic units are the 32 muscles that express facial emotions and 14 Action Descriptors (ADs), which describe facial actions not expressed through muscles, such as the movement of the eyes, tongue and jaw.

AUs are divided into Upper Face (above the nose) and Lower Face (from nose to chin) and into additive (their appearance is independent of the rest of the face) and non-additive (their appearance may be affected by other non-additive AUs, which are in the same facial region). The 32 AUs can form more than 7000 combinations. AUs may manifest voluntarily or involuntarily, which affects the duration of their manifestation and their symmetry. Involuntary AUs are used to detect micro-expressions. AUs have different degrees of intensity, usually divided into five levels of expressiveness.

3   WiSARD and ClusWiSARD Architectures

3.1   WiSARD Models

Weightless artificial neural networks (WANNs) use RAM-based structures as theirs neurons. In these models, learning takes place through writing in memory and classification through reading. So, WANNs avoid the calibration of synaptic weights and have a far superior training speed in comparison with traditional models.

The pioneering implementation of WANNs is called WiSARD, a n-tuple classifier, composed by multiple class discriminators [2]. Each discriminator is a set of N RAM nodes having 2^n address lines each. All discriminators have a structure called *retina*, from which a pseudo-random mapping of its N * n bits composes the input addresses of its RAM nodes.

WiSARD handles only binary data, using groups of n bits of data to access the memory locations formed by them. Each position accessed has a counter that is incremented in the training phase. In the classification phase, each RAM contributes to the score of a given discriminator if its memory position accessed by the input to be classified has a counter with a value greater than a threshold. This threshold, called *bleaching*, is initialized with value zero and increased in cases of tie between discriminators.

WiSARD has a variation capable of dealing with semi-supervised learning called ClusWiSARD [6]. This model applies the classification algorithm to an example without a label and trains it in the discriminator with the highest score. This also creates more than one class discriminator if the example is not sufficiently similar to the discriminators already in existence during your training. In this way, ClusWiSARD can separate examples from the same class by their common characteristics, avoiding undue generalization in their discriminators, creating sub-profiles for the classes.

Another peculiarity of ClusWiSARD's supervised learning is that more than one discriminator of the same class can learn the same example, which would intuitively apply to a data that has characteristics of more than one sub-profile. ClusWiSARD has two parameters used for this check: s, minimum score, and φ, threshold growth interval. When an example o is presented to the network, it is sorted by all discriminators d of its class and case $score(d, o) \geq min(1, s + size(d)/\varphi)$, so the discriminator learns the example o.

3.2   WiSARD-Based Multilabel Classification Systems

Since WiSARD uses a set of discriminators to infer a single class that a given input is more likely to belong to, two traditional multilabels strategies have been adapted to work with this paradigm:

- **Label Powerset:** In this approach a combination of classes is considered as a new class. When the number of classes increases much in relation to the single-label problem, and to circumvent memory spending, new discriminators are instantiated when a new class is presented in the training phase.

One problem with this solution is that a misclassified AU will induce other erroneous classifications, since the network can only find a single group of AUs.

– **Binary Relevance:** The idea is to use a set of WiSARDs where each one is related to an AU, all with two discriminators indicating the presence or the absence of AU. In the training phase, when an example is submitted, all the WiSARDs are trained in the appropriate discriminator. In the classification phase, AUs activation will be predicted according to the response of each of the WiSARDs. The disadvantage of this method over the Label Powerset is the fact that, since the combination of non-additive AUs is extremely idiosyncratic, it may not be captured by the WiSARDs responsible for its elements. On other hand, this method has the advantage of making classification of Upper and Lower Face AUs independents.

4 Experimental Results

4.1 Experimental Setup

The Extended Cohn-Kanade dataset [11] was chosen for the experiments. It is worth mentioning that of 10558 images present in the dataset, only 588 have annotations indicating which AUs, and with what intensity, are present.

The preprocessing methods used were Adaptive Mean, Adaptive Gaussian and Sauvola binarization [14]. The first two techniques binarize the image according to a local threshold for each pixel defined by the mean luminance of the neighborhood and the weighted-sum of Gaussian window, respectively, while Sauvola method uses integral images for computation of the threshold.

The experiments were run on a machine with the following configuration: 7.7 GiB, Intel Core i7-6500U CPU @ 2.50GHz x 4, GeForce 920MX/PCIe/SSE2, 64-bit, Ubuntu 18.04.1.

4.2 Experiments with Supervised and Semi-supervised WiSARD

Both networks (WiSARD and ClusWiSARD) were tested in combination with both methods (Binary Relevance and Label Powerset) using only annotated CK+ images in a 10-fold cross-validation. The landmarks information provided in the dataset was used to obtain the box used to generate the input from the network. Table 1 presents the description of the AUs present in CK+, with their frequency. One of the great difficulties of this dataset can be perceived here, by the imbalance of the classes. Another difficulty is due to the fact that additive AUs modify completely when they mutually manifest, so that the combination of AUs can practically be considered new classes (with many different features of the classes that compose it).

In these experiments, the accuracy was calculated as: $acc = \frac{tp+tn}{tp+tn+fp+fn}$. Other metrics considered here were F1-score, recall and precision.

Figures 1, 2, 3, 4, 5, 6, 7, 8, 9, 10, 11 and 12 show results of accuracy, F1-Score, precision, recall, training time mean and classification time mean for the Binary

Table 1. Frequency of AUs in CK+ dataset

AU	Name	N	AU	Name	N
1	Inner Brow Raiser	173	18	Lip Puckerer	9
2	Outer Brow Raiser	116	20	Lip Stretcher	77
4	Brow Lowerer	191	21	Neck Tightener	3
5	Upper Lip Raiser	102	23	Lip Tightener	59
6	Cheek Raiser	122	24	Lip Pressor	57
7	Lid Tightener	119	25	Lips Part	287
9	Nose Wrinkler	74	26	Jaw Drop	48
10	Upper Lip Raiser	21	27	Mouth Stretch	81
11	Nasolabial Deepener	33	28	Lip Suck	1
12	Lip Corner Puller	111	29	Jaw Thrust	1
13	Cheek Puller	2	31	Jaw Clencher	3
14	Dimpler	29	34	Cheek Puff	1
15	Lip Corner Depressor	89	38	Nostril Dilator	29
16	Lower Lip Depressor	24	39	Nostril Compressor	16
17	Chin Raiser	196	43	Eyes Closed	9

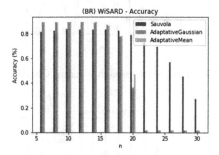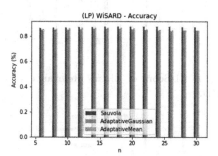

Fig. 1. Accuracy of Binary Relevance vs Label Powerset approaches using WiSARD.

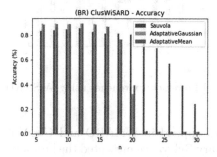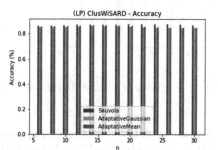

Fig. 2. Accuracy of Binary Relevance vs Label Powerset approaches using ClusWiS-ARD.

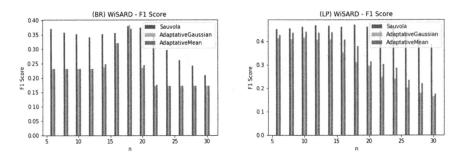

Fig. 3. F1-Score of Binary Relevance vs Label Powerset approaches using WiSARD.

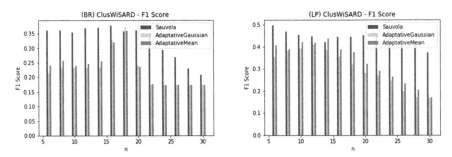

Fig. 4. F1-Score of Binary Relevance vs Label Powerset approaches using ClusWiS-ARD.

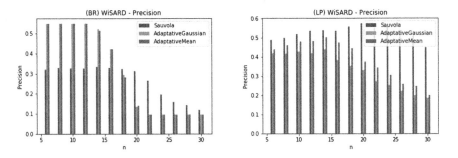

Fig. 5. Precision of Binary Relevance vs Label Powerset approaches using WiSARD.

Relevance and Label Powerset approaches applied in WiSARD and ClusWiS-ARD, respectively. ClusWiSARd with Binary Relevance presented the best accuracy and the same net with Label Powerset presented the best F1-Score. Label Powerset presented a better result for precision, and Binary Relevance presented better results for recall, in both cases independently of the network. This behavior is explained by the fact that Label Powerset minimizes the amount of false positives, when trying to validate the combination of classes, and Binary Relevance minimizes false negatives by checking each class independently, which

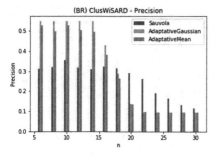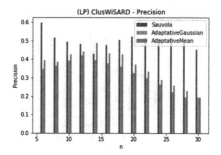

Fig. 6. Precision of Binary Relevance vs Label Powerset approaches using ClusWiS-ARD.

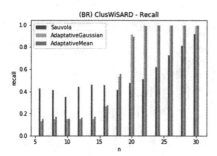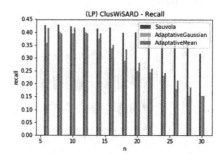

Fig. 7. Recall of Binary Relevance vs Label Powerset approaches using WiSARD.

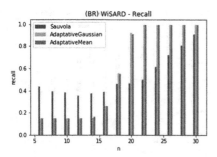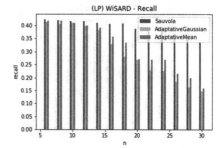

Fig. 8. Recall of Binary Relevance vs Label Powerset approaches using ClusWiSARD.

shows that the Label Powerset approach is more stringent when accepting a class.

In terms of training speed, Label Powerset is faster, independent of the network, because it needs to train in only one discriminator per input. In terms of classification speed, Binary Relevance with WiSARD was more efficient due to the lower number of classes than Label Powerset and due to the smaller number of discriminators compared to ClusWiSARD.

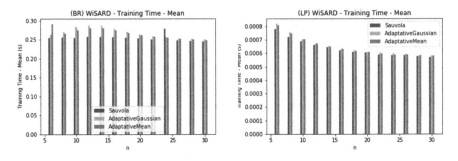

Fig. 9. Training time mean of Binary Relevance vs Label Powerset approaches using WiSARD.

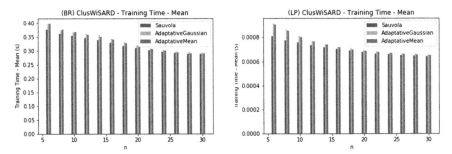

Fig. 10. Training time mean of Binary Relevance vs Label Powerset approaches using ClusWiSARD.

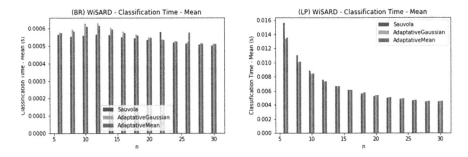

Fig. 11. Classification time mean of Binary Relevance vs Label Powerset approaches using WiSARD.

In relationship to accuracy, Adaptive Mean and Adaptive Gaussian preprocessings worked better with Binary Relevance, while Sauvola provided better results with Label Powerset. The speed in the training and classification phases had similar performances to all preprocessing methods. Smaller addressing values had better F1-Score and precision results with Binary Relevance and recall with Label Powerset, while higher bit-addressing values resulted in better F1-

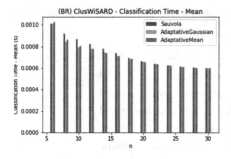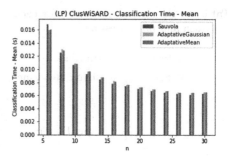

Fig. 12. Classification time mean of Binary Relevance vs Label Powerset approaches using ClusWiSARD.

Score and precision scores with Label Powerset and recall with Binary Relevance, besides better training speed and classification, regardless of method.

The best result obtained in terms of accuracy was 89.66%, using ClusWiS-ARD with 6 bits of addressing, approach Binary Relevance and Adaptive Mean preprocessing. The confusion matrix of best scored AUs in this result is expressed in Table 2. Table 3 shows the best accuracy for each network type combination, multi-label approach and preprocessing.

Table 2. Multi-label confusion matrix for best scored classes (ClusWiSARD, Adaptive Mean, Binary Relevance): AUs 10 and 31, respectively; $M_{0,0}$ is the count of true negatives, $M_{0,1}$ is false positives, $M_{1,0}$ is false negatives and $M_{1,1}$ is true positives.

AU 10		AU 31	
347	41	360	37
182	18	169	22

The main difficulties encountered in the classification of AUs with WANNs were: (a) WiSARD and Label Powerset: few examples per discriminator; (b) ClusWiSARD and Label Powerset: most non-annotated examples were trained by discriminators who already had many examples; (c) WiSARD and Binary Relevance: many instances of absolute tie between discriminators; depending on the adopted policy has low accuracy or low recall; high sensitivity to combinations of AUs; (d) all approaches: many false negatives.

In the literature [3,9,12], other relevant results of classification of AUs in CK+ do not use all AUs or use other techniques to increase the available information. In [5], transfer-learning is used and validation is all-against-all, with only 8 AUs, obtaining accuracy of 98.62%. In [1] a synthetic dataset is used to extend the amount of data and 11 AUs are used and accuracy is 97.87%. [13] validates with 12 AUs and maximum accuracy is 82.5%. There is no indication of which metric was used to calculate the accuracy in these works.

Table 3. Best accuracy results for each combination of type of network, multilabel approach and preprocessing.

Network	Multilabel	Preprocessing	Accuracy (%)
WiSARD	Binary Relevance	Sauvola	83.94
		Adaptive Mean	89.54
		Adaptive Gaussian	89.54
	Label Powerset	Sauvola	87.8
		Adaptive Mean	86.03
		Adaptive Gaussian	86.88
ClusWiSARD	Binary Relevance	Sauvola	85.67
		Adaptive Mean	**89.66**
		Adaptive Gaussian	89.54
	Label Powerset	Sauvola	87.85
		Adaptive Mean	86.21
		Adaptive Gaussian	87.02

Given the low occurrence of some AUs and their combinations, so unique if compared to their combinations, two tests were done using subsets of AUs. A test was performed with ClusWiSARD, $n = 6$, by removing all AUs that do not have sufficient examples in the dataset, reducing to 324 images for the AUs 1, 2, 4, 5, 6, 7, 9, 12, 15, 17, 20, 25 and 27, with 33.33% of perfect matches between classifications and labels, F1-score of 61.46%, precision of 67.13% and recall of 56.67%. The accuracy obtained was 83.02%. With the same configuration of ClusWiSARD: 11 AUs - acc = 86.77%, F1-score = 74.09% (removing AUs 9 and 20 of previous subset); 9 AUs (removing AUs 15 and 17) - acc = 85.71%, F1-score = 76.65%. This represented a significant improvement in the F1-Score and the number of perfect matches, but a slight drop in accuracy.

In order to increase the classification quality, another test was performed using all annotated images and 4242 images without annotation in a ClusWiS-ARD with $n = 25$, minimum score = 0.1, growth interval = 10 and three maximum discriminators per class, in a Label Powerset approach with Sauvola preprocessing, obtaining accuracy = 32.8% and F1-score = 34%, representing a drop in performance on both attributes.

To verify if the problem of that approach was the ability of ClusWiSARD to select the best discriminator for non-annotated data, another test was done using a ClusWiSARD in unsupervised mode. Here, the net has one class and no restrictions on the number of discriminators, and each example was trained exclusively in a discriminator. In this mode, an example is learned by a discriminator if it is the one with the highest score in classification mode among all discriminators that satisfy ClusWiSARD's criterion for learning. In case of ties between discriminators, the tie-breaking policy is to increase the bleaching and if this cancels the score of all discriminators candidates before the tie breaker occurs, the larger discriminator is elected to learn the example. If no discriminator satisfies the learning criterion, a new discriminator is created to learn the example.

All the annotated images were used without their labels, which were then used to evaluate the clustering potential with Rand, Jaccard, and Folkes-Mellow metrics. $Rand = \frac{a+d}{a+b+c+d}$, $Jac = \frac{a}{a+b+c}$ and $FM = \frac{a}{\sqrt{(a+b)(a+c)}}$, where a are the number of pairs that belong to the same class and even cluster, b the quantity of those belonging to the same class and different clusters, c the number of those belonging to different classes and even cluster and d the quantity of those belonging to different classes and different clusters, and each multi-label example being decomposed into several single labels. The results using a ClusWiSARD with $n = 5$, $s = 0.1$ and $\varphi = 1000$ were Rand = 95.7%, Jac = 95.7% and FM = 97.8%, which indicate good performance of ClusWiSARD for unsupervised, and consequently, semi-supervised learning, thus leading to the conclusion that the non-annotaded CK+ data did not have expressive enough AUs, having it probably been obtained in moments of transition of emotions, when AUs were far from their appex.

5   Conclusion

This work presented novel approaches for classifying AUs activation with weightless neural networks. A relevant contribution is the explotation of the WiSARD model in a hard multi-label problem, an yet non observed feat in the literature, to the best of our knowledge. The best values found for accuracy and F1-score are, respectively, 89.66% and 49.11%. The speed of the proposed WANN architectures, both in training and classification phases, was of very low order of magnitude, but a proper state-of-the-art comparison can not be provided because most other works do not provide data related to the speed of their models and use black boxes in their architectures, preventing proper reproduction of them. Another contribution was a new way of using ClusWiSARD in unsupervised learning (others were presented in [7] and [8]), and the proof of its vocation for this type of task, even in a dataset where each example is highly idiosyncratic. Some related ongoing works are: use of co-occurrence rules, ensemble between different approaches, separate upper and lower face AUs, other preprocessing techniques, non-annotated data filtering policy and optimization of discriminator mapping.

References

1. Abbasnejad, I., et al.: Using synthetic data to improve facial expression analysis with 3d convolutional networks. In: 2017 IEEE International Conference on Computer Vision Workshops (ICCVW) (2017)
2. Aleksander, I., Thomas, W., Bowden, P.: Wisard, a radical new step forward in image recognition. Sensor Rev. 4(3), 120–124 (1984)

3. Almaev, T., Martinez, B., Valstar, M.: Learning to transfer: transferring latent task structures and its application to person-specific facial action unit detection. In: IEEE International Conference on Computer Vision (ICCV), pp. 3774–3782 (2015)

4. Bettadapura, V.: Face expression recognition and analysis: the state of the art. arXiv:1203.6722

5. Breuer, R., Kimmel, R.: A deep learning perspective on the origin of facial expressions (2017)

6. Cardoso, D.O., et al.: Financial credit analysis via a clustering weightless neural classifier. Neurocomputing **183**, 70–78 (2016)

7. Cardoso, D., De Gregorio, M., Lima, P., Gama, J., França, F.: A weightless neural network-based approach for stream data clustering. In: Yin, H., Costa, J.A.F., Barreto, G. (eds.) IDEAL 2012. LNCS, vol. 7435, pp. 328–335. Springer, Heidelberg (2012). https://doi.org/10.1007/978-3-642-32639-4_40

8. Cardoso, D.O., Lima, P.M.V., de Gregorio, M., et al.: Clustering data streams with weightless neural networks. In: ESANN 2011, 19th European Symposium on Artificial Neural Networks, Bruges, Belgium (2011)

9. Chu, W.S., la Torre, F.D., Cohn, J.F.: Learning spatial and temporal cues for multi-label facial action unit detection (2016)

10. Ekman, P., W.V.F.: Manual for the facial action coding system (1977)

11. Kanade, T., Cohn, J.F., Tian, Y.: Comprehensive database for facial expression analysis. In: Proceedings of IEEE International Conference Face and Gesture Recognition (AFGR 2000), pp. 46–53 (2000)

12. Martinez, B., Valstar, M.F., Jiang, B., Pantic, M.: Automatic analysis of facial actions: a survey. IEEE Trans. Affect. Comput. (2018). https://doi.org/10.1109/TAFFC.2017.2731763

13. Pons, G., Masip, D.: Multi-task, multi-label and multi-domain learning with residual convolutional networks for emotion recognition (2018)

14. Sauvola, J., Pietikainen, M.: Adaptive document image binarization. Pattern Recognit. **33**, 225–236 (2000)

Automatic Estimation of Dog Age: The DogAge Dataset and Challenge

Anna Zamansky[1]([⊠]) [iD], Aleksandr M. Sinitca[2][iD], Dmitry I. Kaplun[2][iD],
Luisa M. L. Dutra[3], and Robert J. Young[3][iD]

[1] Information Systems Department, University of Haifa, Haifa, Israel
`annazam@is.haifa.ac.il`
[2] Saint Petersburg Electrotechnical University "LETI", Saint Petersburg, Russia
`siniza.s.94@gmail.com, dikaplun@etu.ru`
[3] School of Environmental and Life Sciences, University of Salford,
Greater Manchester, UK
`lulu.mascarenhas@gmail.com, R.J.Young@salford.ac.uk`

Abstract. Automatic age estimation is a challenging problem attracting attention of the computer vision and pattern recognition communities due to its many practical applications. Artificial neural networks, such as CNNs are a popular tool for tackling this problem, and several datasets which can be used for training models are available.

Despite the fact that dogs are the most well studied species in animal science, and that ageing processes in dogs are in many aspects similar to those of humans, the problem of age estimation for dogs has so far been overlooked. In this paper we present the DogAge dataset and an associated challenge, hoping to spark the interest of the scientific community in the yet unexplored problem of automatic dog age estimation.

Keywords: CNN · Computer vision · Applications of deep learning · Age estimation

1 Introduction

Ageing is attracting increasing attention in the modern society. Biologically, ageing results from the impact of the accumulation of a wide variety of molecular and cellular damage over time. One of the most fascinating features of ageing attributes is that it is neither linear nor consistent, and they are only loosely associated with a person's age in years, thus the speed of ageing varies significantly between individuals. Automatic age estimation is a challenging problem attracting attention of the computer vision and pattern recognition communities. It has many practical applications for biometrics, age control, security and surveillance, age simulation and many more; see [2] for a comprehensive survey. Some features automatically detectable from images and useful for evaluation of biological age in humans are wrinkles, sagginess, pigmentation alterations such

© Springer Nature Switzerland AG 2019
I. V. Tetko et al. (Eds.): ICANN 2019, LNCS 11729, pp. 421–426, 2019.
https://doi.org/10.1007/978-3-030-30508-6_34

Fig. 1. Examples of a young and senior dog

Table 1. Image count by classes and datasets

		Adult	Senior	Young	Total
Expert data	Train/Val	370	495	223	1088
	Test	x	x	x	285
Petfinder	Train/Val	15083	2233	8874	15747

as freckles and age spots, etc. [1,6]. Artificial neural networks, such as CNNs have been applied in many recent works to tackle this problem, see, e.g. [7,10,12].

Despite the fact that dogs are a well studied species in animal science, and that ageing processes in dogs are in many aspects similar to those of humans, the problem of age estimation for dogs has so far been overlooked. Yet it presents some interesting challenges not present in the human version of the problem: dogs' skin is covered with fur and so cannot be used as an indication of ageing. Also, the vast variety of dog breeds makes automatic detection much more difficult than in the human case. However, some studies on dog ageing point out some important features related to dogs appearance that can be used when assessing dogs ageing health such as texture of skin, hyperpigmentation alopecia, cataracts, and greying hair [3,9]. Figure 1 shows example images of a young and a senior malinois.

Studying this problem in dogs has several interesting aspects, for instance as individuals who look older than their chronological age tend to have more health problems related to their apparent age than to their chronological age [4,6], the same correlation is expected for dogs. Thus dog's apparent age estimation could be a potential tool to assess life quality in animal welfare.

2   The DogAge Dataset

For sparking the interest of the scientific community in the challenge of dog age estimation, we present and make publically available the DogAge dataset that has been carefully collected in a collaboration between animal and computer scientists. It contains images of dogs, mapping them to one of the three classes young (0–2 years), adult (2–5 years) or senior (>6 years).

Fig. 2. Example images from expert data

The dataset currently consists of two parts (see Table 1 and Figs. 2 and 3):

1. Expert data: contains 1373 images collected by animal scientists, sampling pet dogs, shelter dogs, laboratory dogs, working dogs and commercial kennel dogs. Their age and division into the three groups was carefully verified. The images are mostly high-quality portraits with the dog facing upwards forward. See Fig. 2 for examples.
2. Petfinder data: contains 26190 images collected using the APIs of Petfinder[1], a portal for pet adoption. The division of dogs into groups is not verified, and there is a diversity of angles and distances of the photos. The raw data has been cleaned, removing photos with more than one dog, containing ther pets or large parts of humans, with resolution less then 500 px on any dimension, and signboard photos. See Fig. 3 for examples.

3   Challenge Announcement

We announce the challenge of developing models for automatically estimating dog's age based on the DogAge dataset (the use of other datasets, or expanding the DogAge dataset are also encouraged). Further details on the challenge can be found at our website http://tech4animals.haifa.ac.il/dogchallenge. We provide there three archives with folders containing class definitions. The dataset is

---

[1] https://www.petfinder.com/.

Fig. 3. Example images from Petfinder

provided in three archive folders: expert data and Petfinder data, both divided into three classes (Young, Adult and Senior), and test data which is not divided. The raw dataset from Petfinder, which contains more images and additional annotation such as breeds upon request. Test subset will be taken from the expert data, and will be blind, i.e., the sample distribution will hidden from challenge participants.

Evaluation: The following three metrics will be used for evaluation of performance of solutions.

1. An adaptation of one of the standard performance measures in human age estimation called Mean Absolute Error (MAE) [5]. This metric is standardly defined as follows:

$$MAE = \sum_{k-1}^{N} |\widehat{l_k} - l_k|/N \tag{1}$$

where l_k is the ground truth age for the kth test image, $\widehat{l_k}$ is the estimated age, and N is the total number of test images.

To adapt the MAE metric to our context, we convert the classes of young (0–2 yrs), adult (2–5 yrs) and senior (>6 yrs) to the (average) ages of 1, 4 and 8 years respectively.

2. Average recall (AR), defined as follows:

$$AR = \frac{R_{adult} + R_{senior} + R_{young}}{3} \tag{2}$$

where

$$R_x = \frac{TP_x}{TP_x + FN_x}$$

$x \in \{$Young,Adult,Senior$\}$, and TP_x and FN_x is the number of true positives and false negatives for class x.

3. Categorization accuracy (CA) defined as follows:

$$CA = \frac{\text{Number of correct predictions}}{\text{Total number of predictions}} \tag{3}$$

4   Baseline Solutions

To provide some baseline, we combined convolutional neural networks (CNNs) for feature extraction with classifiers based on the extracted features. We tried different combinations based on two different CNN architectures: SqueezeNet ([8]) and Inception v3 ([11]), and six different well-known classifiers: kNN, SVM, Logistic Regression (LR), Naive Bayes(NB), Random Forest (RF) and feed-forward neural network (NN). Table 2 presents the accuracy of all the 10 solutions using the three metrics described in the previous section.

Table 2. The accuracy of solutions in terms of CA/recall/MAE

	SVM	kNN	LR	NB	RF	NN
Squeezenet						
CA	0.31	0.26	0.31	0.33	0.32	0.32
RA	0.31	0.26	0.32	0.33	0.31	0.32
MAE	3.20	3.73	3.17	3.05	3.24	3.21
Inception v3						
CA	0.28	0.30	0.26	0.31	0.32	0.34
RA	0.32	0.33	0.31	0.32	0.32	0.34
MAE	3.24	3.04	3.43	3.15	3.21	3.04

5   Summary

While age estimation using neural networks is an active research area for humans, this problem for dogs has been so far overlooked. Yet dogs' ageing processes are in many aspects similar to human, which may lead to cross-fertilization between these areas. Moreover, age estimation of dogs may be a useful tool for welfare evaluation. In this paper we made available the DogAge dataset which contains thousands of images classified into three groups of young, adult and senior, and proposed ten different baseline solutions, analyzing their accuracy. We hope that these results will be the starting point for future explorations of automatic dog age estimation. We also invite the research community to contribute to expanding the DogAge dataset and improving its quality.

Acknowledgement. This work has been supported by the NVIDIA GPU grant program.

References

1. Mauger, E., Russell, R.: Anxiety and impulsivity: factors associated with premature graying in young dogs. PLoS ONE **8**(3) (2013)
2. Angulu, R., Tapamo, J.R., Adewumi, A.O.: Age estimation via face images: a survey. EURASIP J. Image Video Process. **2018**(1), 42 (2018)
3. Bellows, J., et al.: Defining healthy aging in older dogs and differentiating healthy aging from disease. J. Am. Vet. Med. Assoc. **246**(1), 77–89 (2015)
4. Borkan, G.A., Norris, A.H.: Assessment of biological age using a profile of physical parameters. J. Gerontol. **35**(2), 177–184 (1980)
5. Geng, X., Zhou, Z.H., Smith-Miles, K.: Automatic age estimation based on facial aging patterns. IEEE Trans. Pattern Anal. Mach. Intell. **29**(12), 2234–2240 (2007)
6. Gunn, D.A., Murray, P.G., Tomlin, C.C., Rexbye, H., Christensen, K., Mayes, A.E.: Perceived age as a biomarker of ageing: a clinical methodology. Biogerontology **9**(5), 357 (2008)
7. Huerta, I., Fernández, C., Segura, C., Hernando, J., Prati, A.: A deep analysis on age estimation. Pattern Recognit. Lett. **68**, 239–249 (2015)
8. Iandola, F.N., Han, S., Moskewicz, M.W., Ashraf, K., Dally, W.J., Keutzer, K.: Squeezenet: alexnet-level accuracy with 50x fewer parameters and <0.5mb model size. arXiv:1602.07360 (2016)
9. King, C., Smith, T.J., Grandin, T., Borchelt, P.: Anxiety and impulsivity: factors associated with premature graying in young dogs. Appl. Anim. Behav. Sci. **185**, 78–85 (2016)
10. Liu, H., Lu, J., Feng, J., Zhou, J.: Label-sensitive deep metric learning forfacial age estimation. IEEE Trans. Inf. Forensics Secur. **13**(2), 292–305 (2018). https://doi.org/10.1109/TIFS.2017.2746062
11. Szegedy, C., Vanhoucke, V., Ioffe, S., Shlens, J., Wojna, Z.: Rethinking the inception architecture for computer vision. In: Proceedings of the IEEE Conference on Computer Vision and Pattern Recognition, pp. 2818–2826 (2016)
12. Wang, X., Guo, R., Kambhamettu, C.: Deeply-learned feature for age estimation. In: 2015 IEEE Winter Conference on Applications of Computer Vision, WACV 2015, Waikoloa, HI, USA, 5–9 January 2015, pp. 534–541 (2015). https://doi.org/10.1109/WACV.2015.77

Motion Analysis

Neural Network 3D Body Pose Tracking and Prediction for Motion-to-Photon Latency Compensation in Distributed Virtual Reality

Sebastian Pohl, Armin Becher, Thomas Grauschopf, and Cristian Axenie[(⊠)]

Electrical Engineering and Computer Science,
Audi Konfuzius-Institut Ingolstadt Lab, Technische Hochschule Ingolstadt,
Esplanade 10, 85049 Ingolstadt, Germany
{sebastian.pohl,armin.becher,thomas.grauschopf}@thi.de,
cristian.axenie@audi-konfuzius-institut-ingolstadt.de

Abstract. Distributed Virtual Reality (DVR) systems enable geographically dispersed users to interact in a shared virtual environment. The realism of the interaction is crucial to increase the feeling of co-presence. Latency, produced either by hard- or software components of DVR applications, impedes reaching high realism levels of the DVR experience. For example, the time delay between the user's motion and the corresponding display rendering of the DVR system might lead to adverse effects such as a reduced sense of presence or motion sickness. One way of minimizing the latency is to predict user's motion and thus compensate for the inherent latency in the system. In order to address this problem, we propose a neural network 3D pose tracking and prediction system with latency guarantees for end-to-end avatar reconstruction. We evaluate and compare our system against multiple traditional methods and provide a thorough analysis on real-world human motion data.

Keywords: Neural networks · Distributed VR systems ·
3D body tracking · Timeseries prediction · Motion-to-photon latency

1 Introduction

Since high-quality consumer-level VR headsets and systems have become commodity there has been a proliferation of novel immersive and interactive VR applications. Although these systems are lightweight, high-resolution and high frame-rate, a remaining obstacle is how to get the user to feel truly immersed in the experience, especially in collaborative scenarios.

In a VR system, when a motion occurs, the motion detection unit samples the orientation data for the view generation. After the motion detection, the visual processing unit renders a 3D image. Finally, the rendered image is outputted to a display corresponding to the head orientation of the user. As these steps

© Springer Nature Switzerland AG 2019
I. V. Tetko et al. (Eds.): ICANN 2019, LNCS 11729, pp. 429–442, 2019.
https://doi.org/10.1007/978-3-030-30508-6_35

take time, the delay results in latency. In this case, the image does not exactly correspond to the actual head orientation of the user, due to the mismatch between visual and vestibular systems, thereby causing the user to experience motion sickness [20].

Motion-to-photon latency, also known as the end-to-end latency, is the delay between the movement of the user's head and the change of the display of VR device reflecting the user's movement. As soon as the user's head moves, the VR scenery should match the movement. The more delay between these two actions, the more unrealistic the VR world seems. To make the VR world realistic, VR systems need low latency of ≤20 ms [11] and even really low latency of ≤7 ms [14]. This values should hold even if two or more users share the same virtual environment and remote latencies occur between different worldwide VR locations [19,23].

Conventional motion-to-photon latency measurement methods can measure the latency only at the beginning of the physical motion. On the other hand, there are more advanced methods can measure the latency in real-time at every sample [6]. Our previous study [4] supports this idea and estimates that the underlying latency can in theory completely compensated if the system benefits from a precise prediction of position and orientation of the user in 3D. In practice, however, this is not easily achievable because human movements are non-deterministic [14].

The contribution of this paper is a neural network based body pose 3D tracking and prediction system for capturing of avatars with: minimal hardware requirements, an efficient learning system and fast processing time. Correlated with the known latency thresholds, [4,11], the proposed system is able to predict the position of the HMD and the two VR hand controllers for continuous time-based (i.e. timeseries) motion representation subsequently fed to VIRTOOAIR [5], in order to learn the inverse kinematics of the upper-body, global rotation and position of a user inside VR.

2   Related Work

Due to considerable practical relevance in DVR, there is renewed interest in 3D pose tracking and prediction, with impressive preliminary results [17]. Similar works use all the known user skeleton joints. With the kinematic information from the joints, neural networks can predict and generate human motion sequences [18,24]. Yet, in order to be able to track all the joints of the body, one needs expensive motion capture systems. They are accurate for extracting 3D full-body models [9]. However they are very expensive, need long acquisition time (up to minutes), require extensive computing resources and/or take several minutes of processing. Some methods have been proposed to acquire dynamic human models [8] and obtained impressive results but using 106 synchronized cameras and several minutes processing per frame.

On the other end of the spectrum, [13] proposed a method for monocular videos where the body shape can be manipulated in videos. Such systems required expert human intervention, whereas our aim is a learning system capable to exploit the motion data correlations and extract the underlying kinematic temporal aspects within the motion of the HMD and the hand VR controllers autonomously. The common commercially available VR devices, such as the HTC Vive or the Oculus Rift, cannot provide precise external tracking. These devices provide only the tracking information for the head-mounted display, via which the head position and orientation is calculated, and the data from the two hand controllers. Closer to our approach and taking advantage of parametric models some methods have been proposed to estimate the 3D body from a single picture [25] or from shape variations in range scans [3]. These approaches can provide exciting results and a deformable body model, but they require additional hardware (e.g. range scanners), data representations and complex models (e.g. model-based body-aware image warping). Instead, we look at a learning based approach which runs in a fully automatic manner after training.

Finally, in contrast to other works, our aim is to compensate for latency using the data that VR devices offer. A latency compensation system must be highly real-time capable. In order to benefit from latency compensation, the introduced latency of the predictor should not be larger than the horizon of the prediction. Yet the time the predictive model needs to calculate the next values, depends on the model itself, as we will see later in the experiments section.

3   System Setup and Description

The neural network tracking and prediction system proposed in the paper is a component of VIRTOOAIR: VIrtual Reality TOOlbox for Avatar Intelligent Reconstruction[1] processing pipeline [5]. This is a novel, inexpensive approach to achieve high-fidelity multimodal motion capturing and avatar representation in VR. By fusing an inverse kinematics learning module for precise upper-body motion reconstruction, with single RGB camera input for lower-body estimation the system obtains a rich representation of user's motion. The learning capabilities allow natural pose regression with cheap and affordable marker-less motion capturing hardware.

4   Experiments and Discussion

4.1   Technical Setup

For all the experiments we acquired data from the HTC Vive system [2], that contains an HMD and two hand controllers data, using OpenVR API [1]. The training dataset was further extended with data from Human 3.6M [12]. This online database is composed of 3.6 Million accurate 3D Human poses, acquired by recording the performance of 5 female and 6 male subjects, under 4 different

---

[1] An overview on the VIRTOOAIR framework is available at: https://audi-konfuzius-institut-ingolstadt.de/category/akii-microlab/current-projects.

viewpoints, for training realistic human sensing systems for pose estimation. The HTC Vive system captures for both the hand controller and the HMD speed and acceleration data via internal sensors, as well position and rotation data via an inside-out tracking system [21]. The implementation of the analysis, predictor models and neural networks was done in Python with Scikit-Learn and Keras API [7]. Tensorflow was used as back-end, which together with CuDNN dispatched the calculations of the networks to an nVidia GTX-1080Ti GPU.

4.2   Data Representation and Pre-processing

The data available from the HTC Vive is in form of a 3×4 transformation matrix T. This matrix is composed of a 3×3 rotation matrix R and the position vector p in 3D space.

$$T = \begin{bmatrix} R\ p \end{bmatrix} = \begin{bmatrix} r_{00} & r_{01} & r_{02} & x \\ r_{10} & r_{11} & r_{12} & y \\ r_{20} & r_{21} & r_{22} & z \end{bmatrix}$$

From this matrix we can calculate the Euler angles, but one of the challenges with Euler rotation angles in R^3 space is that they are not unique and suffer from incontinuities. In order to overcome this limitation we use quaternions. A quaternion can be used to represent unambiguously 3D-rotations as a point on a hypersphere in a R^4 space. The quaternion representation $q = (w, x, y, z)$ or $q = w + ix + jy + kz$ is more informative offering a continuous representation, where w, x, y and z are a system of four scalars and i, j and k are three right versors, respectively. In such a representation one needs to consider that human

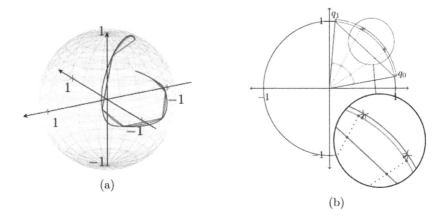

(a)

(b)

Fig. 1. Visual representation of quaternions on spheres after interpolation: (a) Visual representation of interpolation using *linear interpolation* (red), the *slerp* method (green) and the *squad* (blue), (b) Comparison between linear interpolation (red) and the slerp method (green) between points q0 and q1. (Color figure online)

motion data includes inherent information about the speed and acceleration of a body. Interpolating the data in a realistic form assumes that abrupt changes in the speed, or the acceleration, need to be avoided. In order to achieve this, we explored multiple interpolation methods, such as the linear interpolation, Spherical Linear Interpolation (slerp) and Spherical Spline Quaternion Interpolation (squad), as shown in Fig. 1. Such a step is highly relevant in order to maintain in the training data of our model those subtle changes and informative variance of the motion parameters encoded in the quaternions. As previously mentioned, the data acquired from the tracking system is in the form of time indexed sequences, or timeseries. Choosing quaternions to represent rotations, we performed an initial timeseries correlation analysis to check if there is any interesting effect in the user's head and hands motion that we can exploit with our neural network system. In the correlation matrix in Fig. 2 one can observe that with respect to the absolute positions (Fig. 2, left panel) there is a correlation only between the hand and head positions, but not between the axes themselves. The only correlation visible is the correlation in the first derivative (i.e. the speed) (Fig. 2, right panel). Using the input from the correlation analysis, Fig. 3, we investigated the temporal depth (i.e. lag) to which the position components from both head and hands are correlated, in order to define the prediction horizon in the motion-to-photon latency compensation. We observed that for the position, the autocorrelation of the y position (red) approaches zero but stays positive despite the large lag, whereas the x axis (blue) and z axis (green) become anticorrelated.

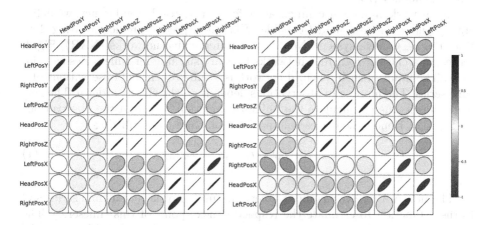

Fig. 2. Motion components correlation analysis. Blue codes for degree of correlation, whereas red anti-correlation of the various 3D motion components. The size of each matrix entry is proportional to the covariance of considered pair of motion components. Left panel: correlation w.r.t. left hand coordinate system; Right panel: correlation w.r.t. right hand coordinate system. (Color figure online)

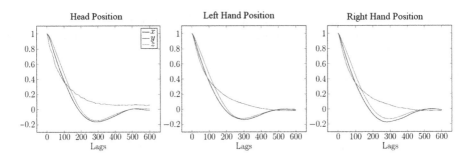

Fig. 3. Position autocorrelation analysis. (Color figure online)

4.3 Neural Network Tracking Model

Human motion prediction aims to understand behaviors of a subject on the observed sequences and to generate future body poses. Most of the models are focused on image data as input instead of other source of data (e.g. inertial, inside-out tracking). Recurrent Neural Networks (RNN) have shown exciting results in: learning 3D motion temporal dynamics in a sequence [10,24], to automatically learn the image-dependent structural and temporal constraints using long short-term memory (LSTM) units [16], and up to LSTM-based deep learning architectures for 3D depth reconstruction by learning the intrinsic joint interdependency [15].

In our work, aiming at compensating for motion-to-photon latency, we deliberately chose a neural model capable of fast and precise prediction using data from the HTC Vive system. Nonlinear autoregressive networks (NAR), Fig. 4, represent a class of recurrent networks that are suitable for time series calculations. The input of such a neural network is a sub-sequence of observations of a time series. The number of observations depends on the chosen order p. The network thus learns to calculate the unknown function $f(\cdot)$ from the observations x_n to x_{n-p}. Hence, the corresponding function can be described as

$$\hat{x}_{n+1} = f(x_n, x_{n-1}, \cdots, x_{n-p}). \tag{1}$$

The network receives as input a certain number of lags of a time series and learns a function to estimate the respective next point of this timeseries. The computation can be implemented as open-loop as well as closed-loop. In the open-loop, the real value of x_{n+1} is used next, and the remaining values x_{n-1} to x_{n-p} are delayed by one input neuron. The oldest value x_{n-p} drops out and will not be used any further. Since there are no explicit feedback connections within the network, the horizon of the timeseries over which dependencies can be learned is limited to the chosen order of autoregression. The closed-loop approach is analogous to the open-loop, with the only difference being that instead of the true value for x_{n+1}, the previously estimated value $\hat{x}_{n+1}$ is used. Depending on how far the forecast should reach into the future, this procedure can be repeated

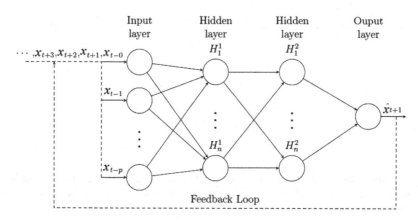

Fig. 4. Neural network model architecture.

as often as desired. In such a network the core assumption is that subsequent measurements are intrinsically spatio-temporally correlated. In order to evaluate the performance of the proposed neural model the prediction of the next point $t+1$ is done using the open-loop prediction with the real data as input. Further predictions with for $t+k$ with $k > 1$ are made via closed-loop operation. Note that in some of the literature, the terms "pose prediction" and "pose estimation" are used interchangeably, both referring to the task of estimating a pose (usually skeleton-based joint locations). In this work, we use the term "prediction" to refer to the specific task of predicting/forecasting 3D user pose at time $t+1$ in a sequence, assuming the 3D poses were already estimated at time t.

4.4   Evaluation

In order to provide a complete and fair analysis of our proposed neural network model, we evaluated state-of-the models for timeseries prediction (i.e. Vector Autoregressive (VAR) Models) as well as machine learning regression techniques (i.e. Ridge Regression). For evaluation, we explored multiple multivariate time-series metrics due to the nature of our input data and found that the Mean Absolute Scaled Error (MASE) would be a good candidate. From the basic MASE formulation, because there is no restriction on the mean, we divide the prediction of a model by the mean, allowing us to also extract more statistics (e.g. median)

$$q_j = \frac{e_j}{\frac{1}{T-1} \cdot \sum_{t=2}^{T} |y_t - y_{t-1}|} \tag{2}$$

so

$$MASE = \frac{1}{N} \cdot \sum_{j=1}^{N} q_j. \tag{3}$$

This metric is very easy to interpret. As Fig. 5 shows, when applied to a model in comparison to the naive forecast (or another benchmark model), for

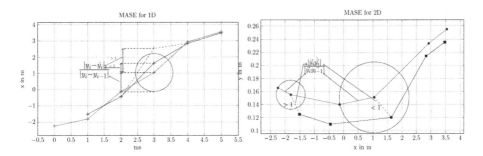

Fig. 5. Evaluation of MASE metric. Blue curve is the true motion, whereas red is the prediction of the system. The equations describe the way the metric is constructed in each dimension. (Color figure online)

values < 1 the model is better, for values be > 1 the model is worse. Since the MASE metric is designed for univariate timeseries, we update the formulation, instead of the absolute deviation between two points of the time series we will use the Euclidean distance

$$|y\hat{y}| = EE = \sqrt{\sum_{i=1}^{d}(y_i - \hat{y}_i)^2} \Rightarrow MEE = \frac{1}{T}\sum_{t=0}^{T}\sqrt{\sum_{i=1}^{d}(y_{i,t} - \hat{y}_{i,t})^2}. \quad (4)$$

For a univariate time series, this procedure is equivalent to normal calculation of the MASE, since the Euclidean distance in the one-dimensional space is equal to the absolute distance. Finally, we formulate MESE (Mean Euclidean Scaled Error) as a second metric that looks at position changes in time

$$MESE = \frac{1}{T} \cdot \sum_{t=1}^{T} \frac{|y_t\hat{y}_t|}{\frac{1}{N-1}\sum_{n=2}^{N}|y_n y_{n-1}|}. \quad (5)$$

In order to guide the reader through the evaluation in Fig. 3 we mention that, in practice, a deviation of almost 2 cm is acceptable for DVR setups. For rotation prediction, we convert quaternions in rotation angles through a nonlinear transformation (assuming unitary quaternions)

$$cos(\theta) = \hat{q} \cdot q, \theta = arccos(\hat{q} \cdot q). \quad (6)$$

The first evaluated model is the VAR model, a multivariate autoregressive model for which the prediction is given by

$$\hat{\boldsymbol{y}}_{t+1} = f(y_{1,t}, \cdots, y_{k,t}, y_{1,t-1}, \cdots, y_{k,t-1}, y_{1,t-p}, \cdots, y_{k,t-p}). \quad (7)$$

For this relatively simple approach we analyse, in Table 1, the MEE, the MESE, and the angular deviation of the quaternions for VAR models with predictions of up to 25 ms in 5 ms intervals. The model input are the last 6 lags of the respective position axes or the four scalar values of the quaternions of the

Table 1. Evaluation of VAR prediction.

VAR						
	Metric	5 ms	10 ms	15 ms	20 ms	25 ms
Head position	MEE	0.0005	0.0070	0.0138	0.0207	0.0274
	MESE	0.0937	1.0230	2.0144	3.0043	3.9882
Left Hand Position	MEE	0.0011	0.0101	0.0195	0.0290	0.0383
	MESE	0.1224	1.0541	2.0420	3.0235	3.9932
Right Hand Position	MEE	0.0015	0.0115	0.0221	0.0328	0.0433
	MESE	0.1489	1.0694	2.0517	3.0272	3.9940

hands and of the head. This value was chosen as significant (i.e. cut-off lag) in the Auto-Correlation Function plot (ACF), Fig. 3, considering 95% confidence interval. As one can see, there is an error in the estimate of the position of the head. After 5 ms the error is half a millimeter and is only after 5 ms that reaches about an inch. The error of the hand positions already exceeds one centimeter after 10 ms and are at over one millimeter at 5 ms. If the input vector consists of several variables, it can lead to multi-collinearity between the descriptive variables. This can lead to a poor estimate of the model parameters [22]. Ridge Regression solves this problem by extending the least squares method using a $L2$ regularization term

$$\sum_{i=1}^{n}(y_i - x_{ij}\beta_j)^2 + \lambda\|\beta\|_2^2. \tag{8}$$

In multivariate cases the estimation of the β parameters is performed by

$$\hat{\beta} = (X^TX + \lambda I)^{-1}X^TY. \tag{9}$$

Similarly to the VAR model, we evaluate the Ridge Regression model, as shown in Table 2. As we can observe, we have nearly identical to the errors of the VAR model. The position of the head is with a mean error of half a millimeter

Table 2. Evaluation of Ridge Regression prediction.

Ridge Regressor						
	Metric	5 ms	10 ms	15 ms	20 ms	25 ms
Head Position	MEE	0.0005	0.0070	0.0138	0.0206	0.0274
	MESE	0.0939	1.0237	2.0142	3.0037	3.9881
Left Hand Position	MEE	0.0011	0.0100	0.0195	0.0290	0.0383
	MESE	0.1229	1.0542	2.0421	3.0232	3.9926
Right Hand Position	MEE	0.0014	0.0115	0.0221	0.0328	0.0433
	MESE	0.1479	1.0698	2.0506	3.0272	3.9934

Table 3. Evaluation of Neural Network prediction.

Neural Network						
	Metric	5 ms	10 ms	15 ms	20 ms	25 ms
Head Position	MEE	0.0064	0.0073	0.0088	0.0107	0.0135
	MESE	1.1288	1.3052	1.5890	1.9593	2.4957
Left Hand Position	MEE	0.009016	0.008784	0.009181	0.011064	0.014852
	MESE	0.944028	0.939354	1.008508	1.233179	1.650189
Right Hand Position	MEE	0.0108	0.0105	0.0110	0.0131	0.0175
	MESE	0.9588	0.9672	1.0405	1.2617	1.6679

better prediction. From 15 ms the error is increasing over one centimeter. The hand positions deviate from 10 ms by over one centimeter. We complete our analysis with the evaluation of our neural network model performance. Similarly to state-of-the-art model, we analyse, in Table 3, the MEE and MASE as well as the statistics of the prediction. This will emphasize the advantages of the proposed system. Similarly to the Ridge Regression, the estimated position of the head is better than that of the hands. The error of the head position is after 5 ms at something more than 0.5 mm. At the same prediction horizon, the hand positions already deviate about an inch. Nevertheless, the MESE metric for the hands is lower than that of the head. This is explained by the fact that the hands move much more than the head does. Therefore, the counter for the MESE metric is larger for the hands than for the head, whereby the total value decreases. In terms of a thorough statistical evaluation of the prediction at various horizon sizes, the neural network model is excelling at horizon levels between 5 and 10 ms, as shown in Table 4. These values are consistent with the interval of interest in motion-to-photon compensation, [4]. This work shows that the prediction of human movements for DVR is difficult. The best prediction was achieved using a neural network model (i.e. NAR) with a global error that lies however after 10 ms in over 25% of the predictions, at over 1 cm deviation. This is still under the guarantees of compensating the motion-to-photon latency and achieved with a simple model (i.e. NAR) compared to other approaches employing LSTMs or other such computationally expensive methods. The used combination of data representation and the neural network model provide a good match for the problem of predicting 3D pose in VR. The errors of the neural network model are on average lower for the prediction for the time steps $t+1$, but not over the entire range of prediction horizons. Table 6 shows the coefficients of variation ($\frac{std}{mean}$) for the head position estimated by the neural network and the Ridge Regression estimate. Here it can be seen that for the first time steps, the variation relative to the mean value for the ridge regression is almost twice as high as that of the neural network. It can be seen from the Tables 3 and 4 that, despite the higher mean error, the maximum error in the neural network model is lower than that of a ridge regression. For prediction horizons larger

Table 4. Evaluation of Neural Network prediction.

		Std	Min	25%	50%	75%	Max
Head	5 ms	0.006138	0.000026	0.001614	0.004255	0.009721	0.052726
	10 ms	0.006847	0.000044	0.002014	0.005024	0.010839	0.064883
	15 ms	0.008053	0.000040	0.002647	0.006258	0.012710	0.086756
	20 ms	0.009730	0.000082	0.003433	0.007806	0.015189	0.123706
	25 ms	0.012079	0.000062	0.004575	0.010032	0.018925	0.162462
Right Hand	5 ms	0.010157	0.000022	0.003026	0.008582	0.015398	0.261596
	10 ms	0.011207	0.000077	0.003373	0.008108	0.014211	0.430261
	15 ms	0.013530	0.000108	0.003997	0.007916	0.013682	0.659150
	20 ms	0.016923	0.000054	0.005132	0.009362	0.015498	0.821064
	25 ms	0.021201	0.000067	0.007047	0.012942	0.021082	1.022083
Left Hand	5 ms	0.008447	0.000024	0.002343	0.006984	0.012944	0.148632
	10 ms	0.008700	0.000023	0.002750	0.006589	0.011913	0.267453
	15 ms	0.009972	0.000074	0.003412	0.006587	0.011584	0.362364
	20 ms	0.012425	0.000058	0.004415	0.007987	0.013395	0.451241
	25 ms	0.015777	0.000144	0.006147	0.011124	0.018236	0.549077

than 15 ms, the errors of the neural network model are consistently lower than is the case with a ridge regression. With an upper quantile limit of 1.89 mm, the errors after 25 ms are still lower than the errors of the Ridge Regression after 15 ms, as shown in Table 5. As previously mentioned, a deviation of almost 2 cm is acceptable for the DVR setups we are considering.

Table 5. Evaluation of Ridge Regression prediction.

		Std	Min	25%	50%	75%	Max
Head	5 ms	0.000911	8.613443e-07	0.000219	0.000379	0.000636	0.091600
	10 ms	0.006241	7.789306e-06	0.001705	0.004993	0.011511	0.124571
	15 ms	0.012349	6.221113e-06	0.003302	0.009812	0.022824	0.171270
	20 ms	0.018467	2.252768e-05	0.004897	0.014620	0.034124	0.189392
	25 ms	0.024569	2.397779e-05	0.000473	0.019391	0.045408	0.251757
Right Hand	5 ms	0.002222	0.000003	0.000333	0.000651	0.001210	0.106050
	10 ms	0.009895	0.000007	0.002373	0.007526	0.014565	0.163459
	15 ms	0.019207	0.000015	0.004519	0.014631	0.028474	0.315861
	20 ms	0.028501	0.000013	0.006642	0.021697	0.042239	0.462435
	25 ms	0.037669	0.000024	0.008729	0.028683	0.055882	0.G03335
Left Hand	5 ms	0.002821	0.000004	0.000444	0.000827	0.001539	0.140264
	10 ms	0.010495	0.000011	0.003057	0.009175	0.016775	0.175692
	15 ms	0.020177	0.000009	0.005757	0.017663	0.032617	0.266510
	20 ms	0.029895	0.000024	0.008430	0.026088	0.048387	0.378546
	25 ms	0.039513	0.000017	0.011057	0.034422	0.064057	0.477469

Table 6. Variation coefficient of Ridge Regression vs. Neural Network.

Variation coefficient (sd/mean)					
	5 ms	10 ms	15 ms	20 ms	25 ms
NN	0.9590	0.938	0.909	0.909	0.895
Ride	1.822	0.891	0.895	0.892	0.896

The thorough evaluation and comparative analysis provided in this section emphasize some advantages the proposed neural network model has in predicting head and hand position and orientation under the constraint of motion-to-photon latency. This is also visible in the quatitative analysis of variation coefficients in Table 6.

Such a system can bring benefits in actively compensating for latency and complete the end-to-end pipeline towards a realistic VR avatar reconstruction in DVR systems such as the one proposed in VIRTOOAIR[2].

5 Conclusions

DVR is still in infancy but will definitely require digital alter egos of the users' physical selves, virtual replicas termed avatars. Such embodied interfaces to the artificially generated environments provide a means of direct interaction with the environments based on the simulation of physical properties. Motion tracking and prediction is a key ingredient for a realistic immersion. Yet, motion-to-photon latency must be compensated taken into account the variability of human motion. The proposed neural network system exploits the underlying correlations in the upper body kinematics and provides latency guarantees for a natural VR experience. As such avatars are our proxies in the DVR, they are the direct extension of ourselves into the virtual domain, hence their digital representations should be tightly bound to our motion, our self-perception, and, why not, our personality.

References

1. Openvr sdk (2015). https://github.com/ValveSoftware/openvr
2. Vive vr system (2018). https://www.vive.com/us/product/vive-virtual-reality-system/
3. Allen, B., Curless, B., Popović, Z., Hertzmann, A.: Learning a correlated model of identity and pose-dependent body shape variation for real-time synthesis. In: Proceedings of the 2006 ACM SIGGRAPH/Eurographics Symposium on Computer Animation, SCA 2006, pp. 147–156. Eurographics Association, Aire-la-Ville (2006). http://dl.acm.org/citation.cfm?id=1218064.1218084

---

[2] Source code available at: https://gitlab.com/akii-microlab/virtooair.

4. Becher, A., Angerer, J., Grauschopf, T.: Novel approach to measure motion-to-photon and mouth-to-ear latency in distributed virtual reality systems. In: GI VR/AR WORKSHOP 2018 (2018)
5. Becher A., Axenie C., Grauschopf, T.: VIRTOOAIR: virtual reality toolbox for avatar intelligent reconstruction. In: Multimodal Virtual and Augmented Reality Workshop (MVAR) at 2018 IEEE International Symposium on Mixed and Augmented Reality (ISMAR) (2018)
6. Choi, S.W., Lee, S., Seo, M.W., Kang, S.J.: Time sequential motion-to-photon latency measurement system for virtual reality head-mounted displays. Electronics 7(9), 171 (2018)
7. Chollet, F., et al.: Keras (2015). https://github.com/fchollet/keras
8. Collet, A., et al.: High-quality streamable free-viewpoint video. ACM Trans. Graph. 34(4), 69:1–69:13 (2015). https://doi.org/10.1145/2766945
9. Daanen, H., Ter Haar, F.: Review. Displays 34(4), 270–275 (2013)
10. Du, X., Vasudevan, R., Johnson-Roberson, M.: Bio-LSTM: a biomechanically inspired recurrent neural network for 3-d pedestrian pose and gait prediction. IEEE Robot. Autom. Lett. 4(2), 1501–1508 (2019)
11. Elbamby, M.S., Perfecto, C., Bennis, M., Doppler, K.: Toward low-latency and ultra-reliable virtual reality. IEEE Netw. 32(2), 78–84 (2018)
12. Ionescu, C., Papava, D., Olaru, V., Sminchisescu, C.: Human3.6m: large scale datasets and predictive methods for 3D human sensing in natural environments. IEEE Trans. Pattern Anal. Mach. Intell. 36(7), 1325–1339 (2014)
13. Jain, A., Thormählen, T., Seidel, H.P., Theobalt, C.: Moviereshape: tracking and reshaping of humans in videos. In: ACM SIGGRAPH Asia 2010 Papers, SIGGRAPH ASIA 2010, pp. 148:1–148:10. ACM, New York (2010). https://doi.org/10.1145/1866158.1866174
14. Jerald, J., Whitton, M., Brooks Jr., F.P.: Scene-motion thresholds during head yaw for immersive virtual environments. ACM Trans. Appl. Percept. 9(1), 4:1–4:23 (2012)
15. Lee, K., Lee, I., Lee, S.: Propagating LSTM: 3D pose estimation based on joint interdependency. In: Ferrari, V., Hebert, M., Sminchisescu, C., Weiss, Y. (eds.) ECCV 2018. LNCS, vol. 11211, pp. 123–141. Springer, Cham (2018). https://doi.org/10.1007/978-3-030-01234-2_8
16. Lin, M., Lin, L., Liang, X., Wang, K., Cheng, H.: Recurrent 3D pose sequence machines. In: 2017 IEEE Conference on Computer Vision and Pattern Recognition (CVPR) (2017)
17. Malleson, C., et al.: Rapid one-shot acquisition of dynamic VR avatars. In: 2017 IEEE Virtual Reality (VR), pp. 131–140 (2017)
18. Martinez, J., Black, M.J., Romero, J.: On human motion prediction using recurrent neural networks. In: 2017 IEEE Conference on Computer Vision and Pattern Recognition (CVPR), pp. 4674–4683 (2017)
19. Meehan, M., Razzaque, S., Whitton, M.C., Brooks, F.P.: Effect of latency on presence in stressful virtual environments. In: IEEE Virtual Reality 2003, pp. 141–148, 22–26 March 2003
20. Munafo, J., Diedrick, M., Stoffregen, T.A.: The virtual reality head-mounted display oculus rift induces motion sickness and is sexist in its effects. Exp. Brain Res. 235(3), 889–901 (2017)
21. Niehorster, D.C., Li, L., Lappe, M.: The accuracy and precision of position and orientation tracking in the HTC vive virtual reality system for scientific research. i-Perception (2017)

22. Shih, S., Shih, W.: Application of ridge regression analysis to water resources studies. J. Hydrol. **40**(1), 165–174 (1979)
23. St. Pierre, M.E., Banerjee, S., Hoover, A.W., Muth, E.R.: The effects of 0.2hz varying latency with 20–100ms varying amplitude on simulator sickness in a helmet mounted display. Displays **36**, 1–8 (2015)
24. Tang, Y., Ma, L., Liu, W., Zheng, W.S.: Long-term human motion prediction by modeling motion context and enhancing motion dynamics. In: Proceedings of the Twenty-Seventh International Joint Conference on Artificial Intelligence (2018). https://doi.org/10.24963/ijcai.2018/130
25. Zhou, S., Fu, H., Liu, L., Cohen-Or, D., Han, X.: Parametric reshaping of human bodies in images. ACM Trans. Graph. **29**(4), 126:1–126:10 (2010)

Variational Deep Embedding with Regularized Student-t Mixture Model

Taisuke Kobayashi$^{(\boxtimes)}$ (iD)

Division of Information Science, Graduate School of Science and Technology,
Nara Institute of Science and Technology, Nara, Japan
kobayashi@is.naist.jp
https://kbys_t.gitlab.io/en/

Abstract. This paper proposes a new motion classifier using variational deep embedding with regularized student-t mixture model as prior,
named VaDE-RT, to improve robustness to outliers while maintaining
continuity in latent space. Normal VaDE uses Gaussian mixture model,
which is sensitive to outliers, and furthermore, all the components of
mixture model can freely move in the latent space, which would lose the
continuity in the latent space. In contrast, VaDE-RT aims to exploit a
heavy-tailed feature of student-t distribution for robustness, and regularize the mixture model to standard normal distribution, which is
employed in a standard variational autoencoder as prior. To do so, three
reasonable approximations for (i) reparameterization trick, (ii) Kullback-
Leibler (KL) divergence between student-t distributions, and (iii) KL
divergence of the mixture model, are introduced to make backpropagation in VaDE-RT possible. As a result, VaDE-RT outperforms the
original VaDE and a simple deep-learning-based classifier in terms of
classification accuracy. In addition, VaDE-RT yields both continuity and
natural topology of clusters in the latent space, which make robot control
adaptive smoothly.

Keywords: Variational autoencoder · Student-t mixture model ·
Human motion classification

1 Introduction

Prediction of the motion intention is useful to adjust parameters in robot controllers [9], and is regarded as classification with sequential data. If resolving it by
a direct classifier, whose outputs are directly given as the predicted results from
inputs (e.g., recurrent neural networks with long short-term memory (LSTM)
and relatives [2,8]), three issues would be caused as below.

1. Appropriate annotation (segmentation) is difficult because the human motion
   seamlessly changes.
2. A classifier using softmax function as an output layer tries to allocate data
   into prepared clusters even if they are outliers.

© Springer Nature Switzerland AG 2019
I. V. Tetko et al. (Eds.): ICANN 2019, LNCS 11729, pp. 443–455, 2019.
https://doi.org/10.1007/978-3-030-30508-6_36

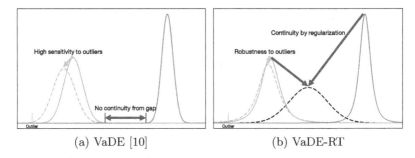

(a) VaDE [10]   (b) VaDE-RT

Fig. 1. Proposal of variational deep embedding with regularized student-t mixture model: robustness of outliers can be given by student-t distribution; continuity in the latent space would be obtained by regularization to standard normal distribution.

3. Such a classifier forcibly separate clusters to achieve high classification accuracy even if they are similar to each other.

These three would make the classifier sensitive to outliers and risky for using the outputs to switch, combine, or optimize the robot controllers.

Alternative methodology to resolve them is based on semi-supervised or unsupervised learning with a generative model of measured data, like Gaussian mixture model (GMM) [14]. Data with unconfident annotation (segmentation) can be used for learning in an unsupervised manner. Outliers can be ignored according to likelihood of data. Similar clusters would be placed on close locations on (input or latent) space since classification is not main purpose in the generative model.

Jiang et al. [10] have proposed variational deep embedding, named VaDE, which assumes that inputs are stochastically generated from stochastic latent variables and GMM is given as prior of the latent variables It can adjust the control strategy according to continuous latent variables, not discrete (or stochastic) classified results. Continuity in control parameters (i.e., the latent variables) would enable robots to adjust the control strategy seamlessly, e.g., at transition between motions. However, two improvements in VaDE are still raised (see Fig. 1(a)). First is to employ a robust model to outliers instead of GMM, which is known to be sensitive to outliers. Another is that the continuity in latent space, where interpolation between latent variables corresponds to one between inputs, is not inherited in VaDE unlike variational autoencoder (VAE) [11] because each component of GMM can freely move over the latent space.

Hence, this paper proposes a new model, VaDE with regularized student-t mixture model (SMM) shown in Fig. 1(b), named VaDE-RT, to achieve the raised improvements. Instead of normal distribution and GMM, employing student-t distribution and its mixture as prior makes classification (i.e., deciding their locations) robust to outliers due to heaviness of tails, as known from previous work [12,19]. In addition, the prior is regularized by standard normal distribution, like VAE, to achieve the continuity in latent space by constraining the clusters' locations. This regularization is also expected to avoid over fitting. Here, it should be noticed that closed-form solutions of these two implementations are not exactly derived, and therefore, approximated forms proposed in previous work [4,6,20] are exploited in this paper.

To verify the performance of VaDE-RT, an experiment with a dataset for motion classification [15] are conducted. As a result, VaDE-RT outperforms the original VaDE and a simple classifier with GRUs [2] in terms of classification accuracy. In addition, it yields both continuity and natural topology of clusters in the latent space, which make controllers of robots adaptive smoothly.

2   Preliminaries

2.1   Variational Autoencoder

Let us briefly introduce the variational autoencoder (VAE) [11] to derive the variational deep embedding (VaDE) [10] in next section. Now, a generative model of inputs x from latent variables z is considered. It is called as a decoder and approximated by (deep) neural networks with parameters θ: $p(x \mid z; \theta)$. A purpose of VAE is to maximize the log likelihood of the generated inputs, $\log p(x)$, although its solution cannot be derived directly. Instead, evidence lower bound (ELBO) $\mathcal{L}_{ELBO}(x)$, which is derived by using Jensen's inequality and an encoder with parameters ϕ, $q(z \mid x; \phi)$, is maximized. $\mathcal{L}_{ELBO}(x)$ is derived below.

$$
\begin{aligned}
\log p(x) &= \log \int p(x \mid z; \theta) p(z) dz \\
&= \log \int \frac{q(z \mid x; \phi)}{q(z \mid x; \phi)} p(x \mid z; \theta) p(z) dz \\
&\geq \mathbb{E}_{q(z \mid x; \phi)} \left[\log \frac{p(x \mid z; \theta) p(z)}{q(z \mid x; \phi)} \right] \\
&=: \mathcal{L}_{ELBO}(x)
\end{aligned}
\tag{1}
$$

where $p(z)$ is a prior of latent variables.

Here, $\mathcal{L}_{ELBO}(x)$ can be summarized as follows:

$$
\mathcal{L}_{ELBO}(x) = \mathbb{E}_{q(z \mid x; \phi)}[\log p(x \mid z; \theta)] - \mathrm{KL}(q(z \mid x; \phi) \,\|\, p(z))
\tag{2}
$$

The first term corresponds to the negative reconstruction error in the autoencoder and the second term, i.e., Kullback-Leibler (KL) divergence between the posterior and the prior, is the regularization term to try to $z = p(z)$.

In the normal VAE, $p(z)$ is given as standard normal distribution $\mathcal{N}(0, I)$. To analytically solve the second term, the encoder $q(z \mid x; \phi)$ is also given as normal distribution $\mathcal{N}(\mu_z, \sigma_z^2 I)$ (its solution is described in Eq. (10)).

2.2   Variational Deep Embedding

In VaDE, the prior is given as Gaussian mixture model (GMM) with K components: $p(z) = \sum_{c=1}^{K} p(c) p(z \mid c)$. Here, $p(c)$ is the probability of each component, given as $\text{Cat}(c \mid \boldsymbol{\pi})$, and $p(\boldsymbol{z} \mid c)$ denotes the distribution in the latent space corresponding to each component, given as $\mathcal{N}(\boldsymbol{z} \mid \boldsymbol{\mu}_c, \sigma_c^2 I)$. Namely, a new latent variable c, which represents the cluster $\boldsymbol{z}$ belongs to, is added.

To solve $\mathcal{L}_{ELBO}(\boldsymbol{x})$ in this case, the encoder is firstly approximated by following mean-field approximation.

$$q(\boldsymbol{z}, c \mid \boldsymbol{x}; \boldsymbol{\phi}) = q(\boldsymbol{z} \mid \boldsymbol{x}; \boldsymbol{\phi}_z) q(c \mid \boldsymbol{x}; \boldsymbol{\phi}_c) \tag{3}$$

where $\boldsymbol{\phi}_z$ is the parameters of (deep) neural networks for the encoder, and $\boldsymbol{\phi}_c$ denotes $\{\boldsymbol{\pi}, \boldsymbol{\mu}_c, \boldsymbol{\sigma}_c\}$, $c \in \{1, \ldots, K\}$. Note that, unlike the normal VAE, the prior with $\boldsymbol{\phi}_c$ also be learned for appropriate classification.

Using the above approximation, $\mathcal{L}_{ELBO}(\boldsymbol{x})$ is derived as follows:

$$\mathcal{L}_{ELBO}(\boldsymbol{x}) = \mathbb{E}_{q(\boldsymbol{z}, c \mid \boldsymbol{x}; \boldsymbol{\phi})}[\log p(\boldsymbol{x} \mid \boldsymbol{z}; \boldsymbol{\theta})]$$
$$- \beta \sum_c \gamma_c \left\{ \log \frac{\gamma_c}{\pi_c} + \text{KL}(q(\boldsymbol{z} \mid \boldsymbol{x}; \boldsymbol{\phi}) \parallel p(\boldsymbol{z} \mid c)) \right\} \tag{4}$$

where a gain β is multiplied to cover β-VAE [7] for generality, so the original VaDE has $\beta = 1$. γ_c denotes $q(c \mid \boldsymbol{x}; \boldsymbol{\phi}_c)$, although it cannot be derived directly. In the original paper [10], therefore, γ_c is assumed to be the same as $p(c \mid \boldsymbol{z})$ to maximize $\mathcal{L}_{ELBO}(\boldsymbol{x})$, and is defined as follows:

$$\gamma_c := q(c \mid \boldsymbol{x}; \boldsymbol{\phi}_c) \simeq p(c \mid \boldsymbol{z}) = \frac{p(c) p(\boldsymbol{z} \mid c)}{\sum_{c'} p(c') p(\boldsymbol{z} \mid c')} \tag{5}$$

That is why $q(c \mid \boldsymbol{x}; \boldsymbol{\phi}_c)$ has the parameters $\boldsymbol{\phi}_c$. In this paper, semi-supervised learning is used for classification tasks. That is, please notice that γ_c is sometimes consistent with 1-of-K representation of the given label.

2.3 Weak Data Allocation to Components

The approximation of γ_c in Eq. (5) should be limited only when the relationship between $\boldsymbol{x}$ and $\boldsymbol{z}$ are clarified, ultimately as injective function. In real use cases, however, the encoder and the prior (and the decoder) are learned simultaneously from the gradient of $\mathcal{L}_{ELBO}(\boldsymbol{x})$, and therefore, it is clear that misclassification by this approximation, in particular in early-stage learning, adversely affects final classification performance. The original paper [10] used pre-training the encoder and the decoder and initializing the prior after that to suppress the misclassification, but it is not practical (e.g., infeasible in incremental learning).

Instead of it, the gain β introduced in β-VAE [7] is now simply designed. To this end, a feature in this system is paid attention: the samples of $\boldsymbol{z}$ in early-stage learning would have large variance, and they would concentrate on their mean $\boldsymbol{\mu}_z$ as learning progresses. That is, β can simply be designed from $q(\boldsymbol{z} \mid \boldsymbol{x}; \boldsymbol{\phi}_z)$ as follows:

$$\beta = \begin{cases} \beta_{\max} & \text{If label is given} \\ \beta_{\max} \frac{q(\boldsymbol{z} \mid \boldsymbol{x}; \boldsymbol{\phi}_z)}{p_{\max}} & \text{Otherwise} \end{cases} \tag{6}$$

where $\beta_{\max}$ is maximum strength of regularization (1 in this paper for simplicity) and $p_{\max}$ is the normalization term for integrating probability density function as 1 (e.g., $((2\pi)^d|\Sigma|)^{-1/2}$ in d-dimensional multivariate normal distribution with variance Σ). By multiplying β to the KL divergence in $\mathcal{L}_{ELBO}(\boldsymbol{x})$, the adverse effect of misclassification is expected to be suppressed.

3   Proposed Method

3.1   Variational Deep Embedding with Student-t Mixture Model

In VAE (and VaDE), the prior of the latent variables is assumed as (mixture of) normal distribution. Two main reasons for this assumption are raised: easy implementation of reparameterization trick, which enables the gradient from the decoder to backpropagate into the encoder [11]; and closed-form solution of KL divergence between normal distributions (see Eq. (10)). In terms of clustering, however, a more robust stochastic model, e.g., SMM [19] is desired since GMM is sensitive to outliers.

Hence, the use of student-t distribution instead of normal distribution would be effective in VaDE, although VAE with the prior of student-t distribution has not been implemented so far. This paper then introduces two approximations to the reparameterization trick and KL divergence between student-t distributions. Here, they are approximated to naturally include normal distribution, which is a special case of student-t distribution (i.e., when degrees of freedom ν is ∞).

Approximated Reparameterization Trick. Samples drawn from probability distribution directly would cut computational graphs since chain rule is no longer applied. The reparameterization trick, which draws samples by combining the parameters of probability distribution and random variables independent from them, can avoid this problem [11]. In the case of diagonal normal distribution $\mathcal{N}(\boldsymbol{\mu}_z, \sigma_z^2 I)$, which is employed in VAE and VaDE, the sample by the reparameterization trick, $\boldsymbol{z}$, is given as follows:

$$\boldsymbol{z} = \boldsymbol{\mu}_z + \boldsymbol{\sigma}_z \odot \boldsymbol{\epsilon} \qquad (7)$$
$$\boldsymbol{\epsilon} \sim \mathcal{N}(\boldsymbol{0}, I)$$

where $\odot$ is element-wise multiplier.

On the other hand, the sampling from student-t distribution $\mathcal{T}(\boldsymbol{\mu}_z, \sigma_z^2 I, \nu_z)$ is generally given as follows:

$$\boldsymbol{z} = \boldsymbol{\mu}_z + \sqrt{\frac{\nu_z}{\tau}} \boldsymbol{\sigma}_z \odot \boldsymbol{\epsilon} \qquad (8)$$
$$\boldsymbol{\epsilon} \sim \mathcal{N}(\boldsymbol{0}, I), \ \tau \sim \mathrm{Chi}(\nu_z)$$

where $\mathrm{Chi}(\nu_z)$ denotes chi-squared distribution with the degrees of freedom ν_z. As can be seen in this equation, chi-squared distribution depends on ν_z, that means backpropagation with regard to ν_z would be inappropriate if this goes on.

Hence, (approximated) reparameterization trick for chi-squared distribution is needed. Actually, several studies have proposed the approximation of chi-squared distribution to standard normal distribution [1,20], and recent one combined them to improve approximation accuracy [1]. Since approximation accuracy and calculation efficiency are in a tradeoff, one should be chosen from them. This paper therefore prioritizes calculation efficiency and chooses third root transformation proposed by Wilson et al. [20], as shown in below.

$$\mathcal{N}(0,1) \sim \epsilon_\tau \simeq \frac{\frac{\tau^{\frac{1}{3}}}{\nu_z} - \left(1 - \frac{2}{9\nu_z}\right)}{\sqrt{\frac{2}{9\nu_z}}}$$

$$\therefore \tau \simeq \nu_z \left(\sqrt{\frac{2}{9\nu_z}}\epsilon_\tau + 1 - \frac{2}{9\nu_z}\right)^3 \tag{9}$$

This approximation enables us to draw samples while keeping computational graphs. Note, however, that clipping is required if $\tau \simeq 0$ to stabilize calculation, although τ has its domain $[0, \infty)$. By substituting Eq. (9) into Eq. (8), the approximated reparameterization trick for student-t distribution is realized. In addition, Eq. (8) converges to the one for normal distribution in Eq. (7) when $\nu_z \to \infty$ since $\tau \to \nu_z$ (see Eq. (9)) and $\sqrt{\nu_z/\tau} \to 1$.

Approximated Kullback-Leibler Divergence. VaDE requires to compute $\mathrm{KL}(q(z \mid x; \phi) \| p(z \mid c))$ for its optimization. If both of the probability density functions are normal distributions, KL divergence has closed-form solution as follows:

$$\mathrm{KL}(\mathcal{N}(\mu_1, \Sigma_1) \| \mathcal{N}(\mu_2, \Sigma_2))$$
$$= \frac{1}{2}\left\{(\mu_2 - \mu_1)^\top \Sigma_2^{-1}(\mu_2 - \mu_1) + \mathrm{tr}(\Sigma_2^{-1}\Sigma_1) - \log|\Sigma_1||\Sigma_2|^{-1} - d\right\} \tag{10}$$

where d is dimension size of the latent space.

On the other hand, if both of them are student-t distributions, KL divergence, in particular its cross entropy component, has no closed-form solution. To solve it approximately, a naive approach is Monte Carlo method with many samples of z. This is infeasible to achieve sufficient accuracy and has no consistency with the normal VaDE with normal distribution.

Instead, an asymptotic form of KL divergence, which converges to the closed-form solution of the case with normal distribution when degrees of freedom is ∞, is employed. Reyes has proposed an following approximation by exploiting Taylor expansion to the cross entropy [4].

$$\mathrm{KL}(\mathcal{T}(\mu_1, \Sigma_1, \nu_1) \| \mathcal{T}(\mu_2, \Sigma_2, \nu_2))$$
$$= \frac{1}{2}\left\{C_2(\mu_2 - \mu_1)^\top \Sigma_2^{-1}(\mu_2 - \mu_1) + C_1 C_2 \mathrm{tr}(\Sigma_2^{-1}\Sigma_1) - \log|\Sigma_1||\Sigma_2|^{-1} - d_1\right\} \tag{11}$$

where,

$$C_1 = \nu_1/(\nu_1 - 2), \ C_2 = (\nu_2 + d)/\nu_2, \ d_1 = (\nu_1 + d)\{\psi((\nu_1 + d)/2) - \psi(\nu_1/2)\}$$

and $\psi(\cdot)$ is digamma function. Here, note that $\nu_1 > 2$ due to using the variance of student-t distribution, $\nu/(\nu - 2)\Sigma$, in the process of approximation. When $\nu_1, \nu_2 \to \infty$, $C_1, C_2 \to 1$ and d_1 converges to d, that is, Eq. (11) is consistent with KL divergence between normal distributions in Eq. (10).

3.2   Regularization to Prior

As a feature of VAE, interpolation of the latent variables z can generate interpolation of inputs x since almost z are aggregated within the range of standard normal distribution in the process of learning the reconstruction of x. Such a continuous latent space is useful. For instance, a method, which has supposed dynamics in the latent space as linear Gaussian state space model, has been proposed [5]. VaDE, however, has the variable prior of GMM, and therefore, continuity between clusters would not be guaranteed, although continuity in the same cluster may be obtained.

Hence, a soft constraint is added to the prior, $p(z) = \sum_c p(c)p(z \mid c)$, toward standard normal distribution given in VAE, $p_0(z) = \mathcal{N}(0, I) = \mathcal{T}(0, I, \infty)$. Specifically, this constraint is given as KL divergence between them as follows:

$$\mathrm{KL}(p(z) \parallel p_0(z)) \simeq \sum_c \pi_c \log \frac{\sum_{c'} \pi_{c'} e^{-\mathrm{KL}(p(z|c)\|p(z|c'))}}{e^{-\mathrm{KL}(p(z|c)\|p_0(z))}}$$

$$= \sum_c \pi_c \left\{ \log \sum_{c'} \pi_{c'} e^{-\mathrm{KL}(p(z|c)\|p(z|c'))} + \mathrm{KL}(p(z \mid c) \parallel p_0(z)) \right\}$$

$$(12)$$

where variational approximation [6] is exploited since KL divergence between mixture models are difficult to solve analytically. KL divergence between components (e.g., $\mathrm{KL}(p(z \mid c) \parallel p(z \mid c'))$) can be solved by Eq. (10) or Eq. (11) in accordance with the stochastic model, normal or student-t distribution.

This soft constraint is added into Eq. (4), and finally following $\mathcal{L}(x)$ will be maximized in learning process.

$$\mathcal{L}(x) = \mathbb{E}_{q(z,c|x;\phi)}[\log p(x \mid z; \theta)]$$

$$- \beta \sum_c \gamma_c \left\{ \log \frac{\gamma_c}{\pi_c} + \mathrm{KL}(q(z \mid x; \phi) \parallel p(z \mid c)) \right\}$$

$$- \beta \sum_c \pi_c \left\{ \lambda_n \log \sum_{c'} \pi_{c'} e^{-\mathrm{KL}(p(z|c)\|p(z|c'))} + \lambda_d \mathrm{KL}(p(z \mid c) \parallel p_0(z)) \right\}$$

$$(13)$$

where λ_n and λ_d denote hyperparameters. Actually, they should be the same as each other, but giving different values would enhance their own roles: the

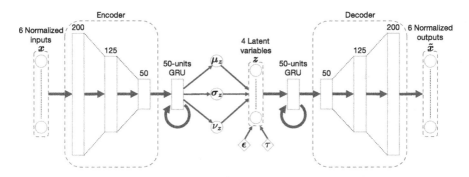

Fig. 2. Designed network structure: sequential data are encoded to the latent space with probability modeled as student-t distribution; the approximated reparameterization trick enables the whole network to learn parameters by backpropagation of $\mathcal{L}(x)$.

numerator is repulsive forces between components, making classification more prominent and; the denominator is attractive forces to standard normal distribution acting on all the components, resulting in continuity of the latent space. Therefore, $\lambda_n < \lambda_d$ is better for the tasks requiring continuity in the latent space, and $\lambda_n > \lambda_d$ is better for the tasks requiring classification only.

When $\lambda_n = \lambda_d = 1$, chained KL divergence [16] is established for minimization of $\beta\{\mathrm{KL}(q(z \mid x; \phi) \parallel p(z)) + \mathrm{KL}(p(z) \parallel p_0(z))\}$. In that case, the encoder is regularized to $p_0(z)$, which is the prior in the normal VAE, with weaker constraint than regularization in the normal VAE. Such a weakened constraint would give room to form clusters in the latent space.

4   Experiment

4.1   Dataset

As a dataset of human motion classification, the dataset including seven activities, i.e., bending1, bending2, cycling, lying, sitting, standing, and walking, is used (details are in ref. [15]). It can be downloaded from UCI Machine Learning Repository. Six inputs are given from three beacons, i.e., means and variances of received signal strength of respective sensors. This dataset is divided into 75% training data and 25% test data.

Each sequence of motion is annotated by hand, namely all the classification labels are actually correct. Hence, although this experiment assumes that only 50% of labels are correct and others are not used in learning process, it is possible to evaluate the classification accuracy for all the inputs. Note that learning with labels is conducted from 25% at the beginning and to the 75% at the end of sequences.

Table 1. Parameters for VaDE-RT in the experiment

Symbol	Meaning	Value
d	Dimension size of the latent space	4
K	The number of components	7
$\lambda_{n,d}$	Gains for regularization to standard normal distribution	1.0
γ_{norm}	Smoothness for online normalization	0.999
N_{trunc}	Mean of truncation length of backpropagation through time	10
ν_0	Minimum degree of freedom in student-t distribution	3.0
α_w	Learning rate for networks	1e-3
α_p	Learning rate for prior	1e-5
$\beta_{1,2}$	Hyperparameters for AMSGrad	[0.9, 0.999]
ϵ	Small number for computational stabilization	1e-6

4.2 Network Design

For generality, inputs x is normalized in online as follows:

$$\sigma_x \leftarrow \gamma_{\text{norm}}\sigma_x + \gamma_{\text{norm}}(1 - \gamma_{\text{norm}})(x - \mu_x)^2$$
$$\mu_x \leftarrow \gamma_{\text{norm}}\mu_x + (1 - \gamma_{\text{norm}})x \tag{14}$$
$$x \leftarrow \frac{x - \mu_x}{\sigma_x}$$

where μ_x and σ_x^2 are means and variances of inputs, respectively. γ_{norm} denotes the hyperparameter for update speed. Note that outputs of the decoder aim to reconstruct inputs after this normalization.

Since all x in the used dataset are given as real values, Laplace distribution with fixed scale I is employed as the decoder $p(x \mid z; \theta)$, although normal distribution with fixed scale $I/2$ is common. In that case, outputs from the decoder $\tilde{x}$ correspond to location and $\mathbb{E}_{q(z,c\mid x;\phi)}[\log p(x \mid z; \theta)]$ in Eq. (13) is approximated by Monte Carlo method as negative L1 norm.

$$\mathbb{E}_{q(z,c\mid x;\phi)}[\log p(x \mid z; \theta)] \simeq -\|x - \tilde{x}\|_1 \tag{15}$$

With the benefit of L1 norm, the reconstruction is robust to outliers, in particular, reconstructed from extreme z drawn by student-t distribution.

To handle the sequential data, two 50-units GRUs [2] as recurrent networks are inserted before and after the latent space, respectively. In addition, truncated backpropagation through time [17] is employed to reduce computational cost, although new truncation lengths are drawn from Poisson distribution with a mean of N_{trunc} every after truncation.

The above network structure is illustrated in Fig. 2, and related parameters are described in Table 1. Learning of the prior is performed directly, unlike learning of outputs via weights of connections between neurons, hence, it is desirable

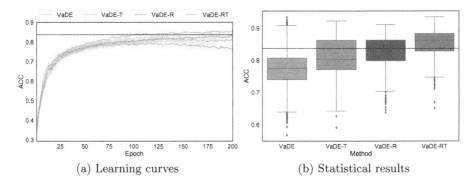

(a) Learning curves   (b) Statistical results

Fig. 3. Learning results: dashed lines denote the mean accuracy of the case using a direct classifier with two 50-units GRUs; SMM improved the classification accuracy, while the regularization allowed the networks to avoid over fitting, that was implied by reducing variance; as a result, VaDE-RT using both of them outperformed the baseline and even the direct classifier.

for stable learning to set the smaller learning rate α_p than the one for the weights α_w. The latent space size d is set to be four-dimensional, that is smaller than the input dimension (i.e., six dimensions) and sufficient to represent human motions empirically, although the rule to define the latent space is still one of the open problems. Note that ELU [3] and AMSGrad [18] are employed as activation function in the networks and stochastic gradient decent for learning, respectively. The initial states of components are determined by variational Bayesian GMM [14] for latent variables generated from the training data given to the untrained network.

For comparison, VaDE as a baseline, VaDE-T only with SMM, and VaDE-R only with the regularization to standard normal distribution learn the same dataset. Note that their parameters are the same as the proposal, i.e., VaDE-RT. 50 trials with each method are conducted to evaluate the statistical classification accuracy.

4.3   Results

Learning curves and statistical box plots, which are evaluated from the last 10 epochs in all the trials, are depicted in Fig. 3. Note that dashed lines in both figures denote the mean accuracy of the case using a direct classifier (i.e., its outputs correspond to the probabilities of respective classes) with two 50-units GRUs. It is inappropriate for future purpose to utilize the latent space for the robot control, thereby only drawing the dashed lines as a reference record. As can be seen, both SMM and the regularization to standard normal distribution improved the classification accuracy, and naturally, the proposal, VaDE-RT with both of them outperformed the other methods including the direct classifier.

To visualize the latent space, a nonlinear dimensionality reduction method, named UMAP [13], which is good at preserving aspects of global structure of the

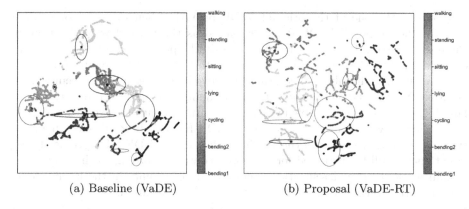

(a) Baseline (VaDE)   (b) Proposal (VaDE-RT)

Fig. 4. Visualization of the latent space: nonlinear dimensionality reduction, named UMAP [13], which is good at preserving aspects of global structure of the data, was applied to visualize the latent space; a red circle with a star on its center denotes standard normal distribution, and the other circles denote the components of the prior; (b) in VaDE-RT, the clusters of the classified motions were placed on natural topology while shrinking the gaps between them to achieve continuity in the latent space. (Color figure online)

data, is applied (see Fig. 4). Please note that circles in the figures are drawn by $\mu_z \pm 2\sigma_z$, so they would be actually distorted due to the nonlinear dimensionality reduction, although they would sufficiently help our understanding. Although both sampled cases achieved over 90% classification accuracy, their latent spaces were obviously developed to different shapes. In VaDE, dissimilar clusters were partially placed on next to each other with gaps: e.g., walking and bending2 that is more similar to cycling than walking. In contrast, VaDE-RT developed more natural topology than VaDE. Namely, static motions (i.e., standing, sitting, and lying) were on the left, periodic motions (i.e., walking and cycling) were on the upper right, and bending motions were on the lower right. Furthermore, the similar motions with sitting posture in such groups (i.e., sitting, cycling, and bending2) were connected on the center. As another feature, the latent space developed by VaDE-RT had small gaps between the clusters, in other words, it may have continuity.

5   Conclusion

This paper proposed a new variational autoencoder for motion classification, which employed the regularized SMM as the prior, named VaDE-RT. To this end, the three approximations were introduced: (i) approximation of chi-squared distribution using standard normal distribution for reparameterization trick; (ii) approximation of KL divergence between student-t distributions for robust classification; and (iii) approximation of KL divergence of the mixture model for regularization to achieve continuity in the latent space. All the approximations converge to the one of the original VaDE or VAE when $\nu_z \to \infty$ or $c = 1$. Namely, the proposal, VaDE-RT, is regarded as the natural generalization of the previous work. In the experiment to verify the performance of VaDE-RT, it outperformed the baselines. In particular, both SMM and the regularization to standard normal distribution certainly improved the classification accuracy. In addition, VaDE-RT could achieve both continuity and natural topology in the latent space, which are suitable for using the optimal control for versatile robots.

As future work, the performance of VaDE-RT will be confirmed in many types of datasets to increase the validity. After that, VaDE-RT, specifically its latent space, will be exploited for the robot control according to the respective human motions. The classification accuracy and continuity in the latent space will make the controller properly and smoothly be optimized.

References

1. Canal, L.: A normal approximation for the chi-square distribution. Comput. Stat. Data Anal. **48**(4), 803–808 (2005)
2. Chung, J., Gulcehre, C., Cho, K., Bengio, Y.: Empirical evaluation of gated recurrent neural networks on sequence modeling. arXiv preprint arXiv:1412.3555 (2014)
3. Clevert, D.A., Unterthiner, T., Hochreiter, S.: Fast and accurate deep network learning by exponential linear units (ELUs). In: International Conference on Learning Representations (2016)
4. Contreras-Reyes, J.E.: Asymptotic form of the Kullback-Leibler divergence for multivariate asymmetric heavy-tailed distributions. Phys. A **395**, 200–208 (2014)
5. Fraccaro, M., Kamronn, S., Paquet, U., Winther, O.: A disentangled recognition and nonlinear dynamics model for unsupervised learning. In: Advances in Neural Information Processing Systems, pp. 3601–3610 (2017)
6. Hershey, J.R., Olsen, P.A.: Approximating the Kullback Leibler divergence between Gaussian mixture models. In: IEEE International Conference on Acoustics, Speech and Signal Processing, vol. 4, pp. 317–320. IEEE (2007)
7. Higgins, I., et al.: Beta-VAE: learning basic visual concepts with a constrained variational framework. In: International Conference on Learning Representations (2017)
8. Hochreiter, S., Schmidhuber, J.: Long short-term memory. Neural Comput. **9**(8), 1735–1780 (1997)
9. Itadera, S., Kobayashi, T., Nakanishi, J., Aoyama, T., Hasegawa, Y.: Impedance control based assistive mobility aid through online classification of user's state. In: IEEE/SICE International Symposium on System Integration, pp. 243–248 (2019)
10. Jiang, Z., Zheng, Y., Tan, H., Tang, B., Zhou, H.: Variational deep embedding: an unsupervised and generative approach to clustering. In: International Joint Conference on Artificial Intelligence, pp. 1965–1972 (2017)
11. Kingma, D.P., Welling, M.: Auto-encoding variational bayes. In: International Conference on Learning Representations (2014)
12. Kobayashi, T.: Student-t policy in reinforcement learning to acquire global optimum of robot control. Applied Intelligence (2019). Online first
13. McInnes, L., Healy, J., Saul, N., Grossberger, L.: UMAP: uniform manifold approximation and projection. J. Open Source Softw. **3**(29), 861 (2018)

14. Nasios, N., Bors, A.G.: Variational learning for Gaussian mixture models. IEEE Trans. Syst. Man Cybern. Part B (Cybern.) **36**(4), 849–862 (2006)
15. Palumbo, F., Gallicchio, C., Pucci, R., Micheli, A.: Human activity recognition using multisensor data fusion based on reservoir computing. J. Ambient Intell. Smart Environ. **8**(2), 87–107 (2016)
16. Pavlichin, D.S., Weissman, T.: Chained Kullback-Leibler divergences. In: IEEE International Symposium on Information Theory, pp. 580–584. IEEE (2016)
17. Puskorius, G., Feldkamp, L.: Truncated backpropagation through time and Kalman filter training for neurocontrol. In: IEEE International Conference on Neural Networks, vol. 4, pp. 2488–2493. IEEE (1994)
18. Reddi, S.J., Kale, S., Kumar, S.: On the convergence of Adam and beyond. In: International Conference on Learning Representations (2018)
19. Svensén, M., Bishop, C.M.: Robust Bayesian mixture modelling. Neurocomputing **64**, 235–252 (2005)
20. Wilson, E.B., Hilferty, M.M.: The distribution of chi-square. Proc. Natl. Acad. Sci. U. S. A. **17**(12), 684 (1931)

A Mixture-of-Experts Model for Vehicle Prediction Using an Online Learning Approach

Florian Mirus[1,2]([⊠])[iD], Terrence C. Stewart[3], Chris Eliasmith[3][iD],
and Jörg Conradt[4][iD]

[1] Research, New Technologies, Innovations, BMW Group,
Parkring 19, 85748 Garching, Germany
florian.mirus@bmwgroup.com
[2] Department of Electrical and Computer Engineering,
Technical University of Munich, Theresienstr. 90, 80333 Munich, Germany
[3] Applied Brain Research Inc.,
118 Woodbend Crescent, Waterloo, ON N2T 1G9, Canada
{terry.stewart,chris.eliasmith}@appliedbrainresearch.com
[4] Department of Computational Science and Technology,
KTH Royal Institute of Technology, Stockholm, Sweden
jconradt@kth.se,
http://www.bmwgroup.com

Abstract. Predicting future motion of other vehicles or, more generally, the development of traffic situations, is an essential step towards secure, context-aware automated driving. On the one hand, human drivers are able to anticipate driving situations continuously based on the currently perceived behavior of other traffic participants while incorporating prior experience. On the other hand, the most successful data-driven prediction models are typically trained on large amounts of recorded data before deployment achieving remarkable results. In this paper, we present a mixture-of-experts online learning model encapsulating both ideas. Our system learns at run time to choose between several models, which have been previously trained offline, based on the current situational context. We show that our model is able to improve over the offline models already after a short ramp-up phase. We evaluate our system on real world driving data.

Keywords: Vehicle prediction · Online learning ·
Long short-term memory · Spiking neural networks

1 Introduction

Predicting future behavior and positions of other traffic participants from observations is essential for collision avoidance and thus safe motion planning. Such prediction needs to be performed by human drivers and automated vehicles alike

© Springer Nature Switzerland AG 2019
I. V. Tetko et al. (Eds.): ICANN 2019, LNCS 11729, pp. 456–471, 2019.
https://doi.org/10.1007/978-3-030-30508-6_37

to reach their desired goal. Most state-of-the-art approaches to behavior prediction in an automotive context are data-driven and apply neural networks to learn to predict future motion from a large number of examples. Typically, such models employ LSTM (Long Short-Term Memory)-based network architectures [13] to forecast future vehicle motion based on a sequence of prior positions, and are trained offline on a substantial amount of data. In contrast, human drivers make predictions about potential future motion of other vehicles around them continuously based on the currently perceived behavior, by incorporating prior experience about vehicle motion in general. In previous work [19], we investigated several instantiations of LSTM-based models by varying the representation of the input data, and compared them to simpler prediction approaches. We found, that the prediction performance (i.e., which model performs best) changes significantly depending not only on the current driving situation but also on the prediction horizon.

In this paper, we therefore investigate a mixture-of-experts online learning model to select between several offline trained models to achieve the best possible forecast. Importantly, this model is intended to be trained online, i.e., continuously updating its weights based on the data received at run time. One of the advantages of such an approach is that instead of starting the model from a completely blank state, the individual predictors used as inputs for the mixture model already learned a consistent prior during their offline training. Furthermore, the possibility of the offline models being validated in advance and serving as a fallback option in case the online model fails during deployment, is an additional advantage in a safety-critical domain such as automated driving. Finally, the implementation of our approach employing the classic delta rule as well as the possibility to use spiking neuron models allows future deployment on dedicated neuromorphic hardware, which offers interesting possibilities regarding energy efficiency, especially in mobile applications and automotive context. However, any online learning system making predictions about the future poses additional challenges. For instance, the actual motion of the target vehicle and thus the error signal to update the neural weights is unknown at prediction time, but rather becomes available while the agent continues driving. The temporally delayed error signal potentially introduces long lags between the prediction and the update of the corresponding weights. In this paper, we address this issue through a temporal spreading of the error signal, i.e., we use the error of earlier prediction steps to update the weights of predictions further into the future. We evaluate our online learning model on real-world driving data and show, that the model is able to improve over the individual offline models already after being presented just a few vehicles.

1.1 Related Work

Motion prediction for intelligent vehicles in general has seen extensive research in recent years, as it is a cornerstone for collision-free automated driving [20]. Typically, vehicle trajectory prediction approaches are classified into three categories, namely *physics-based*, *maneuver-based* and *interaction-aware* [15]. *Physics-based* and *maneuver-based* motion models consider the law of physics and the intended driving maneuver respectively as the only influencing factors for future vehicle motion and ignore inter-dependencies between the motion of different vehicles. On the other hand, there exist a growing number of different *interaction-aware* approaches to account for those dependencies and mutual influences between traffic participants. Probabilistic models like cost maps [3] account for physical constraints on the movements of the other vehicles. Classification approaches categorize and represent scenes in a hierarchy [5] based on the most generic ones to predict behavior for a variety of different situations. Data-driven approaches to behavior prediction mainly rely on LSTM neural network architectures [13], which have proven to be a powerful tool for sequential data analysis. LSTM-models are currently the most successful approaches and therefore the state-of-the-art regarding trajectory prediction. The authors in [2] use a LSTM network and account for interactions by including distances between the target vehicle and other agents directly in the training data. The authors of [8] combine LSTM networks with an additional maneuver classification network to predict future vehicle motion. In [7], there are several LSTM networks used to encode vehicle trajectories, (convolutional) social-pooling layers to account for interactions between the vehicles, and a maneuver-based LSTM decoder to predict vehicle trajectories in highway situations.

Common to all the aforementioned approaches is the fact that the models are trained offline on batched data and remain unchanged during deployment. In contrast, incremental or online learning approaches, which attempt to tackle learning tasks by processing sequential data one at a time, gained growing interest as an attractive alternative to update learning models during deployment. This approach is particularly interesting in the context of big data and in situations, where the system needs to learn from continuously incoming data streams and a complete data set during offline training is not available. There exists an increasing number of online learning approaches in several problem domains (see [11, 16] or [14] for a comprehensive overview of the field). However, such models adapting their (neural) weights at run time through online learning are rather rarely investigated in automotive context due to safety considerations, issues with convergences time as well as the lack of proofs/guarantees that the models converge at all. The model presented in [18] uses self-supervised online learning to recognize, classify and add new maneuvers of the ego-vehicle at run time. The approach employed in [12] uses case-based reasoning to learn to predict driving behavior for specific driving situations, namely intersection scenarios. In [17], the authors employ incremental learning to personalize maneuver prediction at intersections. An alternative approach to combining several weak learning models such as stumps or smoothing splines through an averaging scheme is boosting [21], which offers superior performance over the individual learners. While the type of online learning approach employed in this paper has been shown to be successful in adaptive robot arm control [9], to the best of our knowledge, our approach is the first trajectory prediction model to be trained during deployment for choosing from several pre-trained prediction models to achieve the best possible forecast.

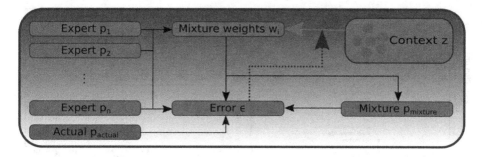

Fig. 1. Schematic visualization of the architecture of our mixture-of-experts online learning model. The red arrow indicates the learning connection with changing decoder values $\mathbf{d}_{p,t,i}$, whereas the dotted green arrow indicates that the error signal ε is temporally delayed and is used to update the decoders $\mathbf{d}_{p,t,i}$ of the red connection. (Color figure online)

2   Mixture-of-Experts Models

The online training we are investigating in this paper does not involve re-training the individual offline models in any way. Rather, we combine their predictions using a simple weighted sum, and we apply online training to learn these weights and how they differ depending on the context. That is, in some conditions one expert should be weighted more highly than in other conditions, and we want to adapt this weighting based on experience. The core weighting algorithm is given by

$$\mathbf{v}_{mix,t} = \sum_p \mathbf{W}_{p,t} \mathbf{v}_{p,t}, \tag{1}$$

where $\mathbf{v}_{p,t}$ is the predicted value for time t into the future from offline model p (i.e., the position of the target vehicle at time t as anticipated by model p), and $\mathbf{W}_{p,t}$ is the weight for expert p for a prediction time of t. Note that the weighting between the expert predictions may be different depending on how far into the future we are predicting. Crucially, we believe that the ideal weights will depend on some aspects of the current situation (i.e., the current context). Now our goal is to use this context information $\mathbf{z}$ to generate the weights $\mathbf{W}$. To do this, we use a simple single hidden-layer neural network. That is, we input the $\mathbf{z}$ values into N neurons (encoding), and the output of the network (decoding) will be the $\mathbf{W}$ values for the current context. The encoding process (the input weights for the neural network) is given by

$$\mathbf{a}_i = \mathbf{G}\left(\sum_j \mathbf{e}_{i,j} \mathbf{z}_j + \beta_i\right) \tag{2}$$

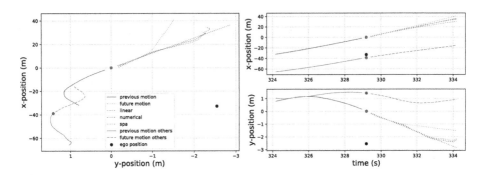

Fig. 2. One example from the *On-board* data-set depicting a particular driving situation as well as the predictions made by each individual offline model used as input for our mixture-of-experts model. The dots indicate the position of the vehicles and color-code the vehicle type (red = motorcycle, green = car, blue = truck, black = ego-vehicle), the solid blue and dotted orange line show past and future motion of the target vehicle, dotted colored lines visualize the predictions of the offline models whereas gray lines depict the other vehicles' motion. (Color figure online)

converting $\mathbf{z}$ into the activity $\mathbf{a}_i$ of the ith neuron. $\mathbf{G}$ is the neuron non-linearity, $\mathbf{e}_{i,j}$ and β_i are randomly generated to produce a uniformly distributed range of maximum firing rates and intercepts (the $\mathbf{z}$ value at which the neuron starts firing), as per [10]. This has been shown to be a good distribution of values for a wide variety of situations, and is consistent with what is observed in mammalian brains [10]. Unlike most neural network models, since these input weights are a reasonable distribution, we do not change $\mathbf{e}_{i,j}$ and β_i at any time, leaving them at their initial randomly generated values. In other words, we only adjust the weights between the hidden layer and the output layer, and leave the other set of weights at their initial randomly generated values. This greatly reduces the computation cost of performing the online learning. Given the neural activity $\mathbf{a}_i$, we now use

$$\mathbf{W}_{p,t} = \sum_i \mathbf{d}_{p,t,i} \mathbf{a}_i \qquad (3)$$

to decode the $\mathbf{W}$ values for the current context $\mathbf{z}$. We initialize the $\mathbf{d}$ values such that there is an equal weighting across all the expert predictions (i.e., $\mathbf{W}_{p,t} = 1/N_p$ where N_p is the number of prediction models being combined, for all context $\mathbf{z}$). The $\mathbf{d}$ values achieving this equal weighting are found using least-squares minimization.

Now that we have this system for generating context-dependent weights, we can use online learning to adjust $\mathbf{d}$ to change the weights $\mathbf{W}$ based on the accuracy of the predictions. While any neural network learning algorithm could be used to do this, we adapt the classic delta learning rule, which is the basis of all gradient-descent learning algorithms, for the sake of simplicity and ease of implementation:

$$\Delta \mathbf{W}_{p,t} = \kappa \nu_t \mathbf{v}_{p,t} \underbrace{\left(\mathbf{v}_{observed,t} - \mathbf{v}_{mix,t} \right)}_{= \varepsilon_t} = \kappa \nu_t \mathbf{v}_{p,t} \varepsilon_t. \tag{4}$$

Equation (4) shows the classic delta learning rule that would determine how much to adjust $\mathbf{W}$ given the current error ε_t between the mixture-of-experts prediction and the observed actual position of the vehicle (i.e., the error in $\mathbf{v}$). κ is the learning rate and ν_t is a factor to scale the learning rate κ differently for each prediction time step. However, rather than applying that change to $\mathbf{W}$ directly, we instead use that as the error signal for the delta rule applied to the decoding network, turning an adjustment to $\mathbf{W}$ into an adjustment to $\mathbf{d}$:

$$\Delta \mathbf{d}_{p,t,i} = \kappa \mathbf{a}_i \nu_t \mathbf{v}_{p,t} \varepsilon_t = \mathbf{a}_i \Delta \mathbf{W}_{p,t} \tag{5}$$

Figure 1 shows a schematic visualization of our model's architecture. The solid red line indicates the connection to decode out the weights $\mathbf{W}_{p,t}$ for the individual expert predictors from the neural population encoding the context $\mathbf{z}$. The dotted green line indicates the (delayed) error signal ε_t used to update the decoders $\mathbf{d}_{p,t,i}$ of the connection between the context population and the expert weights.

2.1 Temporal Spreading of the Error Signal

One extremely important consideration for any online updating of a predictive model (i.e., one where it is generating anticipated future observations) is that the error signal is only available in the future. That is, we can only apply Eq. (5) after the amount of time t has occurred. This introduces a long lag into the learning process. We illustrate this issue using an example situation showing the predictions of the individual offline models depicted in Fig. 2. In this example, all individual models predict the target vehicle's motion in y-direction almost perfectly until a prediction horizon of roughly 2.5 s when the predictions start to deviate from the actual motion. Assuming a similar situation for a model employing an online learning approach, the weights for the current prediction 2.5 s into the future can only be updated after 2.5 s have passed. For all prediction time-steps further into the future, we have to wait even longer while the error between the prediction and the actual motion potentially increases even more. In the meantime, the model is doomed to make predictions for these future time-steps based on sub-optimal weights based on past learning updates. However, the example depicted in Fig. 2 also hints, that the error at 2.5 s could already be used to update weights further into the future as, although the error increases, the general *direction* of the deviation between predictions and actual motion remains the same. In other words, we assume that if our system is currently predicting too large a value at time t, then it is likely also to be predicting too large a value at time $\tilde{t} > t$. That is, whenever we have an observation at time t that we compare with the prediction made t time steps ago, we can also apply Eq. (5) for all the larger values as well, i.e., we apply Eq. (5) for all $\tilde{t}$ with $\tilde{t} > t$ once the amount of time t has passed. Since this is just an estimation, we want the predictions for time steps $\tilde{t}$ further into the future than t be less influenced by the error at t. Hence, we exponentially scale down the amount of adjustment of $\mathbf{d}$ by the difference in time $\tilde{t} - t$, leading to our final learning rule:

$$\Delta \mathbf{d}_{p,\tilde{t},i} = \kappa \mathbf{a}_i \nu_t \mathbf{v}_{p,t} (\mathbf{v}_{observed,t} - \mathbf{v}_{mix,t}) e^{-(\tilde{t}-t)/\tau} \quad \text{for all } \tilde{t} \geq t. \quad (6)$$

3 Experiments

There are two subsequent algorithmic steps in this paper, namely motion prediction using offline trained models and online learning employing our mixture-of-experts model. Here, we describe the data-sets and both, the preprocessing steps conducted to prepare the data for the offline models and the input data to the online mixture-of-experts model. In this paper, we use the output of three different prediction models as input for our mixture-of-experts online learning model. Each offline model's output is anticipated positions of the target vehicle in x- and y-direction for the next 5 s into the future. The individual predictors are a simple *linear* prediction model based on a constant velocity assumption and two LSTM-based neural networks, referred to as *SPA* and *numerical*, consisting of one encoder and one decoder cell each. These models differ in the encoding of the input data: the *numerical* model uses raw numerical values of the target vehicle's position during the past 5 s, whereas the other employs a semantic vector encoding based on the SPA (Semantic Pointer Architecture) using convolutive vector-powers. Hence, the input to the *SPA* model is a sequence of vectors encapsulating the positions of the target vehicle as well as other vehicles within a certain distance to the target vehicle during the past 5 s (see [19] for details).

We present results from two variants of our mixture-of-experts model. Firstly, we evaluate a simplified version (cf. Sect. 3.2), which applies Eq. (5) directly at prediction time assuming that the error signal, which is future data, is actually available already at prediction time. The benefit of this prior evaluation is twofold: on the one hand, we get an impression what benefits can be expected from using context information over the context-free variant before employing the more sophisticated, timing-sensitive model. On the other hand, a model having immediate access to the future error signal serves as an upper bound for the performance to be expected from models that have to deal with temporally delayed error signals (cf. Sect. 3.3). Both versions are implemented using the neural simulator Nengo [4], which is typically used for constructing large-scale biologically realistic neural models [10], but also allows for traditional feed-forward artificial neural networks using either spiking or non-spiking neurons. Here, we use the rate-approximation of the Leaky Integrate and Fire neuron, although we expect any other neuron model to have similar behavior. Spiking neurons are of considerable interest for automotive applications due to the potential for reduced power consumption when deployed on dedicated neuromorphic hardware.

3.1 Data and Preprocessing

In this paper, we use two different data-sets for training and evaluation of our system, which we refer to as *On-board* or D_1 and *NGSIM* or D_2. The *On-board*

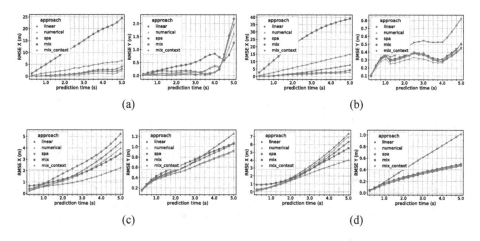

(a)   (b)

(c)   (d)

Fig. 3. Visualization of the RMSE of the timing-agnostic mixture-of-experts model variants on both data-sets. (a) shows the performance at the start of the training process on the *On-board* data-set. (b) shows the performance at the start of the training process on the *NGSIM* data-set. Similarly, (c) shows the models' performance on the first 70 vehicles of the *On-board* data-set, whereas Fig. (d) show the models' performance on the first 92 vehicles of the *NGSIM* data-set.

data-set contains real-world data gathered using the vehicle's on-board sensors (see [1] for details on the vehicle's sensor setup) during test drives mainly on highways in southern Germany for a total of 3891 vehicles, which yield a total length of roughly 28.3 h. The NGSIM (Next Generation Simulation) US-101 data-set [6] is a publicly available trajectory data-set extracted from video footage recorded with cameras observing traffic from rooftops on a segment of the US-101 freeway in Los Angeles, California. It consists of 5930 vehicles and therefore a total time of roughly 91.3 h when adding up the time each individual vehicle is visible. Both data-sets contain object lists with information about motion and behavior of the dynamic objects in the scene such as position, velocity and acceleration as well as the type and the current lane for each vehicle. The main difference between the data sets is that the *NGSIM* data-set is recorded with external stationary cameras instead of on-board sensors of a driving vehicle as in the *On-board* data-set. Thus, there is no ego-vehicle present in the *NGSIM* data-set and all information are available in absolute coordinates, whereas all information in the *On-board* data-set are measured relative to the ego-vehicle and its coordinate system.

Preprocessing for Offline Models. The offline models predict positions of dynamic objects 5 s into the future based on their positions 5 s prior to their current location. As the two data-sets are sampled at different frequencies, we interpolate the available data over 20 equidistant steps to achieve intervals of 0.25 s to improve consistency and comparability. Furthermore, we translate the current position of the target vehicle (the vehicle to be predicted) into the origin, i.e., position $(0,0)$, to prevent our models from treating similar trajectories

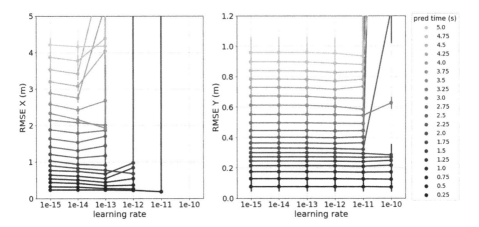

Fig. 4. Visualization of the RMSE performance of our mixture-of-experts model with 100 neurons in the context population for different learning rates κ and learning scale factors ν_t linearly decreasing from 1 down to 0.001 over the 20 prediction steps. The figures show the RMSE performance for each prediction time step into the future on two test runs evaluating a different randomly chosen set of test vehicles for longitudinal (x) and lateral (y) direction separately.

differently due to positional variations. Finally, to improve suitability of the data as input for neural networks, we divide all x-positions by a factor of 10 such that x-/y-values are scaled to a similar order of magnitude. We split both data-sets into training $T_i \subset D_i$ and test data $V_i \subset D_i$ containing 90% and 10% of the objects respectively with $T_i \cap V_i = \varnothing$, where only vehicles in T_i have been used to train the individual offline predictors.

Input to the Mixture-Model. The output of each individual offline prediction model is anticipated positions in x- and y-direction at 20 equidistant time steps t_i for $i = 1, \ldots, 20$ for 5 s into the future, i.e., $t_1 = 0.25, t_2 = 0.5, \ldots, t_{20} = 5.0$, which we use unaltered and without any further preprocessing as input for our mixture model. Figure 2 shows one data sample from the *On-board* data-set depicting the input data to the offline models (previous motion) as well as each model's individual predictions, which are the input to the mixture model. In other words, the dotted lines in Fig. 2 depicting the predictions of the *linear*, *SPA* and *numerical* models form the input of the mixture-of-experts online learning model. During the evaluation runs of our mixture models, we only use vehicles from the test sets V_1 and V_2 to avoid presenting vehicles to the system the individual offline predictors have already been trained on.

Contextual Information Used in the Mixture-Model. In contrast to the anticipated positions predicted by each offline model we use as input to our mixture-of-experts model as described in the previous section, here we present the information used to describe the current driving situation, i.e., the contextual information encoded in the context population of our model. While this context could be described in many different ways, we focus on the following three pieces of information for the context-sensitive models in this work:

- z_1: the current distance from the car to the ego-vehicle (if available)
- z_2: the current distance from the car to the nearest other car (including the ego-vehicle)
- z_3: the number of cars currently visible

In earlier work [19], we found that this contextual information shows significant differences depending on which of the offline models performs best. Hence, we use these values in this work to describe the context of the current driving situation and leave a more in-depth evaluation of potential alternatives regarding the contextual input to the mixture models for future work. Finally, we use the training data to normalize the context values and use their z-scores as context for our online learning model.

3.2 Evaluation of the Timing-Agnostic Model Variant

Experimental Setup. In this section, we evaluate a simplified version of our mixture-of-experts online learning model, which ignores the fact that the actual vehicle motion and thus the error signal for the weight updates is not available at prediction time. Instead, we assume that Eq. (5) can be applied directly at prediction time to update the weights. The context-free version updates its weights solely based on the prediction error, which is equivalent to the context-sensitive model if the context is kept constant. The context-sensitive model variant evaluated in this section contains 3000 neurons in the neural population encoding the driving context. To limit the simulation time, we exposed only a subset of 70 vehicles from the *On-board* test set V_1 and 92 vehicles from *NGSIM* the test set V_2 to the models.

Results. Figure 3 shows the results of the timing-agnostic variants of the context-free and context-sensitive mixture-of-experts online learning models on both data-sets. Figure 3a and c show the models' performance on the *On-board* data-set at the start of training (3a) and for the complete set of 70 evaluation vehicles from V_1 (3c), whereas Fig. 3b and d similarly depict the models' performance on the *NGSIM* data-set at the start of training and for all 92 evaluation vehicles respectively. We observe in Fig. 3a and b that both, the context-free and context-sensitive mixture models perform poorly at the start of training (which makes sense due to the randomly initialized weights), but improve significantly and consistently on both data-sets (Fig. 3c and d) after having received more data. The context-free version yields mild improvements over all individual predictors in x-direction without improving over the best individual model in y-direction. The context-sensitive variant outperforms all other models (including the context-free version) in x-direction while being on par with the best individual predictors in y-direction, hence we focus our efforts for the timing-sensitive mixture models on this variant.

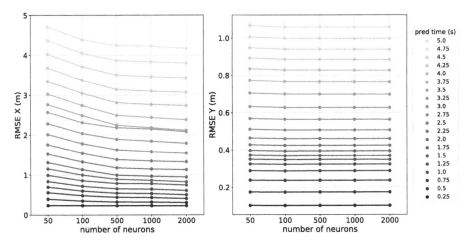

Fig. 5. Visualization of the RMSE performance of our context-sensitive mixture-of-experts model using temporal spreading for varying numbers of neurons in the context population on 30 test vehicles after being exposed to 5 vehicles. The learning rate used in this evaluation is set to $\kappa = 10^{15}$ and scaling factors ν_t decreasing linearly from 1 down to 0.001 over the 20 prediction time steps. The figure shows the RMSE performance for each prediction time step into the future and longitudinal (x) and lateral (y) direction separately.

3.3   Evaluation of the Context-Sensitive Model Variant with Temporal Spreading

In this section, we proceed with evaluating the more sophisticated variant of our mixture-of-experts model having to deal with temporally delayed error signals and therefore employing the temporal spreading proposed in Sect. 2.1 and Eq. (6). To evaluate feasibility and performance of our mixture-of-experts model, we conduct several experiments evaluating different parameter setups of the mixture model and compare the model with the best parameters to the performance of the individual offline models.

Experimental Setup. We conducted all experiments shown in this section in the following way: after randomly initializing the weights of the mixture model, we present the data of 5 randomly chosen vehicles to the model to make sure the weights depart reasonably from their initial values. After this ramp-up phase, during which we conduct no evaluation, the model is presented with 30 more

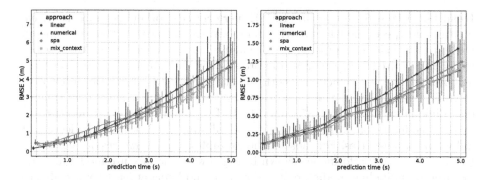

Fig. 6. Visualization of the RMSE performance of all individual expert predictors as well as our context-sensitive mixture-of-experts model employing temporal spreading with 2000 neurons in the context population, evaluated on 30 vehicles after the mixture model has been trained on 5 vehicles in advance to make the weights depart reasonably from their random initialization. The figures show the RMSE performance for longitudinal (x) and lateral (y) direction separately.

randomly chosen vehicles to be evaluated on. During the presentation of these 30 test vehicles, the mixture model continues to adapt its weights depending on the current error and context.

Parameter Analysis. To find the best possible variant of our mixture-of-experts model, we first analyzed the adjustable parameters of the model. In this paper, we focus on scaling factors ν_t decreasing linearly from 1 to 0.001 over the 20 prediction times with 1 corresponding to the earliest prediction step. Figure 4 shows a visualization of the RMSE performance of our mixture-model with 100 neurons in the context population with for different values of the learning rate κ. In general, we found that a rather low learning rate κ is necessary as higher learning rates tend to let the model overfit the current vehicle, which leads to large errors and even complete failure when switching from one vehicle to the next. We observe that issue in particular in x-direction when already a learning rate of $\kappa = 10^{-13}$ leads to large errors and even failure. Although a learning rate of $\kappa = 10^{-14}$ seems to be sufficiently low, we use $\kappa = 10^{-15}$ as our learning rate in this work. As the evaluation shown in Fig. 4 included only 30 test vehicles, we chose this rather conservative learning rate to make sure our model does not overfit when using a different set of vehicles.

Furthermore, we investigated the influence of the number of neurons in the context ensemble on the model's performance employing the aforementioned values for the learning rate κ and scaling factors ν_t. Figure 5 shows the RMSE of the model for varying numbers of neurons in the context population. In y-direction, the influence of the number of neurons is nearly invisible, whereas in x-direction increasing the number of neurons results in lower RMSE values. Thus, we focus our further investigations on models with 2000 neurons in the context population.

Results. Figure 6 shows the RMSE performance of our context-sensitive mixture-of-experts model employing temporal spreading with 2000 neurons on the 30 test vehicles in comparison to the individual input predictors. We observe, that our mixture-of-experts model improves over the individual models on average over all 30 test vehicles in both directions without clearly outperforming them. To further investigate these results, we evaluate the model's performance on individual vehicles. Figure 7 shows the RMSE performance of our mixture-of-experts model in comparison to the individual input predictors on a selection of individual test vehicles. For most of the examples, we observe results similar to the overall, mean performance shown in Fig. 6 with the mixture model improving over all individual predictors in x-direction and being at least comparable to the best individual predictor in y-direction (cf. Fig. 7a, c, d, e). However, there are also vehicles such as the one shown in Fig. 7b, where we observe improvements of the mixture model over the individual predictors in y-direction with no improvements shown in x-direction. For the vehicle shown in Fig. 7f, the mixture model does not yield any improvements over the input models in either direction. For that particular vehicle however, we also observe for both directions, that one of the offline models achieves a remarkably low RMSE performance, namely the linear predictor in x-direction and the LSTM models in y-direction, leaving little room for improvement. However, it would be desirable that our online learning model detects such situations and at least learns to approximate the best available individual offline model.

4   Discussion

In this paper, we have presented a mixture-of-experts model meant for training at run time based on the current driving context to perform a weighting of several available offline models for vehicle prediction. We investigated the differences between a context-free and context-sensitive variant using a temporally simplified version of this mixture model with the result, that we actually get improved performance by providing contextual information to the model. This prior evaluation also served as an upper bound for the performance to be expected if the model has to deal with temporally delayed error signals. Furthermore, we analyzed a more sophisticated variant of the model propagating the prediction error back in time to update the system's neural weights. To deal with potentially long delays between prediction and weight update, we employed temporal spreading of the error signal, i.e., using the error of earlier prediction steps to already adjust the weights of later predictions. Our evaluation on real world driving data showed that our approach is able to achieve improvements over the individual offline models already after being presented with only a few example vehicles. However, the mixture-of-experts model did not outperform the individual offline models as clearly as the performance of the timing-agnostic model variant, which serves as an upper bound for the performance to be expected, suggested. This performance gap leaves room for improvement in future work for instance experimenting with a different set of parameters, another set of vehicles in the evaluation and maybe also alternative contextual information.

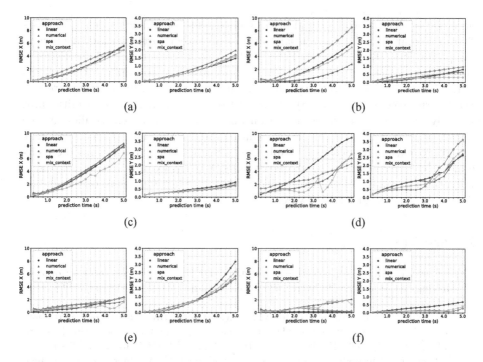

Fig. 7. Visualization of the RMSE of our mixture-of-experts model on 6 different test vehicles in comparison to the input predictors' performance. Each figure shows the RMSE performance on one test vehicle for longitudinal (x) and lateral (y) direction separately.

4.1 Future Work

Although the approach proposed in this paper shows promising results, there are several possible directions for future research. In this paper, we solely used linearly decreasing scaling factors of the learning rate, which should be further investigated in future work to evaluate if the model can be improved by using a different set of scaling factors. Furthermore, we used rather low learning rates, which makes sense as for the x-direction the online learning model tends to fail for higher learning rates, while on the other hand, the predictions in y-direction seem to benefit from higher learning rates (cf. Fig. 4). Hence, we also could investigate an improved model with separate learning rates and scaling factors for predictions in lateral and longitudinal direction. Another possibility would be to evaluate how much the model at hand can be further improved by increasing the number of neurons in the context population.

On the other hand, we aim to conduct a deeper analysis of the results presented here by investigating other selections of vehicles to better understand in what sorts of situations our model is beneficial and, more importantly, where it fails. For instance, we could focus on training/evaluating the online learning model on vehicles, where "interesting" behavior such as lane changes of sudden acceleration occurs, which could be problematic for the offline models to capture due to similar situations potentially appearing rather rarely during their training phase. Since we investigated the model variant using temporal spreading in this paper on the *On-board* data-set only, we also aim to evaluate the model's performance on the *NGSIM* data-set. Furthermore, we aim to investigate potential alternatives to the contextual information used in this paper. Additionally, we only trained our mixture model on one vehicle at a time. To allow actual deployment in a driving vehicle, we aim to investigate an advanced version of our approach, which spawns multiple model instantiations to be trained on several vehicles in parallel using shared weights. Finally, we also aim to investigate potential run time and energy-efficiency benefits when deploying our model on dedicated neuromorphic hardware.

References

1. Aeberhard, M., et al.: Experience, results and lessons learned from automated driving on Germany's Highways, **7**(1), 42–57. https://doi.org/10.1109/MITS.2014.2360306
2. Altche, F., de La Fortelle, A.: An LSTM network for highway trajectory prediction. In: 2017 IEEE 20th International Conference on Intelligent Transportation Systems (ITSC), pp. 353–359. IEEE (2017). https://doi.org/10.1109/itsc.2017.8317913
3. Bahram, M., Hubmann, C., Lawitzky, A., Aeberhard, M., Wollherr, D.: A combined model- and learning-based framework for interaction-aware maneuver prediction. IEEE Trans. Intell. Transp. Syst. **17**(6), 1538–1550 (2016). https://doi.org/10.1109/TITS.2015.2506642
4. Bekolay, T., et al.: Nengo: a python tool for building large-scale functional brain models. Front. Neuroinform. **7**(48) (2014). https://doi.org/10.3389/fninf.2013.00048
5. Bonnin, S., Kummert, F., Schmüdderich, J.: A generic concept of a system for predicting driving behaviors. In: 2012 15th International IEEE Conference on Intelligent Transportation Systems, pp. 1803–1808 (2012). https://doi.org/10.1109/ITSC.2012.6338695
6. Colyar, J., Halkias, J.: US Highway 101 Dataset (2017). https://www.fhwa.dot.gov/publications/research/operations/07030/index.cfm
7. Deo, N., Trivedi, M.M.: Convolutional social pooling for vehicle trajectory prediction. CoRR abs/1805.06771 (2018). http://arxiv.org/abs/1805.06771
8. Deo, N., Trivedi, M.M.: Multi-modal trajectory prediction of surrounding vehicles with maneuver based LSTMs. In: 2018 IEEE Intelligent Vehicles Symposium (IV), pp. 1179–1184. IEEE (2018). https://doi.org/10.1109/ivs.2018.8500493
9. DeWolf, T., Stewart, T.C., Slotine, J.J., Eliasmith, C.: A spiking neural model of adaptive arm control. Proc. R. Soc. B **283**(48), 20162134 (2016). https://doi.org/10.1098/rspb.2016.2134
10. Eliasmith, C.: How to Build a Brain: A Neural Architecture for Biological Cognition. Oxford University Press, Oxford (2013)
11. Gomes, H.M., Barddal, J.P., Enembreck, F., Bifet, A.: A survey on ensemble learning for data stream classification. ACM Comput. Surv. **50**(2), 1–36 (2017). https://doi.org/10.1145/3054925

12. Graf, R., Deusch, H., Seeliger, F., Fritzsche, M., Dietmayer, K.: A learning concept for behavior prediction at intersections. In: 2014 IEEE Intelligent Vehicles Symposium Proceedings, pp. 939–945 (2014). https://doi.org/10.1109/IVS.2014.6856415
13. Hochreiter, S., Schmidhuber, J.: Long short-term memory. Neural Comput. 9(8), 1735–1780 (1997). https://doi.org/10.1162/neco.1997.9.8.1735
14. Hoi, S.C.H., Sahoo, D., Lu, J., Zhao, P.: Online learning: A comprehensive survey abs/1802.02871. http://arxiv.org/abs/1802.02871
15. Lefèvre, S., Vasquez, D., Laugier, C.: A survey on motion prediction and risk assessment for intelligent vehicles. ROBOMECH J. 1(1), 1 (2014). https://doi.org/10.1186/s40648-014-0001-z
16. Losing, V., Hammer, B., Wersing, H.: Incremental on-line learning: a review and comparison of state of the art algorithms. Neurocomputing 275, 1261–1274 (2018). https://doi.org/10.1016/j.neucom.2017.06.084
17. Losing, V., Hammer, B., Wersing, H.: Personalized maneuver prediction at intersections. In: 2017 IEEE 20th International Conference on Intelligent Transportation Systems (ITSC), pp. 1–6. IEEE (2017). https://doi.org/10.1109/ITSC.2017.8317760
18. Maye, J., Triebel, R., Spinello, L., Siegwart, R.: Bayesian on-line learning of driving behaviors. In: Proceedings of The International Conference in Robotics and Automation (ICRA) (2011). https://doi.org/10.1109/ICRA.2011.5980414
19. Mirus, F., Blouw, P., Stewart, T.C., Conradt, J.: Predicting vehicle behaviour using LSTMs and a vector power representation for spatial positions. In: 27th European Symposium on Artificial Neural Networks, ESANN 2019, Bruges, Belgium (2019)
20. Polychronopoulos, A., Tsogas, M., Amditis, A., Andreone, L.: Sensor fusion for predicting vehicles' path for collision avoidance systems, 8(3), 549–562. https://doi.org/10.1109/TITS.2007.903439
21. Taieb, S.B., Hyndman, R.: Boosting multi-step autoregressive forecasts. In: Xing, E.P., Jebara, T. (eds.) Proceedings of the 31st International Conference on Machine Learning. Proceedings of Machine Learning Research, vol. 32, pp. 109–117. PMLR. http://proceedings.mlr.press/v32/taieb14.html

Analysis of Dogs' Sleep Patterns Using Convolutional Neural Networks

Anna Zamansky[1]([envelope]) [ORCID], Aleksandr M. Sinitca[2] [ORCID], Dmitry I. Kaplun[2] [ORCID],
Michael Plazner[1], Ivana G. Schork[3], Robert J. Young[3] [ORCID],
and Cristiano S. de Azevedo[4]

[1] Information Systems Department, University of Haifa, Haifa, Israel
annazam@is.haifa.ac.il
[2] Saint Petersburg Electrotechnical University "LETI", Saint Petersburg, Russia
[3] School of Environmental and Life Sciences, University of Salford,
Greater Manchester, UK
[4] Department of Biodiversity, Evolution and Environment,
Federal University of Ouro Preto, Ouro Preto, Brazil

Abstract. Video-based analysis is one of the most important tools of animal behavior and animal welfare scientists. While automatic analysis systems exist for many species, this problem has not yet been adequately addressed for one of the most studied species in animal science—dogs. In this paper we describe a system developed for analyzing sleeping patterns of kenneled dogs, which may serve as indicator of their welfare. The system combines convolutional neural networks with classical data processing methods, and works with very low quality video from cameras installed in dogs shelters.

Keywords: Convolutional neural networks · Animal science · Animal welfare · Computer vision

1 Introduction

Video-based analysis is one of the most important tools of animal behavior and animal welfare scientists. For instance, it is very useful for measuring *time budget* of animals, a common ethological and welfare parameter, indicating the amount or proportion of time that animals spend in different behaviors [1]. In this case the data to be analyzed may amount of hundreds of hours of data, and is a tedious and error-prone task. Naturally, automatic video analysis has the potential to revolutionize the work of animal scientists in terms of precision, nature and number of behavioral variables that can be measured, and volumes of video data that can be processed. Automatic video-based systems already exist for different species: wild animals [2], pigs [3,4], poultry [5], insects [6], and many more. Moreover, well-developed commercial systems for rodent tracking such as Ethovision [7,8] are widely used in behavioral research.

Dogs are a widely studied species in animal science. While video analysis is widely applied in the context of dogs (see, e.g. [9,10]), very few works address

© Springer Nature Switzerland AG 2019
I. V. Tetko et al. (Eds.): ICANN 2019, LNCS 11729, pp. 472–483, 2019.
https://doi.org/10.1007/978-3-030-30508-6_38

automatic video-based analysis of dog behavior [11–13]. All of these works use video from 3D Kinect camera, the installation and use of which is not trivial and also quite expensive.

Our approach takes a different strategy, using the simplest web or security cameras footage, and paying a "computational" price instead for the system's learning. It is a part of our ongoing multi-disciplinary project for automatic analysis of dog behavior, based on video footage obtained from simple cameras (an overview of the project can be found in [14]; preliminary ideas were presented in [15]). In this paper we present a system developed for supporting an ongoing research project in animal science, investigating sleeping patterns of kennelled dogs as indicators of their welfare. Our system was developed for automatically quantifying dogs' sleeping patterns. It combines convolutional neural networks with classical data processing methods; it works with very low quality video data, and supports detecting multiple dogs in a frame. In what follows we describe in further details the research problem and the developed solution.

2   Related Work

Automatic tracking and behavior analyzing systems are used for wild animals [2], pigs [3,4], poultry [5], insects [6], and many more. Well-developed systems for rodent behavior recognition such as Ethovision [7,8] are widely used in behavioral research. In the context of dogs, automatic quantification of animal activities have mostly been explored in relation to pet wearables. These include a plethora of commercially available canine activity trackers (such as FitBark[1], Whistle[2] or PetPace[3]). While such devices can measure activity and sleep patterns, none of them has yet been scientifically validated, and thus are not always appropriate to be used in clinical and scientific settings. Wearables have been investigated in the context of predicting the success of future guide dogs ([13,16]), impacting the bonding between dog and owner [17,18], and supporting the relationship between guide dog centers and puppy raisers ([19]). van der Linden et al. [20] provide a comprehensive overview of commercially available dog trackers, discussing also their privacy implications. yet ripe to be used for scientific research or clinical settings. Fair accuracy was achieved for several self-developed sensor-based activity trackers [21–23], which are limited to a small number of basic positions and postures.

Barnard et al. addressed a similar problem of automatic behavioral analysis of kennelled dogs using 3D video monitoring [11]. Dog body part detection was done using standard Structural Support Vector Machine classifiers, and automatic tracking of the dog was also implemented. However, as discussed in the introduction, this approach requires expensive equipment and non-trivial installation of 3D cameras (such as Microsoft Kinect). Our approach, on the other

---

[1] See: https://www.fitbark.com/.

[2] See: https://www.whistle.com/.

[3] See: https://petpace.com/.

hand, can use video footage of very low quality, obtained from simple, cheap and easily available cameras.

3 Problem Definition

The above mentioned animal science study[4] is a collaboration between the University of Salford and the Animal Science Center of Universidade Federal de Ouro Preto in Brazil. It focuses on analyzing sleep patterns of breeding stock kenneled dogs as welfare indicators. The dogs, bred and maintained by the Animal Science Center in Brazil, were captured for eight consecutive months using simple security cameras installed in their kennels (using night vision at night). The collected video data is of size 2.1 TB and contains 13,668 videos, comprising over 4,000 hours of footage. Each of the kennel rooms house either one or two dogs. The cameras are able to capture videos in two modes: full-color mode, where the space is illuminated by the sun or a lamp, and gray-scale mode, where the space is illuminated by infrared camera light. Despite their HD resolution (1280x720), the video footage is of a very low quality.

The main problem consists of automatically computing the following sleep parameters for each dog, which have been recognized as important in the study:

- total amount of sleep – the number of frames in the video where the dog is asleep (i.e., lying down, eyes closed);
- sleep interval count – the number of blocks of consecutive frames where the dog is asleep in every frame;
- sleep interval length – the number of frames in a given sleep interval.

Our aim is to automatically compute these parameters for each dog by (i) localization of the dog in each frame, and (ii) classification of its state as awake or asleep. We henceforth focus on these two tasks and evaluate the performance of the system in relation to the final task (ii).

4 System Description

An overview of the system's client/server architecture is provided in Fig. 1. The input to the system is a video, and its output is a summary of the sleep parameters for that video. The video is processed by the client, and sent to the server frame by frame. The frames serve as input to a neural network, which has two main tasks: marking the dog's position, and classifying the sleep/awake state of each dog that was identified. The images are fed to the model in a sequence, which the network processes one-by-one without keeping state.

In what follows, we describe in further detail the dataset used to train the neural network, our experiments with the networks' different architectures, the post-processing methods applied to correct the network's outputs, and, finally, the calculation of the sleep parameters.

---

[4] The study was approved by the ethical panels of both institutions; protocol numbers: University of Salford Ethical Approval Panel - STR1617-80, CEUA/UFOP (Brazil) - 2017/04.

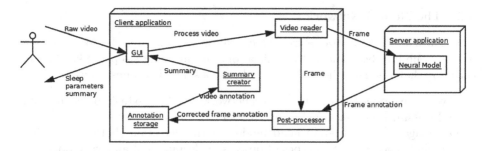

Fig. 1. System architecture.

Fig. 2. Example of frames.

4.1   The Dataset

Our training dataset consisted of 8000 frames extracted from the videos (see Fig. 2).

The obtained frame annotations included two attributes for every dog visible in the frame: (i) bounding box: an axis-aligned box surrounding each identified dog, and (ii) state of the identified dog: awake or asleep.

The annotation was performed by the first three authors independently, reaching a consensus via discussion in controversial situations (e.g., when the dog's eyes are not visible), and consulting with the last three authors who are animal experts. Frames where the dog was not clearly seen or hidden behind objects were discarded.

4.2   The Neural Network

The neural network has two tasks: (i) localization, i.e., marking the dog's position with a bounding box, and (ii) classification, i.e., marking sleep/awake state of each dog that was identified. To this end we considered two possibilities:

- Two-stage model: two distinct neural networks for the two tasks of localization and classification, packaged as one model (see Fig. 3).
- One-stage model: an end-to-end model for the detection (both localization and classification) of two types of objects: a sleeping and an awake dog.

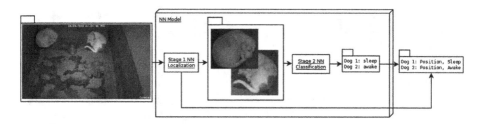

Fig. 3. Two stage model.

We decided to experiment with both types of models, comparing them using the following two criteria.

1. Intersection over union (IoU) is a standard evaluation metric in object detection. Similarly to the approach taken in [24], we calculated the widely used detection accuracy measure, mean Average Precision (mAP), based on a fixed IoU threshold, i.e. 0.5.
2. Number of unrecoverable network errors, i.e., classification errors which are impossible to recover from using the post-processing module (which will be described below). One particularly problematic error is continuous false classification of a non-moving sleeping dog.

While both approaches had comparable results with respect to the first criterion (around 0.75 mAP@0.5IoU on the evaluation set), the second approach performed much better with respect to the second criterion. Therefore, we decided to use the end-to-end architecture[5].

For object detection we used the TensorFlow Object Detection API [25].

Due to a low level of variety in training data we have chosen to use transfer learning based on state-free neural networks pretrained on the COCO dataset

---

[5] It should be noted that the chosen end-to-end architecture has a drawback of simultaneous detection of the same dog as sleeping and awake due to its detection of two objects (sleeping and awake dog) independently. However, this happens in very rare cases and can be overcome by using a higher confidence level for classification.

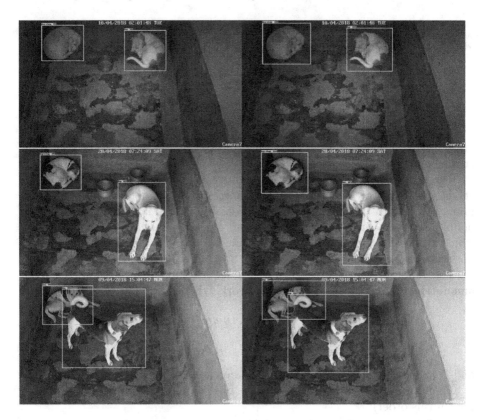

Fig. 4. Example of predicted boxes.

[26]. Initially for better performance we tried to use ssd_mobilenet_v1 [27], but it could not provide sufficient accuracy due to a number of factors, such as a small input dimension. Due to the above, we currently use faster_rcnn_resnet101 [28].

We show some samples of predicted bounding boxes of dogs in the validation set as Fig. 4 where the left column contains the model's prediction, while the right one is the ground truth as annotated by humans.

The output of the neural network consists of N tuples of the form $< x_1, y_1, x_2, y_2, R_{sleep}, R_{awake} >$, where x_1, y_1, x_2, y_2 are the bounding box coordinates, and R_{sleep}, R_{awake} are confidence scores for sleeping and awake dog respectively. This output is then transformed to $< Ind, x_1, y_1, x_2, y_2, R, Type >$, where $Type$ can be "sleep" or "awake" and $R = \max(R_{sleep}, R_{awake})$, Ind is the dog's index.

4.3   Post-processing

The main idea behind post-processing the network's outputs is compensating for possible errors produced by the network in the tasks of localization and classification. The possible errors include: double detection, random detection

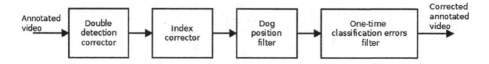

Fig. 5. Post-processing filter sequence.

order, high frequency noise in bounding box coordinates, one-time classification errors, and false-positive sleep detection (in some cases).

The post-processing module consists of a sequence of filters handling a variety of tasks, related to the above mentioned errors. The order of the filters is important due to their non-linearity. For example, it is important to eliminate double detection first, as it may result in a wrong number of detected dogs, which affects further tasks. Figure 5 presents an overview of the data flow in the post-processor module.

The input of the post-processor is a sequence of images paired with the annotations predicted by the neural network, where:

$$A = \; <\overline{A^{dog}}, Image> \tag{1}$$

$$\overline{A^{dog}} =\; < Ind, x_1, y_1, x_2, y_2, Rate, State > \tag{2}$$

and $Image$ is a $1280 \times 720 \times 3$ matrix. A_i denotes an annotated pair for frame i.

The correction tasks performed by the post-processing module as the following (in this order):

1. *Double detection correction* - based on the assumption that the euclidean distance $D(C_i, C_j)$ as in Eq. (3) between the centers C of detected boxes calculated as per (4) in the instance of double detection (between box i and j) is smaller than some ϵ, and that the probability of this situation for different dogs is quite small. The ϵ parameter is tunable.

$$D(C_i, C_j) = \sqrt{(x_i^c - x_j^c)^2 + (y_i^c - y_j^c)^2} \tag{3}$$

$$C = (x^c, y^c), x^c = \frac{x_1 + x_2}{2}, y^c = \frac{y_1 + y_2}{2} \tag{4}$$

We calculate D on all pairs of detected boxes for the current frame, and if $D(i, j) < \epsilon$ we compare the detection rate R_i and R_j of these two boxes and delete the one with the smaller rate.

2. *Index correction* - intended for correcting random order of dog indexes Ind in the frame annotation. The index corrector works in the time domain.

The first step of index correction is calculating the centers of bounding boxes, this data is provided by the previous step.

The second step is calculating distance as Eq. (3) between boxes on step k and $k - 1$. At this moment we have a square matrix of distances:

$$\overline{D} = \begin{bmatrix} D(C_1^k, C_1^{k-1}) \ ... \ D(C_n^k, C_1^{k-1}) \\ D(C_1^k, C_2^{k-1}) \ ... \ D(C_n^k, C_2^{k-1}) \\ ... \qquad ... \qquad ... \\ D(C_1^k, C_n^{k-1}) \ ... \ D(C_n^k, C_n^{k-1}) \end{bmatrix} \tag{5}$$

For each column of this matrix we look for the minimal element and obtain a row of new indices $\overline{Ind_{new}}$. Then the the Ind values in frame annotations are overwritten with new values from $\overline{Ind_{new}}$.

3. *Dog position filtering.* Video can contain different high frequency noises, but the typical neural network is not totally noise invariant, therefore we should use a low frequency filter for position outputs to compensate for the shaking effect of bounding boxes on the output video.

   We use a moving average (MA) filter which s widely used as an indicator in technical analysis that helps smooth out values by filtering out the "noise" from random fluctuations. It is a trend-following, or lagging, indicator because it is based on past values. In our case we use the following difference equation:

$$P[k] = \frac{1}{n} \sum_{i=0}^{n-1} P[k-i] \tag{6}$$

   where $P = [x_1, x_2, y_1, y_2]$ are bounding box coordinates, n is the filter order (we are using $n = 5$) and all operations are element-wise.

   For an example of filtering, we can look at a plot of the x_1 coordinate for a sleeping dog in Fig. 6, where the orange line represents the non-filtered value, and the blue line is the value after filtering.The same effect applies to the values of the remaining coordinates. This transformation eliminates the jittering effect, providing the user with a more comfortable watching experience.

4. *One-time classification errors filtering.* One of the fundamental features of deep neural networks is the presence of singular points where the output value may be incorrect. Often these points can be artificially obtained by adding manually crafted noise-like signals.

   To compensate for this effect, we use two approaches. The first one is related to motion analysis. We use motion analysis techniques based on classical computer vision methods like Gaussian blur, frame delta calculation, finding contours, etc.

   For detecting movement we use a threshold based method containing the following steps: (a) crop current and previous image to dog bounding box (with coordinates from last frame); (b) convert to gray-scale; (c) calculate absolute difference between cropped images; (d) binarize image by threshold; (e) apply dilation procedure to the image for filling holes; (f) find contours on dilated image.

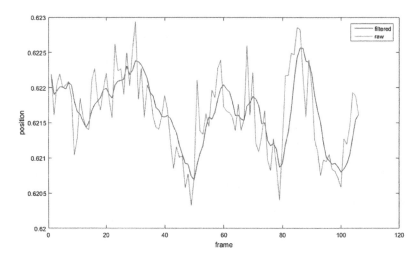

Fig. 6. Example of filter effect.

If a sufficiently large contour was found, we interpret that as evidence that the dog moved and change the dog's state to awake. This helps fixing false positives in sleeping state classification.

The second approach is filtering states. This algorithm aims to correct sequences of one state type (i.e. only sleep or only awake), that are shorter than a certain threshold. In most situations this kind of wrongly classified sequence is shorter than 3 frames. This is based on the assumption that the frequency of alternating between asleep/awake states in animals cannot be too high.

We use an approach based on remembering the currently active state of a frame sequence and switching to a new state only after seeing N frames with that state. At first glance, it may seem that this can corrupt the statistics about dog sleeping patterns, but the algorithm is symmetric in regards to states, thus the loss of the previous state's points in the beginning of a new state sequence (we had to wait N frames until toggling the state) is compensated by additional state points after the end of the sequence.

4.4   Sleep Parameters Calculation

Next we describe the calculation of the following parameters: (i) total amount of sleep, (ii) sleep interval count, and (iii) sleep interval length.

We represent a vector of dog states $State$ for dog j as follows:

$$State^j[k] = \begin{cases} 1 \text{ if } A_k[A_j^{dog}][State] = \text{``sleep''} \\ 0 \text{ if } A_k[A_j^{dog}][State] = \text{``awake''} \end{cases} \tag{7}$$

where k is the frame index.

The total amount of sleep for dog j is obtained as follows:

$$Length_j = \sum_{k=0}^{len(State^j)} State^j[k] \tag{8}$$

Sleep interval count is calculated as follows:

$$Count_j = \sum_{k=0}^{len(State^j)} \max(\Delta State^j[k], 0) \tag{9}$$

where $\Delta State^j[k]$ is defined as:

$$\Delta State^j[k] = \begin{cases} State^j[k] & \text{if } k = 0 \\ State^j[k] - State^j[k-1] & \text{if } k > 0 \end{cases} \tag{10}$$

5 Evaluation

We evaluated the system on 10 videos of total length 600 s. The video set included videos with 0–2 dogs, day/night time and different dogs and rooms. The videos were processed by the system and a testing set of 6,000 frames annotated with the system's predictions were manually checked for correctness by the authors; in controversial cases consensus was reached by discussion between the authors. The manual revision process yielded a result of 5,340 correct frame classifications.

6 Summary and Future Work

Despite dogs being a well studied species in animal science, very few works addressed so far the challenge of automatic analysis of dog behavior. In this paper we presented a system for automatic quantification of sleeping patterns of kennelled dogs, which is being currently used to measure welfare indicators in an ongoing research project. Due to the immense amount of video footage collected in the project, manual analysis is an extremely time consuming, tedious and error-prone task, to which our system, based on convolutional neural networks, provides an efficient and accurate solution. The approach presented here is based on frame vt frame analysis. One of the future research directions is to investigate more sophisticated approaches in which dependencies over time can be modelled (e.g., recurrent systems or modelling dog sleeping-states and frame dependencies using probabilistic models).

More generally speaking, behaviour analysis plays a major role in animal welfare science [29]. Our system demonstrates the potential of using neural networks for revolutionizing the way animal scientists work today. The development of automatic systems for behavior analysis has the potential for impacting the welfare of companion, farm and zoo animals, which is a problem of increasing interest for the modern society. Therefore, an important direction for future research is making the suggested approach generalizable to other types of behavior analysis and other types of animals. Some first steps were already taken in [14].

Acknowledgement. This work has been supported by the NVIDIA GPU grant program.

References

1. Arney, D.: What is animal welfare and how is it assessed?. Sustainable Agriculture, p. 311 (2012)
2. Burghardt, T., Ćalić, J.: Analysing animal behaviour in wildlife videos using face detection and tracking. In: IEE Proceedings-Vision, Image and Signal Processing, vol. 153, no. 3, pp. 305–312 (2006)
3. Ahrendt, P., Gregersen, T., Karstoft, H.: Development of a real-time computer vision system for tracking loose-housed pigs. Comput. Electron. Agric. **76**(2), 169–174 (2011)
4. Tillett, R., Onyango, C., Marchant, J.: Using model-based image processing to track animal movements. Comput. Electron. Agric. **17**(2), 249–261 (1997)
5. Sergeant, D., Boyle, R., Forbes, M.: Computer visual tracking of poultry. Comput. Electron. Agric. **21**(1), 1–18 (1998)
6. Noldus, L.P., Spink, A.J., Tegelenbosch, R.A.: Computerised video tracking, movement analysis and behaviour recognition in insects. Comput. Electron. Agric. **35**(2), 201–227 (2002)
7. Van de Weerd, H., et al.: Validation of a new system for the automatic registration of behaviour in mice and rats. Behav. Process. **53**(1), 11–20 (2001)
8. Spink, A., Tegelenbosch, R., Buma, M., Noldus, L.: The ethovision video tracking system–a tool for behavioral phenotyping of transgenic mice. Physiol. Behav. **73**(5), 731–744 (2001)
9. Valletta, J.J., Torney, C., Kings, M., Thornton, A., Madden, J.: Applications of machine learning in animal behaviour studies. Anim. Behav. **124**, 203–220 (2017)
10. Palestrini, C., Minero, M., Cannas, S., Rossi, E., Frank, D.: Video analysis of dogs with separation-related behaviors. Appl. Anim. Behav. Sci. **124**(1), 61–67 (2010)
11. Barnard, S., et al.: Quick, accurate, smart: 3D computer vision technology helps assessing confined animals' behaviour. PloS One **11**(7), e0158748 (2016)
12. Pons, P., Jaen, J., Catala, A.: Assessing machine learning classifiers for the detection of animals' behavior using depth-based tracking. Expert Syst. Appl. **86**, 235–246 (2017)
13. Mealin, S., Domínguez, I.X., Roberts, D.L.: Semi-supervised classification of static canine postures using the microsoft kinect. In: Proceedings of the Third International Conference on Animal-Computer Interaction, p. 16, ACM (2016)
14. Kaplun, D., et al.: Animal health informatics: towards a generic framework for automatic behavior analysis. In: Proceedings of the 12th International Conference on Health Informatics (HEALTHINF 2019) (2019)
15. Amir, S., Zamansky, A., van der Linden, D.: K9-blyzer-towards video-based automatic analysis of canine behavior. In: Proceedings of Animal-Computer Interaction 2017 (2017)
16. Alcaidinho, J., Valentin, G., Yoder, N., Tai, S., Mundell, P., Jackson, M.: Assessment of working dog suitability from quantimetric data. In: NordiCHI 2014, Helsinki, Finland, 26–30 Oct 2014. Georgia Institute of Technology (2014)

17. Alcaidinho, J., et al.: Leveraging mobile technology to increase the permanent adoption of shelter dogs. In: Proceedings of the 17th International Conference on Human-Computer Interaction with Mobile Devices and Services, pp. 463–469. ACM (2015)
18. Zamansky, A., van der Linden, D., Hadar, I., Bleuer-Elsner, S.: Log my dog: perceived impact of dog activity tracking. IEEE Computer (2018)
19. Zamansky, A., van der Linden, D.: Activity trackers for raising guide dogs: challenges and opportunities. IEEE Technol. Soc. **37**(4), 62–69 (2018)
20. van der Linden, D., Zamansky, A., Hadar, I., Craggs, B., Rashid, A.: Buddy's wearable is not your buddy: privacy implications of pet wearables. In: Forthcoming in IEEE Security and Privacy
21. Ladha, C., Hammerla, N., Hughes, E., Olivier, P., Ploetz, T.: Dog's life: wearable activity recognition for dogs. In: Proceedings of the 2013 ACM International Joint Conference on Pervasive and Ubiquitous Computing, pp. 415–418. ACM (2013)
22. Brugarolas, R., Loftin, R.T., Yang, P., Roberts, D.L., Sherman, B., Bozkurt, A.: Behavior recognition based on machine learning algorithms for a wireless canine machine interface. In: 2013 IEEE International Conference on Body Sensor Networks (BSN), pp. 1–5. IEEE (2013)
23. Gerencsér, L., Vásárhelyi, G., Nagy, M., Vicsek, T., Miklósi, A.: Identification of behaviour in freely moving dogs (canis familiaris) using inertial sensors. PloS One **8**(10), e77814 (2013)
24. Everingham, M., Eslami, S.A., Van Gool, L., Williams, C.K., Winn, J., Zisserman, A.: The pascal visual object classes challenge: a retrospective. Int. J. Comput. Vis. **111**(1), 98–136 (2015)
25. Huang, J., et al.: Speed/accuracy trade-offs for modern convolutional object detectors. CoRR, vol. abs/1611.10012 (2016)
26. Lin, T., et al.: Microsoft COCO: common objects in context. CoRR, vol. abs/1405.0312 (2014)
27. Howard, A.G., et al.: Mobilenets: efficient convolutional neural networks for mobile vision applications. CoRR, vol. abs/1704.04861 (2017)
28. He, K., Zhang, X., Ren, S., Sun, J.: Deep residual learning for image recognition. CoRR, vol. abs/1512.03385 (2015)
29. Dawkins, M.: Using behaviour to assess animal welfare. Anim. Welf. **13**(1), 3–7 (2004)

On the Inability of Markov Models to Capture Criticality in Human Mobility

Vaibhav Kulkarni[1]([envelope]) [ID], Abhijit Mahalunkar[2] [ID], Benoit Garbinato[1] [ID], and John D. Kelleher[2] [ID]

[1] UNIL-HEC Lausanne, Lausanne, Switzerland
`vaibhav.kulkarni@unil.ch`
[2] ADAPT Research Center, Technological University Dublin, Dublin, Ireland

Abstract. We examine the non-Markovian nature of human mobility by exposing the inability of Markov models to capture criticality in human mobility. In particular, the assumed Markovian nature of mobility was used to establish an upper bound on the predictability of human mobility, based on the temporal entropy. Since its inception, this bound has been widely used for validating the performance of mobility prediction models. We show that the variants of recurrent neural network architectures can achieve significantly higher prediction accuracy surpassing this upper bound. The central objective of our work is to show that human-mobility dynamics exhibit criticality characteristics which contributes to this discrepancy. In order to explain this anomaly, we shed light on the underlying assumption that human mobility characteristics follow an exponential decay that has resulted in this bias. By evaluating the predictability on real-world datasets, we show that human mobility exhibits scale-invariant long-distance dependencies, bearing resemblance to power-law decay, contrasting with the initial Markovian assumption. We experimentally validate that this assumption inflates the estimated mobility entropy, consequently lowering the upper bound on predictability. We demonstrate that the existing approach of entropy computation tends to overlook the presence of long-distance dependencies and structural correlations in human mobility. We justify why recurrent-neural network architectures that are designed to handle long-distance dependencies surpass the previously computed upper bound on mobility predictability.

Keywords: Predictability limits · Human-mobility · Criticality

1 Introduction

Real-time user locations are typically collected using the Global Positioning System (GPS), Call Detail Record logs (CDR) and Wireless-LAN (WLAN); they can be used to study and model user mobility behaviors, beneficial to a variety of applications such as traffic management, urban planning and location-based advertisements. An application of mobility modeling consists of formulating predictive models to forecast individual trajectories, for which various

© Springer Nature Switzerland AG 2019
I. V. Tetko et al. (Eds.): ICANN 2019, LNCS 11729, pp. 484–497, 2019.
https://doi.org/10.1007/978-3-030-30508-6_39

methods have been proposed, including Markov chains [6] and neural networks. Formally, mobility modeling can be defined as estimating the probability distribution over a user's location traces by minimizing the negative log-likelihood over the training sequences. Existing research relies upon several datasets differing with respect to their spatiotemporal granularity, resulting in vastly contrasting prediction accuracies ranging from over 90% to under 40% [5].

1.1 Related Work

In this context, the seminal paper by Song et al. [27] laid the foundations for computing an upper bound on the maximum predictability of human mobility. This work establishes a benchmark for quantifying the performance of different algorithms and generalizes its approach across various datasets. It defines the *maximum predictability*, noted π^{max}, as the temporally correlated entropy of information associated with an individual's trajectory. π^{max} is estimated by first computing the entropy based on the Lempel-Ziv data compression [34] and then by solving the limiting case for Fano's inequality [24], an information-theoretical result used to compute lower bounds on the minimum error probability in multiple-hypotheses testing problems. The proposed theoretical upper bound ($\pi^{max} = 93\%$) is empirically validated using a CDR dataset consisting of 50,000 users collected by a telecommunications operator for a duration of three months. It should be noted however that CDRs are a rather rough approximation of human mobility. Song et al. [27] also show that π^{max} is independent of radius of gyration and movement periodicity, hence observe an insignificant level of variation across a heterogeneous population.

Several subsequent works either redefine this theoretical upper bound or perform empirical validations with different mobility datasets. Lu et al. [18] re-estimate π^{max} to be 88% and use Markov chains to empirically verify this redefined upper bound. They analyze another CDR dataset consisting of 500,000 users, collected for a duration of five months and achieve an average predictability of 91% with an *order-1* Markov chain. They also show that higher-order Markov chain models do not improve prediction accuracy. Their interpretation behind surpassing their own estimated theoretical bound is that trajectories exceeding this bound are non-stationary, whereas the accuracy of stationary trajectories prevails within the bound. A trajectory is considered to be stationary when people tend to remain still during short time-spans. This conclusion directly contradicts findings of Song et al. [27], because non-stationary trajectories should by definition have a higher entropy. Additionally, Cuttone et al. [5] show that the stationary nature of trajectories plays a significant role in the higher accuracies resulting from Markov models [5] as they often predict the user will remain in the previous location, i.e., self-transitions. Lin et al. [16] also show that π^{max} is independent of the data sampling rate which was later questioned by Smith et al. [26] ($\pi^{max} = 81 \pm 4\%$) and Cuttone et al. [5] ($\pi^{max} = 65\%$). Smith et al. [26] and Cuttone et al. [5] use mobility datasets containing GPS trajectories and empirically show that predictability has a direct correlation with the temporal resolution and an inverse correlation with the spatial resolution.

Human mobility varies under time translations, therefore the entropy not only depends on the duration of past observations but also on number of visited locations, these factors tend to be hidden in such datasets [1,2]. Additional inconsistencies become evident due to the fact that the authors in [18,27] group the user locations into one hour bins when constructing the historical trajectory of a user. Further inspection suggests that these models can foresee future locations at π^{max}, only when an individual is present in one of the top n bins [5]. The first two works [18,27] thus consider the last location of each day, consequently predicting only the user's home place. Under such a scenario, Ikanovic et al. [11] and Cuttone et al. [5] show that the predictability of the true next location is significantly lower ($\pi^{max} = 71.1 \pm 4.7\%$) than the predictability of the location in the subsequent bin. They further show that an individual's mobility entropy is directly proportional to the number of visited locations. The authors also point out that the generating function behind the stochastic mobility behavior is often unknown. Therefore the bounds cannot be estimated theoretically and require empirical derivation. Cuttone et al. [5] achieve an even lower bound on π^{max} of 65% on the same datasets with the same methods as Ikanovic et al. [11].

Based on the research literature discussed above, we observe a discrepancy regarding the maximum predictability bound, π^{max} and disagreements on the impact of entropy, the number of uniquely visited locations and the spatiotemporal resolution of the trajectory on π^{max}. In order to gain a deeper understanding about this discrepancy, we construct next-place prediction models by using seven different approaches. We compute the empirical maximum accuracy and compare it with the theoretically derived π^{max}, considering three large-scale real-world datasets containing GPS trajectories. We find that recurrent-neural architectures [25] significantly surpass π^{max} on datasets compiled for long timespans.

The current approaches [18,27] estimate π^{max} by first computing the true entropy of user mobility, denoted by S^{real} using Lempel-ziv compression [34], followed by the computation of the minimum error probability by leveraging Fano's inequality [24]. Fano's inequality is based on the assumption that the system is governed by a Markovian process and computes the conditional entropy of a random variable X, relative to the correlated variable Y, to the probability of incorrectly estimating X from Y, thus yielding the minimum error probability, noted p_e. In practice, p_e is computed by segmenting the entire trajectory into sub-strings, where the length of the shortest substring beginning at index i does not appear previously [11,18,26,27]. The predictability π^{max} is thus the complement of the average of error probabilities of individual substrings.

1.2   Contributions

We show that when a trajectory is split into substrings, the entropy associated with the individual substring increases, thus increasing S^{real}. This occurs as Fano's inequality, rooted in information theory [24], is intended for a data source with known probability distribution [7]. Human mobility prediction however, is based on the discretization of the trajectories, where the probability distribution

Table 1. Dataset specifications along with their respective S^{real} and π^{max}.

Datasets	#users	Duration (months)	Avg. trajectory length	Distinct locations	Avg. spatio-temporal granularity	S^{real}	π^{max}
PrivaMov [21]	100	15	1560000	2651	246 m, 24 s	7.63	0.7646
NMDC [14]	191	24	685510	2087	1874 m, 1304 s	6.08	0.8323
GeoLife [32]	182	36	8227800	3892	7.5 m, 5 s	9.77	0.6219

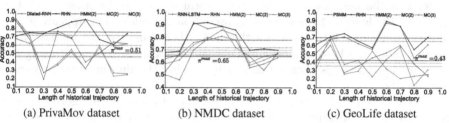

(a) PrivaMov dataset   (b) NMDC dataset   (c) GeoLife dataset

Fig. 1. Comparison of π^{max} with the maximum predictability achieved using models from each category. The dotted lines indicate the predictability by each approach (indicated with the same color). (Color figure online)

is not known *a priori*. Furthermore, the estimation of entropy by using Lempel-Ziv coding [34] was originally constructed to provide a complexity measure for finite sequences, i.e., input sequence displaying exponential decay in long-range correlations (memoryless structure). Such sequences, when further split, changes the true distribution of the data and increase the associated entropy; and the derived π^{max} thus acts as a limit on the Markov model. We argue that this is due to ignoring the presence of long-distance dependencies and structural correlations present in human trajectories.

The current π^{max} computation is thus based on the widely used assumption that human mobility is Markovian (memoryless), i.e., the movements are independently distributed, as testified by the numerous research works relying on Markov models to characterize mobility [13,18,28]. In opposition to this widely used assumption, we show the presence of non-Markovian character in human mobility dynamics by empirically showing that the drop in the mutual information [17,24] follows a power law function of the distance between any two points in a trajectory. We also show the state-dependent nature of mobility by illustrating the presence of scaling laws in the distribution of location dwell times and the rank associated with location visits. Using real-datasets, we show that these underlying mechanisms that govern human mobility are consistent across disparate mobility behaviors.

2 Experiments

In this section, we first present the values of S^{real} and π^{max} computed using the approach mentioned in the works of Song et al. [27] and Lu et al. [18] as per Eq. 1 which is based on Lempel-Ziv data compression [34].

$$S^{real} = (\frac{1}{n}\sum_{i=1}^{n}\lambda_i)^{-1}ln(n) \qquad (1)$$

where, n is the length of the trajectory (total number of locations) and λ is defined as the length of the shortest substring at an index i not appearing previously from index 1 to $i - 1$. Furthermore, their length is set to zero upon reaching index i, when no more unique substrings can be computed using the above method. π^{max} is then estimated by solving the limiting case of Fano's inequality [24].

We then discuss the accuracy results estimated using seven algorithms and compare them with respect to the theoretical upper bound. To investigate the presence of memory in human mobility, we conduct several experiments and use the results to illustrate the reason for surpassing the upper bound. Finally, we investigate the existing approach and discuss their failure to compute the true entropy (S^{real}) of mobility trajectories. We conduct the experiments by using three mobility datasets whose specifications, along with the estimated values of S^{real} and π^{max}, are shown in Table 1. The computation of S^{real} and π^{max} at the aggregate level for the dataset is based on our observation of independence of predictability on travel distance (radius of gyration r_g) in human mobility, which is consistent with previous studies [18,27,30].

2.1 Mobility Prediction and Algorithms

We define mobility prediction as forecasting the transitions between places, after eliminating all self-transitions [5,26]. A preliminary step in achieving this consists of transforming the raw GPS locations into a sequences of points of interest. A point of interest is defined as any location where an individual visits with an intentional purpose with a perceived priority for e.g., home/work place, gym, train station etc. We then convert the raw GPS trajectory of a user into a sequence of temporally ordered points of interest, $s(t) = \langle(poi_1, t_1), (poi_2 t_2)...(poi_n, t_n)\rangle$, where poi_i is the point of interest at index i. The mobility prediction task is thus formulated as: given a sequence $s(t)$ up to a timestamp n, predict the next point of interest at timestamp $n + 1$. The prediction accuracy is then estimated by following the approach stated by Lu et al. [18].

We estimate the empirical predictability using seven different approaches: (1) Markov chains [6] (order 1–5), (2) Hidden Markov model(HMM), (3) Vanilla Recurrent Neural Network [9] (Vanilla-RNN), (4) Recurrent Neural Network with Long Short-Term Memory [10] (RNN-LSTM), (5) Dilated Recurrent Neural Network [3] (Dilated-RNN), (6) Recurrent Highway Network [33] (RHN), and

Table 2. Prediction accuracy achieved by the best performing models for each dataset.

Datasets	$\pi^{MC(2)}$	$\pi^{MC(3)}$	$\pi^{HMM(2)}$	π^{RHN}	π^{RNN}
PrivaMov	0.47	0.46	0.60	0.76	0.72 (Dilated-RNN)
NMDC	0.70	0.68	0.66	0.78	0.72 (RNN-LSTM)
GeoLife	0.40	0.36	0.43	0.70	0.66 (PSMM)

(7) Pointer Sentinel Mixture Model [20] (PSMM). We use the standard imple-mentations of the predictive algorithms and hyper-parameters as described in their respective papers. Vanilla-RNN, RNN-LSTM and dilated-RNN are based on predicting the next character (language modeling) in the text, whereas RHN and PSMM, model the prediction task as multivariate classification. We find that higher order Markov chains (typically > 3) do not contribute to increase predic-tion accuracy, as also observed by Lu et al. ([18]). The prediction accuracy for the Markov chain models and the best performing recurrent-neural architectures for each dataset is shown in Fig. 1.

2.2 Conforming Prediction-Accuracy Discrepancy

We observe that the accuracy of Markov models lie in the vicinity of the the-oretical π^{max}. It is also clearly evident that recurrent-neural architectures sig-nificantly outperform Markov models with respect to their average accuracies. Recurrent-neural architectures are a class of artificial neural networks, which use their hidden memory representation to process input sequences. The variants of these architectures differ in their capacity to manipulate this memory and prop-agate gradients along the network. For instance, RHN's are built to account for short and long-range correlations present in a sequence, which explains their superior performance as compared to the other architectures. Whereas, PSMM's weigh long-range dependencies much higher than short-distance correlations in the sequence. In Table 2, we show the maximum predictability achieved by using the best performing models from each algorithm, and in Fig. 1 we compare their performance with the theoretical upper bound.

The prediction accuracies of recurrent-neural architectures also surpass the theoretical upper bound for the respective dataset. This anomaly in computing π^{max} is puzzling, even more so considering the diversity of the datasets with respect to their collective time spans, visited number of locations, demograph-ics and spatiotemporal granularity. This lets us question the assumption that human mobility follows a Markov process. Here, we conduct extensive analysis to empirically prove its non-Markovian nature.

2.3 Statistical Tests to Evaluate Markovian Assumption

In order to gain insight into the datasets, we first analyze the rank distribution of the locations, according to the visit frequency at individual and aggregated

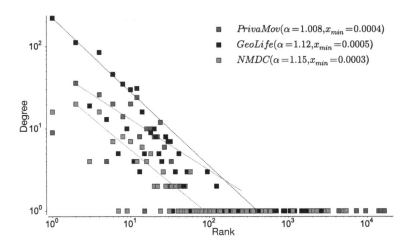

Fig. 2. Rank distribution of location visits at the collective level for aggregated dataset. The data is binned into exponentially wider bins and normalized by the bin width. The straight line represents the fitting through least squares regression (α and x_{min}, computed through maximum likelihood estimation).

levels. An individual visits different locations depending on a perceived priority attached to the location [1]; this results in a heterogenous location frequency distribution [31]. To study the location-rank distribution we rank the locations according to their collective magnitude at the aggregate level. Figure 2 shows the existence of power-law scaling (Zipf's law) (Verified with KS test [19]) in the rank distribution of visited locations in human mobility. We also observe a convergence and robustness at the individual level, which clearly indicates non-uniform mobility behavior and its effect on entropy, hinting at the non-Markovian nature of human mobility.

Next, we analyze the criticality property of human-mobility. Criticality is defined as the property of dynamic systems to regulate their microscopic behavior to be spatiotemporally scale-independent [16]. As a result, critical behavior implies scale invariance; and when criticality is involved, the effects at distances much longer than microscopic lengths are crucial to study. Criticality characteristics are often corroborated by a metric known as Mutual Information I, that quantifies the measure of information provided by a symbol/location coordinate (Y) about another symbol/location coordinate (X). Equation 2 gives mutual information, I, between two discrete random variables X, Y jointly distributed according to the probability mass function $p(x, y)$.

$$I(X, Y) = \sum_{x,y} p(x, y) \log(\frac{p(x, y)}{p(x).p(y)}) \tag{2}$$

In case of human mobility, mutual information between two location instances is the realization of a discrete stochastic process, with separation τ in time [16]. Lin et at. [16,17] express I, as a function of the number of symbols (locations)

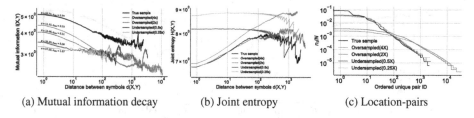

(a) Mutual information decay   (b) Joint entropy   (c) Location-pairs

Fig. 3. Figure 3a and b show the mutual information decay and joint entropy for the GeoLife dataset at different sampling rates. Figure 3c shows the location-pair occurrences across all the sampling rates of the true sample. Here, the x axis represents the unique pair ID in the descending order of their frequency of occurrence. The y axis is the ratio between the unique pairs and the total number of pairs contained in the an individual trajectory.

between any two symbols and state that it would decay with a power-law for any context-free grammar and hence must be non-Markovian. In order to perform this validation on human mobility, we first estimate mutual information as a function of distance for the GeoLife dataset [32]. This choice is based on uniformly sampled location points in the dataset. To validate the emergence of power-law at distinct sampling rates, we under-sample and oversample the dataset by a factor of two and four and show the resulting trend in Fig. 3a. We estimate I by computing the entropy of the marginal distribution of discrete random variables X and Y, and the joint entropy of discrete random variables X and Y.

$$I(X,Y) = H(X) + H(Y) - H(X,Y) = D_{KL}(p(XY)\|p(X)p(Y)) \qquad (3)$$

where $H(X)$ is the entropy of a random variable X and $H(X, Y)$ is the joint entropy of X and Y. D_{KL} is the Kullback-Liebler Divergence [23]. Thus, Mutual Information is same as the Kullback-Leibler Divergence between distributions of X and Y. In order to compensate for insufficient samplings, we use the following adjustment proposed by Grassberger et al. [8] to compute $H(X)$, $H(Y)$, $H(X,Y)$.

$$H(X) = \log N - 1/N \sum_{i=1}^{k} N_i \psi((N_i)) \qquad (4)$$

As suggested by Lin et al. [16], we observe a power-law decay at all the sampling rates. Contrary to our assumption that I would increase and decrease by the factor of under/over sampling, we observe a decrease in I for all the contexts in which the true distribution of the data is altered. We also observe that the reduction is proportional to the Kullback-Leibler divergence between their respective distributions. The reduction in I stems from the fact that a change in the distribution results in the alteration of the true correlation between the location pairs. The true distribution will therefore show maximum I, compared to the cases when either artificial pairs are introduced (oversampling) or true

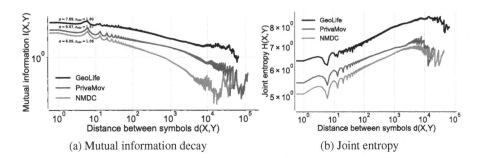

(a) Mutual information decay

(b) Joint entropy

Fig. 4. Mutual information decay and joint entropy for all the datasets. The dataset consists of stacked sequences of temporally arranged individual points of interest.

pairs are removed (under-sampling) from the dataset. To verify our hypothesis, we also calculate the joint entropy for all the cases and observe an increase in $H(X,Y)$ for the altered distributions as shown in Fig. 3b. We see that the increased entropy is due to an increase in the ratio between unique pairs in the dataset over the total number of pairs. The introduction of spurious pairs scrambles the true distribution as it leads to introduction of data points in the true sequence, thereby changing the random variables sampled at distance D, hence reducing I. This occurrence was confirmed after computing the area under the curve (ROC), which was maximum for the true data distribution in the first quartile as compared to the rest, as shown in Fig. 3c. This explains our observation of higher joint entropy for the oversampled and the under-sampled case.

To analyze the long-range correlations present in each of the datasets, we compute their respective mutual information decay. This information will serve as basis for the difference in accuracy for each dataset and the performance difference between the prediction algorithms. Again, we observe a power-law decay across all the datasets and their respective joint entropy, as shown in Fig. 4a and b. We further explore the Markov transition matrices for these datasets and observe that they are reducible and periodic, resulting in the decay of I to a constant. It has been shown that such a characteristic of the transition matrix cannot result in an exponential decay by Lin et al. [16]. They show that an irreducible and aperiodic Markov process, with non-degenerate eigenvalues, cannot produce critical behavior because I decays exponentially. This phenomenon is seen in a number of cases, including hidden and semi-Markov models [16,17]. In the literature, such behavior is superficially dealt with by increasing the state space to include symbols from the past, which does not address the main issue [17] with Markov models; lack of memory. This analysis shows that GeoLife dataset consists of considerably higher number of long-range correlations, compared to the PrivaMov dataset and the NMDC dataset. This should be self-evident from their respective data collection durations. However, the lower dependencies in the NMDC dataset, compared to PrivaMov, is due to the smaller area of the data collection region, which generally results in lower entropy of movement [18,27].

Here, we reason about the accuracy variation within and between the datasets and about the performance differences between the prediction algorithms. We observe that the NMDC dataset provides higher accuracy as compared to the other datasets, and witness a lower variation within the accuracies of different algorithms. This stems from the presence of very short dependencies in the individual trajectories present in the dataset, as seen in Fig. 4. The lower correlations also result in roughly equivalent prediction accuracies within the predictive models. The lower accuracies of recurrent-neural architectures, compared to Markov chain at some time-steps are due to the models tendency to actively seek for long-range dependencies. However, if the dataset does not contain such dependencies, the model underperforms, unless it is weighted to account for such an existence. This underperformance is evident from the behavior of dilated-RNN's, where an increase in dilations (to account for longer dependencies) results in dropping accuracy. Such a phenomenon has also been observed in language modeling tasks, which suggests that this is not a domain specific occurrence [12]. The performance drop in the recurrent-neural architectures at different time steps is due to capturing the long-distance dependencies to different degrees, resulting in either under/over fitting. An additional reason for higher accuracy in NMDC dataset is due to a lower number of unique locations and smaller variations in the dwell-times, as compared to the PrivaMov and GeoLife datasets. These aspects directly correlate with the entropy and thus affect predictability [27]. We also observe that PSMMs, perform better on GeoLife dataset, compared to other two, due to its ability to search for dependencies at longer distances.

Entropy and Predictability Estimation. The current method [11,18,27,31] uses Lempel-Ziv data compression scheme [34] to compute the mobility entropy. This approach segments the complete trajectory into substrings, where a substring is defined as the shortest length element subsequence yet to be encountered. As observed by Lesne et al. [15], a vast majority of substrings are of length one or two, which are the dominant contributors to the entropy. The estimated entropy is thus the outcome of finite-size fluctuations; and the total count of the substrings and of the elements in a substring does not represent the true probability distribution. Furthermore, in this process the structural correlation between the individual substrings is ignored, based on the argument that the probability of joint occurrences is weak [15]. This argument stems from the reasoning that the parsed substrings are independently and identically distributed (iid) according to Gaussian distribution, that does not apply to mobility trajectories. Finally, the correlated features can be compressed only by memorizing all the cases of intervening random variables between the correlated instances [29]. It has thus been proved that Lempel-Ziv approach fails to capture redundancies in the data sources with long-range correlations [15].

More importantly, Storer et al. [29] shows that standard data compression approaches, such as the Lempel-Ziv approach cannot truly capture long-range dependencies, as the information carriers of a sequence lie in its structural origin. However, these approaches limit the entropy estimation process at the sub-string level. Given that entropy is the complete quantitative measure of the dependency relations (including many point correlations), the computation of higher-order entropy is non-trivial. Therefore, it is flawed to assume that the π^{max} derived from such an approximate estimation of S^{real} should act as an upper bound of predictability on trajectories compiled for long time-spans.

3   Discussion

The previous research [18,27] estimated S^{real} and π^{max} by using CDR datasets spanning a period of three to five months. Such datasets do not truly capture features such as the total number of unique locations visited by an individual, due to its low granularity (typically 4–5 km [11]). This results in a dataset with a masked entropy and mobility patterns ignoring long-range correlations. An important point to note is that for very short distances, power-law decay and exponential decay may not be trivial to differentiate [22]. This was due in part to the unavailability of high granularity GPS datasets and the fact that previous works [18,27] were only studied for short distances of human mobility. Therefore, the assumptions underlying the computation of S^{real} and π^{max} would have been fairly easy to overlook.

The aforementioned inadequacies would reinforce the empirical validation of π^{max} using Markov chains, however, as mentioned above this would result in an error-prone estimation of the predictability. As seen in other domains of sequential-data modeling such as natural language processing, it has been shown that Markov chains are fundamentally unsuitable for modeling such processes [4]. Our empirical observations, backed by theoretical foundations, indicate that human mobility will be poorly approximated by Markov chains. This is particularly afflictive for trajectories that satisfy criteria such as long time-span of collection and large radius of gyration of movement.

Our choice to rely on mutual information was based on its triviality and its domain independence. As shown by Lin et al. ([16]), the mutual information decay offers some insights into why recurrent-neural architectures exceed probabilistic models in terms of capturing criticality. As for a Markov process, the observations at t_n depends only on events at previous time step t_{n-1} or on previous n time-steps for an n-order Markov chain. Under such a context, the maximum possible predictive information is given by the entropy of the distribution of states at one time step, which is in turn bounded by the logarithm of the number of accessible states. Unlike Markov chains, the recurrent-neural architectures, such as RHN's, approach this bound while maintaining the memory long enough, that the predictive information is reduced by the entropy of transition probabilities.

We expect to provide a more sophisticated description of the underlying phenomenon as more of the trajectory is observed. Consequently, increasing the number of parameters in the model. That is, when we examine trajectories on the scale of individual coordinates, we learn about the rules of combining these points into points of interest and the transition paths between them. At the next level, if we consider several of these points of interest and the paths, we learn the rules for combining these points into semantic patterns. Similarly, when we look at semantic patterns, we learn about the visitation periodicities and circadian rhythms associated with the mobility behaviors. Therefore, longer traces have increasing number of long range structural correlations that are non-trivial to be captured by the currently available entropy measure. Moreover, the current approximation implies that the substrings have the same compressibility factor [34], hence the results derived from this approach would coincide with the average. Thus, the current computation will result in higher estimates of entropy, consequently resulting in a lower predictability bound.

Even though Markov models tend to underperform in modeling, their use in mobility prediction is not entirely without precedent. In fact, considering their low computational complexity, it might be advantageous to opt for a Markov model when a dataset contains short-distance dependencies and low number of unique locations. However, in datasets exhibiting criticality, long-range correlations appear in the vicinity of the critical point, which necessitate recurrent-neural architectures to accurately model human mobility. We argue that precise quantification of long-distance dependencies present in mobility datasets can lead to selection of appropriate prediction models.

4   Conclusion

In this paper, we have shown that human mobility exhibits scale-invariant long-range correlations which can be quantitatively measured by a power-law decay of mutual information. We highlight that the exponent characterizing the power-law decay of the correlations is well defined for infinite sequences. For mobility trajectories, however, the accuracy of the analysis is restricted by the length of the substrings and their entropy, which results in an incorrect estimation of maximum predictability. This explains why the empirical results obtained using recurrent neural network variants surpass the theoretical upper bound in several previous research works and in our own experiments.

Acknowledgements. This research work was partially supported by the Swiss National Science Foundation grant 157160. This research was also supported by the ADAPT Research Centre, funded under the SFI Research Centres Programme (Grant 13/ RC/2106) and is co-funded under the European Regional Development Funds. The research was also supported by an IBM Shared University Research Award.

References

1. Barabasi, A.L.: The origin of bursts and heavy tails in human dynamics. Nature **435**(7039), 207 (2005)
2. Bialek, W., Tishby, N.: Predictive information. arXiv preprint cond-mat/9902341 (1999)
3. Chang, S., et al.: Dilated recurrent neural networks. In: NIPS (2017)
4. Chomsky, N.: On certain formal properties of grammars. Inf. Control **2**(2), 137–167 (1959)

5. Cuttone, A., Lehmann, S., González, M.C.: Understanding predictability and exploration in human mobility. EPJ Data Sci. **7**(1), 2 (2018)
6. Gambs, S., Killijian, M.O., del Prado Cortez, M.N.: Next place prediction using mobility Markov chains. In: Proceedings of the First Workshop on Measurement, Privacy, and Mobility, p. 3. ACM (2012)
7. Gerchinovitz, S., Ménard, P., Stoltz, G.: Fano's inequality for random variables. arXiv preprint arXiv:1702.05985 (2017)
8. Grassberger, P.: Entropy estimates from insufficient samplings. arXiv preprint physics/0307138 (2003)
9. Grossberg, S.: Recurrent neural networks. Scholarpedia **8**(2), 1888 (2013)
10. Hochreiter, S., Schmidhuber, J.: Long short-term memory. Neural Comput. **9**(8), 1735–80 (1997)
11. Ikanovic, E.L., Mollgaard, A.: An alternative approach to the limits of predictability in human mobility. EPJ Data Sci. **6**(1), 12 (2017)
12. Khandelwal, U., He, H., Qi, P., Jurafsky, D.: Sharp nearby, fuzzy far away: how neural language models use context. arXiv preprint arXiv:1805.04623 (2018)
13. Krumme, C., Llorente, A., Cebrian, M., Moro, E., et al.: The predictability of consumer visitation patterns. Sci. Rep. **3**, 1645 (2013)
14. Laurila, J.K., et al.: The mobile data challenge: big data for mobile computing research. In: Pervasive Computing, No. EPFL-CONF-192489 (2012)
15. Lesne, A., Blanc, J.L., Pezard, L.: Entropy estimation of very short symbolic sequences. Phys. Rev. E **79**(4), 046208 (2009)
16. Lin, H.W., Tegmark, M.: Critical behavior from deep dynamics: a hidden dimension in natural language. arXiv preprint arXiv:1606.06737 (2016)
17. Lin, H.W., Tegmark, M.: Critical behavior in physics and probabilistic formal languages. Entropy **19**(7), 299 (2017)
18. Lu, X., Wetter, E., Bharti, N., Tatem, A.J., Bengtsson, L.: Approaching the limit of predictability in human mobility. Sci. Rep. **3**, 2923 (2013)
19. Massey Jr., F.J.: The Kolmogorov-Smirnov test for goodness of fit. J. Am. Stat. Assoc. **46**(253), 68–78 (1951)
20. Merity, S., Xiong, C., Bradbury, J., Socher, R.: Pointer sentinel mixture models. CoRR abs/1609.07843 (2016)
21. Mokhtar, S.B., et al.: PRIVA'MOV: analysing human mobility through multi-sensor datasets. In: NetMob 2017 (2017)
22. Newman, M.E.: Power laws, pareto distributions and Zipf's law. Contemp. Phys. **46**(5), 323–351 (2005)
23. Pérez-Cruz, F.: Kullback-Leibler divergence estimation of continuous distributions. In: 2008 IEEE International Symposium on Information Theory, pp. 1666–1670 (2008)
24. Prelov, V.V., van der Meulen, E.C.: Mutual information, variation, and Fano's inequality. Probl. Inf. Trans. **44**(3), 185–197 (2008)
25. Schmidhuber, J.: Deep learning in neural networks: an overview. Neural Netw. **61**, 85–117 (2015)
26. Smith, G., Wieser, R., Goulding, J., Barrack, D.: A refined limit on the predictability of human mobility. In: 2014 IEEE International Conference on Pervasive Computing and Communications (PerCom), pp. 88–94. IEEE (2014)
27. Song, C., Qu, Z., Blumm, N., Barabási, A.L.: Limits of predictability in human mobility. Science **327**(5968), 1018–1021 (2010)
28. Song, L., Kotz, D., Jain, R., He, X.: Evaluating next-cell predictors with extensive Wi-Fi mobility data. IEEE Trans. Mob. Comput. **5**(12), 1633–1649 (2006)

29. Storer, J.A.: Data Compression: Methods and Theory. Computer Science Press, Inc., Rockville (1987)
30. Yan, X.Y., Han, X.P., Wang, B.H., Zhou, T.: Diversity of individual mobility patterns and emergence of aggregated scaling laws. Sci. Rep. **3**, 2678 (2013)
31. Zhao, Z.D., Cai, S.M., Lu, Y.: Non-Markovian character in human mobility online and offline. Chaos: Interdisc. J. Nonlinear Sci. **25**(6), 063106 (2015)
32. Zheng, Y., Xie, X., Ma, W.Y.: Geolife: a collaborative social networking service among user, location and trajectory. IEEE Data Eng. Bull. **33**(2), 32–39 (2010)
33. Zilly, J.G., Srivastava, R.K., Koutník, J., Schmidhuber, J.: Recurrent highway networks. In: ICML (2017)
34. Ziv, J., Lempel, A.: Compression of individual sequences via variable-rate coding. IEEE Trans. Inf. Theory **24**(5), 530–536 (1978)

LSTM with Uniqueness Attention for Human Activity Recognition

Zengwei Zheng[1], Lifei Shi[1,2], Chi Wang[1,2], Lin Sun[1(✉)], and Gang Pan[2]

[1] Hangzhou Key Laboratory for IoT Technology and Application,
Zhejiang University City College, Hangzhou, China
{zhengzw,sunl}@zucc.edu.cn
[2] College of Computer Science and Technology, Zhejiang University,
Hangzhou, China
{shilf,cwangup,gpan}@zju.edu.cn

Abstract. Deep neural network has promoted the development of human activity recognition research and becomes an indispensable tool for it. Deep neural networks, such as LSTM, can automatically learn important features from the data of human activities. But parts of these data are irrelevant and correspond to the Null activity [3], which can affect the recognition performance. Therefore, we propose a uniqueness attention mechanism to solve this problem. Every human activity consists of many atom motions. Some of these atom motions only occur in one single human activity. This kind of motion is more effective to discriminate human activities, and should therefore receive more attention. We design a model, named LSTM with Uniqueness Attention. When we identify the category of an unknown activity, our model first discover unknown activity's atom motions which are unique to a known activity, and then use these motions to discriminate this unknown activity. In this way, irrelevant information can be filtered out. Moreover, by discovering an activity's unique atom motion, we can get more insights to understand this human activity. We evaluate our approach on two public datasets and obtain state-of-the-art results. We also visualize this uniqueness attention, which has an excellent interpretability and goes pretty well with common sense.

Keywords: LSTM · Uniqueness attention ·
Human activity recognition · Interpretability

1 Introduction

The research of human activity recognition (HAR) aim to extract knowledge from the data acquired by sensors [1]. It's a significant research field, due to its potential in providing personalized support for many applications such as smart environments, surveillance and homeland security. In earlier studies, researchers used traditional machine learning methods to deal with this problem. But these methods' ability to handle raw data was limited [2]. Therefore, it is necessary

© Springer Nature Switzerland AG 2019
I. V. Tetko et al. (Eds.): ICANN 2019, LNCS 11729, pp. 498–509, 2019.
https://doi.org/10.1007/978-3-030-30508-6_40

to extract features from the collected sensor data and convert the raw data into an appropriate internal representation. This internal representation is then sent to various classifiers for training. These methods require researchers to have skills of feature engineering, and deep understanding on the differences between activities to be identified in order to design good features. Deep learning frees us from designing features, and the rise of it provides us with a new way to study human activity recognition.

Deep learning is a kind of representation learning methods that allows researchers to obtain excellent features without knowing professional background knowledge. RNNs is a kind of deep learning method. It can process time series data one by one according to its time, and maintain a 'state vector' in their hidden units, which contains information of the past elements of the input data [2]. In addition, HAR's data is a kind of time series data. Therefore, it is quite appropriate for RNNs to process the sensor data of human activity. However, when dealing with HAR, RNNs also has some problems: In HAR, only a few parts of time-series data are relevant to human activities, while the dominant parts are irrelevant [3]. This makes it difficult for RNNs to capture important parts of human activity. We combined an attention mechanism with the LSTM, a type of RNNs, so that it can focus on the more important parts.

Every human activity consists of many atom motions, such as running and walking. Some of these atom motions are common to both running and walking, and thus not appropriate for distinguishing human activity. There is also motion that only happens when you are running, which is suitable for classification. Our definition of atom motion is very broad. Every movement for a short period can be considered as atom motion. Since LSTM's state vector is mainly affected by the input of a short period from the current to the recent past, this state vector can represent the current atom motion. The degree to which an atom motion uniquely belong to one single activity is called uniqueness of this motion in this paper. We use LSTM's state vector to calculate this uniqueness, and then determine how much attention our model should pay to these atom motions.

Our main contribution in this paper is that we design a model, which called LSTM with Uniqueness Attention. This model derives from our understanding on the relationship between human activity and the atom motions that make up it. And it treats the uniqueness of the current motion as its attention weight. In addition, we visualize our uniqueness attention. Then we show this attention's noteworthy characteristics, and explain why these characteristics are reasonable.

2 Related Work

In the earlier study of HAR, the common process was to extract features from the raw data and then carry out machine learning. Usually two kinds of features were extracted: (i) time-domain features, such as mean, variance, interquartile range (IQR), mean absolute deviation (MAD), correlation between axes, entropy, and kurtosis [4,6–11]; and (ii) frequency-domain features, such as Discrete Cosine Transform (DCT) [13] and Fourier Transform (FT) [9,10]. Some works also introduced Principal Component Analysis (PCA) [13,14] and Linear Discriminant Analysis (LDA) [10] to reduce the dimension of features in order to select the most important information for classification.

Due to the great representation potential of deep learning and its ability to automatically learn features, more and more efforts have been made to combine HAR with deep learning in recent years, which not only allows researchers to avoid extracting features, but also greatly improves the performance of identifying human activities. Plotz et al. [14] combined restricted Boltzmann machine (RBM) with HAR. It stacked up multiple layers of RBM to form a deep belief networks (DBN), which can be used for feature extraction. Alsheikh et al. implemented hidden Markov models (HMMs) above the RBM layers [15], so that we can utilize HMM's ability to stochastic model temporal sequences. What's more, a large number of unlabeled acceleration samples were used for unsupervised feature extraction, which solved the problem of scarcity of labeled training data [15]. However, HMM is limited by the number of hidden states, it is therefore impractical to model long-term dependencies in a large context window [16].

There were two works that introduced convolutional neural networks (CNNs) to HAR [17,18]. Both of these two methods used only one accelerometer. whereas the latter has a deeper CNNs. A CNNs model, proposed in [20], inputted multichannel time series signals acquired from a set of body worn inertial sensors and outputted categories of human activity. Moreover, this works used 2D CNN, which regards the time-series data as an image. In this way, it can fuse different sensor modalities [21].

Since human activity consists of a series of atom motions that follow one another in time, it is very important for HAR to capture this temporal dynamic. RNNs is well suited for this task, and there were already many efforts to combine HAR with RNNs [16,19,20]. Hammerla et al. [19] rigorously explored deep, convolutional, and recurrent approaches across three representative datasets. What's more, this works introduced a novel regularization approach. Ordonez et al. [16] proposed a generic deep framework for HAR using convolutional and LSTM recurrent units [20], which can perform sensor fusion naturally. Murad et al. proposed a deep recurrent neural networks (DRNNs), which can capture long-range dependencies in variable-length input sequences. Their proposed three architectures based on long and short-term memory (LSTM) DRNNs: unidirectional, bidirectional, and cascaded architectures respectively, and evaluate their effectiveness on various benchmark data sets.

However, RNNs may encode irrelevant information. The attention mechanism was derived from human intuition, and proposed to mitigate this problem. This mechanism was then applied to machine translation for automatic token alignment [22–24]. Zeng et al. [21] introduced attention mechanism to HAR problem at the earliest, which included temporal attention and sensor attention. They used LSTM to encode the time-series data and calculate an attention weight of each LSTM's state vector based on the current and the last state vector. To further improve the understandability and mean F1 score, Zeng et al. [21] added continuity constraints, which was consistent with our intuition that our temporal attention to atom motion should be continuous over time. When we designed our model, we did not add any continuity constraints, but the experimental results show that our uniqueness attention is naturally continuous over time, and F_m of our model is also higher than that of [21], which indicates our method may be more suitable for HAR problems than that of zeng et al. [21].

3 Method

The data we obtained are all collected at a certain frequency by sensors worn by volunteers. We assume that the number of data collected at each time is N, which is determined by the characteristics and number of sensors. We use a time window of length T to partition the data, which means that the data collected at continuous time T are combined. We denote the data of time window T as $\mathbf{X} = (x_1, x_2, \cdots, x_T)$, in which x_t denotes a sensor reading at time t. Let's assume $x_t = (x_t^1, x_t^2, \cdots, x_t^N)$, in which x_t^n denotes the n-th data of N data collected at time t. Each $\mathbf{X}$ has a real label $y_r \in \mathbf{A}$, and a predicted label $y_p = model(\mathbf{X}) \in \mathbf{A}$, where $\mathbf{A}$ represents the set of activities to be identified, and $model(\cdot)$ represents model used to map the input $\mathbf{X}$ to a target y_p. Both y_r and y_p are vector whose dimension is equal to the number of activities to be identified. We use cross-entropy as the loss function:

$$L(\mathbf{X}, y_r) = -y_r \log(model(\mathbf{X})) = -y_r \log(y_p). \tag{1}$$

In the following subsections, we introduce a general model from which our model with uniqueness attention can be derived. To demonstrate that our model can indeed focus on important parts of the input data, we derive two benchmark models from this general model. In the following section of experiment, we compare our model with these two benchmark models to prove our model's effectiveness.

3.1 LSTM with Generic Attention

Long short-term memory (LSTM) was proposed to capture the long-term information in time series data [25], and have been successfully applied in HAR [16,20]. In this paper, we also use LSTM as a basic tool to encode time series data into hidden state vector. The structure of this generic model is described in Fig. 1.

In Fig. 1, each line represents data, or the result of processed data; each rectangular module represents an operation, which means that it process the input data and output the corresponding results. The *softmax* module in Fig. 1 represents a fully connected layer with softmax activation function. It takes H as its input and outputs predicted label y_p. The *LSTM* module inputs x_t according to its time and outputs the corresponding state vector h_t. The *genAtt* module will extract the important part of these state vectors h_t's and combine it into H, which has the same shape as h_t. The right elliptic region in Fig. 1 represents

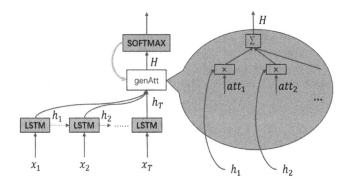

Fig. 1. Structure of LSTM with Generic Attention

the internal structure diagram of its left *genAtt* module. As can be seen from this elliptic region, the *genAtt* module will calculate attention weight att_t for each h_t. All of these h_t, will be multiplied by corresponding att_t, and then added together to form H, which can be defined by the formula below:

$$H = \sum_{t=1}^{T} att_t h_t. \tag{2}$$

We call this model as LSTM with Generic Attention because we don't specify how to calculate attention weights. In order to compare with the attention model proposed below, we specify two way to calculate the attention weight, and thus form two benchmark models: **LSTM with Last Attention**, and **LSTM with Mean Attention**. LSTM with Last Attention only care about the last state vector, so this model sets the attention weight of the last vector to 1 and the rest to 0. LSTM with Mean Attention pays equal attention to each of these state vector, therefore this model gives the same attention weight to all of these vectors.

3.2 LSTM with Uniqueness Attention

Human activity consists of many atom motions. Since the atom motion that is unique to a single activity contain more information in identifying human activities than those that is common to multiple activities, we design a method to measure the uniqueness of atom motions and propose this model: LSTM with Uniqueness Attention. The structure of this model is described in Fig. 2. Notice that all of these *softmax* modules in this figure are exactly the same module. We use *softmax* modules, which will be finally used for discrimination, to determine the uniqueness of the atom motions in advance. The notation in right elliptic region of Fig. 2 can be defined by the following formula:

$$prob_t = softmax(h_t) \tag{3}$$

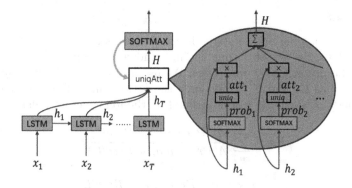

Fig. 2. Structure of LSTM with Uniqueness Attention

$$score_t = max_1(prob_t) - max_2(prob_t) \tag{4}$$

$$att_t = uniq(prob_t) = \frac{score_t}{\sum_{t=1}^{T} score_t} \tag{5}$$

$$H = \sum_{t=1}^{T} att_t h_t, \tag{6}$$

where $prob_t$ is a vector which represents a probability distribution over different human activities. $max_1(\cdot)$ and $max_2(\cdot)$ are used to calculate the largest and second largest value in vector of $prob_t$. $uniq(\cdot)$ represents $uniq$ modules in Fig. 2, which will be used to caculate attention weight of each h_t.

In Fig. 2, each h_t's attention weight is only determined by itself and *softmax* module. h_t is first processed by *softmax* module, and then turned into $prob_t$. If the current atom motion is unique to an activity, the difference between the largest and second largest value in vector of $prob_t$ should be quite large. So $uniq$ module, defined by Equation (9) and Equation (10), use this difference to calculate the uniqueness attention of h_t. Then, we use the calculation defined in Equation (11) to get H, which will finally result in the activity recognition result through the *softmax* module.

4   Experiment

We compare our model, LSTM with Uniqueness Attention, with other methods in two publicly available datasets with the same settings as previous works. The results that our method can achieve the best performance show its effectiveness. In order to test whether our model can pay more attention to important part of the input data, we also compare our model with two benchmark model: LSTM with Mean and Last Attention, whose attention weights are fixed. Finally, we visualize the uniqueness attention obtained by our model on the PAMAP2 dataset, which is in good agreement with human intuition of activity.

4.1   Datasets

Two publicly available datasets are chosen to test our idea. Both of them are time-series data. So we set a time sliding window to segment each dataset so that it can be processed by our model. We use mean F_1 score and weighted F_1 score, denoted as F_m and F_w, to evaluate the performance of our method versus other methods. F_m and F_w can be defined by the following formulas:

$$F_m = \sum_{c=1}^{A} \frac{2 \cdot Precision_c \cdot Recall_c}{A(Precision_c + Recall_c)}. \tag{7}$$

$$F_w = \sum_{c=1}^{A} \frac{2 \cdot n_c \cdot Precision_c \cdot Recall_c}{N(Precision_c + Recall_c)}. \tag{8}$$

where $A = |\mathbf{A}|$ denotes the number of set $\mathbf{A}$. $\mathbf{A}$ represents the set of activities to be identified. n_c is the number of samples in class c, and N is the total number of samples.

The **PAMAP2** (Physical Activity Monitoring for Aging People 2) [27] dataset contains 12 types of activities. And there are 9 subjects participated in the data collection. Each of them wore a Heart-Rate-monitor (HR-monitor) and three inertial measurement units (IMUs), which were bound to the subjects' dominant arm, chest and dominant side's ankles respectively. The sampling frequency of IMUs and HR-monitor are 100 Hz and 9 Hz respectively. Each IMUs gathered 17 data in each moment, which contains one temperature data, six 3D-acceleration data, three 3D-gyroscope data, three 3D-magnetometer data and four orientation data. Thus, the resulting dataset had 52 dimensions. To be consistent with previous work [19,21,28], we choose subject 6 as the test set, subject 5 as validation set, and the rest as training set, and downsample the IMUs data and interpolated HR-monitor data to 33 Hz. The sliding window is 5.12 s, and the adjacent windows have 78% overlap.

The **Opportunity dataset** [26] was collected by four subjects. Each of them perform activity of daily living (termed ADL) five times and a large set of activity instances (termed drill run) one time. There are 7 IMUs mounted on a motion jacket and foot, and 12 3-axis acceleration sensors on the limbs. Following the challenge guidelines, only on-body sensors were taken into account, yielding an input space dimensionality of 113. The recording's sample rate is 30 Hz. The dataset contains two types of labels: Gestures with 18 categories and Locomotion with 5 categories. So there are two kinds of classification tasks. Following the work of predecessors [20,26], we set ADL4 and ADL5 of participants 2 and 3 as testing set, and the rest as training set. We used the 1 s sliding window. In addition, we perform linear interpolation to deal with missing values in these datasets, and normalize all sensor channels to zero mean and unit variance.

4.2   Comparing on the PAMAP2 Dataset

Because of the huge potential of deep learning (DL), in most cases the DL method can achieve better performance than the traditional machine learning

(ML) method when dealing with HAR problem. So we compare our method with other deep learning methods, such as deepConvLSTM [20] and Temporal Attention [21]. Furthermore, to demonstrate that our uniqueness attention is indeed effective, we also compare our method with two benchmark models: LSTM with Mean and Last Attention.

Table 1. F_m results achieved by different DL models

Models	F_m
deepConvLSTM [20]	0.7480
Temporal Attention [21]	0.8052
Continuous + Temporal Attention [21]	0.8629
LSTM with Mean Attention	0.7922
LSTM with Last Attention	0.7568
LSTM with Uniqueness Attention	**0.8796**

The results are shown in Table 1. LSTM with Uniqueness Attention outperforms deepConvLSTM [20], Temporal Attention [21] and Continuous Temporal Attention [21] by as much as 13.16%, 7.44% and 1.67%. This model also achieves around 8.74% and 12.28% improvements in F_m, compared to these two LSTM benchmark models, which indicate that it can indeed focus on the more important parts on the PAMAP2 dataset.

4.3 Comparing on the Opportunity Dataset

Chavarriaga et al. [26] introduced the Opportunity challenge, and provided four well-known classification methods: Linear Discriminant Analysis (LDA), Quadratic Discriminant Analysis(QDA), k-Nearest Neighbours (k-NN), and Nearest Centroid Classifier (NCC), together with nine contributions submitted to this challenge. We use methods of two best contributions, CStar and SStar, and four well-known classification methods mentioned before as baseline to verify our method. We also use a CNN model proposed in [20] for comparison.

The results are shown in Table 2. As can be seen, among methods of [26], CStar can achieve the best performance to classify modes of gesture. But it performs poorly to classify modes of locomotion. The last four methods in Table 2 are deep learning methods. They are all better than the first six methods. LSTM with Uniqueness Attention outperforms two LSTM benchmark models, as expected, indicating that it can focus on important parts on the Opportunity dataset. The fact that LSTM with Uniqueness Attention outperforms any other method also shows its effectiveness.

4.4 Visualizing Uniqueness Attention

The above results show that our uniqueness attention is indeed effective. To better understand how our uniqueness attention work, we visualize the attention

Table 2. F_w results achieved by different methods

Models	Locomotion	Gesture
LDA [26]	0.590	0.690
QDA [26]	0.680	0.530
NCC [26]	0.540	0.510
kNN (k = 3) [26]	0.850	0.850
CStar [26]	0.630	0.870
SStar [26]	0.640	0.840
CNN [20]	0.878	0.883
LSTM with Mean Attention	0.873	0.894
LSTM with Last Attention	0.875	0.889
LSTM with Uniqueness Attention	**0.892**	**0.904**

weight gained from our model. The visualized results are shown in Figs. 3 and 4. All of these two figures represent the walking and running data in a sliding windows time of 5.12s in PAMAP2 dataset.

One noteworthy characteristic of this uniqueness attention in Fig. 3 is that it changes periodically. Walking and running are ideal periodical activity. So if there's an atom motion that's only occur in walking (or running), it should

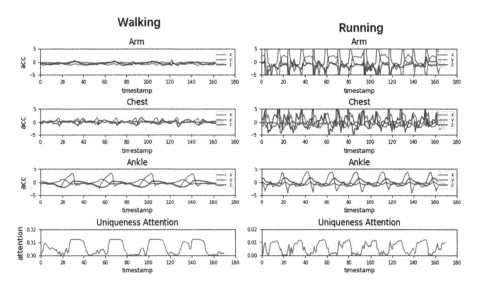

Fig. 3. Walking and running examples on PAMAP2. In either of these two subgraphs, the first three coordinates diagrams describe the acceleration information of the subjects' arms, chest and ankle respectively. The last coordinates diagram describes the corresponding uniqueness attention.

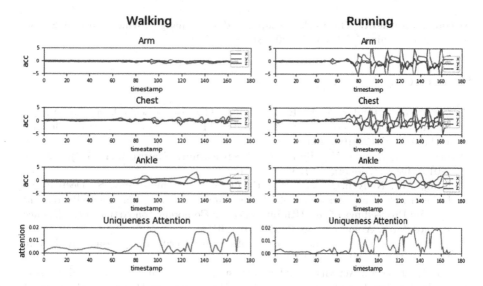

Fig. 4. Another walking and running examples on PAMAP2.

occur periodically as the subjects walks (or runs). Moreover, the cycle time of uniqueness attention should be the same as that of walking (or running). Our visualized results fit perfectly with these ideas.

Noteworthy characteristic in Fig. 4 is that uniqueness attention is almost zero at the beginning. In this figure, the subject start to walk and run at timestamp of 80 and 70, respectively. And this characteristic is reasonable because we shouldn't pay too much attention to the time before the subjects walking or running. Another characteristic is that the peak of uniqueness attention in Fig. 4 is larger than that in Fig. 3. This is because we have normalized attention weights of LSTM's state vector so that the sum of these weights equals to 1. In Fig. 4, the attention weight is small at the beginning. The peak in Fig. 4 needs to be larger so that the sum of all the weights can be equal to 1. This characteristic has an advantage: during an activity, the more atom motions that are irrelevant there are, the more attention our model can give to important atom motions.

5   Conclusion

Based on our understanding on the relationship between atom motion and human activity, we propose a deep learning model: LSTM with Uniqueness Attention. This model outperforms other model on two dataset, which indicates its effectiveness. We also set up two LSTM benchmarks: LSTM with Last and Mean Attention. The fact that our uniqueness attention model is better than these two LSTM benchmarks suggests that the uniqueness attention mechanism does enable our model to focus on the important parts of the input. In the end, by visualizing our uniqueness attention, we show the characteristics of this attention, and explain how similar are these characteristics to human intuition.

Acknowledgement. This work was supported by Zhejiang Provincial Natural Science Foundation of China (NO. LY17F020008).

References

1. Perez, A., Labrador, M.A., Barbeau, S.J.: G-Sense: a scalable architecture for global sensing and monitoring. IEEE Netw. **24**(4), 57–64 (2010). https://doi.org/10.1109/MNET.2010.5510920
2. LeCun, Y., Bengio, Y., Hinton, G.: Deep learning. Nature **521**(7553), 436–444 (2015). https://doi.org/10.1038/nature14539
3. Yang, J.B., Nguyen, M.N., San, P.P., Li, X.L., Krishnaswamy, S.: Deep convolutional neural networks on multichannel time series for human activity recognition. In: Proceedings of the 24th International Conference on Artificial Intelligence, Buenos Aires, Argentina, pp. 3995–4001 (2015)
4. Westerterp, K.R.: Assessment of physical activity: a critical appraisal. Eur. J. Appl. Physiol. **105**(6), 823–828 (2009)
5. Parkka, J., et al.: Activity classification using realistic data from wearable sensors. In: International Conference of the IEEE Engineering in Medicine, vol. 10, no. 1, pp. 119–128(2006). https://doi.org/10.1109/TITB.2005.856863
6. Tapia, E.M., et al.: Real-time recognition of physical activities and their intensities using wireless accelerometers and a heart rate monitor. In: Proceedings of the International Symposium on Wearable Computers, pp. 1–4 (2007). https://doi.org/10.1109/ISWC.2007.4373774
7. Kao, T.P., Lin, C., Wang, J.: Development of a portable activity detector for daily activity recognition. In: Proceedings of the International Symposium on Industrial Electronics, pp. 115–120 (2009). https://doi.org/10.1109/ISIE.2009.5222001
8. Maurer, U., Smailagic, A., Siewiorek, D.P., Deisher, M.E.: Activity recognition and monitoring using multiple sensors on different body positions. In: Proceedings of the Wearable and Implantable Body Sensor Networks, pp. 113–116 (2006). https://doi.org/10.1109/BSN.2006.6
9. Bao, L., Intille, S.S.: Activity recognition from user-annotated acceleration data. In: Ferscha, A., Mattern, F. (eds.) Pervasive 2004. LNCS, vol. 3001, pp. 1–17. Springer, Heidelberg (2004). https://doi.org/10.1007/978-3-540-24646-6_1
10. Chen, Y., Yang, J., Liou, S., Lee, G., Wang, J.: Online classifier construction algorithm for human activity detection using a tri-axial accelerometer. Appl. Math. Comput. **205**(2), 849–860 (2008). https://doi.org/10.1016/j.amc.2008.05.099
11. Ermes, M., Parkka, J., Cluitmans, L.: Advancing from offline to online activity recognition with wearable sensors. In: International Conference of the IEEE Engineering in Medicine and Biology Society, pp. 4451–4454 (2008). https://doi.org/10.1109/IEMBS.2008.4650199
12. He, Z.Y., Jin, L.W.: Activity recognition from acceleration data based on discrete cosine transform and SVM. In: 2009 IEEE International Conference on Systems, Man and Cybernetics, pp. 5041–5044. IEEE, New York (2009). https://doi.org/10.1109/ICSMC.2009.5346042
13. Altun, K., Barshan, B.: Human activity recognition using inertial/magnetic sensor units. In: Salah, A.A., Gevers, T., Sebe, N., Vinciarelli, A. (eds.) HBU 2010. LNCS, vol. 6219, pp. 38–51. Springer, Heidelberg (2010). https://doi.org/10.1007/978-3-642-14715-9_5

14. Plotz, T., Hammerla, N.Y., Olivier, P.: Feature learning for activity recognition in ubiquitous computing. In: International Joint Conference on Artificial Intelligence, pp. 1729–1734 (2011). https://doi.org/10.5591/978-1-57735-516-8/IJCAI11-290
15. Alsheikh, M.A., Selim, A., Niyato, D., Doyle, L., Lin, S., Tan, H.: Deep activity recognition models with triaxial accelerometers. In: National Conference on Artificial Intelligence (2016)
16. Murad, A., Pyun, J.-Y.: Deep recurrent neural networks for human activity recognition. Sensors **17**(11), 2556 (2017). https://doi.org/10.3390/s17112556
17. Zeng, M., et al.: Convolutional neural networks for human activity recognition using mobile sensors. In: 2014 6th International Conference on Mobile Computing, Applications and Services, pp. 197–205 (2014). https://doi.org/10.4108/icst. mobicase.2014.257786
18. Chen, Y., Xue, Y.: A deep learning approach to human activity recognition based on single accelerometer. In: 2015 IEEE International Conference on Systems, Man, and Cybernetics, pp. 1488–1492. IEEE (2015). https://doi.org/10.1109/SMC.2015. 263
19. Hammerla, N.Y., Halloran, S., Plotz, T.: Deep, convolutional, and recurrent models for human activity recognition using wearables. In: Proceedings of the International Joint Conference on Artificial Intelligence, pp. 1533–1540 (2016)
20. Ordonez, F.J., Roggen, D.: Deep convolutional and LSTM recurrent neural networks for multimodal wearable activity recognition. Sensors **16**(1), 115 (2016). https://doi.org/10.3390/s16010115
21. Zeng, M., et al.: Understanding and improving recurrent networks for human activity recognition by continuous attention. In: Proceedings of the 2018 ACM International Symposium on Wearable Computers, pp. 56–63. ACM, Singapore (2018). https://doi.org/10.1145/3267242.3267286
22. Bahdanau, D., Cho, K., Bengio, Y.: Neural machine translation by jointly learning to align and translate, arXiv (2014)
23. Luong, M.-T., Pham, H., Manning, C.D.: Effective approaches to attention-based neural machine translation, arXiv (2015)
24. Hu, D.: An introductory survey on attention mechanisms in NLP problems, arXiv (2018)
25. Hochreiter, S., Schmidhuber, J.: Long short-term memory. Neural Comput. **9**(8), 1735–1780 (1997)
26. Chavarriaga, R., Sagha, H., Calatroni, A.: The opportunity challenge: a benchmark database for on-body sensor-based activity recognition. Pattern Recognit. Lett. **34**, 2033–2042 (2013). https://doi.org/10.1016/j.patrec.2012.12.014
27. Reiss, A., Stricker, D.: Introducing a new benchmarked dataset for activity monitoring. In: ISWC, pp. 108–109(2012). https://doi.org/10.1109/ISWC.2012.13
28. Rueda, F.M. Fink, G.A.: Learning attribute representation for human activity recognition. In: International Conference on Pattern Recognition, pp. 523–528. https://doi.org/10.1109/icpr.2018.8545146

Comparative Research on SOM with Torus and Sphere Topologies for Peculiarity Classification of Flat Finishing Skill Training

Masaru Teranishi$^{(\boxtimes)}$ ⓘ, Shimpei Matsumoto ⓘ, and Hidetoshi Takeno

Hiroshima Institute of Technology, Hiroshima, Japan
teranisi@cc.it-hiroshima.ac.jp

Abstract. The paper compares classification performances on Self-Organizing Maps (SOMs) by torus and spherical topologies in the case of peculiarities classification of flat finishing motion with an iron file measured by a 3D stylus. In case of manufacturing skill training, peculiarities of tool motion are useful information for learners. Classified peculiarities are also useful especially for trainers to grasp effectively the tendency of the learners' peculiarities in their class. In the authors' former studies, a torus SOM are considered to be powerful tools to classify and visualize peculiarities with its borderless topological feature map structure. In this paper, the authors compare the classification performance of two kind of borderless topological SOMs: torus SOM and spherical SOM by quality measurements.

Keywords: Motion analysis · Skill training · Self Organizing Maps · Clustering

1 Introduction

In the technical education of junior high schools in Japan, new educational tools and materials are in development, for the purpose to transfer kinds of crafting technology. When a learner studies technical skills by using the educational tools, two practices are considered to be important: (1) to imitate motions of experts and (2) to notice their own "Peculiarity", and correct it with appropriate aids.

However, present educational materials are not yet effective to assist the practices because most materials consist still or motion pictures of tool motions of experts and have the following drawbacks. It is difficult for learners to imitate detailed experts' motion and postures of the tools due to less image information from fixed viewpoints these materials have. Furthermore, the learners could not recognize their own "peculiarity" because they could not make a difference of motions between the expert's and the learner.

One of the solution for the problem, a new assistant system for a brush coating skill has developed [2,3]. The system presents a learner corrective suggestion

© Springer Nature Switzerland AG 2019
I. V. Tetko et al. (Eds.): ICANN 2019, LNCS 11729, pp. 510–522, 2019.
https://doi.org/10.1007/978-3-030-30508-6_41

by play-backing the learner's motion by using animated 3D Graphics. On the other hand, we are developing a new technical educational assistant system [7–12] that let learners acquire a flat finishing skill with an iron file. The system measures a flat finishing motion of a learner by a 3-D stylus device, and classifies the learner's "peculiarity". The system assists the learners how to correct bad peculiarities based on detected "peculiarity" classified from difference of the motions between the expert and the learner.

In our early studies, we have applied the Self-Organizing Maps (SOMs) with plane topology to classify peculiarities of the learners because the SOMs are available to classify unknown numbers of classes [10,11]. We have also changed the topology of the SOM to torus type to avoid the border effect that deteriorates the classification performance [8]. Additionally, we have introduced an automatic clustering method of the codebooks of the SOM for trainers to get grasp their learners' peculiarity tendency easily [9,12]. Although our recent studies confirmed the effectiveness of the torus SOM as a kind of borderless topological SOM, the effectiveness of the spherical SOM which has another type of borderless topology has not been verified yet.

In this paper, we substitute the topological structure of the SOM to sphere type [1,5]. Then we compare the spherical SOM with the torus SOM in the case of our peculiarity classification result by using several quality measures of SOMs: the quantization error, the topographic error [4], and the cluster map value.

2   Motion Measuring System for Flat Finishing Skill Training

Figure 1(a) shows an outlook of the motion measuring devices of the system for flat finishing skill training. The system simulates a flat finishing task that flatten a top surface of an pillar object by an iron file. The pillar has an area 25 mm width and 25 mm depth, at 80 mm height.

The system measures a 3D + time motion of the file by using a 3D stylus. We use the PHANTOM Omni (SensAble Technologies) haptics device as the 3D stylus. The file motion is measured by attaching the grip of the file to the encoder stylus part of the haptics device. To reduce the mechanical load of force feed back teaching function, we use a light weight mock file made of an acrylic plate which imitates a real 200 mm length iron file [10,11].

When a learner operates the mock file reciprocally in order to flatten the top surface of the work, the system measures the motion including time series of the file position with X, Y, and Z coordinate values, and the posture as the tilt angles along the three axes with Tx, Ty, Tz as the radians. The spatial axes of the operational space and tilt angles of the file are assigned as shown in Fig. 1(b).

Figure 2 shows an example of an expert's motion measured by the system. In these plots, the expert operates the file with reciprocating motion 4 times within 20 s. The main direction of the reciprocating motion is along X axis. Since the file works only in the pushing motion, we focused the pushing motion in the classification task in the rest part of the paper.

(a)

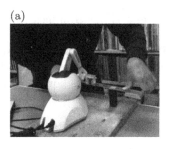

(b)

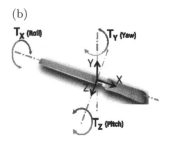

Fig. 1. Flat finishing skill measuring system: (a) outlook, (b) coordinates of measuring.

(a)

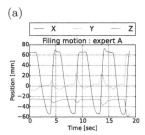

(b)

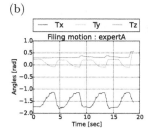

Fig. 2. Filing motion of an expert: (a) tool position, (b) posture of the tool.

We extract same dimensional file-pushing motion patterns from a measured data by using two step data processes: (1) clipping out every pushing motions, and (2) re-sampling the motions. **(1) Clipping:** The clipping is done according to the file-pushing motion range which is defined in X coordinates, beginning with X_{begin}, and ending with X_{end}. **(2) Re-sampling:** The clipped pushing motions have different time lengths. To arrange dimensions of all series to the same number, every series are re-sampled by using the linear interpolation, as shown in Fig. 3(a). Since the stylus samples the motion enough fast, we can use the linear interpolation in the re-sampling with less lose of location precision. Figure 3(b) shows the re-sampled result of the expert motion, Fig. 3(c) is that of a learner. In each plot, all four motions are imposed.

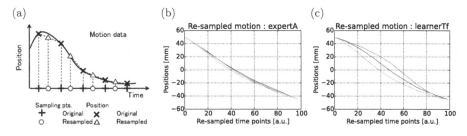

Fig. 3. (a) Re-sampling of a motion pattern, and re-sampled motion:(b) an expert, (c) a learner.

There is relevant differences between the expert's motions and the learner's motions. Every motion of the expert draws almost the same shaped curve, but the learner's don't. Every curve of the same learner's motion differs. Additionally, the expert operates the file by varying its velocity slightly. We call the slight varying velocity "velocity time series (VTS)", and consider it as the important factor of the expert motion.

The difference described above seems to be the main key of the correction in the skill teaching tasks. So we address a classification study of this difference as the starting point of the proposed system. In this paper, we use only the X coordinate values of the measured data for the classification to keep simplicity of data computation. The aim of the classification study is to form the SOMs to organize such different motion curves in the map. After that, taking and using code-books of the learner's motion as the "bad peculiarities".

3   Feature Extraction of Filing Motion Based on Velocity Time Series

Velocity Time Series (VTS)

Although the filing motion obtained the former section have useful information about peculiarities, it is difficult to tell the learner their peculiarities exactly by only using the motion curve. Instead, to display the peculiarities on the basis of velocity time series (VTS) is an effective way. In the system, we obtain a VTS of a motion by computing local velocities at every time point, by using 1st order differential approximation. Figure 4(a) shows VTSs of an expert, and Fig. 4(b) shows VTSs of a learner. Since a VTS represents how velocities were taken at each time point of a filing motion, then learners could recognize and replay their motions more easily than looking raw motion plots. Additionally, learners also can imitate the expert's "model" motion easily. The average of an expert's VTSs is used as the "model" VTS.

Difference of Velocity Time Series (dVTS)

Although the "model" VTS of Fig. 4(a) is the model for learners, a better sign for learners to recognize and to correct the peculiarities is difference of VTSs between the model and the learner. Then, we use difference of VTS (dVTS) as the feature pattern of the peculiarity.

Figure 4(c) shows dVTSs of the expert, Fig. 4(d) shows that of the learner. The proposed system presents a learner dVTS. The dVTS displays a gap of VTSs between the model and the learner: if a learner imitates the model correctly, the dVTS draws a flat line, which means "Your motion is exact. No peculiarity", otherwise, for example, if the former part of the dVTS takes negative values, a trainer could point out the corrective point by telling the learner "You should move the file more fast in the former part of the motion".

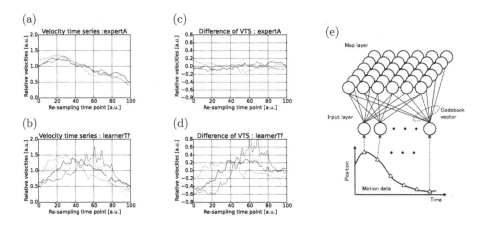

Fig. 4. Velocity time series (VTS) of (a) an expert, (b) a learner, difference of VTS (dVTS) of (c) the expert, (d) the learner, and (e) structure of original SOM.

4   Peculiarity Classification by SOM

We classify the file motion data by using the Self-Organizing Map (SOM). Technical issues about the classification of the file motion are considered in three major points: (1) peculiarities are implicitly existing among the motion data, (2) the number of peculiarity variations, i.e., the number of classes is unknown and (3) every motions are not exactly same even though in the same learner, there are some fluctuation in each motion.

4.1   Structure of Original SOM

SOM is one of effective classification tools for patterns whose number of classes is unknown and whose classification features are implicit. Figure 4(e) shows the structure of the SOM. The SOM is a kind of neural networks which have two layers: one is the input layer, the other is the map layer. The input layer has n neuron units, where n is the dimension of input vector $x = (x_1, x_2, \cdots, x_n)^T$. The map layer consists of neuron units, which is arranged in 2D shape. Every unit of the map layer has full connection to all units of the input layer. The ith map unit u_i^{map} has full connection vector m_i which is called "code-book vector". The SOM classifies the input pattern by choosing the "firing code-book" m_c which is the nearest to the input vector x in the meaning of the distance defined as:

$$\|x - m_c\| = \min_i\{\|x - m_i\|\}. \tag{1}$$

The SOM classifies the high dimensional input pattern vector according to the similarity to the code-book vectors. The map units also arranged in two dimensional grid like shape, and neighbor units have similar code-book vectors. Therefore, the SOM is able to "map" and visualize the distribution of high dimensional input patterns into a simple two dimensional map easily. Since the SOM also could form a classification of patterns automatically by using "Self-Organizing" process described in the later section. Therefore, we need not to consider the number of classes.

The SOM organizes a map by executing the following three steps onto every input pattern: (1) first, the SOM input a pattern, (2) then it finds a "firing unit" by applying Eq. (1) to every code-book vector m_i, (3) and it modifies code-book vectors of the "firing unit" and its neighbors. In the step (3), code-book vectors are modified toward the input pattern vector. The amount of modification is computed by the following equations, according to a "neighbor function" h_{ci} which is defined based on a distance between each unit and the firing unit.

$$m_i(t + 1) = m_i(t) + h_{ci}(t)\{x(t) - m_i(t)\} \tag{2}$$

where t is the current and $t + 1$ is the next count of the modification iterations. The neighbor function h_{ci} is a function to limit modifications of code-book vectors to local map units which are neighbor the firing unit. The proposed method uses "Gaussian" type neighbor function. The Gaussian type modifies code-book vectors with varying amounts that decays like Gaussian function, proportional to the distance from the firing unit as follows:

$$h_{ci} = \alpha(t) \exp\left(-\frac{\|r_c - r_i\|}{2\sigma^2(t)}\right) \tag{3}$$

where $\alpha(t)$ is a relaxation coefficient of modification amount. The standard deviation of the Gaussian function is determined by $\sigma(t)$. We decrease both $\alpha(t)$ and $\sigma(t)$ monotonically as the modification iteration proceeds. The r_c, r_i are the locations of the firing unit and the modified code-book vector unit, respectively. The reason why we use the Gaussian function is based on the assumption that the dVTSs distribute continuously in the feature space.

4.2   Torus SOM and Spherical SOM

When we use the original SOM straightforward, a "border effect" problem often occurs. The problem is observed as over-gathering of input data to code-books which are located borders of the map. Therefore, the classification performance become worth due to the each of the border code-books represents more than one appropriate class of the input data. We have confirmed the problem in the early development of the system [10]. The problem is caused based on the fact that there is no code-book outside the border, therefore the border code-books can't be modified to appropriate direction in the feature space.

In our former works, we have coped the problem [7,12] and improved that by introducing the torus type SOM which has a kind of borderless topology [8,9,12]. In the torus SOM, each code-book has cyclic neighbor relation in the feature map, as shown in Fig. 5. In Fig. 4(e), every code-book at the borders of the map adjoins ones at the opposite borders. Since the torus SOM has no map border, the map is free from border effect. The resulted map is visualized as development plans opened up with any line on the torus. While the visualization is convenient for us because we can choose any codebook as the center of the plan, it often causes misunderstanding of codebooks relations around the borders of the plan. Codebooks around the borders are actually distributed continuously beyond the borders, but the development plans may mislead to regard they are discontinued distribution.

The spherical SOM is another type of borderless topological SOM. In the case of our peculiarity classification that suffers from border effect, the spherical SOM is also considered as another solution. In the spherical SOM, every codebook vector is located nearly equal spaced on a sphere. By using vertices of a geodesic dome [5], code-book vectors can be located in equally spaced, as shown in Fig. 5. The learning algorithm is similar to the original SOM except that distances between two code-book vectors in Eq. 1 are calculated as solid angles or great-circular distances. We can see the spherical SOM result by viewing two hemispheres. There is no viewing dependency like the torus SOM has. On the other hand, the spherical SOM has some inconvenience in choosing map size because geodesic domes have discrete numbers of codebooks.

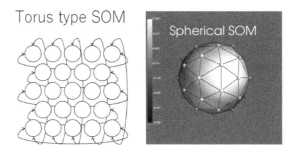

Fig. 5. Structure of a torus SOM(left) and a spherical SOM(right). White circles are location of code-book vectors

5   Automatic Clustering of Codebook Vectors

The distribution of code-books of the SOM help the skill trainers to look out the peculiarities distribution of learners. We think that a grouping facility of the code-books gives the trainers more efficiency in case of many learners they have. Therefore, the resulted code-books of the SOM are divided into some countable clusters. The proposed system could be more helpful for the trainers by providing such clustering information as types of peculiarities. The trainer could teach according to each peculiarity type effectively in short time. Additionally, such clustering result resolves ambiguous boundary of feature map, which one of disadvantage the SOM has. For this purpose, we introduce automatic clustering method of code-books of the SOM [6].

The clustering method divides code-books into clusters automatically according to densities of the code-books in the feature space. The densities of code-book is named "cluster map". A cluster map value $d(i, j)$ of the code-book $m_{i,j}$ is calculated by

$$d(i, j) = \frac{1}{|D(i, j)|} \sum_{(\mu, \nu)} \in D(i, j)(m_{i,j} - m_{i-\mu,j-\nu})^T \times (m_{i,j} - m_{i-\mu,j-\nu}) \quad (4)$$

where $D(i, j)$ is the first order neighbor region of the map location (i, j), which includes six code-books in the case of hexagonal map topology in the case of original and torus SOM, includes five or six ones in the case of spherical SOM. The amount of a cluster map value is in inverse proportion to the density of the code-book.

The clustering is done by labeling code-book location (i, j) based on the cluster map by the following algorithm:

Step 1: Sort all $d(i, j)$ and index them with numbers $q = 1, 2, \cdots$ in ascending order. Let $s(i, j) = q$ and define $(i, j) = s^{-1}(q)$.

Step 2: Set $L = 0$.

Step 3: Iterate Step 3-1 for $q = 1, 2, \cdots$.

    Step 3-1: if $d(s^{-1}(q))$ is the smallest value among its first order neighbor then $L = L + 1$, and assign label $\gamma(s^{-1}(q)) = L$. else assign $\gamma(s^{-1}(q))$ with the same label of neighbor which has the smallest d.

5.1 Comparison Between Torus SOM and Spherical SOM

In this paper, we compare the mapping results of the torus SOM and the spherical SOM with same configuration (i.e. same number of codebooks) and same training parameters, by quality measures: quantization error, topographic error [4], and cluster map value and its clustering result of the codebooks. The quantization error (QE) is computed as mean distance between input data and its fired codebook over all input data. The QE means the goodness of data fitting of every codebook. The topographic error (TE) evaluates the topological preservation between input space and output space of the SOM by simple computation. The TE is computed as follows: first, find the nearest codebook and secondary nearest codebook for an input data. If these codebooks are not in 1st-order neighboring on the feature map, this is counted as topology preservation error. The TE is obtained as sum of the errors for all data and normalized to a range from 0 to 1. The lower TE means good topology preservation. The cluster map value (CMV) defined in the above section means inverse of density of neighboring codebooks at a codebook in the input space. The clustering algorithm of the paper put cluster numbers on every codebooks based on the cluster map value like the labeling algorithms of image processing. The algorithm regards the most dense codebook as the first cluster center, and gives its neighboring codebooks the same cluster index. The low cluster numbers mean dense codebooks.

6   Classification Experiment

To compare the effectiveness of the spherical SOM and the torus SOM, we carried out experiments of the filing motion peculiarities classification. The motion data were measured with an expert and sixteen learners. Every person operated three of four filing motions. Totally we used 66 motion data for classification. Each motion data is clipped out as in range $X_{begin} = 50\,(\text{mm})$, $X_{end} = -45\,(\text{mm})$, and re-sampled at $n = 100$ sampling points.

Both SOMs consist the input layer with 100 units and the spherical SOM consists the map layer with 42 code-book vectors. The torus SOM consists the map layer with 42 code-books, with 7 by 6 hexagonal lattice. The self-organizing process started with initial relaxation coefficient $\alpha = 0.2$. Initial extents of the neighbor functions are chosen to cover whole maps, $\sigma = 4\pi[\text{sr}]$ for the spherical SOM, and $\sigma = 3.5$ for the torus SOM, with the Gaussian type neighbor function. Whole organization process taken 10,000 epochs.

The resulted quality measure values are shown in Table 1. The spherical SOM had better data fitted codebooks (lower QE) and had better topological preservation (lower TE) than the torus SOM. On this point, the spherical SOM is considered to be better topology for our application. In the clustering result, the torus SOM had denser codebooks (lower CMV) but less number of clusters than the spherical SOM.

Table 1. Quality measure of the SOMs.

	Torus SOM	Spherical SOM
Quantization error	0.820	0.693
Topographic error	0.147	0.0735
Minimum cluster map	0.456	0.539
Maximum cluster map	0.905	1.38
Number of clusters	3	6

The distributions of all cluster map values of the both SOMs are shown in Fig. 6. Map locations marked with yellow dotted lines are corresponding expert's motions. Both SOMs mapped the expert's motions at four codebooks, and CMVs at the locations indicated similar tendency in both SOMs: densest codebook and sparsest codebook are in neighborhood.

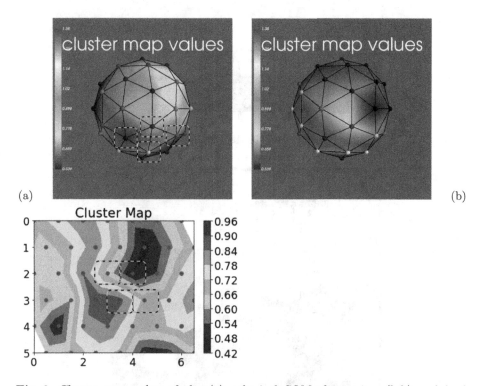

Fig. 6. Cluster map value of the (a) spherical SOM: front view (left) and back view(right) and (b) torus SOM. Low values indicate dense code-book vectors in the feature space. Map locations marked with yellow dotted lines are corresponding expert's motions. (Color figure online)

The dVTS of an expert and learners are classified by the both SOMs as shown in Fig. 7. Codebooks are classified in six clusters by the spherical SOM, and are classified in three clusters by torus SOM. In the both SOMs, the expert's motions are distributed in four neighboring codebooks in a unique cluster. Because the expert's motions are almost similar, the both SOM classified the motion well by mapping them almost similar map locations. By comparing Figs. 7(a) and (b), cluster division accuracy of the spherical SOM seems to be better than that of the torus SOM because the torus SOM has less similarity of classified dVTS especially in cluster 1 and 2. Both clusters 1 and 2 have obviously different dVTS patterns in the upper and lower part of the maps. On the other hand, the spherical SOM's codebooks have less diverse dVTS and well separated cluster boundaries but has over division of clusters at cluster 4 and 5. From these observations, the clustering performance of the spherical SOM seems slightly better than that of the tours SOM. But this evaluation is only qualitative, more quantitative evaluations are required. And other clustering methods [13] should be applied in the future works.

(a)

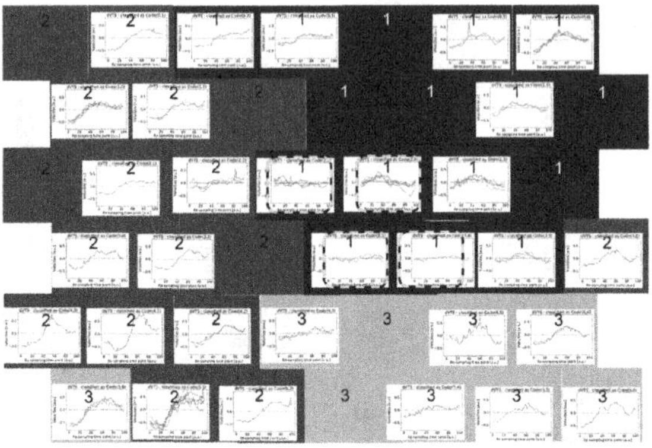

(b)

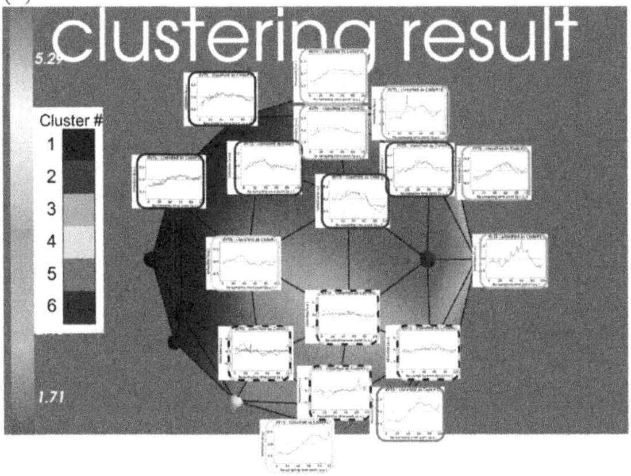

(c)

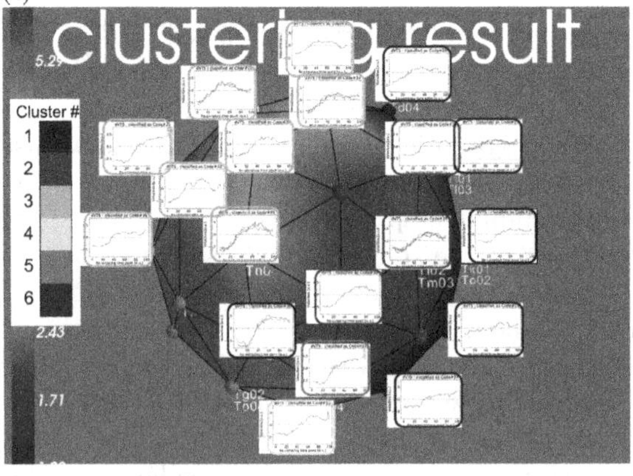

Fig. 7. Classification result of dVTS by (a) torus SOM, (b) spherical SOM: front view (left) and (c) back view(right). Colors of surrounding solid lines on plots correspond cluster number showed at left side of figures. Plots surrounded with dashed yellow lines are the expert's motion. (Color figure online)

7 Conclusion

The paper compared performances of two kinds of borderless SOMs, the torus SOM and the spherical SOM for motion classification of individual learner's "peculiarities" as a part of the development of the new technical educational tool of flat finishing skill. The measured an expert and sixteen learners motion peculiarities are classified by both SOMs with same map size and same learning setups. The classification results are evaluated by quantized error, topographic error, cluster map value, and observation of clustering result of codebooks. The comparison showed the advantages of the spherical SOM in the quantization error and topographic error. The comparative observation of the clustering results showed also slight advantage of the spherical SOM.

To perform more convince comparison, we plan to introduce other topological preserving evaluations [4]. Applications of other automatic clustering method of codebooks [13] and development of quantitative evaluation of clustering results are also future works.

Acknowledgement. The work was supported by JSPS KAKENHI Grant Number 17K04827.

References

1. Kohonen, T.: Self-Organizing Maps. Springer, Berlin (2001). https://doi.org/10. 1007/978-3-642-56927-2
2. Matsumoto, S., Fujimoto, N., Teranishi, M., Takeno, H., Tokuyasu, T.: A brush coating skill training system for manufacturing education at Japanese elementary and junior high schools. Artif. Life Robot. **21**, 69–78 (2016). https://doi.org/10. 1007/s10015-015-0243-8
3. Matsumoto, S., Teranishi, M., Takeno, H.: A training support system of brush coating skill with haptic device for technical education at primary and secondary school. In: Proceedings of International Symposium on Artificial Life and Robotics (AROB 20th 2015), GS10-5 (2015)
4. Pölzlbauer, G.: Survey and comparison of quality measures for self-organizing maps. In: Vortrag: Workshop on Data Analysis, pp. 67–82 (2004)
5. Ritter, H.: Self-organizing maps on non-Euclidean spaces, pp. 97–109. Elsevier (1999). https://doi.org/10.1016/B978-044450270-4/50007-3
6. Tanaka, M., Furukawa, Y., Tanino, T.: Clustering by using self organizing map. J. IEICE **J79–D–I** I(2), 301–304 (1996)
7. Teranishi, M., Matsumoto, S., Fujimoto, N., Takeno, H.: Personal peculiarity classification of flat finishing motion for skill training by using expanding self-organizing maps. Distributed Computing and Artificial Intelligence, 13th International Conference. AISC, vol. 474, pp. 137–145. Springer, Cham (2016). https://doi.org/10. 1007/978-3-319-40162-1_15
8. Teranishi, M., Matsumoto, S., Fujimoto, N., Takeno, H.: Personal peculiarity classification of flat finishing skill training by using torus type self-organizing maps. Distributed Computing and Artificial Intelligence, 14th International Conference. AISC, vol. 620, pp. 231–238. Springer, Cham (2018). https://doi.org/10.1007/978-3-319-62410-5_28

9. Teranishi, M., Matsumoto, S., Takeno, H.: Peculiarity classification of flat finishing motion based on tool trajectory by using self-organizing maps. In: De La Prieta, F., Omatu, S., Fernández-Caballero, A. (eds.) DCAI 2018. AISC, vol. 800, pp. 78–85. Springer, Cham (2019). https://doi.org/10.1007/978-3-319-94649-8_10

10. Teranishi, M., Matsumoto, S., Takeno, H.: Classification of personal variation in tool motion for flat finishing skill training by using self-organizing maps. In: The 16th SICE System Integration Division Annual Conference, 3L2-1, pp. 2655–2669 (2015)

11. Teranishi, M., Takeno, H., Matsumoto, S.: Classification of personal variation in tool motion for flat finishing skill training by using self-organizing maps. In: Proceedings of 2014 Annual Conference of Electronics, Information and Systems Society, I.E.E. of Japan, OS11-8, pp. 1144–1147 (2014)

12. Teranishi, M., Takeno, H., Matsumoto, S.: Peculiarity classification of flat finishing motion training by using torus type self organizing maps. In: Annual Conference of System Integration Division, SICE, pp. 3032–3037 (2017)

13. Ultsch, A.: Clustering with SOM: U*C. In: Proceedings of Workshop on Self-Organizing Maps, pp. 75–82 (2005)

Generating Images

Generative Creativity:
Adversarial Learning for Bionic Design

Simiao Yu[1], Hao Dong[1], Pan Wang[1], Chao Wu[2], and Yike Guo[1(✉)]

[1] Imperial College London, London, UK
{simiao.yu13,hao.dong11,pan.wang15,y.guo}@imperial.ac.uk
[2] Zhejiang University, Hangzhou, China
chao.wu@zju.edu.cn

Abstract. Generative creativity in the context of visual data refers to the generation process of new and creative images by composing features of existing ones. In this work, we aim to achieve generative creativity by learning to combine spatial features of images from different domains. We focus on bionic design as an ideal task for this study, in which a target object (e.g. a floor lamp) is designed to contain features of biological source objects (e.g. flowers), resulting in creative biologically-inspired design. Specifically, given an input image of a design target object, a generative model should learn to generate images that (1) maintain shape features of the input design target image, (2) contain shape features of images from the specified biological source domain, (3) are plausible and diverse. We propose DesignGAN, a novel unsupervised deep generative approach to realising shape-oriented bionic design. DesignGAN employs an adversarial learning architecture with designated losses to generate images that meet the three aforementioned requirements of bionic design modelling. We perform qualitative and quantitative experiments to evaluate our method, and demonstrate that our proposed framework successfully generates creative images of bionic design.

Keywords: Adversarial learning · Bionic design · Image generation · Unsupervised learning · Representation learning

1 Introduction

Achieving generative creativity, i.e. the generation of creative images (in the context of visual data) by composing features of existing ones, is a long-standing challenge in computer vision and machine learning. In this paper, we aim to achieve such generative creativity by learning to combine spatial features of images from different domains. Bionic design [8,23], in which a biologically-inspired object is created by combining the features of a target design object with those of biological source objects, offers an ideal context for our study. In this work, we focus on *shape-oriented* bionic design, which is the crucial step in studying more complicated bionic design problem. More specifically, given an

© Springer Nature Switzerland AG 2019
I. V. Tetko et al. (Eds.): ICANN 2019, LNCS 11729, pp. 525–536, 2019.
https://doi.org/10.1007/978-3-030-30508-6_42

input image of the design target, our objective is to generate biologically-inspired images that (1) maintain the shape features of the input image, (2) contain the shape features of images from the biological source domain, (3) remain plausible and diverse. Figure 1 illustrates examples of bionic design results generated by our proposed model.

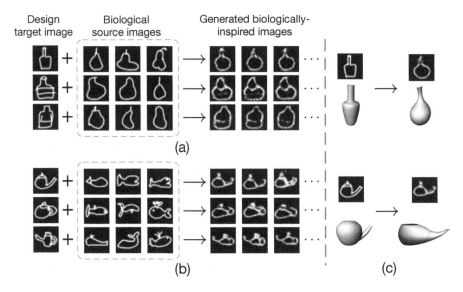

Fig. 1. Given a design target image and biological source images, our proposed model generates varied biologically-inspired images. (a) Wine bottle + pear, generates pear-like bottles. (b) Teapot + whale, generates whale-shaped teapots. (c) Examples of 3D product modelling designed by a designer, inspired by the generated creative images by our proposed model (*top*: a pear-like bottle; *bottom*: a whale-shaped teapot).

Automating the aforementioned process of bionic design is a challenging task due to the following reasons. First, the task is of unsupervised learning, as the nature of creative design implies that there is no or very few available images of biologically-inspired design. In our case, we only have unpaired data of design target images and biological source images. Second, there should be multiple ways of integrating features of biological source images into the given design target image, i.e. bionic design is a one-to-many generation process. Third, the generated biologically-inspired design should preserve key features of both design target image and biological source images, which requires the model to be able to select and combine the features of different sources.

We propose DesignGAN, a novel unsupervised deep generative approach for shape-oriented bionic design. Our method is based on the architecture of conditional generative adversarial networks (cGAN) [4,17], with various enhancements designed to resolve the challenges mentioned above. First, the generator takes as input both an image and a latent variable sampled from a prior Gaussian distribution, which enables the model to generate diverse output images. This is implemented by the introduction of an encoder and a latent loss. Second, our approach employs a cycle loss [12,24,26] and a regression loss to maintain the key features of the design target. Last, an adversarial loss is used to integrate the features of biological source images into the input image.

We conduct both qualitative and quantitative experiments on the "Quick, Draw" dataset [6], and show that our proposed model is capable of generating plausible and diverse biologically-inspired design images. Figure 1(c) presents examples of 3D product modelling designed by a designer who is inspired by the generated creative images.

2   Problem Formulation

The problem of bionic design can be formulated as follows. Given a design target domain D containing samples $\{d_k\}_{k=1}^{M} \in D$ (e.g. floor lamps) and a biological source domain B containing samples $\{b_k\}_{k=1}^{N} \in B$ (e.g. flowers), we have the corresponding latent spaces of D and B (respectively Z_d and Z_b) that contain the representations of each domain. We denote the data distribution of D and B as $p(d)$ and $p(b)$. We then make two key assumptions of the bionic design problem: (1) there exists an "intermediate" domain I containing the generated objects of biologically-inspired design $\{\hat{i}_k\}_{k=1}^{O} \in I$, and (2) the corresponding latent space of I (denoted as Z) contains the *merged* representations of those from Z_d and Z_b.

Based on these two assumptions, the objective of bionic design is to learn a generating function $G_{DB} : D \times Z \rightarrow I$, such that the generative distribution matches the distribution of I (denoted as $p(i)$). Since in our case we do not have any existing samples from I, it is impossible to explicitly learn such generative distribution. Nonetheless, we could still learn it in an implicit fashion via real data distributions $p(d)$ and $p(b)$, and the careful design of the model architecture, as discussed in the next section. Also note that G_{DB} takes as input the latent variable $z \in Z$ sampled from the distribution $p(z)$, the requirement of variations for bionic design is satisfied directly: multiple samples based on a single d can then be generated by sampling different z from $p(z)$.

3   Methodology

3.1   A Path of Evolution from CycleGAN

Our initial choice is to employ the **CycleGAN** architecture directly, where two image-based cGAN models are cascaded and trained jointly (Fig. 2(a)). We use the cycle loss to maintain the features of the given design target image and an adversarial loss to integrate the features of biological source images. Since the images only contain representations of shapes, the two losses will be forced to directly compete with each other, which makes it possible to generate images from the "intermediate" domain that contains shape features of both domains.

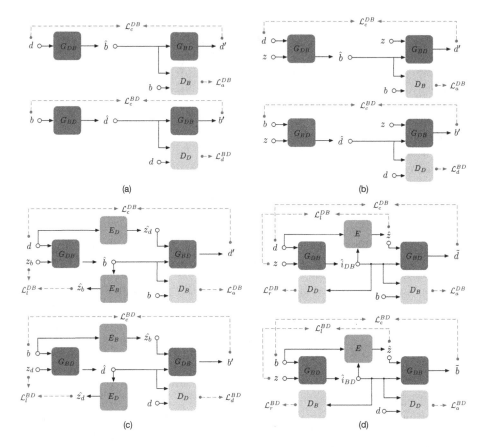

Fig. 2. Schema of investigated and our proposed models. (a) CycleGAN. (b) Cycle-GAN+N. (c) CycleGan+2E. (d) DesignGAN.

However, this model will only learn a deterministic mapping, which will not be able to generate diverse results.

A straightforward way to make the system learn a one-to-many mapping is to inject noise as the input of the system (Fig. 2(b)). The limitation of this approach, as also discussed in [1,9], is that the cycle-consistence restriction would make the generator ignore the noise input. This is because each generator will be under conflicting constraints imposed by each cycle loss (respectively one-to-many and many-to-one mappings), which would eventually be degenerated into one-to-one mappings. We denote this model as **CycleGAN+N**.

We further propose a new architecture to solve the limitation of Cycle-GAN+N by integrating two encoders E_D, E_B into the architecture (Fig. 2(c)). Each encoder takes as input a generated image and encodes it back to the corresponding latent space. The generated latent code is used to compute a latent loss to match the input noise vector, which enforces the generator to generate diverse results. The system will never ignore the noise input because of this latent loss, thus resolves the problem of CycleGAN+N. However, the generated images of this system will heavily depend on the latent variable, without taking into account the input image. More specifically, given an input image d and different noise vectors z_b, diverse $\hat{i}_{DB}$ should be generated by G_{DB} because of the latent loss $\mathcal{L}_l^{DB}$. The problem emerges when calculating the cycle loss $\mathcal{L}_c^{DB}$. G_{BD} is supposed to map all generated diverse images back to the original design target image d. Since d is encoded into a fixed $\hat{z}_d$ by the encoding function E_D, G_{BD} would simply learn a one-to-one mapping from $\hat{z}_d$ to d. In other words, the generators will tend to ignore the input images. We denote this model as **CycleGAN+2E**.

3.2   DesignGAN

To address the problem of CycleGAN+2E, we propose a new model, denoted as **DesignGAN**, as illustrated in Fig. 2(d). Specifically, DesignGAN is comprised of five functions parametrized by deep neural networks (two generators G_{DB} and G_{BD}, two discriminators D_B and D_D, and one encoder E) and four designated loss functions that are discussed in detail as follows. Our model is end-to-end, with all component networks trained jointly.

Adversarial Loss. We employ two sources of adversarial loss $\mathcal{L}_a^{DB}(G_{DB}, D_B)$ and $\mathcal{L}_a^{BD}(G_{BD}, D_D)$ that respectively enforce the outputs of G_{DB} and G_{BD} to match the empirical data distribution $p(b)$ and $p(d)$, as an approach to integrate corresponding features to the generated images.

$$\mathcal{L}_a(G_{DB}, G_{BD}, D_B, D_D) = \mathcal{L}_a^{DB}(G_{DB}, D_B) + \mathcal{L}_a^{BD}(G_{BD}, D_D),$$
$$\mathcal{L}_a^{DB}(G_{DB}, D_B) = \mathbb{E}_{b \sim p(b)}[\log D_B(b)]$$
$$+ \mathbb{E}_{d \sim p(d), z \sim p(z)}[\log(1 - D_B(G_{DB}(d, z)))], \quad (1)$$
$$\mathcal{L}_a^{BD}(G_{BD}, D_D) = \mathbb{E}_{d \sim p(d)}[\log D_D(d)]$$
$$+ \mathbb{E}_{b \sim p(b), z \sim p(z)}[\log(1 - D_D(G_{BD}(b, z)))],$$

where D_B and D_D are discriminators that distinguish between generated and real images from B and D.

Cycle Loss. The problem of bionic design requires the generated images to maintain the features of the input design target. In other words, the generated image should still be recognised as in the class of the design target. For the shape-oriented bionic design problem, it simply implies that the generated images should resemble the input images to a large extent. After all, it would be unreasonable to generate biologically-inspired images that in turn share no relationship to the input design target image. We apply cycle loss $\mathcal{L}_c^{DB}$ and $\mathcal{L}_c^{BD}$ to constrain the generators G_{DB} and G_{BD} to retain the shape representations of the input images:

$$\mathcal{L}_c(G_{DB}, G_{BD}) = \mathcal{L}_c^{DB}(G_{DB}, G_{BD}) + \mathcal{L}_c^{BD}(G_{BD}, G_{DB}),$$
$$\mathcal{L}_c^{DB}(G_{DB}, G_{BD}) = \mathbb{E}_{d \sim p(d), z \sim p(z)}[\|G_{BD}(G_{DB}(d, z), E(G_{DB}(d, z), d)) - d\|_2^2],$$
$$\mathcal{L}_c^{BD}(G_{BD}, G_{DB}) = \mathbb{E}_{b \sim p(b), z \sim p(z)}[\|G_{DB}(G_{BD}(b, z), E(b, G_{BD}(b, z))) - b\|_2^2], \tag{2}$$

where we employ L2 norm in the loss. The inclusion of cycle loss makes our model optimised in a dual-learning fashion [12,24,26]: we introduce an auxiliary generator G_{BD} and train all the generators and discriminators jointly. After training, only G_{DB} will be used for bionic design purpose.

Regression Loss. The cycle loss enforces the generated images to maintain the shape features of the input image only. Another way of maintaining the design target features is to simultaneously force the generated images to contain key features of the design target domain, which directly makes the generated images recognised as the class of the design target. We therefore introduce the regression loss L_r^{DB} and L_r^{BD} imposed by the discriminator D_D and D_B. L_r^{DB} and L_r^{BD} respectively constrains G_{DB} and G_{BD} to maintain representations from the domain of input images. Note that in such a situation D_D and D_B are employed as a regression function only, without competing with the generators as the adversarial loss does. This is why in Fig. 2 (d) there is only one input to D_D and D_B when referring to $\mathcal{L}_r$. The regression loss is one of the major extensions to the CycleGAN architecture.

$$\mathcal{L}_r(G_{DB}, G_{BD}) = \mathcal{L}_r^{DB}(G_{DB}) + \mathcal{L}_r^{BD}(G_{BD}),$$
$$\mathcal{L}_r^{DB}(G_{DB}) = \mathbb{E}_{d \sim p(d), z \sim p(z)}[\log(1 - D_D(G_{DB}(d, z)))], \tag{3}$$
$$\mathcal{L}_r^{BD}(G_{BD}) = \mathbb{E}_{b \sim p(b), z \sim p(z)}[\log(1 - D_B(G_{BD}(b, z)))].$$

Latent Loss. We employ a unified encoder E and a latent loss to model the variation of the bionic design problem:

$$\mathcal{L}_l(G_{DB}, G_{BD}, E) = \mathcal{L}_l^{DB}(G_{DB}, E) + \mathcal{L}_l^{BD}(G_{BD}, E),$$
$$\mathcal{L}_l^{DB}(G_{DB}, E) = \mathbb{E}_{d \sim p(d), z \sim p(z)}[\|E(G_{DB}(d, z), d) - z\|_1], \tag{4}$$
$$\mathcal{L}_l^{BD}(G_{BD}, E) = \mathbb{E}_{b \sim p(b), z \sim p(z)}[\|E(b, G_{BD}(b, z)) - z\|_1].$$

Unlike the encoders of CycleGAN+2E that take as input one image, the encoder E of DesignGAN encodes a pair of images from each domain (either $(\hat{i}_{DB}, d)$ or $(b, \hat{i}_{BD})$) into the latent space Z of domain I, which acts as an encoding function $E : B \times D \to Z$ and corresponds to our assumption of the bionic design problem. The latent loss is computed by the L1 norm distance between the generated latent variable $\hat{z}$ and the input noise vector z, which forces the model to generate diverse output images. More importantly, this choice of encoder ensures that neither the generated images nor the generative latent variable will be ignored under the cycle consistent constraints. This is another major extension to the

CycleGAN architecture that addresses the limitation of both CycleGAN+N and CycleGAN+2E model.

Full Objective. The full objective function of our model is:

$$\min_{\{G_{DB}, G_{BD}, E\}} \max_{\{D_B, D_D\}} \mathcal{L}(G_{DB}, G_{BD}, E, D_B, D_D) =$$
$$\lambda_a \mathcal{L}_a(G_{DB}, G_{BD}, D_B, D_D) + \lambda_c \mathcal{L}_c(G_{DB}, G_{BD}) + \tag{5}$$
$$\lambda_r \mathcal{L}_r(G_{DB}, G_{BD}) + \lambda_l \mathcal{L}_l(G_{DB}, G_{BD}, E),$$

where λ_a, λ_c, λ_r and λ_l control the strength of individual loss components.

4   Experiments

4.1   Experimental Details

Methods. All models discussed in the above section, including CycleGAN, CycleGAN+N, CycleGAN+2E and DesignGAN, were evaluated. We employed the same network architecture in all models for a fair comparison.

Dataset. We evaluated our models on "Quick, Draw!" dataset [6] that contained millions of simple grayscale drawings of size 28×28 across 345 common objects. It is an ideal dataset for the shape-oriented bionic design problem. We selected eight pairs of domains of design targets and biological sources as the varied bionic design problems. We randomly chose 4000 images from each domain of the domain pairs for training.

Network Architecture. For the generators, we adopted the encoder-decoder architecture. The encoder contained three convolutional layers and the decoder had two transposed convolutional layers. Six residual units [7] were applied after the encoder. The latent vector was spatially replicated and concatenated to the input image, where applicable. The discriminators contained four convolutional layers. For the encoder network, the two input images were concatenated and encoded by three convolutions and six residual units. We employed ReLU activation in the generators and encoder, and leaky-ReLU activation in the discriminators. Batch normalisation [10] was implemented in all networks.

Training Details. The networks were trained for 120 epochs using Adam optimiser [13] with a learning rate of 0.0001 and a batch size of 64. The learning rate was decayed to zero linearly over the last half number of epochs. We used the objective functions of Least Squares GAN [16] to stabilise the learning process. The discriminator was updated using a history of generated images, as proposed in [22], in order to alleviate the model oscillation problem [26]. We applied random horizontal flipping and random ± 15 degree rotation to the training images, which were further resized to 32×32 before being fed into the models.

4.2   Qualitative Results

Figure 3 illustrates the qualitative comparison results of our investigated and proposed models. We maintained the same value of the latent variable for the corresponding three generated images for each group of generation, where possible. Specifically, CycleGAN in some cases is able to generate images of bionic design, while in other cases it fails to maintain features of the input design target image (e.g. Fig. 3(d)). Also, since it is a deterministic model, no variation is produced. Similar to CycleGAN, in most cases CycleGAN+N only generates a single result given one input image, which indicates that the input noise vector is completely ignored. Although CycleGAN+2E can generate diverse results, they are either of low-quality (e.g. Fig. 3(b)(c)), or failed to maintain any features of the input design target image. We observe that the input latent variable dominates and the design target image is ignored by CycleGAN+2E, which corresponds to our analysis in the above section. By contrast, DesignGAN is capable of generating plausible and diverse biologically-inspired images that successfully maintain representations of both input design target image and biological source images.

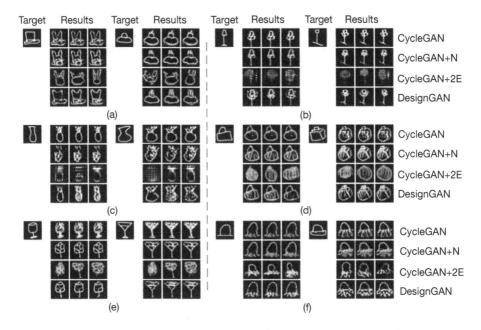

Fig. 3. Qualitative results of our investigated and proposed models for bionic design. (a) Hat + rabbit. (b) Floor Lamp + flower. (c) Vase + pineapple. (d) Suitcase + onion. (e) Wine glass + flower. (f) Hat + octopus.

4.3   Quantitative Results

How to quantitatively evaluate the performance of generative models for creative tasks remains a challenging problem. In this work, we leveraged human judgement to evaluate our investigated and proposed models for bionic design. More specifically, we performed the human evaluation on Amazon Mechanical Turk (AMT). We selected eight domain pairs of design targets and biological sources shown in this paper. For each pair of domains, we used three design target images as the input to the comparison models. For each input image, three biologically-inspired design images were generated by each of the comparison methods. There were twenty subjects recruited, presented all the input and generated images, and required to rank the models, according to the following criteria: whether the generated images (1) maintain the key features of input design target image, (2) contain the key features of biological source domain, (3) are diverse, and (4) are creative and plausible.

Subjects scored 1 for the best and scored 4 for the worst (expect for the evaluation of diversity, in which CycleGAN was not compared and subjects scored 3 for the worst, as CycleGAN is a deterministic model and cannot generate diverse results). We then averaged all the ranking scores over the different criteria.

Table 1. Comparison results of human evaluation between the investigated and our proposed approaches for the bionic design problem. The scores represent the averaged human ranks (1 for the best) according to four specific criteria.

	CycleGAN	CycleGAN+N	CycleGAN+2E	DesignGAN
Design target features	$1.97 \pm .08$	$2.65 \pm .09$	$3.57 \pm .07$	$1.80 \pm .08$
Biological features	$2.28 \pm .09$	$2.70 \pm .09$	$2.73 \pm .11$	$2.29 \pm .09$
Diversity	/	$2.44 \pm .07$	$1.55 \pm .07$	$2.01 \pm .06$
Creativity & plausibility	$2.04 \pm .08$	$2.62 \pm .10$	$3.36 \pm .09$	$1.99 \pm .08$

Table 1 presents the human evaluation results of the comparison methods for the bionic design problem. Specifically, all approaches achieve a comparable ranking score in integrating features of biological source images (CycleGAN and DesignGAN perform better than CycleGAN+N and CycleGAN+2E). In terms of maintaining the features of design target images, DesignGAN performs better than other comparison methods (CycleGAN+2E obtains very poor result in this criterion). For diversity, CycleGAN+2E achieve better rankings than Design-GAN and CycleGAN+N, though it generally fails to preserve any features of design target images. In the aspect of creativity and plausibility, DesignGAN obtains the best ranking score, which indicates that it is capable of generating the most creative and plausible bionic designs. When all the judging criteria are considered, DesignGAN outperforms other comparison approaches.

4.4   Regression Loss vs. Cycle Loss

We studied the effect of regression loss and cycle loss by setting varied values to λ_r and λ_c and generating the corresponding images, which can be seen in Fig. 4(a). Both regression loss and cycle loss are able to improve the generated images by forcing them to contain the features of the input image (e.g. see the area pointed by the red arrow). However, if the cycle loss is applied alone, it is only when setting the weight to a relatively large value that the generated images will resemble the input image. In this case, the results tend to lose the details of features of biological source domain. By contrast, applying the regression loss makes the model generate better images, though the weight of regression loss λ_r needs to be tuned carefully, in order to prevent the generated images from being exactly identical to the input image (i.e. not able to integrate the representations of the biological source domain).

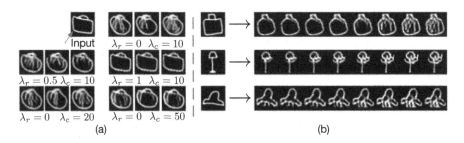

(a)   (b)

Fig. 4. (a) Comparison results of regression loss and cycle loss using an example of Suitcase + onion. (b) Generated biologically-inspired design images by interpolating the input latent variable. (*top*) Suitcase + onion. (*middle*) Floor lamp + flower. (*bottom*) Hat + octopus. (Color figure online)

4.5   Latent Variable Interpolation

Figure 4(b) shows the generated biologically-inspired design images by linearly interpolating the input latent variable z. The smooth semantic transitions of generated results verify that our model learns a smooth latent manifold as well as the disentangled representations for the bionic design problem.

5   Related Work

Deep Generative Networks. Several deep neural network architectures for image generation have been proposed recently, such as generative adversarial networks (GAN) [4], variational autoencoders (VAE) [5,14,21], and autoregressive models [18,19]. Our proposed approach is based on the GAN architecture that learns to approximate the data distribution implicitly, by training a generator and a discriminator in a competing manner. The generator of the original GAN takes as input a noise vector and can be further conditioned by taking as input other conditional information (such as labels [2], texts [20] and images [3]), which forms the conditional GAN architecture (cGAN) [17].

Image-to-Image Generation. When conditioned on images, deep generative networks learn to solve image-to-image generation tasks, many of which can be considered as a domain translation problem, where the goal is to find a mapping function between source domain and target domain. This problem can be of both supervised learning and unsupervised learning settings. In the supervised domain translation problem (e.g. [11,25,27]), paired samples (sampled from the joint distribution of data from two domains) are observed. In the unsupervised counterpart (e.g. [12,15,24,26]), only unpaired samples (sampled from the marginal distribution of data from each domain) are available. Our bionic design problem can be seen as a related task to the unsupervised image-to-image translation, with a key difference: the generating function should be able to combine the key features of images from both domains (rather than finding a mapping function to translate images from one domain to another).

6   Conclusions

In this paper, we proposed DesignGAN as a novel unsupervised deep generative network to (1) combine spatial features of different domains for generative creativity, and (2) enable diverse generation, all done in an unsupervised fashion. We focused on the shape-oriented bionic design problem as an ideal task for our study. We presented a systemic design path of the proposed architecture. We conducted qualitative and quantitative experiments on the methods of our design path and demonstrated that our proposed model achieves results of plausible and diverse biologically-inspired design images.

References

1. Almahairi, A., Rajeswar, S., Sordoni, A., Bachman, P., Courville, A.: Augmented CycleGAN: learning many-to-many mappings from unpaired data. arXiv preprint arXiv:1802.10151 (2018)
2. Chen, X., Duan, Y., Houthooft, R., Schulman, J., Sutskever, I., Abbeel, P.: Info-GAN: interpretable representation learning by information maximizing generative adversarial nets. In: NIPS (2016)
3. Dong, H., Yu, S., Wu, C., Guo, Y.: Semantic image synthesis via adversarial learning. In: ICCV (2017)
4. Goodfellow, I.J., et al.: Generative adversarial nets. In: NIPS (2014)
5. Gregor, K., Danihelka, I., Graves, A., Rezende, D.J., Wierstra, D.: DRAW: a recurrent neural network for image generation. In: ICML (2015)
6. Ha, D., Eck, D.: A neural representation of sketch drawings. In: ICLR (2018)
7. He, K., Zhang, X., Ren, S., Sun, J.: Deep residual learning for image recognition. In: CVPR (2016)
8. Helms, M., Vattam, S.S., Goel, A.K.: Biologically inspired design: process and products. Des. Stud. **30**(5), 606–622 (2009)
9. Huang, X., Liu, M.Y., Belongie, S., Kautz, J.: Multimodal unsupervised image-to-image translation. arXiv preprint arXiv:1804.04732 (2018)
10. Ioffe, S., Szegedy, C.: Batch normalization: accelerating deep network training by reducing internal covariate shift. In: ICML (2015)

11. Isola, P., Zhu, J.Y., Zhou, T., Efros, A.A.: Image-to-image translation with conditional adversarial networks. In: CVPR (2017)
12. Kim, T., Cha, M., Kim, H., Lee, J.K., Kim, J.: Learning to discover cross-domain relations with generative adversarial networks. In: ICML (2017)
13. Kingma, D., Ba, J.: Adam: a method for stochastic optimization. In: ICLR (2014)
14. Kingma, D.P., Welling, M.: Auto-encoding variational Bayes. In: ICLR (2014)
15. Liu, M.Y., Breuel, T., Kautz, J.: Unsupervised image-to-image translation networks. In: NIPS (2017)
16. Mao, X., Li, Q., Xie, H., Lau, R.Y., Wang, Z., Smolley, S.P.: Least squares generative adversarial networks. In: ICCV (2017)
17. Mirza, M., Osindero, S.: Conditional generative adversarial nets. arXiv preprint arXiv:1411.1784 (2014)
18. Oord, A.V.D., Kalchbrenner, N., Kavukcuoglu, K.: Pixel recurrent neural networks. In: ICML (2016)
19. Oord, A.V.D., Kalchbrenner, N., Vinyals, O., Espeholt, L., Graves, A., Kavukcuoglu, K.: Conditional image generation with PixelCNN decoders. In: NIPS (2016)
20. Reed, S., Akata, Z., Yan, X., Logeswaran, L., Schiele, B., Lee, H.: Generative adversarial text to image synthesis. In: ICML (2016)
21. Rezende, D.J., Mohamed, S., Wierstra, D.: Stochastic backpropagation and approximate inference in deep generative models. In: ICML (2014)
22. Shrivastava, A., Pfister, T., Tuzel, O., Susskind, J., Wang, W., Webb, R.: Learning from simulated and unsupervised images through adversarial training. In: CVPR (2017)
23. Shu, L., Ueda, K., Chiu, I., Cheong, H.: Biologically inspired design. CIRP Ann. **60**(2), 673–693 (2011)
24. Yi, Z., Zhang, H., Tan, P., Gong, M.: DualGAN: unsupervised dual learning for image-to-image translation. In: ICCV (2017)
25. Yoo, D., Kim, N., Park, S., Paek, A.S., Kweon, I.S.: Pixel-level domain transfer. In: Leibe, B., Matas, J., Sebe, N., Welling, M. (eds.) ECCV 2016. LNCS, vol. 9912, pp. 517–532. Springer, Cham (2016). https://doi.org/10.1007/978-3-319-46484-8_31
26. Zhu, J.Y., Park, T., Isola, P., Efros, A.A.: Unpaired image-to-image translation using cycle-consistent adversarial networks. In: ICCV (2017)
27. Zhu, J.Y., et al.: Toward multimodal image-to-image translation. In: NIPS (2017)

Self-attention StarGAN for Multi-domain Image-to-Image Translation

Ziliang He[1(⊠)], Zhenguo Yang[1(⊠)], Xudong Mao[2], Jianming Lv[3],
Qing Li[2], and Wenyin Liu[1(⊠)]

[1] School of Computer Science and Technology,
Guangdong University of Technology, Guangzhou, China
ziliangbufer@gmail.com, zhengyang5-c@my.cityu.edu.hk,
liuwy@gdut.edu.cn
[2] Department of Computing, The Hong Kong Polytechnic University,
Hong Kong, China
xudong.xdmao@gmail.com, csqli@comp.polyu.edu.hk
[3] School of Computer Science and Engineering,
South China University of Technology, Guangzhou, China
jmlv@scut.edu.cn

Abstract. In this paper, we propose a Self-attention StarGAN by introducing the self-attention mechanism into StarGAN to deal with multi-domain image-to-image translation, aiming to generate images with high-quality details and obtain consistent backgrounds. The self-attention mechanism models the long-range dependencies among the feature maps at all positions, which is not limited to the local image regions. Simultaneously, we take the advantage of batch normalization to reduce reconstruction error and generate fine-grained texture details. We adopt spectral normalization in the network to stabilize the training of Self-attention StarGAN. Both quantitative and qualitative experiments on a public dataset have been conducted. The experimental results demonstrate that the proposed model achieves lower reconstruction error and generates images in higher quality compared to StarGAN. We exploit Amazon Mechanical Turk (AMT) for perceptual evaluation, and 68.1% of all 1,000 AMT Turkers agree that the backgrounds of the images generated by Self-attention StarGAN are more consistent with the original images.

Keywords: Image-to-image translation · GANs · Multi-domain adaptation · Self-attention mechanism

1 Introduction

The popularity of generative adversarial networks (GANs) boosts the research on the image-to-image translation, which is a representative task of domain adaptation. Although image-to-image translation shows an unprecedented rise in terms of research attention, most of the researchers focus on two-domain adaptation scenarios. Recently, StarGAN [12] is proposed to address the problems of multi-domain image-to-image translation, which takes an image and its target domain information as input and transforms the image into the target domain flexibly. StarGAN can transform images to a number of target domains effectively and efficiently.

© Springer Nature Switzerland AG 2019
I. V. Tetko et al. (Eds.): ICANN 2019, LNCS 11729, pp. 537–549, 2019.
https://doi.org/10.1007/978-3-030-30508-6_43

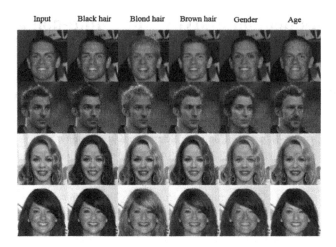

| Input | Black hair | Blond hair | Brown hair | Gender | Age |

Fig. 1. Multi-domain image-to-image translation results of our method on the CelebA dataset

However, StarGAN may suffer from several problems. Firstly, taking the face-to-face translation as an example, we find that StarGAN may pollute the non-interest parts of the facial images, such as non-target attributes, the backgrounds, etc. Specifically, for the task of transforming persons' hair color to black, StarGAN usually results in dark faces and dark backgrounds to some extent. Secondly, StarGAN may result in local regions in the generated images with a target facial attribute (e.g., hair color), where the colors of local regions are not consistent with the colors of the facial attribute. For instance, some generated images in target hair color contain some inconsistent colored regions. The main reason of StarGAN suffering from these problems is that it generates images using cues from spatially local points in lower-resolution feature maps, neglecting the features in distant portions of the images.

To overcome such a problem, we introduce a self-attention mechanism [13] into the convolution layer of the discriminator and generator (denoted as Self-attention Discriminator and Self-attention Generator, respectively) as a complementary to help modelling long-range dependencies among distant image regions. The self-attention mechanism is becoming popular recently in the field of computer vision [13], which can be seemed as a complement to convolution. In the context of multi-domain adaptation, the attention mechanism can use cues from all feature locations to improve the quality of generated images as it does in two-domain adaption [13], which benefits to the consistency between the details of a target facial attribute and keeps the background free from being polluted. In particular, we also introduce spectrum normalization techniques [7] into the Self-attention Discriminator and Self-attention Generator to stabilize the training process. We conduct extensive experiments on the CelebFaces Attributes Dataset (CelebA) [16] to evaluate the perceptual quality of the generated images, reconstruction error, and classification error, etc. Furthermore, the perceptual evaluation performed on AMT shows the superiority of the proposed Self-attention StarGAN, especially for the consistency of the backgrounds during image translation. Intuitively, we show some generated images by the proposed Self-attention StarGAN in Fig. 1. The main contributions of this paper are summarized as follows.

- We propose a Self-attention StarGAN for multi-domain image-to-image translation, which takes the advantages of both local and global feature locations to improve the details of generated images.
- We introduce batch normalization to the upper sampling of the Self-attention Generator, which is beneficial to reduce reconstruction error and improve the quality of the generated images.
- We provide both qualitative evaluation and quantitative evaluation on multiple facial attribute transformation, which demonstrate the high quality of images generated by the proposed Self-attention StarGAN.

2   Related Work

Generative Adversarial Networks for Image-to-Image Translation. Generative adversarial networks (GANs) [1] have made great achievements in various image generation tasks, including image-to-image translation [3, 6], image super-resolution [4] and face image synthesis [5]. A typical GAN model consists of a discriminator and a generator. In the training process of GAN, the discriminator learns to distinguish between real and fake images, while the generator learns to generate fake images to fool the discriminator. Isola et al. [6] proposed the first image-to-image translation framework based on conditional GANs. Although the generated images have high quality, it needs paired training data. To tackle this problem, CycleGAN [8], DualGAN [9] and DiscoGAN [3] leverage cycle consistency to preserve key attributes, which improve the quality of generated images significantly. LS-GAN [2, 15] adopt the least squares loss function instead of cross entropy loss to stabilize the training process and improve the quality of generated images. Recently, StarGAN [12] exploits the auxiliary classifier into the discriminator and proposes to use a shared generator to learn the mappings among multiple domains.

Attention Models. In recent years, self-attention mechanisms have been widely used in the field of computer vision. Zhang et al. [13] first introduced the self-attention mechanism into the convolution layer of the Generative Adversarial Networks and found that the self-attention modules were effective in modeling long-range dependencies. Fu et al. [14] applied the self-attention mechanism to the task of scene segmentation and obtain high performance on Cityscapes dataset.

3   Self-attention StarGAN

3.1   Overview of the Framework

The overall framework of the proposed Self-attention StarGAN is shown in Fig. 2. The Self-attention StarGAN contains a Self-attention Discriminator and a Self-attention Generator, which are shared for the source and target domains. More specifically, real images and their target domain labels are fed into the Self-attention Generator to generate fake images. On the other hand, both fake images and real images are fed into

Self-attention Discriminator, which tries to recognize whether they are real or not, and outputs their domain labels. Finally, the original domain labels and the fake images are fed into the shared Self-attention Generator again to obtain reconstructed images, based on which the reconstruction loss can be calculated by comparing the reconstructed images with the original images.

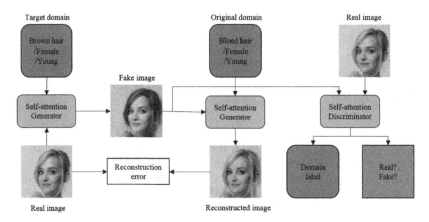

Fig. 2. Overview of the framework

3.2 Self-attention Generator and Self-attention Discriminator

As mentioned previously, StarGAN generates images using cues from spatially local points in lower-resolution feature maps merely, which suffers from two mainly problems. Firstly, the transformation of StarGAN usually has some negative impacts on the non-target attributes. Secondly, there may be some inconsistent colors near the region of the target attribute. To deal with these problems, we introduce the self-attention module [13] to our model in order to model the global dependencies of images. Consequently, our model can select relative context in the light of spatial attention map, generating images with details in high-quality.

(1) **Self-attention Mechanism.** More specifically, the self-attention block is shown in Fig. 3. Given a local feature map $A \in \mathbb{R}^{C \times N}$, we first put it into a 1×1 convolution layer. As a result, it is transformed into three feature maps O, P and Q, where O and P have $C/8$ channels and Q has a number of C channels. Furthermore, we multiply the transpose of matrix O with P, and apply a softmax layer to generate the attention map $S \in \mathbb{R}^{C \times N}$.

$$S_{j,i} = \frac{\exp\big((O_i^T) \cdot P_j\big)}{\sum_{i=1}^{N} \exp\big((O_i^T) \cdot P_j\big)} \tag{1}$$

where $S_{j,i}$ is the influence of the i_{th} position on the j_{th} position.

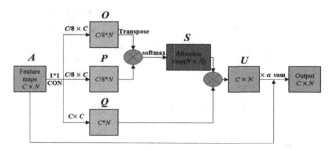

Fig. 3. Self-attention block, where C represents the number of channels and N represents the size of the feature map

Given the attention map, we multiply the matrix S with the matrix Q to get the new feature map $U \in \mathbb{R}^{C \times N}$, which is the same size as A. Next, we multiply the output of the attention layer F by a scale parameter α and add up with the local feature map A. Finally, the output can be obtained as follows:

$$Output_i = \alpha U_i + A_i \tag{2}$$

where α is initialized as 0 and will increase gradually in the training process.

(2) **Self-attention Generator.** In terms of generation, the self-attention module is introduced between the upper sampling convolution layers for the real images as shown in Fig. 4. It can help the generator coordinate the dependences of each position in the image and generate images with fine-grained details. In addition, we feed six residual blocks between the down sampling and the upper sampling processes in the Self-attention Generator for training.

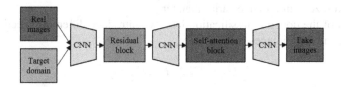

Fig. 4. Self-attention Generator

(3) **Self-attention Discriminator.** Similarly, we introduce the self-attention module to the down sampling process of Self-attention Discriminator. It can help the discriminator apply complex geometric constraints to the global image structure (Fig. 5).

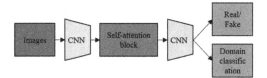

Fig. 5. Self-attention Discriminator

3.3   Loss Function

The objectives of the Self-attention StarGAN for the discriminator and generator are opposite, which follows the principle of adversarial training like regular GANs. In the training stage, the Self-attention Discriminator aims to classify the real images into the original domain and easily identify all the generated images as fake images. In terms of the Self-attention Discriminator, it aims to generate images that can confuse the discriminator, i.e., ideally, the generated images can be labeled as real images by the discriminator. The adversarial training process motivates the Self-attention Generator to generate realistic and high-quality images in the target domain.

To this end, we introduce adversarial loss, domain classification loss, and reconstruction loss [12] into our objective. In terms of the adversarial loss, Wasserstein GAN with gradient penalty is adopted as follows.

$$L_{adv} = \mathbb{E}_x[D^s(x)] - \mathbb{E}_{x,c}[D^s(G^s(x,c))] - \lambda_{gp}\mathbb{E}_{\bar{x}}\left[\left(\|\nabla_{\bar{x}}D^s(\bar{x})\|_2 - 1\right)^2\right] \tag{3}$$

where D^s denotes the Self-attention Discriminator, G^s denotes the Self-attention Generator, c represents target domain label, x represents the input images and $\bar{x}$ is evenly sampled on a line between a pair of a real image and a fake image. The Self-attention Generator G^s tries to minimize L_{adv}, while the Self-attention Discriminator D^s tries to maximize it in an adversarial manner.

In terms of the domain classification loss, we introduce different objectives for the real images and fake images, respectively.

$$L_{cls}^T = \mathbb{E}_{x,\bar{c}}[-logD^s(\bar{c}|x)] \tag{4}$$

$$L_{cls}^F = \mathbb{E}_{x,c}[-logD^s(c|G^s(x,c))] \tag{5}$$

where L_{cls}^T denotes the loss term for the real images, L_{cls}^F is the loss term for the generated images, and $\bar{c}$ represents original domain label.

In terms of the reconstruction loss, it is originally introduced by CycleGAN [8] to guarantee the generated images in the target domain can be transformed back to the images in the original domain. The reconstruction error has been shown to play critical roles in arriving at high-quality images [8]. The reconstruction loss is detailed as follows.

$$L_{rec} = \mathbb{E}_{x,c,\bar{c}}\big[\|x - G^s(G^s(x,c)),\bar{c}\|_1\big] \qquad (6)$$

where G^s takes the generated image and the original label as input to generate the reconstructed image, which is supposed to be as close as the original image. The L1 normalization is adopted as our reconstruction loss. Benefiting from the self-attention modules that can model long-range dependencies across image regions, the reconstruction error is expected to be reduced further. The experimental results will be detailed in Sect. 4 and Table 3.

Consequently, the objective of self-attention GAN can be obtained by combining the aforementioned three loss terms,

$$L_{(D^s)} = -L_{adv} + \lambda_{cls}L_{cls}^T \qquad (7)$$

$$L_{(G^s)} = L_{adv} + \lambda_{cls}L_{cls}^F + \lambda_{rec}L_{rec} \qquad (8)$$

where λ_{cls} and λ_{rec} are the weights that control the importance of domain classification and reconstruction loss terms, $L_{(D^s)}$ and $L_{(G^s)}$ are the total loss of the Self-attention Discriminator and the Self-attention Generator.

3.4 The Stability of Training Self-attention StarGAN

In the context of image-to-image translation, recent research [8, 12] shows that instance normalization (IN) is useful for improving the quality of transformation results. In addition, batch normalization (BN) uses small batches divided from the data for stochastic gradient descent, and applies normalization to each layer before forward propagation of each data batch. It can accelerate the convergence process and be beneficial to the training. Therefore, we use instance normalization in the down sampling of the Self-attention Generator as StarGAN-like approaches. In particular, we adopt batch normalization in the upper sampling of the Self-attention Generator instead of using Instance Normalization like StarGAN.

To stabilize the training process and generate high-quality images, we apply spectral normalization [7] to both Self-attention Generator and Self- attention Discriminator. The computational cost of spectral normalization is relatively small, and it can avoid unusual gradients. Using spectral normalization to the convolution layers prevents the training loss from diverging in practice.

4 Experiments

In this section, we compare our method against StarGAN on the task of facial attribute translation. Both qualitative evaluation and quantitative evaluation are conducted. In particular for the quantitative evaluations, we put the generated images on the Amazon Mechanical Turk (AMT) for perceptual evaluation. Furthermore, we train a hair color classifier on the real images to report the classification error tested on the generated images by the proposed models. In addition, we report the reconstruction loss of our method and StarGAN as well.

4.1   Dataset

In our experiments, we use the public CelebA dataset [16] for evaluations. It contains a number of 202,599 face images and 40 binary attributes annotations per image. We select five of these binary attribute annotations for evaluations, including black hair,

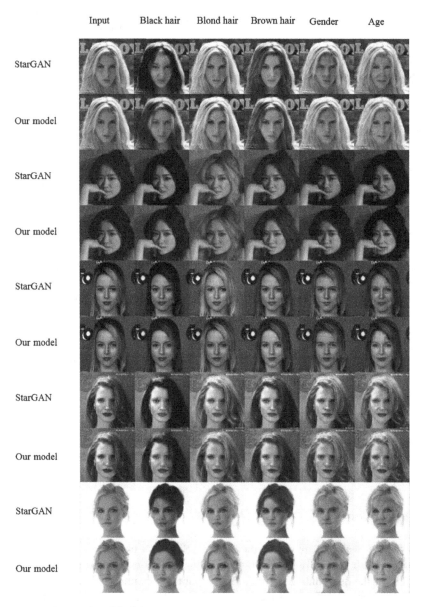

Fig. 6. Transfer results of facial attribute on the CelebA dataset. The first column shows the original images. Other columns show the transfer results on different facial attributes.

blond hair, brown hair, gender and age. The size of the original images is 178*218, we crop them to 178*178 and then resize them to 128*128. We randomly select 2,000 of them as the test set and the rest ones as training set.

4.2 Baselines

StarGAN has shown its superiority on the tasks of face attribute transformation [12]. The quality of the face images generated by their models is significantly higher than the baseline models, including DIAT [10], CycleGAN [8], IcGAN [11]. Consequently, we adopt StarGAN as our main baseline for comparison for the sake of simplicity.

4.3 Implementation Details

In terms of the implementation of Self-attention StarGAN, it is trained by using Adam with $\beta 1 = 0.5$ and $\beta 2 = 0.999$. We train both Self-attention Discriminator and Self-attention Generator with a learning rate of 0.0001. For each time that the Self-attention Discriminator has updated the network parameters for five times, the Self-attention Generator will update the network parameters accordingly. For all the experiments, the batch size is set as 16.

4.4 Qualitative Evaluation

(1) **Transfer results.** Intuitively, we show some transfer results of facial attribute on CelebA in Fig. 6. We can observe that the backgrounds of the images generated by our method have stronger robustness and are more consistent with the original images than the baseline model. Although StarGAN already performs well on facial attribute transfer, yet it may also change image parts that are not related to the target domain, e.g., changing faces when transferring hair colors, and changing backgrounds when transferring facial attributes. In contrast, the image generated by our model alleviates these problems effectively, which benefits from the self-attention modules. The self-attention mechanism keeps the image parts that are not related to the target domain to be consistent with how they are in the original domain.

(2) **Examples of image details.** In Fig. 7, we show some examples by magnifying the partial images generated by the methods to check the difference in details. We can observe that there are uneven color blocks in the images generated by Star-GAN (e.g. a red color block appears in the region of blond hair in Fig. 7-a). In contrast, this is not the case with the images generated by our model, which generates images with fine-grained details. The proposed Self-attention StarGAN benefits from both the self-attention mechanism and BN strategy, improving the quality of generated images.

4.5   Quantitative Evaluation

(1) **Perceptual evaluation.** We have conducted a survey on Amazon Mechanical Turk (AMT) to evaluate the quality of face attribute transfer. Given two images generated by our model and StarGAN respectively, each Turker is instructed to choose one better image based on the quality of transfer on attribute, and also select one image whose background is more consistent with the original image. The results are shown in Table 1, from which we can conclude some observations. (1). In terms of facial attribute transfer, the voting rates between our model and StarGAN are quite close, and our model performs a little bit better in most cases. (2). The background consistency of the images generated by our model is much better than StarGAN. In particular, 68.1% of 1,000 Tuckers agree that the images generated by our model is more consistent with the original images. The proposed method achieves competitive performance on face attribute transfer, and outperforms StarGAN in a large margin in terms of background consistency.

Table 1. AMT perceptual evaluation for different models. Each column sums up to 100%

Method	Black hair	Blond hair	Brown hair	Gender	Age	Background consistency
StarGAN	46.1%	**55.7%**	48.7%	**54.0%**	47.0%	32.9%
Our method	**53.9%**	44.3%	**51.3%**	46.0%	**53.0%**	**68.1%**

(a) Transferring black hair to blond hair

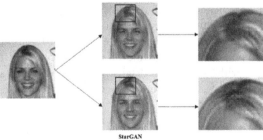

(b) Transferring female to male

Fig. 7. Visualizations by magnifying the generated images partially. (Color figure online)

(2) **Classification error.** Intuitively, the generated images in high quality on facial attribute transfer are expected to be that they can be recognized correctly by a classifier well-trained on real-world images. Such an intuition is widely-used to evaluate the quality of facial attribute transfer in an objective manner. Consequently, we train a hair color classifier on the real images from CelebA dataset by using a ResNet-18 architecture to classify black hair, blond hair, and brown hair. We split 80%/20% of the images for training and testing, respectively. We achieve an accuracy of 93.07% for hair color classification. The testing performance is shown in Table 2, from which we can observe that the classification error of our method is slightly higher than that of StarGAN. There may be two reasons behind it. Firstly, BN normalizes the statistical distribution of each batch samples, narrowing the gap of the different hair colors slightly. Secondly, although the Self-attention StarGAN improves the robustness of background in a large margin (refer to Table 1), yet the high-quality background may not be helpful to the hair color classifier. In particular, the testing results on the images generated by StarGAN and our method are higher than the performance on real images. The reason is that there are quite a few wrong attribute labels in the real image dataset, which reduces the classification accuracy in real images, while the images generated by the models to target attributes are all associated with correct labels.

Table 2. Classification errors [%] of different models.

Method	Classification error
StarGAN	**0.002**
Our method	0.011
Real images	0.0693

Table 3. Reconstruction error of different models.

Method	Reconstruction error
StarGAN	0.04992
Our method (no self-attention)	0.04420
Our method	**0.04191**

(3) **Reconstruction error.** The reconstruction errors are calculated by Eq. 6. A low reconstruction loss is preferred, which indicates the model can recover the original image from transformed image results back well. As shown in Table 3, the reconstruction loss of our method is the lowest, where each model is trained for 300,000 iterations with the same parameters. We also train our model by removing the self-attention modules to evaluate the effectiveness of introducing spectral normalization and batch normalization, as well as the difference compared to StarGAN. The reconstruction error is still smaller than StarGAN. The experimental results demonstrate that spectral normalization, batch normalization and self-attention modules are helpful to improve the quality of generated images in the context of facial attribute transfer.

5 Conclusion

In this paper, we introduce a self-attention mechanism to StarGAN denoted as Self-attention StarGAN, which can model the long-range dependencies among the feature maps at all positions in the context of multi-domain image-to-image translation. Extensive experiments conducted on the CelebA dataset demonstrate that the images generated by our model have robust background and fine-grained texture details. Meanwhile, Self-attention StarGAN decreases the reconstruction error, indicating its ability of transferring facial images across different attributes. Both qualitative and quantitative evaluations show the high quality and effectiveness of the proposed model for multi-domain image-to-image translation.

Acknowledgment. This work is supported by the National Natural Science Foundation of China (No. 61703109, No. 91748107, No. 61876065), the Guangdong Innovative Research Team Program (No. 2014ZT05G157), Natural Science Foundation of Guangdong Province, China (No. 2018A0303130022), Science and Technology Program of Guangzhou, China (No. 201904010200), and a General Research Fund (project no. 1121141) from the Research Grants Council of the Hong Kong Special Administrative Region, China.

References

1. Goodfellow, I., et al.: Generative adversarial nets. In: Advances in Neural Information Processing Systems, pp. 2672–2680 (2014)
2. Mao, X., Li, Q., Xie, H., Lau, R.Y.K., Wang, Z., Smolley, S.P.: On the effectiveness of least squares generative adversarial networks. IEEE Trans. Pattern Anal. Mach. Intell. (2018). https://doi.org/10.1109/tpami.2018.2872043
3. Kim, T., Cha, M., Kim, H., Lee, J.K., Kim, J.: Learning to discover cross-domain relations with generative adversarial networks. In: Proceedings of the 34th International Conference on Machine Learning (ICML), pp. 1857–1865 (2017)
4. Ledig, C., et al.: Photo-realistic single image super-resolution using a generative adversarial network. In: CVPR (2017). https://doi.org/10.1109/cvpr.2017.19
5. Shen, W., Liu, R.: Learning residual images for face attribute manipulation. In: CVPR (2017). https://doi.org/10.1109/cvpr.2017.135
6. Isola, P., Zhu, J.Y., Zhou, T., Efros, A.A.: Image-to-image translation with conditional adversarial networks. In: CVPR (2017). https://doi.org/10.1109/cvpr.2017.632
7. Miyato, T., Kataoka, T., Koyama, M., Yoshida, Y.: Spectral normalization for generative adversarial networks. In: International Conference on Learning Representations (2018)
8. Zhu, J.Y., Park, T., Isola, P., Efros, A.A.: Unpaired image-to-image translation using cycle-consistent adversarial networks. In: ICCV (2017). https://doi.org/10.1109/iccv.2017.244
9. Yi, Z., Zhang, H., Tan, P., Gong, M.: DualGAN: unsupervised dual learning for image-to-image translation. In: ICCV (2017). https://doi.org/10.1109/iccv.2017.310
10. Li, M., Zuo, W., Zhang, D.: Deep identity-aware transfer of facial attributes. In: Computer Vision and Pattern Recognition (CVPR) (2016)
11. Perarnau, G., Van De Weijer, J., Raducanu, B., Álvarez, J.M.: Invertible conditional GANs for image editing. In: Computer Vision and Pattern Recognition (CVPR) (2016)

12. Choi, Y., Choi, M., Kim, M., Ha, J.W., Kim, S., Choo, J.: StarGAN: unified generative adversarial networks for multi-domain image-to-image translation. In: Computer Vision and Pattern Recognition (CVPR) (2018). https://doi.org/10.1109/cvpr.2018.00916
13. Zhang, H., Goodfellow, I., Metaxas, D., Odena, A.: Self-attention generative adversarial networks. In: Machine Learning (2018)
14. Fu, J., Liu, J., Tian, H., Fang, Z., Lu, H.: Dual attention network for scene segmentation. In: Computer Vision and Pattern Recognition (CVPR) (2019)
15. Mao, X., Li, Q., Xie, H., Lau, R.Y.K., Wang, Z.: Least squares generative adversarial networks. In: ICCV (2017). https://doi.org/10.1109/iccv.2017.304
16. Liu, Z., Luo, P., Wang, X., Tang, X.: Deep learning face attributes in the wild. In: ICCV (2015). https://doi.org/10.1109/iccv.2015.425

Generative Adversarial Networks for Operational Scenario Planning of Renewable Energy Farms: A Study on Wind and Photovoltaic

Jens Schreiber$^{(\boxtimes)}$, Maik Jessulat, and Bernhard Sick

University of Kassel, Kassel, Germany
{j.schreiber,mjessulat,bsick}@uni-kassel.de

Abstract. For the integration of renewable energy sources, power grid operators need realistic information about the effects of energy production and consumption to assess grid stability. Recently, research in scenario planning benefits from utilizing generative adversarial networks (GANs) as generative models for operational scenario planning. In these scenarios, operators examine temporal as well as spatial influences of different energy sources on the grid. The analysis of how renewable energy resources affect the grid enables the operators to evaluate the stability and to identify potential weak points such as a limiting transformer. However, due to their novelty, there are limited studies on how well GANs model the underlying power distribution. This analysis is essential because, e.g., especially extreme situations with low or high power generation are required to evaluate grid stability. We conduct a comparative study of the Wasserstein distance, binary-cross-entropy loss, and a Gaussian copula as the baseline applied on two wind and two solar datasets with limited data compared to previous studies. Both GANs achieve good results considering the limited amount of data, but the Wasserstein GAN is superior in modeling temporal and spatial relations, and the power distribution. Besides evaluating the generated power distribution over all farms, it is essential to assess terrain specific distributions for wind scenarios. These terrain specific power distributions affect the grid by their differences in their generating power magnitude. Therefore, in a second study, we show that even when simultaneously learning distributions from wind parks with terrain specific patterns, GANs are capable of modeling these individualities also when faced with limited data. These results motivate a further usage of GANs as generative models in scenario planning as well as other areas of renewable energy.

1 Introduction

Renewable energy sources are by now an essential energy producer of the electrical power grid [1,2]. By integrating these power plants, we introduce a lot of volatile energy. To maintain a stable power grid, power grid operators need realistic information about the effects of energy production and consumption assessing

© Springer Nature Switzerland AG 2019
I. V. Tetko et al. (Eds.): ICANN 2019, LNCS 11729, pp. 550–564, 2019.
https://doi.org/10.1007/978-3-030-30508-6_44

grid stability [2,3]. It is essential to use operational scenario planning [2,4] to evaluate the integration of renewables.

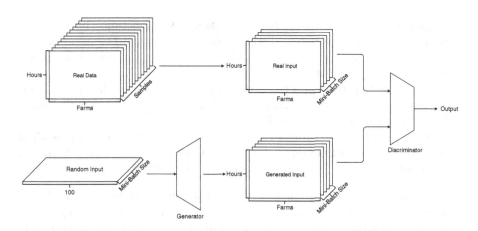

Fig. 1. To train the GANs, samples are selected from the entire dataset according to the batch size. Then, the generator creates a second dataset of the same size from a random input. The shape of the datasets reflects the temporal and spatial relationship. Both datasets need to be distinguished by the discriminator. The output of the discriminator corresponds to how likely a sample of the batch is either real or generated.

Traditionally, generative approaches such as stochastic programming, copula methods, or Monte-Carlo approaches allow simulating the stochastic and intermittent nature of renewable power generation [5–7]. Often, these techniques only allow for modeling either the temporal or the spatial relationship of renewable energy sources. More recently, research in scenario planning shows the strong capabilities of generative adversarial networks (GANs) modeling the temporal as well as the spatial relationship of, e.g., wind and photovoltaic (PV) farms [8–10] simultaneously.

Utilizing GANs for scenario planning is especially interesting because it allows for simulating a large number of realistic power samples after initial training of the GAN. Further, the training, see Fig. 1, emphasizes the spatial relation (of different farm locations) as well as temporal relation (of the simulated hours) through using historical data. However, due to its novel application in the field, there are limited studies on how well GANs can model the underlying power distribution, especially with limited data for training. This analysis is essential because, e.g., extreme situations with low or high power generation are required to evaluate the grid stability.

Besides evaluating the generated power distribution over all farms, it is essential to assess terrain specific distributions, caused by location-specific weather conditions, for wind power scenarios. Often, the average power generation and also the density associated with power values are different for different terrains [11, 12]. To evaluate these effects on the grid in various terrains, the analysis on GANs to generate those distributions is essential.

Therefore, the main contributions can be summarized as follows[1]:

- We provide a comparative study of two different loss functions (binary-cross-entropy loss and Wasserstein distance) on two solar and two wind dataset (with limited historical data for training) to evaluate the underlying power distributions through the Kullback-Leibler divergence (KLD).
- Results show that the Wasserstein distance is superior over the binary-cross-entropy and a Gaussian copula (GC) baseline even when faced with limited data compared to previous studies.
- A study on how location-specific influences and weather conditions (that affect the power distribution) shows that GANs learn those specifics even when only four offshore parks are present in the dataset.

The remainder of this article is structured as follows. In Sect. 2, we give an overview of related work. Section 3 describes two types of loss functions and details the evaluations measures. We continue by describing the experiments and results in Sect. 4. Section 5 summarizes the article and provides an outlook on future work.

2   Related Work

The evaluation of grid stability through operational scenario planning is an essential research topic to integrate volatile renewable energy resources. By creating realistic realizations of stochastic processes in the field of renewable energy, we can analyze their potential impact in real-world scenarios [13]. Often, generating scenarios in the field of renewable energy is done by techniques provided by stochastic programming, copula methods, or Monte-Carlo approaches. In the following, we give a brief overview of these techniques, followed by a summary on utilizing GANs for simulating scenarios.

Already in 2013, [7] developed evaluation methods and algorithms for using stochastic programming in scenario simulations. Further, the authors present a stochastic programming method for portfolio management. Various probabilistic prediction methods are also used to simulate scenarios. These have the advantage that they already model the distribution of power. Besides, they allow modeling temporal relationships as given by the prediction models. This modeling enables the authors in [14] to provide a method for converting probabilistic predictions into multivariate Gaussian random variables. In particular, it focuses on the simulation of scenarios which model the interdependent temporal effects from prediction errors. It is also possible to create scenarios based on probabilistic predictions [15]. For the evaluation of such scenarios, [16] defines criteria

---

[1] Implementation details of the evaluation, the experiment, and the training is available at https://git.ies.uni-kassel.de/scenario_gan/scenario_gan_wind_pv.

measures, such as the energy score, and gives recommendations. However, the implementation of the score is tedious and error-prone.

The authors in [6] use a copula approach to model temporal affects onto forecasts with distinct forecast horizons allowing to distinguish between the uncertainty in wind power forecasts and temporal dependencies. The presented method outperforms all other approaches in their experiments. Recent work in [17] presents a new proposal that models spatial dependence between renewable energy resources. Therefore, the implemented prototype uses Latin hypercube sampling and copula methods and is tested on actual wind power measurements and power forecasts.

A comprehensive study on real-world data in [18] shows the trade-off between computational complexity and the quality of simulated scenarios when using Monte-Carlo techniques. Another method uses a Monte-Carlo approach [5], to study a planning tool that takes various renewable resources from different locations into account – further, the authors consider temporal effects in simulations for load scenarios.

Most of the previous literature either considers temporal or spatial effects. However, recently, utilizing GANs allows simulating wind and solar scenarios that take spatial and temporal relations into account [9]. They also show how to create scenarios with wind ramp events by utilizing conditional GANs. It is shown in [10], that GANs are capable of simulating scenarios conditioned on a previous forecast. In [8], Bayesian GANs create realistic scenarios for wind and PV simultaneously. In a sense, the approach in [8] is similar to ours, as we show the capability of GANs to simulate parks of different terrains together.

The literature review shows that most of the work is focusing on either the temporal or spatial evaluation. Further, a comparison between the historical data and the generated data distribution is not provided using known measures such as the KLD. Besides, none of the articles presents an analysis of whether it is possible to create terrain specific power distribution when simultaneously simulating power distributions of numerous wind farms. Further, previous studies have a large amount of data, e.g., [9] uses 14.728.320 measurements, compared to our datasets with a maximum of 490.752 historical power measurements as detailed in Sect. 4.1.

3   Methodology

After giving a short introduction into the applied GANs, we detail methods to evaluate the simulated power distribution with the distribution from historical data.

3.1   Generative Adversarial Networks

GANs consist of two different neural networks [19]: The discriminator and the generator. In Fig. 1, the generator takes some random values and produces fake samples to imitate the distribution of a real dataset. This imitation enables us to make use of spatial and temporal relations already present in historical data. The discriminator, on the other hand, takes real and fake samples as its input and tries to distinguish between real and generated samples. During the training, the quality of the generated data, as well as the classification accuracy of the discriminator, should increase. The improvement depends on the loss functions used. After training, the generator produces examples from the distribution of the original data. The discriminator, whereas, can detect novelties and outliers in the data [20]. Often, GANs employ the Wasserstein distance [21] or the binary cross entropy (BCE) [22] as loss function. Later on, we refer to the network with the BCE loss function as deep convolutional GAN (DC-GAN) and deep convolutional Wasserstein GAN (DC-WGAN) as the network trained with the Wasserstein distance.

The BCE is defined as follows:

$$BCE = -\left(y \log(p) + (1 - y) \log(1 - p)\right),$$

where y stands for the label if the data is real or generated, and p for the probability that the discriminator assigns (given by the sigmoid function at the final layer). A zero label means that the data is classified as generated, while a one corresponds to the real data.

The Wasserstein distance [21] is a measure that is used to compare two distributions. It is also referred to as earthmover distance and indicates the effort that is required to transform one probability distribution into another distribution. It is defined as follows

$$W_p(\mu, \nu) = \inf E\left[d(X, Y)^p\right], \tag{1}$$

where X and Y are the distributions in the range between μ and ν. Since there is not only one possible solution to convert one distribution into another, the solution chosen for this loss is the one with the least effort, which corresponds to the infimum (inf) in Eq. 1.

3.2   Kernel Density Estimation

The kernel density estimation (KDE) is a statistical method to determine the distribution of a given dataset. In the KDE algorithm, superimposing several Gaussian distributions allows for estimating the probability density function (PDF) for datasets. Applying KDE to the historically measured and generated power data allows comparing them with each other, e.g., by employing the Kullback-Leibler divergence.

3.3   Kullback-Leibler Divergence

The KLD is a non-symmetric statistical measure to determine the difference between the distributions. Later on, we use the KLD to quantify the similarity between the generated and historical data through a KDE. It is defined as

$$D_{KL}(P||Q) = \int_{-\infty}^{\infty} p(x) \log\left(\frac{p(x)}{q(x)}\right) dx \tag{2}$$

with P, Q as the distributions and $p(x)$, $q(x)$ as their PDFs. Due to the non-symmetrical behavior, both $D(P||Q)$ and $D(Q||P)$ are calculated and added together. One interpretation of the KLD is as information gain achieved by replacing distribution Q with P.

4 Experimental Set-Up and Evaluation

This section presents the experimental set-up and evaluation results. Therefore, we detail the different datasets and explain the preprocessing of the data. Further, we describe the architectural set-up of the evaluated DC-GAN and DC-WGAN. Afterward, we evaluate theses GANs concerning a GC baseline. In particular, we evaluate the generated samples regarding their temporal and spatial correlation, their generated distribution, and the creation of high and low-stress power profiles. In the final study on the GermanWindFarm2017 dataset, we assess how different terrains and their location-specific wind conditions (that affect the power distribution) are modeled by the DC-WGAN when trained simultaneously.

4.1 Data

The *EuropeWindFarm2015* and *GermanSolarFarm2015* dataset can be obtained via our website[2]. We further use a *GermanWindFarm2017* and *GermanSolarFarm2017* dataset, which are not publicly available. However, especially the GermanWindFarm2017 dataset allows us to get additional insights into the power distribution relating to terrain-specific conditions. These datasets make our data quite diverse and we cover a broad spectrum of power distribution from the wind as well as solar problems.

Compared to previous studies on GANs for renewable power generation, see, e.g., [9,10] with a total of 14.728.320 measurements and a five-minute resolution, we only have a limited amount of data. The largest of our datasets has 490.752 power measurements, as detailed in Table 1. The solar datasets have a three-hourly resolution totaling in 8 measurements per day. Wind datasets have an hourly resolution with 24 power measurements per day.

To discover relations within the data, we aim at making spatial and temporal relationship available in each training sample. Therefore, we reshape the data to obtain a $P \times H$ shaped matrix for each day (sample), where P refers to the number of parks and H refers to the time steps within the horizon. This matrix is obtained by first creating a list of samples for each farm with its respective time steps (horizon) and afterward combine all individual time steps of all farms. Finally, the reshaping allows the utilized convolutional layers, see Sect. 4.2, to make use of their *receptive field* and discover relations within the data, either temporal or spatial. Respectively, the number samples in Table 1 refer to the number of matrices with shape $P \times H$.

After normalizing and reshaping the data, we randomly select 80% of the data for training and the remaining historical data for testing.

---

[2] https://www.ies.uni-kassel.de.

Table 1. Summary of the evaluated datasets. The samples refer to the number of matrices with shape $P \times H$ (the number of parks times the number of time steps within a datasets horizon).

Name	#Parks	Resolution	Horizon	#Samples	#Measuresments
EuropeWindFarm2015	32	1 h	24 time steps	540	414.720
GermanSolarFarm2015	16	3 h	8 time steps	760	972.80
GermanWindFarm2017	48	1 h	24 time steps	426	490.752
GermanSolarFarm2017	48	3 h	8 time steps	483	185.472

4.2   GAN Training

To discover relations within the data, the applied GANs are designed to make use of the receptive field of convolutional networks. Therefore, the generator utilizes convolutional layers to create samples of the form $P \times H$ subsequently. Depending on the dataset, the generators parameter (kernel size, stride, and padding) are selected to fulfill this requirement as detailed in Table 2. Varying stride and padding allow to almost consistently apply a kernel size of 4 while achieving a receptive field sufficient to cover the complete $P \times H$ matrix.

Table 2. Summary of the generator's configuration for each dataset: The discriminator's parameters are in reverse order. The output shapes of the generator are $[100, 256, 128, 64, 1]$ and in reverse order for the discriminator.

Dataset name	Kernel size	Stride	Padding
EuropeWindFarm2015	$[(4,3), 4, 4, 4]$	$[1, 2, 2, 2]$	$[0, 1, 1, 1]$
GermanSolarFarm2015	$[(2,1), 4, 4, 4]$	$[1, 2, 2, 2]$	$[0, 1, 1, 1]$
GermanWindFarm2017	$[3, 4, 4, 4]$	$[1, 2, 2, (4,2)]$	$[0, 1, 1, (0,1)]$
GermanSolarFarm2017	$[(3,1), 4, 4, 4]$	$[1, 2, 2, (4,2)]$	$[0, 1, 1, (0,1)]$

The discriminator's parameters are reverse to the generators. This (reverse) parameter set-up allows making best use of the joint training and the receptive field of the convolutional layers because the discriminator is capable of detecting missing relations in the generated data and on the other hand the generator is capable of creating those.

In the following, we evaluate two GANs trained with the Wasserstein distance (DC-WGAN) and the BCE loss (DC-GAN). We apply batch normalization inside the discriminator and the generator. As activation function, we use leaky Rectified Linear Units (ReLU). The GANs are trained for 50000 epochs with a learning rate of 2e−5 and a batch size of 64.

4.3   Study on EuropeWindFarm and GermanSolarFarm Dataset

In this section, we highlight the results of the comparative study of the DC-GAN, DC-WGAN, and a GC [23] as the baseline.

Table 3. The table highlights the evaluation results, of the generated distributions after training the different GANs. The KLD is calculated between the created and real distributions for all farms together from each dataset for the DC-GAN, DC-WGAN and the GC.

Location	KLD GC	KLD DC-GAN	KLD DC-WGAN
EuropeWindFarm2015	0.068	0.663	0.029
GermanSolarFarm2015	0.042	0.011	0.011
GermanWindFarm2017	0.062	0.218	0.027
GermanSolarFarm2017	0.034	0.942	0.008

Evaluation Through KLD: To evaluate the generated distributions, we apply a KDE to the test dataset and the samples created by the models. The KDE uses a Gaussian kernel, a Euclidean distance [24], and a bandwidth of 0.01 to reflect 1% of the normalized power. The PDFs from the KDE algorithm are used to examine the similarity between the distributions of real and generated data using the KLD. Table 3 summarizes this comparison of generated samples and historical power data.

Results for all datasets show that the DC-WGAN is superior over the GC baseline. DC-GAN has worse results than GC for all datasets except the GermanSolarFarm2015. The DC-WGAN creates samples with smaller, or at least a similar low, KLDs compared to the DC-GAN and the GC, showing its excellent performance. Note that Fig. 6 provides a representative example of those distributions for the GermanWindFarm2017 dataset.

Interestingly, even though the limiting amount of training data compared to other studies, results of the KLD suggest that generated samples reflect the distribution of the real world. These positive results are potentially due to the combined training and the selected parameters to make the best use of the receptive field.

Evaluation of Temporal and Spatial Relation: Besides creating data of similar distribution, it is essential to examine the spatial and temporal relationship at the same time. As results of the KLD suggest the superior performance of the DC-WGAN over the DC-GAN and GC baseline, we limit the following discussion to the DC-WGAN. Nonetheless, note that results of the DC-GAN and GC are reasonable but outperformed by the DC-WGAN. To restrict the discussion to relevant and non-repetitive results, we limit the following analysis to two representative examples that provide details due to their increased data availability. For example, the wind datasets provide more details about the temporal relation as these include more time steps compared to the solar datasets.

Figure 2 shows typical results using Pearson's correlation matrix to calculate temporal relations for the generated hours [10]. In these results for the EuropeWindFarm2015 dataset, we observe that in real-world as well as in the

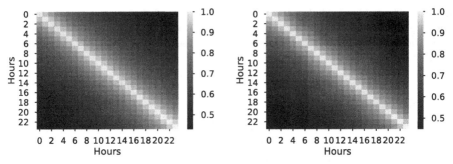

(a) Temporal relation in historical data.   (b) Temporal relation in generated data from DC-WGAN.

Fig. 2. The figures provide a comparison of the temporal relation present in the real-world data and the generated samples using Pearsons correlation matrix [10] of the EuropeWindFarm2015 dataset.

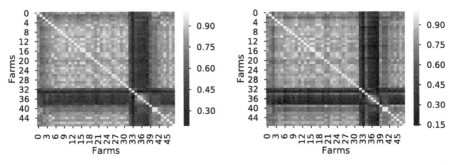

(a) Spatial relation in historical data.   (b) Spatial relation in generated data from DC-WGAN.

Fig. 3. Comparison of the spatial relation present in the real-world data and the generated samples using Pearsons correlation matrix [8,9] of the GermanSolarFarm2017 dataset.

generated samples from the DC-WGAN, the power values have a higher Pearson coefficient for hours related to each other.

Figure 3 shows exemplary results using Pearsons correlation matrix to measure spatial relations between different farms [8,9]. In these results of the GermanSolarFarm2017 dataset, we observe that similar spatial relations, measured by the Pearson coefficient, are present on the historical data as well as the generated samples. In most cases, a high correlation is present and the DC-WGAN captures almost all those spatial relationship compared to the heatmap from historical data. In some examples, the DC-WGAN creates samples with a more substantial spatial relation to each other than present in the historical data.

Interestingly, for some farms, there is a rather modest spatial relation in the historical as well as the generated data. This relation is unlikely in the case of small regions (such as Germany) and can be caused by maintenance problems, shadowing effects, or other problems in the data. As the presented results are representative for all datasets, the above results show that the DC-WGAN is capable of reconstructing the historical power distribution, the spatial relation, and temporal relation for all datasets even for a varying amount of farms, resolutions, and the number of historical power measurements for training.

Evaluation of Generated Power Profile: To asses grid stability, the creation of different stress situations is essential. A typical stress scenario involves large power generation over a long period, as this causes the maximum thermal load on the elements and is therefore relevant for selecting the correct technical characteristics of those elements.

The following section gives insights into the amount of *stress* by calculating the integral over the generated time horizons. E.g., for the wind datasets for each wind farm 24 power values are generated corresponding to 24 h. As the maximum power normalizes the data, the maximum value of the integral is 24 for a single farm of a sample. The maximum value for the solar datasets is about 4 because power is not created at night.

Figure 4 and 5 provide examples of this analysis for the EuropeWindFarm-2015 and the GermanSolarFarm2015 datasets summarized by histograms. Both results show that the generated stress level is similar to the one of the historical data. However, due to the small amount of historical data with high-stress situations, the generated samples contain mostly values below a value of 10 for wind and about 2.5 for solar. The latter results suggest that there are only a small amount of days with intense solar radiation throughout the whole day. The former relates to the fact that wind farms typically are ramped down when working at a maximum level over a long period.

4.4 Study on Location-Specific Distribution Generation

The following study reveals how location-specific influences and their location-specific wind conditions (that affect the power distribution) are modeled by the GANs and GCs when trained simultaneously with different terrains. The evaluation is similar to the previous section but omits the analysis of spatial and temporal relationships as results are identical to the previous study.

In Table 4, we compare the distributions of the generated samples for all models. We calculate the KLDs between the distributions of all real samples and all generated samples. By grouping farms by their terrain, we estimate the location-specific KLD. The results show that both models create a distribution similar to the historical data (also compare Fig. 6). In cases of flatland, the DC-GAN has a smaller KLD, for the forest terrain the values are equal, and for offshore farms, the DC-WGAN has a smaller KLD. Again, the GC achieves smaller KLD values compared to the DC-GAN but larger amounts compared to the DC-WGAN.

Table 4. The table shows the similarity measured by the KLD for terrain specifics power distributions from the GermanWindFarm2017 dataset. In particular outcomes of the offshore and forest terrain are relevant as those have a limited amount of data.

Location	KLD GC	KLD DC-GAN	KLD DC-WGAN	#Farms
Flatland	0.143	0.194	0.037	32
Forest	0.085	0.266	0.018	10
Offshore	0.148	0.304	0.046	4

In Fig. 6, it can be seen that for each terrain and GAN the PDFs are similar to the historical data. For simplicity, we omit the presentation of the GC as we are interested in evaluating GANs for renewable power generation.

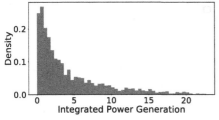
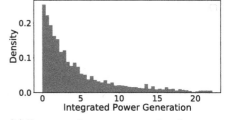

(a) Integrated power generation from historical data.

(b) Integrated power generation from generated DC-WGAN samples.

Fig. 4. Integrated power generation from historical data of the EuropeWindFarm2015 dataset to asses the amount of stress within the considered horizon. A maximum value of 24 is possible as maximum stress level.

The following analysis refers to values from historical data. Both GANs create similar values. However, results of the DC-WGAN are closer to the test dataset. For all terrains, a higher density occurs in the low yield range. The density decreases further for increased yields but rises again slightly in the range of maximum power. Wind farms on flatland have a mean at 0.201. Wind farms near forests have an increased mean at 0.263 in the historical data, resulting in a higher total yield. For offshore wind farms, the average power generation is 0.381, with a higher share in the range of maximum power. Similar differences between the terrains are present in the variance and skewness. Flatland has the most remarkable skewness value, forest the second largest, and offshore the smallest one. The order is the opposite in the magnitude of variance values.

Results of the study confirm that the GANs are capable of modeling the terrain specific power distributions due to site-specific wind conditions even for a limited amount of data as for offshore and the forest terrains. In particular, the GANs create similar PDFs specific to those terrains.

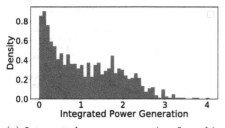 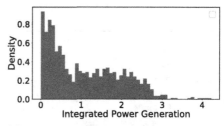

(a) Integrated power generation from historical data.

(b) Integrated power generation from generated DC-WGAN samples.

Fig. 5. Integrated power generation from historical data of the GermanSolarFarm2015 dataset to asses the amount of stress within the considered horizon. A maximum value of about 4 is possible as maximum stress level.

4.5   Discussion

Interestingly, even when training GANs on, e.g., only 16 solar farms and a widely varying amount of capacities, the results of the KLD show that the generated power distribution is similar to historical data. The representative histograms in Fig. 6 confirm those similarities.

Also, in the study of terrain specific distributions, both GANs learn the individualities of each terrain. Statistical values such as mean, variance, and skewness are closer to historical in samples from the DC-WGAN. Impressively in created data of the offshore territory, the large density, in the range of maximum power is also captured by both GANs. This effect might be due to simultaneous learning (similar to a multi-task approach) of the different farms allowing to capture small individualities for each farm and their site-specific conditions.

A critical remark of the analysis needs to be done concerning seasonal effects, which is challenging to consider due to the limited amount of data. Another problem is related to the number of high-stress situations. Due to the limited occurrences in the historical data, the chance of creating those by the GANs are also low. However, they can be created through repeated sampling and rejecting those below a certain threshold of the integrated power value.

Overall, the DC-WGAN is superior in modeling the spatial and temporal relations as well as power distributions even when faced with limited data compared to previous studies.

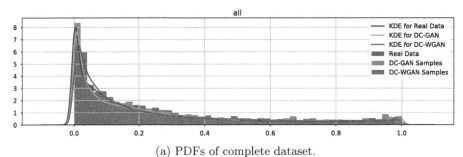

(a) PDFs of complete dataset.

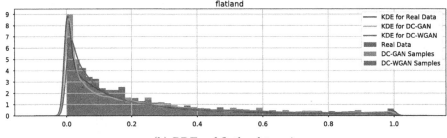

(b) PDFs of flatland terrain.

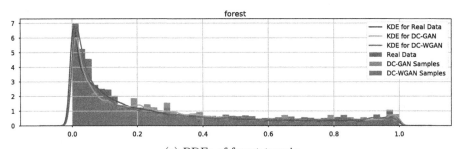

(c) PDFs of forest terrain.

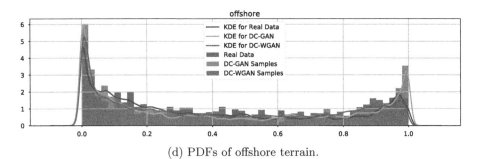

(d) PDFs of offshore terrain.

Fig. 6. The different figures compare PDFs approximated using a KDE for the real and generated data of the GermanWindFarm2017 dataset for each terrain and all farms.

5   Conclusion and Future Work

In this article, we compared the binary-cross-entropy (BCE) loss and the Wasserstein distance to the training of GANs on four different data sets. Results show the superior quality of the Wasserstein distance over the BCE loss and a GC as the baseline to generate the power distribution when taking spatial and relationship and the KLD into account. The publicly available source code, the datasets, and the results provide a basis for comparison when utilizing GANs in the scope of renewable scenario generation. Ultimately, we confirmed that GANs are capable to model different power distributions, including external influences such as terrains even when faced with a limited amount of data compared to previous studies.

A future goal is to utilize GANs to impute missing values or create samples for unknown farms by creating a GAN conditioned on weather events and previous power values. The latter case also allows using the samples in the field of transfer learning.

Acknowledgment. This work was supported within the project Prophesy (0324104A) funded by BMWi (Deusches Bundesministerium für Wirtschaft und Energie/German Federal Ministry for Economic Affairs and Energy).

Additionally, special thanks to Maarten Bieshaar for excellent discussions about Gaussian copulas.

References

1. Fraunhofer-Institut für Energiewirtschaft und Energiesystemtechnik IEE. Windenergie Report Deutschland 2017 (2018)
2. Lowery, C., O'Malley, M.: Wind power scenario tree tool: development and methodology. In: Billinton, R., Karki, R., Verma, A. (eds.) Reliability and Risk Evaluation of Wind Integrated Power Systems. RSEPESM, pp. 13–27. Springer, New Delhi (2013). https://doi.org/10.1007/978-81-322-0987-4_2
3. Schreiber, J., Sick, B.: Quantifying the influences on probabilistic wind power forecasts. In: ICPRE, vol. 3, p. 6 (2018). https://doi.org/10.1051/e3sconf/20186406002
4. Sovan, M.: White paper on scenario generation for stochastic programming. Technical report (2008)
5. Hart, E.K., Jacobson, M.Z.: A Monte Carlo approach to generator portfolio planning and carbon emissions assessments of systems with large penetrations of variable renewables. Renew. Energy **36**(8), 2278–2286 (2011). https://doi.org/10.1016/j.renene.2011.01.015
6. Becker, R.: Generation of time-coupled wind power infeed scenarios using pair-copula construction. IEEE Trans. Sustain. Energy **9**(3), 1298–1306 (2018). https://doi.org/10.1109/TSTE.2017.2782089
7. Kaut, M., Wallace, S.W.: Evaluation of scenario-generation methods for stochastic programming. Pac. J. Optim. **3**(2), 14 (2003). https://doi.org/10.18452/8296
8. Chen, Y., Li, P., Zhang, B.: Bayesian renewables scenario generation via deep generative networks. CiSS **52**, 6 (2018). https://doi.org/10.1109/CISS.2018.8362314

9. Chen, Y., Wang, Y., Kirschen, D.S., Zhang, B.: Model-free renewable scenario generation using generative adversarial networks. IEEE Trans. Power Syst. 33(3) (2018). https://doi.org/10.1109/TPWRS.2018.2794541

10. Chen, Y., Wang, X., Zhang, B.: An unsupervised deep learning approach for scenario forecasts. CoRR, arXiv:1711.02247:7 (2018). https://doi.org/10.23919/PSCC.2018.8442500

11. Pinson, P.: Estimation of the uncertainty in wind power forecasting. Ph.D. thesis, Ecole des Mines de Paris, Paris (2006)

12. Schreiber, J., Buschin, A., Sick, B.: Influences in forecast errors for wind and photovoltaic power: a study on machine learning models. arXiv:1905.13668 (2019)

13. Conejo, A.J., Carrión, M., Morales, J.M.: Decision Making Under Uncertainty in Electricity Markets. ISOR, vol. 153. Springer, Boston (2010). https://doi.org/10.1007/978-1-4419-7421-1

14. Pinson, P., Madsen, H., Nielsen, H.A., Papaefthymiou, G., Klöckl, B.: From probabilistic forecasts to statistical scenarios of short-term wind power production. Wind Energy 12, 51–62 (2009). https://doi.org/10.1002/we.284

15. Iversen, J.E.B., Pinson, P.: RESGen: renewable energy scenario generation platform. In: IEEE PES General Meeting, p. 6 (2016)

16. Pinson, P., Girard, R.: Evaluating the quality of scenarios of short-term wind power generation. Appl. Energy 96, 12–20 (2012). https://doi.org/10.1016/j.apenergy.2011.11.004

17. Wang, T., Chiang, H.D., Tanabe, R.: Toward a flexible scenario generation tool for stochastic renewable energy analysis. In: Power Systems Computation Conference, pp. 1–7 (2016). https://doi.org/10.1109/PSCC.2016.7540991

18. Rachunok, B., Staid, A., Watson, J.P., Woodruff, D.L., Yang, D.: Stochastic unit commitment performance considering Monte Carlo wind power scenarios. In: PMAPS, pp. 1–6 (2018). https://doi.org/10.1109/PMAPS.2018.8440563

19. Goodfellow, I., et al.: Generative adversarial nets. In: Advances in Neural Information Processing Systems, pp. 2672–2680 (2014)

20. Zenati, H., Foo, C.S., Lecouat, B., Manek, G., Chandrasekhar, V.R.: Efficient GAN-based anomaly detection. CoRR, arXiv:1802.06222:7 (2018)

21. Arjovsky, M., Chintala, S., Bottou, L.: Wasserstein GAN. CoRR arXiv:1701.07875 (2017)

22. Radford, A., Metz, L., Chintala, S.: Unsupervised representation learning with deep convolutional generative adversarial networks. CoRR arXiv:1511.06434 (2015)

23. Nelsen, R.B.: An Introduction to Copulas. Springer, New York (2006). https://doi.org/10.1007/0-387-28678-0

24. Pedregosa, F., Varoquaux, G., et al.: Scikit-learn: machine learning in Python. J. Mach. Learn. Res. 12, 2825–2830 (2011)

Constraint-Based Visual Generation

Giuseppe Marra[1,2], Francesco Giannini[2(✉)], Michelangelo Diligenti[2],
and Marco Gori[2]

[1] Department of Information Engineering,
University of Florence, Florence, Italy
g.marra@unifi.it
[2] Department of Information Engineering and Mathematical Sciences,
University of Siena, Siena, Italy
{fgiannini,diligmic,marco}@diism.unisi.it

Abstract. In the last few years the systematic adoption of deep learning to visual generation has produced impressive results that, amongst others, definitely benefit from the massive exploration of convolutional architectures. In this paper, we propose a general approach to visual generation that combines learning capabilities with logic descriptions of the target to be generated. The process of generation is regarded as a constrained satisfaction problem, where the constraints describe a set of properties that characterize the target. Interestingly, the constraints can also involve logic variables, while all of them are converted into real-valued functions by means of the t-norm theory. We use deep architectures to model the involved variables, and propose a computational scheme where the learning process carries out a satisfaction of the constraints. We propose some examples in which the theory can naturally be used, including the modeling of GAN and auto-encoders, and report promising results in image translation of human faces.

Keywords: GANs · Declarative language · Visual generation · FOL

1 Introduction

Generative Adversarial Networks (GANs) [7] have achieved impressive results in image generation. By taking inspiration from the Turing test, a generator function is asked to fool a discriminator function which, in turn, tries to distinguish real samples from generated ones. GANs are known to generate very realistic images when trained properly. A special generation task is image-to-image translation, which learns to map each image for an input domain into an image in a (possibly different) output domain. In most real-world domains, there are no pairs of examples showing how to translate an image into a corresponding one in another domain, yielding the so called UNsupervised Image-to-image Translation (UNIT) problem. In an UNIT problem, two independent sets of images belonging to two different domains (e.g. cats-dogs, male-female, summer-winter, etc.) are given and the task is to translate an image from one

© Springer Nature Switzerland AG 2019
I. V. Tetko et al. (Eds.): ICANN 2019, LNCS 11729, pp. 565–577, 2019.
https://doi.org/10.1007/978-3-030-30508-6_45

domain into the corresponding image in the other domain, even though there exist no paired examples showing this mapping. Unfortunately, estimating a joint distribution of the images in the two domains from the distributions in the original single domains is known to have infinite possible solutions. Therefore, one possible strategy consists in mapping pairs of corresponding images to the same latent space using auto-encoders and then learning to reconstruct an image from its representation in latent space. Combining auto-encoders with GANs has been proposed in [12,21] and outstanding results on image translation have been reported by [13,14,23].

This paper proposes a general approach to visual generation and translation that combines learning capabilities with logic descriptions of the images that are generated. The generation problem is translated into a constrained satisfaction problem, where each constraint forces the generated image to have some predefined feature. A main advantage of this approach is to decouple the logic description level from the generative models. The logic layer is architecture agnostic, allowing to inject into the logic layers any generator model based on deep learning. In particular, expressing the task using logic knowledge allows to easily extend the involved classes to additional translation categories as well as yielding an easier to understand learning scheme. The translations are then interleaved and jointly learned using the constraints generated by the framework that allow to obtain truly realistic images on different translation types.

Integration of learning and logic reasoning has been studied in the past few years, but no framework emerged as generic interface layer. For example, Minervini et al. [17] corrects the inconsistencies of an adversarial learner but the employed methodology is limited in terms of scope and defined ad-hoc for the task. A fuzzy generalization of First Order Logic is used both by Hu et al. [10] and Logic Tensor Networks [22] to integrate logic and learning, but both approaches are limited to universally quantified FOL clauses with specific forms. Another line of research [4,20] attempts at using logical background knowledge to improve the embeddings for Relation Extraction. Also these works are based on ad-hoc solutions that lack a common declarative mechanism that can be easily reused. Markov Logic Networks (MLN) [19] and Probabilistic Soft Logic (PSL) [2,11] are two probabilistic logics, whose parameters are trained to determine the strength of the available knowledge in a given universe. MLN and PSL with their corresponding implementations have received lots of attention but they provide a shallow integration with the underlying learning processes working on the low-level sensorial data. In MLN and PSL, a low-level learner is trained independently, then frozen and stacked with the AI layer providing a higher-level inference mechanism. The framework proposed in this paper instead allows to directly improve the underlying learner, while also providing the higher-level integration with logic. TensorLog [3] is a recent framework to reuse the deep-learning infrastructure of TensorFlow (TF) to perform probabilistic logical reasoning. However, TensorLog is limited to reasoning and does not allow to optimize the learners while performing inference.

This paper utilizes a novel framework, called LYRICS [16] (Learning Yourself Reasoning and Inference with ConstraintS)[1], which is a TensorFlow [1] environment based on a declarative language for integrating prior knowledge into machine learning. The proposed language generalizes frameworks like Semantic Based Regularization [5,6] to any learner trained using gradient descend. The presented declarative language provides a uniform platform to face both learning and inference tasks by requiring the satisfaction of a set of rules on the domain of discourse. The presented mechanism provides a tight integration of learning and logic as any computational graph can be bound to a FOL predicate. In the experimental section, an image-to-image task is formulated using logic including adversarial tasks with cycle consistency. The declarative approach allows to easily interleave and jointly learn an arbitrary number of translation tasks.

2   Constrained Learning and Reasoning

In this paper, we consider a unified framework where both learning and inference tasks can be seen as constraint satisfaction problems. In particular, the constraints are assumed to be expressed by First-Order Logic (FOL) formulas and implemented in LYRICS, a software we developed converting automatically FOL expressions into TensorFlow computational graphs.

Table 1. Fundamental t-norms and their algebraic semantics.

Formula	t-norm		
	Gödel	Łukasiewicz	Product
$\neg x$	$1 - x$	$1 - x$	$1 - x$
$x \wedge y$	$\min\{x, y\}$	$\max\{0, x + y - 1\}$	$x \cdot y$
$x \vee y$	$\max\{x, y\}$	$\min\{1, x + y\}$	$x + y - x \cdot y$
$x \Rightarrow y$	$x \leq y ? 1 : y$	$\min\{1, 1 - x + y\}$	$x \leq y ? 1 : y/x$
$x \Leftrightarrow y$	$x = y ? 1 : \min\{x, y\}$	$1 - |x - y|$	$x = y ? 1 : \min\{x/y, y/x\}$

Given a set of task functions to be learned, the logical formalism allows to express high-level statements among the outputs of such functions. For instance, given a certain dataset, if any pattern x has to belong to either a class A or B, we may impose that $\forall x : f_A(x) \vee f_B(x)$ has to hold true, where f_A and f_B denote two classifiers. As shown in the following of this section, there are several ways to convert FOL into real-valued functions. Exploiting the fuzzy generalization of FOL originally proposed by Novak [18], any FOL knowledge base is translated into a set of real-valued constraints by means of fuzzy logic operators. A *t-norm fuzzy logic* [8] can be used to transform these statements into algebraic expressions, where a t-norm is a commutative, monotone, associative

---

[1] URL: https://github.com/GiuseppeMarra/lyrics.

[0, 1]-valued operation that models the logical AND. Assuming to convert the logical negation $\neg x$ by means of $1 - x$, the algebraic semantics of the other connectives is determined by the choice of a certain t-norm. Different t-norm fuzzy logics have been proposed in the literature and we report in Table 1 the algebraic operations corresponding to the three fundamental continuous t-norm fuzzy logics, Gödel, Łukasiewicz and Product logic. In the following, we will indicate by $\Phi(f(\mathcal{X}))$ the algebraic translation of a certain logical formula involving the task functions collected in a vector f and by $\mathcal{X}$ the available training data.

The constraints are aggregated over a set of data by means of FOL quantifiers. In particular, the universal and existential quantifiers can be seen as a logic AND and OR applied over each grounding of the data, respectively. Therefore, different quantifiers can be obtained depending on the selection of the underlying t-norm. For example, for a given logic expression $E(f(\mathcal{X}))$ using the function outputs $f(\mathcal{X})$ as atoms, the product t-norm defines:

$$\forall x_i \, E(f(\mathcal{X})) \longrightarrow \prod_{x_i \in \mathcal{X}_i} \Phi_E(f(\mathcal{X})) \, , \tag{1}$$

where $\mathcal{X}_i$ denotes the available sample for the i-th task function f_i.

In the same way, the expression of the existential quantifier when using the Gödel t-norm becomes the *maximum* of the expression over the domain of the quantified variable:

$$\exists x_i \, E(f(\mathcal{X})) \longrightarrow \max_{x_i \in \mathcal{X}_i} \Phi_E(f(\mathcal{X})) \, .$$

Once the translation of the quantifiers are defined, they can be arbitrarily nested and combined in more complicated expressions.

The conversion of formulas into real-valued constraints is carried out automatically in the framework we propose. Indeed, LYRICS takes as input the expressions defined using a declarative language and builds the constraints once we decide the conversion functions to be exploited. This framework is very general and it accommodates learning from examples as well as the integration with FOL knowledge. In general terms, the learning scheme we propose can be formulated as the minimization of the following cost function:

$$C(f(\mathcal{X})) = \sum_{h=1}^{H} \lambda_h \mathcal{L}\Big(\Phi_h(f(\mathcal{X}))\Big) \, , \tag{2}$$

where λ_h denotes the weight for the h-th logical constraint and the function $\mathcal{L}$ represents any monotonically decreasing transformation of the constraints conveniently chosen according to the problem under investigation. In particular, in this paper we exploit the following mappings

$$\begin{aligned} &\text{(a)} \;\; \mathcal{L}\Big(\Phi_h(f(\mathcal{X}))\Big) = 1 - \Phi_h(f(\mathcal{X})), \\ &\text{(b)} \;\; \mathcal{L}\Big(\Phi_h(f(\mathcal{X}))\Big) = -\log\Big(\Phi_h(f(\mathcal{X}))\Big) \, . \end{aligned} \tag{3}$$

When the mapping defined in Eq. 3-(b) is applied to an universally quantified formula as in Eq. 1, it yields the following constraint:

$$\mathcal{L}\left(\prod_{x_i \in \mathcal{X}_i} \Phi_E(f(\mathcal{X}))\right) = -\log\left(\prod_{x_i \in \mathcal{X}_i} \Phi_E(f(\mathcal{X}))\right) = \sum_{x_i \in \mathcal{X}_i} -\log\left(\Phi_E(f(\mathcal{X}))\right),$$

that corresponds to a generalization to generic fuzzy-logic expressions of the cross-entropy loss, which is commonly used to force the fitting of the supervised data for deep learners.

Example 1 (From logic formulas to constraints). Let us consider the rule

$$\forall x \forall y \; Married(x,y) \Rightarrow (Republican(x) \Leftrightarrow Republican(y))$$

where *Republican* and *Married* are a unary and a binary predicates indicating if a certain person x votes for a republican and if x is married with a certain person y, respectively. The rule states that, if two persons are married, then they vote for the same party. From a learning point of view, enforcing such a rule allows us to exploit the manifold defined by the predicate *Married* (possibly known) to improve the classification performance about *Republican* predicate by correlating the predictions of married pairs. In this case, the input of the predicates can be any vector of features representing a person (e.g. pixel of images, personal data), while the predicates are generally implemented as deep neural models (e.g. a convolutional neural network). The rule can be converted into a continuous loss function using e.g. the Product t-norm as reported in Table 1 and the previously reported semantics for the quantifiers:

$$\prod_{x,y \in \mathcal{X}} \min\left\{1, \frac{\min\{f_R(x)/f_R(y), f_R(y)/f_R(x)\}}{f_M(x,y)}\right\},$$

where f_R, f_M are the functions approximating the predicates *Republican* and *Married*, respectively and $\mathcal{X}$ is the set of patterns representing the available sample of people[2]. The corresponding loss is obtained by applying Eq. 3-(b):

$$\sum_{x,y \in \mathcal{X}} \max\left\{0, -\log\left(\frac{\min\{f_R(x)/f_R(y), f_R(y)/f_R(x)\}}{f_M(x,y)}\right)\right\}.$$

3 Generative Learning with Logic

This section shows how the discriminative and generative parts of an image-to-image translation system can be formulated by merging logic and learning, yielding a more understandable and easier to extend setup.

Let us assume to be given a set of images $\mathcal{I}$. There are two components of a translator framework. First, a set of *generator* functions $g_j : \mathcal{I} \rightarrow \mathcal{I}$, which

---

[2] For simplicity we do not consider here the case $f_R(x) = f_R(y) = 0$.

take as input an image representation and generate a corresponding image in the same output domain, depending on the semantics given to the task. Second, a set of *discriminator* functions $d_i : \mathcal{I} \to [0,1]$ determining whether an input image $x \in \mathcal{I}$ belongs to class i (i.e. stating if an image has got or not a given property) and, thus, they must be intended in a more general way than in traditional GANs. Interestingly, all learnable FOL functions (i.e. functions mapping input elements into an output element) can be interpreted as generator functions and all learnable FOL predicates (i.e. functions mapping input elements into a truth value) can be interpreted as discriminator functions.

The **discriminator training** corresponds to enforcing the fitting of the supervised examples as:

$$\forall x\, S_i(x) \Rightarrow d_i(x), \quad i = 1, 2, \ldots \tag{4}$$

where $S_i(x)$ is a given function returning true if and only if an image is a positive example for the i-th discriminator. These constraints allow to transfer the knowledge provided by the supervision (i.e. the $S_i(x)$) inside the discriminators, which play a similar role. However, $d_i(x)$ functions are differentiable and can be exploited to train the generators functions. To this end, assuming that a given function has to generate an image with a certain property, we can force the corresponding discriminator function for such a property to positively classify it.

The **generator training** for the j-th class can be performed by enforcing the generator to produce images that look like images of class j, this can be compactly expressed by a rule:

$$\forall x\, d_j(g_j(x)), \quad j = 1, 2, \ldots \tag{5}$$

The logical formalism provides a simple way to describe complex behavior of generator functions by interleaving multiple positive or negative discriminative atoms (i.e $d_i(g(x))$). By requiring that a given image should be classified as realistic, the GAN framework implements a special case of these constraints, where the required property is the similarity with real images.

Cycle consistency [23] is also commonly employed to impose that by translating an image from a domain to another one and then translating it back to the first one, we should recover the input image. Cycle consistency allows to further restrict the number of possible translations. Assuming the semantic of the i-th generator is to generate images of class i, **cycle consistency** can be naturally formulated as:

$$\forall x\, S_i(x) \Rightarrow g_i(g_j(x)) = x \quad i = 1, 2, \ldots, \quad j = 1, 2, \ldots \tag{6}$$

Clearly, in complex problems, the chain of functions intervening in these constraints can be longer.

The images in different domains are typically required to share the same latent space. Let us indicate $e : \mathcal{I} \to \mathbb{R}^n$ an encoding function mapping the image into a latent space. This encoding function must be jointly learned during the

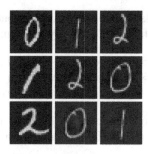

Fig. 1. The first column pictures represents the input images. The second and third column pictures show the outputs of the functions **next** and **previous**, respectively, computed on the input image.

learning phase. In this special case, the generators must be re-defined as decoder functions taking as input the latent representation of the images, namely: g_j : $\mathbb{R}^n \to \mathcal{I}$. The **auto-encoding** constraints can be expressed using FOL as follows:

$$\forall x \; S_i(x) \Rightarrow g_i(e(x)) = x, \quad i = 1, 2, \ldots \tag{7}$$

Up to now, the described constraints are very general and they can be exploited in almost all generative translation tasks. However, the logical formalism (and the LYRICS environment) allows the enforcement of any complex available knowledge about the task at hand. We will see some examples in the following experiment.

Next and Previous Digits Generation. As a toy example, we show a task in which we are asked to learn two generative functions, *next* and *previous*, which, given an image of a $0, 1, 2$ digit, will produce an image of the next and previous digit, respectively. In order to give each image a next and a previous digit in the chosen set, a circular mapping was used such that 0 is the next digit of 2 and 2 is the previous digit of 0. The functions *next* and *previous* are implemented by feedforward neural networks with 50 neurons and 1 hidden layer. Since the output of such functions are still images, the output size of the networks is equal to the input size. A 1-hidden layer RBF with a 3-sized softmax output layer is used to implement the *zero*, *one* and *two* discriminators bound to the three outputs of the network, respectively. The RBF model, by constructing closed decision boundaries, allows the generated images to resemble the input ones. Finally, let *isZero*, *isOne* and *isTwo* be three given functions, defined on the input domain, returning 1 only if an image is a 0, 1 or 2, respectively. They play the role of the $S_i(x)$ in the general description.

The idea behind this task is to learn generative functions without giving any direct supervision to them, but simply requiring that the generation is consistent with the classification performed by some jointly learned classifiers. The problem can be described by the following constraints to learn the discriminators

$$\forall x \, isZero(x) \Rightarrow zero(x), \quad \forall x \, isOne(x) \Rightarrow one(x), \quad \forall x \, isTwo(x) \Rightarrow two(x)$$

and the following constraints to express that the generation functions are constrained to return images which are correctly recognized by the discriminators.

$$\forall x \; zero(x) \Rightarrow one(next(x)) \land two(previous(x))$$
$$\forall x \; one(x) \Rightarrow two(next(x)) \land zero(previous(x))$$
$$\forall x \; two(x) \Rightarrow zero(next(x)) \land one(previous(x))$$

In addition, in order to force the generated images to be similar to at least one digit in the domain, we enforce the following constraints:

$$\forall x \; \exists y \; (isZero(x) \land isOne(y)) \Rightarrow next(x) = y$$
$$\forall x \; \exists y \; (isZero(x) \land isTwo(y)) \Rightarrow previous(x) = y$$
$$\forall x \; \exists y \; (isOne(x) \land isTwo(y)) \Rightarrow next(x) = y$$
$$\forall x \; \exists y \; (isOne(x) \land isZero(y)) \Rightarrow previous(x) = y$$
$$\forall x \; \exists y \; (isTwo(x) \land isZero(y)) \Rightarrow next(x) = y$$
$$\forall x \; \exists y \; (isTwo(x) \land isOne(y)) \Rightarrow previous(x) = y \; .$$

Finally, the cycle consistency constraints can be expressed by:

$$\forall x \; next(previous(x)) = x \qquad \forall x \; previous(next(x)) = x \; .$$

We test this idea by taking a set of around 15000 images of handwritten characters, obtained extracting only the 0, 1 and 2 digits from the MNIST dataset. The above constraints have been expressed in LYRICS and the model computational graphs have been bound to the predicates. Figure 1 shows an example of image translation using this schema, where the image on the left is an original MNIST image and the two right images are the output of the *next* and *previous* generators.

Before proceeding, we want to dwell on the possibilities of this approach after an example has been provided. The declarative nature of the logical formalism and its subsequent translation into real-valued constraints, exploited as loss functions of an optimization problem, enable the construction of very complex generative problems by means of only an high-level semantic description. By exploiting models inherited from the literature, a final user is allowed to face the most different problems with the minimum implementation effort.

In the following section, we show a real image-to-image translation task applying the general setup described in this section, including auto-encoders, GANs and cycle consistency. The declarative nature of the formulation makes very easy to add an arbitrary number of translation problems and it allows to easily learn them jointly.

4   Experiments on Image Translation

UNIT translation tasks assume that there are no pairs of examples showing how to translate an image into a corresponding one in another domain. Combining auto-encoders with GANs is the state-of-the-art solution for tackling UNIT generation problems [13,14,23]. In this section, we show how this adversarial setting can be naturally described and extended by the proposed logical and learning framework. Furthermore, we show how the logical formulation allows a straightforward extension of this application to a greater number of domains.

Fig. 2. Face Gender Translation: male to female. The top row shows input male images, the bottom row shows the correspondent generated female images.

Fig. 3. Face Gender Translation: female to male. The top row shows input female images, the bottom row shows the correspondent generated male images.

The CelebFaces Attributes dataset [15] was used to evaluate the proposed approach, where celebrities face images are labeled with various attributes gender, hair color, smiling, eyeglasses, etc. Images are defined as 3D pixel tensors with values belonging to the $[0, 1]$ interval. The first two dimensions represent width and height coordinates while the last dimension indexes among the RGB channels.

In particular, we used the *Male* attribute to divide the entire dataset into the two input categories, namely male and female images. In the following $S_M(x)$ and $S_F(x)$ (such that $\forall x \; S_F(x) \Leftrightarrow \neg S_M(x)$) are two given predicates holding true if and only if an image x is or is not tagged with the *male* tag. Let e be an encoding function mapping images into the the latent domain $\mathcal{Z} = \mathbb{R}^n$. The encoders are implemented as multilayer convolutional neural networks with res-blocks [9], leaky-ReLU activation functions and instance normalization at each layer (see [13] for a detailed description of the architecture). The generative functions g_M and g_F map vectors of the domain $\mathcal{Z}$ into images. These functions are implemented as multilayer transposed convolutional neural networks (also called "deconvolutions") with resblocks, leaky-ReLU activation functions and instance normalization at each layer. To implement the shared latent space assumption, g_M and g_F share the parameters of the first layer.

The functions d_M and d_F are trained to discriminate whether an image is real or it has been generated by the g_M and g_F generator functions. For example, if x and y are two images such that $S_M(x), S_F(y)$ hold true, then $d_M(x)$ should return 1 while $d_M(g_M(e(y)))$ should return 0.

The problem can be described by the logical constraints that have been introduced in a general form in Sect. 3 and that the encoding and generation functions need to satisfy. First, Eq. 7 is used to enforce the encoder and generator of the same domain to be circular, that is to map the input into itself:

$$\forall x \ S_M(x) \Rightarrow g_M(e(x)) = x \tag{8}$$
$$\forall x \ S_F(x) \Rightarrow g_F(e(x)) = x \tag{9}$$

where the equality operator comparing two images in Eqs. 8 and 9 is bound to a continuous and differentiable function computing a pixel by pixel similarity between the images, defined as $1 - \tanh(\frac{1}{P}\sum_p |x_p - y_p|)$ where x_p and y_p are the p-th pixel of the x and y images and P is the total number of pixels.

Cycle consistency is also imposed as described by the Eq. 6.

$$\forall x \ S_M(x) \Rightarrow g_M(e(g_F(e(x)))) = x \tag{10}$$
$$\forall x \ S_F(x) \Rightarrow g_F(e(g_M(e(x)))) = x \tag{11}$$

where the same equality operator is used to compare the images.

Finally, according to the Eq. 5, the generated images must fool the discriminators so that they will be detected as real ones as:

$$\forall x \ S_M(x) \Rightarrow d_F(g_F(e(x))) \tag{12}$$
$$\forall x \ S_F(x) \Rightarrow d_M(g_M(e(x))) \tag{13}$$

On the other hand, the discriminators must correctly discriminate real images from generated ones by the satisfaction of the following constraints, as stated by Eq. 4:

$$\forall x \ S_M(x) \Rightarrow d_M(x) \wedge \neg d_F(g_F(e(x))) \tag{14}$$
$$\forall x \ S_F(x) \Rightarrow d_F(x) \wedge \neg d_M(g_M(e(x))) \tag{15}$$

Using logical constraints allows us to give a clean and easy formulation of the adversarial setting. These constraints force the generation function to generate samples that are categorized in the desired class by the discriminator. Moreover, the decoupling between the models, used to implement the functions and which can be inherited from the previous literature, and the description of the problem makes really straightforward to extend or transfer this setting.

We implemented this mixed logical and learning task using LYRICS. The Product t-norm was selected to define the underlying fuzzy logic problem. This selection of the t-norm is particularly suited for this task because, as shown earlier, it defines a cross-entropy loss on the output of the discriminators, which is the loss that was used to train these models in their original setup. The e, g_M, g_F functions are trained to the satisfaction of the constraints defined in Eqs. (8) to (13), while d_M and d_F are trained to satisfy Eqs. (14) and (15). Weight learning for the models was performed used the Adam optimizer with a fixed learning rate equal to 0.0001. Some male-to-female and female-to-male translations are shown in Figs. 2 and 3 respectively.

Adding Eyeglasses. Given this setting, we can integrate a third domain in the overall problem adding the corresponding constraints for this class. Let $S_E(x)$ be a given predicate holding true if and only if an image x is tagged with the *eyeglasses* tag in the dataset. Let $g_E(x)$ be the corresponding generator and $d_E(x)$ the corresponding discriminator for this property. The same network architectures of the previous description are employed to implement d_E and g_E. The addition of this third class requires to add the following constraints for the generators, to be integrated with the male and female classes,

$$\forall x\ S_M(x) \Rightarrow d_E(g_E(e(x)))$$
$$\forall x\ S_F(x) \Rightarrow d_E(g_E(e(x)))$$
$$\forall x\ S_E(x) \Rightarrow g_E(e(x)) = x$$
$$\forall x\ S_M(x) \wedge S_E(x) \Rightarrow d_E(g_F(e(x)))$$
$$\forall x\ S_F(x) \wedge S_E(x) \Rightarrow d_E(g_M(e(x)))$$
$$\forall x\ S_M(x) \wedge S_E(x) \Rightarrow g_E(e(g_F(e(x)))) = g_F(e(x))$$
$$\forall x\ S_F(x) \wedge S_E(x) \Rightarrow g_E(e(g_M(e(x)))) = g_M(e(x))$$
$$\forall x\ S_M(x) \wedge \neg S_E(x) \Rightarrow g_M(e(g_E(e(x)))) = g_E(e(x))$$
$$\forall x\ S_F(x) \wedge \neg S_E(x) \Rightarrow g_F(e(g_E(e(x)))) = g_E(e(x))$$

and to add the following for the discriminator:

$$\forall x\ S_E(x) \Rightarrow d_E(x)$$
$$\forall x\ S_M(x) \wedge \neg S_E(x) \Rightarrow \neg d_E(g_E(e(x)))$$
$$\forall x\ S_F(x) \wedge \neg S_E(x) \Rightarrow \neg d_E(g_E(e(x)))$$

We note that in this case, the class eyeglasses is not mutually exclusive neither with male nor female class. This is the reason why we have to consider some constraints with a conjunction on premises. In addition, we have to distinguish how the male and female generators behave in presence of the attribute eyeglasses. In particular we enforce that translating a gender attribute does not affect the presence of eyeglasses. Figure 4 shows some examples of the original face images, and the corresponding generated images of the faces with added eyeglasses.

As we already said, the proposed approach is very general and can be exploited to manage possibly several attributes in a visual generation task combining a high-level logical description with deep neural networks. The most distinguishing property is the flexibility of describing new generation problems by simple logic descriptions, which leads to attack very different problems. Instead of looking for specific hand-crafted cost functions, the proposed approach offers a general scheme for their construction that arises from the t-norm theory. Moreover, the interleaving of different image translations tasks allows us to accumulate a knowledge base that can dramatically facilitate the construction of new translation tasks. The experimental results shows the flexibility of the proposed approach, which makes it possible to deal with realistic face translation tasks.

Fig. 4. Face Gender Translation: male/female to eyeglasses. The top row shows input male/female images whereas the bottom row shows the correspondent generated faces with eyeglasses.

5   Conclusions

This paper shows a new general approach to visual generation combining logic descriptions of the target to be generated with deep neural networks. The most distinguishing property is the flexibility of describing new generation problems by simple logic descriptions, which leads to attack very different problems. Instead of looking for specific hand-crafted cost functions, the proposed approach offers a general scheme for their construction that arises from the t-norm theory. Moreover, the interleaving of different image translations tasks allows to accumulate a knowledge base that can dramatically facilitate the construction of new translation tasks. The experimental results shows the flexibility of the proposed approach, which makes it possible to deal with realistic face translation tasks.

References

1. Abadi, M., et al.: TensorFlow: a system for large-scale machine learning. In: OSDI, vol. 16, pp. 265–283 (2016)
2. Bach, S.H., Broecheler, M., Huang, B., Getoor, L.: Hinge-loss Markov random fields and probabilistic soft logic. arXiv preprint arXiv:1505.04406 (2015)
3. Cohen, W.W.: TensorLog: a differentiable deductive database. arXiv preprint arXiv:1605.06523 (2016)
4. Demeester, T., Rocktäschel, T., Riedel, S.: Lifted rule injection for relation embeddings. arXiv preprint arXiv:1606.08359 (2016)

5. Diligenti, M., Gori, M., Maggini, M., Rigutini, L.: Bridging logic and kernel machines. Mach. Learn. **86**(1), 57–88 (2012)
6. Diligenti, M., Gori, M., Saccà, C.: Semantic-based regularization for learning and inference. Artif. Intell. **244**, 143–165 (2015)
7. Goodfellow, I., et al.: Generative adversarial nets. In: Advances in Neural Information Processing Systems, pp. 2672–2680 (2014)
8. Hajek, P.: Metamathematics of Fuzzy Logic. Springer, Dordrecht (1998). https://doi.org/10.1007/978-94-011-5300-3
9. He, K., Zhang, X., Ren, S., Sun, J.: Deep residual learning for image recognition. In: Proceedings of the IEEE Conference on Computer Vision and Pattern Recognition, pp. 770–778 (2016)
10. Hu, Z., Ma, X., Liu, Z., Hovy, E., Xing, E.: Harnessing deep neural networks with logic rules. arXiv preprint arXiv:1603.06318 (2016)
11. Kimmig, A., Bach, S., Broecheler, M., Huang, B., Getoor, L.: A short introduction to probabilistic soft logic. In: Proceedings of the NIPS Workshop on Probabilistic Programming: Foundations and Applications, pp. 1–4 (2012)
12. Li, C., et al.: ALICE: towards understanding adversarial learning for joint distribution matching. In: Advances in Neural Information Processing Systems, pp. 5501–5509 (2017)
13. Liu, M.Y., Breuel, T., Kautz, J.: Unsupervised image-to-image translation networks. In: Advances in Neural Information Processing Systems, pp. 700–708 (2017)
14. Liu, M.Y., Tuzel, O.: Coupled generative adversarial networks. In: Proceedings of the 30th International Conference on Neural Information Processing Systems, pp. 469–477. Curran Associates Inc. (2016)
15. Liu, Z., Luo, P., Wang, X., Tang, X.: Deep learning face attributes in the wild. In: Proceedings of International Conference on Computer Vision (ICCV), December 2015
16. Marra, G., Giannini, F., Diligenti, M., Gori, M.: Lyrics: a general interface layer to integrate AI and deep learning. arXiv preprint arXiv:1903.07534 (2019)
17. Minervini, P., Demeester, T., Rocktäschel, T., Riedel, S.: Adversarial sets for regularising neural link predictors. arXiv preprint arXiv:1707.07596 (2017)
18. Novák, V.: First-order fuzzy logic. Stud. Logica. **46**(1), 87–109 (1987)
19. Richardson, M., Domingos, P.: Markov logic networks. Mach. Learn. **62**(1), 107–136 (2006)
20. Rocktäschel, T., Singh, S., Riedel, S.: Injecting logical background knowledge into embeddings for relation extraction. In: Proceedings of the 2015 Conference of the North American Chapter of the Association for Computational Linguistics: Human Language Technologies, pp. 1119–1129 (2015)
21. Rosca, M., Lakshminarayanan, B., Warde-Farley, D., Mohamed, S.: Variational approaches for auto-encoding generative adversarial networks. arXiv preprint arXiv:1706.04987 (2017)
22. Serafini, L., d'Avila Garcez, A.S.: Learning and reasoning with logic tensor networks. In: Adorni, G., Cagnoni, S., Gori, M., Maratea, M. (eds.) AI*IA 2016. LNCS (LNAI), vol. 10037, pp. 334–348. Springer, Cham (2016). https://doi.org/10.1007/978-3-319-49130-1_25
23. Zhu, J.Y., Park, T., Isola, P., Efros, A.A.: Unpaired image-to-image translation using cycle-consistent adversarial networks. In: Proceedings of the IEEE Conference on Computer Vision and Pattern Recognition, pp. 2223–2232 (2017)

Text to Image Synthesis Based on Multiple Discrimination

Zhiqiang Zhang[1] , Yunye Zhang[1], Wenxin Yu[1(✉)] , Jingwei Lu[2], Li Nie[1],
Gang He[1], Ning Jiang[1], Gang He[3], Yibo Fan[4], and Zhuo Yang[5]

[1] Southwest University of Science and Technology, Mianyang, China
`yuwenxin@swust.edu.cn, star_yuwenxin27@163.com`
[2] Cadence Design Systems, Inc., San Jose, USA
[3] Xidian University, Xi'an, China
[4] State Key Laboratory of ASIC and System, Fudan University, Shanghai, China
[5] Guangdong University of Technology, Guangzhou, China

Abstract. We propose a novel and simple text-to-image synthesizer
(MD-GAN) using multiple discrimination. Based on the Generative
Adversarial Network (GAN), we introduce segmentation images to the
discriminator to ensure the improvement of discrimination ability. The
improvement of discrimination ability will enhance the generator's generating ability, thus obtaining high-resolution results. Experiments well
validate the outstanding performance of our algorithm. On CUB dataset,
our inception score is 27.7% and 1.7% higher than GAN-CLS-INT and
GAWWN, respectively. On the flower dataset, it further outplays GAN-
CLS-INT and StackGAN by 21.8% and 1.25%, respectively. At the same
time, our model is more concise in structure, and its training time is only
half that of StackGAN.

Keywords: Deep learning · Text to image synthesis · GAN ·
Computer vision · Multiple discrimination

1 Introduce

Automatic image generation from text descriptions has become an active
research topic with tremendous applications, including auxiliary structural
design, scene restoration, etc. Recent advances by Generative Adversarial Networks (GAN) [1] have shown encouraging results in image synthesis and
attracted broad attention. Based on the adversarial training of generator and
discriminator, state-of-the-art methodologies are able to generate images which
are highly correlated with textual information.

However, it remains a headache to generate high-resolution images based on
text description through general GAN, due to the insufficient generation ability
of the generator model. For example, images by GAN-CLS-INT [2] could only
approach at most low resolution, lacking details to produce vivid object content. Instead, Reed et al. [3] proposed the Generative Adversarial What Where

© Springer Nature Switzerland AG 2019
I. V. Tetko et al. (Eds.): ICANN 2019, LNCS 11729, pp. 578–589, 2019.
https://doi.org/10.1007/978-3-030-30508-6_46

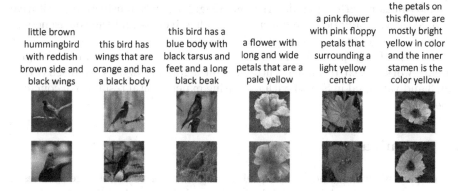

Fig. 1. Some examples of generated images. The first line is the text description, and the next two lines are the corresponding results.

Network (GAWWN) method, which ensures high-resolution images with localized annotations (e.g. bird part keypoints in Caltech-USCD Birds dataset [4]). Despite improved results, such approach highly depends on supporting information beyond the text thus deviate from the original text-to-image scope. Recently, Zhang et al. [5] proposed StackGAN, which successfully realized the generation of high-resolution image from text description without additional annotations. Nevertheless, their two-stage generation method makes the structure more complex and the training time longer.

Through the analysis of the GAN architecture, we find that the generator's generating ability is positively correlated with the discriminator's discriminating ability. Therefore, the generation ability of the generator can be promoted by improving the discrimination ability of the discriminator. It will finally achieve the purpose of improving resolution of the generated image. In this way, the main problem become to improve the discriminating ability. To achieve this goal, we propose the method of multiple discrimination. This method enhances the discriminating ability by adding additional segmentation images to the discriminator. On the one hand, adding segmentation images to the discriminator increases the type of discriminant so that the discriminator can discriminate more types of image and improve the discriminating ability finally. On the other hand, although GAWWN has the above-mentioned problems, it proves that the localized annotations can play guiding role in the generation process for obtaining high-resolution results. Based on this, since the segmentation images contain the localized annotations, adding segmentation image to the discriminator can also promote the generator to generate better.

The contributions to this paper are as follows: (1) We propose a novel and simple method (MD-GAN) for synthesizing images from text descriptions. The generation ability of generator is promoted by a roundabout strategy—adding segmentation image to the discriminator. (2) By multiple discrimination, our method can generate images that are semantically meaningful and higher-resolution with input descriptions (Fig. 1). (3) Extensively quantitative and qualitative evaluations demonstrate the effectiveness and the conciseness of our method in generating high-resolution images.

The rest of this paper is arranged as follows. Section 2 introduces the preliminary work of text-to-image synthesis. Our algorithm details are discussed in Sect. 3 and validated in Sect. 4 with promising experimental results. We conclude in Sect. 5.

2   Preliminaries

In this part we will introduce the preliminary work of text-to-image synthesis, including Generative Adversarial Networks and Joint embedding of text and image.

2.1   Generative Adversarial Networks

Generative adversarial networks learn the distribution of the original data through the game theory and can be used for image generation. The networks are composed of a generator G and a discriminator D. G and D play a game called minimax game: the generator tries its best to generate fake image which makes D believe it. And the discriminator distinguishes between real and fake images as far as possible. The specific process is shown in the Eq. (1):

$$\min_{G} \max_{D} V(D,G) = \sum_{x \sim P_{data(x)}}[\log D(x)] + \sum_{z \sim P_{Z(z)}}[\log(1 - D(G(z)))] \quad (1)$$

It will obtain a global optimal solution when $p_g = p_{data}$, p_g and p_{data} denote the distribution of the generator and original data respectively. The generating ability of G and the discriminating ability of D will perform well enough in this situation. In the process of GAN, the noise z as input to G, and G cheats D by fitting the original data distribution. In order not to be cheated by G, D needs to constantly improve its discriminative power. In this game, if G fails to cheat D, it should learn more to improve its ability to fit the original data. If D is cheated by G, it will have to learn more to improve its judgment. The goal of GAN is to gain a pretty generation model. Assuredly, a fine discrimination model is also obtained when the goal is achieved. This achieves a win-win situation for G and D.

2.2   Joint Embedding of Text and Image

The representation of images can be effectively obtained by CNN encoder. Accordingly, the representation of texts can be obtained through RNN (Recurrent Neural Networks) encoder. In order to realize the effective combination of text and image, they need to be mapped into the same embedding space. We follow the approach of Reed et al. [6], which use CNN and RNN encoders to learn a correspondence function with images and texts. The core of the method is to maximize the compatibility of matched images and descriptions. The structure loss function is as follows:

$$L_{structure} = \frac{1}{N}\sum_{n=1}^{N}\triangle(C_n, f_i(I_n))+\triangle(C_n, f_t(T_n)) \qquad (2)$$

where $\triangle$ is 0-1 loss, I_n and T_n are images and corresponding text descriptions respectively, C_n are the class labels, N is the number of image-text pairs, the goal is minimize this structure loss function. $f_i(I)$ and $f_t(T)$ are image and text classifiers, defined as follows:

$$F(I,T) = \theta(I)^T \varphi(T) \qquad (3)$$

$$f_i(I) = \underset{c\in C}{arg\,max}\sum_{t\sim T(c)}[F(I,t)] \qquad (4)$$

$$f_t(T) = \underset{c\in C}{arg\,max}\sum_{i\sim I(c)}[F(i,T)] \qquad (5)$$

where $F(I,T)$ is the compatibility function, $\theta(I)$ is image encoder, $\varphi(T)$ is text encoder, $T(c)$ and $I(c)$ are the set of text descriptions and images of class C, respectively.

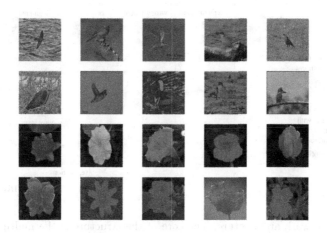

Fig. 2. The result of the segmentation image obtained by the mask R-CNN method, which is used to mark the object of the original images with mask directly.

3   The Proposed Method

In this part we will introduce the way to get the segmentation image, the network architecture and the implementation details. The results of image segmentation and the specific structure diagram will also be shown in this part.

3.1   Obtaining Segmentation Image

The core of the method is to improve the discriminating ability by adding additional segmentation image to the discriminator. Correspondingly, the generator's ability will also be improved with the improvement of discriminating ability. At the same time, the segmentation image contains localized annotations, which are very helpful in generating high-resolution results. Conditioned on this, the quality of segmentation images is particularly important.

We use the mask R-CNN approach [7] to generate the segmentation image. The mask R-CNN approach is the latest proposed algorithm with the best instance segmentation effect. It achieves excellent results by combining the residual network [8] and the feature pyramid network [9]. Based on this, we choose mask R-CNN approach as our image segmentation method. We apply this method to the CUB and Oxford-102 [10] datasets, some results are shown in Fig. 2. It can be seen from the results that mask R-CNN has achieved a near perfect segmentation effect.

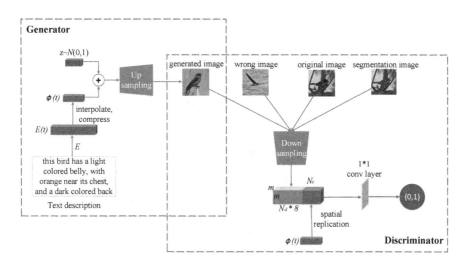

Fig. 3. Our network architecture. The core of the structure is the multiple discrimination in the discriminator. And the wrong image indicates the image that does not match the text information.

3.2   Network Architecture

The network architecture is shown in Fig. 3. In the generator G, first it samples the noise $z \sim N(0,1)$ and encodes the text descriptions using text encoder E. The text vector $E(t)$ is first interpolated to near data manifold [11], and then compressed to a small dimension through a fully connected layer. Next it connects with the noise z, the dimension of z needs to be consistent with the dimension of the compressed text embedding. After the connection is completed, the next step is to up-sample via the de-convolution [12] to generate final fake images.

In the discriminator D, first it down-sample the input image by several convolution layers. The input contains four types, that is, fake image, original image, wrong image and segmentation image. The wrong image here refers to the image that does not match the text information. The feature dimension after down-sampling is $m * m * (N_d * 8)$. Next, the text embedding is compressed to N_t dimension using a fully connected layer and then spatially replicated to form $m * m * N_t$ tensor so that it can concatenate with the image feature map. After the feature map is connected to the text tensor, a $1 * 1$ convolution layer is used to jointly learn feature matching across the image and the text. Finally, the judgment score for each case is calculated by the fully connected layer with only one node.

Algorithm 1.   MD-GAN training algorithm

1: **Input:** text t, original image $I_{original}$, segmentation image I_{seg}
2: wrong image I_{wrong}, number of eopchs N
3: **for** $n = 1$ **to** N **do**
4:    $s = \phi(t)$ {the encoded, interpolated and compressed text vector}
5:    $z = N(0, 1)$ {random noise}
6:    $I_{fake} = G(z, s)$ {the generated fake image}
7:    $d_{original} = D(I_{original}, s)$ {original image, text vector}
8:    $d_{seg} = D(I_{seg}, s)$ {segmentation image, text vector}
9:    $d_{wrong} = D(I_{wrong}, s)$ {wrong image, text vector}
10:   $d_{fake} = D(I_{fake}, s)$ {fake image ,text vector}
11:   $L_{D\_true} = (\log(d_{original}) + \log(d_{seg}))/2$ {Loss function in true case}
12:   $L_{D\_false} = (\log(1 - d_{wrong}) + \log(1 - d_{fake}))/2$ {Loss function in false case}
13:   $L_D = L_{D\_true} + L_{D\_false}$ {Loss function of discriminator}
14:   $D = D - ss * \partial L_D / \partial D$ {Update discriminator}
15:   $L_G = \log(d_{fake})$ {Loss function of generator}
16:   $G = G - ss * \partial L_G / \partial G$ {Update generator}
17: **end**

The specific algorithm is shown in Algorithm 1. Algorithm 1 shows the whole training process, in which ss represents step size. The loss function (lines 11, 12, 15) in the algorithm uses binary cross-entropy. The original image and the segmentation image are regard as true samples, while the false image and the wrong image are regard as false samples.

3.3   Implementation Details

In the process of up-sampling, Batch Normalization [13] is performed after each convolution except the last one. And for text embedding, it performed leaky-ReLU [14] activation after encode the text. In the process of down-sampling, the first one does not have batch normalization. The others performed batch normalization and leaky-ReLU activation after each convolution. In leaky-ReLU, the leaky value is 0.2.

By default, $N_g = N_d = N_z = N_t = 128$, $m = 8$, $W = H = 128$ (N_g, N_d, N_z, N_t denotes the dimension of the generator, discriminator, noise, and text vector, respectively. m is one of the feature dimensions after image down-sampling. W and H denotes the width and height of image). For our model, it trained 600 epochs using the ADAM optimization [15] with initial learning rate of 0.0002 and batch size 64.

4   Experiments

To validate our approach, we perform qualitative and quantitative evaluations on the CUB and Oxford-102 datasets. The CUB dataset contains 11,788 bird images, which are divided into 200 categories. The Oxford-102 datasets contains 8,189 flower images, which are divided into 102 categories. Each image in CUB and Oxford-102 has 10 corresponding text descriptions that will be used for training. Following the Reed et al. [2] experimental setup, we split CUB dataset to 150 train classes and 50 test classes as well as Oxford-102 to 82 train classes and 20 test classes.

Our results are compared with the results of three high-level methods (GAN-CLS-INT, GAWWN and StackGAN). Through quantitative and qualitative results, we prove the effectiveness and conciseness of our method. At the same time, we also demonstrate the generality of our method.

4.1   Evaluation Metrics

In order to evaluate the generated results, we select the recently proposed Inception Score method for quantitative evaluation. The specific evaluation content is shown in Eq. 6:

$$IS = exp(\sum\nolimits_x KL(p(y|x) \parallel p(y))) \tag{6}$$

where x represents generated image, and y is the predicted label gained by the Inception model [16], KL denotes Kullback-Leibler divergence. This method can judge well in the quality and diversity of the generated samples.

To calculate the Inception Score, we use nearly 30k generated images along the advice of Salimans et al. [17].

4.2   Quantitative and Qualitative Results

We compare our results with the state-of-the-art text-to-image synthesis methods GAN-CLS-INT, GAWWN and StackGAN on CUB and Oxford-102 datasets. The results of the comparison are shown in Figs. 4 and 5. In bird results, it shows that the resolution of the results of the GAN-CLS-INT is very low and can only reflect the basic shape and correspond color of the bird. In fact, it can only be recognized as a bird roughly since lacking in detailed information. For the results

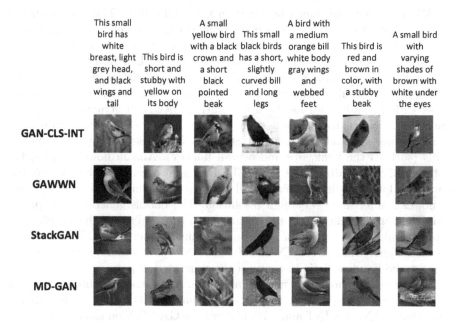

Fig. 4. The corresponding bird results generated by GAN-CLS-INT, GAWWN, Stack-GAN and MD-GAN. By contrast, our results are much better in detail processing. The generated objects are the most vivid and realistic.

Fig. 5. The corresponding flower results generated by GAN-CLS-INT, StackGAN and MD-GAN. It can be seen from the comparison results that our results are far superior to those of method GAN-CLS-INT and better than StackGAN. The flower results generated by our method are almost identical to the real image.

of GAWWN, they look much better than GAN-CLS-INT. The resolution has improved a lot. However, as mentioned before, this method of generating images requires not only text information, but also additional localized annotations. The results of StackGAN look better than both GAN-CLS-INT and GAWWN, but their method is complex in structure and still lacks some details from the results. In contrast, the results generated by our method can generate high-resolution images without additional localized annotations. And our structure is simpler than StackGAN because only one stage is needed. From the comparison results, our results are generally better than StackGAN because they generate better details (such as the beak, eye and overall fluency). And in flower results, the resolution of the results of the GAN-CLS-INT is also very low. StackGAN has improved a lot in resolution, but it still seems to lack some details. In contrast, our flower results show very high resolution. The details generated are pretty good. They are no different from real images in terms of subjective effect.

In general, the resolution of our results is much higher than GAN-CLS-INT. It is also higher than GAWWN and StackGAN. What's more, our results are the most vivid and realistic in terms of the generated objects.

The Inception Score of our method and other comparison methods are shown in Table 1. From this table it can be found that our inception score is 27.8% higher than GAN-CLS-INT and 1.7% higher than GAWWN on the CUB dataset. It is also 21.8% and 1.25% higher than GAN-CLS-INT and StackGAN on the flower dataset. On the one hand, the comparative results present that our method has pretty performance in the quality and diversity of generation. On the other hand, the results also show that our method is more generalization since it has a high score in both CUB and Oxford-102 datasets.

Table 1. Inception Score corresponding to GAN-CLS-INT, GAWWN, StackGAN and MD-GAN on CUB and Oxford-102 datasets.

Dataset	GAN-CLS-INT	GAWWN	StackGAN	MD-GAN
CUB	$2.88 \pm .04$	$3.62 \pm .07$	$3.70 \pm .04$	$3.68 \pm .04$
Oxford-102	$2.66 \pm .03$	/	$3.20 \pm .01$	$3.24 \pm .02$

Table 2. Inception Score and training time corresponding to the stageI and stageII of StackGAN, GAN-CLS-INT on CUB dataset.

	StackGAN (stageI)	StackGAN (stageII)	GAN-CLS-INT
epoch	600	600	600
Training time	2 h	2 days	1 day
Inception Score	$2.66 \pm .03$	$3.70 \pm .04$	$2.88 \pm .04$

In addition, it can be seen from the Table 1 that there is no obvious difference between our method and StackGAN on the Inception Score. However, from

Table 3. Comparison of StackGAN and MDGAN in core training time.

	StackGAN (stageII)	MD-GAN
epoch	600	600
Training time (day)	2	1
Average Time (minutes/epoch)	4.8	2.4

the subjective results, our method can generate better details, such as color processing and fluency. Especially in flower results, they are almost the same as the real image. At the same time, our structure is simpler because it only needs to iterate 600. StackGAN needs two training stages, each of which requires 600 iterations. Table 2 shows the Inception Score and training time corresponding to the stageI and stageII of StackGAN, GAN-CLS-INT on CUB dataset. Obviously, it can be seen that despite the longer training time, Stage II (the core stage) achieved higher score than GAN-CLS-INT. By contrast, our method only has the half of StackGAN training time while achieving almost the same score. As shown in Table 3, the core training stage of StackGAN take 4.8 min to iterate over an epoch, compared to 2.4 min for us, which is half of the time of StackGAN. Therefore, our method is indeed superior to StackGAN in time efficiency when the Incestion Score are about the same. It also demonstrates the simplicity of our structure.

For our model, it can also generate results with different poses or viewpoints based on the same text descriptions. The relevant results are shown in Fig. 6. Furthermore, our model can generate corresponding results when changing 1–

Fig. 6. Generated results with different pose or viewpoint based on the same text description.

Fig. 7. Generated corresponding results by only changing one color word in the text description. (Color figure online)

2 words in the text descriptions (such as color words). The relevant results are shown in Fig. 7. These all show that the model we trained has excellent generalization in generating high-resolution images.

5   Conclusion

This paper discusses a multi-discrimination methodology to synthesize high-resolution images based on text descriptions. The core contribution is a sharpened discriminator by adding segmented images. Our approach is generalized, effective, simple and empirically validated through comprehensive experiments.

Acknowledgement. This research was supported by 2018GZ0517, 2019YFS0146, 2019YFS0155 which supported by Sichuan Provincial Science and Technology Department, 2018KF003 Supported by State Key Laboratory of ASIC & System, Science and Technology Planning Project of Guangdong Province 2017B010110007.

References

1. Goodfellow, I.J., et al.: Generative adversarial nets. In: Advances in Neural Information Processing Systems, pp. 2672–2680 (2014)
2. Reed, S., Akata, Z., Yan, X., Logeswaran, L., Schiels, B., Lee, H.: Generative adversarial text-to-image synthesis. In: International Conference on Machine Learning, pp. 1060–1069 (2016)

3. Reed, S., Akata, Z., Yan, X., Longwaran, L., Schiels, B., Lee, H.: Learning what and where to draw. In: Advances in Neural Information Processing Systems, pp. 217–225 (2016)

4. Wah, C., Branson, S., Welinder, P., Perona, P., Belongie, S.: The Caltech-UCSD Birds-200-2011 Dataset. Technical report CNS-TR-2011-001, California Institute of Technology (2011)

5. Zhang, H., Xu, T., Li, H., Zhang, S., Huang, X., Wang, X., Metaxas, D.: Stack-GAN: text to photo-realistic image synthesis with stacked generative adversarial networks. In: International Conference on Computer Vision, pp. 5908–5916 (2017). https://doi.org/10.1109/iccv.2017.629

6. Reed, S.E., Akata, Z., Lee, H., Schiele, B.: Learning deep representations of fine-grained visual descriptions. In: Computer Vision and Pattern Recognition, pp. 49–58 (2016). https://doi.org/10.1109/CVPR.2016.13

7. He, K., Gkioxari, G., Dollár, P., Girshick, R.B.: Mask R-CNN. In: International Conference on Computer Vision, pp. 2980–2988 (2017). https://doi.org/10.1109/ICCV.2017.322

8. He, K., Zhang, X., Ren, S., Sun, J.: Deep residual learning for image recognition. In: Computer Vision on Pattern Recognition, pp. 770–778 (2016). https://doi.org/10.1109/CVPR.2016.90

9. Lin, Y., Dollár, P., Hariharan, R.B., Belongie, S.J.: Feature pyramid networks for object detection. In: Computer Vision and Pattern Recognition, pp. 936–944 (2017). https://doi.org/10.1109/CVPR.2017.106

10. Nilsback, M.-E., Zisserman, A.: Automated flower classification over a large number of classes. In: Indian Conference on Computer Vision, Graphics and Image Processing (2008). https://doi.org/10.1109/ICVGIP.2008.47

11. Reed, S.E., Sohn, K., Zhang, Y., Lee, H.: Learning to disentangle factors of variation with manifold interaction. In: International Conference on Machine Learning, pp. 1431–1439 (2014)

12. Zeiler, M.D., Fergus, R.: Visualizing and understanding convolutional networks. In: Fleet, D., Pajdla, T., Schiele, B., Tuytelaars, T. (eds.) ECCV 2014. LNCS, vol. 8689, pp. 818–833. Springer, Cham (2014). https://doi.org/10.1007/978-3-319-10590-1_53

13. Ioffe, S., Szegedy, C.: Batch normalization: accelerating deep network training by reducing internal covariate shift. In: International Conference on Machine Learning, pp. 448–456 (2015)

14. Xu, B., Wang, N., Chen, T., Li, M.: Empirical evaluation of rectified activations in convolutional network. In: abs/1505.00853 (2015)

15. Kingma, D.P., Ba, J.: Adam: a method for stochastic optimization. In: International Conference on Learning Representations (2014)

16. Szegedy, C., Vanhoucke, V., Ioffe, S., Shlens, J., Wojna, Z.: Rethinking the inception architecture for computer vision. In: Computer Vision and Pattern Recognition, pp. 2818–2826 (2016). https://doi.org/10.1109/CVPR.2016.308

17. Salimans, T., Goodfellow, I.J., Zaremba, W., Cheung, V., Radford, A., Chen, X.: Improved techniques for training GANs. In: Advances in Neural Information Processing Systems, pp. 2226–2234 (2016)

Disentangling Latent Factors of Variational Auto-encoder with Whitening

Sangchul Hahn[ORCID] and Heeyoul Choi[✉][ORCID]

Handong Global University, Pohang, South Korea
{s.hahn,hchoi}@handong.edu

Abstract. After deep generative models were successfully applied to image generation tasks, learning disentangled latent variables of data has become a crucial part of deep generative model research. Many models have been proposed to learn an interpretable and factorized representation of latent variable by modifying their objective function or model architecture. To disentangle the latent variable, some models show lower quality of reconstructed images and others increase the model complexity which is hard to train. In this paper, we propose a simple disentangling method based on a traditional whitening process. The proposed method is applied to the latent variables of variational auto-encoder (VAE), although it can be applied to any generative models with latent variables. In experiment, we apply the proposed method to simple VAE models and experiment results confirm that our method finds more interpretable factors from the latent space while keeping the reconstruction error the same as the conventional VAE's error.

Keywords: Disentanglement · Deep generative model · Latent variable · Representation · Whitening

1 Introduction

Since variational auto-encoder (VAE) [8] and generative adversarial network (GAN) [5] were proposed in deep learning, various deep generative models have been introduced and they have shown remarkable results in image generation tasks [3,6,7]. Once generative models become successful, disentangling the latent variable of the models has been another major research point. Since the latent variables can play a role as conceptual factors, disentangled latent variables make the models understand our world more conceptually [2,3,6].

As variants of the VAE structure, β-VAE [6] and Factor-VAE [7] change the original objective function to make their latent variable more factorized than the original VAE model. Note that the original VAE model itself enforces the latent variable to be factorized based on the isotropic Gaussian prior. As one of the GAN networks, Info-GAN [3] adds a feature latent code to the original input latent variable to learn independent factors of input data.

© Springer Nature Switzerland AG 2019
I. V. Tetko et al. (Eds.): ICANN 2019, LNCS 11729, pp. 590–603, 2019.
https://doi.org/10.1007/978-3-030-30508-6_47

Although these models show remarkable results in learning an explainable and factorized latent variable, they have drawbacks. For example, β-VAE achieves a better disentangling result [7] at the cost of lower reconstruction quality compared to the original VAE. Factor-VAE overcomes the drawback of β-VAE by introducing a new disentangling method to VAE, but it needs an additional network structure (discriminator). Also, Info-GAN provides good reconstruction quality and disentangling result. However, because of the GAN structure, it has an unstable training issue. Even with W-GAN [1], which provides more stability to training GAN, there are still some issues in hyper-parameter tuning.

In this paper, we introduce a new disentangling method which is simple and easy to apply to any deep generative models with latent variables. The original generative models are good to capture important factors behind the input data, but one problem is that each dimension of the latent variables is correlated to others so that it is hard to figure the meaning of individual dimensions. Therefore, if we can make the latent variables uncorrelated to each other, we could obtain more disentangled or explainable latent variables. Whitening with principal component analysis (PCA) is one of the most frequently used methods that converts a set of correlated variables into a set of linearly uncorrelated variables. In this point of view, we propose to apply PCA whitening to the latent variable of the original VAE.

To verify our method, we compare it to other methods on several image datasets, qualitatively and quantitatively. The qualitative analysis of disentanglement is based on just encoding the input image and generating images while traversing each dimension's value of the latent variables. If the generated images are changing by only one factor of the images when we change one dimension of the latent variables, it means the latent variables are well disentangled or factorized [2]. However, despite the growing interests in research of disentanglement, there is a lack of standard quantitative evaluation metric, although a few papers suggested evaluation metrics recently [4,6,7]. In this paper, we use the evaluation metric proposed in [7] for quantitative verification. We apply our proposed method to the original VAE model and compare to three other models (VAE, β-VAE, and Factor-VAE) on three datasets (MNIST, CelebA, 2D Shapes) [9–11].

The paper is organized as follows. We introduce background knowledge including deep generative models and PCA whitening in Sect. 2.2. In Sect. 2, we review related works like β-VAE, Factor-VAE, Info-GAN. Then, we describe our method to disentangle the latent variables of the models in Sect. 3. The datasets and models that we used in our experiments and the results are presented in Sect. 4. Finally, we conclude this paper with a summary of our work and future works in Sect. 5.

2   Related Work

2.1   Deep Generative Models

Deep generative models are based on deep neural networks and aim to learn a true data distribution from training data in the unsupervised learning manner. If the model can learn the true data distribution, it is possible to generate new data samples from the learned distribution with some variations. However, sometimes it is not possible to learn the true data distribution. Therefore, deep generative models train neural networks to approximate the true data distribution, which leads to model distribution.

In recent deep learning, most deep generative models are variations of VAE or GAN. VAE is an auto-encoder with a constraint on the latent space which is forced to be isotropic Gaussian by minimizing the Kullback-Leibler (KL) divergence between the Gaussian prior and the model distribution. Since the latent space generates samples for the decoder, the reparameterization trick is applied to make the gradient information flow through the latent space. After training the model, the latent space keeps most information to reconstruct input data, as well as it becomes isotropic Gaussian as much as possible. In other words, VAE cannot have perfectly disentangled latent variable even with the isotropic Gaussian prior. Contrary to VAE, in the conventional GAN models, there is no constraint on the latent space. Thus, in both VAE and GAN, the dimensions of the latent space might be entangled with other dimensions.

2.2   Whitening with PCA

Whitening with PCA is a preprocessing step to make data linearly uncorrelated. PCA whitening is composed of two steps. First, it applies PCA to the data samples to transform the correlated data distribution to uncorrelated one. Second, it normalizes each dimension with the square root of the corresponding eigenvalue to make each dimension have the unit variance.

2.3   Disentangling Models

Provided that z is the latent variable of the model and x is the input data, VAE models are trained to maximize the following objective function.

$$\mathcal{L}_{VAE} = \mathbb{E}_{q(z|x)}[\log p(x|z)] - KL(q(z|x)||p(z)), \tag{1}$$

where $KL(q||p)$ means the KL divergence between q and p, and $q(z|x)$, $p(x|z)$ and $p(z)$ are the encoder, decoder, and the prior distributions, respectively. The encoder and decoder are implemented with deep neural networks, and the prior distribution is isotropic Gaussian with unit variance. See [8] for the details.

As variations of VAE, several disentangling models have been proposed [6,7]. β-VAE changes the original objective function of VAE with a new parameter β as in Eq. 2.

$$\mathcal{L}_{\beta\_VAE} = \mathbb{E}_{q(z|x)}[\log p(x|z)] - \beta(KL(q(z|x)||p(z))). \tag{2}$$

When $\beta = 1$, it is exactly the same as the original objective function of VAE as in Eq. 1. However, with $\beta > 1$, it constrains the expression power of the latent variable z, and makes the distribution of z to be more similar to the isotropic Gaussian distribution. That is, KL divergence becomes more important with higher β values. Also, if β becomes larger, the latent variables can be more disentangled by resembling the isotropic Gaussian. That is, the KL divergence term in the objective function of β-VAE encourages conditional independence (or uncorrelatedness) in $q(z|x)$ [6]. However, there is a trade-off between reconstruction error and disentanglement [7]. In other words, the quality of reconstruction is damaged with larger β values, with which the latent variable can be more disentangled.

To overcome the side effect of β-VAE, Factor-VAE proposes another disentangling method based on the VAE structure [7]. In addition to the objective function of original VAE, Factor-VAE adds another KL divergence term to regularize the latent variables to be factorized as in Eq. 3.

$$\mathcal{L}_{F\_VAE} = \mathbb{E}_{q(z|x)}[\log p(x|z)] - KL(q(z|x)||p(z)) - \gamma KL(q(z)||\bar{q}(z)), \quad (3)$$

where

$$q(z) = \mathbb{E}_{p(x)}[q(z|x)], \quad (4)$$

$$\bar{q} = \prod_{j=1}^{d} q(z_j), \quad (5)$$

and d is the dimension of the latent variables. In other words, the second KL divergence term is added to force $q(z)$ to be as independent as possible. Since $\mathbb{E}_{p(x)}[q(z|x)]$ is intractable in practice, it is approximated by sampling N input cases as follows.

$$\mathbb{E}_{p(x)}[q(z|x)] \approx \frac{1}{N} \sum_{i=1}^{N} q(z|x^{(i)}). \quad (6)$$

Note that the first two terms in Eq. 3 are exactly the same as the original VAE objective function, Eq. 1.

2.4   Metrics for Disentanglement

Despite the growing interests about disentangling models, there is no standard evaluation metric and lack of labeled data for evaluation. Therefore, the previously proposed disentangling models verify their disentangling quality based on qualitative analysis. Most commonly used analysis is based on latent variable traversal. If only one factor of generated images is changing while changing the value of one dimension in the latent variable, then the latent variable that the model learned is considered to be well disentangled. This qualitative analysis is easy to understand and intuitive, but we still need quantitative analysis methods to compare the disentangling ability of various models.

Recently several evaluation metrics have been proposed for disentanglement with labeled data for that metrics [4,6,7]. One of these quantitative evaluation metrics proposed by [7] is summarized in Table 1. In experiments, we use this metric to compare models quantitatively. For the details of the metric, see Appendix B in [7].

Table 1. Algorithm: disentangling metric.

1. Select L images $(x_1, x_2, \ldots, x_L)$ from D_{f_k}. D_{f_k} is a set of sample images with a fixed value for the k-th generating factor and random value for the other factors
2. Encode $(x_1, x_2, \ldots, x_L)$ to make latent variables $(z_1, z_2, \ldots, z_L)$, where $z_i \in \mathbb{R}^d$
3. Rescale latent variables with empirical standard deviation $s \in \mathbb{R}^d$
4. Calculate empirical variance in each dimension of the rescaled latent variable
5. Find a dimension, d^*, which has the minimum variance $d^* = \arg\min_d \mathrm{var}(z_d)$
6. Add (d^*, k) into the training set
7. Repeat 1 to 6 for all generating factors to make M training votes. (M is the number of training votes)
8. Making a majority vote classifier with training votes and calculate accuracy of the majority vote classifier for the disentangling score

3   Whitening the Latent Variable

We propose a new disentangling method based on whitening the latent variables with PCA, which leads to *Whitening VAE* (WVAE). We apply PCA to the original latent variables of the trained model, then we rescale the dimensions of the projected variable with the square root of corresponding eigenvalues. This is the process of PCA based whitening method. With the rescaled eigenspace, every dimension in the eigenspace has a unit variance. The reason why we rescale the latent space is to make the scale of control panel to be similar while we control the latent space for the latent variable traversal.

After training a generative model (VAE) with training data **X**, the generative model encodes **X** to **Z** in the latent space. Then the whitening process is applied to **Z**, which is summarized in Table 2. Because our proposed method applies the whitening method to the latent space of the already trained model, it does not change the objective function of the original VAE. That is, the objective function of our model (Eq. 7) is the same as one of the original VAE, and the reconstruction error also does not change. This means that our proposed method does not sacrifice the reconstruction quality while achieving more disentangled latent variables.

$$\mathcal{L}_{WVAE} = \mathbb{E}_{q(z|x)}[\log p(x|z)] - KL(q(z|x)||p(z)). \qquad (7)$$

Table 2. Algorithm: whitening the latent variable.

Given a trained VAE model
1. Apply the encoder to $\mathbf{X}$ to obtain $\mathbf{Z}$
2. Apply PCA to $\mathbf{Z}$ to find the eigenvalue Λ and eigenvector $\mathbf{U}$ of the covariance matrix
3. Project $\mathbf{Z}$ to the eigenspace by $\mathbf{Z}_{PCA} = \mathbf{U}^T\mathbf{Z}$
4. Rescale the eigenspace by $\mathbf{Z}_{PCA\_W} = \Lambda^{1/2}\mathbf{Z}_{PCA}$

Figure 1(a) shows the model structure of our proposed method applied to VAE, and Fig. 1(b) describes how latent variable traversal can be applied. To generate new samples, we control $\mathbf{Z}_{PCA\_W}$ in the rescaled eigenspace.

While β-VAE has a trade-off between disentangling and reconstruction quality as we described above, our proposed method does not sacrifice the reconstruction quality to disentangle the latent variable. Also, Factor-VAE needs sampling and approximation, because $\gamma KL(q(z)||\bar{q}(z))$ term is intractable in practice [7]. Additionally, extra discriminator for the density-ratio trick is necessary to minimize the KL divergence term as in Eq. 8 [12,13].

$$TC(z) = KL(q(z)||\bar{q}(z)) = \mathbb{E}_{q(z)}[\log \frac{q(z)}{\bar{q}(z)}]$$

$$\approx \mathbb{E}_{q(z)}[\log \frac{D(z)}{1 - D(z)}], \qquad (8)$$

where $TC(z)$ is the total correlation [14] and D is the discriminator. However, our proposed method does not need any extra network, sampling or approximation process.

4   Experiments

4.1   Data

We use three different image datasets for our experiments: MNIST, CelebA, and 2D Shapes. These datasets are most frequently used in many papers of deep generative models and disentanglement of latent variable. The first two datasets (MNIST and CelebA) have no label for generative factors, while the 2D shapes dataset has labels for generative factors. MNIST consists of 60 K and 10 K hand written images (28×28) for training and testing, respectively. CelebA (aligned and cropped version) has 202,599 RGB face images ($64 \times 64 \times 3$) of celebrities.

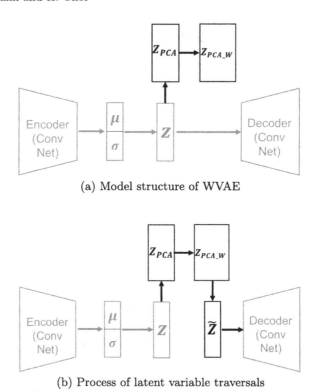

(a) Model structure of WVAE

(b) Process of latent variable traversals

Fig. 1. The proposed model architecture. (a) Model structure of our proposed model with the process of making disentangled latent variable (WVAE) after training the VAE model. (b) process of latent variable traversals on WVAE. When doing latent variable traversals, the dimensions of Z_{PCA_W} are controled and recovered to the $\mathbf{Z}$ space to make changed latent variable $\tilde{Z}$. The VAE model part (in gray color) is fixed after training in advance.

2D Shape has 737,280 images (64×64) that are generated with 6 generative factors (number of values): color(1), shape(3), scale(6), orientation(40), position X(32), and position Y(32). 2D Shape has label of generated factors as the value of each generative factors, so it can be used for quantitative analysis of disentangling performance. Figure 2 shows a few sample images of the datasets. We analyze qualitatively the methods on the three datasets, and analyze quantitatively on the 2D Shapes dataset. We compare our proposed method to three different methods: VAE, β-VAE, and Factor-VAE.

4.2   Models

To compare our proposed method to other models, we use the same VAE architecture of β-VAE, and Factor-VAE. The encoder consists of convolutional neural networks, and the decoder consists of deconvolutional neural networks. For

Fig. 2. Image examples sampled from the three datasets. (Top) MNIST, (Middle) CelebA, and (Bottom) 2D Shapes.

Factor-VAE, we use fully connected layers for the discriminator as in [7]. To apply the whitening process to the latent variable, we calculate eigenvalue and eigenvector with latent variable of the entire training data of each dataset. To disentangle the latent variable, our proposed model does not need any other architecture but need original VAE architecture only. We used RMSprop as an optimizer and set the learning rate to 0.001 at the beginning of the training process. We set the dimension of latent variable to 10 for all three datasets.

4.3   Results

Figure 3 shows that the latent variable of our model is disentangled better than original VAE with MNIST. When we change the value of the dimension of a latent variable which corresponds to the factor of thickness, the generated image from original VAE changes with thickness and shape simultaneously, but the generated image from WVAE model changes with thickness only. As with the thickness, the image from original VAE changes with circle size and thickness when we change the circle factor but the image from WVAE changes with circle size only. This experiment results show that applying whitening method to latent variable can make latent variable more disentangled. Also, comparing to the Factor-VAE and β-VAE, it shows that our WVAE can disentangle the latent variable as good as Factor-VAE and β-VAE.

Figure 4 presents the results of latent variable traversals with four different models. The latent variable of the original VAE model is highly entangled. Factor-VAE ($\gamma = 6.4$) and β-VAE ($\beta = 4$) show more distinct variations than original VAE. Comparing to the other models (VAE, β-VAE, and Factor-VAE), disentangling quality of our proposed method is as good as, if not better than, Factor-VAE and β-VAE, while it is much better than the original VAE. Note that our method is much simpler approach than the others.

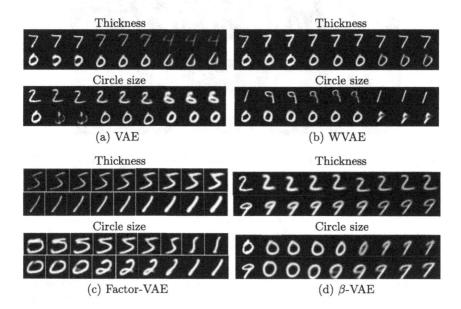

Fig. 3. Qualitative analysis of conventional VAE, WVAE, Factor-VAE, and β-VAE on MNIST. The left-most column of each image is the ground truth image.

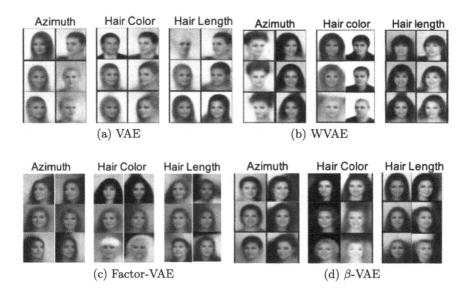

Fig. 4. Qualitative analysis of VAE, WVAE, Factor-VAE, and β-VAE models on CelebA.

Figure 5 presents the results of latent variable traversals with our proposed method. Each image ((a)–(e)) correspond to variations of hair length, background darkness, azimuth, smile, and hair color changing, respectively, and the variations are distinct. It shows that our whitened latent variables have linearly independent factors of the face data.

Table 3. Average disentangling score of models with the disentangling metric proposed in [7].

	VAE	Factor-VAE	WVAE
Disentangling score	80.0	82.0	85.0

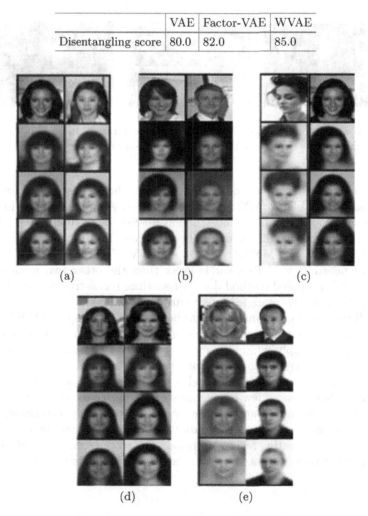

Fig. 5. Qualitative analysis of our proposed method on the CelebA dataset. The top row of each image is the ground truth image. (a–e) show several results of latent variable traversals. The columns correspond to variations of hair length, background darkness, azimuth, smile, and hair color changing, respectively.

Table 3 summarizes the quantitative analysis results on the 2D Shapes dataset from the three different deep generative models (VAE, Factor-VAE, and WVAE) with the disentanglement metric proposed in [7]. The disentangling score is the accuracy of major vote classifer. Therefore, higher disentangling score means the model encodes the generative factors into the dimension of the latent variable more independently. Our proposed model's disentanglement score is higher than ones of original VAE and Factor-VAE. Note that the evaluation metric is the one proposed in the Factor-VAE paper [7], which is described in Table 1.

Fig. 6. Reconstruction results of WVAE on the three datasets. In each image, the top row is original images and the bottom row is the reconstructed ones.

To check reconstruction quality, Fig. 6 shows the reconstruction results of WVAE model for CelebA, MNIST, and 2D Shapes. As we mentioned in Sect. 3, WVAE model has the same reconstruction quality as original VAE. Also, we compare the reconstruction error of three models: Factor-VAE ($\gamma = 6.4$), β-VAE (2D Shape: $\beta = 4$, MNIST: $\beta = 6$), and WVAE during training, as shown in Fig. 7, where our model's error is lower than the other two models'. This proves that our proposed method does not sacrifice reconstruction quality while obtaining the more disentangled latent variable.

In addition to the experiment results above, using our proposed WVAE model has an advantage to interpret the meaning of latent variable and factors of generated images. To apply whitening method to the latent variable, we calculate the eigenvalue and eigenvector of the latent variable. Figure 8 presents the eigenvalues of the latent space for the CelebA training dataset and the 2D Shapes dataset. It is shown that a few latent variables dominate the latent space, meaning that the factors in the latent space by VAE have strong correlation to each other. This eigenvalue analysis can indicate dominant dimensions of the latent variable and the generating factors corresponding to those dominant dimensions. Such knowledge is important to make a model more explainable.

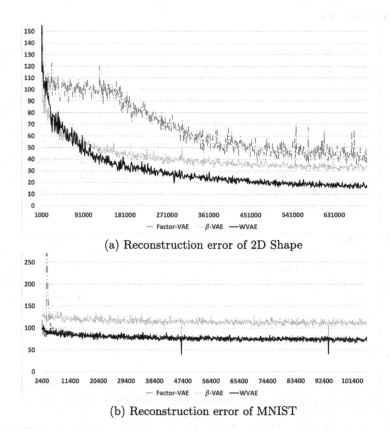

(a) Reconstruction error of 2D Shape

(b) Reconstruction error of MNIST

Fig. 7. Training curves of reconstruction error for the three models on the 2D Shape and MNIST dataset.

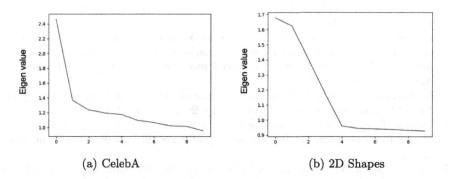

(a) CelebA   (b) 2D Shapes

Fig. 8. Eigenvalue of the latent variable of the CelebA training dataset and the 2D Shapes dataset. The eigenvalues are sorted by descending order. Note that only a few factors are dominant.

5   Conclusion

Learning a disentangled representation of given data set is important for not only deep generative models but also making an artificial intelligence (AI) model to understand our real world more conceptually. We showed that the latent variables can be disentangled by a simple method (PCA whitening) without any change in the objective function or model architecture. The results of qualitative and quantitative analysis show that our proposed method can disentangle the latent variable as good as other disentangling models can, without loss of reconstruction quality. Also, with eigenvalue analysis, we could see that our proposed method makes a more interpretable model. For the future work, we will try other transformation methods like non-negative matrix factorization (NMF) or independent component analysis (ICA).

Acknowledgement. This research was supported by Basic Science Research Program through the National Research Foundation of Korea (NRF) funded by the Ministry of Education (2017R1D1A1B03033341), and by Institute for Information & communications Technology Promotion (IITP) grant funded by the Korea government (MSIT) (No. 2018-0-00749, Development of virtual network management technology based on artificial intelligence).

References

1. Arjovsky, M., Chintala, S., Bottou, L.: Wasserstein generative adversarial networks. In: Proceedings of the 34th International Conference on Machine Learning, ICML 2017, Sydney, NSW, Australia, 6–11 August 2017, pp. 214–223 (2017)
2. Bengio, Y., Courville, A.C., Vincent, P.: Representation learning: a review and new perspectives. IEEE Trans. Pattern Anal. Mach. Intell. **35**(8), 1798–1828 (2013). https://doi.org/10.1109/TPAMI.2013.50
3. Chen, X., Duan, Y., Houthooft, R., Schulman, J., Sutskever, I., Abbeel, P.: InfoGAN: interpretable representation learning by information maximizing generative adversarial nets. In: Annual Conference on Neural Information Processing Systems, pp. 2172–2180 (2016)
4. Eastwood, C., Williams, C.K.I.: A framework for the quantitative evaluation of disentangled representations. In: 6th International Conference on Learning Representations, ICLR 2018, Conference Track Proceedings, Vancouver, BC, Canada, 30 April–3 May 2018 (2018)
5. Goodfellow, I.J., et al.: Generative adversarial nets. In: Annual Conference on Neural Information Processing Systems, pp. 2672–2680 (2014)
6. Higgins, I., et al.: β-VAE: learning basic visual concepts with a constrained variational framework. In: 5th International Conference on Learning Representations (2017)
7. Kim, H., Mnih, A.: Disentangling by factorising. In: Proceedings of the 35th International Conference on Machine Learning, ICML, pp. 2654–2663 (2018)
8. Kingma, D.P., Welling, M.: Auto-encoding variational Bayes. In: 2nd International Conference on Learning Representations, ICLR 2014, Conference Track Proceedings, Banff, AB, Canada, 14–16 April 2014 (2014)

9. LeCun, Y., Bottou, L., Bengio, Y., Haffner, P.: Gradient-based learning applied to document recognition. Proc. IEEE **86**(11), 2278–2324 (1998). https://doi.org/10.1109/5.726791
10. Liu, Z., Luo, P., Wang, X., Tang, X.: Deep learning face attributes in the wild. In: 2015 IEEE International Conference on Computer Vision, ICCV 2015, Santiago, Chile, 7–13 December 2015, pp. 3730–3738 (2015). https://doi.org/10.1109/ICCV.2015.425
11. Matthey, L., Higgins, I., Hassabis, D., Lerchner, A.: dSprites: disentanglement testing Sprites dataset (2017). https://github.com/deepmind/dsprites-dataset/
12. Nguyen, X., Wainwright, M.J., Jordan, M.I.: Estimating divergence functionals and the likelihood ratio by convex risk minimization. IEEE Trans. Inf. Theory **56**(11), 5847–5861 (2010). https://doi.org/10.1109/TIT.2010.2068870
13. Sugiyama, M., Suzuki, T., Kanamori, T.: Density-ratio matching under the bregman divergence: a unified framework of density-ratio estimation. Ann. Inst. Stat. Math. **64**(5), 1009–1044 (2012). https://doi.org/10.1007/s10463-011-0343-8
14. Watanabe, M.S.: Information theoretical analysis of multivariate correlation. IBM J. Res. Dev. **4**(1), 66–82 (1960). https://doi.org/10.1147/rd.41.0066

Training Discriminative Models
to Evaluate Generative Ones

Timothée Lesort[1,2]([✉]) [iD], Andrei Stoian[2][iD], Jean-François Goudou[2],
and David Filliat[1][iD]

[1] Flowers Laboratory (ENSTA ParisTech & Inria), Palaiseau, France
`lesort@ensta.fr`
[2] Thales, Theresis Laboratory, Paris, France

Abstract. Generative models are known to be difficult to assess. Recent
works, especially on generative adversarial networks (GANs), produce
good visual samples of varied categories of images. However, the validation of their quality is still difficult to define and there is no existing
agreement on the best evaluation process. This paper aims at making
a step toward an objective evaluation process for generative models. It
presents a new method to assess a trained generative model by evaluating the test accuracy of a classifier trained with generated data. The test
set is composed of real images. Therefore, The classifier accuracy is used
as a proxy to evaluate if the generative model fit the true data distribution. By comparing results with different generated datasets we are able
to classify and compare generative models. The motivation of this approach is also to evaluate if generative models can help discriminative neural networks to learn, i.e., measure if training on generated data is able
to make a model successful at testing on real settings. Our experiments
compare different generators from the Variational Auto-Encoders (VAE)
and Generative Adversarial Network (GAN) frameworks on MNIST and
fashion MNIST datasets. Our results show that none of the generative
models is able to replace completely true data to train a discriminative
model. But they also show that the initial GAN and WGAN are the best
choices to generate on MNIST database (Modified National Institute of
Standards and Technology database) and fashion MNIST database.

1   Introduction

Generative models are machine learning models that learn to reproduce training
data and to generalize it. This kind of model has several advantages, for example
as shown in [16], the generalization capacity of generative models can help a
discriminative model to learn by regularizing it. Moreover, once trained, they
can be sampled as much as needed to produce new datasets. Generative models
such as GAN (Generative Adversarial Network) [6], WGAN (Wasserstein-GAN)
[1], CGAN (Conditional-GAN) [15], VAE (Variational Auto-Encoder) [10] and
CVAE (Conditional-VAE) [25] have produced samples with good visual quality
on various image datasets such as MNIST, bedrooms [19] or imageNet [17].

© Springer Nature Switzerland AG 2019
I. V. Tetko et al. (Eds.): ICANN 2019, LNCS 11729, pp. 604–619, 2019.
https://doi.org/10.1007/978-3-030-30508-6_48

They can also be used for data augmentation [20], for safety against adversarial example [27], or to produce labeled data [24] in order to improve the training of discriminative models.

One commonly accepted tool to evaluate a generative model trained on images is visual assessment. It aims at validating the realism of samples. However those methods are very subjective and dependent on the evaluation process. One case of this method is called "visual Turing tests", in which samples are visualized by humans who try to guess if the images are generated or not. It has been used to assess generative models of images from ImageNet [5] and also on digit images [11]. Others propose to replace the human analysis by the analysis of first and second moments of activation of a neural network. This method has been used with the output of the inception model for "Inception Score" (IS) [22], or with activation from intermediate layers for "Frechet Inception Score" (FID) [7]. Log-likelihood based evaluation metrics were also widely used to evaluate generative models but as shown in [26], those evaluations can be misleading in high dimensional cases such as images.

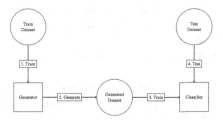

Fig. 1. Proposed method: 1. Train a generator on real training data, 2. Generate labeled data, 3. Train classifier with the generated data, 4. Evaluate the generator by testing the classifier on the test set composed of real data

The solution we propose evaluates generative models by training a classifier with generated samples and testing it on real data. The classifier test accuracy indicates how good the generative model is at reproducing the distribution of the original dataset. The full process of the method is illustrated in Fig. 1. The test data come from the original dataset but have not been used to train the generator.

Our contribution is twofolds: first we propose a method to evaluate generative models on the testing set. Secondly we introduce a quantitative score, *the fitting capacity* (FiC), to evaluate and compare performance of generative models.

2   Related Work

2.1   Generative Models

Generative models can be implemented in various frameworks and settings. In this paper we focus on two kind of those frameworks: variational auto-encoders and generative adversarial networks.

The variational auto-encoder (VAE) framework [10,21] is a particular kind of auto-encoder which learns to map data into a Gaussian latent space, generally chosen as an univariate normal distribution $N(0, I)$ (where I is the identity matrix). The VAE learns also the inverse mapping from this latent space to the observation space. This characteristic makes the VAE an interesting option for generating new data after training. Indeed, thanks to the inverse mapping, new data can be generated by sampling a Gaussian distribution and decoding these samples. The particularity of the latent space comes from the minimization of the KL divergence between the distribution of data in the latent space and the prior $N(0, I)$. For the sake of simplicity, in this paper we will refer to decoder of the VAE as a generator.

Generative adversarial networks [6] are another framework of models that learn to generate data. The learning process is a game between two networks: a generator that learns to produce images from a distribution P and a discriminator which learns to discriminate between generated and true images. The generator learns to fool the discriminator and the discriminator learns to not be fooled. This class of generative models can produce visually realistic samples from diverse datasets but they suffer from instabilities in their training. One of the models we evaluate, the Wasserstein GAN (WGAN) [1], try to address those issues by enforcing a Lipschitz constraint on the discriminator. We also evaluate the BEGAN [2], another variant of the GAN which uses an auto-encoder as discriminator.

Both GANs and VAEs can also be implemented into a conditional setting. Conditional neural networks [25] and in particular Conditional Variational Autoencoders (CVAE) and Conditional Generative adversarial networks (CGAN) [15] are a class of generative models that have control over the sample's class of their training dataset. By imposing a label during training on the generator, a conditional generative network can generate from any class and thus produces labeled data automatically. The conditional approach has been used to improve the quality of generative models and make them more discriminative [18]. They are particularly adapted for our setup because we need to generate labeled datasets to train our classifiers.

2.2   Evaluation of Generated Samples

The evaluation of generative models has been addressed in various settings. [26] show that different metrics (such as Parzen windows, Nearest Neighbor or Log likelihood) applied to generative models can lead to different results. Good results in one application of a generative model can not be used as evidence of good performance in another application. Their conclusion is that evaluation based on sample visual quality is a bad indicator for the entropy of samples. Conversely, the log-likelihood can be used to produce samples with high entropy but it does not assure good visual quality. In this setting, high entropy means high variability in the samples.

More methods exist to evaluate generative networks as described in [3]. In particular, approaches that use a classifier trained on real data to evaluate generative models, [8,30]. [13] proposes to use the two samples test with a classifier to evaluate if generated samples and original one are from the same distribution. Since generative models often produce visual artifacts it may be to easy to discriminate real images from generated one. Different quantitative evaluation have also been experimented in [9] which compares models of GANs in various settings. These quantitative evaluations are based on divergence or distances between real data or real features and generated ones. In our method we don't train the classifier with real data but with generated one.

2.3   Multi-scale Structural Similarity

Multi-scale structural similarity (MS-SIM, [28]) is a measurement that gives a way to incorporate image details at different resolutions in order to compare two images. This similarity is generally used in the context of image compression to compare images before and after compression.

Odena et al. [18] use this similarity to estimate the variability inside a class. They randomly sample two images of a class and measure the MS-SIM. If the value is high, then images are considered different. By operating this process on multiple data points X of the class Y, the similarity gives an insight on the entropy of $P(X|Y)$: if the MS-SIM gives high result, the entropy is high (i.e. variate images); otherwise, the entropy is low. A good generator produces variate classes with variate images. MS-SIM is able to estimate the variability of the generated samples, however, it can not estimate if the sample comes from one or several modes of the distribution $P(X|Y)$. For example, if we want to generate images of cats, the MS-SIM similarity can not differentiate a generator that produces different kinds of black cats from a network that produces different cats of different colors. In our method, if the generator is able to generate in only one mode of the distribution $P(X|Y)$, the score will be low in the testing phase.

2.4   Inception Score

One of the most used approach to evaluate a generative model is Inception Score (IS) [18,22]. The authors use an inception classifier model pretrained on ImageNet to evaluate the sample distribution. They compute the conditional classes distribution at each generated sample x, $P(Y|X = x)$ and the general classes distribution $P(Y)$ over the generated dataset.

They proposed the following score:

$$IS(X) = \exp(\mathbb{E}_X[KL(P(Y|X) \parallel P(Y))], \tag{1}$$

Where KL is the Kullback-Leibler divergence. The KL term can be rewritten:

$$KL(P(Y|X) \parallel P(Y)) = H(P(Y|X), P(Y)) - H(P(Y|X)), \tag{2}$$

Where $H(P(Y|X))$ is the entropy of $P(Y|X)$ and $H(P(Y|X), P(Y))$ the cross-entropy between $P(Y|X)$ and $P(Y)$. The entropy term is low when predictions given by the inception model have high confidence in one class only. The entropy term is high in other cases. The cross-entropy term is low when predictions given by the inception model gives unbalanced classes in the whole dataset and is high if the dataset is balanced.

Hence, the inception score promotes when the inception model predictions have high confidence in varied classes. The hypothesis is that if the inception has high confidence in its prediction the image should look real.

Unfortunately, it does not estimate if the samples have intra-class variability (it does not take the entropy of $P(X|Y)$ into account). Hence, a generator that could generate only one sample per class with high quality would maximize the score.

One important restriction of IS is that the generative models to evaluate should produce images in ImageNet classes because the model required for the evaluation is pretrained on it and can not evaluate other classes.

2.5   Frechet Inception Distance

Another recent approach to evaluate generative adversarial networks is the Frechet Inception Distance (FID) [7]. The FID, as the inception score, is based on low moment analysis. It compares the mean and the covariance of activations between real data (μ and C) and generated data (μ_{gen}, C_{gen}). The activation are taken from a inner layer in an inception model. The comparison is done using the Frechet distance (as if the means and covariance where taken from a Gaussian distribution) (see Eq. 3). The inception model is trained on Imagenet.

$$d^2((\mu, C), (\mu_{gen}, C_{gen})) = \| \mu - \mu_{gen} \|_2^2 + Tr(C + C_{gen} - 2(C * C_{gen})^{\frac{1}{2}}), \quad (3)$$

FID have in particular been used in a large scale study to compare generative models [14]. FID measure the similarities between the distribution of generated feature and the distribution of real features but it does not directly assess the good visual quality. Furthermore, it assumes a gaussian distribution of features over the dataset which introduce a bias in the evaluation.

Our approach is similar to the approach developed in parallel by [23]. However we evaluate all generative models with the same generator architecture, all trained by the same method and not models with their original architecture and training process. We have then a clear comparison of different learning criterion.

3   Methods

We evaluate generators in a supervised training setup. The real dataset D, the *original dataset*, is composed of pairs of examples (x, y) where x is a data point and y the associated label. The dataset is split in three subsets D_{train}, D_{valid} and D_{test} for cross-validation. Our method needs a generative model that can sample conditionally from any given label y, i.e. we can choose from which class we sample the generator. This conditional generative model is trained on D_{train}. Then, we sample the generator to crate a new dataset D_{gen} of samples $\hat{x}$. D_{gen} is sampled with balanced classes. It is used afterwards to train a classifier C implemented as a deep neural network. D_{valid} is used for validation of C. C will then be used to evaluate G.

When C is trained, we evaluate C on D_{test} the accuracy of C on D_{test} is what we call the "fitting capacity" (FiC).

It can be compared with the accuracy of a classifier trained only on real data from D_{train} (the baseline) or with the FiC of another generator. We consider that the baseline is an upperbound to the FiC because no generative models beats it when $\tau = 1$. But it is theoretically possible to have a FiC higher to the baseline.

We can summarize our method as follows:

1. Train a conditional generative model over D_{train}
2. Sample data to produce D_{gen}
3. Train a discriminative model (the classifier) over D_{gen}
4. Select a classifier over a validation set D_{valid}.
5. Iterate the process for several generative models and compare the accuracy of the classifiers on D_{test}.

The protocol presented allows to analyze the performance of a model on the whole test set or class by class. The final accuracy can be compared directly to with the accuracy compute with another generator even if the classifier change. As we will see in results, we estimate the stability of the generators by training them with different random seeds.

The simple act of changing these seeds can have great impact on the generative models training and thus induce a variability in the results. To show that the variability of results comes mainly from the instability of the generator and not from the classifier, we compare our results with results computed with KNN classifiers instead of neural networks. As KNN classifiers are deterministic, if the random seeds produce variability with this kind of classifier, the instability necessarily comes from the generators. The KNN classifier is however not a good option for our evaluation methods because it is not adapted for complex image classification.

The classifier was chosen to be a deep neural network because they are known to be difficult to train if the testing set distribution is biased with respect to the training set distribution. This characteristic is put to good use in order to compare generated datasets and hence generative models. If D_{gen} contains unrealistic samples or samples that are not diverse enough, the classifier will not reach a high accuracy. Moreover, to investigate the impact of generated data into the training process of a classifier, we also experiment the method by mixing real data and generated data. The ratio between generated data over the complete dataset is called τ. If $\tau = 0$ there is no generated data and $\tau = 1$ means only generated data.

We call our final score for a generator G the *fitting capacity* (Noted Ψ_G) because it evaluates the ability of a generator to fit the distribution of a testing set. It is the testing accuracy of the classifier C over D_{Test} trained by a generator when $\tau = 1$.

It is important to note that for fair comparison, whatever τ the total number of datapoint used to train the classifier is constant, i.e. more generated data lead to less real data.

We evaluate models with the generator or discriminator architecture proposed in [4].

4   Experiments

4.1   Implementation Details

Generative models are often evaluated on the MNIST dataset. Fashion MNIST [29] is a direct drop-in replacement for the original MNIST dataset but with more complex classes with higher variability. Thus, we use this dataset in order to evaluate different generative models in addition to MNIST.

As presented in the previous section, to apply our method, we need to generate labeled datasets. We used two different methods for that. For the first one, we train one generator for each class y on D_{train}. This enables us to generate sample from a specific class and to generate a labeled dataset. In this setting, we compare VAE, WGAN, GAN and BEGAN. The second method uses conditional generative models which can generate the whole labeled dataset D_{gen} directly. In this case, we ran our experiments on CVAE and CGAN. The generators are trained with Adam optimizer on the whole original training dataset for 25 epochs on eight different random seeds.

The classifier model trained on D_{gen} is a standard deep CNN with a softmax output (see in Appendix for details). The classifier is trained with Adam optimizer for a maximum of 200 epochs. We use early stopping to stop the training if the accuracy does not improve anymore on the validation set after 50 epochs. Then, we apply model selection based on the validation error and compute the test error on D_{test}. The architecture of the classifier is kept fixed for all experiments.

We performed experiment with values of $\tau = [0.0, 0.125, 0.250, ..., 1.0]$. $\tau = 0$ is used as a baseline (using only real data) to compare other results. However most of the analysis are made on $\tau = 1$ because the results are representative of the full quality of the generator, i.e. generalization and fitting of the distribution of the testing set.

The experiment with various τ makes it possible to visualize if a generator is able to generalize and fit a given dataset. If the method results improve when τ is low ($\tau < 0.5$) it means that the generator is able to perform data augmentation i.e. generalize training data. If the result are as good when τ is high ($\tau > 0.5$) and a fortiori near 1 it means the generator is able to fit D_{test} distribution.

4.2   Adaptation of Inception Score and Frechet Inception Distance

We compare our evaluation method of the generative model with the two most used methods: IS and FID. IS and FID, as originally defined, use a model pre-

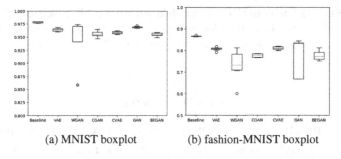

(a) MNIST boxplot   (b) fashion-MNIST boxplot

Fig. 2. Analysis and comparison of fitting capacity for different models when $\tau = 1$

trained on ImagenNet. To apply these methods, it is mandatory to use the exact same model proposed in [22] with the exact same parameter because otherwise results are not comparable with results from other papers. However, as proposed in [12] we can adapt these methods to other setting (for us, MNIST and Fashion-MNIST) to compare several generative models with each other.

We therefore train a model for classification on D_{train}. Then we use it to produce a probability vector to compute IS and an activation vector to compute FID. The activation are from a layer in the middle of the model (details in appendix). The very same formula than IS and FID can then be used to compare models.

4.3 Results

The relevant results presented below are the maximum *fitting capacity* (FiC) of each model over all seeds in order to evaluate what models can achieve and statistics on the results among those 8 seeds to give insight on the stability of each model with regards to the random seed.

First we present boxplots of *FiC* results of each models in Fig. 2a and b. They present the median value along with the first and last quartile limits. Furthermore they display the outliers of each training (values that are outside 1.5 of the interquartile range (IQR) over the different seeds). This representation is less sensible to outliers than mean value and standard deviation without making those outliers disappear[1].

Those results show an advantage for the GAN model as it has the best median value (even if it does not make better than baseline). Unfortunately some of the generator training failed (in particular on Fashion-Mnist), producing outliers in the results. WGAN produce results comparable to GAN in MNIST but seems less stable.

The figures are complemented with the values computed for the mean *FiC* Ψ_G in Table 1 and the values for the best *FiC* in Table 2. We can note that for

---

[1] The Figs. 2a and b are zoomed to be able to visually discriminates models making some outliers out of the plot. Full figures are in appendix.

both MNIST and Fashion-MNIST, models with unstable results, such as GAN and WGAN, have the best Ψ_G. However since some training failed for GAN and WGAN, more stable models, such as VAE and CGAN, have the best *mean fitting capacity* (FiC).

Table 1. Mean Ψ_G

Datasets	**Baseline**	VAE	CVAE	GAN	CGAN	WGAN	BEGAN
MNIST	**97.81%**	96.39%	95.86%	86.03%	**96.45%**	94.25%	95.49%
Fashion	**86.59%**	**80.75%**	73.43%	67.75%	77.68%	73.43%	77.64%

Table 2. Best Ψ_G

Datasets	**Baseline**	VAE	CVAE	GAN	CGAN	WGAN	BEGAN
MNIST	**97.94%**	96.82%	96.21%	97.18%	96.45%	**97.37%**	95.86%
Fashion	**87.08%**	81.85%	81.93%	**84.43%**	78.63%	81.32%	81.32%

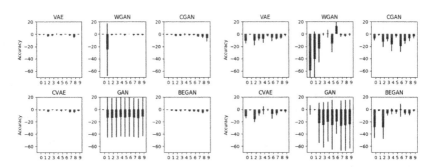

(a) Relative accuracy wrt. baseline on mnist class by class for $\tau = 1$ (b) Relative accuracy wrt. baseline on fashion-mnist class by class for $\tau = 1$

Fig. 3. Plot of the difference between models performance and baseline class by class when $\tau = 1$: Mean and standard deviation over random seeds

In addition, we present in Fig. 3a and b, the *per class fitting capacity*. The figures show the difference between the baseline classes results and the classifier trained on the generator to evaluate. For generative models that are not conditional and trained class by class, those figures show how the generator is successful to generate in different classes of the dataset. For conditional generative models, it evaluates if the models is able to learn each mode of the distribution with the same accuracy.

We can also estimate the stability of each model class by class or from a class to another. For example we can see that WGAN on MNIST is very stable except on class 1 and on Fashion-MNIST it seems to struggle a lot between the first 3 classes. On an other hand we can see that BEGAN has some trouble on Fashion-MNIST on class 0 and 2 (T-shirt and pullover) suggesting that the generator is not good enough to discriminate between those two classes.

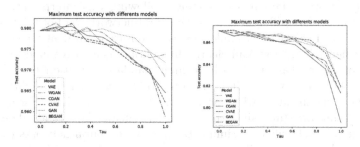

Fig. 4. Representation of the test accuracy of the classifiers trained by each G with various τ on MNIST (left) and Fashion-MNIST (Right). Figures show maximum test accuracy for each models against τ.

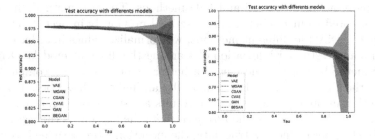

Fig. 5. Representation of the test accuracy of the classifiers trained by each G with various τ on MNIST (left) and Fashion-MNIST (Right). Figures show mean and standard deviation of classifiers test accuracy

In Fig. 4, we present the test accuracy with various τ to represent the impact of generated data on the training process. When $\tau = 0$, there is no generated data, this is the result of the baseline. Figure 4 show result of cherry-picking among seeds the best results for each τ, Fig. 5 show statistics among different seeds and the stability of each model on the trained dataset. Our interpretation is that if the accuracy is better than baseline with a low τ ($0 < \tau < 0.5$) it means that the generator is able to generalize by learning meaningful information about the dataset. When $\tau > 0.5$ if the accuracy is still near the baseline it means the generated data can replace the dataset in most parts of the distribution. When $\tau = 1$, the classifier is trained only on generated samples. If the accuracy is still better than the baseline, it means that the generator has fitted the training distribution (and eventually has learned to generalize if this score is high over the test set).

Our results show that some models are able to produce data augmentation and outperform the baseline when τ is low but unfortunately none of them is able to do the same when τ is high. This show that they are not able to replace completely the true data in this setting. Following this interpretation, Fig. 4 allows us to compare different generative neural networks on both datasets. For example, we can see that all models expectation are equivalent when τ is low. However when τ is high we can clearly differentiate generative models type.

Some of the curves in Fig. 5 have high standard deviation (e.g. for GAN when $\tau = 1$). To show that it is not due to the classifier instability we plot the results of classification with various τ with a KNN classifier (Fig. 6 ($k = 1$)). KNN algorithms are stable since they are deterministic. The standard deviations found with KNN classifiers is similar to those with neural networks classifiers. This proves that the instability does not come from the classifier but from the generative models. This is coherent with the fact that in Fig. 2, the diagrams of the reference classifiers trained with true data on eight different seeds show a high stability of the classifier model.

4.4   Comparison with IS and FID

We compare our results to IS and FID methods. The two methods have been slightly adapted to fit our setting as described previously in Sect. 3. To be able to compare easily the different methods, we normalize values in order to have a mean of 0 and a standard deviation of 1 among the different models. Originally for FID methods, a low value means a better model, for easier comparison we multiply the FID score by -1 to valuate by an higher value a better model as for the other evaluation methods. The results are shown on Fig. 7. We added a baseline for each method, for the *fitting capacity* the baseline is the test accuracy when the classifier trained on true data, the inception score baseline is computed on the test data and the frechet inception distance (FID) baseline is computed between train data and test data.

The results of the IS are completely different between MNIST and Fashion-MNIST and some model radically beat the baseline (as WGAN) when in the other methods, none of the results outperforms the baselines. However, the FID computed between test set and generated data gives coherent results between MNIST and fashion-MNIST. Even if they are not always coherent with our results. As an example, VAE does not perform well with FID when we can see with our *fitting capacity* that it is able to train a classifier quite well with high stability. The FID baseline outperform the other models however there is a small margin between best model and baseline when the margin between best model and baseline is big for the *fitting capacity*. The performances of each model are

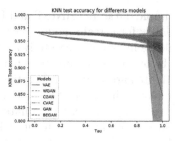 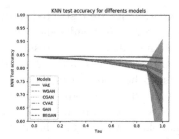

Fig. 6. Comparison of models using a nearest neighbor classifier on MNIST (left) and Fashion-MNIST (Right). Figures show mean and standard deviation of Classifiers Accuracy for 1−NN

unfortunatly specific to each datasets and the experiments made are not sufficient to generalized results to other datasets. This can be seen in models like CGAN or WGAN where results are very different between MNIST and Fashion-MNIST.

5 Discussion

We presented a method to evaluate a generative model: the *fitting capacity*. It assesses how well the generative model learned to generalize and fit a distribution in a conditional setting. Moreover, it gives a clear insight on potential top-down application of generative models.

The use of a discriminative model to evaluate generative models have already be experimented, e.g with IS and FID. However, the model used in those methods is pretrained on true data and can not be replaced with another one. In other case, results are not comparable. Fitting capacity is based on the testing set, which is by definition specifically designed to measure the ability to understand and generalize data distribution. Therefor, it is well adapted to evaluate a learning algorithm as a generative model. On the other hand, relying only on the testing set, make easy comparison between different approaches. Any generators with any classifiers can be compared as long as they evaluate on the same test set.

Moreover, *fitting capacity* gives a more in depth evaluation of generated data. Indeed, IS and FID rely on the analysis of first and second moments of features when *Fitting capacity* rely on data complex hidden variables: labels. Evaluating the joint distribution between labels and images into generated data gives a good insight on if the generative model fits the images distribution.

Our evaluation method requires more computational power with respect to other methods because a classifier needs to be trained. Unfortunately, This computational power, is unfortunately needed to evaluate if the data distribution is well fitted by the generative model. Nevertheless, we can take advantage from simpler approaches as IS and FID for model selection during training and then applying *fitting capacity* for deeper analysis.

Our experiments are restricted to two simple datasets (MNIST and Fashion-MNIST), however our results show a instability for certain models with regards to the random seed. Therefore, results should be interpreted carefully as different initialization could gives different results. In order to disentangle what models can do versus what they actually do, we evaluate and compare generative models on their top performance and on their stability with regards to random seeds.

In order to have a fair comparison we use same classifier to evaluate all generative models. However, any classifier could be used in replacement to improve and complete the results, our focus is on keeping the same test set to compare models. For instance it is obvious that a generator that just learned to reproduce the training set will beat our results, since no generator are able to beat the baseline. However we hope that new generators or better classifier will be able to beat the baseline. We believe that it is simple enough to be easily reproducible to evaluate any generative model. Moreover, *fitting capacity* is well adapted to be used on other kinds of generative models that produce data that are not images.

6   Conclusion

This paper introduces a method to assess and compare the performances of generative models by training a classifier on generated samples. It estimate the ability of a generative model to fit and generalize a testing set. It does not directly assess the realistic characteristics of the generated data but rather if their content and variability contains enough information to classify real data.

This method makes it possible to take into account complex characteristics of the generated samples and not only the distribution of their features. Moreover it does not evaluate generative models by testing if we can discriminate true data from generated one. Our results show that the *fitting capacity* allows to compare easily generative models and estimate their stability and shortcomings. It makes possible to both evaluate on the full dataset and evaluate class by class. In our experiment, the fitting capacity suggest that to get the best results GAN or WGAN approach should be privileged, however to maximize the chance of having a decent result CGAN or VAE are preferable.

We believe that generating data might have numerous application in top down settings: e.g. data-augmentation, data compression, transfer learning... We hope that this evaluation will help to select efficient and powerful generative models for those applications.

Acknowledgement. We really want to thanks Florian Bordes for experiment settings and interesting discussions as well as Pascal Vincent for his helpful advises. We would like also to thanks Natalia Díaz Rodriguez and Anthonin Raffin for their help in proof reading this article.

APPENDIX

A   models

A.1   Generator Architectures

See Table 3.

Table 3. VAE and GAN Generator Architecture

Layer	Architecture
1	FC (20,1024) + BN + relu
2	FC (1024,128*7*7) + BN + relu
3	ConvTranspose2d(128, 64, 4, 2, 1) + BN + relu
4	nn.ConvTranspose2d(64, 20, 4, 2, 1) + sigmoid

A.2   Classifier Architectures

FID Note: The activation vector to compute FID have been taken arbitrary at he ouput of layer 2 for both MNIST and Fashion-MNIST (Tables 4 and 5).

Table 4. MNIST

Layer	Architecture
1	conv(5*5), 10 filters + maxpool(2*2) + relu
2	conv(5*5), 20 filters + maxpool(2*2) + relu
3	dropout(0.5)
4	FC (320, 50) + relu
5	FC (50, 10) + log-softmax

Table 5. Fashion-MNIST

Layer	Architecture
1	conv(5*5), 16 filters + maxpool(2*2) + relu
2	conv(5*5), 32 filters + maxpool(2*2) + relu
3	dropout(0.5)
4	FC (512, 10) + log-softmax

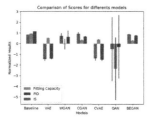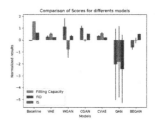

Fig. 7. Comparison between results with mean and standard deviation over random seeds from different approaches on MNIST (left) and Fashion-MNIST (right). Each result have been normalize to have mean = 0 and standard deviation = 1 among all models.

References

1. Arjovsky, M., Chintala, S., Bottou, L.: Wasserstein generative adversarial networks. In: Proceedings of the 34th International Conference on Machine Learning (2017)
2. Berthelot, D., Schumm, T., Metz, L.: BEGAN: boundary equilibrium generative adversarial networks. CoRR abs/1703.10717 (2017). http://arxiv.org/abs/1703.10717
3. Borji, A.: Pros and Cons of GAN Evaluation Measures. ArXiv e-prints, February 2018
4. Chen, X., Duan, Y., Houthooft, R., Schulman, J., Sutskever, I., Abbeel, P.: InfoGan: interpretable representation learning by information maximizing generative adversarial nets. CoRR abs/1606.03657 (2016). http://arxiv.org/abs/1606.03657
5. Denton, E.L., Chintala, S., Szlam, A., Fergus, R.: Deep generative image models using a Laplacian pyramid of adversarial networks. In: Advances in Neural Information Processing Systems, vol. 28 (2015)
6. Goodfellow, I., et al.: Generative adversarial nets. In: Advances in Neural Information Processing Systems, vol. 27 (2014)
7. Heusel, M., Ramsauer, H., Unterthiner, T., Nessler, B., Hochreiter, S.: GANs Trained by a Two Time-Scale Update Rule Converge to a Local Nash Equilibrium. ArXiv e-prints, June 2017
8. Isola, P., Zhu, J., Zhou, T., Efros, A.A.: Image-to-image translation with conditional adversarial networks. CoRR abs/1611.07004 (2016). http://arxiv.org/abs/1611.07004
9. Jiwoong Im, D., Ma, H., Taylor, G., Branson, K.: Quantitatively Evaluating GANs With Divergences Proposed for Training. ArXiv e-prints, March 2018
10. Kingma, D.P., Welling, M.: Auto-encoding variational Bayes. In: Proceedings of the 2nd International Conference on Learning Representations (ICLR) (2014)
11. Lake, B.M., Salakhutdinov, R., Tenenbaum, J.B.: Human-level concept learning through probabilistic program induction. Science **350**(6266), 1332–1338 (2015)
12. Li, C., et al.: Alice: towards understanding adversarial learning for joint distribution matching. In: Neural Information Processing Systems (NIPS) (2017)
13. Lopez-Paz, D., Oquab, M.: Revisiting classifier two-sample tests. arXiv preprint arXiv:1610.06545 (2016)
14. Lucic, M., Kurach, K., Michalski, M., Gelly, S., Bousquet, O.: Are GANs Created Equal? A Large-Scale Study, ArXiv e-prints, November 2017

15. Mirza, M., Osindero, S.: Conditional generative adversarial nets. CoRR abs/1411.1784 (2014)
16. Ng, A.Y., Jordan, M.I.: On discriminative vs. generative classifiers: a comparison of logistic regression and naive Bayes. In: Advances in Neural Information Processing Systems (2002)
17. Nguyen, A., Clune, J., Bengio, Y., Dosovitskiy, A., Yosinski, J.: Plug & play generative networks: conditional iterative generation of images in latent space. In: Proceedings of the IEEE Conference on Computer Vision and Pattern Recognition (2017)
18. Odena, A., Olah, C., Shlens, J.: Conditional image synthesis with auxiliary classifier GANs. In: Proceedings of the 34th International Conference on Machine Learning (2017)
19. Radford, A., Metz, L., Chintala, S.: Unsupervised representation learning with deep convolutional generative adversarial networks. CoRR abs/1511.06434 (2015)
20. Ratner, A.J., Ehrenberg, H.R., Hussain, Z., Dunnmon, J., Ré, C.: Learning to compose domain-specific transformations for data augmentation. stat (2017)
21. Rezende, D.J., Mohamed, S., Wierstra, D.: Stochastic backpropagation and approximate inference in deep generative models. In: Proceedings of the 31th International Conference on Machine Learning (2014)
22. Salimans, T., Goodfellow, I.J., Zaremba, W., Cheung, V., Radford, A., Chen, X.: Improved techniques for training GANs. CoRR abs/1606.03498 (2016)
23. Santurkar, S., Schmidt, L., Madry, A.: A classification-based perspective on GAN distributions (2018). https://openreview.net/forum?id=S1FQEfZA-
24. Sixt, L., Wild, B., Landgraf, T.: RenderGAN: generating realistic labeled data. CoRR abs/1611.01331 (2016)
25. Sohn, K., Lee, H., Yan, X.: Learning structured output representation using deep conditional generative models. In: Advances in Neural Information Processing Systems, vol. 28 (2015)
26. Theis, L., van den Oord, A., Bethge, M.: A note on the evaluation of generative models. In: Proceedings of the 4th International Conference on Learning Representations (ICLR) (2016)
27. Wang, W., Wang, A., Tamar, A., Chen, X., Abbeel, P.: Safer Classification by Synthesis. ArXiv e-prints, November 2017
28. Wang, Z., Simoncelli, E.P., Bovik, A.C.: Multiscale structural similarity for image quality assessment. In: Proceedings of 37th Asilomar Conference on Signals, Systems and Computers (2003)
29. Xiao, H., Rasul, K., Vollgraf, R.: Fashion-MNIST: a novel image dataset for benchmarking machine learning algorithms (2017)
30. Zhang, R., Isola, P., Efros, A.A.: Colorful Image Colorization. ArXiv e-prints, March 2016

Scene Graph Generation via Convolutional Message Passing and Class-Aware Memory Embeddings

Yidong Zhang[1] , Yunhong Wang[1], and Yuanfang Guo[2,3]([⊠])

[1] Beijing Advanced Innovation Center for Big Data and Brain Computing,
Beihang University, Beijing, China
{zhydong,yhwang}@buaa.edu.cn
[2] Laboratory of Intelligent Recognition and Image Processing,
School of Computer Science and Engineering, Beihang University, Beijing, China
andyguo@buaa.edu.cn
[3] Science and Technology on Information Assurance Laboratory, Beijing, China

Abstract. Detecting visual relationships between objects in an image still remains challenging, because the relationships are difficult to be modeled and the class imbalance problem tends to jeopardize the predictions. To alleviate these problems, we propose an end-to-end approach for scene graph generations. The proposed method employs the ResNet as the backbone network to extract the appearance features of the objects and relationships. An attention based graph convolutional network is exploited and modified to extract the contextual information. Language and geometric priors are also utilized and fused with the visual features to better describe the relationships. At last, a novel memory module is designed to alleviate the class imbalance problem. Experimental results demonstrate the validity of our model and our superiority compared to our baseline technique.

Keywords: Visual relationship detection · Scene graph generation · Graph convolutional neural networks · LSTM

1 Introduction

Scene graph, whose nodes are object entities in the image and edges depict the pairwise relationships of the objects, represents a high-level abstraction of an image. It not only contains the geometric and semantic information of objects, but also describes the correlations, i.e., the visual relationships, among the objects. As shown in the scene graph example in Fig. 1, a more advanced representation to an image is acquired by visual relationship detection (VRD) compared to the regular computer vision tasks, such as object detection and segmentation [5,12,13,17]. According to the existing literatures, other complex computer vision tasks such as image retrieval [9,24], image generation [8], image captioning [1,11], etc., can be improved based on the VRD result.

© Springer Nature Switzerland AG 2019
I. V. Tetko et al. (Eds.): ICANN 2019, LNCS 11729, pp. 620–633, 2019.
https://doi.org/10.1007/978-3-030-30508-6_49

Different from the typical object classification task [5,19], VRD is usually more challenging, because different pairs of objects may possess identical relationships. The visual appearances of the relationships are highly depending on the object classes. For example, the relationship "on" may appear as a man walking "on" a road, or a cup "on" a desk, etc. Moreover, relationship datasets usually remain class imbalance problem, which increases difficulties of modeling relationships.

Although the existing techniques have explored various features/priors, such as visual features [21], language priors [14], geometric features [2] and object class prior [23], the VRD performances still desire improvements. Therefore, inspired by [22], we propose an end-to-end VRD approach to generate the scene graphs of the input images. Specifically, ResNet is utilized as the backbone network to extract the visual features. After the feature extraction, attention based graph convolutional network (aGCN) [6,22] is exploited to model the visual cues of the relationships and objects. To better preserve the spatial information, which is essential for relationship predictions, convolution layers are exploited instead of the fully connected layers in the existing aGCN. Then, with the fused features, we construct a memory module, which is based on long-short term memory (LSTM) [7], to reduce the interferences from imbalanced number of samples in different relationship classes.

Our contributions are summarized as follows:

(1) We propose an end-to-end VRD method to generate the scene graphs from images by preserving the spatial information and relieving the class imbalance problem.
(2) We exploit the attention based graph convolutional network to describe the relationship patterns and propose to replace the fully connected layers with convolution layers to maintain more spatial information.
(3) We propose an LSTM based memory module to alleviate the class imbalance problem for VRD task.
(4) Experimental results demonstrate that our proposed network can successfully improve the performances compared to the baseline approach while reduce the negative effects caused by the class imbalance problem.

2   Related Work

In the past decade, many researches have been conducted on VRD and various features/priors have been explored. Relationships are modeled as the visual phrases, i.e., the $\langle sub, pred, obj \rangle$ triplet[1] is employed to represent the objects and their relationships, in [18]. Computing the triplets directly [18] gives poor performance as well as high computational complexity. To improve the performance, [14] predicts the classes of sub, obj and $pred$ individually. Besides, language priors (word vector [15,16]) are also explored in [14]. The visual appearance features

---

[1] In this paper, "obj" denotes the object in relationship triplets $\langle sub, pred, obj \rangle$, and "object" denotes the perceived object in the image.

are also extracted in [21] by a message passing scheme. This scheme jointly considers the objects and the relationships between each pair of the objects. Besides of the visual appearance features and language priors, other features can also be exploited. The relative locations and sizes of the bounding boxes are modeled as binary masks in [2]. [23] concludes that the object classes are important priors in predicting the relationships. LinkNet [20] utilizes contextual features by adopting multi-label classification as their subtask and designs relationship and object embedding module.

Recently, more mechanisms are explored. [11] performs a multi-task learning by jointly tackling the object detection, VRD and image captioning tasks, and proves that these three tasks can benefit from each other. [22] predicts the relationships via an attention based graph convolutional network.

In general, existing approaches have discovered various kinds of mechanisms to solve the VRD problems. Unfortunately, current performances are still relatively low, thus more efforts are desired.

3   Proposed Work

In practice, the nodes of a scene graph usually represent the coordinates of object bounding boxes with object class labels. Meanwhile, the edges usually stand for the class labels of relationships. We denote scene graph as a two-tuple $G = \{O, R\}$. O and R denote objects and relationships, respectively. Given an image I, our objective is to predict the probability of the scene graph as Eq. 1 shows.

$$P(G|I) = P(R|O, I)P(O|I) \tag{1}$$

Note that I in Eq. 1 can be omitted for simplicity. $P(O)$ denotes the probabilities of the object class labels and $P(R|O)$ denotes the probability of the relationship labels given the object class labels.

3.1   Pipeline

The pipeline of our network is shown in Fig. 1. Given the object bounding boxes, each two of the object bounding boxes are combined to form a relationship bounding box. With the object and relationship bounding boxes, the object and relationship features are acquired from the top layer of ResNet [5] with *RoIAlign* [4]. Note that the object and relationship feature maps are cropped from the output of the top layer of the backbone network.

Then, the object and relationship features are iteratively updated by an attention based graph convolutional network in the Message Passing (MP) module. Since the visual appearance features may induce inaccurate predictions of the relationships, the language and geometric priors are fused with visual appearance features in the Message Fusion (MF) module. Then, the preliminary relationship classes are generated. To alleviate the class imbalance problem, the Memory (MM) module is proposed by utilizing the sample frequencies to refine the outputs of MF. At last, the outputs of the MF and MM modules are combined to obtain the final triplets.

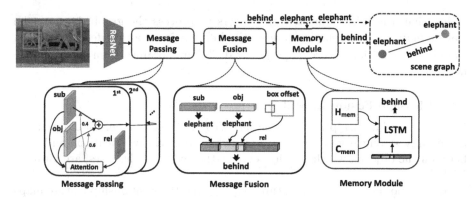

Fig. 1. Pipeline of our network. The "sub", "obj" and "rel" denote subject, object and relationship, respectively. The residual shortcuts are omitted in Message Passing for convenience. The notched arrows denote the softmax outputs.

3.2   Message Passing Module

The message passing scheme has been proven to be efficient in [21]. The model passes the messages, which contains contextual features, among the nodes and edges in a scene graph to refine the object and relationship features. In our work, we exploit an attention based graph convolutional network with residual shortcuts to pass the messages between the objects and relationships. The residual shortcuts can accelerate the training of the network and reduce the degradations [5].

[22] allows the network to pass messages from the relationship features to the object features. Unfortunately, the relationship features usually contain relatively large regions of backgrounds, which are equivalent to noises to the intended object features. Therefore, to avoid potential degradations, we only pass messages from the object features to the relationship features in our MP module.

Let $\boldsymbol{f}_{r,i}^{(t)}$ and $\boldsymbol{f}_{o,j}^{(t)}$ be the ith relationship feature and the jth object feature in the tth iteration. Note that the subscript r represents relationship and o denotes object. $\boldsymbol{W}$ and $\boldsymbol{V}$ stand for the parameters to be trained and α is the attention weight. The operator $\otimes$ stands for the convolution operation. $sub_{r,i}$ and $obj_{r,i}$ respectively denote the sub and obj, which belong to the ith relationship triplet.

With the symbols defined above, the relationship features can be updated by Eq. 2.

$$\boldsymbol{f}_{r,i}^{(t+1)} = \boldsymbol{f}_{r,i}^{(t)} + \boldsymbol{W}_r \otimes \boldsymbol{f}_{r,i}^{(t)} + \sum_{p \in \{sub_{r,i}, obj_{r,i}\}} \alpha_{i,p} \boldsymbol{W}_{o,p} \otimes \boldsymbol{f}_{o,p}^{(t)} \qquad (2)$$

Similarly, the object features can be updated by Eq. 3.

$$\boldsymbol{f}_{o,i}^{(t+1)} = \boldsymbol{f}_{o,i}^{(t)} + \boldsymbol{V}_o \otimes \boldsymbol{f}_{o,i}^{(t)} \qquad (3)$$

Since the spatial information usually serves effectively in the prediction of the relationships (e.g. "on" and "next to"), we utilize the convolution (*conv*) layers rather than the fully-connected (fc) layers to process the graph, because the feature maps tend to contain more spatial information than the feature vectors. Note that the initial feature maps $\boldsymbol{f}_r^{(0)}$ and $\boldsymbol{f}_o^{(0)}$ are obtained from the backbone network.

3.3   Message Fusion Module

In a typical relationship triplets $\langle sub, pred, obj \rangle$, the class labels of obj and sub are usually strong priors for $pred$. Meanwhile, the relative locations and sizes between the objects, which usually serve as the geometric features, are vital for VRD.

In MF module, the object feature maps $\boldsymbol{f}_o$ and the relationship feature maps $\boldsymbol{f}_r$ are transformed into 2048-dim feature vectors. We denote the object feature vectors as $\boldsymbol{v}_o$, and the relationship feature vectors as $\boldsymbol{v}_r$.

The object classes are directly predicted according to $\boldsymbol{v}_o$ with a softmax layer. With these predicted labels, language priors can be constructed in the form of word vectors. The bounding box offsets $\boldsymbol{e}$, which is proposed in [3], are adopted to represent the geometric priors as shown in Eq. 4.

$$\boldsymbol{e} = \left(\frac{x_o - x_s}{w_s}, \frac{y_o - y_s}{h_s}, \log\left(\frac{w_o}{w_s}\right), \log\left(\frac{h_o}{h_s}\right) \right) \tag{4}$$

where the subscript s and o represent the sub and obj in relationship triplets, respectively. After the word vectors and bounding box offset vectors are obtained, they are mapped to higher dimensions with fc layers and concatenated with $\boldsymbol{v}_r$.

The initial relationship class labels can be then calculated from the concatenated features, and the prediction will be refined in the next module.

3.4   Memory Module

The samples with high appearing frequencies usually dominate the network training process when the networks are trained on a dataset with imbalanced classes. Under such circumstances, the learned parameters are less capable of classifying the samples with less appearing frequencies.

To tackle this problem, a Memory (MM) module, which manages memory vectors, is proposed. Each of these vectors, which are essentially the memory embeddings, is updated on one specific class of samples.

These memory embeddings are independent from the parameters which will be trained in the ordinary back propagation process. The memory embedding of class i^{th} intends to remember the information from the samples of class i^{th} in the training stage. Inspired by the hidden and cell states in LSTM, which serve similarly to our proposed memory embeddings, we construct our Memory module based on the standard LSTM structure, as shown in Fig. 2.

Assume the size of each memory embedding is d, and the number of the relationship classes is m. Note that the 0th relationship is denoted as $irrelevant$. In MM module, two matrices $\boldsymbol{H}_{mem} \in \mathbb{R}^{(m+1) \times d}$ and $\boldsymbol{C}_{mem} \in \mathbb{R}^{(m+1) \times d}$ are constructed for storing the memory embeddings. In our design, $\boldsymbol{H}_{mem}$ serves similarly to the hidden state in LSTM, while $\boldsymbol{C}_{mem}$ contributes as the cell state.

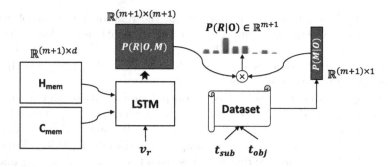

Fig. 2. The inference scheme of our Memory module. v_r denotes the relationship feature adopted from MF module. t_{sub} and t_{obj} denote the classes of subject and object predicted in MF module. m is the number of relationship classes and d is the size of each memory embedding.

Updating. In the training stage, H_{mem} and C_{mem} are indexed with the ground truth labels of the relationships. When a sample v_r is being processed by the MM module, according to the ground truth labels of v_r, the MM module will fetch the corresponding rows of the memory embeddings and feed them into LSTM. After v_r is processed, the hidden and cell states are assigned back to the corresponding locations in the matrices.

With the mechanism of the proposed MM module, the ith row of the memory embeddings will only be updated by the samples of the ith class. Thus the MM module can prevent the information, which is learned from the rare samples, from being corrupted by the information from the frequently appearing samples.

Inference. With the memories of each classes stored in the memory embeddings, we designed a scheme to infer the final relationship predictions as Fig. 2 shows.

After the labels of the objects are acquired, the class labels of the relationships can be computed based on $P(R|O) \in \mathbb{R}^{m+1}$ as shown in Eq. 5.

$$P(R|O) = P(R,O)/P(O) \tag{5}$$

Let M_i represents the memory embeddings of the ith relationship class. Then, $P(R,O)$ can be computed via Eq. 6.

$$P(R,O) = \sum_{i=0}^{m} P(R,O,M_i) = \sum_{i=0}^{m} P(R|O,M_i)P(O,M_i) \tag{6}$$

where $P(O,M_i)$ can be decomposed by the Bayesian formula via Eq. 7.

$$P(O,M_i) = P(M_i|O)P(O) \tag{7}$$

By substituting Eqs. 6 and 7 into Eq. 5, we obtain

$$P(R|O) = \sum_{i=0}^{m} P(R|O,M_i)P(M_i|O), \tag{8}$$

where $P(R|O, M_i)$ denotes the probability of the relationship when objects O are detected and the memory embedding of the ith relationship class is fetched. $P(M_i|O)$ is regarded as the probability of selecting the ith row of the memory embeddings, given the objects O are detected. The $P(R|O)$ in Eq. 8 is the final relationship prediction in MM module.

Obviously, $P(R|O, M_i) \in \mathbb{R}^{m+1}$ is the output probability of LSTM when the ith rows of $\boldsymbol{H}_{mem}$ and $\boldsymbol{C}_{mem}$ are fetched to be the hidden and cell states.

The frequencies of relationships, which are usually provided in the datasets and can be estimated in practice, are adopted to estimate $P(M_i|O)$. We count the probabilities of all possible relationships given two object classes t_{sub} and t_{obj} predicted from the MF module, which are denoted as $\hat{P}(R|t_{sub}, t_{obj}) \in \mathbb{R}^{m+1}$. Then, $P(M_i|O)$ can be approximated by $P(M_i|O) \approx \hat{P}(R_i|t_{sub}, t_{obj})$.

Note that there may not exist any relationship label for some object class pairs t_{sub} and t_{obj} in practice, i.e. $\hat{P}(R|t_{sub}, t_{obj}) \equiv \boldsymbol{0}$, because certain pairs tend to possess no correlations intuitively. Under such circumstances, the initial predicted relationship from the MF module will be considered as the final relationship prediction result instead of $P(R|O)$ in Eq. 8.

4   Experimental Results

Our proposed method was evaluated on the Visual Genome (VG) dataset [10]. Since the original VG dataset was sparsely annotated, we adopted the preprocessed VG dataset, which was filtered and split by [21], as [20–22]. This preprocessed dataset selects the most frequently appearing 150 object classes and 50 relationship classes and contains 75k images for training, 5k images for validating and 32k images for testing. In the experiments, the scene graph classification (**SGCls**) and predicate classification (**PredCls**) tasks were solved and the **Recall@K** metric [14] was employed for assessment. A single edge between each two object nodes was predicted in the scene graph in our experiments.

In **SGCls**, the VRD model is usually given an image with certain object bounding boxes, and classifies the objects and the relationships between these objects. On the other hand, **PredCls** only requires the VRD model to classify the relationships between the objects, because the image, object bounding boxes and the object labels are all given. The **PredCls** metric evaluates the ability to detect relationships among the known objects, while **SGCls** judges the ability to generate the relationship triplets.

Recall@K computes the ratio of true positive triplets $\langle sub, pred, obj \rangle$ to the overall ground truth triplets in the top-K probable relationship outputs as

$$Recall@K = \sum_{i=1}^{N} \frac{|TP_i[: k]|}{|GT_i|}, \tag{9}$$

where N denotes the total number of images, TP_i and GT_i represent the true positive triplets and ground truth triplets, respectively, and $[: k]$ stands for the top-k probable values.

4.1   Implementation Details

The cross-entropy loss was adopted in both the object and relationship classification tasks. The overall loss of our model during the training process is shown as

$$L = L_{object} + L_{rel\_mf} + L_{rel\_mm}, \tag{10}$$

where L_{object} is the object classification loss in MF module, and L_{rel_mf} and L_{rel_mm} represent relationship classification losses in the MF and MM module, respectively.

The input images were reshaped to 592×592. Our network was trained with batch size 6 on a single Nvidia 1080Ti GPU. The learning rate was 1e-3 at the beginning and decayed by the PyTorch ReduceLROnPlateau rule.

We pre-trained the ResNet in faster RCNN [17] on the VG dataset on object detection task. Then, our end-to-end network was trained without fixing any parameters.

4.2   A Study of the MP Module

Number of Iterations. Our model was assessed with different number of iterations of MP on the validation set. As shown in Table 1(left), different numbers of iterations of the message passing tend to give different performances. Inadequate iterations only result in less capability of modeling the contexts and correlations between the objects and relationships. Meanwhile, too many iterations tend to induce overfitting, and thus jeopardize both the performance and the convergence speed of our model. Since 2 iterations of MP introduced the best performance, the latter experiments were performed with this setting.

Table 1. (left) Results of different MP iteration numbers. "iter" stands for the number of iterations of the MP module. (right) Results of different layers employed in the attention based graph convolutional network.

iter	SGCls		
	R@20	R@50	R@100
0	22.56	26.98	29.05
1	25.55	28.82	29.94
2	**26.45**	**30.11**	**31.26**
3	25.91	29.72	31.15

	SGCls		
	R@20	R@50	R@100
fc	24.94	28.11	29.20
$conv$	**26.45**	**30.11**	**31.26**

Conv vs. FC. In previous attention based graph convolutional network, nodes were processed with the fc layers. On the contrary, the $conv$ layers are adopted in our model. Therefore, we compared these two types of layers on the validation set in **SGCls** task to verify the effectiveness of our modification.

In this experiment, only the MP module and the backbone network were employed. Table 1(right) indicates that the *conv* layers outperform the *fc* layers in our MP module, because the *conv* layers can maintain more spatial information for the relationship predictions.

4.3 Ablation Study

Here, the ablation study was conducted to validate each module in our network on the testing set. The results are reported in Table 2.

Table 2. Results of ablation study.

MP	MF	MM	SGCls			PredCls		
			R@20	R@50	R@100	R@20	R@50	R@100
			17.97	21.79	23.29	30.18	38.78	42.44
√			21.09	24.08	25.02	38.85	46.54	49.32
√	√		31.12	**34.41**	35.81	**55.92**	**63.61**	66.34
√	√	√	**31.67**	34.40	**35.90**	55.61	63.54	**66.61**

As can be observed, the MP module gives about 3% gains in **SGCls** and 8% gains in **PredCls** compared to the prediction results of the backbone network. These improvements indicate that the modified attention based graph convolutional network can effectively model the relationships. Note that the gains in **PredCls** are more than that in **SGCls**, which proves that the gains achieved by the MP module are mainly contributed by a more precise modeling of the relationship patterns, rather than optimizing the object classification results. After the MF module is added, the performance raised 8%–15%, which clearly demonstrates the effectiveness of the language priors and geometric information.

Since our MM module only refines the existing prediction results to alleviate the class imbalance problem, the performance gains of the MM module in Table 2 are less obvious, we will further study the validity of our MM module in Sect. 4.4.

4.4 A Study of the Memory Module

We tested our model with/without the MM module on the **PredCls** task, and compared their **R@50** values. The results of the specific relationship prediction improvement are reported in Fig. 3. As shown in Fig. 3, the recall rate of some relationships with certain appearing frequencies decreases while the recall rate of more relationships with relatively less appearing frequencies achieves obvious improvements, with the MM module.

This imbalanced dataset resembles the relationships in reality. Typically, people may employ "on" in a relationship description for thousands of times while "laying on" may only be selected for a few times. If a model simply predicts

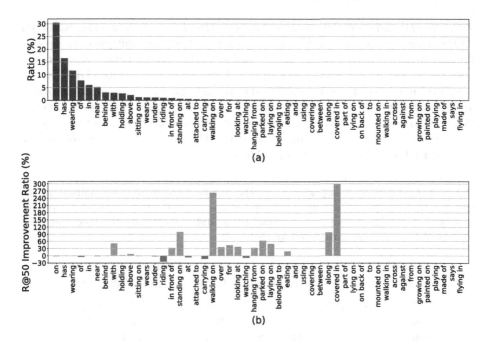

Fig. 3. Results of the specific relationship prediction improvement. (a) Sample distribution of the relationships in VG dataset. (b) The **R@50** improvement ratio (%) for the individual relationship classes with the MM module.

all the relationships to be the frequently appearing relationships such as "on", "above" or "beside", it may achieve a high recall value in assessments. However, these frequently appearing relationships usually contain less semantic information and tend to give superficial descriptions of the images. On the contrary, the less frequently appearing relationships, such as "laying on", "walking in", tend to give a more accurate descriptions of the images.

To generate the scene graph more precisely, we tried to boost the recall rate of our model to enhance the ability of our network to fit the data distribution of the dataset. But we believe that a VRD model should not only achieve a high recall rate in the experiments, but also generate relationships containing more semantic information. It motivated us to design a model to generate more meaningful relationships. As can be observed from the experimental results, we propose a particular memory module to alleviate the class imbalance problem and extract deeper semantic relationship information among the objects, which can aid the VRD problem in the future.

4.5   Objective Results

Since our proposed model is developed based on Graph RCNN [22], we chose Graph RCNN as our baseline technique. We also compared our method to [2,14,21], because our model exploits the language priors [14], message passing structure [21] and geometric features [2]. Note that DR-Net [2] was not evaluated on the same version of VG dataset as ours and it allows multiple-edge predictions between each two of the object nodes. Predicting multiple edges usually gives higher performance as proven in [23]. Thus, we reimplemented DR-Net and evaluated it on the preprocessed VG dataset [21] for fair comparisons. Following the experimental protocols in [22], our method was also compared to motifs frequency model [23], which predicts the relationships according to the frequencies of the potential relationships. In addition, the results of the state-of-the-art method LinkNet [20] are shown in Table 3.

Table 3. Quantitative comparisons. All the numbers are in %. The omitted values indicate that the results are not presented in the original paper. The results of [14] is adopted from [21] because the original paper did not evaluate the model on VG. Results of DR-Net was reproduced by us.

Methods	SGCls			PredCls		
	R@20	R@50	R@100	R@20	R@50	R@100
Language prior [14]	-	11.8	14.1	-	27.9	35.0
IMP [21]	-	21.7	24.4	-	44.8	53.0
DR-Net [2]	27.8	32.0	33.4	37.5	45.4	48.3
Motif-Freq [23]	27.7	32.4	34.0	49.4	59.9	64.1
Graph RCNN [22]	-	29.6	31.6	-	54.2	59.1
Our method	31.7	34.4	35.9	55.6	63.5	66.6
(**SOTA**) LinkNet [20]	38.3	41	41.7	61.8	67.0	68.5

As can be observed, our proposed model obviously outperforms our baseline Graph RCNN. The results of our model also surpass [2,14,21] and the frequency model [23] in both the **SGCls** and **PredCls** task. These results indicate that our model can generate a more precise scene graph comparing with the most of the existing methods which exploit similar structures and features.

Unfortunately, our model generates less decent objective results compared to the state-of-the-art LinkNet. As can be observed, the performance gap between our method and LinkNet is smaller for the **PredCls** task than the **SGCls** task. A potential explanation to this phenomenon is that LinkNet extracts context features from the overall image [20] to improve the object classification while we only focused on refining the relationship features. Besides, since our main objective is to alleviate the class imbalance problem, we spent less efforts on enhancing the overall recall value, which may not be optimized as illustrated in Sect. 4.4.

4.6   Subjective Results

Some subjective results of our model for the **SGCls** task are given in Fig. 4. As can be observed from Figs. 4(a), (b), (c), our model gives excellent predictions when the object classes are accurately classified. On the other hand, as Figs. 4(d) and (e) show, the inaccurate predictions are mainly induced by the misclassifications of the object classes.

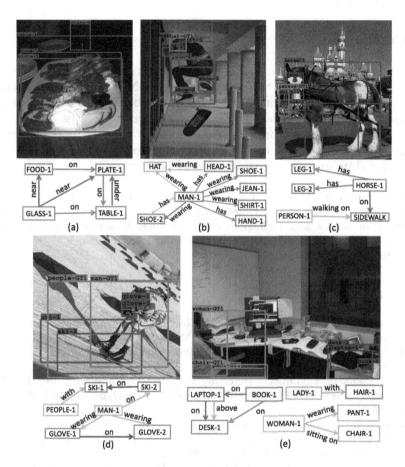

Fig. 4. Subjective results of our method. (a) (b) (c) demonstrate good predictions while (d) and (e) give failure cases. The green color indicate a correct and labelled prediction. The blue color means a correct prediction yet the label does not exist in the dataset. The yellow color represents unpredicted labels in the dataset. The red color is an inaccurate and unlabelled prediction. (Color figure online)

The evaluation results are highly depending on the annotations of the dataset. For example, in Fig. 4(b), our model predicts $\langle man - 1, wearing, shoe - 2 \rangle$ while the ground truth label is $\langle man - 1, has, shoe - 2 \rangle$. Although our prediction predicts a relationship which is different yet more accurate for the descriptions of the image, our recall value decreases because of the mismatch between the output and ground truth label. These ambiguous annotations are one of the main reasons of the class imbalance problem. Since the evaluations are usually depending on the ground truth labels, these ambiguous annotations also jeopardize the correctiveness of the evaluations. Besides, these ambiguous annotations also serve as the obstacles in the training process by deteriorating the convergences of the cross-entropy loss.

5   Conclusion

In this paper, we proposed an end-to-end scheme to tackle the VRD problem. By replacing the fc layers with the $conv$ layers in aGCN, we managed to maintain more spatial information. The proposed model also benefited from the extracted geometric features and the language priors for generating precise scene graphs. At last, the class imbalance problem could be alleviated by the proposed memory module. Extensive experiments verified the validity of the proposed method and demonstrated its superiority against our baseline method.

Acknowledgement. This work was supported in part by the National Natural Science Foundation of China under Grant 61573045 and Grant 61802391, in part by the Foundation of Science and Technology on Information Assurance Laboratory under Grant KJ-17-006, and in part by the Fundamental Research Funds for the Central Universities.

References

1. Anderson, P., Fernando, B., Johnson, M., Gould, S.: SPICE: semantic propositional image caption evaluation. In: Leibe, B., Matas, J., Sebe, N., Welling, M. (eds.) ECCV 2016. LNCS, vol. 9909, pp. 382–398. Springer, Cham (2016). https://doi.org/10.1007/978-3-319-46454-1_24
2. Dai, B., Zhang, Y., Lin, D.: Detecting visual relationships with deep relational networks. In: IEEE CVPR, pp. 3076–3086 (2017). https://doi.org/10.1109/CVPR.2017.352
3. Girshick, R., Donahue, J., Darrell, T., Malik, J.: Rich feature hierarchies for accurate object detection and semantic segmentation. In: IEEE CVPR, pp. 580–587 (2014). https://doi.org/10.1109/CVPR.2014.81
4. He, K., Gkioxari, G., Dollár, P., Girshick, R.: Mask R-CNN. In: IEEE ICCV, pp. 2961–2969 (2017). https://doi.org/10.1109/ICCV.2017.322
5. He, K., Zhang, X., Ren, S., Sun, J.: Deep residual learning for image recognition. In: IEEE CVPR, pp. 770–778 (2016). https://doi.org/10.1109/CVPR.2016.90
6. Henaff, M., Bruna, J., LeCun, Y.: Deep convolutional networks on graph-structured data. arXiv preprint arXiv:1506.05163 (2015)
7. Hochreiter, S., Schmidhuber, J.: Long short-term memory. Neural Comput. **9**(8), 1735–1780 (1997). https://doi.org/10.1007/978-3-642-24797-2_4
8. Johnson, J., Gupta, A., Fei-Fei, L.: Image generation from scene graphs. In: IEEE CVPR, pp. 1219–1228 (2018). https://doi.org/10.1109/CVPR.2018.00133
9. Johnson, J., et al.: Image retrieval using scene graphs. In: IEEE CVPR, pp. 3668–3678 (2015). https://doi.org/10.1109/CVPR.2015.7298990
10. Krishna, R., et al.: Visual genome: connecting language and vision using crowd-sourced dense image annotations. IJCV **123**(1), 32–73 (2017). https://doi.org/10.1007/s11263-016-0981-7

11. Li, Y., Ouyang, W., Zhou, B., Wang, K., Wang, X.: Scene graph generation from objects, phrases and region captions. In: IEEE ICCV, pp. 1261–1270 (2017)

12. Lindh, A., Ross, R.J., Mahalunkar, A., Salton, G., Kelleher, J.D.: Generating diverse and meaningful captions. In: Kůrková, V., Manolopoulos, Y., Hammer, B., Iliadis, L., Maglogiannis, I. (eds.) ICANN 2018. LNCS, vol. 11139, pp. 176–187. Springer, Cham (2018). https://doi.org/10.1007/978-3-030-01418-6_18

13. Long, J., Shelhamer, E., Darrell, T.: Fully convolutional networks for semantic segmentation. In: IEEE CVPR, pp. 3431–3440 (2015). https://doi.org/10.1109/TPAMI.2016.2572683

14. Lu, C., Krishna, R., Bernstein, M., Fei-Fei, L.: Visual relationship detection with language priors. In: Leibe, B., Matas, J., Sebe, N., Welling, M. (eds.) ECCV 2016. LNCS, vol. 9905, pp. 852–869. Springer, Cham (2016). https://doi.org/10.1007/978-3-319-46448-0_51

15. Mikolov, T., Sutskever, I., Chen, K., Corrado, G.S., Dean, J.: Distributed representations of words and phrases and their compositionality. In: NeurIPS, pp. 3111–3119 (2013)

16. Pennington, J., Socher, R., Manning, C.: Glove: global vectors for word representation. In: EMNLP, pp. 1532–1543 (2014). https://doi.org/10.3115/v1/D14-1162

17. Ren, S., He, K., Girshick, R., Sun, J.: Faster R-CNN: towards real-time object detection with region proposal networks. In: NeurIPS, pp. 91–99 (2015). https://doi.org/10.1109/TPAMI.2016.2577031

18. Sadeghi, M.A., Farhadi, A.: Recognition using visual phrases. In: IEEE CVPR, pp. 1745–1752 (2011). https://doi.org/10.1109/CVPR.2011.5995711

19. Simonyan, K., Zisserman, A.: Very deep convolutional networks for large-scale image recognition. arXiv preprint arXiv:1409.1556 (2014)

20. Woo, S., Kim, D., Cho, D., Kweon, I.S.: LinkNet: relational embedding for scene graph. In: NeurIPS, pp. 560–570 (2018)

21. Xu, D., Zhu, Y., Choy, C.B., Fei-Fei, L.: Scene graph generation by iterative message passing. In: IEEE CVPR, pp. 5410–5419 (2017). https://doi.org/10.1109/CVPR.2017.330

22. Yang, J., Lu, J., Lee, S., Batra, D., Parikh, D.: Graph R-CNN for scene graph generation. In: Ferrari, V., Hebert, M., Sminchisescu, C., Weiss, Y. (eds.) ECCV 2018. LNCS, vol. 11205, pp. 690–706. Springer, Cham (2018). https://doi.org/10.1007/978-3-030-01246-5_41

23. Zellers, R., Yatskar, M., Thomson, S., Choi, Y.: Neural motifs: scene graph parsing with global context. In: IEEE CVPR, pp. 5831–5840 (2018). https://doi.org/10.1109/CVPR.2018.00611

24. Zhang, W., Cao, X., Wang, R., Guo, Y., Chen, Z.: Binarized mode seeking for scalable visual pattern discovery. In: IEEE CVPR, pp. 6827–6835 (2017). https://doi.org/10.1109/CVPR.2017.722

Attacks on Images

Change Detection in Satellite Images Using Reconstruction Errors of Joint Autoencoders

Ekaterina Kalinicheva[1] , Jérémie Sublime[1,2](✉) , and Maria Trocan[1]

[1] LISITE - DASSIP Team ISEP,
10 rue de Vanves, 92130 Issy-Les-Moulineaux, France
{ekaterina.kalinicheva,jeremie.sublime,maria.trocan}@isep.fr
[2] LIPN - CNRS UMR 7030, 99 av. J-B Clément, 93430 Villetaneuse, France
jeremie.sublime@lipn.univ-paris13.fr

Abstract. With the growing number of open source satellite image time series, such as SPOT or Sentinel-2, the number of potential change detection applications is increasing every year. However, due to the image quality and resolution, the change detection process is a challenge nowadays. In this work, we propose an approach that uses the reconstruction losses of joint autoencoders to detect non-trivial changes (permanent changes and seasonal changes that do not follow common tendency) between two co-registered images in a satellite image time series. The autoencoder aims to learn a transformation model that reconstructs one co-registered image from another. Since trivial changes such as changes in luminosity or seasonal changes between two dates have a tendency to repeat in different areas of the image, their transformation model can be easily learned. However, non-trivial changes tend to be unique and can not be correctly translated from one date to another, hence an elevated reconstruction error where there is change. In this work, we compare two models in order to find the most performing one. The proposed approach is completely unsupervised and gives promising results for an open source time series when compared with other concurrent methods.

Keywords: Satellite images · Change detection · Autoencoder · Unsupervised learning · Reconstruction loss

1 Introduction

Nowadays, change detection in satellite image time series (SITS) is required for many different applications. Among them, there are numerous ecological applications such as the analysis and preservation of the stability of ecosystems or the detection and the analysis of phenomena such as deforestation and droughts, the studies of economical development of cities, the analysis of vegetation state for different agricultural purposes, etc. While in some applications, we are interested in seasonal changes such as evolutions in agricultural parcels, others require the

© Springer Nature Switzerland AG 2019
I. V. Tetko et al. (Eds.): ICANN 2019, LNCS 11729, pp. 637–648, 2019.
https://doi.org/10.1007/978-3-030-30508-6_50

detection of the permanent changes such as buildings or roads constructions. Nevertheless, due to image resolution and preprocessing level (most of the SITS do not have a correction of the atmospheric factors), properly detecting changes remains a difficult task.

Different algorithms for change detection are proposed in the literature. For example, in [5] the authors use PCA and hybrid classification methods for change detection in urban areas. The authors of [2] propose siamese neural networks for supervised change detection in open source multispectral images.

However, most change detection algorithms are supervised or semi-supervised, and therefore need some labeled data. Providing the labeled data for remote sensing images and especially SITS is a costly and time-consuming task due to the variance of objects present in them and the time needed to produce the large amount of labeled images required to train large models. This lack of labeled data and the difficulty to acquire them is not specific to SITS and remains true for any application with satellite images. This issue has encouraged the use of unsupervised methods to tackle this type of images especially, when the number of features is large or when the images are very complex.

In this paper, we propose an unsupervised approach based on a neural network autoencoder (AE) algorithm for non-trivial change detection in SITS. The algorithm is based on change detection between two bi-temporal images Im_n and Im_{n+1}. Needless to say, it can be also applied to two co-registered images instead of a SITS. In the presented approach, we use joint AEs to create models able to reconstruct Im_{n+1} from Im_n and vice versa by learning the image features. Obviously, the non-changed areas and trivial changes such as seasonal ones will be easily learned by the model, and therefore reconstructed with small errors. As the non-trivial changes are unique, they will be considered as outliers by the model, and thus will have a high reconstruction error (RE). Thresholding on the RE values allows us to create a binary change map (CM). The proposed method has showed promising results on a dataset with high ratio of agricultural areas and outperformed the concurrent approach. Different joint AE models were tested in order to find the most accurate. Our method has a low complexity and gives high quality results on open source high resolution (HR) images.

The remainder of this article is organized as follows: In Sect. 2, we present related works. Section 3 details our proposed approach. Section 4 is dedicated to experimental results and some conclusions and future work perspectives are drawn in Sect. 5.

2   Related Works

The main difficulty with unsupervised approaches to analyze satellite images is that they usually produce lower quality results than supervised ones. To improve the quality of unsupervised change detection between two images, the fusion of results from different algorithms is often proposed [6]. At the same time, automatic methods for selection of changed and unchanged pixels are used to obtain training samples for a multiple classifier system [11]. Following this paper, the authors of [1] propose the improved backpropagation method of a deep belief network (DBN) for change detection based on automatically selected change labels.

Nevertheless, classic feature comparison approaches do not separate trivial (seasonal) changes from non-trivial ones (permanent changes and changes that do not follow seasonal tendency). This weakness can drastically complicate the interpretation of change detection results for regions with high ratio of vegetation areas. In fact, when analyzing two images belonging to different seasons of the year, almost all the area will be marked as change and further analysis will be needed to identify meaningful changes (non-trivial).

In [9], a regularized iteratively reweighted multivariate alteration detection (MAD) method for the detection of non-trivial changes was proposed. This method is based on linear transformations between different bands of hyper-spectral satellite images and canonical correlation analysis. However, spectral transformation between multi-temporal bands is very complex. For these reasons, deep learning algorithms which are known to be able to model non-linear transformations have proved their efficiency to solve this problem [12].

Our method is based on the approach proposed in [12]. In this work, the authors use a Restricted-Boltzmann Machines-based (RBM) model to learn the transformation model for a couple of very high resolution (VHR) co-registered images Im_1 and Im_2. RBM is a type of stochastic artificial network that learns the distribution of the binary input data. When dealing with the continuous data, Gaussian-Bernoulli RBM (GBRBM) is used [8].

The principle of the proposed method to detect changes is the following: most of the trivial changes can be easily modeled from Im_1 to Im_2, at the same time, non-trivial changes will not be properly reconstructed. Therefore, the reconstruction accuracy can be used to detect the non-trivial change areas. The proposed approach consist of the following steps: feature learning, feature comparison and thresholding. During the feature learning step, the algorithm learns some meaningful features to perform transformation of patches of Im_1 to the patches of Im_2. Once the features are learned by the model, Im_1 is transformed in Im_2'. Then the difference image (DI) of Im_2 and Im_2' is calculated. The same steps are performed to create a DI of Im_1 and Im_1'. The thresholding is then applied on an average DI. Obviously, the areas with high difference values will be the change areas.

For the feature learning, the authors use an AE model composed of stacked RBMs layers GBRBM1-RBM1-RBM2-GBRBM2. The authors indicate that the algorithm is sensitive to changing luminosity and has high level of false positive changes in real change data. To our knowledge, the algorithm was tested only on urban areas.

3   Proposed Approach

Our method is similar with the one presented in [12] that we have introduced in the previous section. However, contrary to RBM models that are based on a stochastic approach and distribution learning, we propose to use a deterministic model based on feature extraction. Furthermore, we use patch reconstruction error for every pixel of the image - instead of image difference - as extracting features from every pixel neighborhood is an important step for any eventual subsequent pixel-wise classification task.

Classical AEs are a type of neural network where the input is the same as the output. During the learning process, the encoding pass of the model learn some meaningful representation of the initial data that is being transformed back during the decoding pass. In our work, we test two deterministic AE architectures and assess their performance for change detection in order to pick the best adapted one. The tested models are joint fully-convolutional AEs and joint convolutional AEs.

Fully-convolutional AEs consist of a stack of layers that apply different convolutions (filters) to the input data in order to extract meaningful feature maps (FM) (Fig. 1). Convolutions are often used in image processing as they deal with non-flattened data (2D and 3D). Therefore, unsupervised feature extraction with fully-convolutional AEs has been proved efficient in different remote sensing applications [4]. Convolutional AEs equally contain different convolutional layers that are followed by some fully-connected layers to compress the feature maps. Usually these AEs are used for image clustering as FC layers perform the dimensionality reduction.

3.1   Change Detection Algorithm

Let Im_1, Im_2, ..., Im_{S-1}, Im_S be a SITS made of S co-registered images taken at dates T_1, T_2, ... , T_{S-1}, T_S. Our algorithm steps are the followings (Fig. 2):

- The preprocessing step consists of a relative radiometrical normalization [7]. It reduces a number of potential false and missed change alarms related to the changing luminosity of objects.
- The first step of change detection algorithm consist in model pre-training on the whole dataset (Fig. 2).
- During the second step, we fine-tune the joint AE model for every couple of images (Im_n, Im_{n+1}). Once the model is trained, we calculate the reconstruction error of Im'_{n+1} from Im_n and vise versa for every patch of the images. In other words, the reconstruction error of every patch is associated to the position of its central pixel on the image.

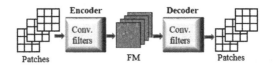

Fig. 1. Fully-convolutional AE model. Pre-training phase.

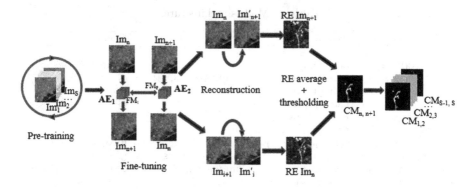

Fig. 2. Change detection algorithm.

- In the last step, we identify areas of high reconstruction error using Otsu's thresholding method [10] in order to create a binary change map $CM_{n,n+1}$ with non-trivial change areas.

3.2 Model Pre-training and Fine-Tuning

In our method, we use deep AEs to reconstruct Im_{i+1} from Im_i. During the model pre-training, the feature learning is performed patch-wise for a sample extracted from the SITS. In our method, we sample $\frac{H \times W}{S}$ patches (H and W represent image height and width, respectively) from every image to prevent the model from overfitting. The patches for the border pixels are generated by mirroring the existing ones in the neighborhood. During the encoding pass, the model extracts feature maps (FM) for the fully-convolutional AE (and feature vector for the convolutional AE) of i, j, m-patch of chosen samples, and then during the decoding pass, it reconstructs them back to the initial i, j, m-patch ($i \in [1, H]$, $j \in [1, W]$, $m \in [1, S]$).

The fine-tuning part consists of learning two joint reconstruction models AE_1 and AE_2 for every patch of a couple of co-registered images (Im_n, Im_{n+1}). The patches are extracted, for every pixel of the images ($H \times W$ patches in total) as the local neighborhood wherein the processed pixel is the central one (i.e., the image i, j-pixel corresponds to i, j-patch central pixel).

Our joint fully-convolutional AEs model is presented in Fig. 2. The joint model for the convolutional AE has the same structure. AE_1 and AE_2 have the same configuration of layers as the pre-trained model, and are initialized with the parameters it learned. In the joint model, AE1 aims to reconstruct patches of Im'_{n+1} from patches of Im_n and AE2 reconstructs Im'_n from Im_{n+1}. The whole model is trained to minimize the difference between: the decoded output of AE1 and Im_{n+1}, the decoded output of AE2 and Im_n, and the encoded outputs of AE1 and AE2.

In our work, we use the mean squared error (MSE) for model optimization and calculation of the patch reconstruction error.

Table 1. Models architecture.

	F-conv.AE	Conv.AE	RBM	Impr. RBM
Encoder		$C(B, 32)+R$		$GBRBM(p^2 \times B,$
	$C(B, 32)+R$	$C(32, 32)+R$		$(p+1)^2 \times B)+S$
	$C(32, 32)+R$	$C(32, 64)+R$	$GBRBM(p^2 \times B, 384)+S$	$RBM((p+1)^2 \times B,$
	$C(32, 64)+R$	$C(64, 64)+R$	$RBM(384, 150)+S$	$(p-2)^2 \times B)+S$
	$C(64, 64)+\ell_2$	$L(64 \times p^2, 12 \times p^2)+R$		
		$L(12 \times p^2, 2 \times p^2)+\ell_2$		
Decoder		$L(2 \times p^2, 12 \times p^2)+R$		
	$C(64, 64)+R$	$L(12 \times p^2, 64 \times p^2)+R$		$RBM((p-2)^2 \times B,$
	$C(64, 32)+R$	$C(64, 64)+R$	$RBM(150, 384)+S$	$(p+1)^2 \times B)+S$
	$C(32, 32)+R$	$C(64, 32)+R$	$GBRBM(384, p^2 \times B)+S$	$GBRBM((p+1)^2 \times B,$
	$C(32, B)+S$	$C(32, 32)+R$		$p^2 \times B)+S$
		$C(32, B)+S$		

C - Convolutional, L - Linear, R - ReLU, S - Sigmoid, ℓ_2 - ℓ_2-norm

Once the model is trained and stabilized, we perform the image reconstruction of Im'_n and Im'_{n+1} for every patch, and we create two images representing their reconstruction errors. We apply Otsu's thresholding [10] to the average reconstruction error of these images in order to produce a binary change map.

4   Experimental Results

4.1   Dataset

Our algorithm was applied to a SPOT-5 SITS of Montpellier area, France, taken between 2002 and 2008. This SITS belongs to the archive Spot World Heritage[1]. This particular SITS was chosen due to its high ratio of agricultural zones and progressive construction of new areas. The preprocessing level of SITS is 1C (orthorectified images, reflectance of the top of atmosphere). We kept only green, red and NIR bands that have 10 m resolution as they are the most pertinent. The original images are clipped to rectangular shapes of 1600×1700 pixels, radiometrically normalized and transformed to UTM zone 31N: EPSG Projection (transformation from geographic coordinate system in degree coordinates to a projected coordinate system in meter coordinates).

4.2   Results

As mentioned in Sect. 3, we propose different architectures: convolutional and joint fully-convolutional AEs, and we compare them in order to assess their strengths and weaknesses. We further compare our approaches with the RBM-based method presented in [12] that we have discussed in Sect. 2 and with improved RBM method. Initially, in [12] the images are clipped in $\frac{H \times W}{p \times p}$ not overlapped patches. In the improved method, we propose to extract patches with neighborhoods of every pixel of the image ($H \times W$ patches). Equally, we

---

[1] Available on www.theia-landsat.cnes.fr.

use the patch reconstruction error instead of the image difference to detect the changes. In other words, the improved RBM method uses the same steps as in our proposed algorithms.

In the experiments, we use the architectures presented in Table 1, where B is the number of spectral bands and p is the patch size (in these reported results, the patch size is 5×5 for all our methods, the patch size is justified later in text). The following parameters were chosen for all convolutional layers: kernel size $= 3$, stride $= 1$, padding $= 1$. Adam algorithm was used to optimize the models. During the pre-training phase, the learning rate was set to 0.0005 and then changed to 0.00005 for the fine-tuning phase.

The RBM model presented in [12] is developed for VHR images, but we have kept the patch size 10×10 pixels and the layer sizes suggested by the authors. In the improved RBM method we use 5×5 pixels patch size as in our methods. We apply ReLU and sigmoid activation functions as well as ℓ_2-normalization to the different layers outputs.

In our approaches and in improved RBM method, before learning the Otsu's threshold, we exclude 0.5% of the highest values under the hypothesis that they correspond to some noise and extreme outliers.

We assess the algorithms performances on two extracts from the SPOT-5 SITS. The image couples were taken between May 2004 and April 2005 for the first extract, and between February 2006 and August 2008 for the second one. To evaluate the proposed approaches, we compare the obtained results with ground truth change maps. These ground truths were created for an extract of the image of size 800×600 pixels ($48 \, \mathrm{km}^2$) for the first couple and for 320×270 pixels ($8,64 \, \mathrm{km}^2$) for the second one. However, the change detection was performed on the full images of 1600×1700 pixels ($272 \, \mathrm{km}^2$).

The following quality criteria were used to evaluate the performances of the different approaches: precision (1), recall (2) and Cohen's kappa score [3].

$$Precision = \frac{TruePositives}{TruePositives + FalsePositives} \tag{1}$$

$$Recall = \frac{TruePositives}{TruePositives + FalseNegatives} \tag{2}$$

The patch size of 5×5 pixels was chosen empirically, however, the correlation between the patch size and the performance of our algorithms is shown in Table 2. We can observe that $p = 3$ gives us poor results for both methods as the patch do not contain enough information about the neighborhood, $p = 7$ gives us slightly better results for fully-convolutional AE than $p = 5$ though learning time is higher. However, we see that for $p = 5$ performance of convolutional AE is much better than for $p = 7$. It can be explained by layer flattening when passing from convolutional layers to linear.

Some change detection results are presented on Figs. 3, 4, 5, 6, 7. All the images are represented in false colors, where red corresponds to vegetation and green to empty fields.

Table 2. Algorithm performance based on patch size p for images taken in 2004 and 2005 years.

Methods	p×p	Classification performance			
		Precision	*Recall*	*Kappa*	*Time*[a], *min*
Fully-Conv.	3×3	0.69	0.73	0.70	**11 + 10**
	5×5	0.67	**0.78**	0.70	14 + 12
	7×7	**0.69**	**0.78**	**0.72**	19 + 16
Conv.	3×3	0.67	0.74	0.69	**12 + 11**
	5×5	**0.68**	0.79	**0.71**	17 + 16
	7×7	0.61	**0.81**	0.69	24 + 22

[a] Pre-training+fine-tuning.

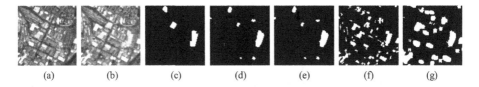

(a)   (b)   (c)   (d)   (e)   (f)   (g)

Fig. 3. Classification results. Image extract 100 × 100 pixels. Example of luminosity sensitivity. a - image taken on May 2004, b - image taken on April 2005, c - ground truth, d - fully-convolutional AE, e - convolutional AE, f - RBM, g - improved RBM.

Figure 3 features changes in an urban area: several buildings were constructed (or started to be constructed). The images extracts have great change in luminosity between the two dates. We observe that both convolutional and fully-convolutional AEs have low ratio of false positive changes while the RBM sensitivity in urban area claimed by its authors is confirmed. At the same time, the improved RBM method has less false positives changes than the initial one. This can also be seen in Figs. 4 and 6.

Figure 4 shows the construction of a new road. The road limits were correctly identified by all the models, except for the improved RBM model that did not detect the narrow part of the road.

Figure 5 displays changes in an agricultural area between May 2004 and April 2005. The overall seasonal change tendency is the following: the vegetation is more dense in May, the empty fields and fields with young crops have different minor changes between the two images. All the models except improved RBM showed relatively high ratio of false positive changes in vegetation. Nevertheless, the improved RBM missed more changes than other algorithms. The high ratio of false positives changes detected by first three architectures can be explained by the fact that vegetation density might be irregular and it is considered by the algorithm as changes. We observe that convolutional AE have slightly better results than other models.

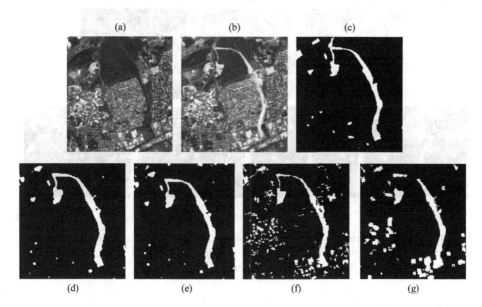

Fig. 4. Classification results. Image extract 180×190 pixels. a - image taken on May 2004, b - image taken on April 2005, c - ground truth, d - fully-convolutional AE, e - convolutional AE, f - RBM, g - improved RBM.

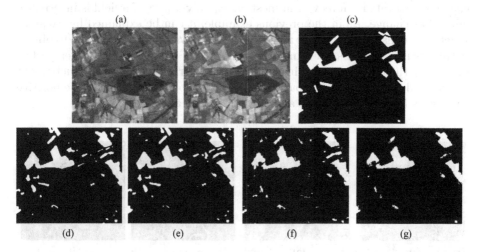

Fig. 5. Classification results. Image extract 230×200 pixels. a - image taken on May 2004, b - image taken on April 2005, c - ground truth, d - fully-convolutional AE, e - convolutional AE, f - RBM, g - improved RBM.

(a)   (b)   (c)

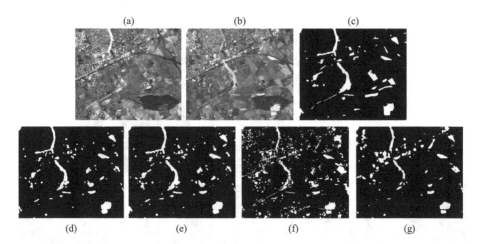

(d)   (e)   (f)   (g)

Fig. 6. Classification results. Image extract 320×270 pixels. a - image taken on February 2006, b - image taken on August 2008, c - ground truth, d - fully-convolutional AE, e - convolutional AE, f - RBM, g - improved RBM.

Figure 6 represents changes in an agricultural area between February 2006 and August 2008 as well as some constructions. The overall seasonal change tendency is the following: the fields that are empty in February have vegetation in August, and vise versa. Forest's vegetation state (bottom right corner) has some minor changes. We can see again that the convolutional AE has slightly better results than the fully-convolutional AE. However, the ratio of false positive changes is elevated. Moreover, in most cases, only a part of a field is incorrectly labeled as change. As in the previous example, it can be explained by irregular vegetation density, and further morphological analysis might be needed to obtain better results. At the same time, the initial RBM model showed better performance for the detection of a linear object that corresponds to constructions at the roadside at the lower left part of the image, though the level of false positive changes is high both in urban and agricultural areas.

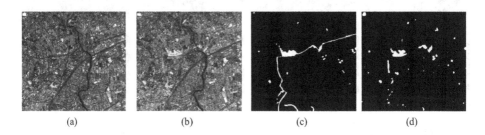

(a)   (b)   (c)   (d)

Fig. 7. Classification results. Algorithm limitations. Image extract 300×280 pixels. a - image taken on May 2004, b - image taken on April 2005, c - ground truth, d - convolutional AE.

Table 3. Performance of change detection algorithms on SPOT-5 images.

Methods		Classification performance			
		Precision	Recall	Kappa	Time[a], min
2004	RBM AE	0.48	0.64	0.52	**8 + 2**
2005	Impr. RBM AE	0.52	0.63	0.54	20 + 10
	Conv. AE	**0.68**	**0.79**	**0.71**	17 + 16
	Fully-Conv. AE	0.67	0.78	0.70	14 + 13
2006	RBM AE	0.40	0.61	0.43	**8 + 2**
2008	Impr. RBM AE	0.50	0.54	0.48	20 + 10
	Conv. AE	0.76	**0.79**	**0.75**	17 + 16
	Fully-Conv. AE	**0.80**	0.71	0.73	14 + 12

[a]Pre-training+fine-tuning.

Figure 7 shows the limitations of the proposed approach for the detection of the construction of a tramway line. Our method have poor quality of change detection for linear objects that can be explained by the patch-wise learning. As a patch reconstruction error determines the change class of its central pixel, changes in 1–2 pixel width linear objects can not be properly detected.

The different approaches performances are presented in Table 3. The algorithms were tested on NVIDIA Titan X GPU with 12 GB of RAM. Based on the presented results and on the performance estimators, we can conclude that joint convolutional AEs slightly outperformed fully-convolutional ones, though the training time stays higher as the model is more complicated. The performance of joint convolutional AEs can be explained by the higher complexity of the convolutional model. At the same time, both models of our approach showed better performances for change detection than the RBM-based models. However, it can be noted that the initial RBM method still has a high recall and the best training time despite a high level of false positive changes in urban areas compared to our approaches. We can equally conclude that methods with pixel-wise extracted patches have higher performance than initial RBM method where patches are not overlapped. Nevertheless, the improved RBM method detected less changes than the initial RBM method, though the number of false positives changes is much lower and overall classification performance characterized by kappa is higher.

5   Conclusion

In this paper, we have presented unsupervised deterministic approaches for change detection in open source SITS based on AE models. Our experiments have shown that our deterministic AE models perform better than state of the art RBM approaches on a large area with various land cover occupation. Among our proposed architectures, the joint fully-convolutional AEs model showed slightly better performances in spite of a longer training time.

In future works, we will focus on developing an algorithm for clustering these changes. Furthermore, we will improve our model by adding the analysis of morphological features, leading to more robust results for images with higher variance of seasonal changes.

References

1. Cao, G., Wang, B., Xavier, H., Yang, D., Southworth, J.: A new difference image creation method based on deep neural networks for change detection in remote-sensing images. Int. J. Remote Sens. **38**(23), 7161–7175 (2017). https://doi.org/10.1080/01431161.2017.1371861
2. Caye Daudt, R., Le Saux ,B., Boulch, A., Gousseau, Y.: Urban change detection for multispectral earth observation using convolutional neural networks. CoRR abs/1810.08468 (2018). https://doi.org/10.1109/IGARSS.2018.8518015
3. Cohen, J.: A coefficient of agreement for nominal scales. Educ. Psychol. Measur. **20**(1), 37–46 (1960). https://doi.org/10.1177/001316446002000104
4. Cui, W., Zhou, Q.: Application of a hybrid model based on a convolutional auto-encoder and convolutional neural network in object-oriented remote sensing classification. Algorithms **11**, 9 (2018). https://doi.org/10.3390/a11010009
5. Deng, J.S., Wang, K., Deng, Y.H., Qi, G.J.: PCA-based land-use change detection and analysis using multitemporal and multisensor satellite data. Int. J. Remote Sens. **29**(16), 4823–4838 (2008). https://doi.org/10.1080/01431160801950162
6. Du, P., Liu, S., Gamba, P., Tan, K., Xia, J.: Fusion of difference images for change detection over urban areas. IEEE J. Sel. Top. Appl. Earth Obs. Remote Sens. **5**(4), 1076–1086 (2012). https://doi.org/10.1109/JSTARS.2012.2200879
7. El Hajj, M., Bégué, A., Lafrance, B., Hagolle, O., Dedieu, G., Rumeau, M.: Relative radiometric normalization and atmospheric correction of a SPOT 5 time series. Sensors **8**(4), 2774–2791 (2008). https://doi.org/10.3390/s8042774
8. Hinton, G.E., Salakhutdinov, R.R.: Reducing the dimensionality of data with neural networks. Science **313**(5786), 504–507 (2006). https://doi.org/10.1126/science.1127647
9. Nielsen, A.A.: The regularized iteratively reweighted MAD method for change detection in multi- and hyperspectral data. IEEE Trans. Image Process. **16**(2), 463–478 (2007). https://doi.org/10.1109/TIP.2006.888195
10. Otsu, N.: A threshold selection method from gray-level histograms. IEEE Trans. Syst. Man Cybern. **9**(1), 62–66 (1979). https://doi.org/10.1109/TSMC.1979.4310076
11. Tan, K., Jin, X., Plaza, A., Wang, X., Xiao, L., Du, P.: Automatic change detection in high-resolution remote sensing images by using a multiple classifier system and spectral-spatial features. IEEE J. Sel. Top. Appl. Earth Obs. Remote Sens. **9**(8), 3439–3451 (2016). https://doi.org/10.1109/JSTARS.2016.2541678
12. Xu, Y., Xiang, S., Huo, C., Pan, C.: Change detection based on auto-encoder model for VHR images. In: Proceedings of the SPIE, vol. 8919, p. 891902 (2013). https://doi.org/10.1117/12.2031104

Physical Adversarial Attacks
by Projecting Perturbations

Nils Worzyk[(✉)], Hendrik Kahlen, and Oliver Kramer

Carl von Ossietzky University Oldenburg, 26129 Oldenburg, Germany
{nils.steffen.worzyk,hendrik.kahlen,oliver.kramer}@uol.de

Abstract. Research on adversarial attacks analyses how to slightly manipulate patterns like images to make a classifier believe it recogises a pattern with a wrong label, although the correct label is obvious to humans. In traffic sign recognition, previous physical adversarial attacks were mainly based on stickers or graffity on the sign's surface. In this paper, we propose and experimentally verify a new threat model that projects perturbations onto street signs via projectors or simulated laser pointers. No physical manipulation is required, which makes the attack difficult to detect. Attacks via projection imply new constraints like exclusively increasing colour intensities or manipulating certain colour channels. As exemplary experiments, we fool neural networks to classify stop signs as priority signs only by projecting optimised perturbations onto original traffic signs.

Keywords: Neural networks · Adversarial computing · Street sign classification

1 Introduction

Convolutional neural networks (CNNs) yield remarkable results in the domain of image classification. A specific usecase is the classification of street signs in the domain of autonomous driving systems. Here, the *German Traffic Sign Recognition Benchmark* (GTSRB) [16] dataset is widely used. Authors have reported accuracies of over 99% over the testset, see, e.g., [4,10].

However, CNNs have been fooled by *adversarial images* – images which are still classified as the original input by humans, but classified wrong by an artificial classifier. One prominent example is to manipulate a stop sign to be detected as a priority sign by the artificial classifier. The first notion of adversarial images in combination with neural networks was made by Szegedy et al. [18] but more recently, other authors showed that it is possible to transfer adversarial images into the physical world like Kurakin et al. [6] or Athalye et al. [1].

Athalye et al. [1] for example introduced a framework to calculate robust adversarial images, enabling a transfer into the physical world. The framework

This research is funded by the German Research Foundation through the Research Training Group DFG-GRK 1765: "System Correctness under Adverse Conditions".

© Springer Nature Switzerland AG 2019
I. V. Tetko et al. (Eds.): ICANN 2019, LNCS 11729, pp. 649–659, 2019.
https://doi.org/10.1007/978-3-030-30508-6_51

will be explained in more detail in Sect. 2.2. After manipulating the image digitally, they print out the manipulated version of the image, or even manipulated 3-D objects, which fool the classifier robustly, after recapturing the image, resp., 3-D printed object.

In addition, in the context of street sign classification, Eykholt et al. [2] proposed to attach stickers to the street signs which look like graffiti. They argue, that graffiti is widely known by humans and considered as normal, and therefore the stickers are not directly noticeable for humans. Another approach of Sitawarin et al. [15] is to manipulate corporate logos or advertisements to be recognised as the desired street sign. A human for example would recognize an advertisement, while the car would stop, because it detected a stop sign.

The current attacks have in common, that the attacker has to manipulate the street sign or the surroundings physically. To fool the classification systems, this requires the attachments to be not torn off or worn-out by weather conditions. Furthermore, at least in the case of an incident, the physical manipulation might be detected by the police or pedestrians. Probably even previous to an incident such that the attack might not work at all.

In this paper, we propose and investigate a different kind of manipulation by projecting the perturbation onto the street sign with a projector. In addition, to simulate the usage of a laser pointer, which would be less noticeable in reality, we also restricted the attack to only manipulate one colour channel, e.g., the green one. Thereby, there is no necessity to physically manipulate the street sign to attack. The projector can be placed somewhere hidden and project the manipulations onto the street sign. In an extended scenario the projector could be controlled via internet and only be activated under certain conditions, e.g., when a passing car is detected. Thereby, the detectability of the manipulation would be impeded.

Using a projector implies additional restrictions like non-decreasing pixel values if projecting the perturbation. This is due to the fact that by projecting something, we only can increase the captured value and not decrease it, i.e., projecting a "shadow" is somewhat impossible at full sunlight. To simulate the usage of a laser pointer, we adapt our attack to only use one colour channel, e.g., the green one, to create the adversarial images.

The remainder of this paper is organised as follows. In Sect. 2 we will give an overview of some attacks used to create adversarial images. Those attacks are basically interchangeable in the later framework. Especially, we line out the Expectation over Transformations (EoT) Framework by Athalye et al. [1]. In Sect. 3 we describe the setup of our experimental study, for which some noteworthy results will be presented in Sect. 4. More detailed information on parameter settings and results, as well as the code, can be found at https://github.com/icebreaker2/AI/tree/master/MA. Section 5 will conclude the paper.

2 Related Work

2.1 Adversarial Attacks

In general, adversarial attacks can be formalised by the following equation:

$$\text{minimise } \mathcal{D}(\boldsymbol{x}, \boldsymbol{x} + \boldsymbol{\delta})$$
$$\text{such that } \mathcal{C}(\boldsymbol{x} + \boldsymbol{\delta}) = t \tag{1}$$
$$\boldsymbol{x} + \boldsymbol{\delta} \in [0, 1]^n$$

Less formal, the attackers goal is to minimise a distance $\mathcal{D}$, e.g., the L_2 difference, between the original input $\boldsymbol{x}$ and the manipulated input $\boldsymbol{x} + \boldsymbol{\delta}$, such that the classification $\mathcal{C}(\boldsymbol{x} + \boldsymbol{\delta})$ of the manipulated input is t, where $t \neq \mathcal{C}(\boldsymbol{x})$. Also, the manipulated input has to be in the acceptable input range of the classifier, here between 0 and 1, as it is often used for image classification.

The task of solving this general formulation is implemented differently and can be categorised according to several criteria (cf. Serban et al. [13]). One of these criteria is the separation into white-box and black-box attacks. For white-box attacks the full target model is accessible, i.e., the architecture, the weights, and especially the gradients of the model with regards to a given input image. For black-box attacks, in general, only the outputs of the model are accessible. Depending on the attack scenario the attacker knows all possible classes of the model and gets the output, i.e., probability for each class. In another scenario the attacker only gets the probabilities for a subset of the classes, e.g., Ilyas et al. [5] consider, among other scenarios, that an attacker only gets access to the classification with the highest confidence. In the following we will give some examples for white and black-box attacks.

White-Box Attacks. One of the first effective white-box attacks, called *fast gradient sign method* (fgsm), was introduced by Goodfellow et al. [3]. They formulated the problem as given in Eq. 2, where in the original formulation ε is some constant value to adjust the permitted perturbation, $\nabla_{\boldsymbol{x}}$ denotes the gradient with respect to the input $\boldsymbol{x}$, L is the loss function, used to train the neural network in the first place, θ are the parameters of the trained model and y_t denotes the target classification:

$$\boldsymbol{x}' = \boldsymbol{x} + \varepsilon \cdot \text{sign}\left(\nabla_{\boldsymbol{x}} L\left(\theta, \boldsymbol{x}, y_t\right)\right) \tag{2}$$

The drawback of this method is, that the ε is a constant and therefore the perturbation can either be too small to fool the target system, or the perturbation is unnecessarily large. Therefore, more recent attacks propose to use iterative attacks to also minimise the amount of perturbation applied to the input. One example, which is the basis to the attack used in this work, is the *basic iterative method* (bim) proposed by Kurakin et al. [6], which implements the iterative equation:

$$\boldsymbol{x}'_0 = \boldsymbol{x}, \ \boldsymbol{x}'_{N+1} = \text{clip}_{\boldsymbol{x}, \varepsilon}\{\boldsymbol{x}'_N + \alpha \cdot \text{sign}\left(\nabla_{\boldsymbol{x}'_N} L\left(\theta, \boldsymbol{x}'_N, y_t\right)\right)\}, \tag{3}$$

where x denotes the original image scaled to range $[0, 1]$, x' is the (intermediate) adversarial image, and $L\left(\theta, x'_N, y_t\right)$ is the loss function, which was used to train the network, depending on the parameters of the neural network θ, x', and the target class of the attack y_t. In this formulation the parameter α is used to control the perturbation at each iteration step, while ε controls the maximally allowed perturbation via the clip function, which is applied element-wise and defined as:

$$\text{clip}_{x, \varepsilon}\left(p, c\right) = \min\{1, x\left(p, c\right) + \varepsilon, \max\{0, x\left(p, c\right) - \varepsilon, x'\left(p, c\right)\}\}, \qquad (4)$$

where p indicates the specific pixel to address, and c indicates the colour channel.

Black-Box Attacks. In contrast to white-box attacks, for black-box attacks the attacker does not have access to the target model parameters. So called *transfer attacks* are based on the observation, that adversarial inputs are (to some extend) transferable between models trained for the same (or similar) purposes [7,11]. If the dataset, the target model was trained on is accessible, the adversary can train his own model and use white-box attacks to create adversarial inputs. Otherwise, for example, Pengcheng et al. [12] propose to query the target model with known images to create a substitute model with a similar classification behaviour as the target model. From there on they can proceed with white-box attacks as previously.

Another direction of black-box attacks utilise techniques from evolutionary computing to create adversarial inputs. For example, in a recent work Ilyas et al. [5] propose to use natural evolution strategies to estimate the gradient of the target model. Based on these estimations they perform a projected gradient descent as proposed by Madry et al. [9]. Hence, they were able to reduce the amount of necessary queries to the target model with respect to earlier work.

2.2 Expectation over Transformations (EoT)

When transferring adversarial images from the digital to the physical world, an adversary faces new problems. For example the distance, as well as the angle, or rotation of the camera recording an image differs from the digital version of the image. Often these transformations lead to classifying the adversarial image not as the target class, but as the original class. For example Lu et al. [8] state that because of this behaviour there is "no need to worry about adversarial examples". However, considering such behaviour, Athalye et al. [1] introduced a framework to make adversarial images more robust to such transformations, called *Expectation over Transformation* (EoT).

The basic idea is to predefine a distribution T over expected transformations t, where t consists of multiple sub-transformations $t_1, \ldots, t_E$ with a defined value range each, e.g., rotation in $[-10°, 10°]$. Those transformations are then applied sequentially to the original, or intermediate adversarial image and afterwards the new (intermediate) adversarial image is calculated. The calculation can be summarised by the following equation, where $m \leq E$ denotes the m-th transformation, and *attack* defines the output of the applied attack:

$$x'_0 = x \qquad\qquad x'^{m=0}_{N+1} = x'_N$$
$$x'^{(0<m\leq E)}_{N+1} = t_m \left(x'^{(m-1)}_{N+1} \right) \quad x'_{N+1} = \text{attack} \left(x'^{(m=E)}_{N+1} \right) \tag{5}$$

By using this framework, the authors were able to print out 2-D or even 3-D objects which were robustly, i.e., recorded in different angles, distances, and other transformations, classified as the desired class. Furthermore, the framework is independent on the attack used to create the adversarial images.

3   Setup

3.1   Adaptation of the Attack

The attack we propose is based on the *basic iterative method* defined in Eq. 3. Furthermore, to make the digital adversarial inputs robust we use the EoT framework explained in Sect. 2.2.

However, our scenario requires some adaptations. The first one is given by the assumption, that we *project* the perturbation onto the street sign. This requires to only allow *increases* in the pixel values, because we can not project shadows. This is achieved by calculating the perturbation $\mathcal{X}$ as the difference between the (intermediate) adversarial image x' and the original image x after each iteration of the attack, and truncate $\mathcal{X}$ to the range $[0,1]$ by:

$$\mathcal{X} = \min\left(1, \max\left(0, x' - x\right)\right) \tag{6}$$

The second adaptation is based on the assumption, that in our scenario the attacker uses, for example, a laser pointer with a specific attachment to project the perturbation. Since laser pointers normally do only have one colour, we use the following equation to restrict the attack to only manipulate one colour channel:

$$RGB_{x,U}\{x'\}(p,c) = \begin{cases} x_{p,c} & c \in U \\ x'_{p,c} & \text{else} \end{cases}, \tag{7}$$

where x, resp. x' denotes the original, resp. adversarial image, p the specific pixel, and c the colour channel of the image. The variable U defines the set of *unwanted* colour channels over the set $\{r, g, b\}$, where r is the red colour channel, g the green, and b the blue one. Thereby, only the *wanted* colour channels are perturbed, the unwanted are left on their original value. Thus, Eq. 3 can then be extended to:

$$x'_0 = x, \; x'_{N+1} = RGB_{x,U}\{\text{clip}_{x,\epsilon}\{x'_N + \alpha \cdot \text{sign}\left(\nabla_{x'_N} J\left(\theta, x'_N, y\right)\right)\}\} \tag{8}$$

where in each iteration the perturbation is clipped according to Eq. 6.

3.2   Experimental Setup

As mentioned in the introduction we used the *German Traffic Sign Recognition Benchmark* (GTSRB) [16], which consists of 39,209 training and 12,630 test images, of more than 40 different classes. Based on this dataset we trained two CNNs—Inception-v3 [17] and VGG-16 (version D) [14], with 95.2% and 94.02% accuracy, respectively. To generate the adversarial examples we used our proposed attack (Sect. 3.1). We always attempt to transfer a stop sign into a priority sign. Furthermore, we only consider an attack to be successful, if the target class is top-1, i.e., is classified with the highest confidence over all possible classes. This explicit assumption differs from other works like [6] where the authors also observe the top-5 success, i.e., the target class is among the classes with the highest 5 confidences.

In a preliminary study we verified our approach in a virtual environment by applying random transformations to the adversarial example digitally. Exemplary, the transformations we consider are rotation, scaling, or salt & pepper. A list of all transformations used and their ranges is given on https://github.com/icebreaker2/AI/tree/master/MA.

To carry out the physical applicability of our attack, we investigated two scenarios. The first one was to project the adversarial image onto a white wall, and track the adversariality, i.e., the percentage of adversarial images classified as the target class, as well as the top-1 confidence of the captured image classification. In the second scenario, we projected only the adversarial perturbation onto a printed stop sign, hanged to a white wall. The second scenario is further referred to as *physical adversarial perturbation* (PAP). This setup is depicted in Fig. 1 in the most left picture. We used a 1080p home projector, a 1080p webcam, and the stop sign was printed on a professional printer. The captured images of the stop sign were then semi-automatically cropped to the necessary area.

Two examples of manipulated images taken by the webcam located at an angle of 45° to the wall are also shown in Fig. 1. The manipulation for the image in the middle was calculated for the Inception model, on the right side we see the resulting manipulation for the VGG model.

4   Results

4.1   Preliminary Virtual Study

To verify our digital setup and reproduce results published in the literature, we allowed the attack to manipulate all colour channels and to increase as well as decrease the pixel value. Thereby, we achieved an adversariality of 99.89% on Inception, respectively 98.36% on VGG. These results are even slightly higher as the reported adversariality of 96.4% on Inception reported by Athalye et al. [1].

In order to verify our concept digitally, we restricted the attack to only manipulate the green colour channel and only to increase pixel values. This is the most restricted scenario in which we consider a green laser pointer as projector. Nevertheless we achieve an adversariality of 72.8% on Inception,

Fig. 1. Left: picture of the setup, Middle: adversarial example for Inception, Right: adversarial example for VGG (Color figure online)

respectively 52.04% on VGG. These results motivated to transfer the attack to the physical world.

4.2 Projection of Adversarial Images

In this subsection we consider the scenario, that an attacker projects the *complete manipulated stop sign* onto, for example, a house wall. In the following figures we use the abbreviation *plain* to indicate that all colour channels may be manipulated, while *rgb_1* expresses that only the green colour channel may be manipulated. Furthermore, *inc* indicates that the attack only increases the pixel values.

In Fig. 2 the results for successful attacks, i.e., the target class is top-1, are shown. In the left figure the results for Inception are shown, in the right figure those for VGG. The x-axis ε indicates the amount of perturbation allowed for the attack, while on the y-axis the top-1 confidence of the projected adversarial images are shown. Each cross indicates the mean confidence of two adversarial inputs for the given ε.

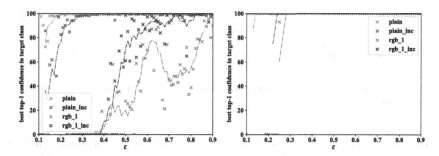

Fig. 2. Top-1 confidence of projected adversarial images on Inception-v3 (left) and VGG-16 (right).

As we can see, if we are allowed to manipulate all colour channels, we get confidences near 100% in the adversarial class (priority sign) with less perturbation, compared to attacks performed only on the green colour channel. But still, if we restrict the attack to manipulate only the green colour channel, we can achieve confidences in the adversarial class above 60% for medium or high perturbation levels. In the case of VGG even confidences of 100% with rather low perturbation levels were achieved. If we further restrict the attack to only increase pixel values, we are still able to achieve high confidences, but again, need higher perturbation levels.

If the attacker is only allowed to manipulate the green colour channel Inception and VGG behave differently. For Inception, if only *rgb_1* applies, the adversariality reduces to 36.42%, where in this case for VGG the adversariality only slightly reduces to 80.66%. If we added the condition to only increase the pixel values, the adversariality for both architectures was 49.59% and 56.79% for Inception and VGG, respectively.

Aside high confidences, if all channels are allowed to be manipulated by increasing and decreasing the pixel values, the adversariality over all perturbation levels ε is 97.94% and 98.35%, for Inception and VGG, respectively. The adversariality reduces, if *plain_inc* applies, to 89.71% and 82.51%, for Inception and VGG respectively. At this point it is noteworthy, that the remaining percentages combine images, where the manipulation already failed in the generation process (failed attack), the manipulated image was still recognised as stop sign (original), or the manipulated image was recognised as a completely different street sign (other top-1), as shown in Fig. 3. For VGG basically an attack was either successful (target top-1) or the attack failed to find an adversarial image at all (failed attack). For inception, however, we can see that, under restriction *rgb_1_inc* 18.31% of the attacks did not bring the target class into top-1, but another class unequal to the original class.

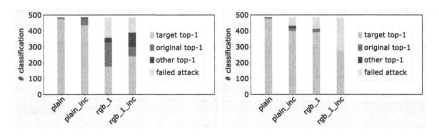

Fig. 3. Top-1 confidence of projected adversarial images on Inception-v3 (left) and VGG-16 (right).

The case, that the manipulated image was classified as something different than the original or target class was not considered as a success in this work, but in a real scenario can still have fatal effects to the traffic.

4.3 Projection of Adversarial Perturbation

In this scenario, only the adversarial perturbations were projected onto a previous printed stop sign, and the top-1 confidence results are shown in Fig. 4.

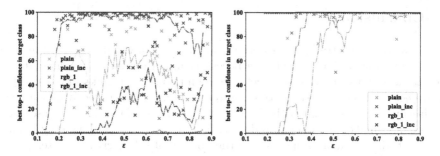

Fig. 4. Top-1 confidence of projected adversarial perturbations on Inception-v3 (left) and VGG-16 (right).

In comparison to the complete projected adversarial images, the confidence levels are worse in almost all cases. But it is noticeable that for VGG the confidence levels are still near 100% if an adversarial attack was successful. Also it is noticeable, that the *inc* variations, i.e., those attacks, which are optimised to only increase the pixel values, achieve better results than the attacks without inc.

For the non-*inc* variations the adversariality for Inception drops from 97.94% to 30.45% under restriction *plain* and from 36.42% to 0.41% under restriction *rgb_1*. For VGG the adversariality drops from 98.35% to 46.50% under restriction *plain* and from 80.66% to 66.67% for restriction *rgb_1*.

If we consider the restriction *plain_inc*, the old adversariality of 89.71% for Inception reduced only to 79.22%. For VGG the adversariality even improved from 82.51% to 88.48%. Considering the restriction *rgb_1_inc* again for Inception the adversariality drops, from 49.59% to 21.61%, but for VGG the adversariality stayed the same at 56.79%.

A detailed overview of the outcome of the attack is given in Fig. 5. Again it is interesting that for VGG an attack is basically successful or fails at all, while for Inception there is a noticeable amount of cases, in which the attack caused a different classification to the original or target label.

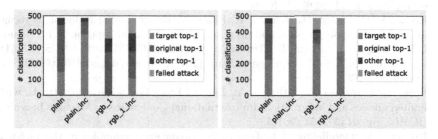

Fig. 5. Top-1 confidence of projected adversarial perturbations on Inception-v3 (left) and VGG-16 (right).

5   Conclusion

Previous attacks on traffic signs were based on direct physical access to the signs or its environment. This is no longer necessary in our approach. We showed that an attacker can use a normal projector, or a limited projector like a laser pointer, to project adversarial perturbations onto street signs, which deceive a classifier to classify the street sign with the adversaries target class. This imposes new dangers and makes the understanding of neural networks and how they behave under attack even more important in the domain of safety critical systems.

To verify the applicability of this threat model we implemented (necessary) restrictions to the basis attack, namely that we (1.) only manipulated one colour channel and (2.) only allowed to increase the pixel values. The presented results show that it is indeed possible to fool neural networks by only projecting adversarial images to a white wall. Even more concerning is that only projecting the perturbations to a printed sign can also lead to a high number of successful attacks.

In future work we consider to use black-box attacks and the classification output of a real car to test adversarial attacks in an even more realistic scenario. In such a scenario the usage of projections is easier and faster than printing out the manipulated version of a street sign each time, or manipulate the street sign physically in any way. In addition, using projections enables to perform a sequence of adversarial attacks which preserves the common sequence of observed traffic signs when, for example, changing from the freeway into the city.

References

1. Athalye, A., Engstrom, L., Ilyas, A., Kwok, K.: Synthesizing robust adversarial examples. In: International Conference on Machine Learning (ICML), pp. 284–293 (2018). http://proceedings.mlr.press/v80/athalye18b.html
2. Eykholt, K., et al.: Robust physical-world attacks on deep learning visual classification. In: IEEE Conference on Computer Vision and Pattern Recognition (CVPR), pp. 1625–1634 (2018)
3. Goodfellow, I.J., Shlens, J., Szegedy, C.: Explaining and harnessing adversarial examples. arXiv:1412.6572 (2014)
4. Hoang, V.-D., Le, M.-H., Tran, T.T., Pham, V.-H.: Improving traffic signs recognition based region proposal and deep neural networks. In: Nguyen, N.T., Hoang, D.H., Hong, T.-P., Pham, H., Trawiński, B. (eds.) ACIIDS 2018. LNCS (LNAI), vol. 10752, pp. 604–613. Springer, Cham (2018). https://doi.org/10.1007/978-3-319-75420-8_57
5. Ilyas, A., Engstrom, L., Athalye, A., Lin, J.: Black-box adversarial attacks with limited queries and information. In: International Conference on Machine Learning (ICML), pp. 2142–2151 (2018)
6. Kurakin, A., Goodfellow, I.J., Bengio, S.: Adversarial examples in the physical world. In: International Conference on Learning Representations (ICLR) (2017)
7. Liu, Y., Chen, X., Liu, C., Song, D.: Delving into transferable adversarial examples and black-box attacks. In: International Conference on Learning Representations (ICLR) (2017)

8. Lu, J., Sibai, H., Fabry, E., Forsyth, D.: No need to worry about adversarial examples in object detection in autonomous vehicles. arXiv preprint arXiv:1707.03501 (2017)
9. Madry, A., Makelov, A., Schmidt, L., Tsipras, D., Vladu, A.: Towards deep learning models resistant to adversarial attacks. arXiv preprint arXiv:1706.06083 (2017)
10. Mao, X., Hijazi, S., Casas, R., Kaul, P., Kumar, R., Rowen, C.: Hierarchical CNN for traffic sign recognition. In: 2016 IEEE Intelligent Vehicles Symposium (IV), pp. 130–135. IEEE (2016)
11. Papernot, N., McDaniel, P., Goodfellow, I.: Transferability in machine learning: from phenomena to black-box attacks using adversarial samples. arXiv preprint arXiv:1605.07277 (2016)
12. Pengcheng, L., Yi, J., Zhang, L.: Query-efficient black-box attack by active learning. In: 2018 IEEE International Conference on Data Mining (ICDM), pp. 1200–1205. IEEE (2018)
13. Serban, A.C., Poll, E.: Adversarial examples-a complete characterisation of the phenomenon. arXiv preprint arXiv:1810.01185 (2018)
14. Simonyan, K., Zisserman, A.: Very deep convolutional networks for large-scale image recognition. In: International Conference on Learning Representations (ICLR) (2015)
15. Sitawarin, C., Bhagoji, A.N., Mosenia, A., Mittal, P., Chiang, M.: Rogue signs: deceiving traffic sign recognition with malicious ads and logos. In: IEEE Deep Learning and Security Workshop (DLS) (2018)
16. Stallkamp, J., Schlipsing, M., Salmen, J., Igel, C.: The German traffic sign recognition benchmark: a multi-class classification competition. In: International Joint Conference on Neural Networks (IJCNN), pp. 1453–1460. IEEE (2011)
17. Szegedy, C., Vanhoucke, V., Ioffe, S., Shlens, J., Wojna, Z.: Rethinking the inception architecture for computer vision. In: IEEE Conference on Computer Vision and Pattern Recognition (CVPR), pp. 2818–2826 (2016)
18. Szegedy, C., et al.: Intriguing properties of neural networks. In: International Conference on Learning Representations (ICLR) (2014)

Improved Forward-Backward Propagation to Generate Adversarial Examples

Yuying Hao[1], Tuanhui Li[2], Yang Bai[1], Li Li[2], Yong Jiang[2(✉)],
and Xuanye Cheng[3]

[1] Tsinghua-Berkely Shenzhen Institute, Tsinghua University, Shenzhen, China
{haoyy17,y-bai17}@mails.tsinghua.edu.cn
[2] Graduate School at Shenzhen, Tsinghua University, Shenzhen, China
lth17@mails.tsinghua.edu.cn, lilihitcs@gmail.com,
jiangy@sz.tsinghua.edu.cn
[3] SenseTime Research, SenseTime, Shenzhen, China
xuanyech@gmail.com

Abstract. Deep neural networks (DNNs) have been widely applied in many areas. However, they are quite vulnerable to well-designed perturbations. Most recent methods of generating adversarial examples fail to limit the perturbations while keeping good transferability. In this work, we propose a new method to address these problems. We combine local attack and gradient descent optimization method to generate adversarial examples. Specifically, in forward propagation, we select sensitive pixels and add perturbations to them. In backward propagation, we propose a novel loss function to reduce the difference between adversarial examples and benign images. Extensive experiments demonstrate that our method achieves strong attack ability with lower distortion.

Keywords: Window filter · Forward derivative ·
Backward gradient propagation · Adversarial attack

1 Introduction

Deep neural networks (DNNs) are widely used in many areas, such as object detection [7,21], natural language processing (NLP) [5]. However, these neural networks are very sensitive to adversarial examples [10], which limits the practical application of deep neural networks [12,15]. Adversarial example is the image which adds quasi-imperceptible noise to benign image and confuses the DNNs. Recent attack approaches usually generate adversarial examples based on the gradient methods, such as [3,8], which add redundant noise on the benign images. Other attack approaches add noise on specific pixels instead of the whole image, such as the extreme example of one-pixel attack [22], but these methods cannot obtain excellent attack ability.

Y. Hao and T. Li—Indicates equal contributions.

© Springer Nature Switzerland AG 2019
I. V. Tetko et al. (Eds.): ICANN 2019, LNCS 11729, pp. 660–672, 2019.
https://doi.org/10.1007/978-3-030-30508-6_52

In this work, we propose an efficient method, which just perturbs the most sensitive pixels rather than the whole image. These pixels can capture the most important structure information of the benign image, thus we can obtain the adversarial examples with less expense. For this purpose, we define a local attack method to detect the sensitive pixels and control the magnitude as well as locations of the perturbations. Specifically, we take the forward derivative to select sensitive pixels and generate perturbations on adversarial examples. This process can be adjusted according to requirements to make the perturbations more targeted and smoother. Besides, in order to make the adversarial examples difficult to perceived by humans, we propose a new loss function to impose a constraint on the number of perturbed pixels, resulting in a sparse attack. Compared to the previous methods, our method obtains higher attack success rate in experiments and demonstrates stronger attack ability.

This paper makes the following contributions:

(1) We firstly propose a method of combining forward and backward propagation to add sparse perturbations and introduce an excellent approach to select sensitive pixels for misclassification.
(2) We introduce a novel loss function for optimization, which is able to smooth and reduce the perturbations and achieve the goals of targeted attack. More specifically, the ℓ_0 norm can be converted into a derivable function.
(3) We generate adversarial examples on MNIST. Our method performs the best in white-box attack against other compared methods. In addition, it reduces the accuracy of convolutional neural networks from 99% to 6.17% in black-box attack. We achieve the goals to limit the magnitude of perturbations and maintain the attack ability.

2   Related Work

This section will briefly introduce various methods to implement adversarial attacks. Adversarial attacks can be roughly divided into 2 categories: white-box attack and black-box attack. White-box attack assumes that attackers know the complete knowledge of the attacked model, and black-box attack assumes that attackers generate adversarial examples without knowledge of the attacked model. For white-box attack, Szegedy et al. [23] firstly discovered and defined the adversarial examples. FGSM [8] aims to mislead neural networks by adding noise in the gradient direction. It is a one step method and does not perform stably. Then Kurakin et al. [22] improved the performances of FGSM by taking the targeted label instead of the original label to compute perturbations.

To make the adversarial perturbations undetectable, Moosavi-Dezfooli et al. [18] simplified the problems of generating adversarial examples to a linear decision function attack problem, and finally detected the perturbations direction of each attack to obtain the final result. Carlini and Wagner [3] proposed to limit the ℓ_∞, ℓ_2 and ℓ_0 norms. Experiments show that defensive distillation [19] can not defend against these three attacks [3]. It also illustrated the best result among the three methods was ℓ_2 norm attack.

Compare with [3], Papernot *et al.* [20] proposed a method by restricting ℓ_0 norm. They used Saliency Map to select the pixels instead of perturbing the entire image. However, the calculation of Saliency Map is more complicated. One-pixel attack [14] based on the genetic algorithm method can be achieved by changing only one pixel value in the image, while the noise is very serious and easy to be perceived. These attacks have limitations on many defense methods of making the numerical estimation unreachable because they introduce a sharp-edged plateau around the samples.

Some studies probed the final decision boundaries by changing the pixels values on purpose [4]. Neither the parameters of the model nor the distribution of training data are required previously in their methods, thus they can achieve black-box attack. However, these methods are selective for images leading to that many images cannot generate the adversarial examples.

Different from above methods of adding specific perturbations on a image to achieve attack goals, Moosavi-Dezfooli *et al.* [17] discover that neural networks exist the universal perturbations with impressive transferability. To generate quasi-imperceptible universal adversarial perturbations, they apply the deepfool method [18] and limit ℓ_∞ and ℓ_2 norms.

For adversarial defenses, research can be classified into two categories: white-box strategies and black-box strategies. For the first category, Shaham *et al.* [24] and Ian *et al.* [2] took learning algorithms and regularization scheme to smooth the inputs, aiming to find the strategies of adversarial attacks. For the second category, Zoubin *et al.* [6] adopted the JPEG compression to remove the perturbations, Evan *et al.* [11] applied the image rescaling. But for the first category, they make strong assumptions on adversarial examples. For the second category, the methods is not efficient for their simplicity. Guo *et al.* [9] achieved the defenses based on the total variation minimization and image quitting, which performs better than other defenses.

Reflection. Different from other researches focused on utilizing backward propagation to generate adversarial examples, our method makes full use of forward propagation information to select sensitive pixels and add sparse perturbations on benign images. Besides, we propose a new loss function to overcome the drawbacks of utilizing the L_p norm to measure image similarity. We add more prior information to the loss function, making the attack more efficiency.

3   Model

In this section, we firstly describe the general definition of adversarial attack and then present the proposed model of our method. Finally, we will demonstrate a complete summary of the whole algorithm.

3.1   Preliminary About Adversarial Attack

As described in [23], a benign image is denoted as $\mathbf{X} \in \mathbb{R}^{w \times h \times c}$, where c represents the channels, and (w, h) denotes the width and height of the image. Assume that the model output probability of $\mathbf{X}$ is $f(\mathbf{X})$, we use $f(\mathbf{X})_i$ to denote the probability of being classified as i-th class label. We denote y_0 as the ground-truth label of $\mathbf{X}$, and the corresponding adversarial example as $\mathbf{X}'$, then the **untargeted attack** can be defined as follows:

$$y_0 \neq \arg\max_i f(\mathbf{X}')_i \tag{1}$$

As shown above, the successful untargeted attack is just required to make the predicted label different from ground-truth label. By contrast, the more strict type is targeted attack of trying to make the predicted label correspond to a target label y_t. We present the targeted attack as follows:

$$y_t = \arg\max_i f(\mathbf{X}')_i \tag{2}$$

In this paper, we only operate the targeted attack, which is more critical to realize. A successful attack for image $\mathbf{X}$ should always be constrained within a limited perturbations. The most popular metric to calculate the difference between the benign image and adversarial example is ℓ_p norm ($p = 0, 1, 2, \infty$), which can be described as:

$$\ell_p = |\mathbf{X} - \mathbf{X}'|_p, \tag{3}$$

In the practical optimization problem, we usually choose ℓ_2-norm. Combining the perturbations constraint and the misclassification object, we present the general optimization function for targeted attack as follows:

$$\min \ \|\mathbf{X} - \mathbf{X}'\|_2^2 + \mathcal{L}(f(\mathbf{X}'), y_t) \tag{4}$$
$$\text{s.t.} \ \mathbf{X}' \in [0, 1]^{w \times h \times c},$$

where the box constraint $\mathbf{X}' \in [0, 1]^{w \times h \times c}$ is utilized to control the adversarial example in the normal range. The previous methods mainly focus on adding dense noise on $\mathbf{X}'$ according to gradient information. By contrast, we propose that the neural network changes the classification result of adversarial images since some important pixels are disturbed. After some few pixels of benign images being changed, these images may separated from the original manifolds when the perturbations propagate in the neural networks. As a result, we adopt a novel sparse attack method which just perturb few pixels in the benign image to reach a competitive attack ability.

3.2   The Proposed Sparse Attack Method

Different from the previous methods of just perturbing the images according to the back propagation gradient, we propose to perturb the benign image via two process: the forward derivative local attack and the backward gradient perturbations.

Forward Derivative Local Attack. To generate more effective adversarial example, inspired by [20], we apply forward derivative to selecting sensitive pixels, and add perturbations on these parts. Assume that $\mathbf{Z}_t(\mathbf{X}')$ is the output of logit layer with $\mathbf{X}'$ as the corresponding input and y_t as target label. The forward derivative can be described as:

$$\nabla \mathbf{Z}_t(\mathbf{X}') = \frac{\partial \mathbf{Z}_t(\mathbf{X}')}{\partial \mathbf{X}'} \tag{5}$$

The value of $\nabla \mathbf{Z}_t(\mathbf{X}')$ presents the contribution of each pixel for $\mathbf{X}'$ being classified to target label y_t. To increase the probability of being classified as y_t, we select the top-k values of $\nabla \mathbf{Z}_t(\mathbf{X}')$ and add perturbations on these pixels (In this paper, we use $[p,q,n]$ to represent the location of selected pixel). The selected values can be denoted as d_i, where $i \in [1 \ldots k]$ and $d_i > 0$. The assigned perturbations of each selected pixel can be described as:

$$\mathbf{Pert}[p,q,n] = d_i / (\sum_{i=1}^{k} |d_i|) \tag{6}$$

To enlarge the difference of selected pixels value, we apply the floor and ceil functions to add perturbations. Floor and ceil functions accurate to 0.01, such that the pixel-values can be changed about 2.5 for each iteration ($0.01/(1/255) \approx 2.5$).

Modeling for Loss Function. The ℓ_2-norm can only measure the difference between the $\mathbf{X}$ and $\mathbf{X}'$, while it can not control the number of perturbed pixels. In this method, we control the intensity of noise added to the most sensitive pixels and obtain a competitive attack ability with smaller disturbance cost. Due to that ℓ_0 cannot be derived, we propose a new metric $\mathcal{D}(\mathbf{X}, \mathbf{X}')$ to denote the number of pixels to be perturbed in the benign image, which can be described as follows:

$$\mathcal{D}(\mathbf{X}, \mathbf{X}') = \sum_{x \in \mathbf{X}} \mathbf{I}(x, x'), \tag{7}$$

where $\mathbf{I}(x, x')$ is a indicator function, we denote it as follows:

$$\mathbf{I}(x, x') = \begin{cases} 0 \ |x - x'| \leq 0.0039 \\ 1 \ |x - x'| > 0.0039 \ . \end{cases} \tag{8}$$

The threshold 0.0039 is derived from the normalization of pixel value $1/255 \approx 0.00392$. The indicator function cannot be optimized, we transfer this term as:

$$\mathbf{I}(|x - x'|) \implies clip\{255 * (|x - x'| - 0.0039), 0, 1\}, \tag{9}$$

where $clip(a, min, max)$ is denoted that the values of a are limited into $[min, max]$. If the value of a is out of range, it will be cliped to $[min, max]$.

Algorithm 1. The propose algorithm for adversarial attack

Input: benign image $\mathbf{X}$; ground-truth y_0; target label y_t; local attack pixel number k; maximum iterations $maxiter$;

Output: $\mathbf{X}'$

  while $iter < maxiter$ **do**

    Compute $\nabla \mathbf{Z}_t(\mathbf{X}')$ according to (5)

    Select the top-k magnitudes in $\nabla \mathbf{Z}_t(\mathbf{X}')$ and record the correspond position $[p, q, n]$.

    Calculate $\mathbf{Pert}[p, q, n]$ according to (6)

    if $m \leq \mathbf{Round}(k/2)$ **then**

      $\mathbf{Pert}[p, q, n] = \text{Floor}\left(\mathbf{Pert}[p, q, n]\right)$

    else

      $\mathbf{Pert}[p, q, n] = \text{Ceil}\left(\mathbf{Pert}[p, q, n]\right)$

    end if

    Compute $\mathbf{Mod} = \nabla F_{loss}(\mathbf{X}')$ according to (10)

    $\mathbf{X}' = \mathbf{X}' - r_1 * \mathbf{Mod} + r_2 * \mathbf{Pert}$

    if $\arg\max\left(\mathbf{Z}(\mathbf{X}')\right) = y_t$ **then**

      Return $\mathbf{X}'$

    end if

  end while

Inspired by [3], we presents the optimization function of our method as follows:

$$\min \quad c_1 \|\mathbf{X} - \mathbf{X}'\|_2^2 \tag{10}$$
$$+ c_2 \sum_{x \in \mathbf{X}} clip\{255 * (|x - x'| - 0.0039), 0, 1\}$$
$$+ c_3 \max\{0, \mathbf{Z}_{max} - \mathbf{Z}_t\}$$
$$+ c_4 \max\{0, \mathbf{Z}_0 - \mathbf{Z}_t\}$$
$$\text{s.t.} \quad \mathbf{X}' \in [0, 1]^n.$$

where $c_i(i = 1, 2, 3, 4)$ is hyper-parameter, $\mathbf{Z}_{max}$ is the maximum logit output, $\mathbf{Z}_t$ is the logit output of target label y_t and $\mathbf{Z}_0$ is the logit output of original label y_0. This model function can guarantee that the logit output of y_t label is able to obtain the maximum value. In other words, $\mathbf{X}'$ can be missclassified.

The Implementation of the Proposed Method. The algorithm of our method is shown in Algorithm 1, we demonstrate the detailed implementation of the proposed adversarial attack method as follows:

(1) Set the WINSIZE, which equals to top-k value and represents the maximum number of pixels changed. Calculate the forward derivative of $\nabla \mathbf{Z}_t(\mathbf{X}')$, and select the k pixels with maximum k forward derivative values.

(2) Add specific perturbations to selected pixels according to the floor and ceil function. Floor and ceil functions are not rounded to integer, but accurate to 0.01. In this way, we can discover the specific pixels and add limited noise in the forward propagation for local attacks.

Fig. 1. Our attack method applied on MNIST performs targeted attacks. The generated images in each row have all labels in order except its original label.(For example, in the first row for 0, adversarial images are listed with targeted label 1-2-3-4-5-6-7-8-9.)

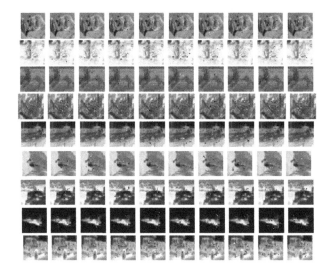

Fig. 2. Our attack method applied on CIFAR-10 performs targeted attacks. The left column is the benign image, followed by adversarial examples with different labels.

(3) In backward propagation, we apply the improved loss function (10) for optimization. The new loss function contains the original label information and the changed pixel information, such that it can better measure the gap between the adversarial example and the benign image, realize the generation of adversarial example and reduce the perturbations on the benign image.

4   Performance Evaluation

4.1   Experimental Setup

Dataset and Implementation Details. In this work, we utilize 2 datasets: MNIST [14] and CIFAR-10 [1]. MNIST contains 60k training images and 10k

Table 1. The performance of white-box attack on MNIST dataset, T and K are different CNN structures.

Model	Method			
	FGSM	Deepfool	C&W $- \ell_2$	Ours
K	43.55	15.58	0.75	0
T	1.32	1.885	1.5	0

evaluation images. CIFAR-10 contains 50k training images and 10k evaluation image. Both of them are distributed into 10 classes. As for the model hyperparameters, the weighting coefficients c_1, c_2, c_3, c_4, r_1, r_2 are set to 2, 0.004, 5, 0.5, 0.3, 2, respectively. For black-box and white-box attack on MNIST, we select WINSIZE as 2. We exploit the toolkit provided by IBM to reproduce the FGSM [8], Deepfool [18] and C&W [3] algorithms for comparision with our proposed method. Compared to other datasets with complex images, adversarial examples on the MNIST are the most difficult to generate. The network has excellent classification ability for simple images, such that the difficulties of attack will increase. Therefore, in this work, we evaluate our white-box attack and black-box attack mainly on MNIST.

Evaluation Model. In order to evaluate the attack ability of the generated adversarial examples, we construct two kinds of network structures: K and T. K and T both have 4 convolution layers, 2 max pooling layers, 1 flatten layer and 3 fully connected layers, while keeping a variety of the number of filters and the size of fully connected layers. The adversarial examples are generated on T structure and attack the K structure. Then we do adversarial training to evaluate the robustness of adversarial examples.

4.2   Experiment Result

White-Box Attack. We firstly apply the pretrained model T and K to generate the adversarial examples, respectively. The results of white-box attack on MNIST are shown on Table 1. The *Acc* implies accuracy of classifiers. Smaller *Acc* value means better performance of attack.

FGSM method performs unstably, because its performance relies tightly on the CNN structure. The performance of Deepfool also relies on CNN structure, since it is mainly based on the assumption of Deepfool that CNN is locally linear. C&W-ℓ_2 attack generates adversarial examples based on optimization and measures the difference between the benign images and the generated images in ℓ_2 norm. C&W behaves well, but can not achieve 100% attacks. Compared to C&W-ℓ_2, our method performs much more stably and obtain the most powerful attack ability, even achieve 100% attack rate. Furthermore, different from the dense attack method of C&W, our method is just required to perturb few pixels to achieve competitive ability, as shown in Table 2. The experiment results indicate that our method has stronger attack ability.

Table 2. We randomly select pictures (the original label is forth) in CIFAR-10 and compare the number of pixels changed between C&W − ℓ_2 and our method.

Label	1	2	3	5	6	7	8	9	10
C&W − ℓ_2	399	538	766	872	320	340	322	499	478
Ours	6	21	1	12	22	4	10	24	19

Table 3. Transferability of 5 different methods on MNIST dataset.

Method	Type	Acc (%)
FGSM	Adversarial training	30.93
	Black-box attack	32.73
Virtual	Adversarial training	33.53
	Black-box attack	36.04
C&W − ℓ_2	Adversarial training	34.83
	Black-box attack	40.24
Deepfool	Adversarial training	6.61
	Black-box attack	11.41
Ours	Adversarial training	6.06
	Black-box attack	6.17

Transferability. Recent studies show that adversarial examples can be transferred in different models. The adversarial examples generated from one specific model can still attack other different neural network structures. We present the transferability of our adversarial examples generated from MNIST dataset on Table 3. For black-box attack, we generate adversarial examples on T structure and attack K structure. For defense method, we refer to [13] to apply adversarial training. As shown on Table 3, FGSM doesn't perform well in adversarial training and black-box attack. Virtual adversarial method [16] doesn't have good transferability. The result of C&W is not good, comparing with the performances of our method in adversarial training and black-box attacks. Table 3 illustrates that our method has the best attack ability among these attack methods. This is because we make full use of local attacks and optimization methods, which not only reduce the change of pixel values, but also stabilize the performance of the adversarial examples against neural networks. Applying the optimal method can essentially change the probability distribution of the adversarial examples, rather than just stay in the pixel-wise space.

In the experiment, we discover that adversarial training is less effective for our attack. We analyze the experiment results and conclude that our method based on the local attack and iterative optimization generates specific attack perturbations on the corresponding benign images. A great diversity of adversarial examples result in that adversarial perturbations do not have a uniform probability distribution. If we retrain the model after correcting the wrong labels of adversarial examples, CNN will break the original balance and lead to the classifiers less effective. Therefore, adversarial training is useless for the images generated in our method.

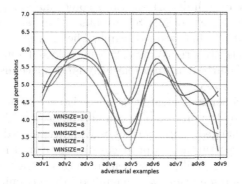

Fig. 3. The effect of WINSIZE on total perturbations in MNIST.

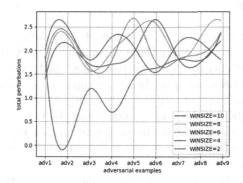

Fig. 4. The effect of WINSIZE on total perturbations in CIFAR-10.

Effect of Local Attack Pixels. To explore the effect of local attack pixels, we randomly select images from MNIST for experiment and generate 9 other adversarial examples by changing the number of local attack pixels. WINSIZE equals to top-k value and represents the maximum number of pixels changed. Figure 3 shows the effect of perturbed pixels of local attack, where WINSIZE denotes the number of selected pixels for local attack. Different WINSIZE shows same tendency in perturbations intensity. This demonstrates that the relative perturbations are required to be stable and able to generate different adversarial examples under the same condition. The perturbations intensity has a growth trend when the WINSIZE increasing. However, opposite situation also occurs in local parts since the size of WINSIZE limit the number of changed pixels.

Thus, it can not exceed the WINSIZE per iteration, but may be smaller than WINSIZE during iterations. We also randomly select images in CIFAR-10 for experiment and generate 9 other adversarial examples by changing the size of WINSIZE as shown Fig. 4. When the WINSIZE equals to 2, our method cannot achieve 100% attacks, this value cannot be selected. When we select a relatively large WINSIZE, the overall distortion will become smaller and is different from MNIST. Because the images of MNIST are binary images. We choose the small WINSIZE equivalent to a fine-grained search. The images of CIFAR-10 are color images. When a relatively large WINSIZE being selected, our method can select relatively smooth perturbations in a relatively large space instead of sharp perturbations in a small space.

The above experiments illustrate that the existence of the adversarial examples may be caused by the process of accumulating errors. After some few pixels of benign images changed, these images may be separated from the original manifolds when the perturbations propagate in the neural networks. Although adversarial examples are similar to the benign images in the pixel-wise, the difference of high-level representations are magnified in the training process, leading to the existence of adversarial examples.

5   Conclusions

Adversarial examples limit the application of convolutional neural networks. Most present attack methods either limit the number of perturbed pixels without outstanding attack ability or add redundant noise which are easy to be detected.

In this work, we proposed a method with combination of forward and backward propagation to generate adversarial examples. Our method provides a impressive balance between the local attack and the overall optimal issue. We utilize the local attack to control the perturbations intensity of each iteration and improve the loss function to adjust the perturbations quasi-imperceptible. The experimental results illustrate that our method performs stably and efficiently. Due to its stable and efficient performance, our method can be utilized to generate the adversarial examples for estimation the robustness of classifiers.

Acknowledgements. This work is supported by Guangdong Province Key Area R&D Program under grant No. 2018B010113001, the R&D Program of Shenzhen under grant No. JCYJ20170307153157440 and the Shenzhen Key Lab of Software Defined Networking under grant No. ZDSYS20140509172959989, and the National Natural Science Foundation of China under Grant No. 61802220.

References

1. Krizhevsky, A.: Learning multiple layers of features from tiny images. CoRR (2009)
2. Goodfellow, I., Kurakin, A., Bengio, S.: Adversarial machine learning at scale. arXiv:1611.01236

3. Carlini, N., Wagner, D.: Towards evaluating the robustness of neural networks. In: IEEE Symposium on Security and Privacy (SP), pp. 39–57 (2017). https://doi.org/10.1109/SP.2017.49

4. Tsipras, D., Schmidt, L., Engstrom, L., Madry, A.: A rotation and a translation suffice: fooling CNNs with simple transformations. CoRR, abs/1712.02779 (2017)

5. Yu, D., Hinton, G., Deng, L., et al.: Deep neural networks for acoustic modeling in speech recognition. The shared views of four research groups. IEEE Sig. Process. Mag. **29**(6), 82–97 (2012). https://doi.org/10.1109/MSP.2012.2205597

6. Ghahramani, Z., Dziugaite, G.K., Roy, D.: A study of the effect of JPG compression on adversarial images. arXiv:1608.00853

7. Girshick, R., Donahue, J., Darrell, T., et al.: Rich feature hierarchies for accurate object detection and semantic segmentation. In: IEEE Conference on Computer Vision and Pattern Recognition, pp. 580–587. IEEE Computer Society (2014). https://doi.org/10.1109/CVPR.2014.81

8. Goodfellow, I.J., Shlens, J., Szegedy, C.: Explaining and harnessing adversarial examples. Comput. Sci. (2014)

9. Guo, C., Rana, M., Cisse, M., et al.: Countering adversarial images using input transformations. arXiv:1711.00117

10. Huang, S., Papernot, N., Goodfellow, I., Duan, Y., Abbeel, P.: Adversarial attacks on neural network policies. arXiv preprint arXiv:1702.02284 (2017)

11. Fabry, E., Lu, J., Sibai, H., Forsyth, D.: No need to worry about adversarial examples in object detection in autonomous vehicles. arXiv:1707.03501

12. Kurakin, A., Goodfellow, I., Bengio, S.: Adversarial examples in the physical world (2017)

13. Bengio, S., Kurakin, A., Goodfellow, I.: Adversarial machine learning at scale. arXiv:1611.01236

14. Cortes, C., Lecun, Y.: The MNIST database of handwritten digits. CoRR (2010)

15. Liu, Q., Liu, T., Liu, Z., Wang, Y., Jin, Y., Wen, W.: Security analysis and enhancement of model compressed deep learning systems under adversarial attacks. In: Asia and South Pacific Design Automation Conference, pp. 721–726 (2018). https://doi.org/10.1109/ASPDAC.2018.8297407

16. Miyato, T., Maeda, S., Koyama, M., Nakae, K., Ishii, S.: Distributional smoothing with virtual adversarial training. Computer Science (2015)

17. Fawzi, A., Fawzi, O., Moosavi-Dezfooli, S.M., Frossard, P.: Universal adversarial perturbations. In: IEEE Conference on Computer Vision and Pattern Recognition (CVPR), pp. 86–94 (2017). https://doi.org/10.1109/CVPR.2017.17

18. Moosavi-Dezfooli, S.-M., Fawzi, A., Frossard, P.: DeepFool: a simple and accurate method to fool deep neural networks. In: IEEE Conference on Computer Vision and Pattern Recognition (CVPR), pp. 2574–2582 (2016). https://doi.org/10.1109/CVPR.2016.282

19. Papernot, N., McDaniel, P., Wu, X., Jha, S., Swami, A.: Distillation as a defense to adversarial perturbations against deep neural networks. In: 2016 IEEE Symposium on Security and Privacy (SP), pp. 582–597. IEEE (2016). https://doi.org/10.1109/SP.2016.41

20. Papernot, N., Mcdaniel, P.: The limitations of deep learning in adversarial settings. In: IEEE European Symposium on Security and Privacy, pp. 372–387. IEEE (2016). https://doi.org/10.1109/EuroSP.2016.36

21. Zisserman, A., Simonyan, K.: Very deep convolutional networks for large-scale image recognition. Computer Science (2014)

22. Vargas, D.V., Su, J., Kouichi, S.: One pixel attack for fooling deep neural networks. IEEE Trans. Evol. Comput. (2019). https://doi.org/10.1109/TEVC.2019.2890858

23. Szegedy, C., et al.: Intriguing properties of neural networks. In: International Conference on Learning Representations (ICLR) (2014)
24. Yamada, Y., Shaham, U., Negahban, S.: Understanding adversarial training: increasing local stability of neural nets through robust optimization. arXiv:1511.05432

Incremental Learning of GAN for Detecting Multiple Adversarial Attacks

Zibo Yi[(✉)], Jie Yu, Shasha Li, Yusong Tan, and Qingbo Wu

College of Computer, National University of Defense Technology,
Changsha, Hunan Province, China
{yizibo14,yj,shashali,yusong.tan,qingbo.wu}@nudt.edu.cn

Abstract. Neural networks are vulnerable to adversarial attack. Carefully crafted small perturbations can cause misclassification of neural network classifiers. As adversarial attack is a serious potential problem in many neural network based applications and new attacks always come up, it's urgent to explore the detection strategies that can adapt new attacks quickly. Moreover, the detector is hard to train with limited samples. To solve these problems, we propose a GAN based incremental learning framework with Jacobian-based data augmentation to detect adversarial samples. To prove the proposed framework works on multiple adversarial attacks, we implement FGSM, LocSearchAdv, PSO-based attack on MNIST and CIFAR-10 dataset. The experiments show that our detection framework performs well on these adversarial attacks.

Keywords: Incremental learning · Generative neural network ·
Adversarial attacks · Jacobian-based data augmentation

1 Introduction

Artificial intelligence nowadays are believed to be powered by neural network based deep learning. Recent research [1,13–15] show that neural networks are vulnerable to adversarial attack. By adding tiny perturbations to a sample, the recognition of neural network classifiers can be misled. This type of attack is called adversarial attack. For example, autonomous vehicles are easily to be misguided by the traffic signs which are perturbed by adversarial attack, resulting in traffic accidents [15]. Unauthorized personnel may hack biometrics identification system with adversarial samples [2]. Adversarial attack is a serious potential problem in many neural network based applications and it is urgent to research the adversarial attacks and it's defense strategies.

There exist various adversarial attacks that demonstrate neural networks can be misled in many ways. Two categories of neural network classifiers are studied, white-box and black-box. A white-box classifier is the one that reveal all the details in the classifier, including network architecture and weights. A black-box classifier is the one that conceal the details in the classifier, and only leave

© Springer Nature Switzerland AG 2019
I. V. Tetko et al. (Eds.): ICANN 2019, LNCS 11729, pp. 673–684, 2019.
https://doi.org/10.1007/978-3-030-30508-6_53

the classification interface to users. Either white-box neural network classifier or black-box is vulnerable. For example, Goodfellow *et al.* [5] propose fast gradient sign method (FGSM), which calculates the gradient of white-box classifier to find adversarial samples. Papernot *et al.* [16] propose Jacobian-based saliency map attack (JSMA), which measures each pixel's influence to the white-box. Modifying the most influential pixels will quickly find adversarial samples. As for the black-box classifier, Papernot *et al.* [15] discover the adversarial attacks' transferability and successfully attack a black-box through attacking its white-box substitute.

Researchers propose several defense [17,20,21] or detection [3,4,10,12] strategies against adversarial samples. Even though the defense strategies improve robustness which makes successfully attacking more difficult, adversarial samples can still mislead classifier with more perturbations. Moreover, the enhancement of robustness may cause less precision of the classifier. As for the existing detection approaches, they usually have difficulty in general utilization for the reason that each of them only considers one kind of adversarial attack. Another challenge of adversarial sample detection is the quantity of samples. Attackers tend to use partial adversarial samples when they conduct a new kind of attack. The detector is hard to train with limited samples.

We propose a Generative Adversarial Network (GAN) based incremental learning framework to tackle the above difficulties. We train the generator and detector in GAN with natural images. The detector can tell apart natural images and fake ones after training. Further, the incremental training is used for learning the pattern of adversarial samples. The detector which learns from specific pattern will recognize the corresponding adversarial samples. By using the Jacobian-based data augmentation technology we solve the problem of limited samples. To test the performance of the proposed framework, we generate adversarial samples of 3 adversarial attack and detect them. In summary, this work makes the following contributions:

- We propose a GAN incremental learning framework to detect multiple adversarial samples. With Jacobian-based data augmentation applied, the problem of learning from limited adversarial samples are solved.
- We implement 3 adversarial attacks (FGSM, LocSearchAdv, PSO-based attack) and generate adversarial samples on MNIST and CIFAR-10 dataset. The experiments show that our framework effectively detect multiple adversarial attacks on multiple image recognition applications.

2   Related Work

Adversarial attacks on neural networks are a hot topic in recent years. In 2013, Szegedy *et al.* [18] point out neural networks are vulnerable to adversarial samples. They formalize the adversarial attack as a constrained optimization problem, and solve it using L-BGFS. The research is followed by Goodfellow *et al.* [5], who propose the fast gradient sign method (FGSM), a simple but effective method to generate adversarial samples. Kurakin *et al.* [8] propose basic iterative method (BIM), which iteratively perturb the sample with "fast gradient sign". All the above methods are white box attack. To attack black box neural networks, Papernot *et al.* [15] propose transferability, using which they can craft a substitute of the black box. Attacking the substitute with white box attack can also generate the adversarial samples that can attack the original neural network.

Several researchers discuss defense technologies as they propose adversarial attack. Szegedy *et al.* [18] find out that the neural networks with less activated neurons are not easily to be perturbed by tiny modifications. It is more robust to quantify the activated neurons and integrate it to the optimization objective. Goodfellow *et al.* [5] propose a defense method after they present FGSM. The original optimization objective function introduces a regularization item, which measures the loss of samples' gradient ascent. Training with new objective function, the robustness is improved.

Several neural networks for defending and detecting adversarial attacks are proposed. Gu *et al.* [6] propose deep contractive network. It aims at decreasing the gradient of layers' outputs, which makes the model more "smoothly". Attackers have to make more modifications to successfully mislead the model. Magnet [11] is a two pronged defending method. For those samples with tiny perturbations, Magnet can denoise them. As for the samples with massive perturbations, Magnet directly report them. Gong *et al.* [4] use a binary neural network classifier to tell apart adversarial samples and the normal ones. Xu *et al.* [19] demonstrate that sample's most features are redundant for classification. Feature squeezing can reduce the degrees of freedom available to an adversary.

3 GAN Based Multiple Adversarial Attacks Detection

In this section, we present our incremental GAN learning approach for adversarial sample detection. Before we present the framework, some preliminary about GAN and it's training are introduced. Then the incremental GAN learning framework are described in detail. The last part of this section is Jacobian-based data augmentation, using which we can train the framework with limited adversarial samples.

3.1 Preliminary

Generative adversarial network consists of generator and discriminator. The generator can generate samples that are similar to real ones through learning the distribution of real samples. We denote a neural network generator with G. G takes a vector z from latent space as input and outputs a fake sample x'. The discriminator D takes sample as input and outputs the possibility that the sample is real. To train G and D, GAN optimize the following objective function with D and G being constant alternately.

$$\min_{G} \max_{D} V(D, G) = \mathbb{E}_{x \sim p_{data}(x)}[\log D(x)] + \mathbb{E}_{z \sim p_z(z)}[\log(1 - D(G(z)))] \quad (1)$$

When we optimize D, the G is constant. Then the objective function becomes

$$\max_D V(D) = \frac{1}{m} \sum_{i=1}^{m} [\log D(\boldsymbol{x}^{(i)}) + \log(1 - D(\boldsymbol{x}'^{(i)}))]. \tag{2}$$

The $\boldsymbol{x}$ and $\boldsymbol{x}'$ are real sample and sample generated by G. The GAN use m samples averaged to substitute expectation value calculation. The D which makes the largest V is the best for distinguishing real samples and the fake ones. When we optimize G, the D is constant. Then the objective function becomes

$$\min_G V(G) = \frac{1}{m} \sum_{i=1}^{m} \log[1 - D(G(\boldsymbol{z}^{(i)}))]. \tag{3}$$

The G which makes the smallest V is the best for generating fake samples.

3.2   The Incremental GAN Learning Framework

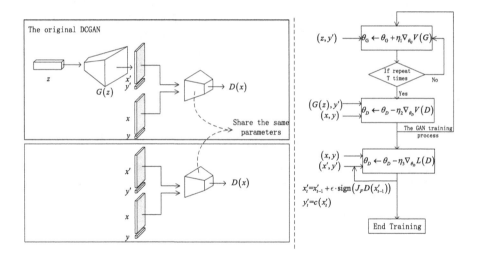

Fig. 1. The incremental GAN learning framework. The left part of the figure depicts the schematic layout of the framework and the right side shows it's flowchart. We implement incremental training of the discriminator by parameters sharing. We trained a preliminary discriminator using the original DCGAN (See the original DCGAN in the layout and the GAN training process in the flowchart). Then the discriminator are incremental trained using (x, y), (x', y'), which are generated with Jacobian-based data augmentation technique.

For image recognition, adversarial samples are fake images that generated through modifying the real images. Thus, the discriminator D shall give a rough judgment on adversarial samples. However, the direct use of D has poor detection performance. The difficulty of using D for detection is that the modification of samples is often very tiny. Besides, D has not learned the modification pattern of adversarial attack.

To solve the above problems, we proposed an incremental training framework of GAN for adversarial samples detection. Figure 1 shows the GAN incremental learning framework. The framework includes a DCGAN and a copy of discriminator D. DCGAN (Deep Convolutional Generative Adversarial Network) is an improved version of GAN for generating better fake images. In our incremental learning framework, label information is also important because it can be used for judging whether an image is fake. The reason is that an adversarial sample always disguise itself to be different from its own label. The original DCGAN can only accept the hidden space sample z and the real sample as input. Our framework provide additional inputs entrance for adversarial samples (x', y') and normal samples (x, y).

The incremental learning framework includes a DCGAN and a copy of discriminator D. Notice that the two discriminators share the same set of parameters and synchronize the other when one changes. The discriminator of the original pre-trained DCGAN has a preliminary ability of adversarial samples detection. Then the incremental training strengthens the discriminating ability on one specific attack through training the model with corresponding attack's samples.

The workflow of our framework includes two parts (see the right side of Fig. 1): the GAN training process and incremental training process. In GAN training process, generator G and discriminator D are trained alternately. Let θ_G and θ_D denote the parameters of G and D. To optimize the objective function in Eqs. 2 and 3, we update θ_G and θ_D with $\theta_G \leftarrow \theta_G + \eta_1 \nabla_{\theta_G} V(G)$ and $\theta_D \leftarrow \theta_D - \eta_2 \nabla_{\theta_D} V(D)$. Note that in GAN training process, θ_D is updated one time while θ_G is updated T times. In incremental training process, the discriminator D is trained with additional normal samples (x, y) and adversarial samples (x', y'). From Sect. 3.1, we learn that G is constant when optimizing D. So G is omitted in D's objective function. The objective function is

$$\min_D \mathcal{L}(D) = -\frac{1}{m} \sum_{i=1}^{m} [\log D(x^{(i)}, y^{(i)}) + \log(1 - D(x'^{(i)}, y'^{(i)}))]. \quad (4)$$

In incremental training process, we update θ_D with $\theta_D \leftarrow \theta_D - \eta_3 \nabla_{\theta_D} \mathcal{L}(D)$. Under real detection circumstances, The adversarial samples (x', y') are usually limited. We propose an iterative method to craft sufficient adversarial samples for incremental training. Let c denote the classifier the adversary tends to attack. In each iteration, the new adversarial samples are crafted with the following equation.

$$x'_t = x'_{t-1} + \epsilon \cdot \text{sign}(J_F D(x'_{t-1}))$$
$$y'_t = c(x'_t) \quad (5)$$

We will describe the dataset augmentation method in detail in Sect. 3.3.

3.3   The Jacobian-Based Data Augmentation for Incremental Training

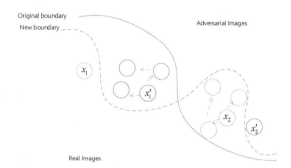

Fig. 2. The illustration of Jacobian-based incremental learning. The discriminator separates the adversarial images and the real images with the classification boundary. x_1, x_2 are adversarial images while x_1' and x_2' are real images. Both x_1' and x_2 are misclassified by the original discriminator. Incremental training adjust the boundary with additional samples. The arrows in the figure represent the data generation process using Jacobian-based data augmentation (See Eq. 5). After incremental training, the boundary is adjusted to obtain the correct classification result.

When attacking deep learning systems, attackers usually use only a few adversarial samples to mislead it. Therefore, the defenders often cannot get a large number of adversarial samples. The problem is how to expand the adversarial sample dataset. We propose a data augmentation method based on Jacobian matrix to expand the incremental training dataset.

The Jacobin matrix of $D(x)$ is the direction of the sample x facing the classification boundary. For each (x, y) in dataset $\mathbb{D}$, we apply Jacobian-based data augmentation with Eq. 5. We demonstrate the data augmentation in Fig. 2, both x_1' and x_2 are misclassified by the original discriminator. After two iterations of incremental training, the new boundary of the discriminator (the dashed line) distinguishes both normal and adversarial samples. The iterative process of two incremental training steps are shown by the yellow arrow in Fig. 2. The first augmentation (the solid yellow arrows) let the two misclassified samples x_1' and x_2 produced new samples. These samples incrementally train the discriminator D to form a new classification boundary. The second augmentation (the dashed yellow arrows) continuing produce new samples. Then the boundary is adjusted again after incremental training. After that the boundary can correctly distinguish the adversarial samples from the normal ones.

Algorithm 1 is the incremental learning part of our framework. This method uses a small number of initial adversarial samples, which will be augmented afterwards. The size of the normal sample set is n times that of the initial adversarial sample set. The reason why we use larger normal sample dataset is that the normal samples are easily obtained and more normal samples for

---

Algorithm 1. Jacobian-based incremental learning of GAN

Input:

The adversarial sample dataset, $\mathbb{D}_A$;

The size of initial adversarial sample dataset, $k = |\mathbb{D}_A|$;

The dataset (only contains normal samples) of GAN, $\mathbb{D}_N$;

The parameters of discriminator, θ_D;

The normal dataset larger than initial adversarial dataset, n;

The number of incremental training rounds, r;

The step size, ϵ;

Output:

The updated parameters of discriminator, θ_D;

1: **for each** t **in** $[1, 2, ..., r]$ **do**

2:     Random split $\mathbb{D}_N$ into $\mathbb{D}_N^{(1)}, \mathbb{D}_N^{(2)}, ..., \mathbb{D}_N^{(n)}$

3:     **for each** j **in** $[1, 2, ..., n]$ **do**

4:         $\theta_D \leftarrow \theta_D - \eta_3 \nabla_{\theta_D}(-\frac{1}{k}\sum_{i=1}^{k}[\log D(\boldsymbol{x}^{(i)}, y^{(i)}) + \log(1 - D(\boldsymbol{x}'^{(i)}, y'^{(i)}))])$,

            where $(\boldsymbol{x}^{(i)}, y^{(i)}) \in \mathbb{D}_N^{(j)}$, $(\boldsymbol{x}'^{(i)}, y'^{(i)}) \in \mathbb{D}_A$

5:     **end for**

6:     Replace each $(\boldsymbol{x}'_t, y'_t) \in \mathbb{D}_A$ with $(\boldsymbol{x}'_{t+1}, y'_{t+1})$

        where $\boldsymbol{x}'_{t+1} = \boldsymbol{x}'_t + \epsilon \cdot \text{sign}(J_F D(\boldsymbol{x}'_t)), y'_{t+1} = c(\boldsymbol{x}'_{t+1})$

7: **end for**

8: **return** θ_D

---

training will reduce the false positive. Line 4 in Algorithm 1 is the incremental training step of discriminator D. The parameters of D are updated with gradient descent. Line 6 in Algorithm 1 is Jacobian-based data augmentation. Equation 5 is applied to generate new adversarial samples for the next incremental training iteration.

4 Experiments

4.1 Dataset and Experiment Setup

We use MNIST and CIFAR-10 as datasets for adversarial sample detection. The MNIST dataset includes 60,000 training and 10,000 testing handwritten digits images. Each image has a label from digit 0 to 9. For MNIST handwritten digits recognition task, LeNet [9] has the best performance. We implement the standard LeNet two convolutional layers architecture with TensorFlow. After training, LeNet has 99.2% accuracy on MNIST digital recognition test set. The CIFAR-10 dataset includes 50,000 training and 10,000 testing images in 10 different classes. We use the open source DenseNet[1] proposed by Huang *et al.* [7] to recognize the CIFAR-10 testing images and achieves 94.8% accuracy. After that, several white box and black box adversarial attacks were implemented to attack LeNet and DenseNet. The attacks include FGSM [5], LocSearchAdv [13] and our proposed PSO-based attack. These attacks are detailed described in Sect. 4.2.

---

[1] https://github.com/liuzhuang13/DenseNet.

After attacking, the adversarial samples are generated. Then we use our proposed framework to test the normal samples and adversarial samples of the above attacks.

The experiments run on a work station with i7-5930k CPU and 2 NVIDIA GeForce TITAN GPU. The operating system is Ubuntu 16.04. TensorFlow 1.4.1 deep learning framework is employed for neural networks construction.

4.2   Adversarial Attacks

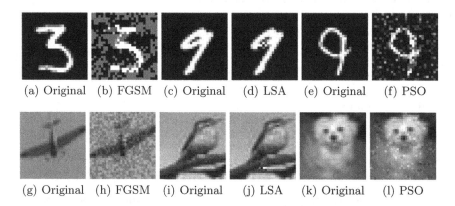

(a) Original   (b) FGSM   (c) Original   (d) LSA   (e) Original   (f) PSO

(g) Original   (h) FGSM   (i) Original   (j) LSA   (k) Original   (l) PSO

Fig. 3. The examples of original images and the three attacks' adversarial samples. The first row shows the images from MNIST while the images in second row are from CIFAR-10. Three adversarial attacks (FGSM, LSA, PSO) are used to perturb the original images. The three attacks use different modification patterns which cause the images are classified incorrectly.

We implemented three adversarial attacks on MNIST and CIFAR-10: FGSM, LocSearchAdv, PSO-based Attack. The implementation of these three attacks are described below.

FGSM uses gradient $\nabla_x \mathcal{L}(x, y)$, where $\mathcal{L}$ represents the loss function of the classifier and y represents the label of x. Let x^* denote the adversarial sample. $x^* = x + \epsilon \cdot \text{sign}(\nabla_x \mathcal{L}(x, y))$. It means that x move along the fastest direction of increasing the loss function. A sample with greater loss function is more easily to be misclassified. In the implementation, TensorFlow's API tf.gradients is used to find the gradient. We apply FGSM to each sample in test set of MNIST and CIFAR-10. Most of the samples are misclassified by LeNet or DenseNet when proper hyper-parameters are set (we set $\epsilon = 0.5$). For the recognition of MNIST and CIFAR-10, the successful rate of FGSM attack is above 90%. We will use FGSM's normal and adversarial samples for detection in Sect. 4.3.

LocSearchAdv is a method based on iterative local search. Images are usually represented by $x \in [0, 255]^{\mathbb{S}}$, where $\mathbb{S} = width \times height \times 3$ (3 means RGB 3 channels). As x is a $\mathbb{S}$ shaped tensor, it need to be flatten into a vector. Let

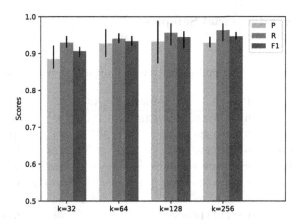

Fig. 4. Detection performance of FGSM's adversarial samples on MNIST dataset. Precision, Recall, and F1-score (P, R, F1) are calculated in 5 times repeated experiments. The macro-averaged P, R, F1 are shown in the figure. The maximum and minimum P, R, F1 in the multiple experiments were also shown. k values in this figure are the number of initial adversarial samples for incremental learning (See Algorithm 1). We can conclude that even with only a small number of adversarial samples, a fine detection performance will be obtained with Jacobian-based data augmentation.

$\sigma(x)$ denote the neighborhood of flatted x. Using $x_{t+1} = \arg\min_{a \in \sigma(x_t)} P_y(a)$ for each iteration to modify x until x can mislead classifier or reach the iteration limitation. P_y is the probability that x is classified to class y. In the implementation, the iteration limitation is set to 50, which means that most images are modified less than 50 iterations until they mislead the classifier.

PSO-based attack is our proposed attack method based on particle swarm optimization. For classifier c, let δ denote the perturbation vector. we need to find the least perturbations to mislead classifier c. Thus, the problem is formalized as an optimization problem: $\min \delta$, subject to $c(x + \delta) \neq c(x)$. We employ PSO to solve the problem. There are multiple $\delta_i \in [-U, U]^{\mathbb{S}}$, which can be regarded as particles, are used for finding $\min \delta$. During the PSO algorithm, the δ_i is recorded if it satisfies $c(x + \delta_i) \neq c(x)$. Note that the perturbation δ_i has a search boundary U and has the same shape $\mathbb{S} = width \times height \times 3$ of x. A greater U has larger perturbations. In our implementation, the search boundary $U = 5$ and 100 particles are used.

Some examples before and after adversarial attacks are shown in Fig. 3. It can be seen from Fig. 3 that different attacks have different modification patterns of samples. FGSM simply modifies every pixel of the image. LocSearchAdv ("LSA" in Fig. 3 refers to "LocSearchAdv", avoiding too long names) tends to modify partial area. PSO-based attack adds some noise to the image. Different modification patterns cannot be identified using the same model parameter. Therefore, the incremental training are needed to continuously modify the model parameters in order to adapt new attacks.

4.3 Detecting Adversarial Samples

Table 1. The performance of multiple adversarial attacks detection on two datasets

Dataset	Attack	k	P	R	F1	Dataset	Attack	k	P	R	F1
MNIST	FGSM	32	0.885	0.929	0.906	CIFAR-10	FGSM	32	0.856	0.937	0.895
		64	0.927	0.940	0.933			64	0.927	0.899	0.913
		128	0.932	0.956	0.943			128	0.928	0.967	0.947
		256	0.929	0.963	0.945			256	0.917	0.968	0.942
		baseline	0.886	0.908	0.896			baseline	0.904	0.834	0.868
	LSA	32	0.865	0.769	0.814		LSA	32	0.834	0.822	0.828
		64	0.837	0.819	0.827			64	0.805	0.869	0.835
		128	0.875	0.846	0.860			128	0.864	0.878	0.871
		256	0.930	0.877	0.902			256	0.899	0.905	0.902
		baseline	0.878	0.800	0.837			baseline	0.909	0.669	0.771
	PSO	32	0.887	0.944	0.914		PSO	32	0.861	0.948	0.903
		64	0.913	0.943	0.927			64	0.867	0.967	0.914
		128	0.906	0.970	0.936			128	0.928	0.967	0.947
		256	0.964	0.982	0.972			256	0.935	0.981	0.957
		baseline	0.895	0.917	0.905			baseline	0.894	0.910	0.902

The samples in MNSIT and CIFAR-10 test sets are attacked by the above attacks, generating adversarial samples. For each attack in each data set, 32, 64, 128, 256 adversarial samples are taken for incremental learning. For example, Fig. 4 is the detection performance of FGSM on MNIST dataset. The adversarial samples recognition precision, recall, and F1-score are calculated. Using Algorithm 1 to train the proposed framework with a small number of adversarial samples and a large number of normal samples on the training set (based on our hypothesis: the adversarial sample is not easy to obtain and the normal sample is easy to obtain). Experiment 5 times and use macro averaging to get the final precision, recall, and F1-score.

$$P_{macro} = \frac{1}{n} \sum_{i=1}^{n} P_i \tag{6}$$

$$R_{macro} = \frac{1}{n} \sum_{i=1}^{n} R_i \tag{7}$$

$$F1_{macro} = \frac{2 \times P_{macro} \times R_{macro}}{P_{macro} + R_{macro}} \tag{8}$$

The final averaged P, R, and F1 of the multiple experiments are shown in Fig. 4. It can be seen from the figure that even if the number of adversarial samples is small, the framework can still recognize adversarial samples well. Under small sample conditions, the performance will be better if more samples were given. For the reason that more examples will let the framework learn more attack patterns.

The macro averaged P, R, and F1 of three attacks on the two datasets are shown in Table 1. This experiment uses incremental training without data augmentation as the baseline. The baseline method use 256 adversarial samples for incremental learning. It can be seen from Table 1 that for FGSM and PSO-based attacks, even a very small number of examples can be better than baseline through data augmentation. This shows that the data augmentation technology can significantly enhance the performance on adversarial sample detection under small sample conditions. The adversarial samples of LocSearchAdv is more difficult to recognize than FGSM and PSO-based Attack, because local modifications to the image may still leave the image in the normal images' probability distribution manifold.

5 Conclusions and Future Work

In this paper, we propose a GAN based incremental learning framework to detect multiple adversarial attacks. The GAN framework is improved to let discriminator learn the modification pattern of adversarial attack. By using the Jacobian-based data augmentation technology we solve the problem of training from limited samples. The experiments show that our incremental learning approach can detect multiple adversarial samples.

It is obvious that more adversarial samples will improve detection performance. However, the recognition performance will not improve further after a certain number of samples are given. Another drawback of our approach is that the detection of LocSearchAdv is not so well. The mainly reason is that the samples generated by LocSearchAdv lie in the manifold of normal sample space. In the future, we will explore more robust approach to detect this kind of attacks and investigate how to get a better performance with more training samples.

Acknowledgments. This work is supported by the NSFC under Grant 61303190.

References

1. Akhtar, N., Mian, A.: Threat of adversarial attacks on deep learning in computer vision: a survey. IEEE Access **6**, 14410–14430 (2018)
2. Biggio, B., Russu, P., Didaci, L., Roli, F., et al.: Adversarial biometric recognition: a review on biometric system security from the adversarial machine-learning perspective. IEEE Signal Process. Mag. **32**(5), 31–41 (2015)
3. Gao, J., Wang, B., Lin, Z., Xu, W., Qi, Y.: DeepCloak: masking deep neural network models for robustness against adversarial samples. arXiv preprint arXiv:1702.06763 (2017)
4. Gong, Z., Wang, W., Ku, W.S.: Adversarial and clean data are not twins. arXiv preprint arXiv:1704.04960 (2017)

5. Goodfellow, I.J., Shlens, J., Szegedy, C.: Explaining and harnessing adversarial examples. arXiv preprint arXiv:1412.6572 (2014)

6. Gu, S., Rigazio, L.: Towards deep neural network architectures robust to adversarial examples. arXiv preprint arXiv:1412.5068 (2014)

7. Huang, G., Liu, Z., van der Maaten, L., Weinberger, K.Q.: Densely connected convolutional networks. In: Proceedings of the IEEE Conference on Computer Vision and Pattern Recognition (2017)

8. Kurakin, A., Goodfellow, I.J., Bengio, S.: Adversarial examples in the physical world. In: Artificial Intelligence Safety and Security, pp. 99–112. Chapman and Hall/CRC (2018)

9. LeCun, Y., Haffner, P., Bottou, L., Bengio, Y.: Object recognition with gradient-based learning. Shape, Contour and Grouping in Computer Vision. LNCS, vol. 1681, pp. 319–345. Springer, Heidelberg (1999). https://doi.org/10.1007/3-540-46805-6_19

10. Lu, J., Issaranon, T., Forsyth, D.: SafetyNet: detecting and rejecting adversarial examples robustly. In: Proceedings of the IEEE International Conference on Computer Vision, pp. 446–454 (2017)

11. Meng, D., Chen, H.: MagNet: a two-pronged defense against adversarial examples. In: Proceedings of the 2017 ACM SIGSAC Conference on Computer and Communications Security, pp. 135–147. ACM (2017)

12. Metzen, J.H., Genewein, T., Fischer, V., Bischoff, B.: On detecting adversarial perturbations. arXiv preprint arXiv:1702.04267 (2017)

13. Narodytska, N., Kasiviswanathan, S.: Simple black-box adversarial attacks on deep neural networks. In: 2017 IEEE Conference on Computer Vision and Pattern Recognition Workshops (CVPRW), pp. 1310–1318. IEEE (2017)

14. Nguyen, A., Yosinski, J., Clune, J.: Deep neural networks are easily fooled: high confidence predictions for unrecognizable images. In: Proceedings of the IEEE Conference on Computer Vision and Pattern Recognition, pp. 427–436 (2015)

15. Papernot, N., McDaniel, P., Goodfellow, I., Jha, S., Celik, Z.B., Swami, A.: Practical black-box attacks against machine learning. In: Proceedings of the 2017 ACM on Asia Conference on Computer and Communications Security, pp. 506–519. ACM (2017)

16. Papernot, N., McDaniel, P., Jha, S., Fredrikson, M., Celik, Z.B., Swami, A.: The limitations of deep learning in adversarial settings. In: 2016 IEEE European Symposium on Security and Privacy (EuroSP), pp. 372–387. IEEE (2016)

17. Papernot, N., McDaniel, P., Wu, X., Jha, S., Swami, A.: Distillation as a defense to adversarial perturbations against deep neural networks. In: 2016 IEEE Symposium on Security and Privacy (SP), pp. 582–597. IEEE (2016)

18. Szegedy, C., et al.: Intriguing properties of neural networks. arXiv preprint arXiv:1312.6199 (2013)

19. Xu, W., Evans, D., Qi, Y.: Feature squeezing mitigates and detects Carlini/Wagner adversarial examples. arXiv preprint arXiv:1705.10686 (2017)

20. Zantedeschi, V., Nicolae, M.I., Rawat, A.: Efficient defenses against adversarial attacks. In: Proceedings of the 10th ACM Workshop on Artificial Intelligence and Security, pp. 39–49. ACM (2017)

21. Zheng, S., Song, Y., Leung, T., Goodfellow, I.: Improving the robustness of deep neural networks via stability training. In: Proceedings of the IEEE Conference on Computer Vision and Pattern Recognition, pp. 4480–4488 (2016)

Evaluating Defensive Distillation for Defending Text Processing Neural Networks Against Adversarial Examples

Marcus Soll$^{(\boxtimes)}$ (ID), Tobias Hinz (ID), Sven Magg (ID), and Stefan Wermter (ID)

Knowledge Technology, Department of Informatics, Universität Hamburg,
Vogt-Koelln-Str. 30, 22527 Hamburg, Germany
{2soll,hinz,magg,wermter}@informatik.uni-hamburg.de
https://www.inf.uni-hamburg.de/en/inst/ab/wtm

Abstract. Adversarial examples are artificially modified input samples which lead to misclassifications, while not being detectable by humans. These adversarial examples are a challenge for many tasks such as image and text classification, especially as research shows that many adversarial examples are transferable between different classifiers. In this work, we evaluate the performance of a popular defensive strategy for adversarial examples called defensive distillation, which can be successful in hardening neural networks against adversarial examples in the image domain. However, instead of applying defensive distillation to networks for image classification, we examine, for the first time, its performance on text classification tasks and also evaluate its effect on the transferability of adversarial text examples. Our results indicate that defensive distillation only has a minimal impact on text classifying neural networks and does neither help with increasing their robustness against adversarial examples nor prevent the transferability of adversarial examples between neural networks.

Keywords: Adversarial examples · Defensive distillation ·
Text classification · Convolutional neural network · Robustness

1 Introduction

One of the main goals in neural network research is the creation of robust models, especially against noise in the input data. A special form of noise are so-called adversarial examples, first discovered by Szegedy et al. [24]. This special type of noise is explicitly crafted to make a classifier misclassify samples without being detectable by humans (up to manipulating the sample so that it is classified to any class the adversary desires). This impact is increased for image classification by a property called transferability [24], which means that adversarial images created for one network have a high chance of being also misclassified by networks with different architectures or training sets.

© Springer Nature Switzerland AG 2019
I. V. Tetko et al. (Eds.): ICANN 2019, LNCS 11729, pp. 685–696, 2019.
https://doi.org/10.1007/978-3-030-30508-6_54

Recently, adversarial examples have also been created for deep neural networks used for text classification [11,22,27]. Such examples are challenging for a lot of cases, such as automatic indexing and text filtering. In automatic indexing, adversarial examples could change the index of a document, e.g. to push an advertising article into a different category, while in text filtering adversarial examples could change the filter outcome, e.g. change a spam e-mail so it is not detected by the spam filter. Since deep neural networks now achieve similar or better results compared to traditional methods for text classification (e.g. decision trees or support vector machines) [9,28,29], adversarial examples can prove problematic for real-world text classification applications.

Consequently, one of the main research goals with respect to adversarial examples is to develop defense mechanisms that make neural networks less susceptible to these adversarial examples. This is especially important for neural networks that are applied in sensitive application areas. The goal is, therefore, to harden these neural networks in order to prevent (adversarial) misclassifications. There already exist methods for hardening (deep) neural networks for image classification, such as defensive distillation [18,19], Batch Adjusted Network Gradients [21], or detecting adversarial examples like in SafetyNet [12]. However, such work is currently missing for deep neural networks for text classification.

In this work, we examine whether it is possible to transfer one popular defense mechanism, called defensive distillation [18,19], for adversarial image examples to the text classification domain in order to increase the robustness of the deep neural network against both adversarial examples and their transferability. We use the algorithm of Samanta and Mehta [22] for generating adversarial examples in the text domain and evaluate the effectiveness of defensive distillation on two datasets. Our experiments show no increased robustness of networks trained with defensive distillation for both, directly generated adversarial examples and adversarial examples generated for a network trained without defensive distillation. Additionally, our results show that defensive distillation is also not effective in preventing the transfer of adversarial examples from one network to another.

2   Related Work

Szegedy et al. [24] introduced adversarial examples for deep neural networks for image recognition. They also added the concept of transferability of adversarial examples between neural networks with different architectures and trained on different datasets. The first proposed method for generating adversarial examples of images is the *fast gradient sign method* (FGSM) by Goodfellow et al. [6]. To find these samples, the sign of the cost function's gradient (with respect to the input) is added to the original image. Because this basic approach of using the gradient is used by many of the current methods, the gradient has an important role for both generating adversarial examples and hardening networks.

As a result, many hardening methods perform *gradient masking* [20]. While this can help against white-box attacks (where the process generating the adversarial examples has access to the model), it does not work for methods based on probability [23] or black-box attacks. In black box attacks, the generating process has no direct access to the model and needs to generate adversarial examples by other means, e.g., by creating them on a different network and exploiting transferability. An overview of the current research on adversarial examples focusing mostly on image classification can be found in a survey by Akhtar and Mian [2], who summarize different popular generation methods (including real-world examples), the current understanding of adversarial examples, and different methods of increasing robustness of neural networks.

Since text is discrete rather than continuous (like images), methods for creating adversarial examples for images cannot directly be applied to the text domain [27]. In addition, small changes can be detected more easily by humans and can easily change the semantics of a sentence [27]. Liang et al. [11] were the first to examine adversarial examples for text-processing deep neural networks. They focused on so-called *Hot Training Phrases (HTP)* and *Hot Sample Phrases (HSP)*, which are phrases which contribute strongly to the determination of the predicted class. Both *HTP* and *HSP* are determined using the cost gradient of the prediction, and both are then used in conjunction for modifying the original sample to generate an adversarial example. Through insertion, modification and deletion as well as combining these three strategies, Liang et al. [11] are able to generate adversarial examples.

Samanta and Mehta [22] extend Liang et al.'s algorithm using the same three basic operations (insertion, modification, deletion). The algorithm works on a current word w_i which changes every round, ordered by the cost gradient (the word with the highest gradient is chosen first):

1. If the current word w_i is an adverb, it is deleted (because this operation often does not change the grammar of the sentence).
2. Else, a word p_i is chosen from a candidate pool P and processed as follows:
   (a) If the chosen word p_i is an adverb and the current word w_i is an adjective, the chosen word p_i is placed before the current word w_i.
   (b) Else, the current word w_i is replaced with the chosen word p_i.

The candidate pool is built from *synonyms, typos* and *genre specific keywords* which are words which can only be found in one class.

This was later followed up by more work as shown in a survey by Zhang et al. [27]. Besides different ways of generating adversarial examples, they also report two ways of increasing robustness used in the literature: data augmentation (where adversarial examples are included in the training set) and adversarial training (changing the learning function to include adversarial examples as additional regularization). However, most current defense mechanisms can be circumvented. Data augmentation sometimes helps to prevent adversarial examples generated with the same method as the augmented adversarial examples but fails to harden the network against adversarial examples generated by methods that were not used for the augmented dataset. Jia and Liang [8] present another example where data augmentation does not help against modified generation algorithms. As a result, developing effective defense mechanisms against adversarial examples in the text domain remains as a challenge for many real-world applications.

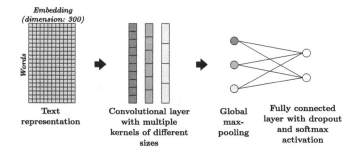

Fig. 1. Single-layer convolutional neural network model with different kernel sizes for text classification.

3   Methodology

3.1   Datasets

We used the following two datasets as the basis for generating adversarial examples in this paper and to evaluate the effects of defensive distillation:

AG's corpus of news articles: The AG's corpus of news articles is a dataset of news article metadata (including URL, title, category, description, and publication date) [1]. The metadata of almost 500.000 articles can be found in the XML version. Given this description, the task is to predict the category of the article. Similarly to Zhang et al. [28] we only consider the four largest categories: *World*, *Entertainment*, *Sports*, and *Business*. Because of the size of the dataset, only the first 4000 articles of each category are used for the training set (total: 16000) and the following 400 (total: 1600) for the test set.

Amazon movie reviews: The Amazon movie reviews dataset [13], taken from the Stanford Network Analysis Project [10], contains Amazon movie reviews from the years 1997-2002. The task is to rate the review as *good* (≥ 4.0) or *bad* (≤ 2.0) based on the text of the review. Because of the size of the dataset, 2000 reviews for each category were taken into consideration (total: 4000), with an additional 200 (total: 400) from each category for the test set.

3.2   Text Encoding

In order to process the text with a neural network, we need an appropriate representation of it. We chose to encode our words with word2vec [14], which encodes each word into a single vector containing continuous values. The resulting vectors are concatenated and used as input for our network. In this paper, we used the model trained by Mikolov et al. [15] on the Google news corpus to encode each word into a 300-dimensional vector.

3.3 Neural Network Model

We use a convolutional neural network (CNN) similar to the ones proposed by Kim [9] and Zhang and Wallace [29]. The architecture (see Fig. 1) consists of a single convolutional layer with multiple kernels, where the kernels have different window sizes (we use window sizes of 3, 4, and 5 in our network). The convolutional layer is followed by a global max-pooling and a fully connected layer with dropout. The advantage of this simple architecture is its fast training and high flexibility due to the different kernel sizes. All networks are trained using categorical cross-entropy as the loss function, as used by Zhang and Wallace [29].

AP - Pau Gasol and Spain won the Olympics' first matchup of NBA stars Sunday, easily beating Yao Ming and China. Gasol, who plays for the Memphis Grizzlies, had 21 points and 10 rebounds despite missing 6 minutes in the first quarter because of a Yukos bloody nose, and Spain won 83-58.

(a) The network's classification changes from *Sports* (correct) to *World* (incorrect) through the insertion of the word *"Yukos"* (highlighted in blue).

Denzel Washington will next direct The Great Debaters, a film based on a true story about an all-black high school debate eventing (team) in 1935, MTV reports

---

(b) The network's classification changes from *Entertainment* (correct) to *Sports* (incorrect) through the modification of the word *"team"* which is replaced by the word *"eventing"* (highlighted in red).

Fig. 2. Generated adversarial examples on the AG dataset.

3.4 Creating Adversarial Examples

Formally, the problem of finding an adversarial example can be defined as following: given a model f (e.g. a neural network) and an input x with the label y, find some noise ϵ so that $f(x + \epsilon) = y'$ with $y' \neq y$. To avoid detection by humans, the noise ϵ should be as small as possible.

In this work, we use a version of the algorithm by Samanta and Mehta [22], where the candidate pool P, from which possible words for insertion and replacement are drawn, was created from the following sources:

- *Synonyms* gathered from the WordNet dataset [5],
- *Typos* from a dataset [16] to ensure that the typos inserted are not recognized as artificial since they occur in normal texts written by humans, and
- *Keywords* specific for one input class which were found by looking at all training sentences and extracting words only found in one class.

Words from the candidate pool were only considered if the part of speech (e.g. *plural noun*) matches the target word. Examples of adversarial samples created in this paper can be seen in Figs. 2 and 3.

> Still haven't got it. I ordered this series a month ago, I received in the mail a ~~completely~~ trivia (different) movie addressed to someone in connecticut (I live in Louisiana) I then payed out of my own pocket to mail it to the address on the slip. I contacted the seller and they said they would work on getting me my product. Then yesterday I sent an email to see what was going on and they told me they have confirmation of delivery a month ago. So now I have to reexplain what happened to what I am assuming is a different employee.

(a) The network's classification changes from *bad* (correct) to *good* (incorrect) through the deletion of the word "*completely*" (crossed out) and the modification of the word "*different*" which is replaced by the word "*trivia*" (highlighted in red).

> Don't buy The quality is horrible. The screen shakes through the whole movie. The title screen excels (is) all in spanish even though the movie is in english. You would be better off recording it off the television.

(b) The network's classification changes from *bad* (correct) to *good* (incorrect) through the modification of the word "*is*" which is replaced by the word "*excels*" (highlighted in red).

> Still enjoy watching. Watching older movies, such as this one, can be quite enjoyable. There is no reliance on special effects, just what is needed to get to points. Otherwise this is a people movie commenting on Welles' vision of what may be. Rod Taylor plays his part well and for once was not the cavalier playboy as in others. A nice piece was the featurette that included an ONLY updated visit of Welles and his friend. Nothing fancy, good watching.

(c) The network's classification changes from *good* (correct) to *bad* (incorrect) through the through the insertion of the word "*ONLY*" (highlighted in blue).

Fig. 3. Generated adversarial examples on the Amazon movie dataset.

3.5   Defensive Distillation

Defensive distillation is a method proposed by Papernot et al. [18,19] and is based on the *distillation* method by Hinton et al. [7]. Both methods are based on the idea that knowledge from one neural network can be transferred to another neural network by using *soft labels* (the output of a previously trained network which represents the probability of the different classes) for the training instead of *hard labels* (where every data belongs to exactly one class). To achieve this effectively, the soft labels have to be calculated according to the following equation:

$$y_i = \frac{e^{l_i/T}}{\sum_i e^{l_i/T}},$$

where y_i is the probability of the i-th class, l_i the i-th *logit* (the inputs to the final softmax level) and T the *temperature*. The temperature is used to control how "soft" the resulting labels are. A high T ($T \to \infty$) means that a sample has a uniform probability of belonging to any class and a small T ($T \to 0^+$) means that the label becomes more similar to a one-hot vector. A special case is $T = 1$, which equals the normal *softmax*.

These soft labels can now be used to transfer knowledge from the original network to a distilled one. The original network is trained as usual and the soft labels are then calculated for the training set using a high temperature (e.g. Papernot et al. [18] suggest a temperature of $T = 20$). These soft labels are then used to train the distilled network, which has to use the same temperature in its last layer during training. After that, the temperature is set back to $T = 1$ and the distilled network can be used normally.

The difference between distillation and defensive distillation is that Hinton et al. [7] use distillation to transfer knowledge from a large neural network to a small one while retaining accuracy, whereas Papernot et al. [18, 19] use defensive distillation to transfer knowledge from one network to another one with the same size with the goal of making it harder to find adversarial examples for the distilled network. In this work, we use the variant described by Papernot et al. [18] and the network is trained on both the hard and the soft labels since this can significantly improve the process according to Hinton et al. [7].

4 Experiment Setup

To examine whether defensive distillation [18, 19] has any effects on adversarial examples for text classification, we trained neural networks with and without defensive distillation. After that, adversarial examples were generated for each of the networks[1]. Since the goal is to determine whether defensive distillation actually increases the robustness against adversarial examples, it is not necessary to find the optimal hyperparameters for each dataset. Therefore, the temperature $T = 20$ chosen for all experiments is the one used by Papernot et al. [18] for the MNIST dataset. To get a better overview over the influence of the temperature, the temperatures $T = 10$, $T = 30$ and $T = 40$ were also tested. For the training, both the soft labels and the hard labels were used, where the loss function consists of 10% of the hard label loss and 90% of the soft label loss. All networks were trained for 10 epochs since no notable improvement of accuracy occurred after that.

The question remains whether transferability is an inherent property of adversarial examples or if transferability can be prevented. Some recent research [26] suggests that it might be possible to prevent transferability, however, at the time of writing more research is needed in this direction. To test whether defensive distillation has any effect on transferability, we use adversarial examples created on the network trained without distillation and investigate whether these are also misclassified by the neural network trained with defensive distillation. An adversarial example is tested on the distilled network if the distilled network predicts the class of the corresponding unaltered input correctly.

---

[1] The software used for the experiments can be found online at https://github.com/Top-Ranger/text_adversarial_attack.

As a baseline, the same examples are tested on retrained networks without distillation.

Table 1. *Accuracies* of defensively distilled networks trained with different Temperatures T against test set of the specified dataset.

Dataset	$T = 10$	$T = 20$	$T = 30$	$T = 40$	w/o distillation
AG	0.733	0.728	0.739	0.744	0.759
Amazon movie	0.798	0.825	0.795	0.780	0.885

5 Results

The accuracies of the networks trained with and without defensive distillation are reported in Table 1. The performance of the networks trained with distillation is slightly worse compared to the networks trained without distillation, which is expected according to Papernot et al. [18]. The accuracy achieved in the experiment is comparable to others for the Amazon movie dataset (0.82−0.95 by Zhang et al. [28]) and slightly lower for the AG dataset (0.83−0.92 by Zhang et al. [28]).

When we look at the success rate of generating adversarial examples (see Table 2), the difference between the distilled and the non-distilled networks is marginal at best. Overall, the success rate of generating adversarial examples is high with 96% to 98% percent, with no visible difference between the different temperatures. This is surprising, since the experiments of Papernot et al. [18] showed improved robustness for image processing networks even for low temperatures.

When looking at the number of changes (Table 3), we can see that distillation makes it slightly more difficult to generate adversarial examples. The mean number of changes went up for all experiments (AG: 3.52 to 3.94 − 4.47, Amazon movie: 14.76 to 17.31 − 19.29). A similar increase can be seen in some instances for the median number of changes (Amazon movie: 3 to 4), however, these seem to be minor. The difference between the mean and the median can be explained if we look at the distribution in Fig. 4: while most generated adversarial examples only need a few changes, a small number of adversarial examples need a large number of changes increasing the mean value.

Table 2. *Success rates* of generating adversarial examples for networks trained with defensive distillation with different Temperatures T.

Dataset	$T = 10$	$T = 20$	$T = 30$	$T = 40$	w/o distillation
AG	0.976	0.981	0.972	0.978	0.982
Amazon movie	0.961	0.966	0.974	0.966	0.984

Table 3. *Number of changes* for generating adversarial examples with defensive distillation and Temperature T. Numbers in brackets are without distillation as comparison.

T	Dataset	Mean length of sentences in successful runs	Mean number of changes	Median number of changes	Mode number of changes
10	AG	32.12 (32.76)	4.47 (3.52)	2 (2)	1 (1)
	Amazon movie	148.85 (139.80)	19.29 (14.76)	4 (3)	1 (1)
20	AG	32.01 (32.76)	4.18 (3.52)	2 (2)	1 (1)
	Amazon movie	143.05 (139.80)	18.39 (14.76)	4 (3)	1 (1)
30	AG	32.00 (32.76)	4.13 (3.52)	2 (2)	1 (1)
	Amazon movie	140.04 (139.80)	18.47 (14.76)	4 (3)	1 (1)
40	AG	31.76 (32.76)	3.94 (3.52)	2 (2)	1 (1)
	Amazon movie	141.24 (139.80)	17.31 (14.76)	4 (3)	1 (1)

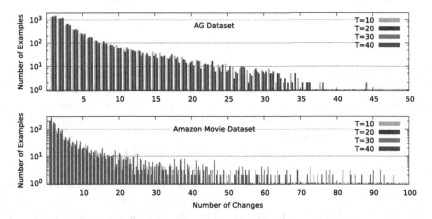

Fig. 4. Distribution of changes for generated adversarial examples for networks trained with defensive distillation; note the logarithmic scale on the y-axis.

Another aspect is robustness against transferability. Table 4 shows that the transferability rate for the AG ($0.323 - 0.337$ compared to 0.369) and Amazon movie ($0.199 - 0.253$ compared to 0.250) datasets is a bit lower in most cases compared to the retrained network without distillation, with a difference of only $0.032 - 0.051$. Based on this, we conclude that defensive distillation has only a small impact on transferability and does not, in fact, prevent it.

6 Discussion

Our results indicate that, at least on the two tested datasets, defensive distillation does not have the same effect for text classification as it has for image classification. The robustness against adversarial examples of networks trained with defensive distillation increases only slightly. One reason for this might be that defensive distillation effectively performs *gradient masking* [20,25], which works against methods which directly or indirectly add the gradient to the input.

Table 4. *Transferability* of generated adversarial examples to networks trained with defensive distillation with Temperature T.

T	Dataset	Number tested	Success rate	Success rate w/o distillation
10	AG	8150	0.323	0.369
	Amazon movie	1157	0.218	0.250
20	AG	8126	0.331	0.369
	Amazon movie	1217	0.199	0.250
30	AG	8141	0.325	0.369
	Amazon movie	1229	0.253	0.250
40	AG	8134	0.337	0.369
	Amazon movie	1195	0.211	0.250

However, in the algorithm used in our experiments the value of the gradient is only used to measure the importance of a given word on the network's final output, not directly added onto the input. The exact characteristics of the gradient are not important and, as a result, the *gradient masking* itself has only a minimal effect on our algorithm.

This hypothesis is further boosted by the results of Carlini and Wagner [4], who were able to generate adversarial examples for networks trained with defensive distillation with a slight modification to the generating algorithm on image classification tasks. They did this by restoring the gradient from the *gradient masking* done by defensive distillation. This shows that the gradient still holds enough information for the generation of adversarial examples for image classification tasks, but it might not be as easily accessible as without defensive distillation. If this hypothesis is true, this might mean that other methods based on gradient masking are also not effective in the text domain.

7   Conclusion

In this paper, we showed that, at least on the two tested datasets, defensive distillation does not work for hardening neural networks for text classification against adversarial examples. This still leaves two questions open: is gradient masking an option for increasing the robustness of neural networks and, if not, how can the robustness of neural networks for text classification be increased? To answer the first question, the effect of *gradient masking* [20,25] for both image classification and text classification should be studied in more detail, especially since similar results for another method of increasing robustness for image classification (saturated networks [17]) were achieved by Brendel and Bethge [3]. For this, different methods of *gradient masking* should be analyzed in future experiments to see if the gradient could be restored in a similar fashion. To answer the second question, different methods of hardening neural networks for text classification need to be examined. The question still remains open whether different methods from image classification can be successfully transferred to text classification or whether completely new approaches must be developed.

Acknowledgments. The authors gratefully acknowledge partial support from the German Research Foundation DFG under project CML (TRR 169) and the European Union under project SECURE (No 642667). The following software libraries were used for this work: Keras, Tensorflow, Gensim, NLTK with the WordNet interface, and NumPy.

References

1. AG's corpus of news articles. http://www.di.unipi.it/~gulli/AG_corpus_of_news_articles.html. Accessed 27 Oct 2017
2. Akhtar, N., Mian, A.: Threat of adversarial attacks on deep learning in computer vision: a survey. IEEE Access **6**, 14410–14430 (2018). https://doi.org/10.1109/ACCESS.2018.2807385
3. Brendel, W., Bethge, M.: Comment on "biologically inspired protection of deep networks from adversarial attacks". CoRR abs/1704.01547 (2017)
4. Carlini, N., Wagner, D.A.: Defensive distillation is not robust to adversarial examples. CoRR abs/1607.04311 (2016)
5. Fellbaum, C. (ed.): WordNet: An Electronic Lexical Database. MIT Press, Cambridge (1998)
6. Goodfellow, I.J., Shlens, J., Szegedy, C.: Explaining and harnessing adversarial examples. In: International Conference on Learning Representations (2015)
7. Hinton, G., Vinyals, O., Dean, J.: Distilling the knowledge in a neural network. In: NIPS Deep Learning Workshop (2014)
8. Jia, R., Liang, P.: Adversarial examples for evaluating reading comprehension systems. In: Proceedings of the Conference on Empirical Methods in Natural Language Processing, pp. 2021–2031 (2017). https://doi.org/10.18653/v1/D17-1215
9. Kim, Y.: Convolutional neural networks for sentence classification. In: Proceedings of the Conference on Empirical Methods in Natural Language Processing, pp. 1746–1751 (2014)
10. Leskovec, J., Krevl, A.: SNAP datasets: stanford large network dataset collection. http://snap.stanford.edu/data (2014)
11. Liang, B., Li, H., Su, M., Bian, P., Li, X., Shi, W.: Deep text classification can be fooled. In: Proceedings of the International Joint Conference on Artificial Intelligence, pp. 4208–4215 (2018). https://doi.org/10.24963/ijcai.2018/585
12. Lu, J., Issaranon, T., Forsyth, D.: SafetyNet: detecting and rejecting adversarial examples robustly. In: IEEE International Conference on Computer Vision, pp. 446–454 (2017). https://doi.org/10.1109/ICCV.2017.56
13. McAuley, J.J., Leskovec, J.: From amateurs to connoisseurs: modeling the evolution of user expertise through online reviews. In: Proceedings of the International Conference on World Wide Web, pp. 897–908 (2013). https://doi.org/10.1145/2488388.2488466
14. Mikolov, T., Chen, K., Corrado, G., Dean, J.: Efficient estimation of word representations in vector space. In: International Conference on Learning Representations (2013)

15. Mikolov, T., Sutskever, I., Chen, K., Corrado, G.S., Dean, J.: Distributed representations of words and phrases and their compositionality. In: Advances in Neural Information Processing Systems, pp. 3111–3119 (2013)
16. Mitton, R.: Corpora of misspellings for download. http://www.dcs.bbk.ac.uk/~ROGER/corpora.html. Accessed 10 Nov 2017
17. Nayebi, A., Ganguli, S.: Biologically inspired protection of deep networks from adversarial attacks. CoRR abs/1703.09202 (2017)
18. Papernot, N., McDaniel, P., Wu, X., Jha, S., Swami, A.: Distillation as a defense to adversarial perturbations against deep neural networks. In: IEEE Symposium on Security and Privacy, pp. 582–597 (2016). https://doi.org/10.1109/SP.2016.41
19. Papernot, N., McDaniel, P.D.: Extending defensive distillation. CoRR abs/1705.05264 (2017)
20. Papernot, N., McDaniel, P.D., Sinha, A., Wellman, M.P.: Towards the science of security and privacy in machine learning. CoRR abs/1611.03814 (2016)
21. Rozsa, A., Gunther, M., Boult, T.E.: Towards robust deep neural networks with bang. In: IEEE Winter Conference on Applications of Computer Vision, pp. 803–811 (2018). https://doi.org/10.1109/WACV.2018.00093
22. Samanta, S., Mehta, S.: Towards crafting text adversarial samples. CoRR abs/1707.02812 (2017)
23. Su, J., Vargas, D.V., Sakurai, K.: One pixel attack for fooling deep neural networks. IEEE Trans. Evol. Comput. (2019). https://doi.org/10.1109/TEVC.2019.2890858
24. Szegedy, C., et al.: Intriguing properties of neural networks. In: International Conference on Learning Representations (2014)
25. Tramèr, F., Kurakin, A., Papernot, N., Boneh, D., McDaniel, P.: Ensemble adversarial training: attacks and defenses. In: International Conference on Learning Representations (2018)
26. Tramèr, F., Papernot, N., Goodfellow, I., Boneh, D., McDaniel, P.: The space of transferable adversarial examples. CoRR abs/1704.03453 (2017)
27. Zhang, W.E., Sheng, Q.Z., Alhazmi, A.A.F., Li, C.: Generating textual adversarial examples for deep learning models: a survey. CoRR abs/1901.06796 (2019)
28. Zhang, X., Zhao, J., LeCun, Y.: Character-level convolutional networks for text classification. In: Advances in Neural Information Processing Systems, pp. 649–657 (2015)
29. Zhang, Y., Wallace, B.: A sensitivity analysis of (and practitioners' guide to) convolutional neural networks for sentence classification. In: Proceedings of the International Joint Conference on Natural Language Processing, pp. 253–263 (2017)

DCT: Differential Combination Testing of Deep Learning Systems

Chunyan Wang⬥, Weimin Ge, Xiaohong Li$^{(\boxtimes)}$, and Zhiyong Feng

College of Intelligence and Computing,
Tianjin Key Laboratory of Advanced Networking (TANK), Tianjin University,
Tianjin 300350, China
{chunyan_wang,gewm,xiaohongli,zyfeng}@tju.edu.cn

Abstract. Deep learning (DL) systems are increasingly used in security-related fields, where the accuracy and predictability of DL systems are critical. However the DL models are difficult to test and existing DL testing relies heavily on manually labeled data and often fails to expose erroneous behavior for corner inputs. In this paper, we propose Differential Combination Testing (DCT), an automated DL testing tool for systematically detecting the erroneous behavior of more corner cases without relying on manually labeled input data or manually checking the correctness of the output behavior. Our tool aims at automatically generating test cases, that is, applying image combination transformations to seed images to systematically generate synthetic images that can achieve high neuron coverage and trigger inconsistencies between multiple similar DL models. In addition, DCT utilizes multiple DL models with similar functions as cross-references, so that input data no longer must be manually marked and the correctness of output behavior can be automatically checked. The results show that DCT can find thousands of erroneous corner behaviors in the most commonly used DL models effectively and quickly, which can better detect the reliability and robustness of DL systems.

Keywords: Deep learning · Differential testing ·
Image transformation · Deep neural networks

1 Introduction

In the past few years, Deep Learning (DL) has made great progress in image classification [11,13], speech recognition [28], etc. These advances have led to the widespread use of DL in safety-related systems, such as self-driving cars [6], automated medical diagnosis [22], etc. Therefore the reliability and robustness of these DL systems are critical. However, DL systems often exhibit unexpected or incorrect behaviors in corner cases. Some incorrect behaviors can lead to catastrophic consequences, such as the fatal collision incident of the Google/Tesla self-driving car. Therefore, DL systems applied in security-related fields need to be tested systematically for different corner conditions.

© Springer Nature Switzerland AG 2019
I. V. Tetko et al. (Eds.): ICANN 2019, LNCS 11729, pp. 697–710, 2019.
https://doi.org/10.1007/978-3-030-30508-6_55

The traditional software and the DL system based on Deep Neural Network (DNN) are fundamentally different. For example, the program logic of traditional software is written manually by software developers. DNN automatically learns its logic from large amounts of data with minimal guidance. Furthermore, the logic of the traditional program is represented by control flow statements, while the DNN uses weights and nonlinear activation functions between different neurons for similar purposes. These differences make automated testing of DL systems challenging.

The standard way to test DL systems is to manually label the real-world test data as much as possible. But this is difficult to achieve, for example, the ImageNet dataset contains more than one million generic images. In addition, data monitoring and manual label processing are also labor intensive and error prone. And we also need to manually provide help and control for the data test result. It is challenging in terms of test data implementation and test result judgment.

In this paper, we solve these problems and propose Differential Combination Testing (DCT) - an automatic and systematic testing tool for DL systems. We systematically explore the DNN logic using neuron coverage proposed by [19]. We give reasonable image transformation types and parameters on the seed inputs. By combining these image transformations, we generate sufficient and reasonable corner test cases. We use multiple DL systems with similar functions as cross-references to eliminate the dependency on manually labeled input data, and also automatically identify the erroneous behavior of systems without manual inspection. Finally, we evaluated DCT in six of the most commonly used DL models. These models are trained using two real-world datasets from ImageNet and MNIST. We demonstrated that the DCT is not only effective in generating test cases and increasing neuron coverage, but also in terms of time efficiency.

The main contributions of this paper are:

(1) We propose a combined search technique guided by differential testing and neuron coverage to automatically synthesize test cases, which can systematically find synthetic images that can achieve high neuron coverage and can trigger inconsistencies between multiple similar DL models.
(2) Our method has demonstrated that combining different image transformations can increase the neuron coverage and obtain more corner test cases. In addition, our test method does not rely on manually labeled input data and can automatically detect the erroneous behaviors of the output without manual inspection.
(3) We tested the six most commonly used DNN models on two popular datasets using the automatic system testing tool DCT. We have found thousands of erroneous behaviors effectively and quickly in these models by DCT.

2   Related Work

Testing of DL Systems. DeepXplore [19] proposed a white-box testing framework to systematically generate adversarial examples that cover all neurons in the DNN. DeepTest [26] used neuron coverage to guide the testing of DNN-driven autonomous vehicles and used specific metamorphic relations to detect erroneous behaviors. DeepCover [25] proposed the MC/DC test criteria for DNNs. The test criteria have been only evaluated on small scale neural networks. DeepMutation [18] explored and proposed the first mutation testing technique for DL systems, it provided a general mutation testing framework, including both model-level mutations testing and source-level mutation testing. However, most testing methods rely heavily on manually labeled data.

Verification of DL Systems. DLV [27] enabled to verify local robustness of DNNs. Reluplex [15] employed an SMT-based approach that verifies robustness and safety of DNNs with ReLU activation functions on a network with 300 ReLU nodes. Ai2 [10] proposed DL systems verification based on abstract interpretation, and designed abstract domains and transformation operators. VERIVIS [20] could verify safety of DNNs when the inputs are modified by given transformation functions. However, most of verification techniques have been demonstrated only on simple DNN network architectures.

Differential Testing. It has been widely used to test traditional software successfully, including mobile applications [14], JVM [7], Web Application Firewall [5], SSL/TLS authentication verification logic [24] and C compilers [29]. The adversarial images generation process is essentially limited to the use of small, undetectable perturbations, as any visible change requires manual inspection. DCT can bypass this problem by using differential testing in DL systems, since it can create many real visible differences (e.g., different lighting, etc.) to interfere with the inputs and automatically detect the erroneous behaviors of DNN models in DL systems.

3 Methodology

In this section, we elaborate the differential combination testing for the DL systems. First, we take an overview of DCT and then describe three key points of DCT - differential testing, neuron coverage and image combination transformations. Finally, we provide a combined search algorithm based on differential testing and neuron coverage to solve the test problem of DL systems.

3.1 Overview of DCT

Figure 1 depicts the overview of DCT. DCT uses the unlabeled test inputs as seeds and eventually generate a set of synthesized test cases. First, DCT gets the seed images with the same label generated by the detection of multiple similar DNN models for unlabeled test inputs. Then, DCT performs combination transformations on same labeled images. Finally, it can generate a large number

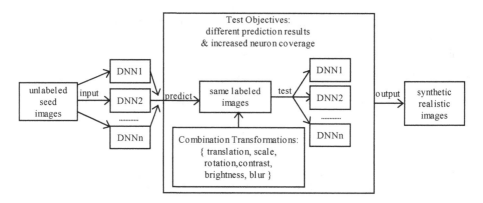

Fig. 1. The workflow of DCT, which leverages combination transformations to generate synthetic realistic images with neuron coverage and prediction feedback as guidance.

of real and effective test cases that cause the DL system to generate erroneous decisions by increasing neuron coverage and different prediction results.

We add specific image transformation constraints to ensure that synthetic images still represent the real world images after modifying the seed inputs. DCT attempts to cover as many neurons as possible by activating the inactive neurons in the hidden layer by image combination transformations.

3.2   Differential Testing and Neuron Coverage

We apply differential testing in DL systems, that is, we use multiple DNNs with similar functions as cross-references, so that the test inputs are not necessarily labeled images and DCT can automatically check the correctness of output behaviors. For example, if an intelligent security system judges a person to be male and all other systems judge a woman for the same input, then one of them may be incorrect.

Some studies have shown that neuron coverage is significantly better than code coverage for measuring the completeness of DNN test inputs. Each neuron in the DNN tends to extract a specific feature of the input independently, rather than collaborating with other neurons for feature extraction [21]. Essentially, each neuron tends to learn rules that are different from other neurons [19]. Therefore, neuron coverage is a good indicator of the comprehensiveness of DNN testing. DCT attempts to generate test cases by maximizing the neuron coverage of DNN. Neuron coverage was originally proposed in [19] to measure the test degree of the internal logic of the DNN. It is defined as follows.

$$Neuron\,Coverage = \frac{|\{n|\forall x \in I, \phi(n, x) > t\}|}{|N|} \tag{1}$$

where $N = \{n_1, n_2,...\}$ represents all neurons of a DL system, $I = \{x_1, x_2,...\}$ represents all test inputs, $\phi(n, x)$ is a function that returns the output value of a neuron $n \in N$ for a given test input $x \in I$ and t represents the threshold at which the neuron is activated.

3.3 Combination Transformations of Images

In this work, we focus on striking a balance between increasing the variability of the transformation and generating more meaningful test cases by applying image combination transformations to the seed images. Image combination transformations also can be used to further increase neuron coverage.

Definition 1. *An image x' is generated after a transformation tr and a corresponding parameter p on x (denoted as $x \xrightarrow{(tr,p)} x'$), where $x \in I$, $tr \in T$, $p \in P$. An image x' is generated after a sequence of transformations ($x \xrightarrow{(tr_1,p_1)} x_1$, $x_1 \xrightarrow{(tr_2,p_2)} x_2$, ..., $x_{n-1} \xrightarrow{(tr_n,p_n)} x'$) (denoted as $x \xrightarrow{(tr_1,p_1),(tr_2,p_2),...,(tr_n,p_n)} x'$).*

By setting the appropriate parameters for different transformations, it is guaranteed that the transformed image is still a meaningful real image. These image transformations mimic different real-world phenomena, such as camera lens distortion, object motion, and so on. To this end, we studied six different real image transformations to increase the variability of the transformation. These transformations can be divided into three groups: linear transformation (changing image brightness, image contrast), affine transformation (translation, scaling, rotation) and convolution transformation (blurring). We describe the details of the transformations as follows.

Linear Transformation - changing brightness and contrast. Its formula is:

$$dst(x,y) = \alpha * src(x,y) + \beta \tag{2}$$

The brightness of the image depends on the size of the pixel value. The brightness of the image can be adjusted by adding/subtracting the constant parameter β to the current value of each pixel. Contrast represents the difference between different pixels in brightness. The contrast of the image can be adjusted by multiplying the value of each pixel with the constant parameter α.

Affine Transformation - translation, scaling and rotation. An affine transformation is a linear mapping of points, lines and planes between two images [2]. In image processing, affine transformation is commonly used to fix distortion due to camera angle changes. In this paper, we use affine transformation to simulate different real-world camera angles or object motions.

Convolution Transformation - Blurring. They perform convolution operations on input pixels with different kernels. We use four different types of blurring filters: Averaging, Gaussian, Median, and Bilateral [1].

If the image transformation without any guidance changes the seed image purposelessly, then it is not known whether the generated test case is desirable. Therefore, we select the results of neuron coverage and DNNs differential testing as feedback to determine if the newly generated synthetic image should be retained.

3.4   Combined Search Based on Differential Testing and Neuron Coverage

To obtain valid and realistic test cases, we provide a combined search technique guided by differential testing and neuron coverage (see Algorithm 1). Algorithm 1 shows the generation process of test cases using a set of seed images I, a set of image transformations T and their corresponding parameters P and a set of DNN models D as inputs. The resulting synthetic images are used as an output. The algorithm obtains synthetic images of higher neuron coverage and differential behavior by adding combination transformations to given seed images. This process is repeated for all images in an iterative manner. Below, we explain the details of the algorithm.

First, we get the seed that is classified into the same class by all DNNs (Line 4–5), and then randomly select the types of image transformations and the corresponding parameters to perform image combination transformations (Line 8–11). Then the transformed image needs to meet two goals. One goal is that the modified seed input needs to be classified differently by at least one DNN; the other is that the transformed seed input is capable of increasing neuron coverage such that the neuron output exceeds the neuron activation threshold. Specifically, comparing the obtained neuron coverage of each DNN model with the activation threshold, as long as there is a DNN model with neuron coverage greater than the threshold, then the transformed seed input can be considered to increase neuron coverage (Line 13). A synthetic image that satisfies both of these conditions is added to the test image set and the neuron coverage is updated (Line 14–15). Repeat the above process for each test image to get the final set of test cases.

In Algorithm 1, the technique of generating test cases by a combined search of differential testing and neuron coverage guidance can be general, without the need to assume specific DNN structures (e.g., activation function types).

4   Experiments and Results

We implement DCT in Python using TensorFlow 1.12.0 [4] and Keras 2.2.4 [8] DL frameworks. DCT is implemented on TensorFlow/Keras but does not need to make any modifications to these frameworks. All our experiments are run on a Window all-in-one running Window10 Version 1803 (one Intel i7-8700 3.20 GHz processor with 2 cores,16 GB of memory).

Algorithm 1: Combined search to obtain synthetic images

Input : Unlabeled seed images I, Transformations T, Parameters P, multiple DNNs D
Output : Generated synthetic images
Variable: Threshold t for determining if a neuron is activated
           Iterations iters for determining the number of iterations for searching
           Kinds k for determining the number of kinds of image transformations

---

```
1   /*main procedure*/
2   genImgs = ∅
3   for x ∈ I do
4          ∀d ∈ D   //randomly select one dnn d from D
5          if d.predict = (D-d).predict(x) then
6                  numIters = 0
7                  While numIters ⩽ iters do
8                          for i from 1 to k do
9                                  ∀tr ∈ T    //randomly select transformation tr from T
10                                 ∀p ∈ P    //randomly select the corresponding parameter p for tr from P
11                                 x = transform(x, tr, p)
12                         end
13                         if covIncreas(x) and d.predict ≠ (D-d).predict(x) then
14                                 genImgs.add(x)
15                                 updateCoverage()
16                         end
17                 end
18         end
19  end
20  return genImgs
```

4.1 Test Datasets and DNNs

We select two popular public datasets, MNIST [17] and ImageNet [9], as the evaluation datasets. For each dataset, we study DCT on three popular DNN models (i.e., a total of six DNNs) that are widely used in other people's previous work. We provide a summary of the two datasets and corresponding DNNs in Table 1. All evaluated DNNs are pre-trained (i.e., we use public weights reported by previous researchers). For each dataset, we use DCT to test three DNNs with different architectures, as shown in Table 1.

4.2 Image Transformations

We use six different types of image transformations. They are translation, scale, rotation, contrast adjustment, brightness adjustment and blur. We implement

Table 1. Details of the DNNs and datasets used to evaluate DCT.

Dataset	Dataset description	DNN description	DNN name	#of Neurons	Architecture
MNIST	Hand-written digits (70,000 data)	LeNet variations	MNI_C1	52	LeNet-1, LeCun et al. [16,17]
			MNI_C2	148	LeNet-4, LeCun et al. [16,17]
			MNI_C3	268	LeNet-5, LeCun et al. [16,17]
ImageNet	General images (over 10,000,000 images)	State-of-the-artImage classifiers from ILSVRC	IMG_C1	14888	VGG-16, Simonyan et al. [23]
			IMG_C2	16168	VGG-19, Simonyan et al. [23]
			IMG_C3	94123	ResNet50, He et al. [13]

Table 2. Transformations and parameters used by DCT for generating synthetic images in ImageNet and MNIST.

Transformations		Parameters	Parameter ranges	
			ImageNet	MNIST
Translation		(t_x, t_y)	$(-20, -20)$ to $(20,20)$	$(-2, -2)$ to $(2,2)$
Scale		(s_x, s_y)	$(0.5, 0.5)$ to $(1.5, 1.5)$	$(0.8, 0.8)$ to $(1.2, 1.2)$
Rotation		(degree)	-20 to 20	-20 to 20
Contrast		(gain)	0.5 to 2	0.5 to 2
Brightness		(bias)	-21 to 21	-21 to 21
Blur	Averaging	kernel size	3 3	3 3
	Gaussian	kernel size	3 3, 5 5	3 3, 5 5
	Median	aperture linear size	3	3
	Bilateral filter	diameter, sigmaColor, sigmaSpace	9, 75, 75	9, 75, 75

these transformations by using OpenCV [3]. Since MNIST and ImageNet are two different types of datasets, the parameters used for each transformation are different. The parameters of the image transformations on the two types of datasets are shown in Table 2.

4.3 Results and Evaluation

In this section, we describe the experiment results and evaluation analysis in detail. We use the principle of minority majority, assuming that most DNN models make the right decisions. In this paper, we set the neuron activation threshold for all experiments to zero, which is selected based on multiple experiences to increase neuron coverage. Specifically, we set the activation thresholds to 0, 0.25, 0.5 and 0.75 respectively for many experiments, and found that when set to 0, the neuron coverage can be significantly increased.

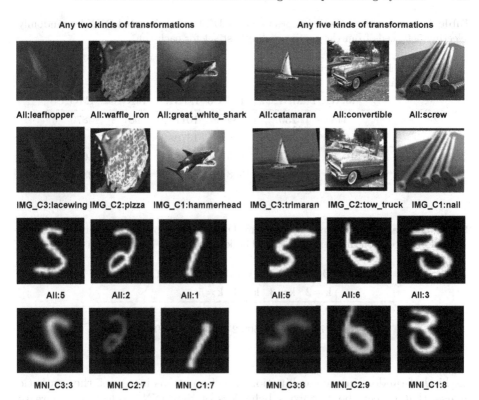

Fig. 2. Odd rows show the seed images and even rows show the synthetic images that represent the erroneous behaviors of DNN models generated by DCT. The first two rows show images for ImageNet and the last two rows are for MNIST. The left three columns show images for applying any two kinds of transformations and the right three columns show images for applying any five kinds of transformations.

Results. DCT found thousands of erroneous behaviors in all tested DNN models. Figure 2 shows some synthetic images and the corresponding erroneous behaviors generated by DCT for MNIST and ImageNet. Table 3 summarizes the number of erroneous behaviors that the DCT found for each tested DNN model, with 500 randomly selected seed images from the corresponding test set as input. Since test sets provide a similar number of samples for each class, these randomly selected 500 samples also follow this distribution. The number of search algorithm iterations of the experimental data in Table 3 is set to 20, and the neuron threshold is set to 0.

We applied the image transformation types and corresponding parameters of Table 2 to the randomly selected seed images. Figure 2 shows that the constraints we added are reasonably efficient, both generating meaningful images and detecting the DNN models. Table 3 shows that by randomly combining six different transforms, we get thousands of valid synthetic images that represent the erroneous behaviors of DNN models. It can be seen from Table 3 that as

Table 3. Number of synthetic images found by DCT for each tested DNN by randomly selecting 500 seeds from the corresponding test set for each run.

Variable k (Algorithm 1)	DNN name					
	MNI_C1	MNI_C2	MNI_C3	IMG_C1	IMG_C2	IMG_C3
2	348	230	284	1017	987	870
3	695	541	556	1370	1358	1127
4	1073	741	845	1988	2035	1616
5	1476	1078	1308	2645	2716	2303

Table 4. Total time(in minutes) taken by DCT and DeepXplore running randomly selected 500 seeds on different test sets. The k is a variable in Algorithm 1.

	DCT Variable k (Algorithm 1)				DeepXplore
	k = 2	k = 3	k = 4	k = 5	
MNIST	2.18	5.5	10.8	21.9	36.7
ImageNet	270.8	361.7	509.2	720.4	943.71

the kind of random image combination transformations increases, the synthetic images that detect the erroneous behaviors of the DNN models also increase significantly. The main reason is that all transformations help to increase the neuron coverage, and the neuron coverage can be further increased by combining different image transformations.

Performance Evaluation. We use two indicators to evaluate the performance of DCT: neuron coverage and execution time of the generated synthetic images.

In this experiment, we compared neuron coverage achieved by randomly selecting 500 samples with the neuron threshold set to zero by four different methods. They are: (1) DCT, (2) DeepXplore [19], (3) adversarial testing [12], and (4) random selection testing. Since some neurons of the fully connected layers of DNNs testing MNIST and ImageNet are very difficult to activate, only neuron coverage on layers other than the fully connected layers is considered. We first obtain the neuron coverage of each DNN model that is greater than the neuron activation threshold, and then take their average to compare the neuron coverage of each method. The results are shown in Fig. 3. We can see from the results that the DCT covers an average of 8.25% and 9.3% more neuron coverage than adversarial testing and random testing, while DCT and DeepXplore are comparable in neuron coverage and can be both used for more thorough testing on neurons.

We further compared the total time taken by DCT and DeepXplore running randomly selected 500 seeds on MNIST and ImageNet. The results are shown in

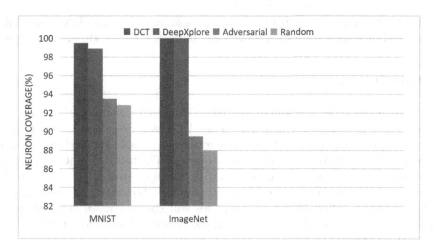

Fig. 3. The neuron coverage achieved by DCT, DeepXplore [19], adversarial testing [12], and random selection testing running randomly selected 500 seeds from the corresponding test set.

Table 4. As can be seen from the table, no matter what kind of image combination transformations the DCT runs, it is much shorter than the execution time of DeepXplore. This indicates that DCT is not only effective in finding test cases and increasing neuron coverage, but also in terms of time efficiency.

4.4   Discussion

For the same input, it can be seen from Table 3 that the number of erroneous behaviors detected by different DNN models is different, and the root cause is that there are differences in the decision logic of different DNNs. The decision logic of DNNs is determined by factors such as training data, DNN architecture, etc. However, the number of erroneous behaviors detected by each DNN model we tested is also considerable, so DCT can effectively find the erroneous behaviors in all tested DNNs. In addition, due to the differences between DNNs, the method in this paper is also effective for other similar DNN models. We have only selected the most commonly used DNN models.

DCT uses differential testing technology to automatically detect erroneous behaviors of DL systems without manual checking. But differential testing also has some limitations. First, the differential testing requires at least two different DNN models with the similar functionality. Our research found that in most cases, developers often customize and train their own DNNs for a given problem to improve accuracy, so multiple different DNNs are readily available. Second, at least one DNN is required to produce a different result than the other DNNs, the differential testing is valid. If all DNNs make the same mistake, DCT will not be able to generate the test cases. But we found that most DNNs are built and trained independently, so all DNNs are unlikely to make the same mistake.

5   Conclusion

In this paper, we presented and evaluated DCT, a tool for automatically testing the reliability and accuracy of DL systems. DCT generates corner test images by applying different combination transformations on a set of seed images and guided by differential testing and neuron coverage. The tool does not need to rely on manual labeled data and can automatically identify erroneous behaviors. We demonstrated the usefulness of DCT on six popular DL models and two datasets, MNIST and ImageNet. In future work, we will conduct more comprehensive research covering more different transformation standards and more DNN models of the DL system.

Acknowledgements. Xiaohong Li is the corresponding authors. This work is supported in part by National Natural Science Foundation of China(Nos. 61872262, 61572349).

References

1. The opencv reference manual release 2.4.9.0 (2014). docs.opencv.org/opencv2 refman.pdf
2. Affine transformation (2015). https://www.mathworks.com/discovery/affine-trans formation.html
3. Open source computer vision library (2015). https://github.com/itseez/opencv
4. Abadi, M., et al.: TensorFlow: a system for large-scale machine learning. In: 12th {USENIX} Symposium on Operating Systems Design and Implementation ({OSDI} 16), pp. 265–283 (2016). https://www.usenix.org/conference/osdi16/technical-sessions/presentation/abadi
5. Argyros, G., Stais, I., Jana, S., Keromytis, A.D., Kiayias, A.: SFADiff: automated evasion attacks and fingerprinting using black-box differential automata learning. In: Proceedings of the 2016 ACM SIGSAC Conference on Computer and Communications Security, pp. 1690–1701. ACM (2016). https://doi.org/10.1145/2976749.2978383
6. Bojarski, M., et al.: End to end learning for self-driving cars. arXiv preprint arXiv:1604.07316 (2016)
7. Chen, Y., Su, T., Sun, C., Su, Z., Zhao, J.: Coverage-directed differential testing of JVM implementations. In: ACM SIGPLAN Notices, pp. 85–99. ACM (2016). https://doi.org/10.1145/2908080.2908095
8. Chollet, F.: Keras. Github repository (2015). https://github.com/fchollet/keras. Accessed 25 2017
9. Deng, J., Dong, W., Socher, R., Li, L.J., Li, K., Fei-Fei, L.: ImageNet: a large-scale hierarchical image database. In: 2009 IEEE Conference on Computer Vision and Pattern Recognition, pp. 248–255. IEEE (2009). https://doi.org/10.1109/CVPR.2009.5206848

10. Gehr, T., Mirman, M., Drachsler-Cohen, D., Tsankov, P., Chaudhuri, S., Vechev, M.: Ai2: safety and robustness certification of neural networks with abstract interpretation. In: 2018 IEEE Symposium on Security and Privacy (SP), pp. 3–18. IEEE (2018). https://doi.org/10.1109/SP.2018.00058
11. Goceri, E., Goceri, N.: Deep learning in medical image analysis: recent advances and future trends. In: International Conferences Computer Graphics, Visualization, Computer Vision and Image Processing (2017)
12. Goodfellow, I.J., Shlens, J., Szegedy, C.: Explaining and harnessing adversarial examples. arXiv preprint arXiv:1412.6572 (2014)
13. He, K., Zhang, X., Ren, S., Sun, J.: Deep residual learning for image recognition. In: Proceedings of the IEEE Conference on Computer Vision and Pattern Recognition, pp. 770–778 (2016). https://doi.org/10.1109/CVPR.2016.90
14. Jung, J., Sheth, A., Greenstein, B., Wetherall, D., Maganis, G., Kohno, T.: Privacy Oracle: a system for finding application leaks with black box differential testing. In: Proceedings of the 15th ACM Conference on Computer and Communications Security, pp. 279–288. ACM (2008). https://doi.org/10.1145/1455770.1455806
15. Katz, G., Barrett, C., Dill, D.L., Julian, K., Kochenderfer, M.J.: Reluplex: an efficient SMT solver for verifying deep neural networks. In: Majumdar, R., Kunčak, V. (eds.) CAV 2017. LNCS, vol. 10426, pp. 97–117. Springer, Cham (2017). https://doi.org/10.1007/978-3-319-63387-9_5
16. LeCun, Y., Cortes, C., Burges, C.: Mnist handwritten digit database. AT&T labs (2010). http://yann.lecun.com/exdb/mnist2
17. LeCun, Y.: The mnist database of handwritten digits (1998). http://yann.lecun.com/exdb/mnist/
18. Ma, L., et al.: DeepMutation: mutation testing of deep learning systems. In: 2018 IEEE 29th International Symposium on Software Reliability Engineering (ISSRE), pp. 100–111. IEEE (2018). https://doi.org/10.1109/ISSRE.2018.00021
19. Pei, K., Cao, Y., Yang, J., Jana, S.: DeepXplore: automated whitebox testing of deep learning systems. In: Proceedings of the 26th Symposium on Operating Systems Principles, pp. 1–18. ACM (2017). https://doi.org/10.1145/3132747.3132785
20. Pei, K., Cao, Y., Yang, J., Jana, S.: Towards practical verification of machine learning: the case of computer vision systems. arXiv preprint arXiv:1712.01785 (2017)
21. Radford, A., Jozefowicz, R., Sutskever, I.: Learning to generate reviews and discovering sentiment. arXiv preprint arXiv:1704.01444 (2017)
22. Rajpurkar, P., et al.: ChexNet: radiologist-level pneumonia detection on chest x-rays with deep learning. arXiv preprint arXiv:1711.05225 (2017)
23. Simonyan, K., Zisserman, A.: Very deep convolutional networks for large-scale image recognition. arXiv preprint arXiv:1409.1556 (2014)
24. Sivakorn, S., Argyros, G., Pei, K., Keromytis, A.D., Jana, S.: HVLearn: automated black-box analysis of hostname verification in SSL/TLS implementations. In: 2017 IEEE Symposium on Security and Privacy (SP), pp. 521–538. IEEE (2017). https://doi.org/10.1109/SP.2017.46
25. Sun, Y., Huang, X., Kroening, D.: Testing deep neural networks. arXiv preprint arXiv:1803.04792 (2018)
26. Tian, Y., Pei, K., Jana, S., Ray, B.: DeepTest: automated testing of deep-neural-network-driven autonomous cars. In: Proceedings of the 40th International Conference on Software Engineering, pp. 303–314. ACM (2018). https://doi.org/10.1145/3180155.3180220

27. Wicker, M., Huang, X., Kwiatkowska, M.: Feature-guided black-box safety testing of deep neural networks. In: Beyer, D., Huisman, M. (eds.) TACAS 2018. LNCS, vol. 10805, pp. 408–426. Springer, Cham (2018). https://doi.org/10.1007/978-3-319-89960-2_22
28. Xiong, W., et al.: Achieving human parity in conversational speech recognition. arXiv preprint arXiv:1610.05256 (2016)
29. Yang, X., Chen, Y., Eide, E., Regehr, J.: Finding and understanding bugs in c compilers. In: ACM SIGPLAN Notices, pp. 283–294. ACM (2011). https://doi.org/10.1145/1993498.1993532

Restoration as a Defense Against Adversarial Perturbations for Spam Image Detection

Jianguo Jiang[1,2], Boquan Li[1,2(✉)], Min Yu[1,2(✉)], Chao Liu[1], Weiqing Huang[1], Lejun Fan[3], and Jianfeng Xia[3]

[1] Institute of Information Engineering, Chinese Academy of Sciences, Beijing, China
{jiangjianguo,liboquan,yumin,liuchao,huangweiqing}@iie.ac.cn
[2] School of Cyber Security, University of Chinese Academy of Sciences, Beijing, China
[3] National Computer Network Emergency Response Technical Team/ Coordination Center of China, Beijing, China
{fanlejun,xiajianfeng}@cert.org.cn

Abstract. Spam image detection is essential for protecting the security and privacy of Internet users and saving network resources. However, we observe a spam image detection system might be out of order due to adversarial perturbations, which can force a classification model to misclassify the input images. To defend against adversarial perturbations, previous researches disorganize the perturbations with fundamental image processing techniques, which shows limited success. Instead, we apply image restoration as a defense, which focuses on restoring the perturbed adversarial images to their original versions. The restoration is achieved by a lightweight preprocessing network, which takes the adversarial images as input and outputs their restored versions for classification. The further evaluation results demonstrate that our defense significantly improves the performance of classification models, requires little cost and outperforms other representative defenses.

Keywords: Defense against adversarial perturbations ·
Spam image detection · Image classification · Deep neural network

1 Introduction

Image classification is widely applied in various domains of cyber security, and one crucial application is spam image detection [1]. Spam images, frequently transmitted by e-mails, refer to the unsolicited images with purposeful information, including terrorism, politics, malicious fraud, commercial advertisements, etc. Spam image detection can filter such harmful information, and thereby can not only protect Internet users' security and privacy but also save network resources. Nevertheless, spammers frequently craft various perturbations to degrade the performance of image classification models (distortion, rotation,

© Springer Nature Switzerland AG 2019
I. V. Tetko et al. (Eds.): ICANN 2019, LNCS 11729, pp. 711–723, 2019.
https://doi.org/10.1007/978-3-030-30508-6_56

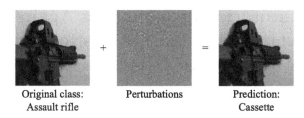

Original class: Perturbations   Prediction:
Assault rifle   Cassette

Fig. 1. By adding imperceptible adversarial perturbations to a spam image with class 'assault rifle' (an image with weapons is commonly deemed as a terrorism-related spam image), a classifier is fooled to output a legitimate class 'cassette'.

changing the background of an image, etc.), thus impacting the detection of spam images [2].

Besides the above perturbations, we observe a new threat which poses even greater challenges to spam image detection, namely the adversarial perturbation [3]. By adding subtle but purposeful adversarial perturbations to a normal image, an adversarial image is crafted which forces classification models (especially deep neural networks) to output incorrect predictions. As the example shown in Fig. 1, such imperceptible perturbations cause the malfunction of a spam image detection system, as well as preserve the spam image unbroken to spread harmful information. The adversarial perturbation can even degrade the precision of image classification to 0% (as verified in Sect. 4.1), which poses a serious threat to the spam image detection system as well as other security-sensitive artificial intelligence systems [4]. Therefore, it is necessary to apply effective defenses against such threats.

For defending against adversarial perturbations, most previous researches focus on modifying classification models to enhance the robustness [5,6]. Nevertheless, a few researches transform the adversarial images into clean ones which can be correctly classified [7]. Compared with the former defenses, the input transformation-based ones require less cost, suit more classification models and are more combinative with other defenses. Existing researches transform adversarial images with fundamental image processing techniques (filters [7], compression [8], Principal Component Analysis [9], etc.) to disorganize the adversarial perturbations. Nevertheless, the legitimate pixels of the images are also destroyed due to the transformations, which leads to a part of the modified predictions still differ from the images' original classes (e.g., the prediction of an adversarial image is modified from 'cassette' into 'binoculars' rather than the original class 'rifle'). Hence such defenses show limited success in improving the precision of image classification.

Based on the above issues, we apply image restoration as a defense against adversarial perturbations. Unlike previous approaches disorganize the perturbations, our defense focuses on restoring the adversarial images to their original versions. Specifically, we employ a lightweight preprocessing network (abbreviated as pre-network) for restoration. The pre-network adopts a convolutional neural network as the basic architecture, which takes an adversarial image as input and outputs a restored version approximating to the original image. The evaluation results demonstrate the effectiveness of our defense, which significantly improves a model's precision of classifying adversarial images (e.g., an average improvement from 10.2% to 81.8% with a 6-layer network), costs little time (e.g., an average restoration cost of 0.19 s per image with a 6-layer network), suits multiple classification models, and outperforms other representative benchmarks.

The main contributions of this paper are summarized as follows:

- We observe a spam image detection system will malfunction due to the adversarial perturbation, which poses new challenges to detect spam images.
- We propose to apply image restoration as a novel defense against adversarial perturbations, which restores an adversarial image to its original version instead of disorganizing the perturbations.
- Our defense significantly improves the performance of multiple classification models, requires little cost, and is superior to other state-of-the-art work.

The reminder of this paper is structured as follows. Section 2 presents a brief introduction to related adversarial perturbations and defenses. Our proposed defense is elaborated on and evaluated in Sects. 3 and 4, respectively. Finally, we conclude this paper in Sect. 5.

2   Related Work

This section briefly presents some existing researches on adversarial perturbations and input transformation-based defenses.

2.1   Adversarial Perturbations

The adversarial perturbations are crafted by an adversary with the aim to force a classification model (termed '*target model*') to produce incorrect outputs. Generally, we input a normal image x to a classifier f, which produces a correct output y (i.e., $f(x) = y$). By applying adversarial perturbations, an adversary generates an adversarial image x' closing to x, which produces an incorrect output (i.e., $f(x') \neq y$). Based on the outputs, two categories of adversarial perturbations are proposed, namely the targeted perturbations and untargeted perturbations.

In the targeted perturbations, the adversary forces the classifier to output an assigned incorrect class, which is termed '*target class*' (i.e., $f(x') = y'$ and $y' \neq y$). Szegedy et al. first observed the imperceptible perturbation by maximizing a neural network's prediction error, namely the *L-BFGS* algorithm. And they termed such adversarial images as '*adversarial examples*' [3]. Papernot et al. proposed a *JSMA* algorithm to perturb inputs with merely little alterations by formalizing the space of adversaries against deep neural networks [10]. Carlini et al. designed one of the most forceful adversarial methods acknowledgedly [11],

Carlini and Wagner perturbation, which successfully made multiple defenses unavailable [12].

In the untargeted perturbations, the adversary merely forces the classifier to output an incorrect class without assigning it (i.e., $f(x')$ is arbitrary except y). Goodfellow et al. proposed a linear view of adversarial perturbations and suggested a fast gradient sign method, namely *FGSM*, which also provided samples for regularizing model training [13]. Moosavi-Dezfooli et al. proposed a *DeepFool* algorithm by designing an accurate method for searching adversarial perturbations, which quantified the robustness of classification models [14].

Taking the typical *FGSM* algorithm as an example, the generation of adversarial perturbations can be described as an iterative process. The perturbation can be expressed as

$$\Delta(x, x') = \epsilon \text{sign}(\nabla_x J(f(x), y)),$$

where ϵ is a small enough positive value for limiting the strength of perturbation, and $J(f(x), y)$ is the loss function for training the classifier f. During the iteration, the direction of $\Delta(x, x')$ is consistent with the gradient of $J(f(x), y)$, which makes $J(f(x), y)$ increase with iteration times. The iteration continues until an incorrect output is produced.

Although multiple novel adversarial methods are still being proposed, our research is primarily based on the above five perturbations on account of their typicality and comprehensiveness.

2.2   Input Transformation-Based Defenses

As aforementioned, the input transformation-based defenses have multifaceted advantages over the model modification-based ones in terms of cost and universality, hence we primarily discuss the former one in this paper.

Xu et al. proposed *Feature Squeezing*, one of the state-of-the-art defenses, which applied spatial smoothing and color depth reduction to reduce the search space available to an adversary [7]. Besides transforming inputs, *Feature Squeezing* also showed excellent performance in identifying the adversarial images. Analogously, Osadchy et al. applied several types of image filters to eliminate adversarial perturbations [15]. In addition, some researches employed image compression as a preprocessing step before classification [8]. With a similar idea of reducing dimensionality, Bhagoji et al. employed *Principal Component Analysis* to transform inputs, which enhanced the resilience of machine learning in both training and evaluating phases [9].

Among all the above defenses, we take the approaches in references [7] and [15] as benchmarks in further experiments due to their representativeness and effectiveness.

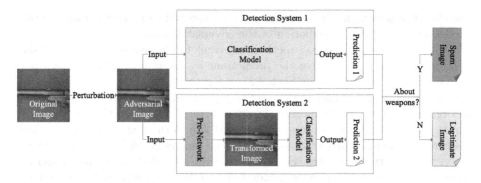

Fig. 2. The framework of a spam image detection system, which determines a spam image by the prediction of the classification model. Detection system 2 has an additional component, the pre-network, to transform an adversarial image before classification.

3   Restoration as a Defense

In this section, we apply image restoration as a defense against adversarial perturbations. We first present the threat in a spam image detection task and its defense strategy. Then we elaborate on the methodology of restoration.

3.1   Threat in Spam Image Detection

The adversarial perturbation is a serious threat to many security-sensitive systems, including road sign recognition of self-driving cars [4], face recognition of access control [16], etc. To investigate the effect of the adversarial perturbation on spam image detection, a weapon-related spam image detection task is simulated (an image with weapons is commonly deemed as a terrorism-related spam image).

As the detection system 1 illustrated in Fig. 2, a spam image is determined by the prediction of an image classification model. After being added adversarial perturbations, a weapon-related image may deceive the classification model into outputting a weapon-unrelated prediction. Meanwhile, those adversarial perturbations are so subtle to be perceived by human eyes. In this way, an adversarial image can avoid being determined as a spam image and successfully spread harmful information to people.

In addition, it is possible that the classification model incorrectly predicts all spam images, which makes the detection system be out of order completely (as verified in Sect. 4.1).

3.2   Defense Strategy

As the detection system 2 illustrated in Fig. 2, for defending against adversarial perturbations, an additional component is appended to the detection system. An adversarial image is transformed by a pre-network before being input to the classification model. The pre-network is expected to make the classification model output a correct prediction of the adversarial image.

As for the transformation methods, several fundamental image processing techniques are used to correct the predictions by disorganizing adversarial perturbations (as introduced in Sect. 2.2). As mentioned above, the adversarial images are crafted by changing merely tiny pixels of normal images, hence such disorganization can partly modify the adversarial pixels. Nevertheless, the legitimate pixels of the images are also destroyed due to the transformations, which leads to the modified predictions of adversarial images are still nonidentical with these images' original classes. For instance, with a 3×3 sliding-window median filter, 34.7% adversarial images (generated by CW_2 algorithm with target class 'cassette') are still predicted as the weapon-unrelated classes (binoculars, dish, etc.) rather than their original weapon-related classes (rifle, assault rifle, etc.). Thus the performance of these defenses is barely satisfactory.

Therefore, we propose a defense approach which aims at not only modifying the adversarial pixels but also restoring the adversarial images into their original versions. Towards that end, a lightweight pre-network is employed for image restoration. The pre-network restores an adversarial image to a cleaner version approximating to the original image. It is noted that the restored image might not be identical to the original image in practice. Nevertheless, in our task, the clean version approximating to the original image is sufficient to correct the misclassification, which achieves the defense goal.

The effectiveness of our defense is attested in Sect. 4. Such a defense can improve the anti-perturbation capacity of a spam image detection system, and also contribute to multiple artificial intelligence systems suffering from adversarial perturbations.

3.3   Restoration Methodology

The process of restoring adversarial images can be described as a mapping function g, which maps an original image I with adversarial perturbation P to its restored version I', i.e., $g : (I + P) \rightarrow I'$. The pre-network is employed to learn this mapping, which devotes to outputting I' approximating to I. Since the mapping from images to images leads to high complexity, an intact image is split into patches so that the mapping can be learned from patches to patches.

It is noteworthy that such mapping merely represents the process of image restoration, which is not associated with adversarial images. Thus P can be any noise besides the highly-cost adversarial perturbations, and the learned pre-network is independent of the classification model.

Architecture of the Preprocessing Network. In the pre-network, a convolutional neural network (CNN) is adopted as the basic architecture. Owing to its local receptive field architecture designed for image data, CNN can achieve superior performance with less training data. Such an advantage of CNN is adequate for various tasks [17,18], and is in accordance with our task of image restoration.

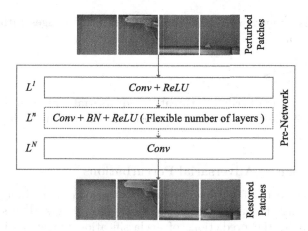

Fig. 3. The architecture of a pre-network, where the number of the intermediate layers (dotted portion) is flexible. The network receives image patches and outputs the restored version of them.

The architecture of the pre-network is illustrated in Fig. 3. The network consists of N convolution layers, each of which is composed of M convolutional filters. The first layer (L^1) adopts a *Conv* (Convolution) operation followed by an activation function of *ReLU* (Rectified Linear Units) [17], where $ReLU(x) = \max(0, x)$. In intermediate layers (L^2 to L^{N-1}), a *BN* (Batch Normalization) [19] operation is set between *Conv* and *ReLU* during the training period, and it is substituted by an affine operation which applies learned normalization during the evaluating period. The last layer (L^N) merely adopts a *Conv* operation. Then, the n-th layer L^n of the network is formulated as

$$L^n = ReLU(BN(\sum_{i=2}^{n} k^i * L^{i-1})),$$

where $n \in [2, N - 1]$, k^i denotes the convolutional kernel of the i-th layer, and $BN(\cdot)$ refers to the *BN* operation in training period (substituted by affine operation during evaluating period). A zero-padding operation is adopted for the inputs of each convolution layer to maintain the spatial size unchanged.

Network Training and Implementation. During training period, the parameters of a pre-network are learned by minimizing the loss between the output (patches of I') and input (patches of I). We randomly collect 1000 color images (I) and split each image into four patches. Then we craft corresponding noisy patches ($I + P$) with the additive white Gaussian noise (a typical random noise), which requires little cost on crafting training data. Based on these patches, five pre-networks in different depths are trained. The implementation of neural network training partly refers to reference [20]. It is worth noting that such restoration is independent of the class of training samples, hence the pre-networks is trained with 1000 random-class color images rather than the weapon-related ones.

4   Experiments

In this section, we first verify the threats of adversarial perturbations. Then, we demonstrate the effectiveness of our defense and compare it with other benchmarks.

4.1   Verification of Adversarial Perturbations

To verify the threats of adversarial perturbations in spam image detection, we simulate a task to detect weapon-related spam images. The spam images are determined by the predictions of a classification model (as illustrated in Sect. 3.1). Thus two evaluation metrics are utilized in our experiments as follows:

- **Classification precision:** The fraction of the correctly classified samples against the total samples. (A sample is said to be correctly classified if its final prediction is same with its original class.)
- **Detection precision:** The fraction of the correctly detected samples against the total samples. (A sample is said to be correctly detected if its final prediction is a weapon-related class.)

First, we collect 800 color weapon-related images from the popular dataset *ImageNet* [21] and apply a pre-trained model *Resnet50* [22] for classification. We classify the 800 spam images and select the first 100 correctly classified ones for the follow-up experiment, ensuring that the misclassification is caused by adversarial perturbations rather than the low performance of the model itself, i.e., the classification precision of original unperturbed images is 100%.

Subsequently, we generate 500 adversarial images by adding three targeted perturbations (*L-BFGS*, *JSMA* and *CW$_2$*) and two untargeted perturbations (*FGSM* and *DeepFool*) to the selected 100 images, respectively. For the three targeted perturbations, we set 'cassette' as the target class. These perturbations are implemented with a python toolbox: *Foolbox* [23].

Finally, we classify these adversarial images and present the results in Table 1. In the table, with the three targeted perturbations, the predictions of total images are changed into the target class 'cassette', which is a weapon-unrelated class, hence the classification precision and detection precision are both 0%. With the other two untargeted perturbations, the predictions of part images are changed (93% and 56%, respectively). The classification precision and detection precision are different because the predictions a part of misclassified images are still about weapons (e.g., class 'assault rifle' is changed into 'rifle'), such images are identified as spam images.

It can be seen that the adversarial perturbation is indeed a serious threat to spam image detection. Especially, the targeted perturbations degrade the classification precision to 0%, leading to the malfunction of the detection system.

Table 1. Verification of adversarial perturbations

Evaluation metrics	Adversarial images						Original images
	Targeted			Untargeted		Average	
	L-BFGS	JSMA	CW$_2$	FGSM	DeepFool		
Classification precision	0%	0%	0%	7%	44%	**10.2%**	100%
Detection precision	0%	0%	0%	71%	81%	**30.4%**	100%

Table 2. Evaluation of precision and cost

Evaluation metrics	Conv layer depth	Restored images					
		Targeted			Untargeted		Average
		L-BFGS	JSMA	CW$_2$	FGSM	DeepFool	
Restoration cost (s)	24	0.92	0.92	0.92	0.91	0.92	0.92
	12	0.44	0.43	0.44	0.44	0.44	0.44
	6	**0.19**	**0.20**	**0.19**	**0.19**	**0.20**	**0.19**
	3	0.08	0.08	0.08	0.08	0.08	0.08
Classification precision	24	81%	73%	76%	82%	79%	78.2%
	12	72%	66%	73%	73%	74%	71.6%
	6	**84%**	**79%**	**81%**	**82%**	**83%**	**81.8%**
	3	80%	73%	75%	81%	80%	77.8%
Detection precision	24	92%	89%	88%	94%	91%	90.8%
	12	90%	85%	89%	90%	90%	88.8%
	6	**93%**	**90%**	**91%**	**92%**	**92%**	**91.6%**
	3	92%	88%	88%	93%	90%	90.2%

4.2   Evaluation of the Proposed Defense

In this part, we evaluate the effectiveness of our defense in terms of precision, cost and universality.

Precision and Cost. To evaluate the effect of our defense against such threats, we apply five pre-networks in different depths to restore the above 500 adversarial images. The time cost of restoring each image is also recorded and is counted on a server with an i7-7820X 3.60 GHz CPU, a 32 GiB memory and a GeForce GTX 1080Ti graphics card. Subsequently, we input these restored images into the *ResNet50* model and present the classification precision and detection precision in Table 2.

Comparing the results in Table 1 with that in Table 2, all five pre-networks significantly improve both the classification precision and detection precision with little time cost. Taking the 6 *Conv*-layer pre-network as an example, the classification precision is improved from 10.2% to 81.8% on average, and the average time of restoring each image is only 0.19 s. The detection precision is averagely improved from 30.4% to 91.6%, which nearly restores the detection

Table 3. Evaluation of universality

Evaluation metrics	Restoration	Classification models		
		ResNet50	ResNet18	VGG19
Classification precision	Before	0%	0%	0%
	After	81%	81%	70%
Detection precision	Before	0%	0%	0%
	After	91%	92%	84%

capability of the system. Owing to its effectiveness, we apply the 6 *Conv*-layer pre-network for further experiments.

It is noted that the CW_2 perturbation is acknowledgedly difficult to defend [11], whereas our defense still shows excellent performance. Moreover, a deeper pre-network do not show better performance than a shallower one, hence a lightweight network is qualified for the defense task.

Universality. To attest that our proposed defense is suitable for multiple classification models, we apply the *ResNet50* and two more typical classifiers, *ResNet18* [22] and *VGG19* [24], as target models.

Again, we apply the three models to classify the 800 weapon-related images and select the first 100 correctly predicted ones for the follow-up experiment.

For each target model, we generate 100 adversarial images with the CW_2 algorithm (with 'cassette' as the target class) and then restore these images with the 6 *Conv*-layer pre-network. Finally, we apply the three models to classify these adversarial images before and after restoration and record the results in Table 3.

As expected, for each model, the classification precision and detection precision are significantly improved (e.g., the classification precision of *ResNet18* and *VGG19* is improved from 0% to 81% and 70%, respectively), which attests the universality of our defense.

4.3   Comparison with Benchmarks

We apply five typical and effective defenses proposed in reference [7] (*Feature Squeezing*, which is one of the state-of-the-art work.) and reference [15] as our benchmarks.

Specifically, we reproduce these transformation approaches with the parameters in the two references, namely the median filters (sizes of 2×2, 3×3 and 5×5), the median filters (sizes of 2×2 and 5×5), the Gaussian filters (standard deviations of 0.5 and 1), the non-local means denoising algorithms [25] (patch sizes of 3 and 6, patch distances of 11 and 4) and the wavelet denoising algorithm [26] (standard deviation of 3 and level of 1), as well as compare them with the 6 *Conv*-layer pre-network.

Firstly, we select the first 300 correctly classified images with the *ResNet50* model, and apply the CW_2 (targeted) and *FGSM* (untargeted) algorithms to

Table 4. Comparison with benchmarks

Defenses		Classification precision		Detection precision	
Transformations	Parameters	CW_2	FGSM	CW_2	FGSM
Median smoothing	2 × 2	46.7%	53.7%	70.7%	74.7%
	3 × 3	65.3%	69.0%	**83.3%**	84.7%
	5 × 5	30.0%	35.0%	54.3%	59.3%
Mean smoothing	2 × 2	42.0%	45.0%	78.7%	85.7%
	5 × 5	20.7%	17.7%	64.3%	68.3%
Gaussian smoothing	$\sigma = 0.5$	50.7%	61.0%	79.0%	**90.3%**
	$\sigma = 1$	31.0%	27.0%	73.3%	78.7%
Non-local means denoising	s = 3, d = 11	56.0%	60.7%	79.0%	82.7%
	s = 6, d = 4	**68.3%**	**70.7%**	82.0%	81.3%
Wavelet denoising	$\sigma = 3, l = 1$	36.7%	35.7%	79.3%	83.0%
Pre-network	Conv layer = 6	*79.7%*	*81.7%*	*91.0%*	*91.0%*

generate 300 adversarial images, respectively. Furthermore, we transform these adversarial images with the 6 *Conv*-layer pre-network as well as the five transformation approaches. Finally, we input the restored images to the *ResNet50* model again for classification.

As the results represented in Table 4, our restoration defense outperforms all of these benchmarks. Compared with the best-performance results of the benchmarks (bold results in the table), our defense (slanted results in the table) achieves a classification precision gains of 11.4% and 11.0% for the two perturbations, respectively. Further, an excellent detection precision of 91.0% is achieved with our defense for both perturbations, which is superior to any setting of these defenses.

We further analyze the detailed predictions of the CW_2 algorithm-generated adversarial images and obtain some facts. Take the median smoothing defense as an example, the predictions of all adversarial images are modified to the classes different from 'cassette'. But a part of these predictions (e.g., 34.7% with the 3 × 3 median filter) are still nonidentical with the images' original classes, which remain as threats to some security-sensitive system. Such observations verify that such transformations (with fundamental image processing techniques) cause a contingency on correcting the misclassification. Thus the approach towards restoring the adversarial images is necessary and provides a better idea to defend against adversarial perturbations.

5   Conclusion

In this paper, we applied image restoration as a defense against adversarial perturbations for spam image detection. The restoration was achieved by a lightweight pre-network, which took an adversarial image as input and output its restored version for classification. The experimental results verified the effectiveness of our defense. With a 6 *Conv*-layer pre-network, our defense improved the classification precision from 10.2% to 81.8% on average, behaved well in three typical classification models, as well as outperformed five representative defenses including the state-of-the-art *Feature Squeezing* approach.

Acknowledgement. This work is supported by National Key R&D Program of China (No.2018YFB0803402).

References

1. Mehta, B., Nangia, S., Gupta, M., Nejdl, W.: Detecting image spam using visual features and near duplicate detection. In: 17th International Conference on World Wide Web (2008). https://doi.org/10.1145/1367497.1367565
2. Gao, Y., et al.: Image spam hunter. In: International Conference on Acoustics, Speech and Signal Processing (ICASSP) (2008). https://doi.org/10.1109/ICASSP.2008.4517972
3. Szegedy, C., et al.: Intriguing properties of neural networks (2014)
4. Evtimov, I., et al.: Robust physical-world attacks on deep learning models. In: IEEE Conference on Computer Vision and Pattern Recognition (CVPR) (2018). https://doi.org/10.1109/CVPR.2018.00175
5. Papernot, N., McDaniel, P., Wu, X., Jha, S., Swami, A.: Distillation as a defense to adversarial perturbations against deep neural networks. In: IEEE Symposium on, Security and Privacy (SP) (2016). https://doi.org/10.1109/SP.2016.41
6. Madry, A., Makelov, A., Schmidt, L., Tsipras, D., Vladu, A.: Towards deep learning models resistant to adversarial attacks. arXiv preprint arXiv:1706.06083 (2017)
7. Xu, W., Evans, D., Qi, Y.: Feature squeezing: detecting adversarial examples in deep neural networks. In: Network and Distributed Systems Security Symposium (NDSS) (2018). https://doi.org/10.14722/ndss.2018.23210
8. Dziugaite, G.K., Ghahramani, Z., Roy, D.M.: A study of the effect of JPG compression on adversarial images. arXiv preprint arXiv:1608.00853 (2016)
9. Bhagoji, A.N., Cullina, D., Sitawarin, C., Mittal, P.: Enhancing robustness of machine learning systems via data transformations. In: Annual Conference on Information Sciences and Systems (CISS) (2018). https://doi.org/10.1109/CISS.2018.8362326
10. Papernot, N., McDaniel, P., Jha, S., Fredrikson, M., Celik, Z.B., Swami, A.: The limitations of deep learning in adversarial settings. In: IEEE European Symposium on Security and Privacy (EuroS&P) (2016). https://doi.org/10.1109/EuroSP.2016.36
11. Xu, W., Evans, D., Qi, Y.: Feature squeezing mitigates and detects Carlini/Wagner adversarial examples. arXiv preprint arXiv:1705.10686 (2017)
12. Carlini, N., Wagner, D.: Towards evaluating the robustness of neural networks. In: IEEE Symposium on Security and Privacy (SP) (2017). https://doi.org/10.1109/SP.2017.49
13. Goodfellow, I.J., Shlens, J., Szegedy, C.: Explaining and harnessing adversarial examples. arXiv preprint arXiv:1412.6572 (2015)
14. Moosavi Dezfooli, S.M., Fawzi, A., Frossard, P.: DeepFool: a simple and accurate method to fool deep neural networks. In: IEEE Conference on Computer Vision and Pattern Recognition (CVPR) (2016). https://doi.org/10.1109/CVPR.2016.282

15. Osadchy, M., Hernandez-Castro, J., Gibson, S., Dunkelman, O., Pérez-Cabo, D.: No bot expects the deepcaptcha! introducing immutable adversarial examples, with applications to captcha generation. IEEE Trans. Inf. Forensics Secur. **12**(11), 2640–2653 (2017). https://doi.org/10.1109/TIFS.2017.2718479

16. Sharif, M., Bhagavatula, S., Bauer, L., Reiter, M.K.: Accessorize to a crime: real and stealthy attacks on state-of-the-art face recognition. In: ACM SIGSAC Conference on Computer and Communications Security (2016). https://doi.org/10.1145/2976749.2978392

17. Krizhevsky, A., Sutskever, I., Hinton, G.E.: ImageNet classification with deep convolutional neural networks. In: Advances in Neural Information Processing Systems, pp. 1097–1105 (2012). https://doi.org/10.1145/3065386

18. Wang, X., Jiao, J., Yin, J., Zhao, W., Han, X., Sun, B.: Underwater sonar image classification using adaptive weights convolutional neural network. Appl. Acoust. **146**, 145–154 (2019). https://doi.org/10.1016/j.apacoust.2018.11.003

19. Ioffe, S., Szegedy, C.: Batch normalization: accelerating deep network training by reducing internal covariate shift. arXiv preprint arXiv:1502.03167 (2015)

20. Kai, Z., Zuo, W., Lei, Z.: FFDNet: toward a fast and flexible solution for CNN based image denoising. IEEE Trans. Image Process. **27**(9), 4608–4622 (2018). https://doi.org/10.1109/TIP.2018.2839891

21. Russakovsky, O., et al.: ImageNet large scale visual recognition challenge. Int. J. Comput. Vis. (IJCV) **115**, 211–252 (2015). https://doi.org/10.1007/s11263-015-0816-y

22. He, K., Zhang, X., Ren, S., Sun, J.: Deep residual learning for image recognition. In: IEEE Conference on Computer Vision and Pattern Recognition (CVPR) (2016). https://doi.org/10.1109/CVPR.2016.90

23. Rauber, J., Brendel, W., Bethge, M.: Foolbox: a Python toolbox to benchmark the robustness of machine learning models. arXiv preprint arXiv:1707.04131 (2017)

24. Simonyan, K., Zisserman, A.: Very deep convolutional networks for large-scale image recognition. arXiv preprint arXiv:1409.1556 (2014)

25. Buades, A., Coll, B., Morel, J.M.: A non-local algorithm for image denoising. In: IEEE Conference on Computer Vision and Pattern Recognition (CVPR) (2005). https://doi.org/10.1109/CVPR.2005.38

26. Mihcak, M.K., Kozintsev, I., Ramchandran, K.: Spatially adaptive statistical modeling of wavelet image coefficients and its application to denoising. In: International Conference on Acoustics, Speech and Signal Processing (ICASSP) (1999). https://doi.org/10.1109/ICASSP.1999.757535

HLR: Generating Adversarial Examples by High-Level Representations

Yuying Hao[1], Tuanhui Li[2], Li Li[2], Yong Jiang[2(✉)], and Xuanye Cheng[3]

[1] Tsinghua-Berkely Shenzhen Institute, Tsinghua University, Shenzhen, China
{haoyy17,lth17}@mails.tsinghua.edu.cn
[2] Graduate School at Shenzhen, Tsinghua University, Shenzhen, China
lilihitcs@gmail.com,jiangy@sz.tsinghua.edu.cn
[3] SenseTime Research, SenseTime, Shenzhen, China
xuanyech@gmail.com

Abstract. Neural networks can be fooled by adversarial examples. Recently, many methods have been proposed to generate adversarial examples, but these works mainly concentrate on the pixel-wise information, which limits the transferability of adversarial examples. Different from these methods, we introduce perceptual module to extract the high-level representations and change the manifold of the adversarial examples. Besides, we propose a novel network structure to replace the generative adversarial network (GAN). The improved structure ensures high similarity of adversarial examples and promotes the stability of training process. Extensive experiments demonstrate that our method has significant improvement on the transferability. Furthermore, the adversarial training defence method is invalid for our attack.

Keywords: Adversarial example · Perceptual module · High-level representations

1 Introduction

Deep neural networks have enabled great advances in many artificial intelligence fields. However, these networks are susceptible to adversarial examples. Recently, many methods have been proposed to generate adversarial examples, but most of them only concentrate on the pixel-wise information, which limits the transferability of adversarial examples.

Different from these existing methods, we focus on the high-level representations of adversarial examples. High-level representations are the extracted output response of the high-level layers from the network model [4]. These output response contains guidance information for classification. Our goal is to generate adversarial examples with similar pixel-wise information corresponding to the benign images, but different on high-level representations. This characteristic can improve the transferability for the generated adversarial examples. To this

© Springer Nature Switzerland AG 2019
I. V. Tetko et al. (Eds.): ICANN 2019, LNCS 11729, pp. 724–730, 2019.
https://doi.org/10.1007/978-3-030-30508-6_57

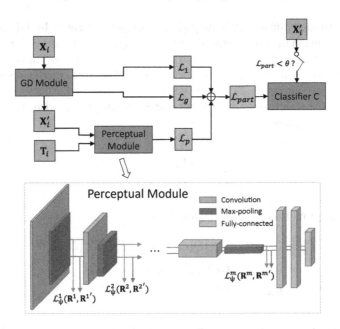

Fig. 1. The overall model structure of the HLR attack method. $\mathbf{X}_i$ is the benign image, $\mathbf{X}_i'$ is generated image and $\mathbf{T}_i$ is reference image. GD module produces losses $\mathcal{L}_1$ and $\mathcal{L}_g$, perceptual module generates loss $\mathcal{L}_p$. Classifier C is the state-of-the-art classifier.

end, we propose a novel structure shown on Fig. 1, which mainly consists of three parts: GD module, perceptual module and classifier C.

The main contributions of this paper can be summarized as follows: we use the GD module instead of GAN to generate adversarial examples, reducing the difficulty of training process while preserving the quasi-imperceptible properties of generated images. We introduce a perceptual loss to evaluate the high-level representations difference between benign images and the adversarial examples, which is more efficient than the pixel-wise ℓ_p-norm.

2 The Proposed HLR Attack

GD Module. We propose a GD module which is modified from the GAN structure. On the one hand, we preserve the generator of GAN structure in our method to generate examples with imperceptible perturbations. On the other hand, we abandon the discriminator, but directly use the ℓ_1 norm to simplify this problem. Compared to the original discriminator, the ℓ_1 norm in our GD module can measure the magnitude of perturbations and control the number of disturbance pixels. The $\mathcal{L}_1$ loss between $\mathbf{X}_i$ and $\mathbf{X}_i'$ can be described as:

$$\mathcal{L}_1 = ||\mathbf{X}_i' - \mathbf{X}_i||_1. \tag{1}$$

We denote distribution of $\mathbf{X}$ as $p_{\mathbf{X}}$, the images generated by GD module as $\mathbf{X}'$, the distribution of the generated images as $p_{\mathbf{X}'}$. To compare GD module with GAN, we denote the generator framework as G, the distribution of the images produced by generator as $p_{G(\mathbf{X})}$ and discriminator framework as D, discriminator output as $D(\cdot)$. When the $\mathcal{L}_1$ loss is greater than the perturbation intensity ϵ, the output of discriminator is the generated image. Otherwise, the output is normal image, as presented as follows:

$$D(\mathbf{X}_i') = \begin{cases} 1, & \mathcal{L}_1 \geq \epsilon \\ 0, & \mathcal{L}_1 < \epsilon \end{cases}. \tag{2}$$

And GAN loss function $\mathcal{L}_g$ can be described as:

$$\begin{aligned} \mathcal{L}_g &= E_{G(\mathbf{X}_i) \sim p_{G(\mathbf{X})}}[D(G(\mathbf{X}_i))] - E_{\mathbf{X}_i \sim p_{\mathbf{X}}}[D(\mathbf{X}_i)] \\ &= E_{\mathbf{X}_i' \sim p_{\mathbf{X}'}}[D(\mathbf{X}_i')] - E_{\mathbf{X}_i \sim p_{\mathbf{X}}}[D(\mathbf{X}_i)] \\ &= E_{\mathbf{X}_i' \sim p_{\mathbf{X}'}}[D(\mathbf{X}_i')] \end{aligned} \tag{3}$$

Perceptual Module. We define $\mathbf{R}^l \in \mathbb{R}^{N^l \times W^l \times H^l}$ as the input response of a single reference image $\mathbf{T}_i$ in layer l and $\mathbf{R}^{l'} \in \mathbb{R}^{N^l \times W^l \times H^l}$ as the input response of a single generated image $\mathbf{X}'_i$. N^l, W^l and H^l denote the input channels, the kernel width and height, respectively. The perceptual loss of layer l can be represented as follows:

$$\mathcal{L}_p^l = \frac{1}{N^l W^l H^l} ||\psi(\mathbf{R}^l) - \psi(\mathbf{R}^{l'})||^2, \tag{4}$$

where $\psi(\cdot)$ is denoted as the pooling operation. The perceptual loss of the whole network can be represented as follows:

$$\mathcal{L}_p = \frac{1}{m} \sum_{l=1}^{m} \mathcal{L}_p^l, \tag{5}$$

where m denotes the selected pooling layers in the perceptual module.

Classifier C and Loss Function. To facilitate the proposed method, we define a combined loss as $\mathcal{L}_{part}$, which can be described as:

$$\mathcal{L}_{part} = \lambda_1 * \mathcal{L}_p + \lambda_2 * \mathcal{L}_g + \lambda_3 * \mathcal{L}_1. \tag{6}$$

Our training process consists of two stages. In the first stage, we take $\mathcal{L}_{part}$ as the loss function for generating the images to fit high-level representations of reference images. When GD module is stable in the state $\mathcal{L}_{part} < \theta$, we take $\mathcal{L}_{HLR} = \mathcal{L}_{part} + \mathcal{L}_{KL}$ as the loss function to increase the misclassification probability of classifier C. $\mathcal{L}_{KL}$ serves as an indicator for measuring the output

Table 1. Fooling rates across different attack methods on CIFAR-10. We generate adversarial examples on VGG-16, VGG-19 and Resnet-18, and attack 3 different unknown models.

g-model	Fooling rates	d-model		
		Model1	Model2	Model3
VGG-16	NOISE	7.12	7.75	5.76
	PGD [6]	21.19	23.50	19.17
	CW-L2 [1]	32.56	37.20	32.82
	FGSM [2]	24.29	26.24	23.55
	VIRTUAL [7]	30.97	32.27	28.46
	Ours	**43.62**	**40.78**	**55.74**
VGG-19	NOISE	1.97	3.49	0.75
	PGD [6]	8.26	13.24	6.90
	CW-L2 [1]	21.95	29.43	21.88
	FGSM [2]	24.07	27.44	23.85
	VIRTUAL [7]	28.95	35.14	28.26
	Ours	**43.33**	**37.35**	**29.09**
ResNet-18	NOISE	6.62	6.84	5.98
	PGD [6]	12.68	29.85	11.88
	CW-L2 [1]	30.26	**34.90**	14.46
	FGSM [2]	18.83	20.22	17.6
	VIRTUAL [7]	27.48	31.06	25.51
	Ours	**38.01**	33.87	**30.85**

distance between the generated images $\mathbf{X}'$ and reference images $\mathbf{T}$. We introduce $\mathcal{L}_{KL}$ in the second training stage to accelerate the process of generating adversarial examples. $\mathcal{L}_{KL}$ can be described as:

$$\mathcal{L}_{KL}(p\|q) = \sum p(C(\mathbf{T}_i))log\frac{p(C(\mathbf{T}_i))}{q(C(\mathbf{X}'_i))}, \qquad (7)$$

where $C(\cdot)$ denotes the output of classifier C in Fig. 1, $p(C(\mathbf{T}_i))$ is the distribution of $C(\mathbf{T}_i)$, $q(C(\mathbf{X}'_i))$ is the distribution of $C(\mathbf{X}'_i)$.

3 Experiments

3.1 Experiment Setting

In the experiment, we initialize the perturbation intensity ϵ with 0.03 on CIFAR-10 and ϵ with 0.07 on ImageNet to implement untargeted attacks. We normalize the pixel values of images to [0, 1]. The hyper-parameters $\lambda_1, \lambda_2, \lambda_3, \lambda_4, \theta$ are set to 0.5, 0.2, 0.5, 0.1, 0.4, respectively. During the training process, the maximum

Table 2. Fooling rates across different attack methods on ImageNet. Each row indicates the network for generating adversarial examples, and each column indicates the fooling rate for corresponding architecture.

g-model	Fooling rates	d-model		
		VGG-16	VGG-19	ResNet-152
VGG-16	UAP [8]	78.30	73.10	63.40
	FFF [9]	47.10	41.98	–[a]
	OPT [5]	100.00	–	**78.00**
	FGA [5]	99.00	–	–
	SA [3]	52.00	60.00	–
	NAG [10]	73.25	**77.50**	54.38
	Ours	**100.00**	66.05	67.8
VGG-19	UAP [8]	73.50	77.80	58.00
	FFF [9]	38.20	–	43.62
	OPT [5]	–	–	–
	FGA [5]	–	–	–
	SA [3]	48.00	60.00	–
	NAG [10]	80.56	83.78	65.43
	Ours	**83.30**	**100.00**	**82.20**
ResNet-152	UAP [8]	47.00	45.50	84.00
	FFF [9]	–	–	–
	OPT [5]	81.00	–	100.00
	FGA [5]	80.00	–	96.00
	SA [3]	–	–	–
	NAG [10]	52.17	53.18	87.24
	Ours	**84.00**	**80.80**	**100.00**

[a] Denotes that the data is not reported in paper.

epoch is 1000. We use VGG-19 as perceptual module and extract high-level representations from layers 12, 16. In the training process, the parameters of perceptual module and classifier C are frozen.

3.2   Comparing with State-of-the-art Methods

Adversarial examples have shown the attack ability for different neural networks. Some adversarial examples generated from a certain model also have the attack ability to other unknown models [8]. In order to evaluate the attack ability under different models, we compare our method with state-of-the-art methods on CIFAR-10 and ImageNet. In Tables 1 and 2, 'g-model' is the model of generating adversarial examples and 'd-model' is model being attacked. In Table 2, the entries where 'd-model' matches with 'g-model' represent white-box attack, and others represent black-box attack.

Results on CIFAR-10. We attack 3 different networks Model1, Model2, Model3, which have different convolutional layers and full connected layers. The fooling rates are shown in Table 1. Our goal is to explore the attack ability under the weak perturbations. We generate adversarial examples via the same network for different methods and attack three unknown networks. Compared with other attack methods, our method achieves the best fooling rates when generated on VGG-19 and VGG-16 and competitive results on ResNet-18. That means the adversarial examples generated by our method have better transferability than those of other compared methods. The experiments show that under the weak perturbations, the adversarial perturbations generated according to high-level representations provide more manifold information than the perturbations generated by pixel-wise information.

Results on ImageNet. We compare our method with latest state-of-the-art methods, UAP [8], FFF [9], OPT [5], FGA [5], SA [3] and NAG [10]. The results of fooling rates among different attack models are shown on Table 2. Our method generates specific perturbations for each image. The adversarial examples cannot be produced via 'g-model' until they are misclassified by 'g-model', such that our method can achieve 100% of fooling rates for white-box attack. As for black-box attack, our method achieves competitive performance, compared with other methods. For example, when VGG-19 serves as 'g-model', NAG achieves fooling rates of 80.56% on VGG-16 and 65.43% on ResNet-152, while our method achieves fooling rates of 83.30% on VGG-16 and 82.20% on ResNet-152. If adversarial examples are generated in complex network structure, the fooling rates of our method tends to have a significant improvement. The experiment results prove that attack ability of adversarial examples are more correlative to high-level representations. We conclude that high-level representations align well for different model structures, thus our method can achieve excellent attack ability.

4   Conclusion

We propose an effective method of combining the GD module and perceptual module to generate adversarial examples. We utilize GD module to ensure that the perturbations are quasi-imperceptible to humans. We utilize perceptual module to extract the high-level representations, other than just pixel-wise information. We found that the depth and the complexities of the network structures applied to our attack directly affect the transferability of adversarial examples. The experiment results prove that the high-level representations are more robust than pixel-wise information for different models and have great effects on attack ability of adversarial examples. In the future work, we will explore how to use the high-level representations to generate targeted adversarial examples.

Acknowledgements. This work is supported by Guangdong Province Key Area R&D Program under grant No. 2018B010113001, the R&D Program of Shenzhen under grant

No. JCYJ20170307153157440 and the Shenzhen Key Lab of Software Defined Networking under grant No. ZDSYS201405091729599989, and the National Natural Science Foundation of China under Grant No. 61802220.

References

1. Carlini, N., Wagner, D.: Towards evaluating the robustness of neural networks. In: IEEE Symposium on Security and Privacy (SP), pp. 39–57 (2017). https://doi.org/10.1109/SP.2017.49

2. Goodfellow, I.J., Shlens, J., Szegedy, C.: Explaining and harnessing adversarial examples. In: International Conference on Learning Representations (ICLR) (2015). arXiv:1412.6572

3. Khrulkov, V., Oseledets, I.: Art of singular vectors and universal adversarial perturbations. In: IEEE Conference on Computer Vision and Pattern Recognition (CVPR), pp. 8562–8570 (2018). https://doi.org/10.1109/CVPR.2018.00893

4. Liao, F., Liang, M., Dong, Y., Pang, T., Hu, X., Zhu, J.: Defense against adversarial attacks using high-level representation guided denoiser. In: Proceedings of the IEEE Conference on Computer Vision and Pattern Recognition (CVPR), pp. 1778–1787 (2018). https://doi.org/10.1109/CVPR.2018.00191

5. Liu, Y., Chen, X., Liu, C., Song, D.: Delving into transferable adversarial examples and black-box attacks (2017)

6. Madry, A., Makelov, A., Schmidt, L., Tsipras, D., Vladu, A.: Towards deep learning models resistant to adversarial attacks (2017). stat, 1050:9

7. Miyato, T., Maeda, S.-I., Koyama, M., Nakae, K., Ishii, S.: Distributional smoothing with virtual adversarial training (2015). arXiv preprint arXiv:1507.00677

8. Fawzi, A., Fawzi, O., Moosavi-Dezfooli, S.M., Frossard, P.: Universal adversarial perturbations. In: IEEE Conference on Computer Vision and Pattern Recognition (CVPR), pp. 86–94 (2017). https://doi.org/10.1109/CVPR.2017.17

9. Garg, U., Mopuri, K.R., Babu, R.V.: Fast feature fool: a data independent approach to universal adversarial perturbations. In: British Machine Vision Conference (BMVC) (2017). https://doi.org/10.5244/C.31.30

10. Mopuri, K.R., Ojha, U., Garg, U., Babu, R.V.: NAG: Network for adversary generation. In: Proceedings of the IEEE Conference on Computer Vision and Pattern Recognition (CVPR), pp. 742–751 (2018). https://doi.org/10.1109/CVPR.2018.00084

Author Index

Printed in the United States
By Bookmasters